Cecil Collins

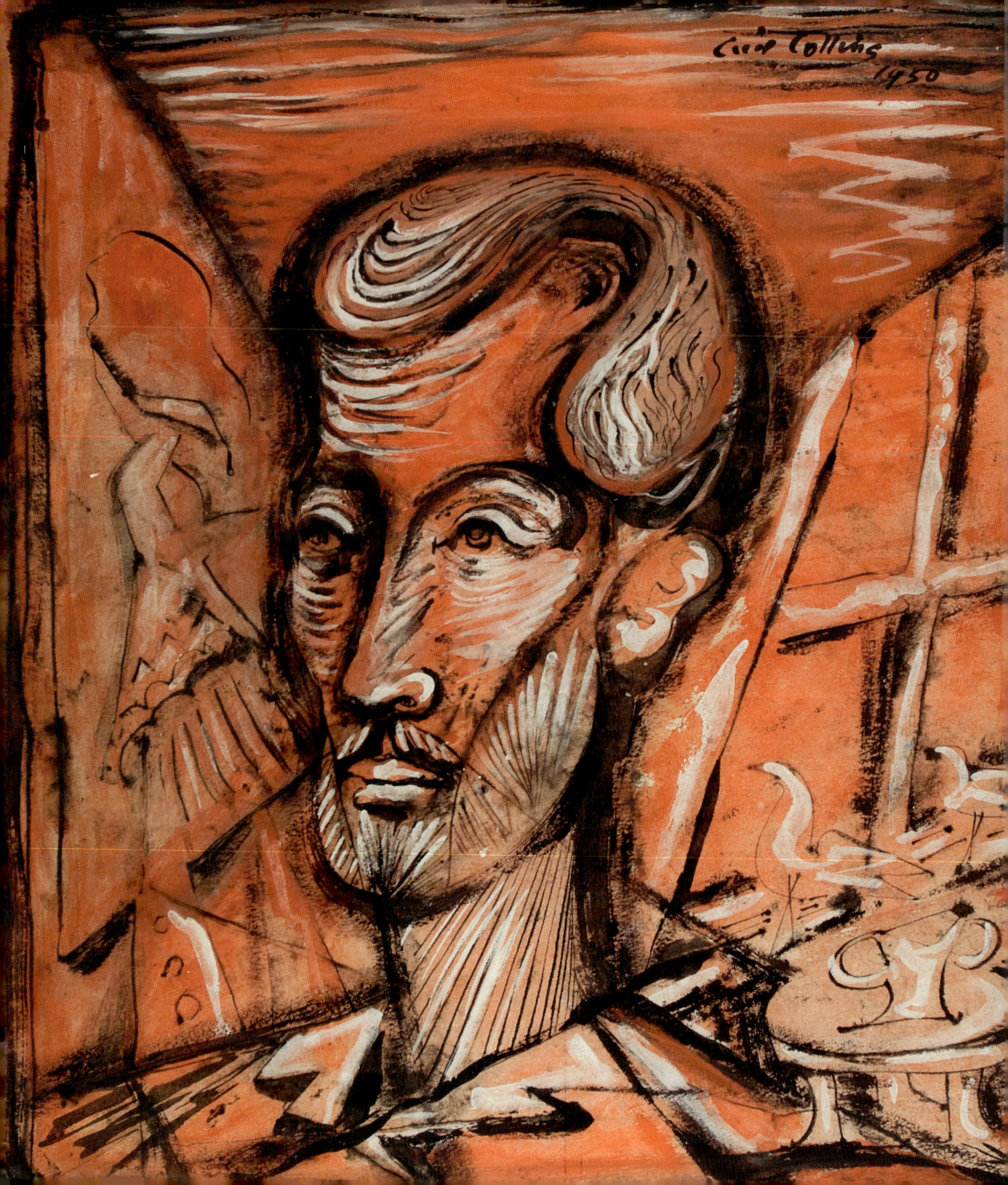

IN CELEBRATION OF

Cecil Collins

VISIONARY ARTIST AND EDUCATOR

Dedicated to Cecil and Elisabeth Collins

First published in the United Kingdom in 2008 by
FOOLSCAP
Distributed by Paul Holberton Publishing
89 Borough High Street
London SE1 1NLT
T: 020 7407 0809
E: books@paul-holberton.net

Copyright © 2008 Tate, London; Nomi Rowe

Grateful acknowledgment is made to copyright holders of material reproduced in this book, but if any have been inadvertently overlooked the publishers would be glad to hear from them to make good in future editions any errors or omissions brought to their attention.

For legal purposes the Acknowledgments and Credits pages constitute a continuation of this copyright page.

Publisher: FOOLSCAP
Editor and compiler: Nomi Rowe
Designer: Jonathan Raimes

Any copy of this book issued by the publisher as a paperback is sold subject to the condition that it shall not by way of trade or otherwise be lent, resold, hired out, or otherwise circulated without the publisher's prior consent in any form of binding or cover other than that in which it is published and without a similar condition including sthese words being imposed on a subsequent purchaser.

British Library Cataloguing-in-Publication Data
A catalogue record for this book is available from
the British Library

ISBN 978 1 872458 99 0

All rights reserved. No part of this publication may be reproduced or used in any form, or by any means – graphic, electronic, or mechanical, including photocopying, recording, or information storage-and-retrieval systems – without the prior permission of the publisher.

Printed and bound by HSW Print, Tonypandy, Rhondda CF40 2XX

For more information on this title please visit:
www.paul-holberton.net

Title page:
Cecil Collins
Self Portrait
1950
Gouache
17.8 x 23cm

CONTENTS

PREFACE	7
FOREWORD	8
CHRONOLOGY	10
INTRODUCTION	14
TATE GALLERY TALK 1981	24
ABOUT CECIL BY ELISABETH COLLINS	28
CURATORS & GALLERY OWNERS	34
STUDENTS, MODELS & COLLEAGUES	52
FRIENDS & OTHER RELATIONSHIPS	206
INDEX	316
ACKNOWLEDGEMENTS & CREDITS	320

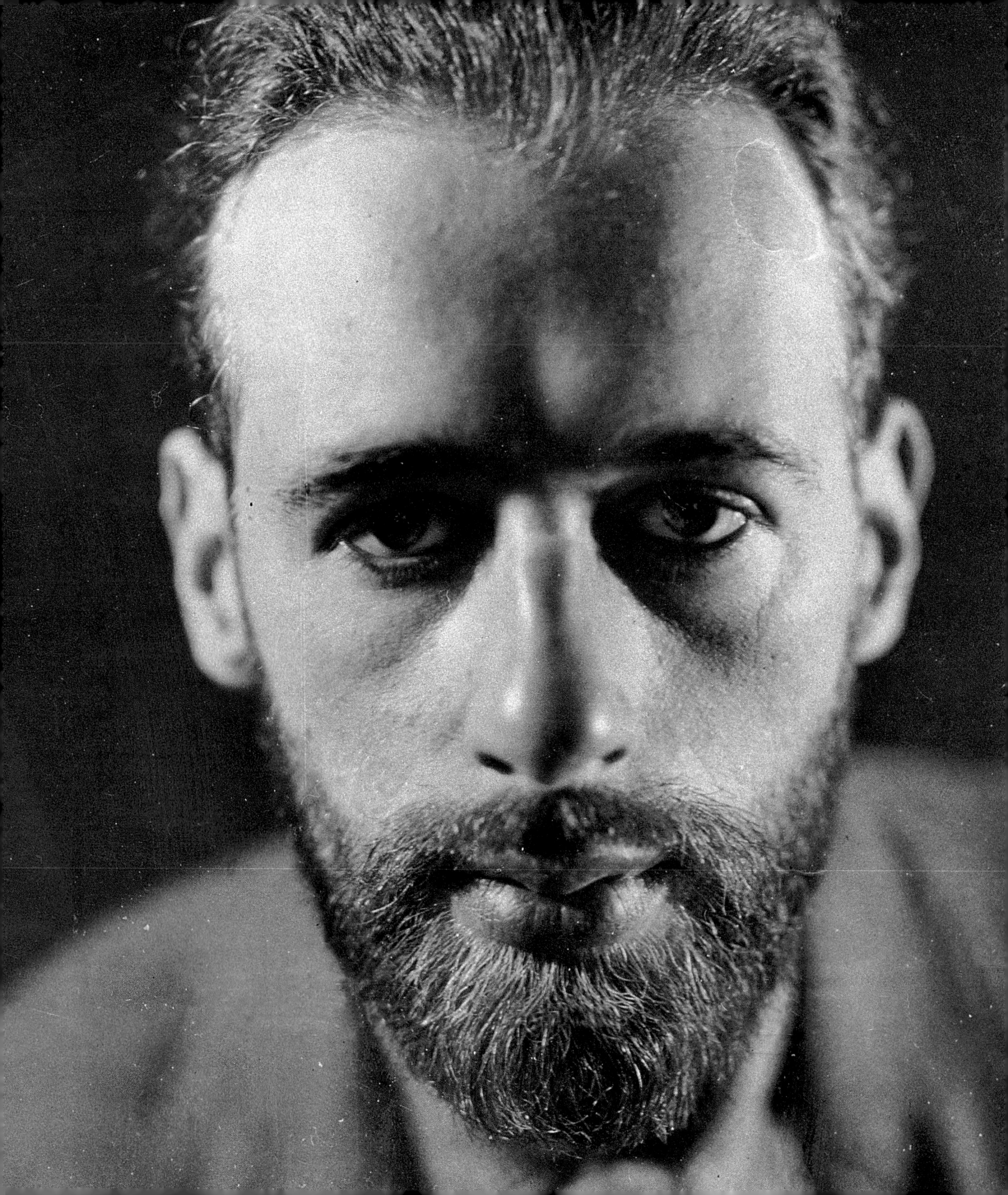

PREFACE

There is only one voice in the universe. We do not even own our own voices.
Cecil Collins

Even though you tie a hundred knots, the string remains one.
Jelaluddin Rumi

This book consists of my edited versions of informal recorded conversations with Cecil Collins' friends, students, curators and contemporaries. From their memories a composite portrait of him develops; a mosaic in word form. Their recollections also included his wife, Elisabeth, since she and Cecil were inseparable for over sixty years.

I have created a written version of their vivid accounts, in the rhythms of natural speech. The material was collected over the last decade and the book represents a collage of undated snapshots rather than a more formal studio portrait. These are candid spoken words not polished literary essays or attempts at art-historical analysis. The pieces reflect the views held at the time and in some cases, perhaps, would not be the same or would not be expressed in the same way if the contributors were interviewed today. There were many people I could not reach so this is only a small selection of those whom Cecil and Elisabeth came into contact with and affected so deeply.

In Celebration of Cecil Collins has collected together these very personal accounts in order to preserve the vitality of Cecil's presence and to make his legacy known to a wider public.

My grateful thanks to all those who gave so generously of their time for without their support and encouragement this project would not have been possible.

Cecil Collins
c. 1940

FOREWORD

Anthony d'Offay is a pre-eminent British art dealer and owner of the eponymous gallery, London (1980–2002). His art collection was bought for the nation in 2007 and since 2006, his son, Timothy, runs Postcard Teas from the former gallery premises in Dering Street, selling exclusively-sourced teas and exhibiting postcards from Anthony's personal collection.

It's highly likely that it was Richard Morphet who suggested Cecil for the gallery. He took an interest in suggesting things to us because he liked the shows that we did. He talked about the house in Paultons Square, 'Go and see a magic house in London filled with geniuses,' and he arranged a meeting. There was Kathleen Raine on the ground floor and Winifred Nicholson in the basement and the Collinses at the top.

I have found that it's very important, in terms of understanding art, to meet the artist. When you meet the artist, then everything falls into place. You understand what the art is about in a much more real way, otherwise you sometimes can't quite get it.

It was impossible to meet Cecil and not to fall in love with him. He cared deeply about making pictures that he felt would make a difference to people's lives and he cared so much for other people. Another fact which made him so loveable was that he'd been a great teacher and his students loved him. When there was a question of his retiring, they all came out in protest and managed to get him re-instated. The Japanese venerate age: very often people come into their own in their fifties, sixties, seventies and even eighties. In Japan, Cecil would have been a National Living Treasure.

We loved working with him and I liked that he had very decided views. I enjoyed arguing with him and having a dialogue, yet he was also a very spectral figure. He looked like somebody you'd hardly have glimpsed as they disappeared into a doorway and in his pictures the figures were almost disembodied. They were all to do with heaven really. Angelic figures without any corporeal presence. I've probably got two or three drawings of Cecil's that were given to me by him which would have been typical of him. I always believed that my job was to make sure that things went to good collections. I never bought pieces unless they proved impossible to sell. With Cecil's work, people rushed in and bought them immediately.

Cecil had paintings and drawings which felt very personal. They were perhaps related to the very beautiful love affair with his wife, Elisabeth. You felt that this was some sort of lovely fragile miracle you were witnessing and you'd wake up one day and it wouldn't be there anymore, as indeed happened.

The artist is like an endless stream: everything flows through the artist and away. That was true of Cecil. He was always giving and he cared very much about students and shy people and would turn serious situations into a hilarious joke. I remember saying to him once, 'Cecil, you're looking very serious. What are you thinking about?' He said, 'Money. I'm thinking about money.' It was the last thing you expected him to say.

Anthony d'Offay

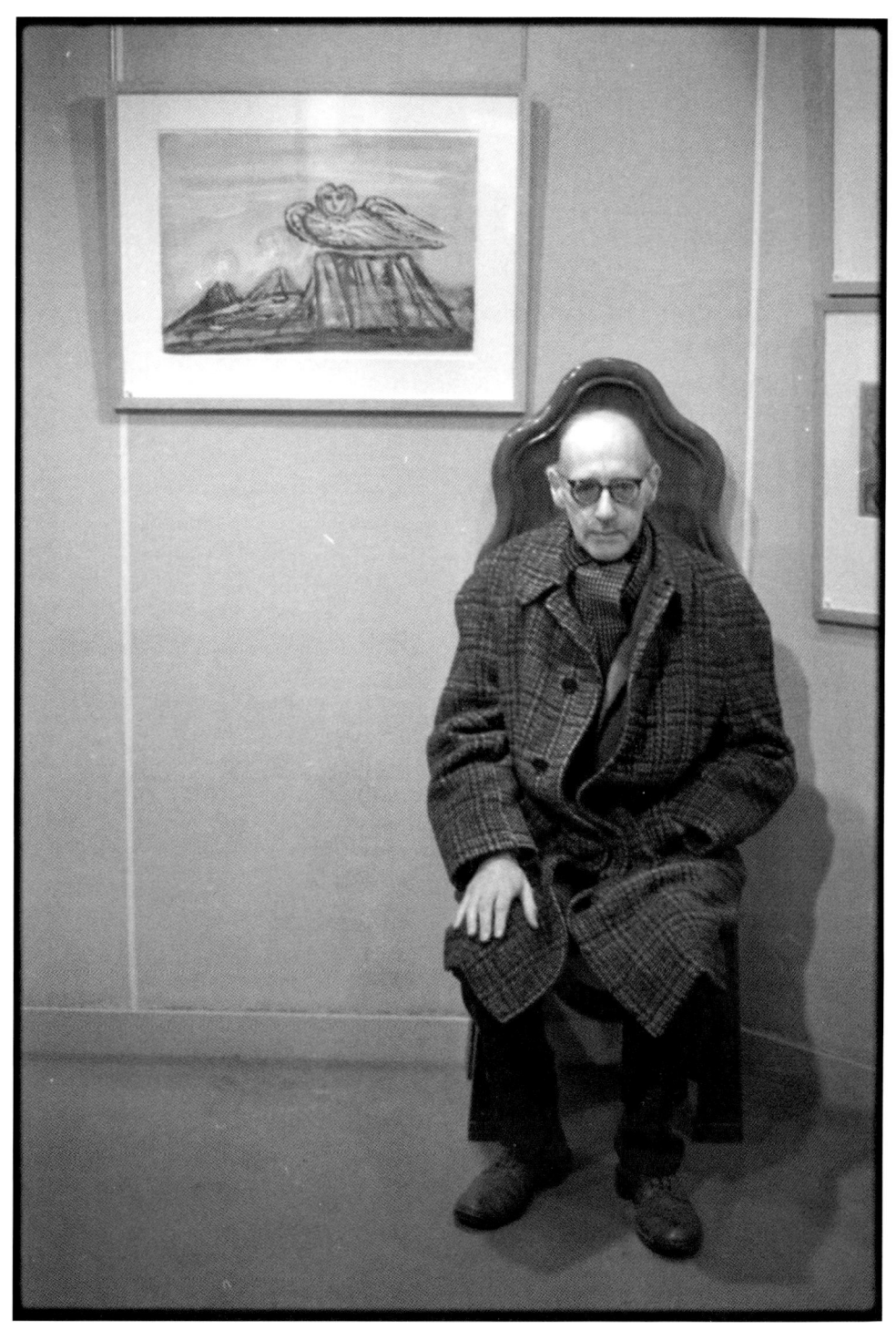

Photograph by Jane Bown
Cecil Collins in Anthony d'Offay Gallery, seated on replica Knossos throne
1988

CECIL COLLINS & CONTEMPORARY EVENTS 1908-1952

1908
- James Henry Cecil Collins is born on 23 March at 2 Bayswater Terrace, Plymouth.
- His childhood is a time of connecting with woodland and seascape near his home.

Venus of Willendorf is discovered (now in Naturhistorisches Museum, Vienna); G.K. Chesterton, *The Man Who Was Thursday*; Kenneth Grahame, *The Wind in the Willows*; Beatrix Potter, *The Tale of Jemima Puddle-Duck*.
Births: Simone de Beauvoir, Henri Cartier-Bresson, Claude Lévi-Strauss, David Oistrakh.

1909
Pablo Picasso and Georges Braque create Analytical Cubism.
Births: Francis Bacon, Isaiah Berlin, Eugène Ionesco.

1910
First exhibition of Post-Impressionism in London, organised by Roger Fry; Igor Stravinsky, *The Firebird*; Ralph Vaughan Williams, *Fantasia on a Theme of Thomas Tallis*.
Births: Jacques-Yves Cousteau, Alicia Markova, Peter Pears.
Deaths: Henri Rousseau, Leo Tolstoy, Mark Twain.

1911
Roald Amundsen's expedition reaches the South Pole.
Births: William Golding, Mervyn Peake, Tennessee Williams.
Death: Gustav Mahler.

1912
Sinking of the RMS Titanic.
Birth: Lawrence Durrell.

1913
Armory Show opens in New York; première of Stravinsky's *Rite of Spring* in Paris.
Birth: Albert Camus.

1914
Beginning of World War I.
Births: Marguerite Duras, Dylan Thomas.

1915
T.S. Eliot, *The Love Song of J. Alfred Prufrock*; publication of final (12th) volume of James Frazer's *The Golden Bough*; Carl Jung's *Theory of Psychoanalysis*.

Births: Saul Bellow, Terry Frost, Thomas Merton, Edith Piaf.

1916
Births: Pir Vilayat Khan (Sufi mystic master); Yehudi Menuhin.
Death: Odilon Redon.

1917
Births: Ella Fitzgerald, John Minton.
Death: Edgar Degas.

1918
Tsar Nicholas II of Russia and his family murdered in Ekaterinberg.
Births: Ingmar Bergman, Leonard Bernstein, Nelson Mandela.

1919
The Ballets Russes gives world première of Manuel de Falla's ballet The Three-Cornered Hat, London; Bauhaus founded by Walter Gropius, Weimar, Germany.
Births: Prunella Clough, Margot Fonteyn, Doris Lessing, J.D. Salinger.

1920
Births: Federico Fellini, Patrick Heron.

1921
Première of Sergei Prokoviev's *The Love for Three Oranges*.
Births: Radha Krishna Choudhary, Humphrey Lyttelton.

1922
- Begins apprenticeship at a motor engineering firm at Millbay in Plymouth Docks, which he leaves in 1923.

T.S. Eliot, *The Waste Land*; James Joyce, *Ulysses*; Lord Carnarvon and Howard Carter enter the tomb of Tutankhamun.
Births: Lucian Freud, Richard Hamilton, Philip Larkin.
Death: Marcel Proust.

1923
- Studies at Plymouth School of Art.
- Hears performance of the St Matthew Passion in St Andrew's Church, Plymouth.

E. M. Forster, *Passage to India*.
Birth: Roy Lichtenstein

1924
André Breton publishes the Surrealist Manifesto.
Births: Anthony Caro, Eduardo Paolozzi.
Deaths: Vladimir Lenin, Cecil Sharpe.

1925
F. Scott Fitzgerald, *The Great Gatsby*, P. G. Wodehouse, *Carry on Jeeves*, Virginia Woolf, *Mrs Dalloway*.
Birth: Peter Sellers.

1926
- Believed to have exhibited his first painting (now lost) at a mixed exhibition in Plymouth.

Franz Kafka, *The Castle*.
Births: Michel Foucault, Allen Ginsberg, Leon Kossoff, Joan Sutherland.

1927
- Collins' father, Harry Collins, dies.
- Wins scholarship to the Royal College of Art, London; studies there until 1931.
- Wins William Rothenstein Life Drawing Prize.

Publication of seventh and final volume of Marcel Proust's *In Search of Lost Time*; Thornton Wilder, *The Bridge of San Luis Rey*; Virginia Woolf, *To the Lighthouse*.
Death: Isadora Duncan.

1928
- Meets Elisabeth Ramsden, his future wife.
- Submits his only three-dimensional work (now lost), the subject of which was the Deposition, to the Victoria and Albert Museum.
- Studies the works of Italian Renaissance masters, as well as medieval and Italian sculpture, at the Victoria and Albert Museum.

Stravinsky, *Apollon Musagète*; publication of D. H. Lawrence, *Lady Chatterley's Lover*; Alexander Fleming discovers penicillin.
Birth: Andy Warhol.
Death: Emmeline Pankhurst, suffragette.

1929
Luis Buñuel's *Un Chien Andalou*, with Salvador Dali; American Depression begins.
Birth: Claes Oldenburg.
Death: Sergei Diaghilev.

1930
Buñuel's *L'Age d'Or*; W. H. Auden, *Poems*.
Births: Elizabeth Frink, Ted Hughes, Harold Pinter.

1931
- Marries Elisabeth Ramsden.
- Lives between London and Monk's Cottage, Highwood Bottom, Buckinghamshire (where he meets Eric Gill and David Jones).
- Enters an introspective, meditative period at Monk's Cottage, reading mystics Meister Eckhart (c. 1260-1327/8); Jacob Böhme (1575-1624) and poets Thomas Traherne (1637-1674) and Henry Vaughan (1622-1695).
- Becomes interested in the scientific world and in the research of Arthur H. Compton (director of the World Survey of Cosmic Rays until 1933) and others. This is reflected later in such works as *A Song* (1934).

Salvador Dali, *The Persistence of Memory*, Virginia Woolf, *The Waves*.
Births: Frank Auerbach, Bridget Riley.

1932
Aldous Huxley, *Brave New World*; first production of Karl Jooss's ballet, *The Green Table*.
Births: Peter Blake, Howard Hodgkin, R.B. Kitaj, Sylvia Plath, John Updike.

1933
- Visits Paris. Sees work of Paul Klee.
- Becomes interested in Surrealism.

Gertrude Stein, *The Autobiography of Alice B. Toklas*; Stravinsky, *Persephone*.

1934
- Meets Mark Tobey at Tobey's exhibition of paintings and drawings at the Beaux Arts Gallery in London and they become friends.
- Theme of love and figure of Angel first appear in his work.
- Introduces bone forms into his works around this time.

Pamela Travers, *Mary Poppins*; Adolf Hitler becomes head of state in Germany.
Birth: Tenzin Gyatso, the fourteenth Dalai Lama.
Death: Edward Elgar.

1935
- First one-man exhibition of 56 works is held at the Bloomsbury Gallery in London (16 – 29 October). Foreword to his exhibition (which appears in *The Vision of the Fool and other writings*, Golgonooza Press, 1994) indicates the origin of a number of ideas that run through the rest

of his life's work, such as a rejection of the modern movement's 'isms', and a belief in art's sacred purpose to serve and awaken each person's inner divinity.
• Around this time, writes *The Artist in Society*, in which he explores and confronts his artistic navigation of Surrealism.
• Crystalline and cellular forms enter his paintings, inspired by the publication of *The World Beneath the Microscope* by Wilfred E. Watson-Baker.

Enid Welsford, *The Fool*.

1936
• Collins' first poem published in *New England Weekly*.
• Two of his works exhibited in the International Surrealist Exhibition (11 June – 4 July) at Burlington Galleries in London.
• Moves with Elisabeth to Totnes, Devon and attends Mark Tobey's classes at Dartington Hall, Devon.

Abdication of Edward VIII; release of documentary film *Night Mail*, narrated by John Grierson with commentary by W.H. Auden and music by Benjamin Britten. Federico Garcia Lorca shot dead near Granada, Spain.

1937
• Exhibits 65 paintings and drawings in the Barn Studio at Dartington Hall (17 – 29 June).

Pablo Picasso, *Guernica*; John Steinbeck, *Of Mice and Men*; J.R.R. Tolkien, *The Hobbit*.
Births: Philip Glass, David Hockney, John Ogden, Tom Stoppard.

1938
• Teaches painting at Dartington Hall Summer School. Other tutors included Hein Heckroth, Bernard Leach, Willi Soukop.

Neville Chamberlain declares 'Peace in our Time'; Daphne du Maurier, *Rebecca*; C.S. Lewis, *Out of the Silent Planet*; George Orwell, *Homage to Catalonia*; Jean-Paul Sartre, *La Nausée*.

1939
• Moves to Dartington Hall at the outbreak of war, staying with Margaret Isherwood.
• *A Spring Tale*, a ballet-drama, is performed at Dartington Hall by the Ballet Jooss (an avant-garde German ensemble). The influence of crowned heads and certain gestures from this production can be seen in Collins' works.
• In March, Elisabeth Collins produces a drawing showing three figures watching a wounded fool whose heart is penetrated by a spear.

World War II declared; end of Spanish Civil War; James Joyce, *Finnegan's Wake*; John Steinbeck, *The Grapes of Wrath*.

1940
• Exhibits work with Roland Penrose and Hein Heckroth in the Barn Studio at Dartington (5 – 25 August).
• Meets dancer, choreographer and ballet master Rudolf von Laban at Dartington Hall. Laban confirms for Collins his 'deepest intuitions about movement being a form of knowledge'.
• Poems written by Collins from 1940 to 1941 betray his despair in the face of contemporary events and a world at war (*Cecil Collins: Meditations, Poems, Pages from a Sketchbook*, Golgonooza Press, 1997).

Deaths: Eric Gill, Paul Klee.

1941
• Introduces Herbert Read's lecture on *The ABC of Art* at Dartington on 25 May.
• Reads Milton and Coleridge's *Biographia Literaria*.

Arthur Koestler, *Darkness at Noon*.
Birth: Michael Craig-Martin.
Deaths: James Joyce, Rabindranath Tagore, Virginia Woolf.

1942
• Exhibits at the Toledo Museum of Fine Art in USA.
• Begins to write essay *The Vision of the Fool*.
• A medical examination in Exeter reveals that he is physically not fit enough to fight in the war.

Albert Camus, *L'Étranger*.
Death: Walter Sickert.

1943
• Collins' mother, Mary (née Bowie), dies.
• Becomes acquainted with John Piper at Dartington.
• John Rothenstein buys *The Sleeping Fool* for the Contemporary Art Society.

Jean-Paul Sartre, *Being and Nothingness*; première Ralph Vaughan Williams' *Fifth Symphony* in London.

1944
• Exhibits 50 paintings and drawings in February at the Lefevre Gallery in King Street, London. His paintings are blown off the walls when King Street is hit in an air raid, but are mainly undamaged.
• Moves to Cambridge in July, lodging with the poet Robert Nichols.
• In December, Paul Nash asks Collins to write text for his illustrated book.

Death: Wassily Kandinsky.

1945
• Moves to Chelsea in October.
• Exhibits 67 watercolours and drawings at the Lefevre Gallery in December.
• The periodical *Transformation* prints his first essay on the Fool, entitled *The Anatomy of the Fool*.

Germany surrenders; atom bomb dropped on Hiroshima; George Orwell, *Animal Farm*; Bertrand Russell, *A History of Western Philosophy*; première of Benjamin Britten's opera *Peter Grimes*; release of Marcel Carné's film *Les Enfants du Paradis*.

1946
• Meets poet Alex Comfort and composer/publisher Conrad Senat in Oxford.
• First book on Collins is published, written by Alex Comfort: *Cecil Collins; Paintings and Drawings* 1935-45.

Release of Jean Cocteau's film *La Belle et la Bête*; Mervyn Peake, *Titus Groan*.
Deaths: Gertrude Stein, H.G. Wells.

1947
• *Vision of the Fool* is published by Grey Walls Press, Collins' essay, drawings and paintings on the theme of the archetypal figure of the Fool.
• Moves back to Cambridge.

India gains independence; exhibition of William Blake's pictures at the Tate Gallery.
Birth: Salman Rushdie.

1948
• Exhibits 32 paintings at the Lefevre Gallery, London, in March.
• Commissioned by the Edinburgh Tapestry Company to create a tapestry design.

Assassination of Mahatma Gandhi; première of Laurence Olivier's film version of *Hamlet* in London; release of Michael Powell and Emeric Pressburger's film *The Red Shoes*.
Birth: Bill Woodrow.

1949
• Designs his first tapestry, commissioned and woven by the Edinburgh Tapestry Company, entitled *The Garden of Fools*.

Founding of COBRA (avant-garde art movement); George Orwell, *Nineteen Eighty-Four*.
Death: George Gurdjieff.

1950
• Exhibits 18 paintings at the Heffer Gallery in Cambridge, with works by Francis Rose and Merlyn Evans, organised by Bryan Robertson (January to February).

E. H. Gombrich, *The Story of Art*; release of Buñuel's film *Los Olvidados*; release of Jean Cocteau's film *Orphée*.
Birth: Antony Gormley.

1951
• Exhibits 46 works in the Leicester Galleries with Mary Potter (30 October – 20 November).
• Commutes to London to teach life drawing with Mervyn Peake at the Central School of Art.
• Tate Collection acquires *The Sleeping Fool*.

Opening of Festival of Britain; Ustad Vilayat Khan plays Festival of India in Britain; *The Goon Show*, broadcast on BBC Home Service; Graham Greene, *The End of the Affair*; J.D. Salinger, *The Catcher in the Rye*; C.P. Snow, The Masters.
Birth: Julian Schnabel.

1952
• Travels to south of France with Michael Rothenstein.

Publication in English of *The Diary of Anne Frank*; Samuel Beckett, *Waiting for Godot*; Ernest Hemingway, *The Old Man and the Sea*; John Steinbeck, *East of Eden*.
Death: George VI.

1953
• Exhibits 23 works in October at the Ashmolean Museum in Oxford. Also exhibits as part of the Society of Mural

CECIL COLLINS & CONTEMPORARY EVENTS 1953-1989

Painters at the Royal Institute of British Architects, London, in April.

Coronation of Queen Elizabeth II; first successful ascent of Mount Everest by Sir Edmund Hillary and Tenzing Norgay; Dylan Thomas, *Under Milk Wood*; Francis Bacon, *Study after Velazquez's Portrait of Pope Innocent X*; Francis Crick and James D. Watt publish work on the DNA double helix.
Deaths: Joseph Stalin, Dylan Thomas.

1954
• Collins designs *The Fools of Summer*, woven by Edinburgh Tapestry Company.

Jiddu Krishnamurti, *The First and Last Freedom*; release of Akira Kurosawa's film *The Seven Samurai*.
Birth: Anish Kapoor.
Death: Henri Matisse.

1955
• Around this time, his painting technique changes to using oil paint thinned with turpentine. He starts to develop his 'matrix' process, a new style of painting drawing on the unconscious. It involves using a brush loaded with a different colour in each hand, and then a gestural striking with the paint on to the canvas, with eyes shut

Vladimir Nabokov, *Lolita*; J.R.R. Tolkien, *The Lord of the Rings*; release of Satyajit Ray's first film, *Pather Panchali* (Song of the Little Road).
Deaths: Albert Einstein, Thomas Mann.

1956
• Exhibits 37 works at the Leicester Galleries (February-March), along with Eliot Hodgkin and Terry Frost.
• Edinburgh Weavers produce two linen fabrics by Collins entitled *The Herdsman and The Fools*.

Suez Crisis; Ravi Shankar conducts solo tour of Europe and America.
Birth: Andy Galsworthy.
Death: Jackson Pollock.

1957
• Hears the New Music Ensemble: music composed and conducted by Cornelius Cardew.

Jack Kerouac, *On the Road*; Boris Pasternak, *Dr Zhivago*; Michael Flanders and Donald Swann's two-man revue *At The Drop Of A Hat* opens at the Fortune Theatre, London. Release of *The Seventh Seal* and *Wild Strawberries*, both directed by Ingmar Bergman.
Birth: Mark Wallinger.
Deaths: Constantin Brancusi, O.G.S. Crawford (pioneer in use of aerial photography for archaeological mapping); Wyndham Lewis, Diego Rivera, Jack Butler Yeats.

1958
• Wins £100 prize for his *Christ Before the Judge* in the first John Moores Liverpool Exhibition.
• Visits Aix en Provence in France.
• Hears *Les Dialogues des Carmélites* by Francis Poulenc, libretto by Georges Bernanos, Rafael Kubelik conducting at the Royal Opera House.
• Hears Wagner's *Tristan and Isolde*.
• Hears Wagner's *Die Walküre*, conducted by Rudolph Kemp.

First protest march for the Campaign for Nuclear Disarmament; Aldous Huxley, *Brave New World*; Primo Levi, *If This is a Man*; Claude Levi-Strauss, *Structural Anthropology*.
Birth: Julian Opie.
Death: Rudolf von Laban.

1959
• Designs fabric, commissioned by the Ministry of Works, for the curtains of the new Conference Hall at the British Embassy in Washington, USA. The fabric, entitled *Avon*, is a mix of rayon and cotton, and depicts eight Shakespearean characters.
• Stays in London.
• Collins' first major retrospective: he exhibits 227 works from the years 1928 to 1959 at the Whitechapel Gallery in London (November – December).
• Sir John Rothenstein, *Modern British Painters*, essay on Collins.

Solomon R. Guggenheim Museum designed by Frank Lloyd Wright opens in New York.
Deaths: Jacob Epstein, Stanley Spencer.

1960
• Becomes an official of the Cambridge Society of Painters and Sculptors (founded 1955).
• Introduced to lithography (1960-1965) and helped by Ernest Dalglish.
• Hears Melos Ensemble perform Shostakovitch *Quintet 57 for Piano and Strings* in Cambridge.

The CERN Proton Synchroton particle accelerator inaugurated in Geneva, Switzerland.
Deaths: Albert Camus, Boris Pasternak.

1961
• Meets the poet George Seferis (Greek Ambassador to GB). Exhibits 54 works at the Gallery Zygos, Athens.

Beyond the Fringe opens at the Fortune Theatre; Joseph Heller, *Catch 22*; first English production of Bertolt Brecht's *The Resistible Rise of Arturo Ui*; Yuri Gagarin is first man in space;
Deaths: Ernest Hemingway, Augustus John.

1962
Thomas Kuhn, *The Structure of Scientific Revolutions*; Doris Lessing, *The Golden Notebook*; The Beatles release first single *Love Me Do*.
Deaths: E.E. Cummings, Yves Klein, Franz Kline.

1963
• Gives talk on *Art and Modern Man* at the annual conference of the Centre for Spiritual and Psychological Studies.
• Exhibits in the Carnegie International Exhibition, Pittsburgh, USA.
• Hears the London Mozart Players.

Martin Luther King Jr delivers his 'I have a dream' speech; Karl Popper, *Conjectures and Refutations*; assassination of John F. Kennedy.
Birth: Rachel Whiteread.
Deaths: Georges Braque, Robert Frost, Aldous Huxley, Sylvia Plath.

1964
• Hears the Allegri String Quartet: Mozart, Shostakovich and Beethoven.
• Hears Jehan Alain: *Two Chorals* (1934); Dorien Phrygien organ recital, King's College, Cambridge.

Death: Giorgio Morandi.

1965
• Exhibits 31 works at Arthur Tooth & Sons, London (23 February -13 March).
• Exhibition of his pencil drawings at the Anthony d'Offay Gallery, London.

American combat units deployed to Vietnam.
Birth: Damien Hirst.
Deaths: Winston Churchill, T.S. Eliot.

1966
• Exhibits 57 works at Robin's Croft Chilham Canterbury.
• Hears Segovia at the Royal Festival Hall.
• Hears Oxford Choral Songs by Wilf Mellers.
• Hears the English Opera Group sing *Noye's Fludde* at Southwark Cathedral.
• Hears Nadia Boulanger's Master Classes at the Royal College of Music.
• Attends Beethoven Lectures – symphonies in relation to sketches by Dennis Matthews at British Institute of Recorded Sound.
• Attends Ceremony of Whirling Mevlevis at the Oriental Centre, Carlton House Terrace.

Truman Capote, *In Cold Blood*; Tom Stoppard, *Rosencranz and Guildenstern are Dead*.
Death: Alberto Giacometti.

1967
• Exhibits 26 works at the Crane Kalman Gallery, London.

World premiere of Karlheinz Stockhausen's *Hymnen in Cologne*; Alan Garner, *The Owl Service*; Gabriel Garcia Marquez, *One Hundred Years of Solitude*; Pink Floyd release debut album *The Piper At The Gates Of Dawn*.

1968
• Commissioned by Oxford University Press to make pencil drawings to illustrate *Psalms, The Book of Ezekiel and Song of Solomon* for the Oxford Illustrated Old Testament.

Martin Luther King Jr shot dead in Memphis, Tennessee; anti-Vietnam war demonstration in London; student protests in Paris; anti-Soviet demonstrations in Prague.
Deaths: Marcel Duchamp, Mervyn Peake.

1969
• Attended International Congress convened by Pir Vilayat Khan (Sufi teacher) at the Royal Overseas League.

Apollo moon landing; first broadcast of *Monty Python's Flying Circus* on BBC; International Interfaith Congress convened by Pir Vilayat Khan (Sufi mystic master) at the Royal Overseas League.
Deaths: Otto Dix, Walter Gropius, Ludwig Mies van der Rohe.

chronology

1970
- Starts teaching drawing at the City Literary Institute, London.
- Gives lecture on *My Week as an Artist* to slides of his painting at the College of Psychic Studies. Moves to London.

Concorde makes first supersonic flight.
Deaths: Hein Heckroth, Mark Rothko, Bertrand Russell.

1971
- Exhibits 30 paintings at Arthur Tooth & Sons (28 September -16 October).
- Exhibits as part of Britain's Contribution to Surrealism at the Hamet Gallery, London (among the exhibitors are Eileen Agar, Julian Trevelyan, Humphrey Jennings, Ceri Richards, Edward Burra, Henry Moore and Paul Nash).

John Updike, Rabbit Redux.

1972
- Exhibits 62 works in his retrospective at the Hamet Gallery (1 -25 November).
- Meets composer Karlheinz Stockhausen.
- Visits Mark Rothko exhibition at the Hayward Gallery, London
- Hears concert of Steve Reich's *Drumming*.
- Hears Messiaen's *Vingt regards sur l'enfant Jesu* at Queen Elizabeth Hall.

1972-73
- Attends various lectures at the British Institute of Recorded Sound: on Debussy; on Webern by Peter Stadlen; on preserving wildlife sounds; on Ravel by Angus Morrison.

Bloody Sunday: 13 unarmed marchers killed in Derry, Northern Ireland.
Death: Ezra Pound.

1973
- Attends meeting of Research Into Lost Knowledge Organisation (RILKO)
- On 3 November, his altarpiece, *The Icon of Divine Light* is consecrated in the Chapel of St Clement in Chichester Cathedral. His wife Elisabeth designed the kneelers for the chapel.
- Attends Dalai Lama service for all faiths at West London Synagogue.
- Attends Royal College of Music Master Classes.
- Attends English Bach Festival.
- Attends Lennox Berkeley's 70th Concert.

United Kingdom, Republic of Ireland and Denmark enter European Community, which later becomes the European Union; Pink Floyd release Dark Side of the Moon.
Deaths: W.H. Auden, Pablo Neruda, Pablo Picasso.

1974
Watergate scandal; President Nixon resigns.

1975
- The Central School of Art asks him to retire, but their decision is rescinded after students' demonstrations. Henry Moore organises an official petition in his support.
- Lectures at Tate and Dartington Hall.
- Attends Mahmud Mirza all night concert.

Ruth Prawer Jhabvala, *Heat and Dust*; release of first Monty Python film, *Monty Python and the Holy Grail*.
Death: Barbara Hepworth.

1976
- Exhibits 26 works at the Anthony d'Offay Gallery in London (24 June -23 July).

1977
J.M. Coetzee, In the Heart of the Country; Pompidou Centre opens in Paris.
Deaths: Max Ernst, Man Ray, Mark Tobey.

1978
- Arts Council commission film on Collins, *The Eye of the Heart* by Stephen Cross.

Iris Murdoch, *The Sea, The Sea*; David Hare, *Plenty*.
Death: F.R. Leavis.

1979
- Awarded MBE.
- Publication of *Cecil Collins: Painter of Paradise* by Kathleen Raine.

Margaret Thatcher becomes prime minister.

1980
Deaths: Oskar Kokoschka, Henry Miller, Jean-Paul Sartre.

1981
- Exhibits 55 prints at the Tate Gallery, London (5 August – 1 November).
- Exhibits 73 works at the Anthony d'Offay Gallery (21 October – 14 November).
- Interviewed by Edward Lucie-Smith for the BBC Radio Programme, *Conversations with Artists*.
- Reissue of *Vision of the Fool*.
- Publication of Collins' book of poems (1940-1981), *In The Solitude Of This Land*.
- *Temenos* publishes a conversation with the artist entitled *Theatre of the Soul*.
- Exhibition at the Tate Gallery, *The Prints of Cecil Collins* curated and catalogue by Richard Morphet.

Lady Diana Spencer marries Charles, Prince of Wales; Salman Rushdie, *Midnight's Children*.
Death: Queenie Leavis.

1982
Falklands War (2 April – 14 June).
Death: Ben Nicholson.

1983
- Exhibits 40 works at the Plymouth Arts Centre (November – December).

Deaths: Nikolaus Pevsner, Joan Miró.

1984
- Exhibits 44 works at the Festival Gallery in Aldeburgh, Suffolk (9 – 24 June).

Turner Prize awarded for the first time: Malcolm Morley wins; Provisional IRA attempts to assassinate British cabinet in the Brighton hotel bombing; Anita Brookner, *Hotel du Lac*; Marguerite Duras, *L'Amant*; Milan Kundera, *The Unbearable Lightness of Being*.
Death: Lee Krasner.

1985
- On 1 November, consecration of his side windows commissioned for All Saints Church, Basingstoke, Hampshire.
- Hears Harmonic Choir of New York: *Hearing Solar Winds* by David Hykes, director and composer.

Mikhail Gorbachev becomes leader of Soviet Union; Margaret Atwood, *The Handmaid's Tale*; Gabriel Garcia Marquez, *Love in the Time of Cholera*.
Deaths: Marc Chagall, Robert Graves.

1986
- Lectures at Dartington, Devon.
- Exhibits in The Temenos Exhibition at Dartington, Devon.
- Hears Olivier Messiaen, *Bel canto*, London.

Turner Prize awarded to Gilbert and George; Musée d'Orsay opens in Paris; Richard Dawkins, *The Blind Watchmaker*.
Deaths: Georgia O'Keefe, Henry Moore.

1987
- Exhibits 19 works in *A Paradise Lost: The Neo-Romantic Imagination in Britain, 1935-55* at the Barbican Art Gallery, London.

Bruce Chatwin, *The Songlines*; Penelope Lively, *Moon Tiger*; Tom Wolfe, *The Bonfire of the Vanities*.
Deaths: William Coldstream, Ernö Goldfinger, Andy Warhol.

1988
- Collins' eightieth birthday is celebrated at the Central School of Art, Chelsea Arts Club and the Royal College of Art. Elected to Royal Academy.
- Exhibits 32 paintings at the Anthony d'Offay Gallery (1 -23 June).
- On 26 May, consecration of his west window, *The Mystery of the Holy Spirit*, commissioned for All Saints Church, Basingstoke, Hampshire.
- Publication of *Cecil Collins: The Quest for Great Happiness* by William Anderson.
- February: *Sacrum Convivium* for four-part choir
- Hears *Hymn to the Holy Spirit* by John Tavener, London.

Anti-government demonstrations in Burma; Benazir Bhutto becomes Prime Minister of Pakistan; Paulo Coelho, *The Alchemist*; Umberto Eco, *Foucault's Pendulum*; Stephen Hawking, *A Brief History of Time*; Salman Rushdie, *The Satanic Verses*.

1989
- Exhibits 147 works in the Tate Gallery, London, *Cecil Collins: A Retrospective Exhibition;* curated and catalogue by Dr Judith Collins.
- Dies in London on 4 June.

1989
Martin Amis, *London Fields*; Tiananmen Square massacre in Beijing, known in Chinese as the June 4th Incident.
Deaths: Bruce Chatwin, Salvador Dali, Daphne du Maurier, Stella Gibbons.

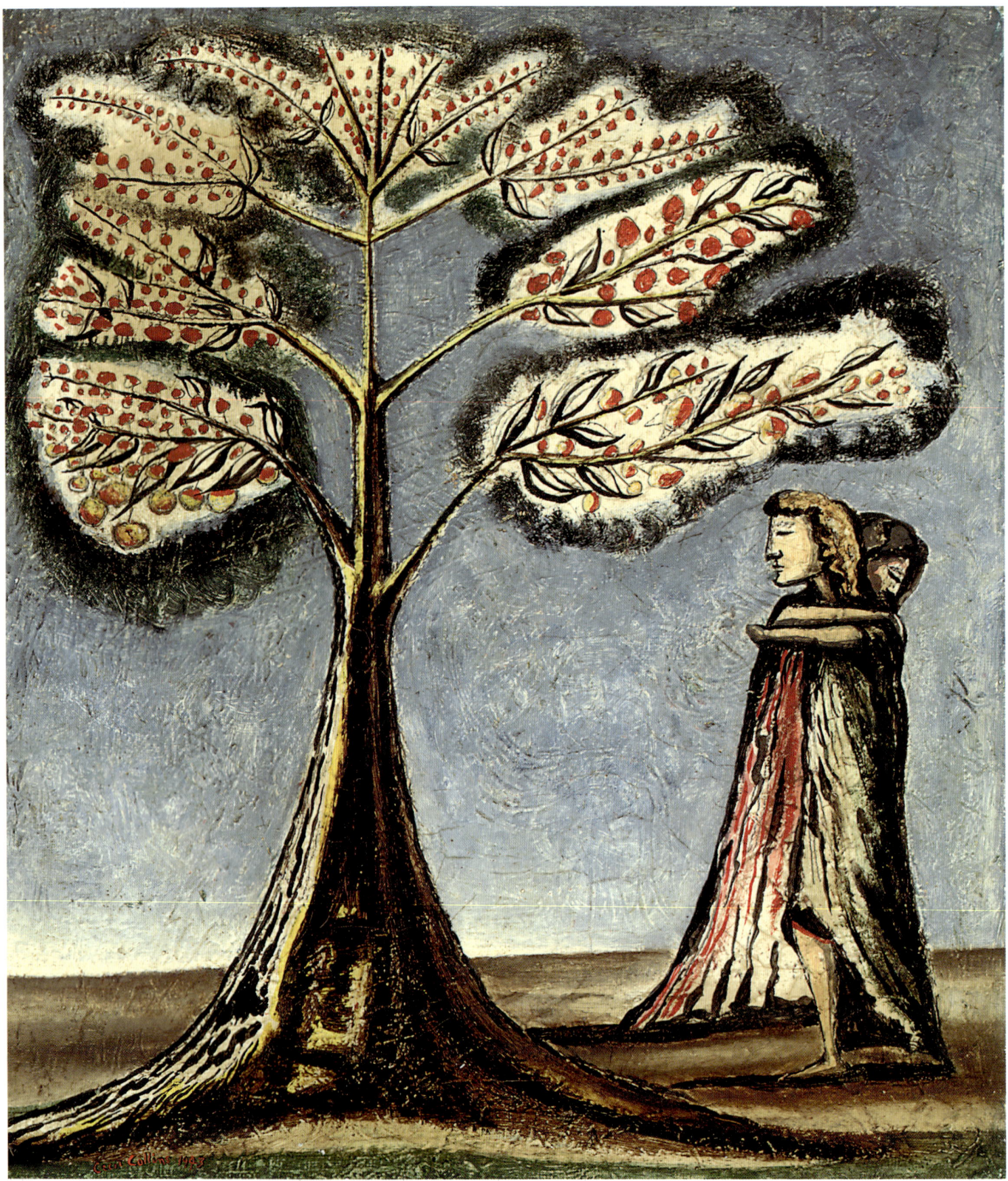

INTRODUCTION

I am extremely timid, sensitive, impressionable, with a great sense of mortality, lazy. Yet inside me there is another self completely unmoved by all this, full of power and light.
Cecil Collins

Cecil Collins was extraordinary, not only as a man and visionary artist but also as an original and inspiring educator. This portrait of him, in the words of his admirers, colleagues, critics, curators, friends and students, bears witness to his importance and the continuing relevance of his art and teaching.

I never supposed I would be creating a book about Cecil, (as he was known to us all). The project started when my own students were told I was retiring and asked if there was anything they could read about the Cecil Collins' system of teaching to which I'd introduced them in my classes. I thought I might put something together for them from my own abundant notes of many years teaching art, according to what I had learnt during my five years' study with Cecil.

The idea of making a portrait, a mosaic in words, with the reflections and memories of his students and friends, arose from an experience I'd had after my mother died. We had organized a tea party to celebrate her ninety-year life. More than a hundred and fifty friends and family of all ages had come from the four corners of the world. At one moment, looking at them all, I had the sense that each one who had known and loved her was, like a hologram, a fragment reflecting the whole woman, as if her presence or spirit having left her frail body had now expanded into all the people united there that day.

There are a number of excellent books on Cecil, as well as scholarly catalogues for his various exhibitions, but I felt this compilation was the way to convey his vitality of spirit and sense of fun. Like many of his students, I thought it was important to preserve our experiences of him for the future in gratitude for all this exceptional, humorous and humane being had given us.

Even when people were resistant or felt doubts about him, their contact with him had a distinct impact on their lives. The reactions and experiences were by no means uniform. They ranged from adulatory or grateful to disillusioned or angry, but never indifference. Most striking of all was the outpouring of love and respect for Cecil expressed by almost everyone.

The structure of this book in some ways emulates Cecil's approach to his paintings: the pictorial elements organized as musical chord progressions and the development in his art of a theme with variations. His presence is recreated by a chorus of voices: the many contributors. Each person's remembrance of Cecil constitutes an act of imaginative re-creation, of identifying his qualities within their own experience and self-knowledge. Most of them continue to speak of Cecil in the present tense; he is still alive in us, although it is almost twenty years since he died. For myself, I wish that I could talk to him again, now that I have a little more understanding of what I learnt through him.

James Henry Cecil Collins was born on 23 March 1908, in Plymouth of Cornish parents. His mother encouraged her only child's creativity, and in later years, she herself took to making bold drawings directly onto the walls of her flat.

Cecil suffered much ill-health as a child, and consequently, spent very little time, if any, at school. He was free to wander in the woods and fields behind their house on the edge of the city. A boy of great sensitivity and imagination, he learnt to read with his mother from the Bible, so his intellectual development was formed by and steeped in the wisdom of these spiritual stories. Although untutored, he spent time playing the piano in the front parlour and listening to the sounds fade into silence. This, he thought, 'was another world into which it might be possible to enter.'

Cecil Collins
Morning
1943
Oil on canvas
35.5 x 30.5cm

When he was very young and had to rest in the afternoons, he remembered once watching a white cloud pass across the window. The cloud seemed reflected in his white counterpane and became, for him, an entrance to Paradise. Such symbolic small white clouds, which enhance the perfection of an otherwise cloudless sky, often occur in his art.

By the age of fourteen, he was a superb draughtsman and drew a self-portrait of astonishing precocity. His determination to become an artist had been disapproved of by his father, who worked in a Plymouth laundry and had apprenticed Cecil to a motor engineering firm at the docks, which Cecil very quickly abandoned to pursue his art.

Fortunately, his artistic gifts were recognised early. He won scholarships to the Plymouth School of Art and subsequently to the Royal College of Art. There he was considered a genius by his contemporaries and the 'golden boy' of the principal, William Rothenstein. Cecil said that although at Plymouth art college he had learnt about art, he learnt how to be an artist from Rothenstein.

At the RCA Cecil met Elisabeth Ramsden. She was the eldest daughter of a Yorkshire newspaper proprietor and had overcome her parents' objections to her studying sculpture. In 1931, the year Cecil graduated, Elisabeth defied her parents and married Cecil. His mother opposed the match (his father had died in 1927) partly out of her Cornish suspicion of the English. All this would have enhanced the young couple's lifelong rejection of authority and conventionality.

Elisabeth was Cecil's muse and support throughout his life. As one contributor expressed it, 'Cecil was Elisabeth's vocation.' She devoted herself to caring for him and enabling him to continue manifesting his visionary works of art. Elisabeth only developed her own art with great success in the last decade of her life, after Cecil's death. She exhibited at the Jane England Gallery who sold four of her works to the Tate Gallery when she was ninety-four years old.

Elisabeth and Cecil had nicknames for each other. Elisabeth called Cecil 'Parc', short for parcel, because she thought, 'he looked like a badly done up parcel with bits of string falling off it'. Cecil's nickname for Elisabeth was 'Bell', but no one could remember what it stood for. Then I finally found my jotted note from when Elisabeth had told me it was short for Bell-buoy. This seems to indicate Cecil's acknowledgment of the role Elisabeth played in his life, since it has the connotation of buoyed up; keeping afloat; serving as a navigation mark or for mooring.

On leaving college Cecil enjoyed immediate success with his first solo exhibition in 1935 at the Bloomsbury Gallery in London. Already, at this early stage, Cecil articulated what remained his life-long orientation, 'My works are visual music of the kingdoms of the imagination. There is in all human beings a secret personal life – untouched, protected – won from communal life ... It is this sensitive life which my art is created to feed and sustain, this real life deep in each person. Thus my art is truly functional.'

Cecil continued to exhibit regularly for most of his life and was never without a circle of devoted admirers and discriminating collectors. These included Lord Kenneth Clark, Sir Stephen Spender and Bryan Robertson, Director of the Whitechapel Gallery, who gave him a retrospective show there in 1959. Awarded an MBE in 1979 and elected Royal Academician in 1988, he had to wait until just before he died in 1989 for his Tate Retrospective. In 2008, his birth centenary year, he is being honoured again by Tate Britain with a room display. Cecil did not fit easily into the categories beloved by art historians. Frances Spalding could find no a slot for him in her survey of British Art since 1900, so she left him out. She now admits this was a grave omission and says, 'It is hard to think of [Collins'] equal in contemporary art, in terms of poetic concentration'.

Though his art and life were so concerned with paradise, Cecil was skilled at living in the world. He was very much in the world, even if he was an outsider. Although he has been relatively neglected by the art establishment, he had the necessary 'shard of steel' which his contemporary, the novelist Graham Greene, claimed

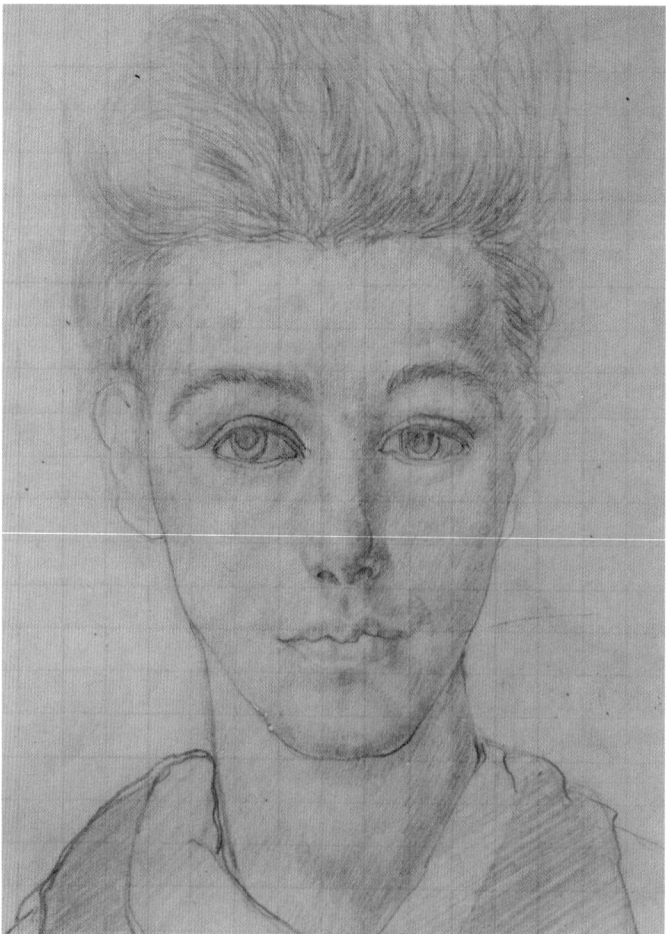

Cecil Collins
Self Portrait
c.1922
Pencil on paper

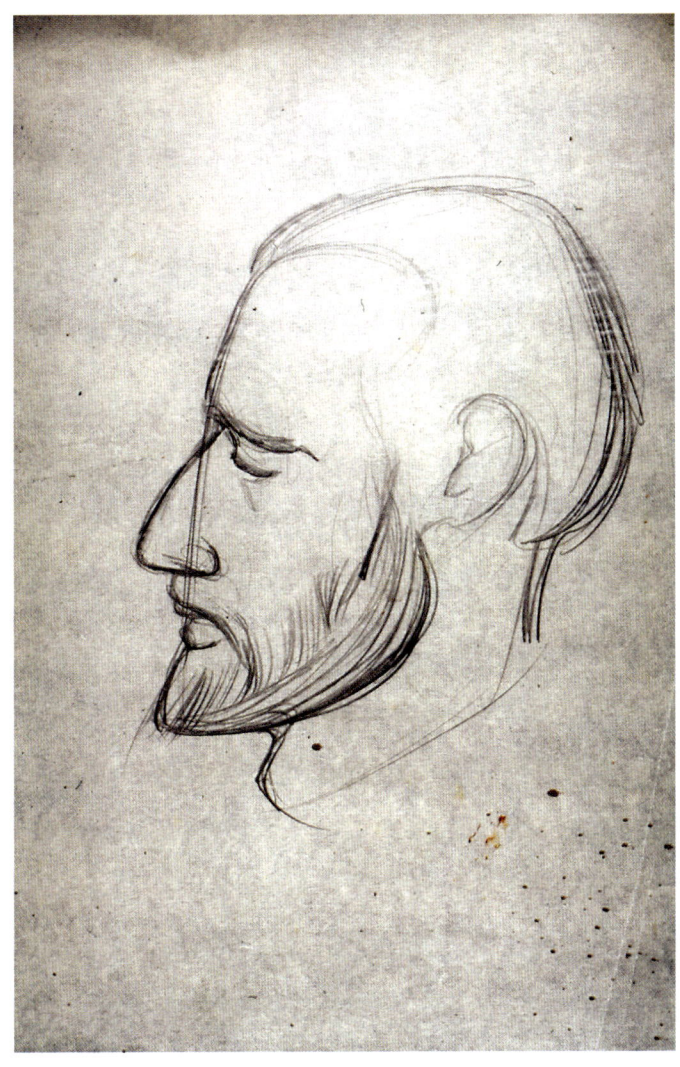

Mark Tobey
Portrait of Cecil Collins
1938
Pencil on paper

was essential for bringing creative work into the public sphere.

Cecil Collins' art often has an extraordinary luminosity, although it is not sensually seductive. Instead, his pictures evoke another kingdom beyond the five senses. This other dimension is accessible to everyone as it contains, and is the fundamental basis of, the illusory world we habitually assume is all there must be to reality. This is neither necessarily comfortable, nor safe. Cecil invites viewers to step out of their small, egotistical concerns and to become involved in what he presents in his work. His paintings, prints and drawings are not illustrative, as some have claimed, but visual, metaphorical narratives comparable to the great tradition of sacred art. Such images focus on reminding us of our connection in the smallest particulars to the divine mystery of life. Cecil has brought to such intimations a pictorial idiom for today, drawn from his own experience and transmutation of personal suffering. Cecil stated that his 'paintings were a theatre of the soul. ....an evocation of [the] inner world, the fragrance of it. A painting ... is a metaphysical experience – it re-enacts the mystery of life.'

Several factors played an important role in Cecil's life. He was six when World War One broke out and in his twenties when World War Two occurred although because of his frail physique he was never called up.

He was deeply troubled by the turbulence of his times. His response was the work for which he is best known, the *Holy Fool* series of paintings, drawings and an essay which he later re-titled *The Vision of the Fool*. This was begun early in 1940, a few months after war was declared. In it, Cecil lays out his vocation as an artist and his belief in the sacred role of artists in society. 'The Saint, the artist and the poet are all one in the Fool, but the Fool is more than this, he is the sorrow of life. ... I believe that there is in life and in the human psyche, a certain quality, an inviolate eternal innocence, and this quality I call the Fool. It is a continuous wisdom and compassion that heals with fun and magic.'

Another source of importance for Cecil was the ancient Celtic culture in which he was embedded as a child. Cecil would have been familiar with such tales as the Cornish love story of Tristan and Iseult. Elisabeth was, for Cecil, a version of this beautiful heroine, whose name means 'she who is to be gazed upon'. While he, like Tristan, meaning sadness, was often melancholy:

'How often, have we, in secret,

wept over you,

O Face of Paradise.'

The Grail legend had great significance for Cecil. A chalice symbolizing the Grail occurs in many of his paintings and he also knew the lovely poem of Sir Gawain and the Green Knight. The valour, loyalty and love of Sir Gawain are tested by the enigmatic Green Knight whose source may be Khidr, or the Green Ancient, who represents the vital inner dimension which transcends form. In one of Cecil's most important paintings, *The Artist and his Wife*, 1939, there is a chalice on the sacramental table between the couple and he has depicted himself wearing a green suit. When Judith Collins, the curator of his Tate Retrospective, asked whether he had, in fact, owned such a suit, Cecil replied, 'I had the suit made from cloth specially woven in Scotland to my specification, because I wanted to be the Green Man.'

In 1943 Cecil completed the relatively small, but powerful, painting *The Pilgrim Fool*. This was made in reaction to the terrible bombings of Plymouth. It shows a Fool with the Pilgrim's shell emblem of St James of Compostello on his tight fitting trousers. He leads a small girl away from a burning city on the horizon. For Cecil, 'the female child represented his own soul, his anima, the most valuable of his possessions which he is saving from destruction and violence.' The Anima figure in Cecil's work was for him the sacred mystery of the soul, represented by the form and energy of the feminine. She also appears as the Sybil, the High Priestess and the

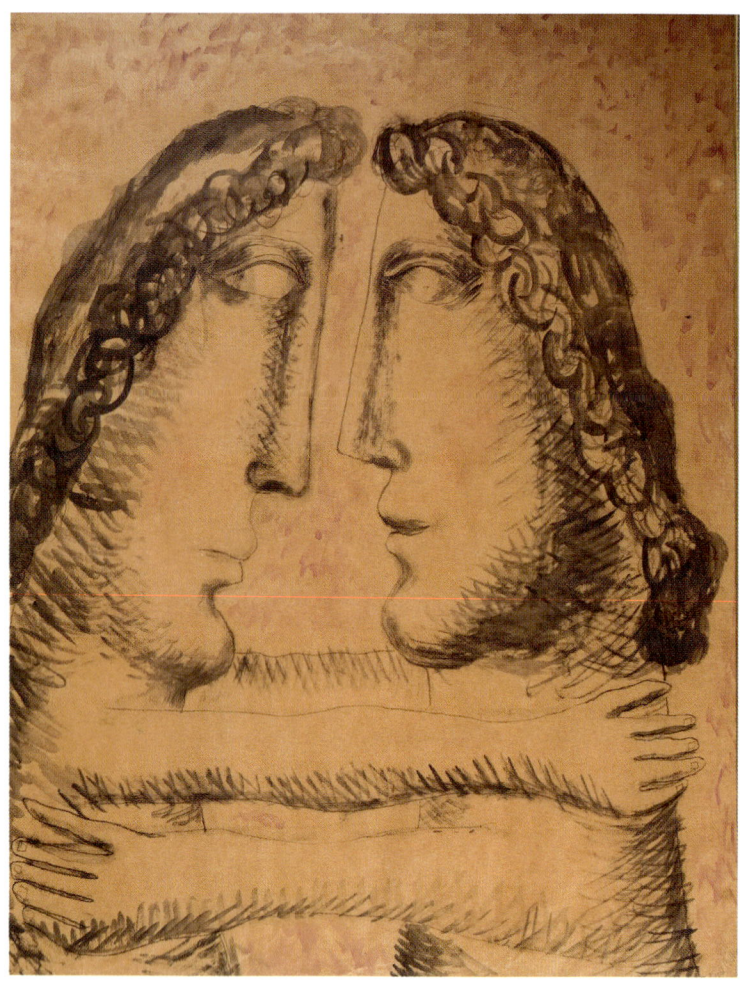

ancient Tarot symbols, particularly the Fool. His theme of the unifying force of love mirrors the charming image, *In Concordiam Populi*, reproduced here, from a later fifteenth century English popular pocket calendar. The wonderful altar frontal *The Icon of Divine Light*, created by Cecil in 1973 for Chichester Cathedral, shows correspondences to, and certain awareness of, the encyclopaedic *Utriusque Cosmi* of 1617 by the mystic physician Robert Fludd, also illustrated here. For Cecil, as for Fludd, Divine Light was a transformative and active principle of creation.

He was fully aware of the many contemporary art movements and shared with the Rumanian sculptor, Constantin Brancusi (1876-1957), not only a love of traditional art, but also a resilience to passing art fashions and a mystical concentration on finding the divine essence behind appearances. Both men worked with a few themes developed over time, as is expressed in the 1907 version of *The Kiss* by Brancusi and Cecil's *Anima and Animus* created in 1933. These are images of complete unity, eternal oneness, through and beyond the duality of union or differences of gender.

Cecil was extremely well read and, what he did not read himself, he absorbed from listening to his wide circle of friends. These included the poet and William Blake scholar, Kathleen Raine, with whom, from 1970, he and Elisabeth shared a house in Chelsea in south-west London. Another friend was Philip Sherrard the scholar, theologian and translator of modern Greek poets. The physicist Glen Schaefer, drew Cecil's attention to the convergence of scientific thought with ancient mystic understanding. The composers John Tavener and Karlheinz Stockhausen were also close friends.

Like many brilliant people, Cecil had the ability to absorb information at such speed that later it was not always possible for him to distinguish where his ideas had originated. When appropriate, he enjoyed creating a mystery about his sources and painting techniques.

Cecil had also read widely in the metaphysical poets and studied many of the mystic traditions of Buddhism, Christianity, Hinduism, Jewish Kabala wisdom, the Neo-Platonic tradition and Sufism. He admired in particular the Bahá'í Faith of universal oneness to which he was introduced by the American artist, Mark Tobey, considered the founder of Abstract Expressionism. Cecil had the highest regard him although he dismissed Jackson Pollack as puerile.

Cecil and Elisabeth had become friends with Tobey in 1934 after meeting him at his exhibition in London. Following their visit to

Angel. Cecil said Angels 'are the winged thoughts of the Divine Mind.' All carried the face of Elisabeth.

Cecil's art could be seen as an extended declaration of the love inspired in him by Elisabeth during their union of almost sixty years, but at a subtler level his paintings and drawings also depicted the unfolding development of his spiritual quest rather as Dante described in relation to his beloved Beatrice.

Cecil's work is often compared to that of Blake and Palmer because they are all English visionary artists. In fact, Cecil's drew inspiration from a much wider and more archaic field of art and mystical references. These included Byzantine sacred art, which can be seen in his use of disembodied hands and heads with rays emanating from them, as well as in the iconic and hieratical nature of much of his work. Cecil's deep concern with the underlying unity of all apparently opposing energies is beautifully expressed in his painting *Morning* of 1943, which reflects his love of early Renaissance art. It shares a quality of visual poetry with the painting by the Sienese unknown master, shown here, of the hermit St Anthony meeting St Paul.

Cecil was very interested in folk art and familiar with the

Cecil Collins
Anima and Animus
1933
Pen and ink with watercolour wash on paper
71 x 53cm

Constantin Brancusi
(1876-1957)
The Kiss,
1907
stone
© ADAGP, Paris and DACS, London 2008.

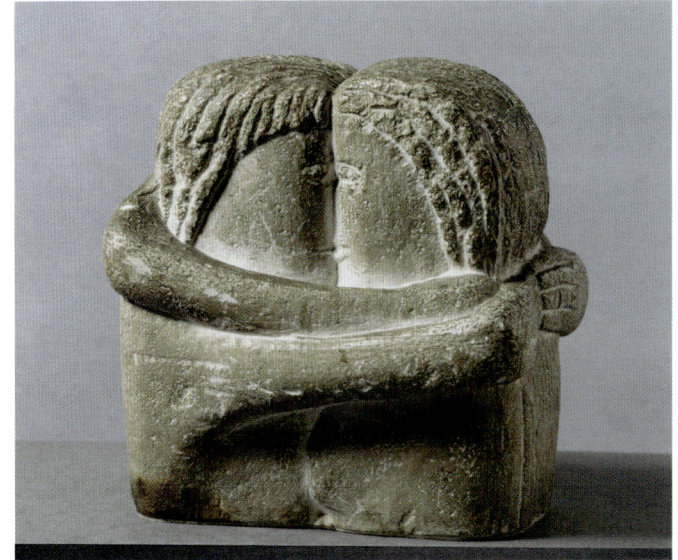

him at Dartington Hall, Devon, where he was teaching art, they settled in nearby Totnes in 1936. Three years later, at the outbreak of World War Two, Cecil and Elisabeth moved to Dartington. The owners, Dorothy and Leonard Elmhirst, had created a vibrant centre for the arts and ran their estate on Utopian ideals greatly influenced by their friend, the Bengali polymath, Rabindranath Tagore (1861-1941). Cecil would have been familiar with their collection of Tagore's paintings. Cecil may also have come into contact with the writings of Tagore through Sir William Rothenstein to whom Tagore had dedicated his 1913 Nobel Prize-winning poem, *Gitanjali (Song of Offerings)*. This had been translated by Tagore into English with an introduction by William Butler Yeats. Cecil learnt about Eastern philosophy, literature and art through Tobey, as well as another school staff member, the potter, Bernard Leach, and from a frequent visitor to Dartington, Arthur Waley, the translator of Chinese poetry.

Cecil and Elisabeth benefited from the stimulating company of the wide variety of creative European exiles at Dartington, including the innovative dance company, Ballet Jooss, co-founded by Kurt Jooss and the theatre designer, Hein Heckroth. Cecil and Elisabeth took part in the preparations for productions and assisted at rehearsals. One of the props, a paper crown made for one of the characters, appears frequently in Cecil's images of Fools.

The former teacher of Jooss, the dance choreologist Rudolf van Laban, also joined the Dartington community. From him Cecil learnt about the relationship of creativity to rhythm and gestural movement. Later this and music, which was of central importance throughout Cecil's life, were incorporated into his teaching.

As a result of the outbreak of the war, all the refugees left or were interned. Cecil was invited to take over the art teaching and so began to develop this most important aspect of his creative life. In the beautiful grounds of the estate, Cecil had a visionary confirmation of his childhood awareness of what he called 'the eternal in the particular'. He related how late one afternoon, after a shower, the light of the setting sun shone through the raindrops on the leaves of a small tree on top of which a thrush was singing. Cecil realized that the tree was the shape of the birdsong. This numinous experience inspired several of Cecil's most beautiful drawings.

During this period in Devon, Cecil also produced some of his greatest paintings, including *The Artist and his Wife, The Quest, The Voice* and *Dawn*. Elisabeth, freed from domestic chores, took up painting and produced an image of a wounded Fool during a class with Tobey. Hein Heckroth saw Elisabeth's painting and 'was enchanted'. As she later described, 'He eagerly talked about the Fool and its implications, about the need for magic in our time, and from that day Cecil's Fool work started.'

In 1943, the Collinses left Dartington for London and Cecil's painting, *The Sleeping Fool,* was bought by Sir John Rothenstein for the Contemporary Art Society. This 1943 work was later presented by the Society to the Tate Gallery. It was their first acquisition of Cecil's work. They now own seventy-five.

Cecil and Elisabeth became acquainted with the Apocalypse group of poets in Oxford, which included Alex Comfort and the composer/publisher Conrad Senat. In 1946, under the imprint Counterpoint Publications, Senat published the first book on Cecil's work, written by Comfort. On revisiting the city years later Cecil commented to a friend, 'Cambridge is so hygienic; Oxford is redolent of evil. I think I could really work here.' He added, 'Do you realise that owing to the absence of moral standards, the student today can't even sin?'

In Concordiam Populo
English calendar
c.1350-90s

Instead by 1948, Cecil and Elisabeth at last settled in Cambridge and became friends with Bryan Robertson, director of the Heffer Gallery. There, in 1950, Cecil exhibited his work. Robertson later remembered Elisabeth's gaiety and how they both seemed unworldly and yet sophisticated. Although initially Robertson thought Cecil was almost stiflingly self-centred, Robertson soon found him totally engaging because of his wide reading, multiplicity of interests, his sweet nature and, above all, his distinctive, lunatic sense of humour. Robertson recalled that at parties Cecil, spectacled and bearded, would perform what appeared to be an amazing trick. He would put his head round the door wearing a pith helmet and look goggle-eyed at the company. An arm, apparently disembodied but in fact his own, would shoot round from behind the door and pull his head out of sight, like a failed cabaret turn being hauled off-stage.

Robertson also remembered that as soon as Cecil saw a friend in the street, he would start to slink against the wall like a mad burlesque of a Bolshevik spy with his hat pulled even further down over dark glasses, collar pulled up. With conspiratorial backward glances, he would clutch his attaché case to his chest as if it contained a bomb. It probably contained a sandwich and a book.

In 1950, Cecil was invited by William Johnston, Principal of the Central School of Art, to teach there part-time. Cecil commuted weekly to London for the next twenty years until he and Elisabeth moved to Paultons Square in Chelsea. At first, Cecil was joint tutor of life classes with Mervyn Peake. A contributor, who was one of their models, remembers Cecil doing all the teaching and Peake sitting drawing.

In the Tate Archive I found the copious preparatory notes Cecil had made in his earliest years of teaching. These included instructions to himself such as:

'Don't go round often looking at the students' work. Try and make it once in the morning, once in the afternoon, near the end of each class.'

'Don't stand about talking, sit as much as possible. Stay seated in the corner.'

'Give the students tasks to do to concentrate on; good solid, long-lasting tasks, not many ideas.'

'Don't teach, it's as bad for you as for them, encourage only.'

I was fascinated by this evidence that Cecil had so consciously developed his exceptional method of education.

My first experience of Cecil's classes happened after the artist, Jacqueline Warner, told me that he was teaching round the corner from my studio in Covent Garden. I attended the six- week summer course Cecil gave on colour, held in a rather chaotic studio on the top floor of the City Lit building. I remember well the bewilderment and excitement of those first lessons. The sensation of 'coming home' is often described by other students. For me it was the feeling of freedom, of a re-connection to childhood delight in an adventure into the unknown which overlaid all other impressions. I felt that I had found a sanctuary, an understanding and permission to relate to colour as song, which was my earliest relationship to it. I had felt obliged to hide this attitude of love and joy in the 'Kitchen Sink' climate prevailing at St Martin's School of Art in the late 1950s.

When I first saw Cecil he looked like a heap of old clothes in the corner of the room on a worn out studio chair. Even so he emanated great authority and an atmosphere of intense concentration and attention. His voice was rather quiet with a trace of an indefinable country burr. At the beginning of each class, he stood up to give a short talk and an explanation of the colour triads to be worked with that day. He described colours in terms of families, parents, children and grandchildren, and wrote diagrammatically on the blackboard the sequence we were to follow in mixing up the colours. This was to allow us to explore their relationships in a series of discs with various combinations. The astonishing fact about the mixtures we created with the same very basic powder gouache paint was how varied were the shades we produced and how completely individual their

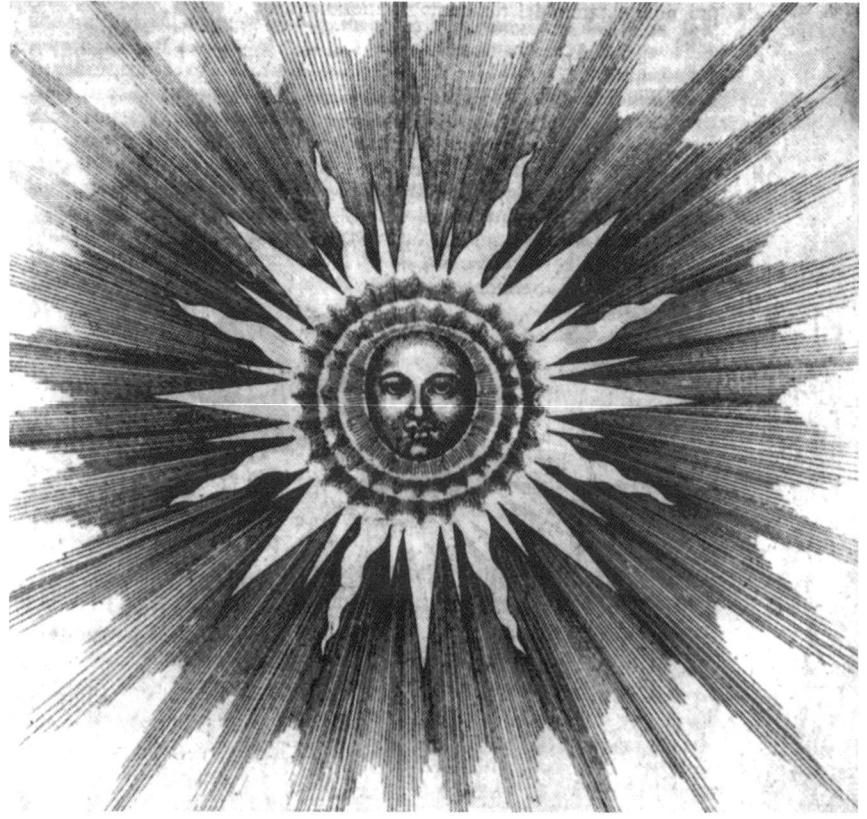

Robert Fludd
Utriusque Cosmi
1617

Sienese Master of the Osservanza
The Meeting of Saint Anthony and Saint Paul
c.1420-1440s
Tempera on panel
47 x 33.5cm

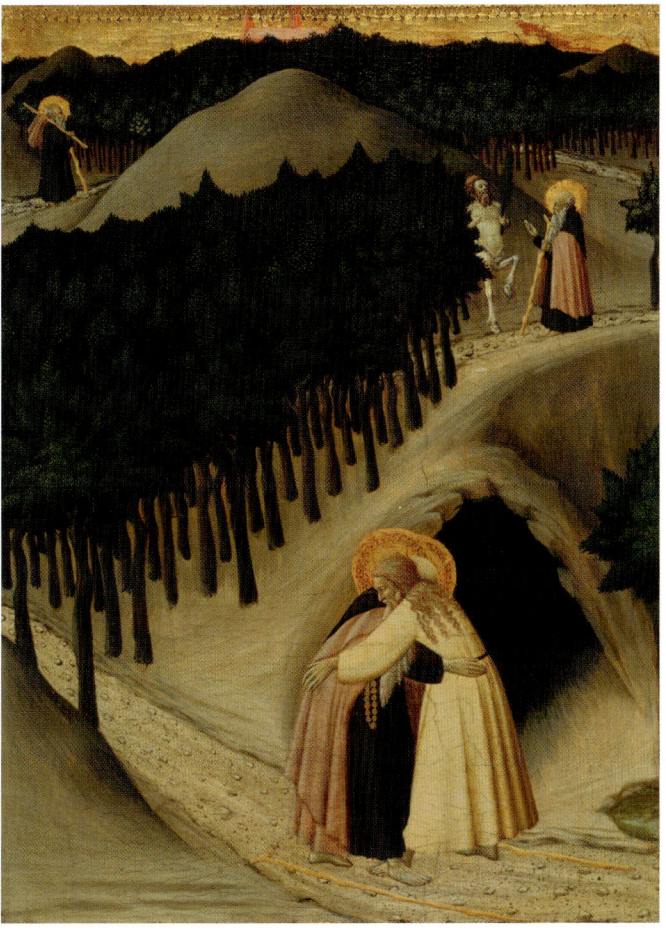

positions they were to be held in. In addition he stipulated exactly which of the gradation of seven tones, mixed from black ink and water, we were to use for each instrument. We were also told how to hold the instruments with not only one or both hands, but also toes or mouth and sometimes all together. This induced much laughter. Sometimes we used simply our fingers or the side of our hands with the particular movement he indicated.

Cecil emphasised the unity of all energies that appeared in opposition: feminine or masculine, horizontal or vertical, crystallised and rigid or flowing and gentle, light or heavy and dark. These were related to the instruments, how we held them what gestures we used and the marks they made. The feather end of the quill was feminine, the nib end masculine, as was the reed pen; the pencil could be both, and the Chinese brushes were feminine. The charcoal could be used with a masculine gesture, but was generally more feminine; the red Conté crayon like charcoal could be used in either mode and also added a note of colour. Each class, although intense and inspiring, was also immense fun and full of lovely surprises.

We learnt about courtesy and its etymological root in cor, the Latin word for 'heart'; the importance of vulnerability instead of defensiveness and greed, the beauty and primacy of relating to each other, to the instruments and paper, to ourselves and to everything. Cecil often instructed us to lie face down on the dirty floor, surrendering to something greater than our petty self-regarding concerns. When he made us work in pairs, we learnt to accept our limitations and failings, as well as those of others.

Throughout the lessons, Cecil encouraged us to move and be moved by music he had carefully selected. This music was almost all based on the perfect harmonies of the Golden Ratio, which gave it an otherworldly symmetry. We listened, among others, to Chopin's *Nocturnes*, Debussy's *La Mer*, Eric Satie, Barber, du Parc songs, Lily Boulanger, Rachmaninov, Vaughan Willliams, the *tintinnabulation* of Arvo Pärt and the birdsong of Olivier Messiaen. All this, too, we absorbed.

Cecil rarely made comments on our work and didn't explain his system; it unfolded in our own experience of it, according to our stage of development. He had a compelling presence and shared truthfully his own hard-won discoveries. His humour and quick wit came not from cleverness, but from a completely different direction: unpremeditated, spontaneous, never destructive or for effect simply a response to something he'd seen as absurd.

His teaching was always based on his own experiences of art and life; what he said could be trusted. His way of being and acting and his certainty of vision exemplified what he taught us about creativity. It was a spiritual training about the necessity of whole-hearted attention, through the discipline of our art practice, to find our own connection with the unity of all life.

presentation on the paper. It was like the signature of each student.

The vibrations inherent in colours, Cecil taught us, evoked atmospheres relating to different times of the day and night and could be grouped according to their affinities with the masculine or feminine qualities and energies. Cecil's colour spectrum was all-inclusive, unlike the scientific one which excluded black and white. These he always insisted were not 'exercises' but explorations of their harmonies and transformations in relation to each other. In the ensuing classes he would always ask if any 'discoveries' had been made as a result of the previous week's explorations. The whole course was like an Advent calendar, with each week's theme opening a window onto a new and yet, once opened, familiar vision of deep inner meaning.

Cecil's drawing course was so popular and over-subscribed that I had to queue outside the City Lit from four in the morning until the doors opened at half past nine. Then having been given a ticket had to queue again and was fortunate to have my application accepted. In these classes I found a completely different universe from the summer course. Although as before he remained quietly in his corner, his instructions were so varied and fast that one had no time to think or to judge. It was an effort to keep up and not misunderstand the precise combination of instruments and precise

When I told him that I would like to own one of his works, Cecil chose an image for me that came as a shock. When I looked at *A Song*, also called *The High Priestess*, from 1960, I wondered if he didn't like me. I'd hoped for one of his dreamy heads or sublime fools. Practically speaking, it was probably all a poor student like me could afford, as it was number thirty of fifty prints drawn from a lithography plate. His choice, however, was also intuitive and wise; it reflected what I needed. I have since observed that this is true of the images he chose for others.

As I respected and trusted him completely, I had it framed and have lived with it daily. Slowly I began to see that this image shows the power of the feminine, the positive qualities inherent in every woman and very much lacking in me at the time of the transaction. The priestess holds lightly on one finger of her right hand, the circling universe with its myriad stars. In her left hand, she grasps 'the sword of discrimination' which cuts away the veils of illusion and the darkness of ignorance. Many other universes float around her as she stands and faces an enormous black shape that may be her shadow. I am sure Cecil would have delighted in the recent cosmological research which indicates that new universes are born from imploded black holes. As Cecil taught us, and is now scientifically confirmed, everything is one interrelated vibration; there is no solid matter as we think of it, all is in a constant state of continual regeneration.

I have come to feel that this book is the consequence of accepting the subliminal challenge of Cecil's image to 'own' my creative power and face with equanimity the shadow of my personal history and the conditioning of our society.

Cecil's works are visual poems and, like all good poetry, they require attention over time to reveal themselves. His art performs its magic only when you are ready. His pictures are not obscure or coded fantasies, they have a deeper meaning and profound life. The pictorial language he devised was based on universally understood symbolic images. He was impelled to communicate in the most direct manner possible his insights and inner metaphysical experiences. His work is like a magic vehicle which invites the viewer to enter and travel on their own journey of the spirit. It is the means for consciousness to expand, to become light-hearted and to participate, as Shelley said, 'in the eternal, the infinite and the one.'

In London Cecil attended a lecture given by Pir Vilayat Inayat Khan on the mystic Sufi tradition. I found a treatise by him on meditation amongst Cecil's papers in the Tate Archive. Later, Cecil was also introduced by one of his students, Maria Lancaster to her Sufi teacher, Irina Tweedie. According to her, Cecil was a 'god-realised' human being. He, in turn, recognised Mrs Tweedie as a great spiritual teacher and they used to send their students to each other. Cecil adopted the Sufi concept of 'the eye of the heart' and it became pivotal to his art and teaching. He taught us about the importance of awakening and opening this inner eye to see (with God's eyes) *through* the physical eyes, rather than using the eyes to look superficially or graspingly.

Rumi, the great thirteenth-century Sufi, said that 'God enters through the wound' and psychiatrists are often referred to as 'the wounded healer'. In the experience of many of his students, Cecil was a healer; his focus was always on the person. Art was not the goal, but the means to heal and sustain the soul. Cecil always insisted, however, that this was not a psychological therapy of the personality. He was a spiritual teacher through art: a healer through creativity. 'My own art,' he said, 'is concerned to give man peace and joy and harmony and to orientate his consciousness that he may have some experience of that great happiness which is forever, through the transmission of the mystery of love, through the mystery of beauty.'

Cecil foresaw many of today's urgent concerns. In the 1989 catalogue for his Retrospective at the Tate, he insisted these lines should be included: 'There is a growing awareness that modern culture is approaching a severe crisis and that sooner or later it will have to undergo a ruthless revaluation. That revaluation must reveal the cause of the disorientation of contemporary culture which for so long now has been made a virtue of, or has been accepted without intelligent criticism or questioning. This revaluation will quicken the realisation of the necessity to focus man's consciousness upon the creative centre of Life, which the great cultures of the world have named the Sacred. And with all its urgency, it is in this act of orientation towards the Sacred centre of Life that contemporary culture will find confirmation of that universal Reality, the rediscovery of which, alone, will save our civilisation.'

His vision and art are of particular relevance now. Cecil's legacy is becoming more generally recognised as truly revelatory and its importance increasingly acknowledged. I'll conclude by quoting from the prophetic and hopeful words at the end of Cecil's essay, *The Vision of the Fool*. 'I do believe in [the], universal and eternal, above and beyond the world of the intellect and the senses; but not beyond the reach of the humility and hunger of the human heart. ...The Saint, the artist, the poet and the Fool are one. They are the eternal virginity of spirit, which in the dark winter of the world, continually proclaims the existence of a new life, gives faithful promise of the spring of an invisible Kingdom, and the coming of light.'

Nomi Rowe
2008

introduction

Cecil Collins
A Song
1960
Lithograph
55.5 x 40cm

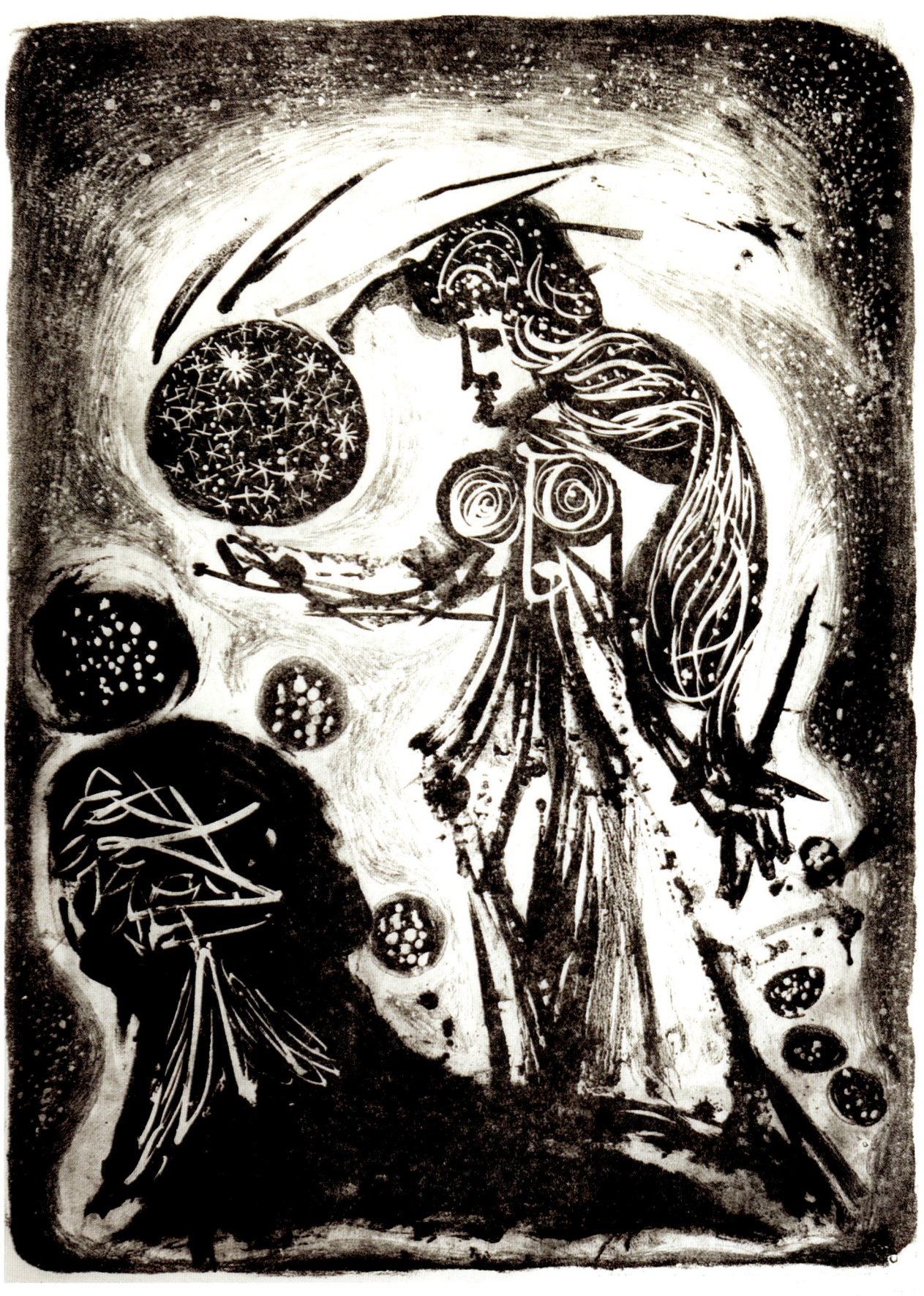

Cecil Collins

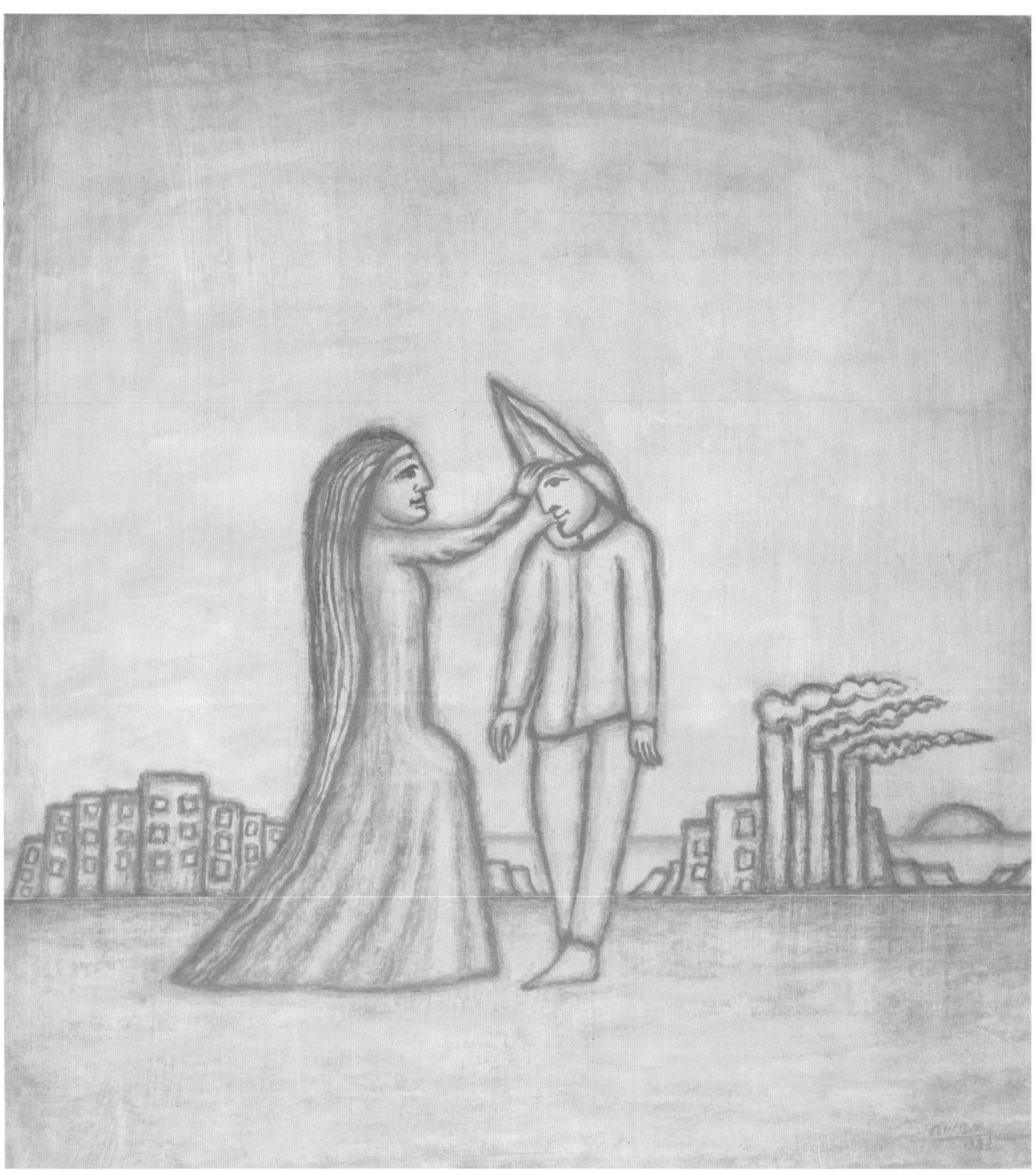

CECIL COLLINS GAVE THIS TALK AT THE TATE GALLERY 22 OCTOBER 1981

(Recorded and transcribed by Helena Drysdale)

I was brought up by the sea with the cry of the curlew crying the exile of the inner heart. What is that exile? 'The only paradise that we know is the paradise that we have lost.' All cultures, even the most primitive, are haunted by a longing for this lost paradise. This is the basic theme of my painting, of all my art and teaching. Creativity is that act of remembering, the recollection of perfection haunting us once our inner nature is awoken. Painting is a kind of pilgrimage, a quest.

The ancient universe saw the world as a kind of living being. Man was created to live in harmony with that being. Everything was a symbol: form and colour, the sun, the moon, the stars, the trees, the flowers, water, all manifesting a metaphysical reality. Later on in history, possibly with Aristotle, another faculty began to develop which said, yes, a tree is a symbol, but it is also something that can be weighed and measured. So the knowledge 'the thing in itself' or 'process knowledge' was born. Science was one of the great achievements of the human mind, but it has proved two-edged, not only because of the Pandora's box of its destructive powers, but also because of the assumption that this is the only form of knowledge, an assumption on which we have based our environment, from which the human heart and the psyche is banished.

For this rejection of the soul, this inner dimension of man, I believe we are going to pay a very high price: mental suffering, caused by 'that organised crime, modern education', which is dominated by a narrow, reductionist, banal rationalism where students are over-pressurised by a vast amount of external education which neither they or anyone else can possibly assimilate, an education dominated by 'process knowledge'. Descartes' celebrated statement, 'I think therefore I am,' sums up the basic illusion of this type of knowledge when it is made absolute. In this context, I remember the Buddhist saying, 'Because I think, I am not.' Large areas of modern education leave man's inner nature untouched and unawakened and, if this condition continues, men and women will become mere empty shells motivated only by external stimuli. As an artist, I sense that one of the main causes of our crisis and what is missing from our education is the feminine principal, the feminine psychology, the loving, caring, feminine genius for relationship. It is no accident that the archetype of the soul is woman.

All the great civilizations and cultures for 20,000 years were based on a metaphysical reality. Ours is the only civilization in the known history of man not to be based on a metaphysical reality. We must be considered, in this sense, abnormal.

This idea of process knowledge, of process for its own sake, has seeped through everything, including art, becoming the idea of 'art for art's sake', the idea of the process of painting becoming the subject of painting. Is this what the loneliness of Cezanne and the suffering of Van Gogh has come to? Is this what the early hopes of modern art, now seventy years old, have ended up with? And all wrapped and packaged with the word 'revolution' written on it. That very intelligent cynic, Marcel Duchamp, hit the mail on the head when he said, 'Revolution is big biz'. When one considers the activity called 'self-expression' or 'the medium is the message' and one compares that with works created by some of the great cultures of the world: Chartres Cathedral, ancient Egypt, the Buddhist temples, one has to admit that it is a bit of a come down.

The feeling of external emphasis has produced in many of us a kind of lassitude and sadness, a sense of unfulfilment because it does not come from the life which is deep within us. True education is based on self-knowledge and the education not based on self-knowledge is based on self-deception; there we have the crux of the matter. The Indian philosopher, Krishna, said, 'If we think that our nature is limited to the small wave of consciousness of our surface self, we are ignorant of our true being and of the relationship of our life to a world which shows itself to us in our craving for beauty and longing for perfection.'

Of the betrayal of our souls and the effects on our culture, we have the words of one of the most influential and successful of all modern artists, Mr Andy Warhol: 'I want to be a machine. I want to be anti-human. Everything is pretty; everything is false.' I should like to contrast this with the words of Alexander Solzhenitsyn, a man of deep sensibility who has suffered: 'Artists can do more. They can vanquish the lie.' That is the voice of a real man. How refreshing: a human being after the inane baby talk of a successful whiz kid. Our civilisation has a brilliant technological surface, but beneath that surface there is a great emptiness. We speed about, filling our days with ceaseless activity in crowds to escape this emptiness, but

Cecil Collins
Woman and Fool
1988
Tempera on canvas
45.7 x 40.6cm

when we return to our rooms, when we are alone, this emptiness comes back to us. If we wish to change the world, we must first change ourselves. And of course that is the last thing we want to do; anything but this. The world is as it is because we are as we are. After the crucifixion, the followers of Christ found the tomb guarded by an angel. When they asked for Christ the angel replied, 'Why seek thee the living among the dead?' That is: why seek the living, creative spirit of life among dead ideas, dead structures, dead organisations.

I want to speak about the Fool, one of the main archetypal images in my painting. Krishna said, 'In the last judgement, we do not hear the voice of God except through the mask of a child, a mad man or some such person.' That person in our time would be the Fool. Look at the mirth of the Fool: foolish humour, innocent, vulnerable, yet full of mysterious joy. The Fool is an image of the lost ones of this world, the misfits, the inarticulate, the failures, the lonely. A society concerned solely with success is a mediocre society. The Fool is not interested in success and its bitter fruit. The Fool is interested in life. It is not the product of intellectual achievement, but a creation of the culture of the heart. The Fool in an ecstasy of happiness bows down, down into the dust, with a humility which touches the bottom of the abyss of life.

This leads to the archetype of the soul which is woman. Crucial to the rediscovery of the soul is the rediscovery of beauty. Beauty is not aesthetic sensation or a commodity to be exploited. As Plato says, 'Whoever desires the beautiful must endure much.' Beauty is the mystery of the spiritual life surrounded by hardship. It has to be won. Beauty will only reveal her secrets to those who have endured the quest, otherwise beauty is betrayed and becomes a prostitute. In case it may be thought that we are idealising the woman, it is salutary to remember that the great cultures were fully aware of woman's connection with the demonic, but it did not prevent them from reaffirming her cosmic function as an archetype of the soul.

I can only speak as a poet because these things are indescribable. I believe today that we are experiencing a major shift of consciousness and that a new spirit is moving in us like an image of the divine sun rising upon the horizon of the world and melting all the hard crystallisations, dogmas and fixations, the ice of winter and of sleep down into the river of life.

What then is the function of art? To give man peace, to set his soul in harmony with the music of the universe, to orient his consciousness towards the primal source of life and, therefore, to affirm the unity of life. And what is the language of the soul? The language of the inner life is poetry, dance, the image symbol, music and excitement. In this language, the nature of the symbol plays a great part. There is a great deal of misunderstanding about the symbol owing to a later rationalisation: iconography. This banality is repulsive to the inner life and ultimately sterile. The symbol is an instrument of evocation. Symbols are like notes of music.

My painting is about that secret life which is very deep in us and which is in danger of being destroyed by conventional education of the modern world. My painting is about transformation which is very difficult to put into words. But, roughly, there are four levels: the small happiness (two toothbrushes in the bathroom), the small unhappiness, the great unhappiness, and the great happiness. The small unhappiness means that you are frightened of losing the small happiness. The great unhappiness means that you see the great happiness and, if you can't experience that, you refuse everything else. This explains the profound melancholy and sadness of so many great works of art. But there is more happiness in the melancholy of Chopin than in the small happiness. [When we have had] ... a vision of the great happiness, paradise, immortal life [and] then that vision fades ... we again enter into a state of exile and loneliness, but with a difference: in our loneliness henceforth the memory of radiance is printed on us. All true creativity and art is an act of remembering. Vision is a journey into that part of ourselves that we have rejected. It is a receiving back into ourselves of that rejected part. In that reconciliation we weep, we cry, not the tears of sadness, but the tears of joy because we have returned to our souls; we have come home. The eye of the heart is open. It is a kind of journey, a journey that we will all have to make sooner or later, each in our own way and according to our own destiny. It is a journey from darkness into light. We have to make this journey because deep down in the secret recesses of our being we carry a heart, wounded by the memory of a lost paradise.

Tate Gallery talk

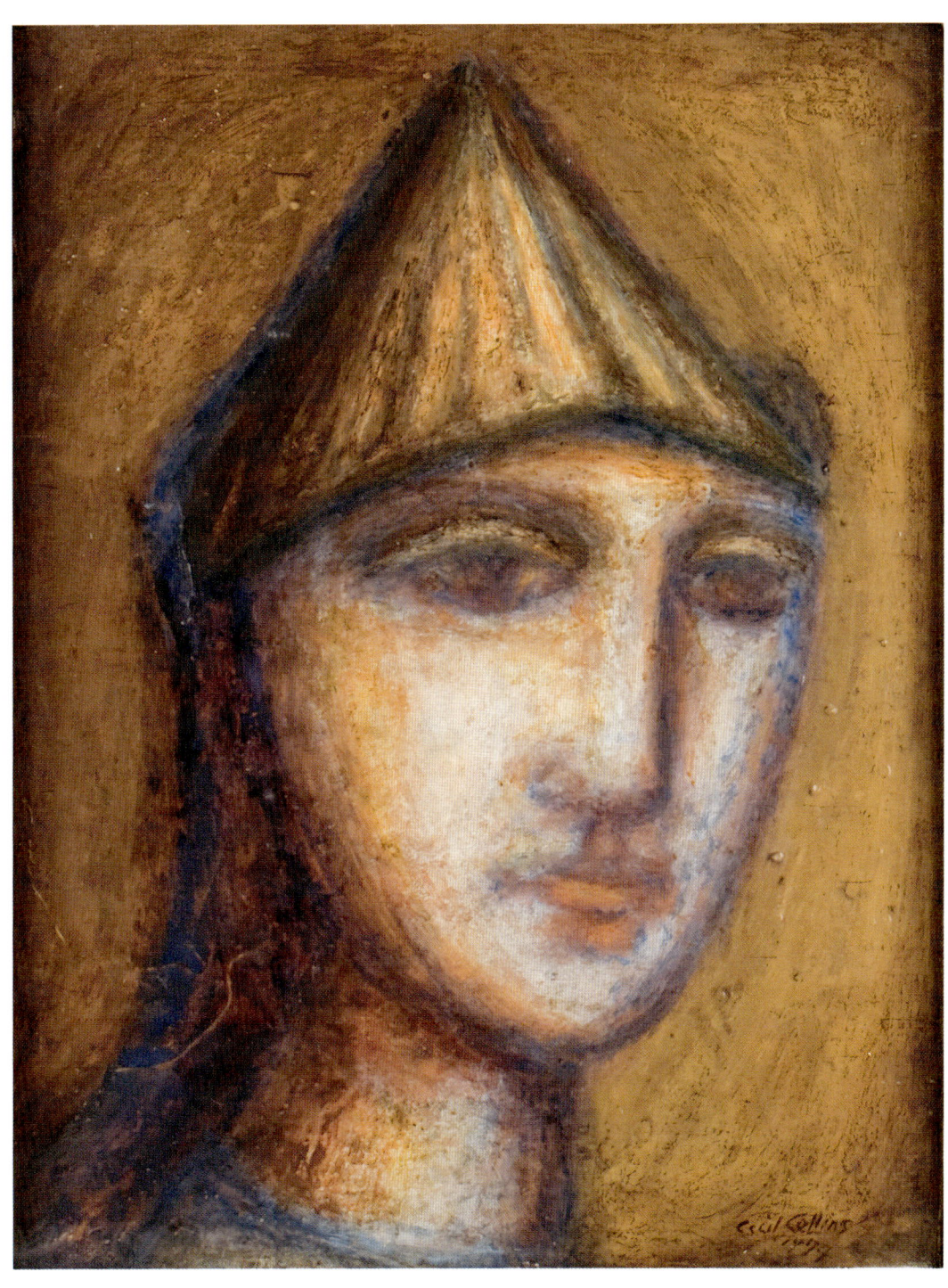

Cecil Collins
Head of a Fool
1974
Oil and other media
on board
20.3 x 15.2 cm

ELISABETH COLLINS

Elisabeth Collins (née Ramsden) was born 1904, in Yorkshire, where her father, Clifford Ramsden, was proprietor of the Halifax Courier. She had an American mother, Nellie (née Ward), and two sisters and a brother. During her childhood, she spent part of every year in Virginia. She studied sculpture with Henry Moore, first at Leeds School of Art and then at the Royal College of Art, London, where she met Cecil Collins. Despite her parents' disapproval, they were married in 1931 and she dedicated herself to his art and the vision they both shared. After Cecil died in 1989 she continued to promote his art and had a creatively productive decade until her death in 2000, including the purchase of her own art by the Tate Gallery when she was ninety-four.

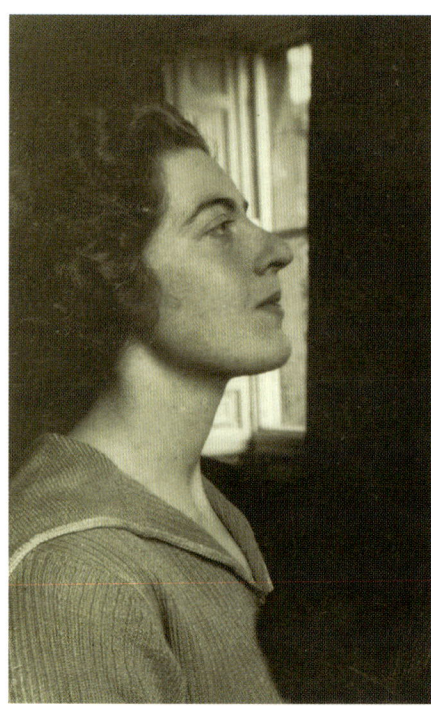

Unknown photographer
Elisabeth Collins
c. 1930

ABOUT CECIL

When I'm in the midst of recollections it appears to me that all is so complicated, so mixed up with the sacred and profane, with what came before Cecil, what has come since he died and with my present perception of that time. I could write a more reverend piece, [but] too much reverence is a big block. It is adoration that upsets our contact with divine things and divine beings.

Cecil, with all his vision, idealism and fastidiousness, had also a good bit of the other side in his nature. Though it seemed out of place in the general pattern of things, he liked to eat tremendously stoking-up-kind-of-food; big, rough food with plenty of greasy chips and sausages, oxtail and stew. When he was unhappy he ate cold ham, but not with any pleasure.

When first in London, he used to eat at a taxi-men's café in Earl's Court. Towards the end of his life, he loved pub food. He used to go to The Man in the Moon pub for lunch until he found a fly in his soup.

He painted with great concentration; often for a short time only. Cecil worked between tea and supper in London. He must have drawn the blinds as the sun came streaming in. He didn't like to go away from home; he wanted to make cups of tea and felt he needed to be at home while I cooked supper.

He loved the ceremony of Christmas and birthdays: the opening of presents at such occasions. He loved to make paper images and to colour them brightly.

Cecil was an only child and didn't go to school; he was too ill and the family were too poor. His mother was a strong character and possessive. She made drawings onto the wall of her home which were marvellous and obsessive. After his mother was bombed out of her home in Plymouth, she lived in a caravan on a hill. Cecil paid the rent, but didn't visit his mother.

I'd never learnt to drive but, after Plymouth was bombed, I went to a garage and bought a two-seater car and went to rescue people. I found Cecil's mother and took her to a café in Totnes. I phoned Cecil, but he didn't want to see his mother or have her brought to our home. Cecil was a good navigator, a back-seat-driver.

This, in some ways, was a life of frailty, but it contained the essence of what he needed to sustain *reality* and to carry out his work. Cecil was good at the theoretical side, but not really on the ground; he was physically unaware, there was a lack of presence. He was enigmatic. Alongside his pompous pronouncements, Cecil had a great sense of humour. He had a parlour trick that he would perform if the guests were boring. He would poke his head round the door and bring his hand round as if it belonged to someone else and mime being choked or strangled. It was very funny.

He loved walking at a certain time of the day, particularly

Photograph by Judy Goldhill
Elisabeth Collins,
Paultons Square
1997

Elisabeth Collins

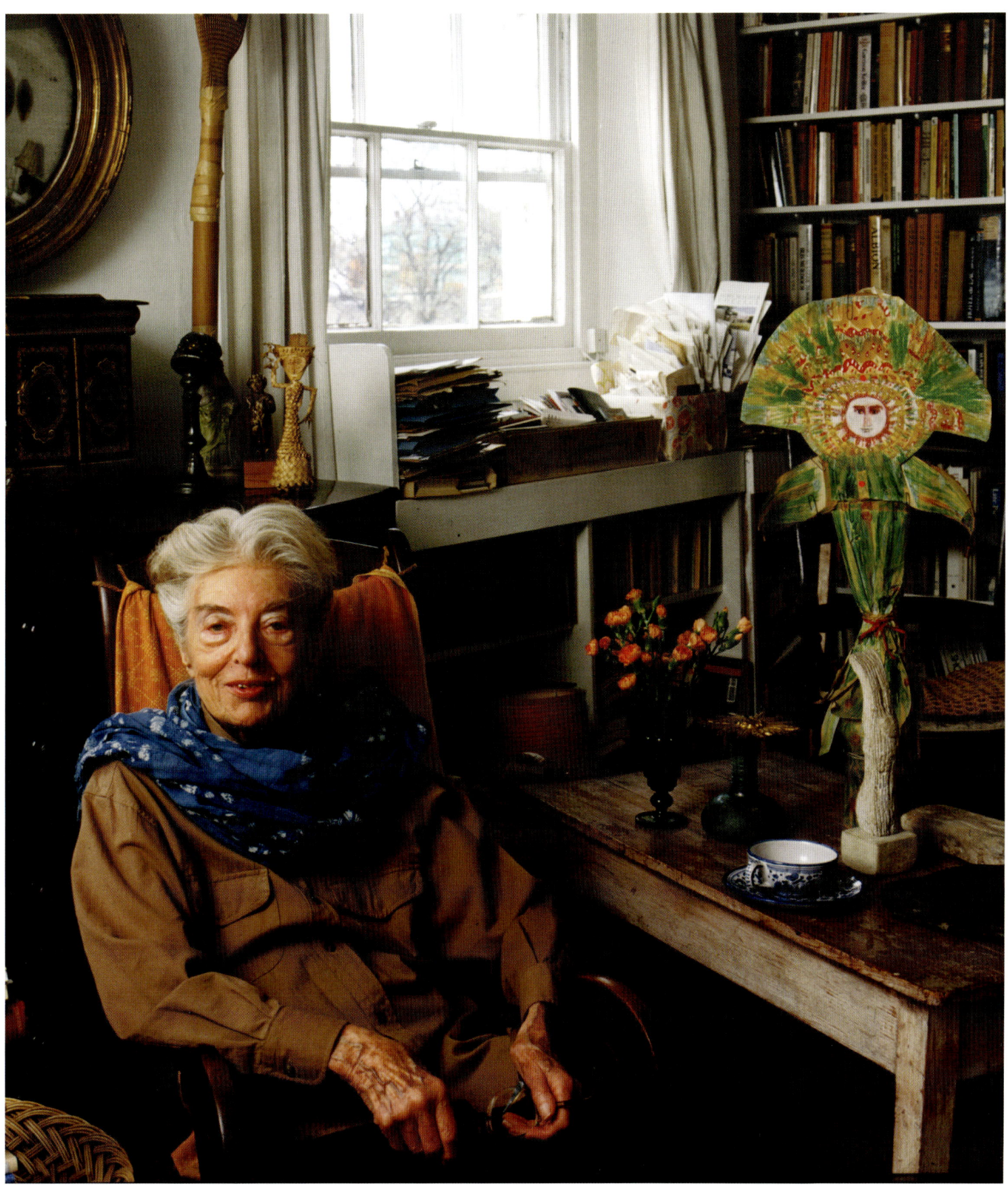

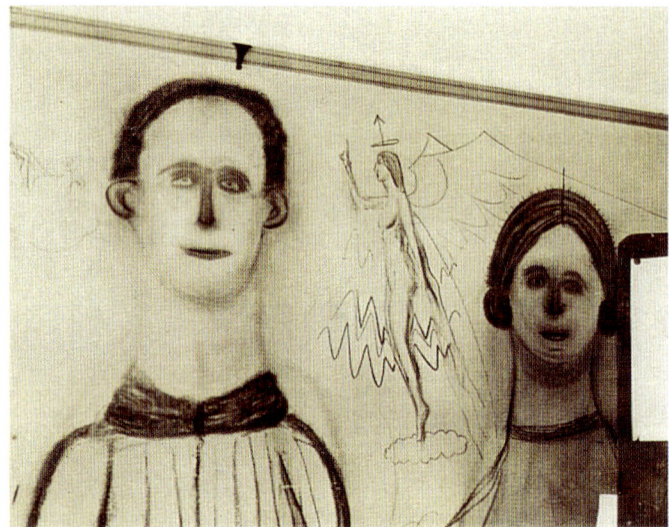

Mary Collins (Cecil's mother) *Murals* 1940s

twilight, when one doesn't know what may appear. It was a time for seeing things undisguised. What one may hear is actually very strange because one is on the edge of illusion and of dream. A cat may pass, the silent birds may be sitting in trees and at that hour when anything might happen, it sometimes did or, by mistake, a rabbit might speak or even a bird might sing in unity with the world. One knows, but cannot be sure of, these things and yet they are the most true things ever. Sometimes Cecil heard voices of an unknown source which reassured him greatly.

We met in 1928 at the Royal College of Art when I was in the sculpture school and Cecil was in the painting school. All students ate together in the canteen and I think that's where we first met. Cecil was surrounded by adoring ladies who all wanted to convert him to the Christian faith and, of course, he was against it at that time. Cecil had been there at least a year before I was and was a well known figure by then because he was quite an exhibitionist. After making a good painting, he used to limp; it was the sign. He walked everywhere, limping and everybody said, 'Ah! He must have done a good painting!'

He was very thin, rather haggard and very, very short of money. He wore terrible clothes, that's why I called him 'Parce', a badly tied up parcel with lots of bits of string falling off. He was dressed in fearful rags and he smelt horrible, but he was somehow rather attractive, partly because he was a very good painter, even then. Also he used to play the piano, by ear, in the Common Room in a wild way with anguish, which was interesting to me. People used to cry 'For heaven's sake! Can't you get him to stop? I can't eat my lunch.' He always had a quality which is very rare and one doesn't often see in people. He wasn't the usual person that one sees around all the time. He was a person and when you're that age, you don't often become a person till a bit later in your life, I think.

We married in 1931, living as students do in rooms or flats and often moving for one reason or another. We did not appeal to landladies. I remember a good deal of trouble caused by a game we played with friends, where someone draws a head and folds the paper and then someone draws the body. These were sometimes wonderful drawings, but often they could be quite rude. Friends of ours used to put these drawings through the front door without a proper envelope. The landlady would find them and be scandalised.

At one time we had a wonderful primitive attic room where Herbert Read visited us, but he never liked the paintings. Cecil stood a painting in front of him for far, far too long waiting for the appreciation that did not come.

Somewhat later we rented Monk's Cottage near High Wycombe, Buckinghamshire. We loved this cottage which was deep in a hollow, wonderfully romantic, but damp. It belonged to an eccentric and kindly man called Mr Monk who had painted it white inside and out. It had four rooms and a big open fireplace, but no conveniences, no gas or electricity, the loo miles down the garden and the garden was full of weeds and raspberries and rain. It was a wonderful cottage. It is still there. We spent our whole time at the cottage becalmed in solitude and happiness, but lonely sometimes for friends. The only people we could see or who wanted to see us were Eric Gill and his family. The Gills became bored with us, I fear. Perhaps we walked the long miles

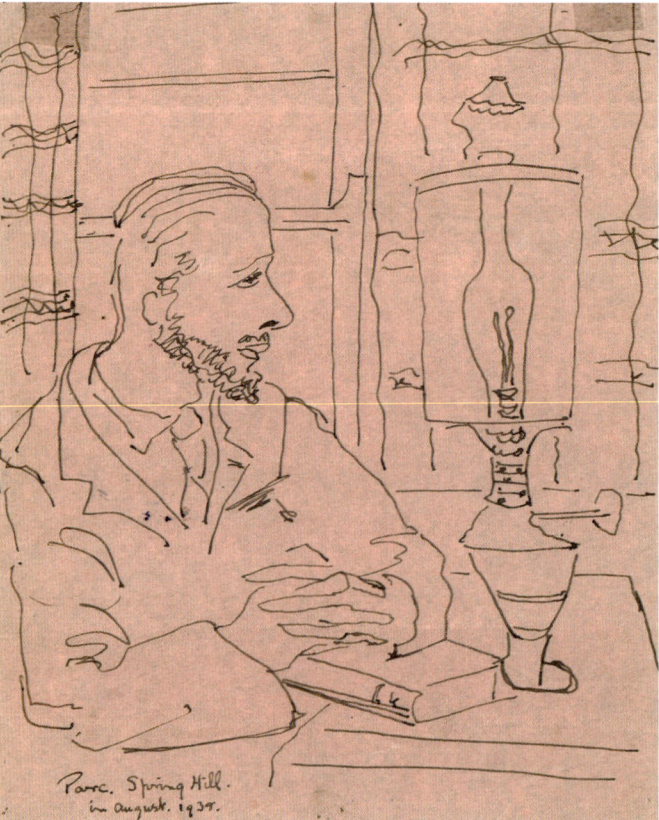

Elisabeth Collins *Cecil Collins* 1939 Ink on paper 25.5 x 20cm

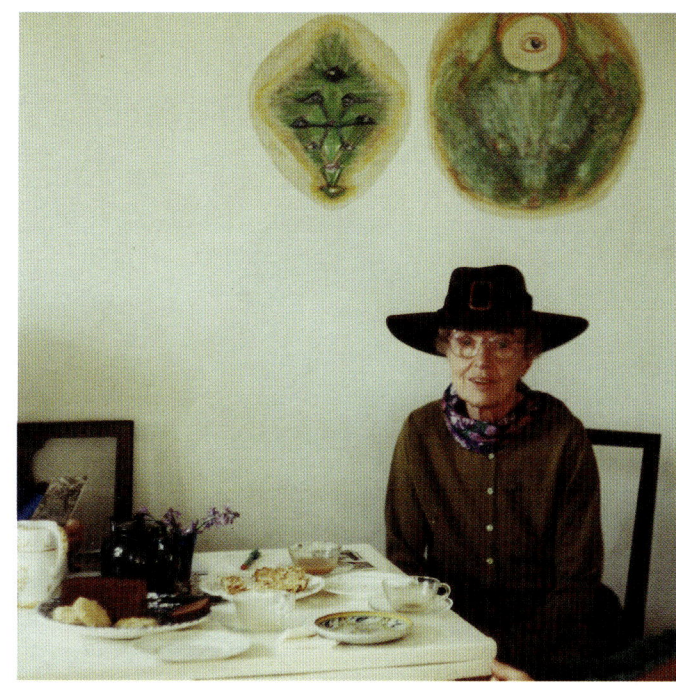

Photograph by Lily Corbett
Elisabeth at tea, Paultons Square (with her murals, *Eyes and Chalices* above)
c.1990

Elisabeth Collins
Sculpture
c.1928-31

to see them too often, but we felt that the only way to happiness was making contact with distinguished and creative contemporaries.

We were present at the great Surrealist party in 1936 in London. It was a dazzling experience: André Breton and his beautiful wife with a raw chop on her shoulder and Salvador Dali getting caught in his diving helmet. Herbert Read stood on a couch to make his speech and it collapsed. This was intended, I think. Cecil, though never really in tune with the Surrealists, was deeply intrigued by them at the time.

In 1937 the painter, Mark Tobey, visited us at Spring Hill, our second cottage in Buckinghamshire. He was a great gourmand and one day cooked an immense omelette. Unwisely, he ate most of it and it made him sick. He also was very uncomfortable amid the disadvantages of cottage life. But we had many good times and good talks which led to our journey later on in that same year to Totnes and Dartington Hall where Mark was then living.

Mark Tobey held 'open' lessons for everyone at Dartington before the war: servants, estate workers, children and staff. He was a wonderful teacher. He would put all the paintings of the class up on the wall. He then talked and gave interpretations, including my *Fool* painting which I did in one of his classes.

Cecil didn't acknowledge his sources, but it was Mark who first brought the Fool to life for Cecil. Later, Cecil and I went to Hein Heckroth's studio sessions up a tower at Dartington. Hein saw my Fool painting and was very excited and thrilled by it. He eagerly talked about the Fool and its symbolic implications, about the need of its magic in our time and inspired Cecil with the Fool theme; from that day Cecil's Fool work started.

When the Second World War started, the owners of Swan Cottage, our Totnes home, wanted it back so we moved to Dartington Hall. Visitors like Stephen and Natasha Spender and Arthur Waley used to come down for weekends. Everyone met at meals in the big refectory. The visitors would walk in the gardens and visit Cecil in his studio. Cecil always painted indoors, but only when he felt like it. He would be in his studio, maybe the whole day, but only paint for an hour, otherwise he would seem to do nothing; reading or thinking.

At the beginning of the war Cecil became very apprehensive. He wanted to get to America and often telephoned our influential friends for help about getting out of the country, but it all came to nothing. Even in as remote an area as Dartington, the war was terrifying, especially at night as the great fleets of bombers flew over on their way to Plymouth or when we watched the bombing of Exeter from Dartington Heath. Dartington was wrecked by the war. The place had been wonderful, full of life and purpose, a home for artists of all kinds and many nations. All this ended with the outbreak of war. Suddenly, Dartington was empty. Everyone had left or been interned. Later, the whole place was taken over by East End children and their teachers.

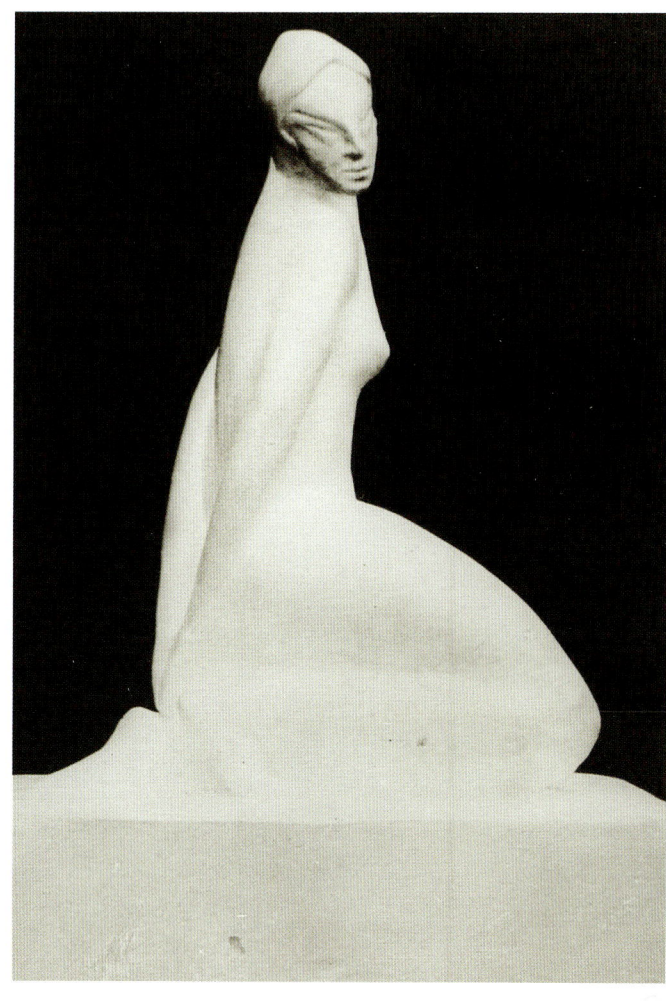

In 1942 Cecil began his essay *The Vision of the Fool*. We were in London and Wrey Gardiner of the Grey Walls Press had the brilliant idea of a book. Cecil spoke terrible English at that time. He came to speak and write beautifully, but then his grammar was abysmal. We had much difficulty with his manuscript. It was a great, great effort, although Cecil was always very clear about what he wanted to say. Very shortly after this, Wrey Gardiner went to Timbucktu and was unheard of for years.

John Rothenstein bought *The Sleeping Fool* from Cecil, in 1943, the year it was painted. There was a tremendous battle about its acquisition. The Tate Trustees said 'No, no, no!' But John persisted. For many years it was the only painting of Cecil's in the Tate. John was a great champion of Cecil's. Later that year we moved to Cambridge. We had been lent a flat in Royal Avenue, Chelsea, but owing to bombing it was impossible to remain there. At that time Cecil had an exhibition at the Lefevre Gallery which also suffered from bomb damage. However, Cecil's paintings were mostly unhurt. We went to stay with my family in Yorkshire for a short time. Later we lived in Cambridge for more years than I can think of.

Nicholas Moore, commissioned some drawings from Cecil for his book of poems and the cover drawing for his booklet *Buzzing Around With A Bee*. This was enjoyed by Cecil since he had worked without appreciation for many years. He was delighted. We got to know Leavis who was marvellous because he was so prejudiced. He loved Dickens and gave a very good lecture on him. He and his wife, Queenie, who was lovely, had a son who was a genius, very musical

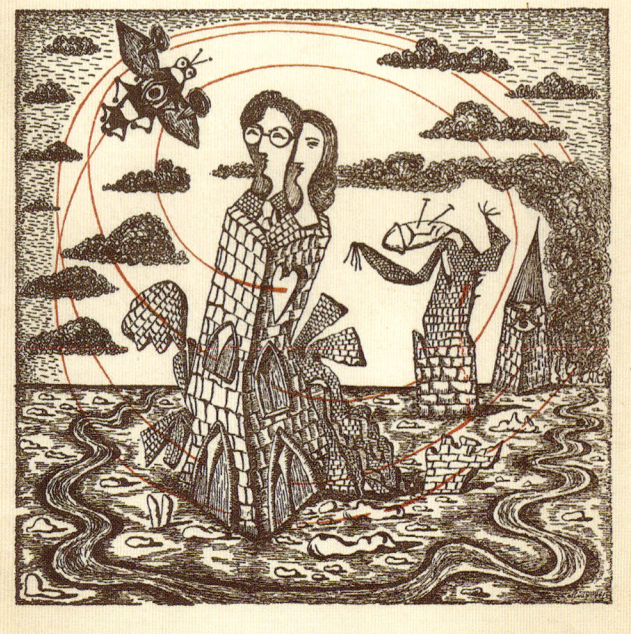

Cecil Collins
Buzzing Around with a Bee
Cover design
1940s

and who knew ten languages. Bryan Robertson, the director of the Heffer Gallery in Cambridge became a friend and in 1950, he gave Cecil an exhibition. For a while Cecil rented the stable belonging to Enid Welsford as a studio in Cambridge.

In 1951 William Johnston, Principal of the Central School of Art in London, asked Cecil to teach there. Cecil drew back from the idea at first, but later he discovered a great joy in teaching. It focused and expanded his ideas enormously; his contact with other painters working at the Central School gave him great companionship. Cecil loved all that adoration from his students there and later at the City Lit. When his ardent young women students lit a candle for him on some occasion, Cecil said to me, 'Isn't that moving?' and I said, 'Not really.'

We didn't intend to come to London from Cambridge, although Duncan MacDonald at the Leicester Galleries had said to Cecil, 'I'll make your reputation,' three or four years before we decided to move into the house in London we share with Kathleen Raine. She is not really creative, but rather an interpreter and organiser. There

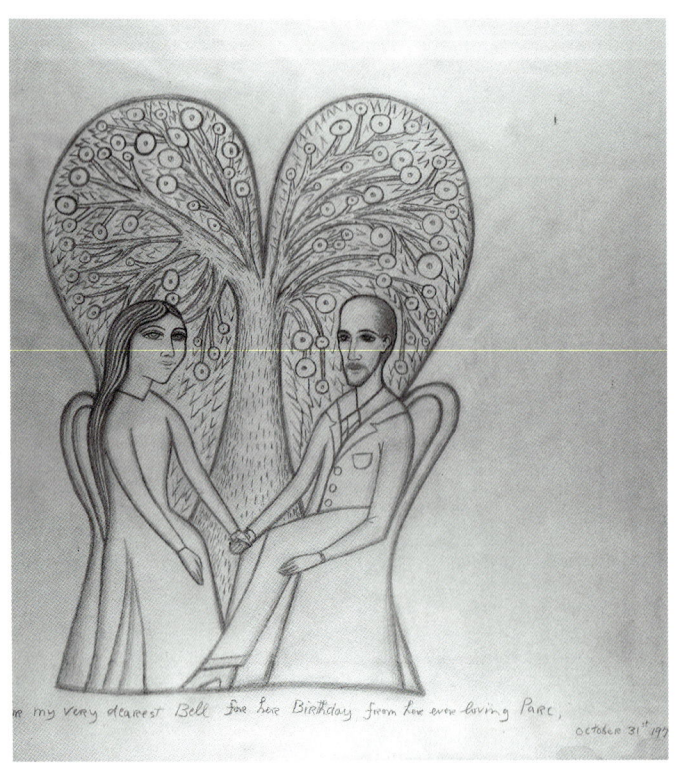

Cecil Collins
Birthday Card for Elisabeth
31 October 1974
Pencil on paper
56 x 46cm

was Winifred Nicholson living in the basement. She and Cecil had an exhibition at the same time at the Lefevre Gallery and there was a huge opening party and no-one came to look at Cecil's work. The lovely writer and poet, David Jones, wanted to live in the house too, but we couldn't cope with him being wildly neurotic so he went to Hampstead to be near his doctor.

Cecil didn't want his life or his painting to be too much interrupted by all the things that do impinge on one's life all the time. So I did all of that, but he changed quite a lot in that way in the last years, because I think he quite enjoyed going round the corner to the local shop and buying things, which he never would have done in the past. All that sort of thing he really found a pleasant change and rather interesting. Also towards the end of his life, Cecil got a good camera and loved taking portraits of people in our living room when they came to visit.

Cecil always said exactly all the things I'm supposed to represent [in his work] angels or the other symbols, which is rather a heavy burden I must say, but nevertheless, I suppose at different times, everyone has different aspects.

The life and thought of my husband, his painting, teaching and writings, all were based and illuminated by a contact (and sometimes, agonisingly a lack of contact) with the spiritual world of our being. Within that world he knew a happiness, a joy and above all a *reality* near, and yet fearfully illusive in this, our everyday world. He experienced much unhappiness as well as, at times, joy.

Remembering is the kind of thing that breaks one's heart. My life doesn't glow in a rosy light; it was not a gloriously happy life, but there is the interest in it clearly. Perhaps it was an illusion that my heart had about the quality of perception which caused marvels to be in existence, to be present, like daily bread; not blessed or anything special, but just to *be* loved and treasured. Marvels could be seen through the windows of a train journey or in the night, awakened I could see, through the window, earth and heaven secretly having a game in the fullness of their separation.

Personal information given to the editor with additions adapted from *The Vision of the Fool: Early Drawings by Cecil Collins* 1991 Anthony d'Offay catalogue

Elisabeth Collins
Carrying the Prince
Gouache

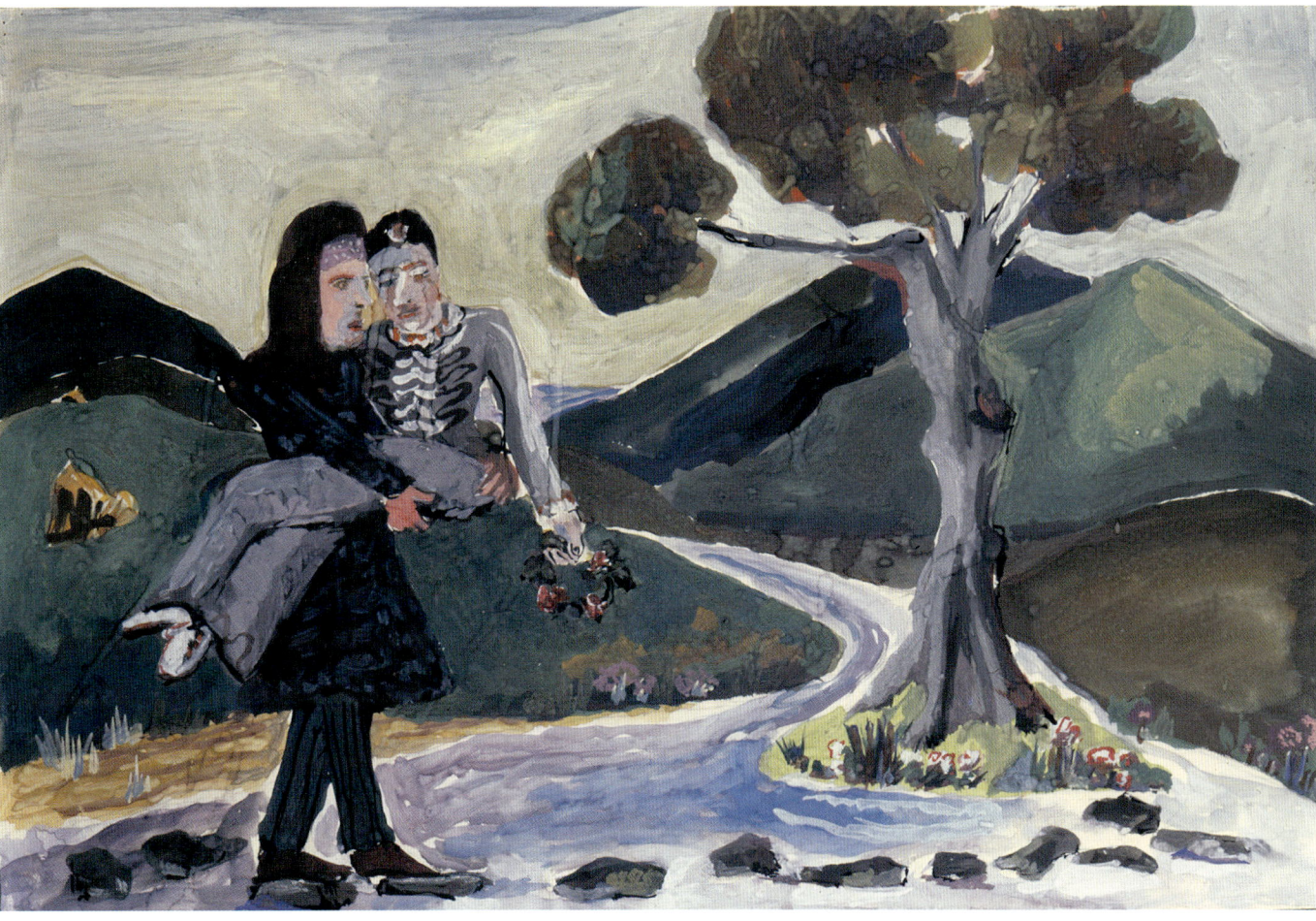

The ego as a source of stimulus for art is finished. Art must transcend the ego again; it must again identify with eternity, with the archetypal world. Our civilisation is based on the ego, identified with time which means with death.

Cecil Collins

The purpose of art is to worship and praise life though wonder and magic.

Cecil Collins

The fundamental innocence of my vision, this is what baffled the critics...

Cecil Collins

photograph by
James Mortimer
Cecil Collins
Avon
1959
Cotton and rayon mix fabric
(Edinburgh Weavers)

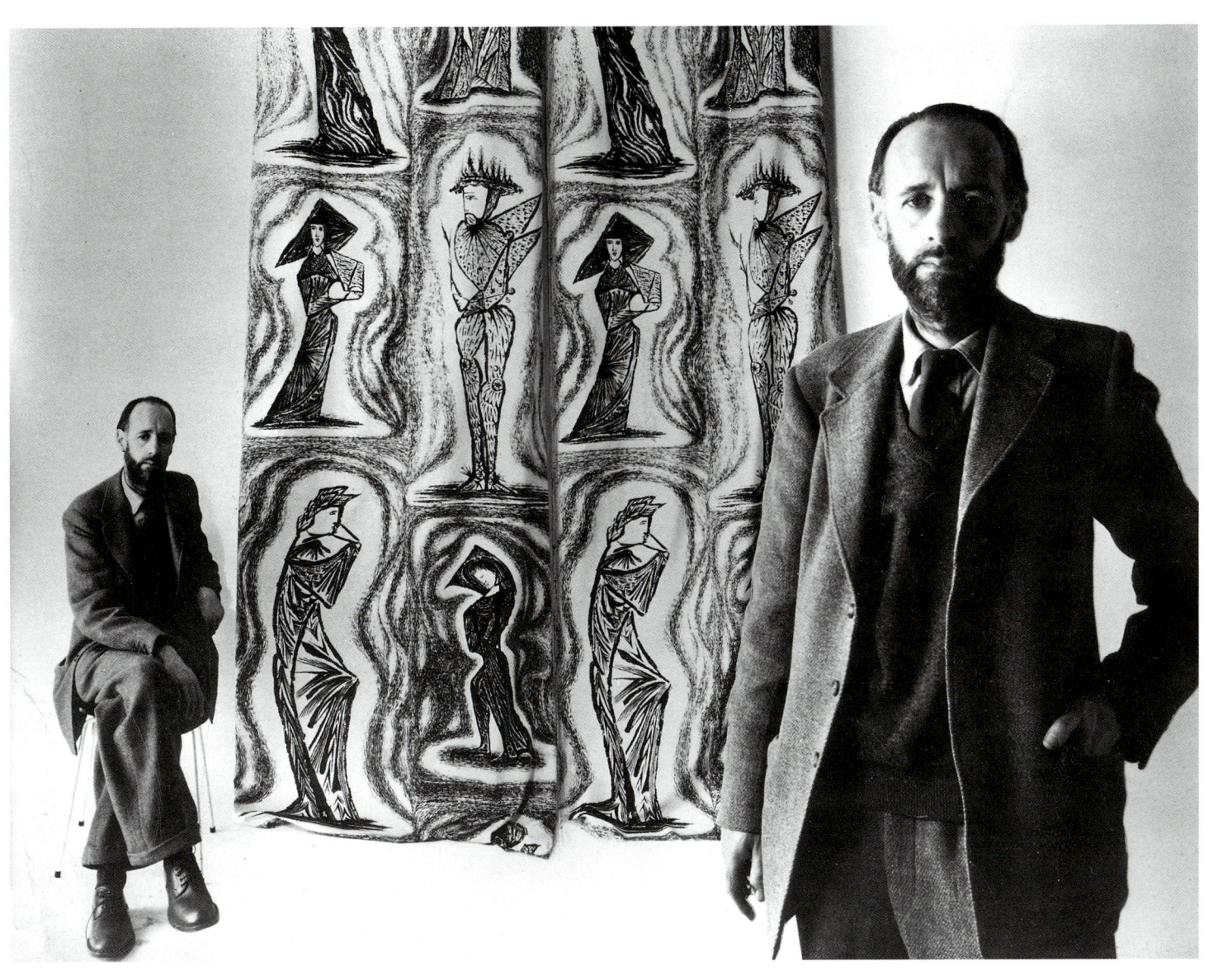

CURATORS & GALLERY OWNERS

SIR NICHOLAS SEROTA

Sir Nicholas was Director of the Whitechapel Gallery, London, and the Museum of Modern Art, Oxford, before becoming Director of the Tate Gallery in 1988.

When I arrived at the Tate in the summer of 1988, there was a commitment in principle to do a show for Cecil. I'd known Cecil as a figure in the London art world and, as Director of the Whitechapel Gallery, I'd met him on a number of occasions during the 1970s and '80s.

The Whitechapel had a particular association with Cecil because of his show there in 1959. One of the things I did when I was director of the Whitechapel was to try to renew the relationships that had existed between the Gallery and those artists who'd shown there. I had enormous admiration for the way in which Bryan Robertson had run the Gallery but, when I arrived, there had been three directors in eight years and the continuity, the memory and the relationships within the institution had been lost. I wanted to repair and then renew those relationships. There were many people in London, both of my generation and also of a slightly older generation, who had been influenced by Cecil or been taught by him and he was someone whom I'd admired for a long time. When I was a student at Cambridge, I remember acquiring his little book, *The Vision of the Fool* and being aware of his work and his vision. Cecil was always an artist whose particular vision was very appealing to the young.

People have sometimes found it surprising that I was interested in Cecil's work because I had a reputation for being much more interested in the avant-garde. I visited Cecil once during the time I was at the Whitechapel. I can't remember what the occasion was, it might have been after an opening, and we went back to Paultons Square and I met both him and Elisabeth. So when I came to the Tate I had a sense not just of who he was as an artist, but also what he was like as a person. There was a commitment to put on a show of his work, but without a clear date being given. Then I discovered that he was seriously ill and it wasn't known how long he would live. It seemed sensible to try and bring the show to the point where it could be done during his lifetime.

When I came to London in the late 1970s, there was a renewal of interest in those artists who had persisted in their attachment to the figure, but also with the idea of the spirit and visionary values in art and that encouraged me to look again at Cecil's work. It could be seen at Anthony d'Offay and I think I met him at one of the openings at Anthony's.

By the time I got to know Cecil properly, he was already quite old and the overwhelming impression I had was of his physical form, the way he held his head and his shoulders always slightly inclined; he was almost looking in on himself, which was, of course, exactly what he did in relation to his own work. You would ask him a question and his response always seemed to be the result of deep thought. You had this sense of the inner workings of a mind that had great depth to it. Every answer he gave was a considered one. There was never anything in the slightest way glib. Although he must have been restating his views and his beliefs, in a way repeating himself, you never had the sense that he was. You had the impression that it was a fresh thought, freshly conceived, freshly put together because it came from this deep sense of inner enquiry. He was by no means an innocent, but he retained the innocence of youth in that he never became cynical. People who do as much teaching as Cecil did and who have worked through successive generations of students often become rather formulaic and even cynical, but I don't think Cecil ever did.

Cecil knew very clearly what he was doing in his work and where he was going. The remarkable thing about his early paintings is that they're so fully formed as statements. There was nothing tentative about them. Much of the expression in the early paintings drew on the achievements of other artists, but there came a moment, especially in the late works where he'd freed himself of all that, when he was able simply to express the spirit residing within himself rather than something that grew out of other people's language. The images became more dependent on painting and less on drawing in the sense that, although he remained a significant draughtsman and printmaker, he became more comfortable with the brush. At the end, as one sees from some of the very late works, he was going towards the light; he was searching for that vision. So the later works, apart from anything else, have a greater sense of imminent light in them and that comes partly from the fact that they're softer and the contour is less sharply defined. I suspect that he began by trying to capture and get down on paper or canvas the fairly clear vision that was always in his mind, whereas later, and I'm talking about much later, he was reaching and searching for it in the act of making the painting; the painting was a way of finding it for himself.

Of course in the 1950s and '60s there were other artists who explored spiritual values and significance, but they weren't using the sort of language that Cecil was. The dominant culture, as seen in the major exhibitions and in associations like the Independent Group and so on, was very much the culture of commodity and the material culture of the world in which the artists moved. For some, Cecil's vision undoubtedly did seem, if not backward looking, at least as coming from someone living in a sheltered part of the garden.

curators & gallery owners

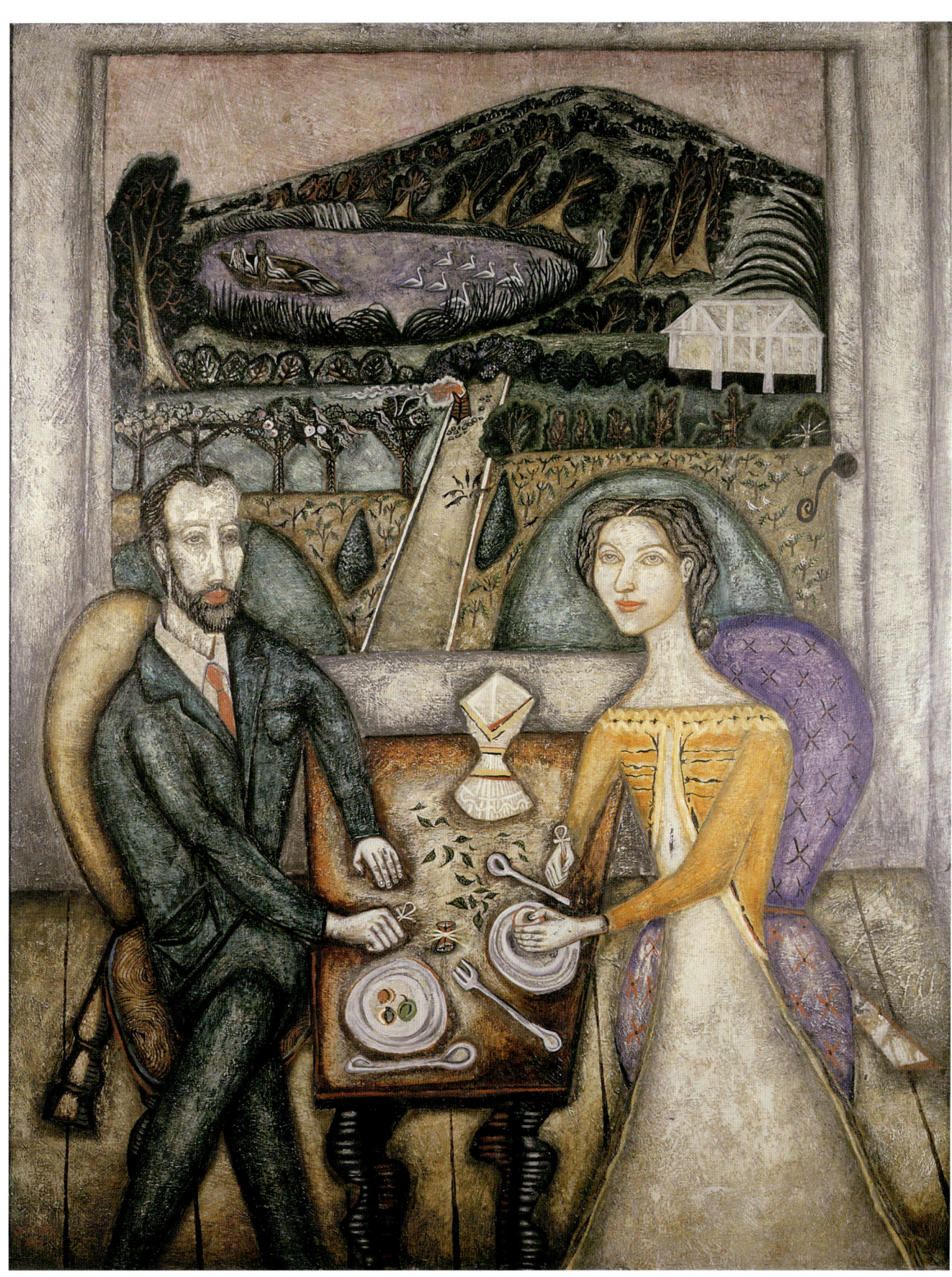

Cecil Collins
The Artist and his Wife
1939
Oil on canvas
43 x 57cm

There were few critics who took an interest. It changed, of course, with the generation of critics and artists who came to maturity in the late 1960s and early '70s. The way in which someone like Peter Fuller, for instance, developed his critical position is indicative of what was happening.

Conversation with Cecil was a kind of master class. In a way, he's closer to a tradition where pupils assemble around a teacher, a practice that is stronger in somewhere like Germany. An interesting connection with Cecil in that respect is Dartington. Important though Dartington was in the 1930s and '40s, by the '60s and '70s it wasn't really regarded as a major centre, not for the visual arts. It seemed as though all of that had been rather Utopian and rural and had somehow lost contact with the harsh, urban world, the world, as we knew it, of the 1960s and '70s. Then something did begin to change and people began to look for a different kind of meaning in art.

I went to see Cecil and Elisabeth several times during the preparation of the exhibition. The visits were mainly during the day and not for a meal, more for a cup of tea or whatever. I remember going with Judy [Judith Collins, curator] on a couple of occasions. Elisabeth was becoming quite shaky by that point, but she had an eagle eye and continued to have an eagle brain for a long time. She was very perceptive and she would, if your attention wandered, catch you quite quickly. She could be sharp, but in a very kindly way. I think the reason that both she and Cecil continued to be so loved and admired by younger people was that they had this great curiosity about the young.

When Cecil was listening to you, you felt that the conversation was, to a surprising degree, one from which he was learning rather than simply imparting. I suppose that's true of all the best teachers; you have this sense that your views, even though you know them to be insignificant, are nevertheless being taken into account. There's an exchange of ideas.

If I had to conjure up a particular image of Cecil's, it wouldn't be the Fool, but that wonderful early double portrait of Cecil and Elisabeth and then one of the very last works showing an angel or a priestess such as *The Music of Dawn*.

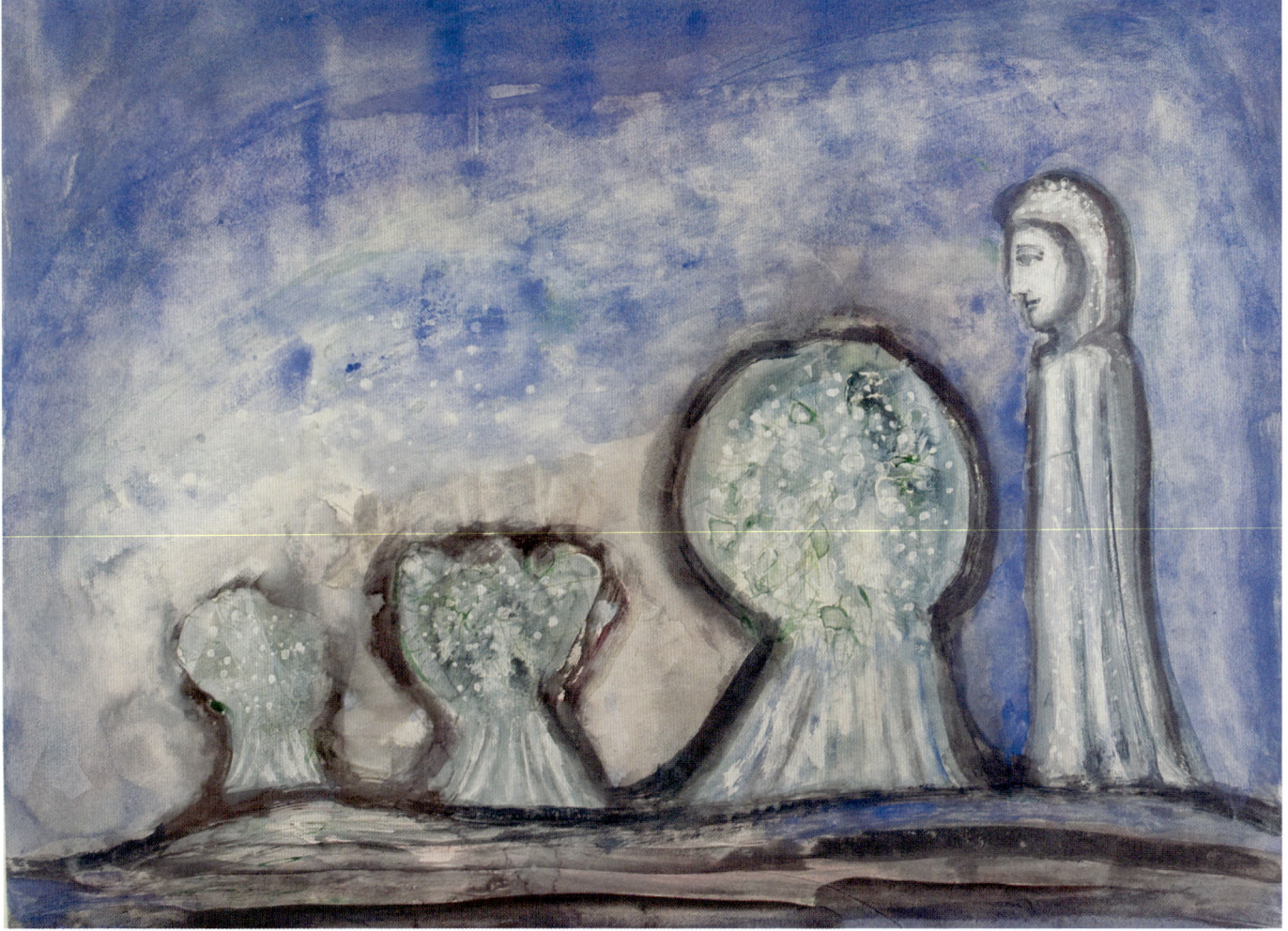

Cecil Collins
The Companion of Light
1980
Gouache
36.8 x 45.7cm

RICHARD MORPHET

Born 1938. Tate Gallery curator 1966 – 98 (Keeper of the Modern Collection 1986 – 98). Curator of The Hard-Won Image (Tate, 1984) and Encounters: New Art from Old (National Gallery, 2000) and of retrospectives ranging from Meredith Frampton and Cedric Morris to Richard Hamilton, William Turnbull and R.B.Kitaj. Has written extensively on twentieth century British and modern western art from Sickert and Bloomsbury to minimal and conceptual art. Writings on Cecil Collins include the catalogue of his 1981 prints retrospective (Tate Gallery) and 'Kingdoms of the Imagination' in Quarterly (magazine of National Art Collections Fund), Summer 2001.

I probably visited Cecil's exhibition at Arthur Tooth and Sons in 1971 and certainly went to the exhibition, *Britain's Contribution to Surrealism of the 30's and 40's* at the Hamet Gallery in the same year. The Tate bought Cecil's, *The Cells of the Night*, 1934, from that show and the reason for my first visit to him and Elisabeth in February 1972 was to embark on the process of interviewing him about this painting. This was my first contact with them. I had a wonderful conversation with them over tea in their flat at Paultons Square. Afterwards Cecil showed me his studio and we got on like a house on fire. The conversation was all about his work and his vision. I felt it was absolutely overwhelming. I was learning more with every minute he spoke.

After having been there maybe two hours, I looked at my watch and realized I had to leave immediately because I was going to the preview of a film about Andy Warhol. I had curated the London showing of the Warhol Retrospective at the Tate in 1971 which had started in the USA and then toured various museums around the world.

When the Collinses gave me my overcoat, it was obvious we had masses more to say to each other, but I had to go which was frustrating. Elisabeth asked me, 'What is this thing you have to rush off to?' When I said, 'It's a film on Andy Warhol,' Cecil's face was an absolute picture. It was obvious he could hardly believe that this young person who'd been deeply responsive to his vision should have been involved with, of all artists, Andy Warhol.

Although Cecil was momentarily taken aback, what mattered to him was people being interested in his work and he could see that this was happening with me. I'm delighted to say our friendship flourished.

Elisabeth was much more open minded about a wide range of art than Cecil was. She was interested in all kinds of art that Cecil hated, as well as sharing all his admirations very intensely. I admired Bacon tremendously and Elisabeth did too, but Cecil felt that Bacon and Warhol, in his quite different way, were consumed by the negative side to the exclusion of the positive and their art was unbalanced in that sense. He thought they were giving expression to aspects of modern life and personal experience that were the very ones Cecil was campaigning against through his work.

Art reflects human experience which is extraordinarily diverse and complex so it's not surprising that some very distinctive art will reflect unpleasant things. Some of Cecil's does too, intentionally on his part. There are scenes of anger and great suffering in his work. It was part of my job as curator at the Tate to be aware of the whole field of current art. As a curator, my attitude towards Bacon and Warhol was the same as to Cecil, though I felt towards his art an intensely personal response as well as an intellectual one.

I'd become curator in 1966 and my work centred on the British and American avant-garde. I feel that art has always thrown up work of lasting significance in every period. I've always maintained that there's an inner affinity in some ways between Cecil's painting and Abstract Expressionism in the 1940s. This is hardly surprising because he was born in 1908 so he's the right generation.

Abstract Expressionism was concerned with an inner subject vital to the painter, but also universal in its meaning, articulated through the act of painting. This came out openly in Cecil's work from about 1957 or '58 onwards. It would be interesting to know whether this was partly because of the sudden exposure to Abstract Expressionist art in England through two shows at the Tate, the first in 1956 and then a much bigger one in 1959. There were also individual exhibitions like the Jackson Pollock in 1958 at the Whitechapel. This aspect was already latent in Cecil's art, as we can see by looking at his work from earlier decades.

Through the late 1960s, I slowly became aware of what a distinctive vision he had and found myself pulled towards this extraordinary world he was able to evoke. A mysterious world, just outside one's ken and yet curiously recognisable at the same time. I wanted to see more and more.

Every time one went to visit, there was a relationship growing, very warm love and friendship, but it was also like being a student sitting at the teacher's feet. He was a extraordinary teacher in my opinion, not just of how to paint, but of his vision. To my mind, he was a national and international treasure. It seemed entirely natural for anyone to take this attitude to him, and especially for me, as part of my job as a curator was to discover what an artist was trying to achieve.

In my teens I had been steeped simultaneously in the Anglican tradition and in Quakerism and I drew strength from both. Cecil always stressed his complete independence of the formal structures of religion, but nevertheless his concern with the sacred, with ritual and with a kind of permanence were all points of contact for us.

I'd arrive at, say, half past two and ring the wonderful bell push. Elisabeth would always be the person who answered. She'd call down and say, 'Hello, do come up.' You'd go up, making sure the door slammed behind you, then say good afternoon on the ground floor to Kathleen. Halfway up the house, you'd come to the curtain that you'd have to pull to one side to move from the Raine section into the Collins one. The staircase would get more and more crowded with paintings hanging on the walls and there'd be this welcoming Elisabeth at the top of the stairs and I'd have a lovely chat with her in the sitting room.

Then I'd go down to Cecil's studio in the room below and it would be very cheerful, lots of chuckles, but essentially he gave profoundly serious revelation and exposition of whatever work was in progress and what it was that he was trying to achieve in it. He was preoccupied by archetypes and used them wonderfully. Cecil would be explaining everything, but he'd be particularly welcoming of any input or observation about what the picture evoked for me. When I was talking about art with him, it was not so much about general ideas as about specific images: how physically they were made and what every tiny detail in the picture meant as they called across to one another. Many of the details had multiple meanings. They were not just decorative flourishes, but were expressing emotional or iconographic ideas.

Very occasionally, I felt I couldn't fully grasp what Cecil was saying, but that was because of my lack of knowledge, not having his wide reading in such fields as philosophical and religious writings, as well as knowledge of distant cultures and all sorts of esoteric thinking. However, I was one hundred percent convinced by the completeness and the consistency of the vision he was articulating, both in visual art and in writing and speech.

What he had to say about his paintings, much of which survives in print, is an invaluable expansion of one's awareness of what the picture's about, but the central point about his art is that it addresses you absolutely directly and goes straight to the heart. It lives and breathes in a completely realised, convincing world of Cecil's own creation.

After about an hour and a half in the studio, it would be upstairs for a delightful tea. There were delicious cakes and the conversation and laughter flew backwards and forwards. Cecil would sit at the end of the table nearest the window, Elisabeth always at the other end, by the door, and I sat in the middle.

It was a marvellous room painted white, but so many of the things on the walls were in bright, jewel-like colours. It was radiantly light, despite the fact that the windows were relatively small because it was at the top of the house and it looked out over the treetops. There was a wonderful exuberance and a delight in the handmade, such as the decorated folded paper lampshades and Elisabeth's mysterious sculptures. At the same time, everything was so soft: the rugs on the floor, the upholstery and, of course, that chaise longue on which Elisabeth spent so much time. It was the most extraordinary creation in its own right. You felt enclosed with affection when you were in that room.

I loved the way Cecil wore old sports jackets that had been interestingly and lovingly mended by Elisabeth. There were patches at the cuffs and at the elbows and shirts in surprisingly bright colours with the collars turned. Elisabeth was, as Cecil always said, his muse. I don't see how he could have achieved what he did without her practical and unswerving emotional support.

During the long period of my friendship with the Collinses, I couldn't get to know Kathleen properly because of the rift between Elisabeth and her. I never understood or dared ask about its origin. You could talk about anything with Elisabeth except what she called 'Downstairs' by which she meant Kathleen. I always thought it strange because the implicit ban seemed so out of character with Elisabeth's attitude to almost everybody. Cecil frequently mentioned Kathleen and her views about his art when one was talking with him about his work.

When Elisabeth had a one-artist exhibition at the Albemarle shortly before Cecil died, I'm delighted to say Cecil was supportive of her work, as he certainly should have been. Marcia and Michael Blakenham gave a lovely supper for them afterwards and Cecil, who was very far from well at the time, made a delightful off-the-cuff speech expressing not only his profound love for Elisabeth, but his great admiration for her achievement as an artist.

I think Elisabeth's life changed dramatically after Cecil died. In a way it was a liberation, although not one she would have sought because it was a terrible loss for her, but it did mean she was freer to travel and her art flowered in her last decade.

Elisabeth had a sense of adventurousness and I remember that everything with her was fun. For example, when she was very old, Peter rang and said that he and his wife were about to go for a few days to their house in northern France and that it was rather primitive, but they'd love it if she would like to come. Although she must have been over ninety years old, she drove with them to this house lacking in modern conveniences without batting an

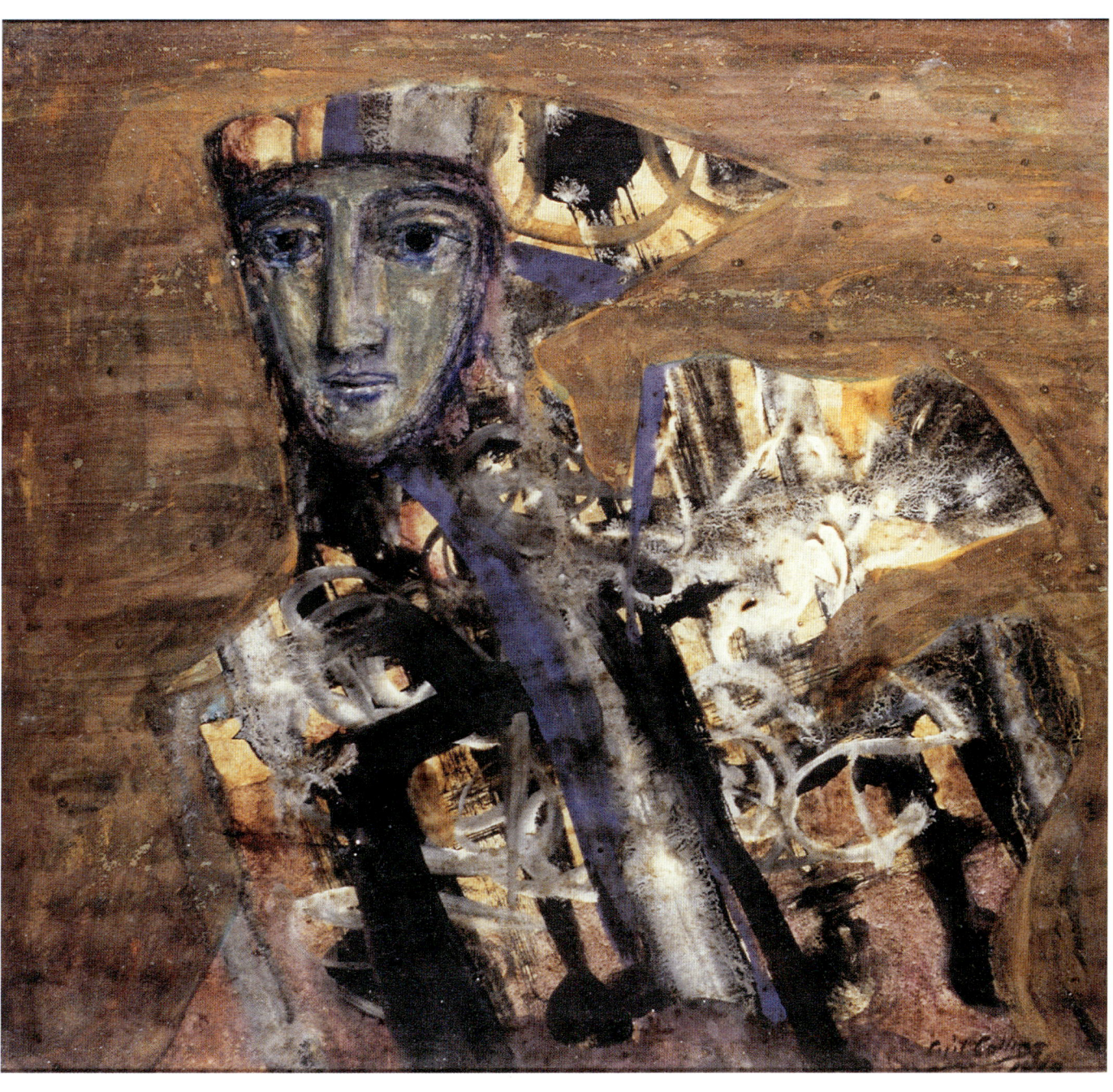

Cecil Collins
Angel of the Apocalypse
1969
Mixed media on board
29.25 x 30.5cm

eyelid. Many women in their seventies would have blanched at the prospect, but she was in her element.

I thought Elisabeth produced delightful, original and very personal work, combining an acute observation of people's behaviour in real life with her own fantasy. There was the sense of a contemporary world with distant periods in history simultaneously represented and frequently containing a strong sense of humour. However, some of her works are quite solemn and profoundly mysterious, particularly expressions of single heads. I admire those very much indeed.

It is my view and it was Elisabeth's view, and I think it's objectively true, that Cecil was the greater artist. Cecil's expressive range was very much greater than hers and the concentration and intensity of his work were also much more pronounced.

People who didn't know Cecil personally and just read his wonderful writings on art and looked at his pictures would have no idea of how intensely aware he was of all the everyday things going not only in London, but also world-wide. I felt that his studio, indeed their section of the house, was slightly withdrawn from the hustle and bustle, but from it they would make forays to pick up information. The two of them weren't cut off in the slightest from the world and were exceedingly gregarious in their quite different ways.

While Cecil was alive, there were often meals with six, eight or ten people round their big table. Cecil's taste in food was unadventurous and Elisabeth would cook delicious, simple food on the old cooker that stood on the top landing. It was a wonder that Elisabeth was able to produce anything from such a tiny kitchen. My wife and I often went there and everything was crackling with life in their entire circle. Other times they came to us for a meal and were always very lively guests.

Cecil was an artist completely taken up with a very distinctive vision and a deep-seated impulse to realize that vision in the medium of painting and drawing. Cecil's absolutely compelling imagery had to find expression. The sheer urgency and concentrated application never failed him at all.

I felt very strongly that the National Collection, and the community as a whole, had a responsibility to take account of anything that was really distinctive and intense, whatever direction it might have come from. Such work ought to be fully represented publicly. I did encourage the Tate to acquire paintings by Cecil and so did other curators, for example, David Brown. We were certainly not alone in our interest in Cecil's work; other curators like Anne Seymour and Simon Wilson were too. The previous Director of the Tate, John Rothenstein, had been an ardent enthusiast of Cecil's work and, under him, the Tate acquired *The Sleeping Fool* which is a marvellous work and two or three other works.

I responded to Cecil's work throughout his career, but one was able to make headway in the Tate acquisitions with Cecil's work of the 1930s because, superficially, there is a feeling in common with Surrealism about the idiom of his work from that period. He had exhibited in the International Surrealist show in London in 1936 before he had his terminal bust-up with the Surrealists.

In those days, a museum was rather heavily predicated in its acquisitions' policy on the notion of the succession of 'isms' historically so a link with Surrealism would make people sit up and that was fine in itself but, of course, it was only part of the essence. No acquisitions could have been made without the crucial support of my predecessor as Keeper of the Modern Collection, the head of our department, Ronald Alley, and above him, the Director who in those days was Norman Reid. We'd been trying to get a Cecil retrospective at the Tate from the mid 1970s onwards. There had been a considerable push all the time.

Cecil's achievement was admired and he was considered to be a significant British artist who certainly should be represented in the Tate, although he wasn't avant-garde or a big name like Henry Moore, Barbara Hepworth or Ben Nicholson. I think that at the very end of his directorship, Alan Bowness had committed the Tate to doing a Cecil Retrospective, although it would be the Trustees' decision through their exhibition sub-committee on which the Director was a key figure.

When Nick Serota became Director in September 1988, he fairly quickly brought the date forward. If he hadn't, Cecil wouldn't have lived to see it. Nick was very supportive of Cecil even before he became Director. I think he may have made a speech at Cecil's eightieth birthday celebration. He had a very good relationship with Cecil and Elisabeth and that was all very happy.

Judy Collins curated Cecil's Retrospective at the Tate. I would have loved to be curator of it but, by then, I was head of the department and it was impossible to combine my duties with the very detailed work on the exhibition. She's a terrific enthusiast for Cecil, a very articulate writer on him and she worked closely with him. Cecil was in considerable physical pain by then and getting more cadaverous looking, but driven by single-minded determination. He never wavered one jot.

It was marvellous to see Cecil in his wheelchair at the private view of this exhibition which he'd looked forward to, and fought for, with people of all generations there to pay homage to him. He was weeping with joy at finally seeing his life's achievement laid out. It was a kind of miracle that he was still alive to see it.

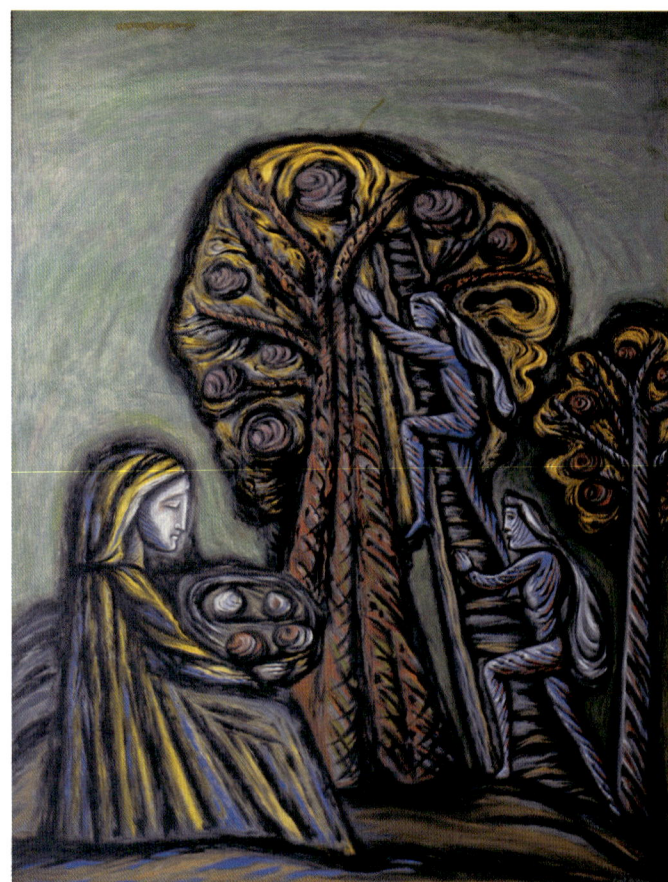

Cecil Collins
The Gatherers of the Fruit
1955
Oil on board
122 x 93cm

JUDITH COLLINS

Dr Collins is an international authority on sculpture, and worked with the Arts Council and the Hayward Gallery before becoming Senior Curator at Tate, 1985 – 2000, London. In 1989, she curated and wrote the catalogue for the Cecil Collins Retrospective Exhibition. She is the author of a wide range of books on modern sculptors, including Eric Gill and Andy Goldsworthy. She lectures throughout Europe and the United States.

The Tate decided that I would do the Cecil Collins' Retrospective. I have no idea why Richard Morphet didn't do it. He had proposed it, but perhaps because I was a new young curator it was given to me. I was taken to tea, at Paultons Square. Cecil took one look at me and said, 'Have you read Ananda Coomaraswamy?' The very first question, no 'Hello.' I said I'd recently read *The Dance of Shiva*, and that was it. He said to Richard, 'This girl's all right.' I had read Coomaraswamy because I was doing work on the sculptor, Eric Gill, who they knew and we talked about that. That first meeting went terribly well.

My surname is Collins and I told them I was a Welsh witch. For a while, we discussed whether we might be related, then we intuitively understood we were not, but it was a nice notion. In a way, I became a relative and that was quite satisfactory for Elisabeth.

The naughty little imp which was on the tea table in her wonderful sitting room was the only sculpture Elisabeth made that was cast into bronze. I always fingered it and asked her, 'What's going to happen to that? Please, could I have it?' She said, 'Yes', and put the instructions in her will. When she died she left me £37,000. Altogether she left two million. I also got a blue and white plate and a straw basket from France, which fell apart very quickly.

The imp is a kind of satyr because he's got furry trousers on and has a shoulder bag. He's in ecstasy: such a divine face with a big secret and a grin hidden there. In fact, I think it's a female face and figure with a little knapsack. It's one of my favourite things and every day I say hello to it. Elisabeth told me that when she was in Henry Moore's class, he used to say to her, 'When you've made a clay figure, hit it with a stick.' She said she learnt quite a lot from smacking things. At the end of my life I'll give the sculpture to the British Museum. They can find a place for it in some ethnographic corner. It has something archaic about it.

It was Richard Morphet who always insisted that because Elisabeth was the muse and the instigator, she should be represented in the Tate's collection. He was the driving force in their acquisition of her painting, *Prince of Aquitaine*, and three lovely drawings of her, but they don't come out on display very often.

I wasn't sure that Elisabeth was good enough for a national collection. She was an absolutely fabulous woman with a great talent, but a national collection of art is another thing. She didn't have enough time to practise and develop her art. She hadn't shown enough, I think she's had one at the Albemarle and another at Jane England, but she needed much more work. It wasn't enough. She'd only got ten years after Cecil died and a good artist needs twenty to twenty five years and she didn't have it. There was a lot she wanted to do which she knew she couldn't. She'd go to Harrods and have a facial. She liked the presentation of self and that bit worked well for her. As a woman she was perfectly all right, but as a creator, she was denied. Whether she was good enough, I'm not sure and I don't think she was given enough innate talent. I think she knew that. She must have thought, I'm not going to make it, but Cecil is, and that's why she dedicated herself to him.

I suppose because Cecil's work had been shown, had knocked around in the marketplace, his had got a larger market and this gave his work the more obvious strength. It's being in the market that gives you the depth, the significance. It's awful really, but it's the way the art world functions.

The Tate said to me, 'When you do this show, you've got to do this, this and this,' and I answered, 'Cecil's teaching at the Central School of Art, I must go to his drawing classes,' and they said, 'No, you can't possibly go,' but I went anyway.

I always got to his class late because I had to run from the Tate so I was invariably at the back and could never hear a word he said. I just had to imagine what he was saying because these menopausal women in macramé tops pressed themselves up against him. Cecil had power there. I found at those classes that I was terribly good with my left foot and it was wonderful. He'd say, 'Draw with the other hand, draw with your mouth, draw with your foot.' In the Sunday newspapers recently they wrote about how to extend your life and your memory, by brushing your teeth with your other hand and Cecil was saying that much earlier.

Bryan Robertson, who'd hung Cecil's exhibition at the Whitechapel, told me that Cecil would be a complete nightmare. 'He'll walk all over you. You'll get the paintings organised. You'll get the catalogue organised and he'll come in wearing that filthy mac which has pockets in the front, and when you've almost got the show hung, he will open the mac and say, 'A jewel. You have to hang that there,' Bryan added, 'Don't let him do this to you.' So I told Cecil very early on, in Richard's presence, 'Do not come to me when I've nearly hung your exhibition with things in your pockets, demanding they be included, I can't accommodate it because we've got hundreds of things.' Richard nearly died.

Concerning the catalogue, Richard said to me, 'Cecil will need to see every word and you can't mention Francis Bacon. You can't mention lots of things,' so I didn't show the catalogue to Cecil.

I think Cecil was jealous of Francis Bacon. Not envy of his paintings. Envy of his success, and how evil could get that high, whereas good was sort of wandering down in the lower foothills. I don't think he could bear that this man who painted such terrible things had got that high. Cecil told me, 'If you put the words Francis Bacon in this catalogue, the show is off.'

I wasn't to mention Blake, but I think I did. In the Tate archive, there are sheets and sheets of Cecil's poems, which aren't terribly good, but then Blake's poetry isn't either, although *Tiger, Tiger Burning Bright* is pretty good. Cecil's work was a second-level Blake.

For the catalogue I had to make a decision as to whether something was gouache or whatever. Cecil wouldn't tell you what the technique was. His secretiveness about his paintings was about trying to hold power. I used to ask him, 'What is this painting made of?' to which he'd reply, 'I'm not going to tell you.' It had to be a mystery. In the end, I think I just put mixed media.

Cecil used to give me these handwritten notes saying, 'These quotes have to go in,' but he never gave the source and I never asked. He wanted to choose the image for the front and back cover and I reversed them. We had a stand-off. He said, 'I shall ring Nick Serota because it's got to go to press and you're not showing me what you're doing,' and I said, 'You'll just have to trust me.' Richard Morphet was on his knees praying and then when the catalogue came out, Cecil said, 'Oh, it's all right.' Cecil didn't believe in God or Christ, but he believed he'd got a very clear line to the Divine and therefore you shouldn't cross him because he knew. You could be completely overwhelmed by that man. One of the reasons was that he spoke very quietly and you are extremely powerful if you speak quietly.

Any artist is a one-man business and their only job is to promote themselves. So knowing there are another four thousand artists, they have to say, I am great, this is my work, show it. You expect them to ask you to promote them.

One day Cecil rang up and said, 'Call up the Prado. I would like the Tate show to go to the Prado.' I told him there was absolutely no way it'd go there. He said, 'Of course it will.' I said, 'We're not even going to ring them.'

He thought he should take his angels to America, and I can remember thinking Los Angeles, would have accepted I'm sure, if we'd really pushed, but there wasn't enough Tate money. I was surprised about Cecil wanting to go to the West coast of America. Something had got into his head that his angels would be well received there. Maybe John Tavener had suggested it. He'd had some concerts there and probably thought Los Angeles or San Francisco would appreciate Cecil. I'm quite sure they would if he'd gone on *Good Morning America*, but Nick Serota wasn't in the mood.

Cecil also suggested that the show go to Russia. I thought it probably would go down well there, that the Orthodox Church would probably appreciate it, but there hadn't been any preparatory group work to have an exhibition. You can't just slap that down on administrators of museums and galleries. Given enough time, one could have probably promoted a show which would have worked, but it's not the Tate's way.

When Cecil died, the Tate decided that we should take the papers from Cecil's studio in their Paultons Square flat. A colleague of mine at the Tate, Caroline Cuthbert, and I spent months because the studio was a rabbit-run, chest high in papers. We worked our way archaeologically into the room to get to the windows, which Cecil had never opened. You don't open windows if you're Cecil Collins. We sifted through single sheets of paper, six feet high and torn from a notepad. It was remarkable that most of them had the same message, 'Praise Bell', which he must have written to himself every three minutes.

He wrote in red, because Cecil and Elisabeth always used to write in red. Other sheets had, 'Wash neck,' written on them. Elisabeth once told me he had no concept of living in the material world. He didn't know how to make a meal or even how to wash. There were some instructions for when he was going to make a telephone call to order a taxi, which had, 'Hello, this is Chelsea 8358. My name is Cecil Collins.' There was another one, which had 'When going out of Paultons Square, look both sides, step off the pavement carefully'. Reading these, you realised what Elisabeth had had to put up with. I liked her more than I liked him.

Cecil and Elisabeth were quite Jungian, but I never thought they were too lost in the wilderness. I thought their adoption of the animus and anima idea was perfectly all right. I thought they were quite embedded, particularly when they were in the Cambridge atmosphere and at Dartington with Mark Tobey and the Baha'i faith and the Jooss Ballet, all that was very conducive and friendly. I didn't feel that Cecil was a single voice and I'm not absolutely sure what is original in Cecil. I think he stole everything in a way, and he took an awful lot from Elisabeth, I would imagine. She provided the money and I think she was the first one to paint the Fool. A lot of art historians had to tell him that this was how it came about. I always thought that Elisabeth's nickname for Cecil, 'Parce,' came from Parcival, who is a fool, but Cecil was no fool. All that preparation, all that writing down the phone call before you make it, all that getting everything right.

After Cecil died, Elisabeth said to Caroline and me, 'Now I don't

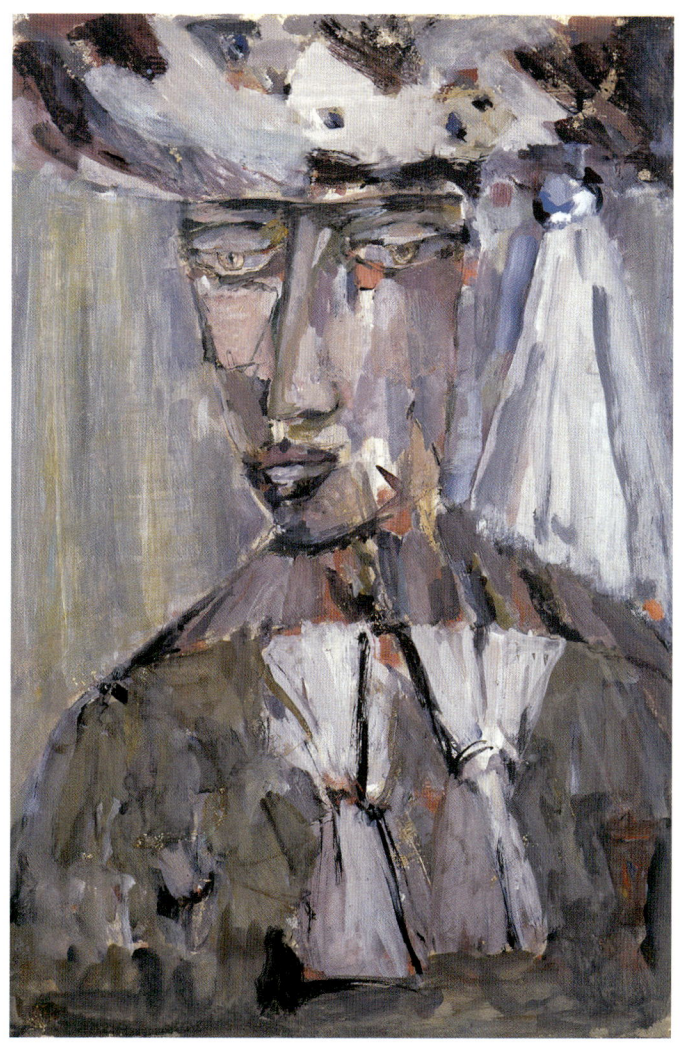

Elisabeth Collins
Prince of Aquitaine
Gouache on paper

who Elisabeth didn't get on with, on the ground floor and Winifred Nicholson used to live in the basement.

I had done an exhibition on Winifred Nicholson who was a significant painter with her early still lives. She had a very short period of importance, but as David Sylvester used to say, any good artist in a huge career will only do ten good works and I think Winifred probably did about five. Her later work was poor and the family should not continue to promote it. I'd love to own one of Winifred's very early still-lifes.

Elisabeth once told me they loved music and that Cecil had been listening to Arvo Pärt. For some reason, I suppose through John Tavener, they decided they'd like to invite Arvo Pärt to tea in Paultons Square. They did the cakes and tea and Arvo Pärt and Cecil talked for two hours. Arvo spoke only Estonian, Cecil spoke in English. They chatted away happily, never exchanging a word in common or understanding each other. It was a very nice kind of communication with Elisabeth presiding. I thought that sort of thing to be quite wonderful really.

Speaking of Tavener reminds me of Cecil's funeral. It was in June and one of the hottest days of the year. They had bought a plot in Highgate, a deep one because Elisabeth was going to be buried on top of him. There weren't many people at the funeral, about six of us. I think it was about 80 or 90 degrees, very hot and I remember holding on to Elisabeth who was more upset than I thought she'd be. John Tavener announced that he'd composed a little song for Cecil's burial. So there we were, standing in the heat with the sweat pouring off us and John started to sing.

What he hadn't told us was there were forty-nine verses. After about eleven Elisabeth and I were starting to sway and after thirty-three verses, I began to think we'd soon be joining Cecil down there. I kept looking over at John and coughing. There were forty-nine verses and me holding on to support Elisabeth. It was a trial, but John absolutely did not notice a ninety year old woman was swaying in front of an open grave. I promise you it had forty-nine verses.

Later John organized Elisabeth's funeral in that Orthodox church. You had to kiss her. I didn't want to. I thought that by doing that we would just sully that completely divine being. I can remember being pushed towards the coffin by a lot of people and thinking I won't kiss her. I think she had one of her hats on. It was weird, but if John hadn't arranged her funeral, I don't know who would have. She probably misses us.

Elisabeth once wrote me a letter saying I was like a little horse that ran across the hills in the wind and she wished she were like me. She was just spectacular. There was absolutely nobody like her. She probably was an angel actually. I never saw her angry or troubled, fuming or distressed. Yes, I think she was an angel.

have to cook two meals a day of meat and two veg or have lunch at a set time and dinner at a set time.' She did have a renaissance for ten years of not washing his neck.

I remember the obituary John Tavener wrote mentioned that he'd asked Elisabeth if she had ever wanted a child. She had replied, 'No, I had Cecil.' She used to say to me that her large family, the Ramsdens, were wonderful, and she'd got lots of nephews and nieces. I don't think she felt diminished, it was part of her wonderful innocence and being Cecil's muse. Elisabeth was still outstandingly beautiful at ninety-six.

Her family were probably quite prominent and owned the *Halifax Courier*. I've always wanted to go to Hollins, her home near Halifax which, in photographs, looks like a great castle. I'm sure her early life was very elegant, but she didn't talk about it.

Elisabeth created the whole lovely effect of their home, the way she did that was very good, the wonderful china, the decorations and she allowed this man to be the artist. Elisabeth loved the house and what an extraordinary house it was. There was Kathleen Raine,

DAVID MELLOR

Professor of History of Art (Film & Visual Arts), Sussex University, Chair of Photography & New Media panel, Arts Council of England and international independent curator.

I first met Cecil in 1987 through organising an exhibition called 'Paradise Lost' which was about British painting of the 1940s and 50s.

In 1970, when I finished my first degree at Sussex, which is where I've ended up, I did an MA on the 40s or in neo-romantic art which nobody was very interested in at that time. I realised that I'd got masses of information, but it went into a special hoard that could be buried in the back garden and brought out at will. Pragmatically I was drawn to photography in the 70s and half of my life is still spent dealing with that. I've always believed that the best painting and the best photography should be together. This is probably beginning to happen, although it comes at a time when art is becoming debased. I had done an exhibition on Cecil Beaton, in 1986, for John Hoole, because he knew that I'd written about Beaton.

Hoole told me that he had booked an exhibition from America and needed something to go with it. 'I was thinking about the neo-romantics,' he said, and I replied, 'I'd just love to do that. I'll do it for free if you want.' I had less than a year to do it in, but I managed it and I did get paid.

I got hold of Cecil's address, probably through Anthony d'Offay who was representing him then. I had been entranced by Cecil's *Vision of the Fool* when I had seen it in the Victoria and Albert Museum library while doing my MA.

For me the crucial thing about Cecil was his ability to see through you. There have only been one or two people who've done that, people whom I regard as senior, authoritative figures.

When you're doing an exhibition you become an impresario. Cecil was a brake on that in a very interesting way. He suggested that the more pragmatic, brutal and professional way of doing things might not be the best way. He acted rather like a good fortune-teller. Most fortune-tellers are charlatans, but they can divine from how you present yourself to the world what you are. Cecil's spiritual radar was turned on fully and so he could go much further in detecting covert clues. He would point out things about you that you had tried to disguise.

There's one remark of Cecil's that I still puzzle about and if he were here I'd ask him about it again. Let me put it in context. He probably made the comment when we were talking about the idea of the daemon in William Blake or one of the late eighteenth-century romantics. After some monologue of mine, Cecil said, 'You have a daemon and you must learn how to use it and you must be careful how you do.' In other words, he was observing that there's always something quite negative about power. At least that's what I deduced from this utterance. A negative force is not necessarily a force for evil, but it certainly would be a force for selling oneself short.

When I had to organise an exhibition recently, I wanted to say, 'For God's sake do that.' This is where the demon comes in. At such a point, I would sometimes say, 'You have no alternative, we have to do this or we won't get the thing out on time and if that happens, I'm in trouble.' There's a whole set of self-serving reasons for me to say, 'Plough on regardless, just get this thing done,' but Cecil had shown me how to spot the bad me. I could see it that morning when we had to make a change and I realised this was the me that gets over-excited in the pursuit of my goal.

I was shocked when Cecil said it was something to do with my laughter. I found that very hard and felt it was a rebuke. Cecil detected this daemon in me. You learn as a curator to be extremely manipulative, that's the daemon, and I think that's what Cecil was warning me against. The bit that's difficult for me to resolve still, is that this was somebody I thought very highly of. His example was not quite a moral example, but an aesthetic one which had moral force to it. It was so strong that one wondered whether one could live up to it, whether one could pass the test. Although Cecil could see through me, I may have given him the impression of being more invulnerable than I was.

I wasn't in a teacher/student relationship with Cecil yet I felt his power very strongly. With most artists I don't feel that. I'm impressed by their example or I have the problem of how I deal with them; why they are as they are, or why they behave so badly. Cecil never behaved badly in that sense. Part of the process was him testing you to see how base your materialism was, your base metal or something like that. He didn't use the words 'A young man like you,' but there was a kind of provocation there. Probably I was cowardly and mollified him. Later I obviously passed the test.

I went to tea at Cecil's flat in Paultons Square and it was magical. Samuel Palmer, in his notebooks, refers to visiting Blake as 'going to the house of the interpreter.' I had a similar feeling on visiting Cecil. I felt that I was entering a kind of magical space that connected two worlds. I may have the topology of the house wrong but I do remember rising up, to the very top.

Cecil was a fierce man. There was nothing airy-fairy about him. He was a very shrewd operator in the world. The way he dealt with me at first was with caution. He probably thought, 'Who is this person?' I talked to him a little bit about how I was going to do the exhibition, but more about himself. There were all sorts of things I wanted to know. You don't need to have questions, it comes from a conversation.

He talked a lot about Dartington Hall and a little bit about his childhood. My impression was that he came from quite a rigid Protestant background and that he only blossomed through contact with other artists, other creative artists generally, including musicians and poets. Dartington Hall was crucial in all of that.

I had to convince Cecil that the exhibition I was putting on was serious enough to merit his work, and also that it would contain art that he probably wouldn't like at all, such as Francis Bacon. I wanted Cecil to select his pictures. I kicked the ball back into his court. I had nothing in mind. In most cases, once you see an artist's work, you realise that your presumptions were nonsensical because you only saw this tiny bit of it. That's part of the process of getting to know an artist, to get them to lead you. They will always know better than you. I really do believe that. They can be complete bastards, but nevertheless they, by definition, will know their work better and I think the problem for most curators is that they won't accept that. It's a great pity. We've now entered an 'age of tin' with art, and with curating. I can't believe what's going on. I don't know that it can be remedied now because of the bureaucratisation of art and curating. I'm often asked whether one should set up an MA in curating to which I give the Gary Cooper answer, 'If you don't know I can't tell you, you won't be able to do it.'

In a sense the exhibition was like somebody giving you a wonderful group of books you hadn't read; I really did learn from those pictures. Nowadays thousands and thousands of pounds are spent either on computer simulations prior to the exhibition or on making models and moving little things around, but we knew what was going to hang in each room; we did the laying out within a matter

Cecil Collins
The Quest
1938
Oil on canvas
109 x 145cm

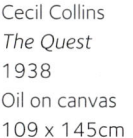

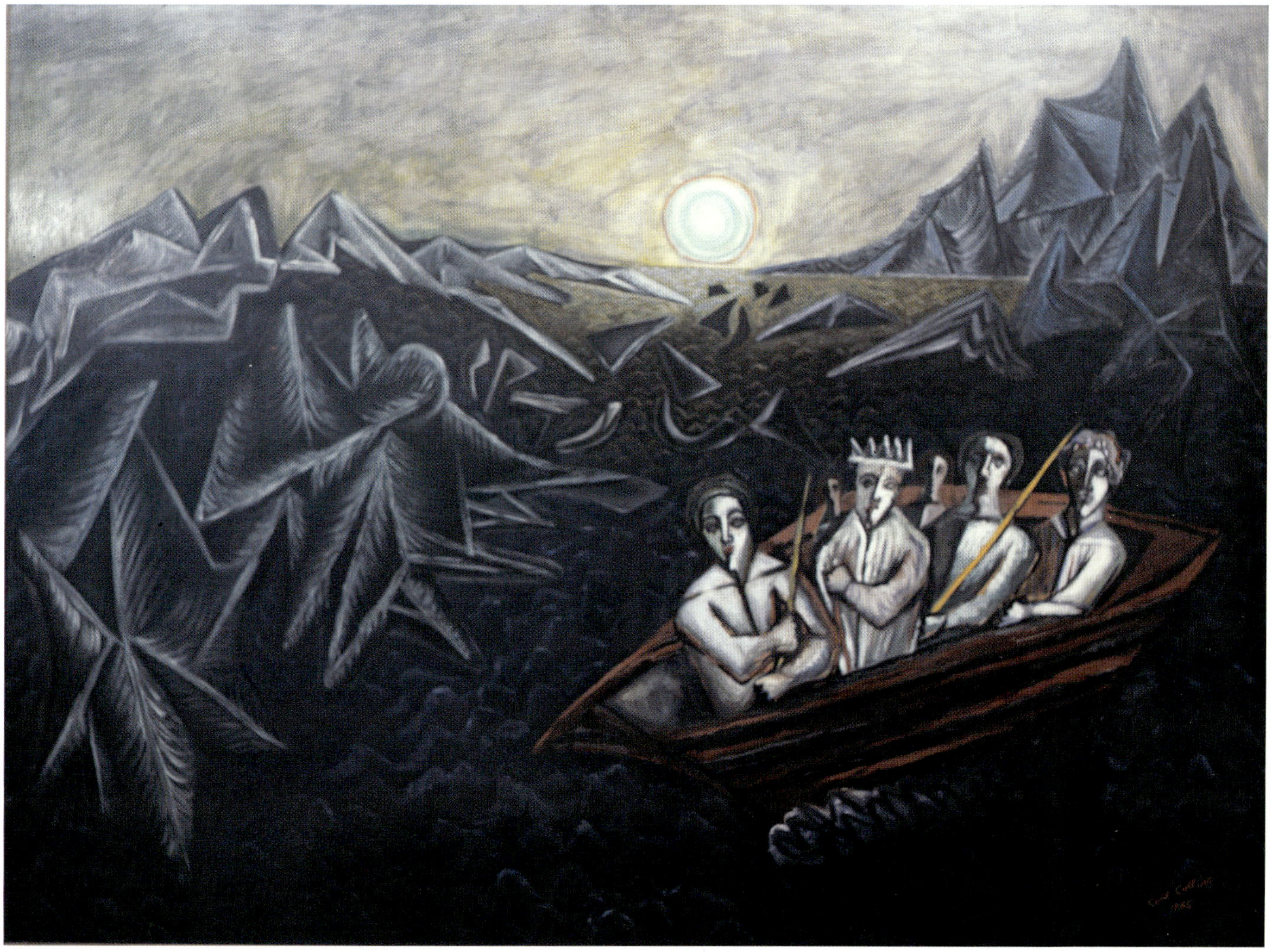

of minutes for each room. It was completely intuitive: this goes here, that goes there. I think it upset a lot of people because we double hung and triple hung and we did all kinds of interesting things.

Cecil invited me to tea again, after the exhibition. That was the second of the tea party occasions. I regret that I never had an independent relationship with Elisabeth. She was such a graceful person. I wish I'd been able to talk to her. I think she gave up her art to promote Cecil's. If there is enough generosity and reciprocity at the deepest level then some partnerships may be blessed. Cecil talked about his favourite music, particularly Fauré, and then he talked about the sublime nature of hearing music, in your dreams. Oddly enough I had heard music in my dream only a few weeks before. I thought this was very striking, that it had happened to me. I was able either to whistle the tune or sing it, and I said, 'God knows what this is?' Then a few days later I realised it was Elmer Bernstein, one of those very underrated, but absolutely marvellous Hollywood composers. Cecil was very excited that this dream-world music was Hollywood music. I don't see Hollywood music as not being transcendental. In fact I spend all my life trying to get rid of that kind of snobbery.

I can't remember Cecil's exact words, but we were talking about the devaluation of the coinage of art and culture and the sanctity of art or something like that, and then we switched to religion and he said, 'What will happen next will be religion itself will become debased. Even spirituality will become part of this process.' The moment he said it, I realised, even though it was shocking, that it was true. He was so far ahead of his time.

Cecil blessed me implicitly. It was completely non-verbal. I think he was inviting me to think more about an inner grace. He was kind enough to give me a couple of pictures. He asked me to pick one and I chose an angel standing in the sun. It was clearly done within the last five or ten years, but it was peeling and falling to pieces and he said, 'You don't want that, it's falling to bits.' I said, 'But it's the image'. Then he said, 'Have another one.' I chose a drawing of a Fool regarding an oil lamp it's quite Picassoesque. The Fool's got very beady eyes looking at the light. In a way, it's a bad drawing; it's very unpretty, very stark and obviously done with a hard pencil. I was delighted with it. What I find interesting about it is the hardness, the crudeness of it. I find it hard to meet the Fool's gaze.

I've got a group of pictures where I work, including an Eileen Agar, a Humphrey Jennings, and a Turner engraving. The Fool is placed the highest and to the left of this group and you can't look at it easily. Your eye can travel over all the other ones and they're wonderful pictures. Cecil's Fool is another kind of rebuke. The picture that's falling to pieces is on another wall. It's behind glass and will eventually disintegrate, but it doesn't matter. When Cecil said, 'Choose another one,' he seemed to be directing me towards one of his dreamy heads, but I didn't want that.

Cecil had an inner vision. At times it was a struggle for him to put down what he had seen. At other times he would start manipulating the paint and let the image come through. Some of those paintings were vehicles for his message, as much as paintings in their own right, and that's one of the problems if I were to be very analytical and cold. The best of his work can be quite epic in its suggestion, quite fabulous.

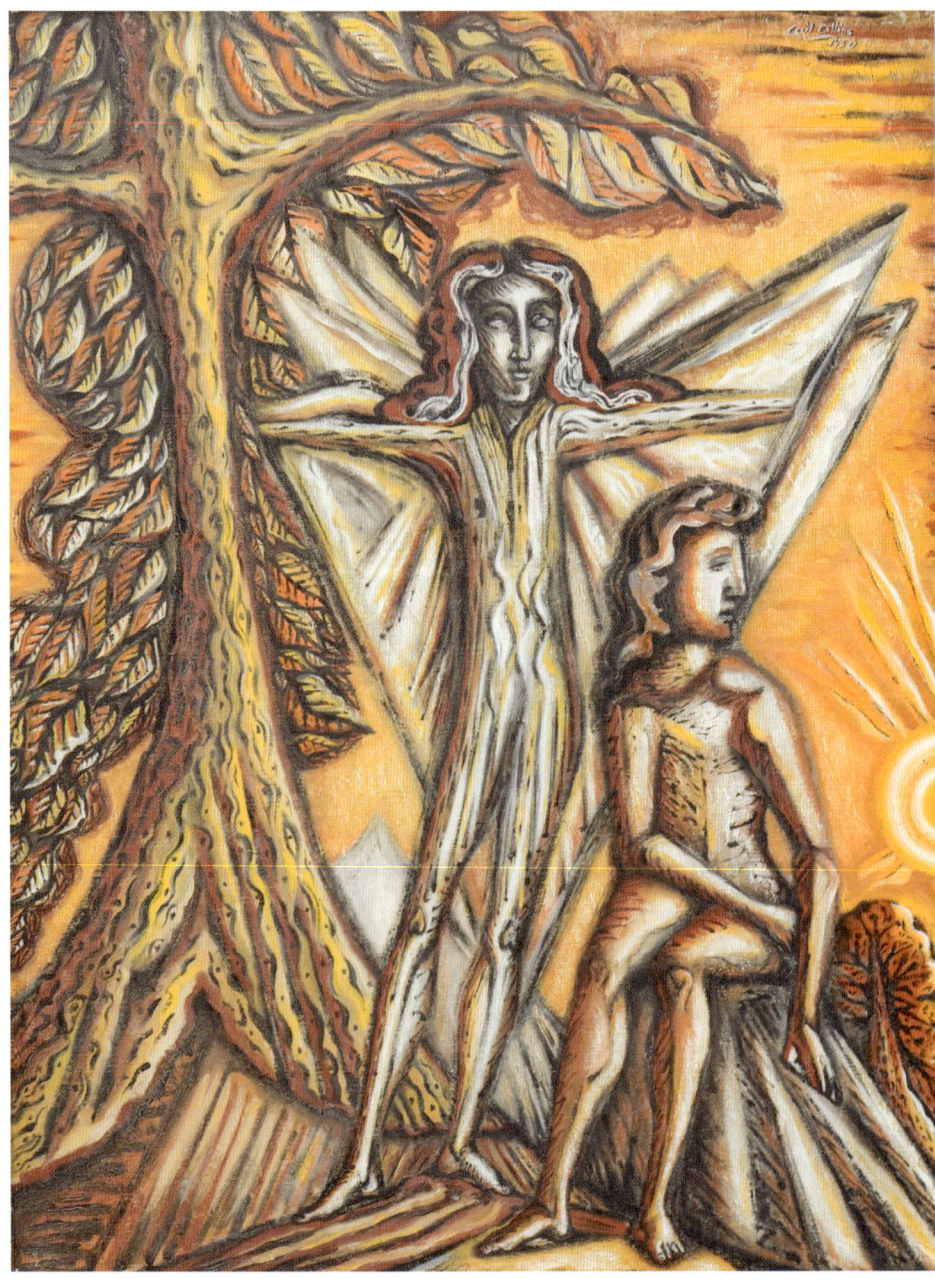

Cecil Collins
The Angel with Adam
1950
Oil on canvas
80 x 61cm

PETER NAHUM

Director with his wife, Renate, of The Leicester Galleries, London, specialist dealers in Victorian, Pre-Raphaelite, Symbolist and Visionary nineteenth and twentieth century art; author, lecturer and television personality.

Cecil, as an artist, hadn't entered my consciousness for many years because there were only scraps around on the market by him of no consequence and so I didn't even think about him. Then somebody brought me a transparency of *The Voice*, which was coming up for sale in America and I thought, 'If this is a good and important picture, then I should buy it.'

When *The Voice* arrived I hung it and eventually Cecil found out where it was and he and Elisabeth arrived at the gallery; this was in 1984. They sat in front of the picture and I was not sure how this spiritual visionary would view a commercial dealer, but we got on very well. People are either special in your lives or they're not. If they're special, as Cecil and Elisabeth became, they're very precious and to be cherished.

Cecil told me later that he knew we would get on because there is a reason why people buy works. If I show Cecil's paintings and somebody who hasn't heard of him is attracted to one of the pictures, I know that there is a reason. We sell a lot of symbolist and spiritual paintings so these are precisely the sort of people I deal with. The sensibilities they hold are not necessarily obvious. The people who have them can be quite tough in other ways.

If as a dealer you are not just a trader, then you buy paintings basically in the same way as choosing friends, not that you necessarily choose friends, it's a mutual thing. If you are true to what you like, you buy those that belong to you somehow, belong to a little bit of you. That's what I think when people buy pictures. Even if they're just doing a decorating job, they've personally chosen that object because it reflects something within them. We don't always achieve the right result for the obvious reason.

When you go to an exhibition, you are seeing a collage of the artist put together by the curator displaying his piecemeal vision of another's life; and every exhibition will be different. Just as when you look at a painting, you may be seeing a collage of a lot of different ideas, some taken from art of other ages. This is the way that art and ideas are formed, not out of a vacuum; they're formed out of living in life and the curiosity of being in life. Cecil's major retrospective at the Tate in 1989, pioneered by his friend Richard Morphet and curated by Judy Collins, was a *tour de force* and immensely moving and powerful. It was for this very reason that it frightened even the more respected of our critics and failed to get many decent reviews. The accessibility of the spirituality seemed to terrify them.

In the sale catalogue of my collection of twentieth century British artists, I described Cecil and Elisabeth as an extraordinary visionary couple, but the visionary aspect is perhaps not the most important, as in Cecil's case that's taken for granted. What perhaps is more important is the couple. So many people talk about artists as a single person and, basically, people who live together all their lives are a couple, not a single entity. They're a unit. I think that's very important. It's often ignored, but it is part of the structure of life. That's the way you are. I mean you might be an isolated human being, that's fine, but I find that if you are happily married, you tend to gravitate towards couples and single people. As a tight unit you probably won't gravitate towards, for instance, a serial philanderer because their philosophy and your philosophy won't fit together.

For me, Cecil and Elisabeth were an island of sanity in a particularly insane era. Maggie Thatcher created a climate where, we all made a lot of money, but we had to work like hell to do it. When you were in the middle of what I call that maelstrom, you couldn't work it out, you had to use all your energy just to stay with it. I used to think of myself as a sort of madly spinning disc.

Cecil and Elisabeth were independent from the present mess that is life. They could observe it, but just as another blip in time. They did what they were in the world to do with all the integrity they had. They never had anything to do with the Maggie Thatchers, Tony Blairs, Ted Heaths or John Majors. Spiritually their lives were on another plane. Artists and all human beings need integrity and that has nothing to do with making mistakes or being honest or dishonest, it means doing your very best with what you have been given and not doing it for the wrong reasons.

Integrity is very important, because we are all given talents to get through life and the main talent for getting through life is getting through life. The next most important talent is discipline. If you don't have discipline, you can, for instance, be the greatest footballer in the world, but fail to live up to your talent and die of drink and drugs, as we've seen many times.

We have to do the best with the talents we're given and Cecil and Elisabeth were very steadfast in their vision and talents. When they removed themselves to an isolated cottage, Cecil could come out and talk clearly and eruditely with great thought off the top of his head for hours, which was an extraordinary talent and to be on the receiving end was a great privilege. They were both great communicators. If Cecil said something, you would listen very carefully because he had stood back and worked it all out a long time ago. He didn't waste his energy. He knew there was no point in being totally spiritual because what's that got to do with life? It's only a part of it.

Almost every artist will tell you that the communication, the painting itself, was not as successful as he would have liked. You may have a vision in your head, but finding the words or finding and creating the image to communicate that vision is a completely different thing. There are quite a number of second-rate Cecil works around, often because he wouldn't sell the great images. Frequently, he had to let go of the stuff that was less successful, which didn't necessarily do him any good in market terms. If you want to fault him, you might say, 'Cecil, rather than letting them go, you should have burnt them.'

When Kenneth Clark made a pilgrimage to Cambridge and stood in Cecil's studio and said, 'I'd like these four for the National Gallery', Cecil told him they weren't for sale. They were far too personal. Kenneth went away mightily pissed off, and I can understand it. Here was this lordly, upper-class, autocratic person and Cecil had cut completely through the bullshit. Basically, he was saying 'Why should I sell to you, and who do you think you are? You're just another human being.' They had no money and here was one of 'the great and the good' offering not only money, but also to put Cecil's paintings in the most important place in the world and Cecil took one look at him and refused. Perhaps if Kenneth Clark had been a humbler person, Cecil might have said, 'I really don't want to part with them', but then he might well have parted with just one.

Peter Bowles, the actor, who is a committed collector, used to come to the gallery and gradually I got to know him. He told me that, as a young student, he'd bought a Cecil for which he had six months to pay, but couldn't make the payments and had to return it. I thought it would be wonderful to get him together with Cecil, so we had a dinner in our very small house and it so happened that a friend, Evan Turner, director of the Cleveland Museum of Art, was also attending.

Cecil and Elisabeth were sitting on this tiny sofa in our tiny room with Evan squeezed near them on a chair, but Peter and his wife, Sue, were late because they couldn't find our house. When that happens to me, I think, 'Why am I driving round this bloody town looking for this house?' and I would have arrived mightily pissed off, but Peter came in and immediately went down before Cecil on one knee. Evan whispered to me, 'He must be an actor.' Cecil is very important to Peter who has his own spiritual vision. Cecil treated it as though it were the most normal thing in the world, which it was.

Cecil's picture that I really care about and which means most to me, not his finest painting in execution but emotionally, is the great statement of the second World War, *The Pilgrim Fool*, and should have been in my collection. It belonged to Lady Spender who should have sold it to me because Elisabeth had recommended that she did. I wrote Lady Spender a very gentle letter, but she gave the painting to d'Offay to sell. 'Why did she do that?' I asked Elisabeth, who replied, 'She didn't take your letter seriously.' I should have simply written, 'Sell me the picture.' It wasn't a question of price. The composition is of the innocent Fool and the untainted little girl as they walk hand-in-hand toward the viewer away from the burning landscape that is the madness of war (and 'civilisation'). It encapsulates the whole folly of humankind. In fact, the painting went to very special collectors whose vision and Cecil's matched. I am a great believer in results like this happening for all the right reasons.

The influence of Dartington, where Cecil painted this picture, was very powerful. It had that extraordinarily spiritual energy. (Unlike the energy in Soho around the same time which was, of course, at the other end of the spectrum, totally decadent, but an artistic energy nonetheless with its poets and writers, who were often drunk and disorderly.) Dartington is a spiritual community and you do feel this special atmosphere when you go there, probably because it's placed on certain ley lines; some places are imbued with this energy and some aren't. It's not the people; rather that sympathetic people are drawn to these places.

There's no question that Cecil was the great visionary artist, but Cecil was also Cecil because of Elisabeth. She sacrificed her whole life to him, as women often do. I say 'sacrificed' but I don't mean sacrificed in a painful way. She kept up her painting, her reading and her interests, but she stepped backwards and allowed him to go forward, which was fine and quite right.

When Cecil died she rang me up and said, 'Would you please drive me out to look for cemeteries.' So we went down to Putney and then to Highgate where we saw the keeper, or whatever he's called, and he said, 'Yes I read your husband's obituary in the papers today and I do think there are one or two places left.' We went to see one place and he said, 'We can put him under this tree.' I said to Elisabeth, 'No, I don't think he should be under the tree, I think he should be in the sunlight.' So we settled on the sunlit grassy patch where the foxes played. Elisabeth felt that Cecil was still there; that he was still with her. They were so close together spiritually, that it gave her strength to go on, and I think it was normal to go on because they were still a couple.

Cecil's art, his teaching, his writings, his poetry and the ability to talk to a group, were all ways of communicating. For me it is his paintings that are the most lasting and accessible legacy of his thoughts. As Cecil said more than once, the process of painting was boring and laborious a lot of the time, but he had to do this to get his visions and his ideas out. The gentle conveyance of his feelings and ideas was important. The teaching to his students was like rearing and

curators & gallery owners

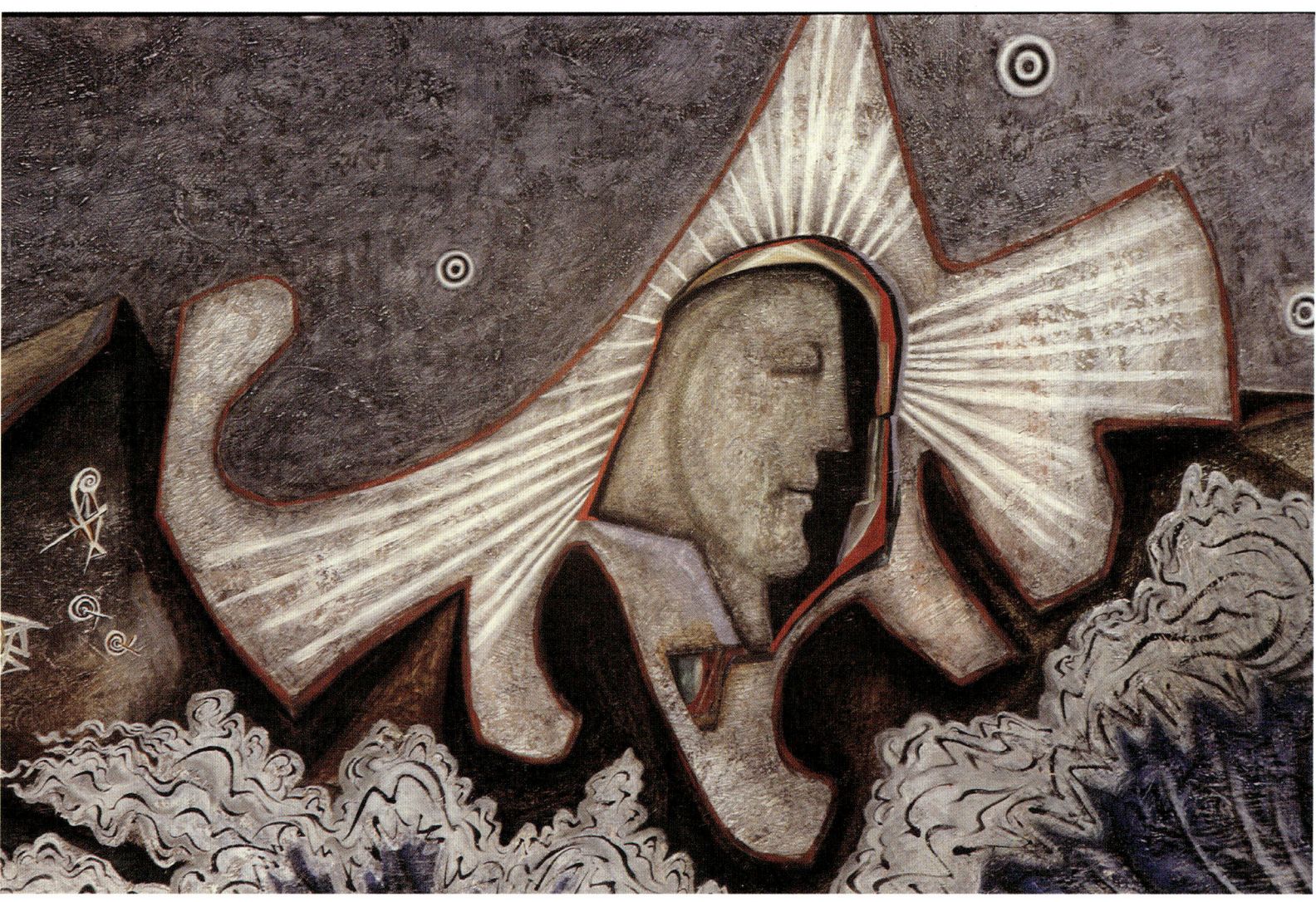

Cecil Collins
The Voice
1938
Oil on canvas
122 x 152cm

inspiring children, and his verbal message was forthright and moving - it hit the spot (many spots). You give children information from your genes and they take it on in a different way, but that's not the same as the immediate vision which is in these paintings and is a message that we all can continue to respond to deeply and emotionally.

The more in tune the viewer is with the painter's point of view, the more they will get out of it. The artist paints an image and the viewer walks into that picture and relates to that vision, that visual message in their own way. Artists give you a very special privilege, they give you their dreams. You walk into their dream and you should make of their dream what you will.

Paintings last. All paintings and the feelings within them, feelings very often put there quite subliminally, exist permanently. As long as there are human beings, then a proportion of those human beings will relate to the sensibilities within an individual work of art. It's not just Cecil's paintings, it's all works of art. There are people who will completely pass by a particular work that speaks to you, but then they will connect with something else.

All art communicates and all art has a value. For me the greatest spiritual artist in the twentieth century is Barnett Newman; his spirituality is unfathomable. It's much more interesting than Rothko's. Rothko is quite deliberate in his spirituality and also rather suicidal later on, so ultimately not very rewarding to me. There's no question that Cecil is the most spiritual artist in Britain of the twentieth century, especially in a very British way of looking at life which comes out in his own personal visionary landscape.

Cecil had a head full of pictures that he didn't have enough time to paint. That's why he was so frustrated by the process of painting because some works took a long time. When he painted with what he called tempera, there was this great liquid mess which few but him could control. His glazes took an enormous amount of time. So there he was, bursting with images and knowing that there weren't enough lifetimes to paint them, but he didn't take shortcuts. He loved the craft of painting.

Music is central to my way of teaching. I'm only concerned with unsealing the flow within the pupils.

Cecil Collins

My painting is about that secret life which is very deep in us and which is in danger of being destroyed by conventional education of the modern world.

Cecil Collins

Rhythm is the most vital primordial element in the creative spirit. The universe is made up of vibrations, only the mind thinks it's matter.

Cecil Collins

Photograph by Jane Bown
Cecil Collins teaching
1988

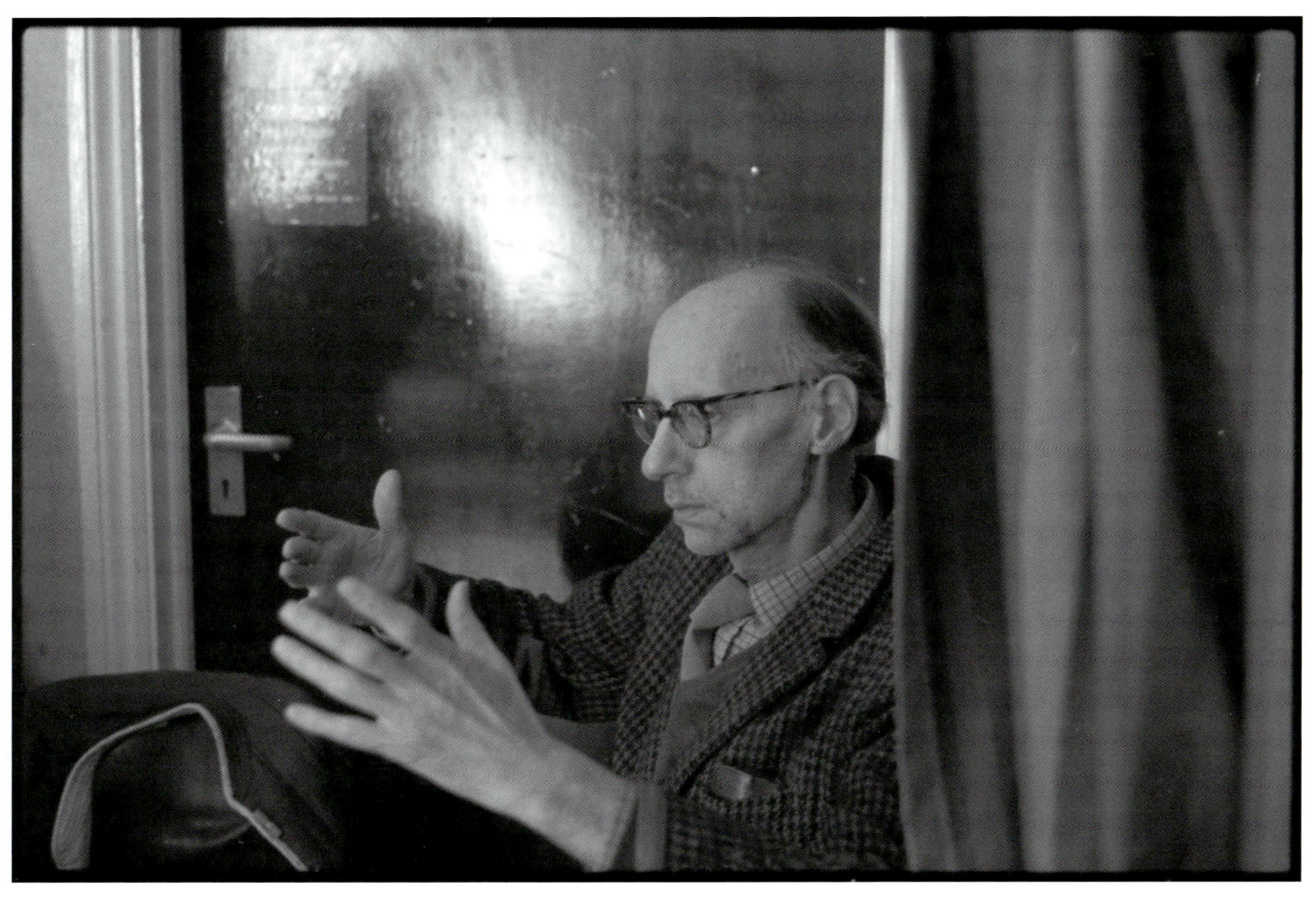

STUDENTS, MODELS & COLLEAGUES

STUDENTS

CLARE ALLEN

Clare Allen studied at the Slade School of Fine Art, has degrees in Embroidered Textiles, History of Art, Art Therapy and an MA in Practical Traditional Arts from the Prince's Foundation. She teaches, restores traditional embroidery, paints, makes jewellery and is a trained counsellor. She is married with twin daughters.

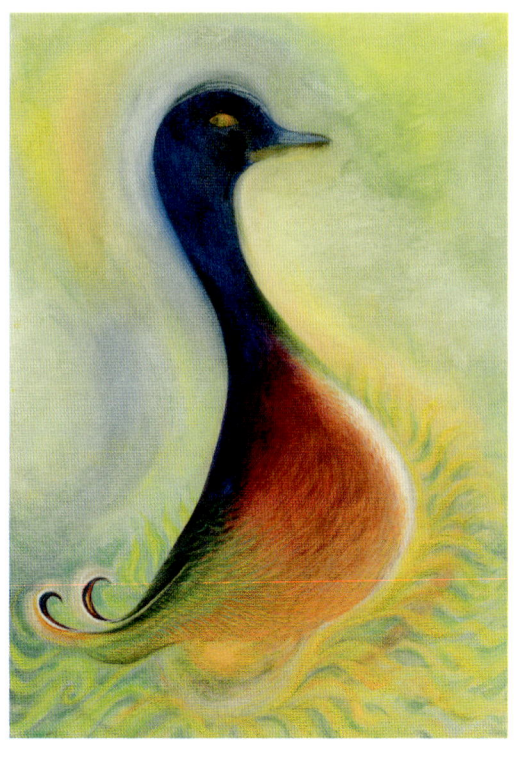

Clare Allen
Golden Egg
1997
Oil on paper
17.5 x 25cm

The first time I met Cecil was in 1981 at the Anthony d'Offay Gallery where he had an exhibition. I'd already fallen totally in love with his work on a previous visit and I went up to him and just said, 'Are you Cecil Collins?' I had tears in my eyes when I then told him, 'This is absolutely wonderful.' He said, 'The reason you feel that is that you are a child of paradise. I do a class on a Tuesday, can you come?'

He was so practical. I'd been doing a lot of searching of all kinds, but suddenly here was this heaven on earth. Then I had to find out where it was because he didn't tell me. I followed it up and so I came for about a year to his class at the City Lit. I felt I'd come home, absolutely come home, because I'd been looking for something in my own painting, in my own life, and I'd found it in his work.

It was as if Cecil knew that in what we think is the worst of ourselves is actually the source of the best. All the things that we most reject or dislike about ourselves are in fact what we need to embrace in some measure. It's like those moments when you feel at your most vulnerable and the other moments when you suddenly realise that you've got enormous strength, those two polarities that one tends not to acknowledge.

In lots of classes we moved to music. We all moved together so we got used to it, but I never liked being picked to lead the movement for the class and model and I only did it a couple of times.

There would be times in his classes when perhaps I was doing the movements, or perhaps if a drawing had gone terribly badly and I'd made a right old mess so in the end I just didn't care, then sometimes I'd burst into tears. On one occasion I was so moved I just couldn't believe it. I went to him at the end of the class and said something like, 'That was the most amazing class,' and I was still blubbing. It wasn't the only time I felt praised or acknowledged or seen, but it was the only time he ever used a phrase like, 'Well done.' He put his arm momentarily around me and said, 'Good for you, good for you,' as if to get in touch with this vulnerable and wounded side was a far richer experience than to feel you'd done a super drawing that looked great.

Looking back, those of my drawings that I was consciously pleased with were probably the ones that were slick, rather than the ones that allowed something extraordinary to happen in the form of a blotch and a line where one had felt the model's heart beat like a chakra and had seen that without putting the words to it. You were in the experience and you didn't have to know with your brain or with your self-appraisal. You didn't even have to know you were in a Cecil Collins class, you just had to surrender somewhere and be yourself.

Immediately before starting a drawing, when all the students were ready poised with the instruments Cecil had instructed us to use, he would say, 'We'll start with a clap.' If it sounded ragged, he'd say, 'You aren't in tune,' or, 'You aren't in touch,' or, 'You aren't ready. Now, again, one, two, three!' Until we all clapped as one. For me this was his way of bringing the energy together, both in each student and in the class as a whole. The clap was a way of shattering the distractions we'd brought in with us and creating intentionality, creating a sacred focus, *the temenos*. The room became a pregnant emptiness. There was a feeling of absolute oneness.

I never felt that going to his classes was about being a good artist, rather it was about this other thing that was happening. Any dreams I've ever had about him have always been about this aspect. In fact, Cecil was certainly my first deep spiritual teacher and I also went to the Sufi teacher, Mrs Tweedie. They both held the pole of the world between them: the masculine and the feminine.

I remember one dream very vividly. I was sitting somewhere in a room that had two entire walls of mirrors, and Cecil was there with a group of people around us and he simply said to me, 'There is no duality. You remember that, don't you?' and I said I did.

When I had to leave London and Cecil's class, it wasn't hard because it was quite clear to me that I had been changed forever. I was having an interesting year, but it wasn't a career and I needed to go somewhere else and do some work. I needed to put things into practice. I moved to Yorkshire and after a couple of weeks, discovered that the husband in the household where I was staying was a close friend of Cecil's. Boy, did I ever feel taken care of!

When I went back to London, I started going to Cecil again because I knew I had to. It was pretty intense. I hardly talked to people after the classes. I would often leave carrying the whole atmosphere inside me. I remember there was a time when I painted at the most extraordinary hours in the dawn and very late at night, feeling this extraordinary atmosphere, which I felt was very much from Cecil's classes, given by Cecil. It had to do with contacting my own sensitivity. For a powerful and short period I was completely aware that what we see of the outside world is but a stage, a theatre setting for something far more than just our human lives. Beyond that, there is something else quite extraordinary pervading and permeating all that's being expressed. I don't know that I can find the words for this experience.

You couldn't possibly be competitive and vulnerable to what was going to happen in the moment. There was nothing to be touchy or edgy about because if you were feeling like that you couldn't be open. I was very aware whenever I felt like that it was as if a hardness was suddenly there. It was much more important not to care how much of a mess one got into or whether one's instruments got muddled up with somebody else's. There wasn't any time for that from the moment you entered the room. It was simply about being there one hundred percent. You just had to sit down and get your stuff out, realising you were being vulnerable, realising you hadn't a clue what was going on, didn't know when he was going to walk in, didn't know if you liked the other people, didn't even know them very well at first, and none of that was really important. It was only about attentiveness.

Often I somehow ended up sitting quite close to him, somewhere towards the edge of the room where he would be sitting near the door. I had the feeling that he could look inside me and as if, from the moment he came into the room, he knew precisely what state everybody was in and exactly what was going on. There was nowhere to hide, but loving him so much, it didn't matter whether you ever spoke to him or not. I think that was a spiritual training in itself. You were forced out of your habitual self. There simply wasn't space to get involved in thinking, I'd like to do this, or what about that, or look at the line of that back. There wasn't time to get into any of our conditioning about life drawing. It was learning that this is a discipline: do what you're told. If you didn't, you got in a muddle, but that didn't matter either, you just did your best to catch up as quickly as possible. There was no question of I'll skip the toe or the little finger, because you knew the teacher knew you were doing that so you were just there, doing exactly what everybody else had to.

In the end, I kept very few drawings from the class. I went through the whole pile a half a dozen times on different occasions, first of all thinking, keep every single thing, never let any of it go. The next time it was, what a load of crap, chuck half a dozen out. Then the next time I'd get rid of more, but I never threw away any of the sheets with drawings of the 'Matrix' which Cecil taught us about. He quoted from Goethe's *Faust*, the part about 'The Mothers' which was linked to the 'Matrix' and the quality of chaos and darkness. It describes this extraordinary cauldron of the feminine, where you are drawn down and down into matter, this dark, never-ending web. In order not to be sucked down into it one has to have the masculine, to differentiate, to make an incision, a cutting to come up out of this web.

Cecil would instruct us to draw with the feminine flow of a continuous line to create a web of lines, a completely undifferentiated scribble over the whole page. Then we'd work with the masculine energy to bring the form out of this matrix.

I wrote down all the quotes, all the instructions and all the instruments in little notebooks that I knew I would always love to go back to. I kept these notebooks because I always felt that I would teach and I have started to teach using his techniques. Towards the end of his life, he once said to me something like, 'Put all this on a back burner. Don't even worry if it's not simmering.' I had this wonderful image of an enormous, grubby black iron stove with a huge pot of my love for him and the work, the painting, the art and the possibility of teaching from depth rather than superficially. It was very much on the back burner, but since then I've been able to dip into that pot, re-warm it and see that it's still simmering.

Cecil Collins

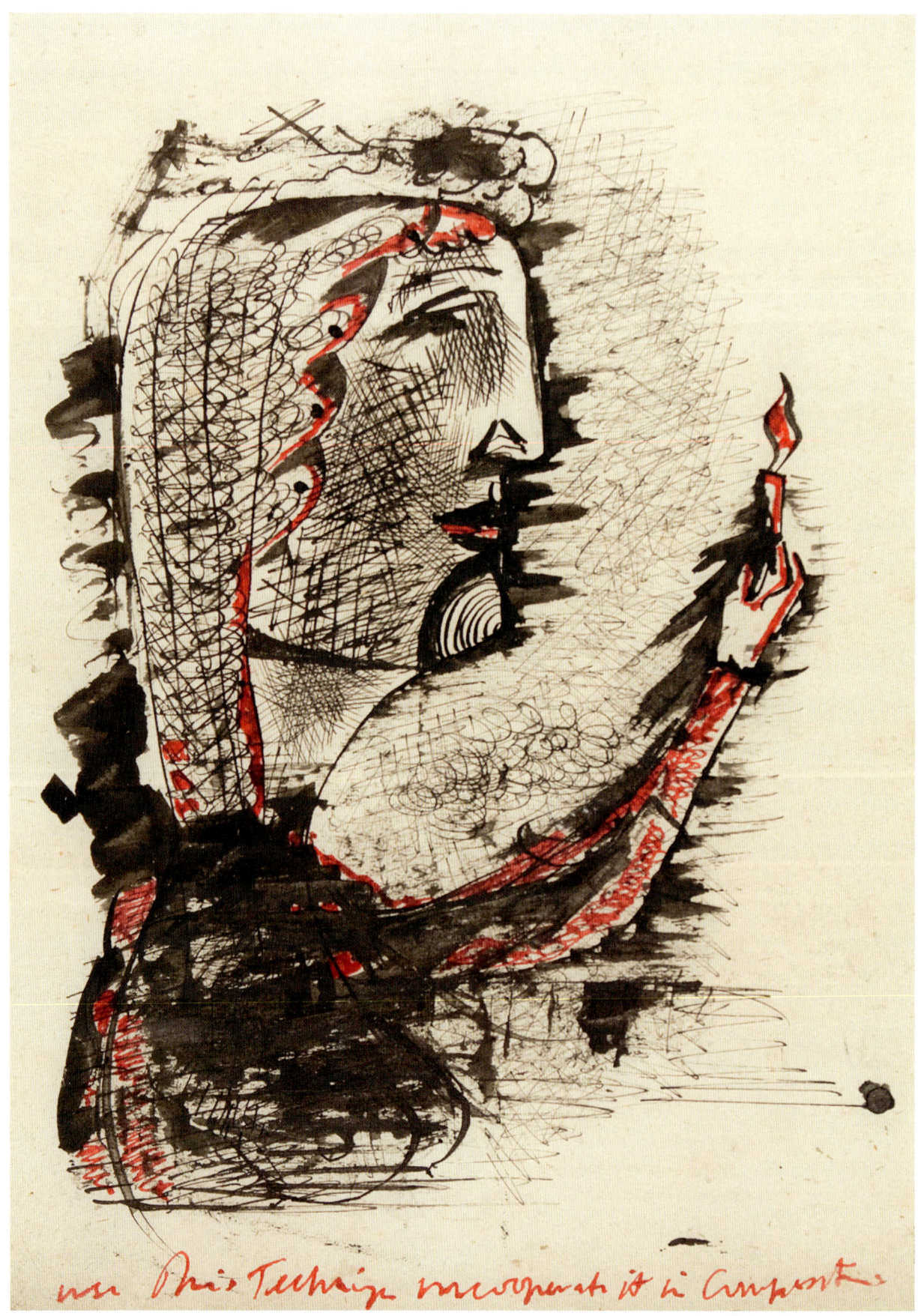

Cecil Collins
Woman with Candle
ink and wash

MELISSA ALLEY

Melissa Alley, born in 1962, attended Wimbledon School of Art and Central St Martins where she studied under Cecil Collins. She has exhibited widely, lives in London and is a trained hypnotherapist. She is married to the artist Paul Tecklenberg and they have one son, Jasper.

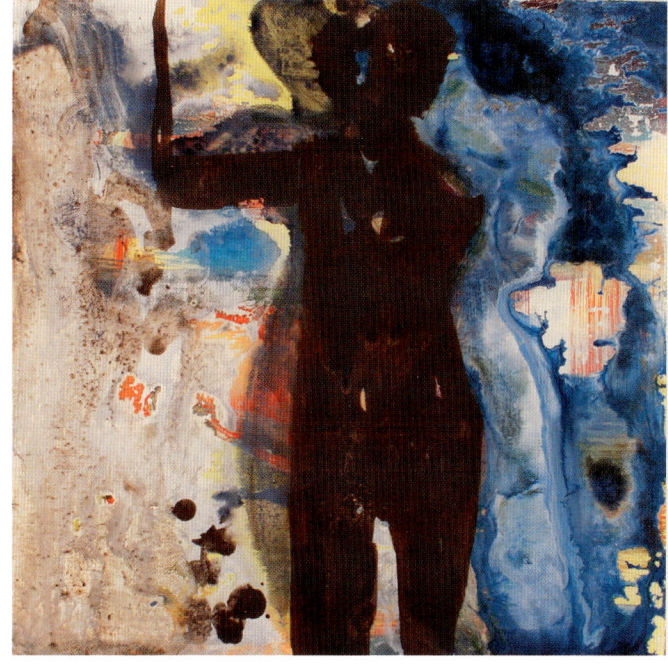

Melissa Alley
Trinity
2007
Mixed media on wood
30 x 30cm

My father, who died in 1999, was a Bevin boy in the war. After that, he studied history of art and was in Paris for a while. He became Keeper of Modern Art at the Tate, retiring when he was sixty in 1986. Obviously that meant we used to have lots of art at home. People like Sydney Nolan lived with us for a while in our top flat and we had Paula Rego and Victor Willing. We also had one of the Nicholson triplets and Paul Jenkins who is my godfather.

My mother, Anthea, died in 1993. She studied art at Chelsea. We used to go to St Ives every summer. We would call in for tea at Barbara Hepworth's and we used to go off to Patrick's house. There were always these amazing people around our table. It was fascinating, but also intimidating. When your mother's an artist and very brave (she taught herself to weld in her fifties which was very unusual) and her best friends were these strong, powerful women, then you think that everything that you do has got to be good enough to hang in the Tate. It was a lot to live up to.

I was studying Fine Art at Central in 1985 and I was on the same floor as the life room that, on Fridays, was taken over by Cecil and his students. There was somebody in my painting group who went to Cecil's classes and he said, 'Everybody's doing very beautiful drawings,' and although he was a bit snotty about it, he did produce some quite interesting work. At that time, there was a degree of distrust of Cecil. All our tutors were wary of him, particularly the trendy young teachers. They thought that his influence would do something strange to students' artwork. Everybody at art school knew my mother and had taught with her at different places so when they said, 'Don't go to Cecil Collins' classes,' I felt I was doing something a bit rebellious by going.

My small space at college had a door on it so I was working in a box and, at the same time, I was doing paintings of a box that was split into four sections. It was a thick corrugated cardboard box with big flaps opened out at the top. It was very deep and when you put it on its side, it had four compartments and it was like looking at a house. I had different 'elements', different kinds of figures that I put inside: a little vase which was very much like a bust and a tall, elegant glass that had broken in such a way that its structure was still there, despite half of it having disappeared, but it created this amazing movement like an arm. There was also a little Indian figure and a marvellous piece of lead I'd picked up from the stained glass department which I trailed out through one of the flaps. I was looking at ideas of space and light, at how you make paint work. I lit them from behind and they took on an extraordinary theatrical quality. I was very disciplined about working, but I had kind of painted myself into a corner.

I was looking for freedom and fluidity and I knew there was something within me that I wasn't touching and I felt a huge degree of frustration with my work. I felt there might be something in Cecil's classes for me, but it was very tentative to begin with and it didn't feel completely comfortable. I did some drawings in the class and I was really pleased with them. After a while, I saw something else in other people's drawings, a fluidity that I didn't have in mine and I could see that if I wanted that, then I had to let go of something. For me, that was a massive thing and it took some time.

Cecil used to talk about it as being like dissolving the ego and it's also a dissolving of what you hold dear which is your armour, part of what you consider your identity, but by letting go of that, you gain so much more. It's like jumping off a cliff, you have to trust and have faith and by doing that, you end up with something that is dynamic and holds fresh life that is not confined. Then later, you go through another crisis when you see the beautiful paintings or drawings that you're doing and you hang on to that as your recipe. As soon as you do that, you have to go through the process of letting it go again.

Cecil was so ingenious in considering different techniques that one could use to break free, to get into that flow: all those things like using both the left and right side of your brain by using both hands. If you're right-handed, you might be able to draw a line in a very purposeful way, but instead you were asked to use your pencil in your left hand. This produced something which potentially could be clumsy, but in a way was much more expressive and innocent. Once you've done that in class for long enough and you're freed up, you're able to do it for yourself and it doesn't matter what medium you're doing it in either. After a while, I got very free with what I was doing and Cecil said, 'Now you're in the flow.' Once that happened, that was it; I've never looked back. Then Cecil said, 'I suggest you go off and have some more formal drawing classes.'

I'll never forget one woman at Central who, in the middle of the class, started bringing out sandwiches. Cecil told her she was very lazy which I thought was entertaining. He didn't say it in a particularly tactless way; he just said it as it was. To me he said, 'You are not lazy at all, but thinking for you is quite dangerous. You're better when you don't have time to think.'

Cecil was pretty old by that stage; it wasn't long before he died. I stayed with him for about two or three years and after I left college I went back to Central to do Ruth's classes till about 1995. Ruth is quite imposing and she was like a terrier defending Cecil's classes at Central which were constantly under threat when they were trying to sack him. That's what frightened the other tutors.

I absolutely loved Ruth's classes. I modelled as a means of paying for them and that was one of the best things I could have done as it moved my drawing along immensely. You really get into the poses, into that state of being and the relationship between you and the students. I think that gives you a greater humility when you then draw another person. It creates a depth to the relationship. You'd know what was happening skeletally and in the muscles so it made a massive difference. I never modelled for Cecil. It would have been too intimate to be on the same floor as the one on which I'd been studying at my art school. I modelled at St Martin's and that was near enough.

I would have particularly loved to get to know Elisabeth better. I did a bit when I was working at England & Co and Elisabeth was having her exhibition there. I helped address all her envelopes. She had an immense elegance and such a presence as well. It didn't matter that she was in her eighties; she was absolutely stunning. I think that she and I might have become good friends, but I was slightly inhibited. I made an unfortunate comment when I said, 'I really enjoyed your husband's paintings,' and it was like, 'It's my time now.' Actually, I thought she was the better painter. There was such freshness about everything that she did, a beautiful naïve quality that was less knowing than Cecil and I think that's why Cecil thought that she was the real painter. There was an amazing depth to what he did, but she had something about her that was just extraordinary. She was so present in her work while Cecil was more contrived. I've always been very resistant to Cecil's paintings which is weird. I have become more attracted as time has gone on and I can see elements that are fantastic.

Cecil was somebody who thought a great deal. I remember some of the things he used to say, that he walked around in total emotional pain because of being in contact with the rawness of life and that you can't be an artist and be happy. He seemed to think that to truly be an artist, you take on board so much of the misery of the world that you cannot help but feel the pain because by unmasking yourself to that degree, you are taking down your defences. I think that by painting, you are opening yourself up and you also get into that river of pure joy which is essential to who we all are so I don't agree with him on that. I feel that he was hampered by his own thoughts. On the other hand, he brought so much knowledge to what he did and one bounced off that.

When you took on Cecil's classes, if you really gave yourself over to the experience of it, you had a kind of religious experience which is possibly what people got freaked out about when I was at college. You were getting through to something that was very essential and you were unclothing yourself. Coming from my background and being inhibited in the way that I was, here I was provided ostensibly with another family insofar as we were all in the same boat with a figurehead who was teaching us. It was an opportunity to get back to the core of who we were.

They used to talk about 'the disciples' and this was something that was ridiculed a lot. I think people did give Cecil a lot of authority, but I never found it intrusive. You longed for his comments so maybe, in that respect, you were a bit of a disciple, but for an essential shift in your being, you need that feedback. He only commented when there was a shift so when he did you thought, 'Yes, I'm doing the right thing.' I never felt as though I was dependent upon him. His class was very much a learning tool.

Because we were using all these different instruments at the same time, we got so discombobulated. That chimes with hypnotherapy where you often end up confusing the conscious

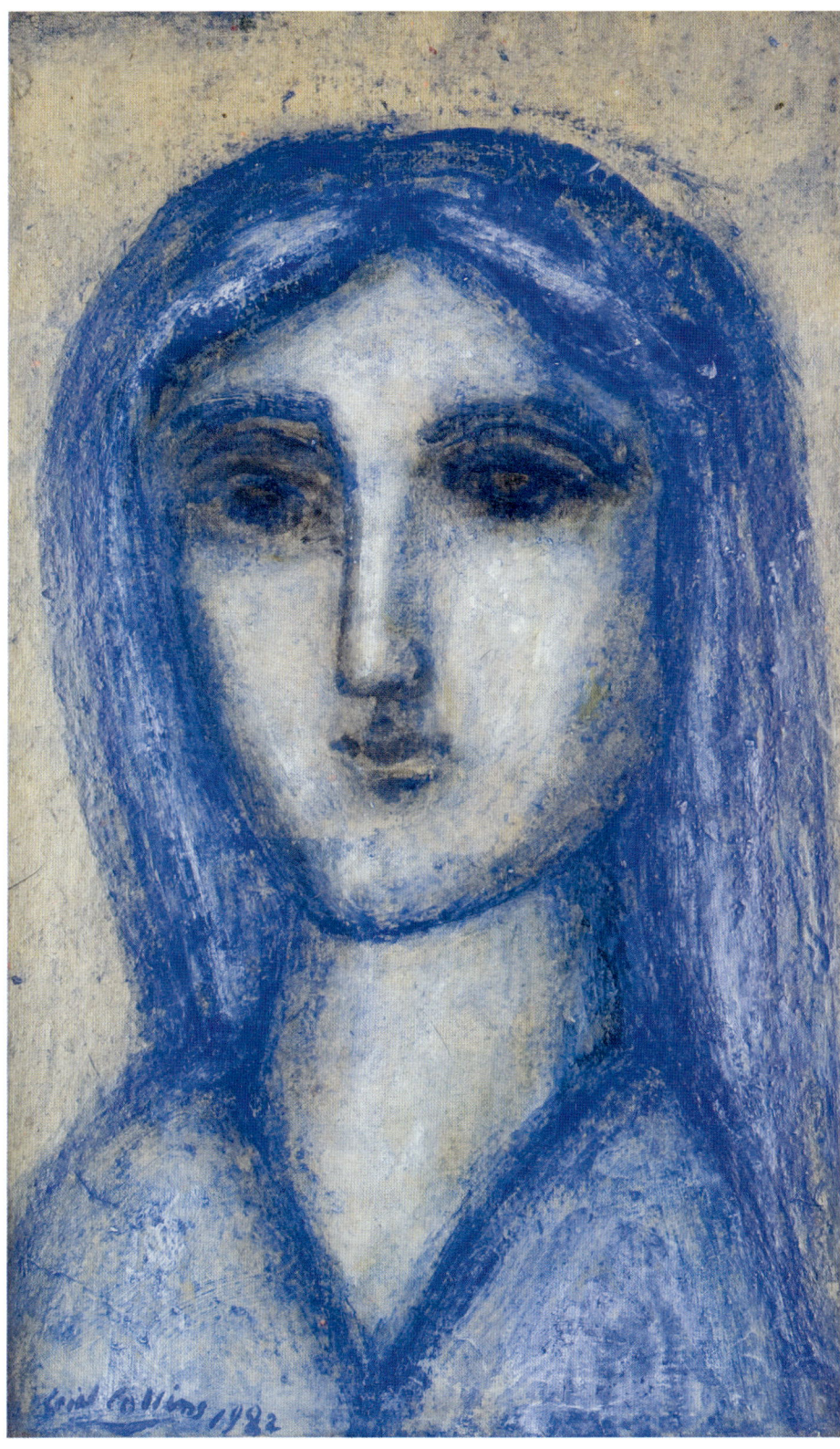

Cecil Collins
Girl in Blue
1982
Mixed media on board
20.3 x 12.7cm

mind so much that you can then communicate directly to the subconscious mind. This is where all the habits lie and all the information. People in Cecil's classes were relinquishing control and that terrified the tutors. They were frightened of you going off into that environment because something weird might happen to you, like in a cult. They felt that he was interfering with us, but we were never hypnotised from that point of view. It was much more that things were drawn out of us than things were put in.

Cecil had a certain luminosity that attracted people to him. I'm not sure whether he really enjoyed that because he was a solitary figure and quite detached, not somebody who would have sought out a huge amount of company. Maybe that was what people who were wary of Cecil picked up on. Maybe they saw that the people who were attracted to him were a bit lost and in need, people whose critical faculty wasn't properly in place and they were worried that they would get absorbed into something. I think it was the people around him who created that kind of mythology about him.

Cecil provided various keys that helped us to unlock our inner potential. If I feel that something's becoming too mannered, too gestural, too confined, if it's stuck or I'm trying too hard, then I go back into the subconscious and it becomes a key that unlocks another world. If I did it consciously it would be leaden, but because it just emerges and I allow it to be, it contains energy.

Ever since I was tiny, colour has been my biggest thing and I used to go to the City Lit every year to do Cecil's summer colour course. There was an amazing exercise where you'd listen to a piece of music and walk around as though you were being priestesses on a shore. There would be a certain moment within the music where you would get down on your knees. You would wait and it would change again and then you would stand up and continue walking round. It was profoundly moving and I cried so much. I said to Cecil, 'I think I was a priestess on the shore once,' and he looked at me and said, 'Yes, I think you were.' It was like coming home to something that was very pure and simple and there was a degree of humility about it. It was a very powerful experience and it had a huge resonance for me. I felt very strongly that it altered me quite deeply, because it gave me something that I needed to create for myself again. It was a bizarre experience. When you're young, you're so caught up in an image of what people expect of you and then you have an experience at a deep organic level that is out of this world, out of time, which is so much more essential to who you are, you never go back. It was quite epic for me.

STELLA ASTOR

After finishing a Foundation Course in 1968, Stella Astor was disillusioned by the approach to education in art schools until she met Cecil Collins in the 1980s and became one of his dedicated students. In 2004 she launched Fools' Press and published *Angels*, a pocket-size introduction to Collins' vision. Having raised a family, she completed a Masters Degree at the Prince's School of Traditional Art in 2007 and now has the time to focus on her art.

I have a passion for drawing and painting and found the consensus of opinion on art and how to teach it in the 1970s and 80s very confusing. Then I met Lily who talked enthusiastically about Cecil Collins and his classes. She showed me a copy of *Vision of the Fool*. The paintings meant very little to me and there wasn't enough time to read the text so I was introduced to Cecil with no real idea of what kind of artist he was.

'Appearances are deceptive,' Cecil often said. He looked rather like a bird, a crane in a tweed overcoat with a hump back, enormous flat feet, thick spectacles and long, sensitive fingers. He had a deep, clear voice and never wasted a word; there was absolutely no waffle and he was often humorous. One of his tweed jackets had incongruous floral patches at the elbows. For the first year or more, I found it hard to remember his face. He would come into the classroom almost unnoticed and settle into the corner as everyone mixed their inks. His soft word was absolute authority. 'Can we begin, please?' and at once there was silence and concentration.

After the first class, though I enjoyed it all very much, I was not at all sure what he was doing. 'That's unimportant at this stage,' he said. In my heart of hearts I felt wary of him, fearing he might rob me of something. Drawing with two hands, sometimes simultaneously, I often made apologies over what I thought to be an inadequate drawing. 'There are no mistakes,' he would say. 'Everything is about valuing the experience.' What was he up to with his unusual approach?

I settled into the class, realising that he was utterly benign and knew exactly what he was doing, even if I didn't. My trepidation turned to respect as I realised he could see exactly where people were coming from and where they were at. He had a very clear understanding of the nature of creativity and its function. This was thrilling to hear and extraordinarily refreshing. He had a keen intelligence and the effect of his teaching was to dismantle my preconceptions, which shackled me before I'd even begun, and to free my hand and my eye. His instruction to leap into the unknown was, at times, an exhausting process. My ego was reluctant to put aside what I already knew. I was clinging to the rational approach and to an insecurity around his teaching and its enhancement of my abilities. Nevertheless, the class was good, I studied with him for six years until his death. 'Don't follow the path of least resistance,' he might remark and then again, 'Don't chase it.' He also taught me how to mix colour.

To talk about the teaching in detail is really quite futile as it is about doing it and learning through the process. I asked him more than once whether he might write it all down. 'The letter killeth,' he answered. His teaching was not a formula, not a crystallised thing.

An approximation of what it involved is to say that it explored empathy with the instruments, 'They are an extension of yourself, of your perception,' with the model, 'Please take the position of the model and feel the atmosphere of the pose,' and with the marks on the paper, 'Relationship is an important part of creativity.'

We used seven different tones. 'Why seven?' I asked. 'Ah haa!' His enigmatic twinkle. 'There are seven steps to heaven.'

We would experiment with rhythm and speed. 'Pattern, Rhythm, Vitality, Sensitivity,' he would write on the blackboard.

We would explore the climate of different postures from the horizontal to the vertical.

We would move to sound and move to silence.

We would sit, stand, kneel at our work.

We would experience the difference between masculine and feminine energy.

Sometimes he would explain things with simple diagrams. His

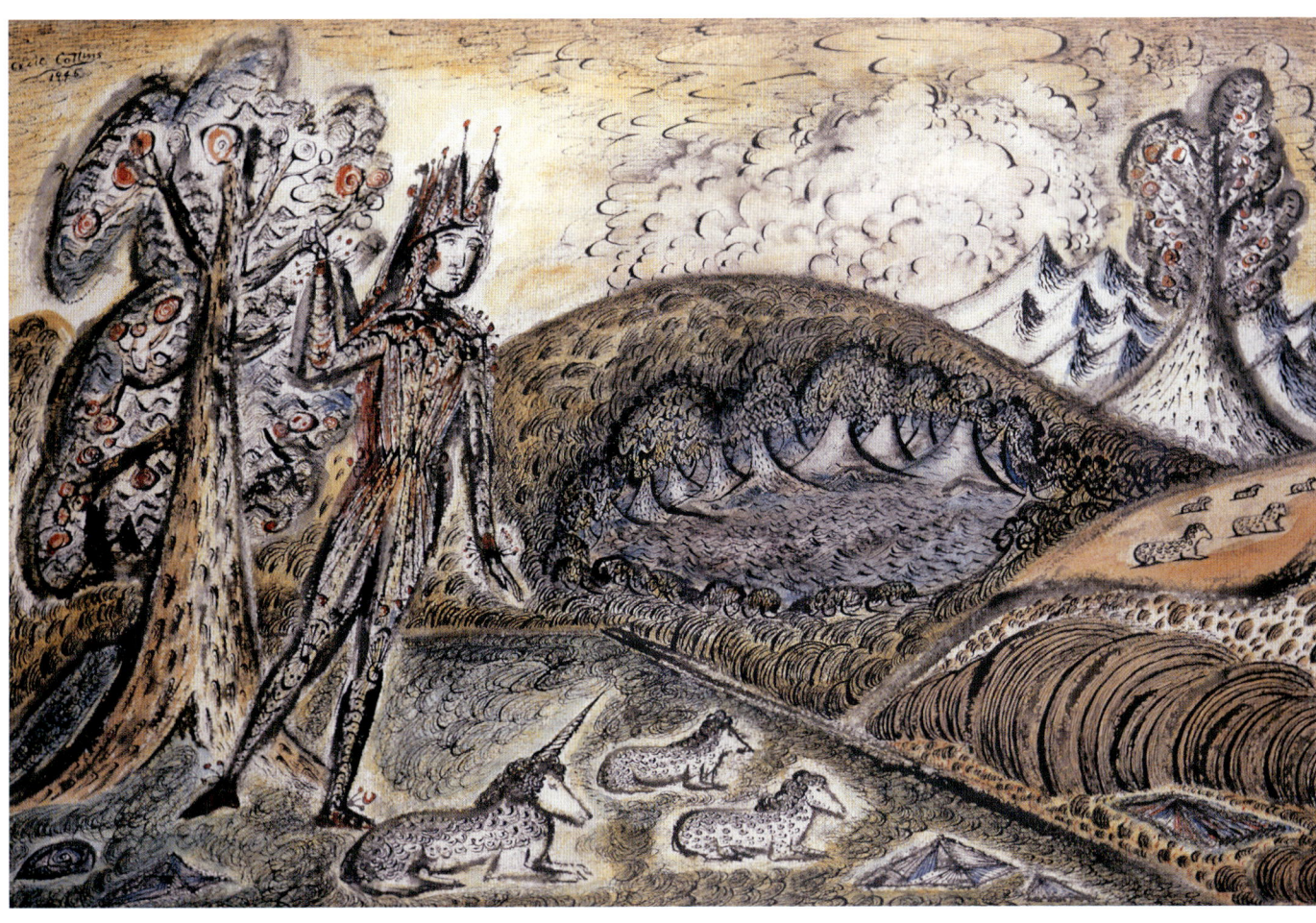

Cecil Collins
Shepherd Fool
1945
Ink and watercolour on paper
38 x 57cm

lessons would open wide horizons. 'It's only drawing I'm teaching,' he would say playfully.

Of course, some people thought he was quite mad. I remember the clatter of an indignant student who did archaeological drawing for a living, leaving in a hurry after he asked us to lie face down on the floor for a moment before beginning each drawing.

There was method to Cecil's madness. Sometimes the class was directed towards one particular person to help them 'dissolve blocks' and everyone would benefit.

Cecil inspired great devotion in his students and attracted all kinds of creative people. 'I am concentric,' he would say; he wasn't interested in eccentricity. He was talking from the perspective of the bigger picture.

He once went around the room, asking each person what the most important lesson was that we'd learnt from him. My answer was that he'd taught me the value of the imagination. He taught that the imagination needs to be educated, otherwise it becomes destructive, that is, it does not regenerate you. Imagery ignites within the imagination, hence the value of the language of symbol. The Ancients understood the role of the imagination: 'In Greek tragedy, murder and fornication were never performed on stage because they were understood to be an offence to the Gods,' evoking something overwhelming inside the spectator. 'Beware of the guests you invite inside your house.' It was important to keep your house clean and ready for the welcome guests. 'You become what you contemplate.'

We have only to look at the society in which we live to understand what he meant and to notice the knock-on effect of a diet of prurience and violence via the media and cinema. It creates an appetite for greater sensation and desensitises us to what is really being said. 'The world of the daemonic is hypnotic.'

Cecil often said, 'Creativity is about the transformation of consciousness.' He also repeated frequently, 'Creative imagination is centred. Uncreative imagination is expanded; it is explosive. It doesn't transform consciousness; it disperses consciousness.'

His favourite thing was 'innocence regained.'

His teaching was profound and greatly enriched my life.

He was an enlightening influence and very good fun. I cannot thank Cecil enough for our acquaintance, for the synchronicity which brought him into my life. I have never looked back.

SHERRY BALLANTINE

Born and raised in Miami, Florida, Sherry Ballantine studied art in Miami, Mexico and Switzerland. She now lives with her husband in London. Sherry works with children in a variety of settings, including television, film, schools and theatre.

My children were very young when I first started going to Cecil's. I didn't understand *why* I needed to be there, but against all odds, I was always there for those Wednesday morning classes. It was the highlight of my week and even the children would notice if I missed class. My youngest, Shawn, especially was very sensitive to my energy and he'd say, 'You didn't go to your art class, did you?'

One day I was rushing to Cecil's class and I grabbed what I thought were all my supplies, but when I got to the class I found that I hadn't brought any of my instruments with me. I'd brought paper and some of the inks, but nothing else. I was shocked and thought, 'How could I come to an art class without my instruments?' Of course, everybody in the class said, 'I've got some extras.' The very strong awareness for me, however, was that I had everything I needed because I was the instrument and I used my hands that day like I hadn't before. I began to understand what Cecil was saying about using the nail, the palm and the side of the hand. After the initial embarrassment over forgetting my instruments, using the chaotic energy that I came in with was very liberating. I remember him saying, 'Use the feet. Put an instrument in your mouth. Use your fingers.' That day literally all I had was my hands and it taught me a lot. The things that people loaned me were a bonus.

It was a turning point for me when I realised that all of these things and even the instruments he had us becoming acquainted with were held by my energy. We had to work on the knots within ourselves, the relationship with ourselves, our relationship with the paper, with our instruments and with the class as a whole. I used to feel that I was getting tuned, becoming in tune, with the tones. It was as if we were all playing instruments in an orchestra and Cecil was the conductor.

I had done figures in clay and wanted to get back to sculpture because I like working three-dimensionally. I had taken some photographs of these things to show Cecil in his last year of teaching and told him I wanted to integrate the energy and flow that he was talking about in the drawing with the clay work so I could find that movement there.

A young woman, blind since birth, asked me if I would teach her how to do a figure in clay. I spent time meditating and imagining my space at home and how I could impart something to her that would be helpful. Finally I said, 'Yes,' and she came for the day with her seeing-eye dog. I set up a table with some of my own sculpture figures. I put out shells and lots of things with different textures that she could feel. I had some music in the background. I had her feeling herself around her head and shoulders and I had her touch me to see where things fit. Then we rolled out the clay and she did two things that day, a figure of a young woman seated with a drum. It was lovely, primitive, beautifully shaped. Then she rolled out clay around the big shells and made a pencil holder out of it with lots of textures. She was moving out of London and wanted help to set up her studio so in the afternoon we went to Tiranti's together. She asked would I help her choose the tools. With each individual instrument drawer, I had her hold out her hand and I rubbed the different instruments along her palm and explained to her what she could use them for and she said, 'I hope you won't mind because it'll take me a little longer to see things here.'

For me, it highlighted something in Cecil's teachings: seeing with the 'eye of the heart'. This was a big part of his teaching. We were on a journey together in uncharted territory. Cecil was a guide, but he also said that he gave us what we gave him. He didn't plan his classes; they would evolve so that we were exploring together. At the end of each session he would say, 'Any discoveries?' It was a whole different way of learning. He was a teacher who gave us so much. After all these years, I'm still processing what I learnt with him.

It may have been through Ros Beeton that I came to hear about Cecil. I've known Ros for a very long time. I met her first when we did some art classes at the Camden Institute. I had also studied person-centred art therapy with Liesl, based on the teachings of Carl Rogers. My parents were the first guinea pigs, so to speak, of Fritz Perls, and I was called the original Gestalt baby. It was in my background and it felt like something I could do. I wasn't going to be an art therapist, but I wanted to use some of this in my work and see how it integrated for me. I always had this conflict in my mind about therapy as such. I remember when Cecil took us around the *Paradise Lost* exhibition he talked about Francis Bacon and said that for Bacon, painting was more like a therapy and that wasn't what art was about. Cecil said art was more about life, the wind, the sea and the movement of energies.

After I finished my training with Liesl, she asked me to work on a project with children. I tailor-made a series of sessions to work with

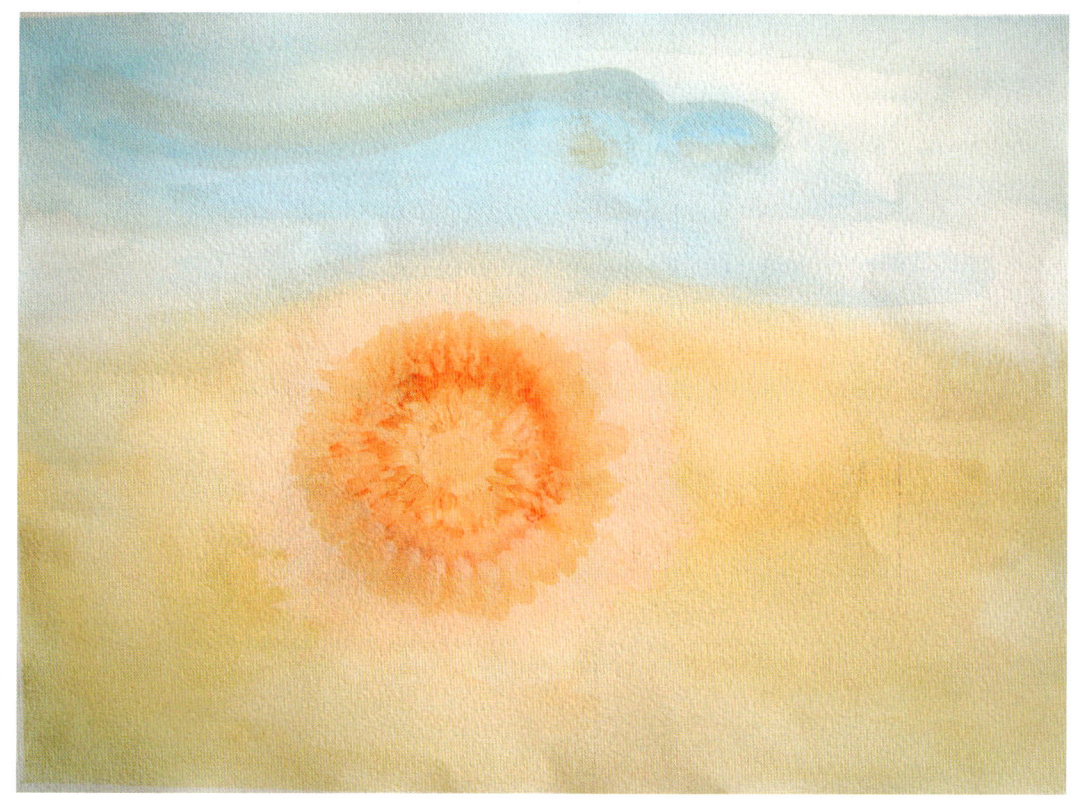

Sherry Ballantine
Coalescence
1991
Watercolour
40 x 30cm

these children, along the lines of Cecil's teachings. We had music and I did a range of things: clay work, making our own inks and working with both the left hand and the right, doing murals and puppet shows. Over a period of two years friendships developed and behaviour improved. It seemed to be an integration of what I'd learned with Cecil and Liesl. I was finding a way of communication and it was therapeutic.

I feel very privileged to have worked with Cecil up until six weeks before he died. I have this image of him over in the corner with his hump, changing the music and orchestrating us with the model. At that time, I still didn't understand what was going on; all I knew was that he talked about entering the creativity, that it was a gift and wasn't my ego. Sometimes he would come up and say something about my work that I didn't understand. What I saw as scribbles, he said, 'You know, the energy is there.' It didn't look like much to me on the page, but gradually I began to feel, more than see, it myself. You want something to show at the end of the day, not just a lot of scribbles, but it was breaking down some of the barriers. I did his colour workshop in the summer as well and listened when he talked to us about the masculine and feminine energies, then marrying them up.

Just to be able to set the palette was a revelation to me, to do studies of dawn and dusk and night. It was a new way of working that felt very centred, very meditative. I think when I was younger it was very chaotic, 'I'll just slap this colour here and put that there and see what comes.' With Cecil, it was all about setting the palette first, which was more disciplined. He used to say there was a part of oneself that was dormant, like seeds in the ground. That is something that has really helped me, to remind myself that, even though something's not sprouting, there's still a lot gestating and growing.

When I was a student at the University of Miami, I remember sitting by the lake and I saw a vision of people ascending a mountain on different levels. I saw it as clear as day. I had my sketchbook with me and I drew it. Somebody came up to me from behind and said, 'What are you drawing?' I said, 'I'm drawing this image.' They said, 'I can't see it anywhere. I see the lake and the ducks, the swans, but where is your image?' There was a moment of panic. Am I going mad? I thought. Am I seeing things that aren't there? I did a whole series of oil paintings on that theme. That was another seminal point in my life when I realised that I had to trust what I see, not look for validation.

That's why I chose to apprentice myself to people I felt I could learn from and be with, who wouldn't interfere. Cecil was brilliant at never interfering. I always try to honour that, not to interfere in my work with adults or children in any kind of capacity. It seems so right, and is similar to how we have brought up our children: that they've come through us. There's never this feeling; they're mine. I am the caretaker and the privilege is that they've come through me.

I didn't know Cecil well personally, but I remember just before he died he was sitting in his wheelchair at his exhibition in the Tate Gallery. I began to see him as being in a different position, in the same way that he'd talked to us about standing and kneeling and lying down. I felt a reverence and respect. I wanted him to sign my copy of the book about him, but I was very cautious; I didn't want to take his energy because I knew he wasn't well. That sums up how I felt towards him. I always respected him. He always had a presence for me. I wanted to make a gesture towards him, which I didn't of course. I felt what a privilege it was to have this in his lifetime, to have his students here with him and to have his book out. I said, 'Do you mind signing it?' He did, very happily. He put his name and the date. It still means a lot to me, his signature on my book. That reminds me of how he talked about drawing being handwriting, that it was our signature. It's interesting that that should end my time with him, having his signature on something.

Cecil Collins

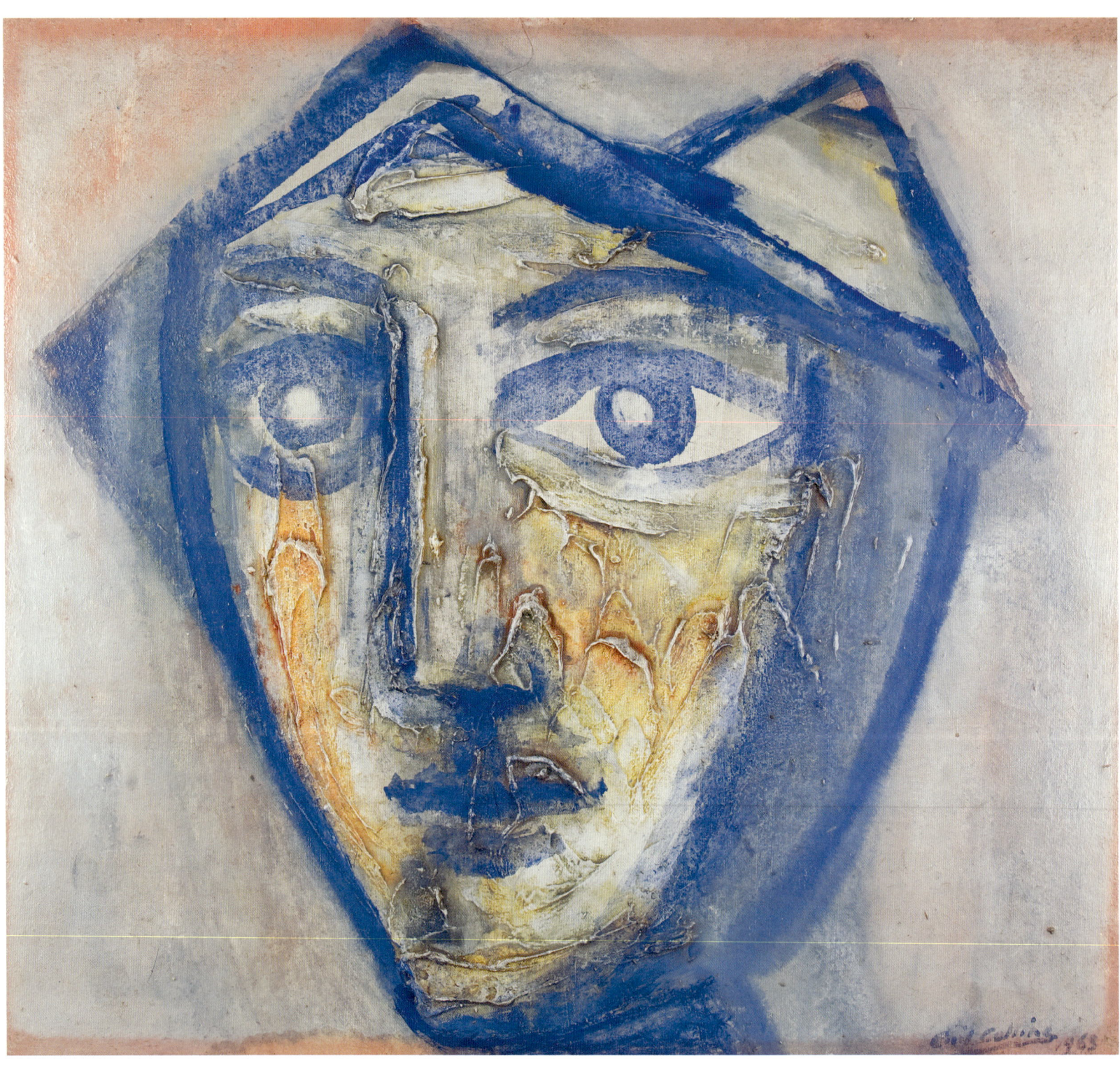

Cecil Collins
Head of a Fool
1963
Oil on board
30.5 x 32cm

ROSALIND BEETON

Rosalind Beeton has a B.Ed degree in Music and Philosophy. She also studied art in the 1960s and with Cecil at the Central School for three years in the late 1980s and has exhibited her work. She is an acupuncturist, herbalist and cranio-sacral therapist and is currently writing poetry and her autobiography.

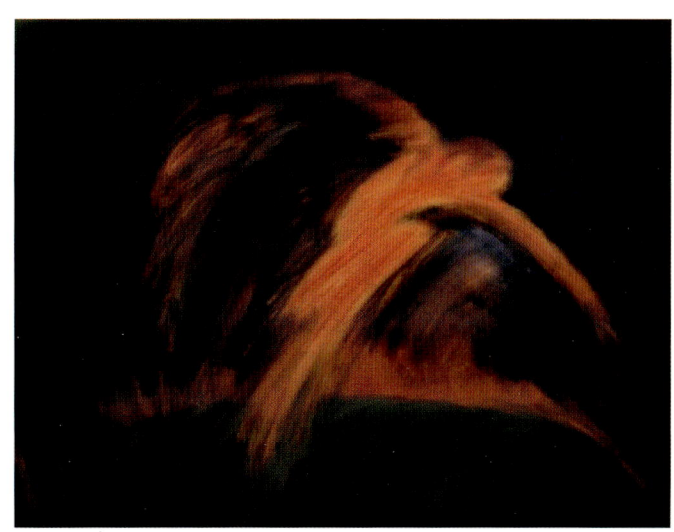

Rosalind Beeton
Holy Spirit
2005
Oil on canvas
87 x 108cm

It was Mrs Tweedie who told me I should go to Cecil's classes. I had been umming and ahhing about it for some time: should I go, shouldn't I go. I came to Mrs Tweedie through my therapist who lent me a book by her, *The Chasm of Fire*, which made a huge impression on me. I then found out that Mrs Tweedie was in London so I started to go to her. When she told me to go to Cecil, I went to the Central and booked in straightaway.

I was completely enamoured the first few weeks of his classes. It was like when I first went to Mrs Tweedie. My whole heart was laid bare and was jumping around. I can remember the tremendous excitement of his classes and the passion about this work, this man, this environment, this opportunity. I also loved it when he made us respond to the movements of the model. Quite often he asked me to lead. If anybody had asked me to speak out in front, I wouldn't have done it, but I was all right with the movement because I love dancing. I really enjoyed that aspect of the class. It helped you to enter the drawing. It was so unusual and completely novel.

For me, the first year with Cecil was the most powerful, although I did gain something when he repeated the lessons in later years and the repetition didn't worry me, it was more a question of time. I was rushing down to the Central in the week, then rushing back because I was doing both part-time teaching and building up an acupuncture practice. I was only at Central for half a day, but it was so intense I don't think I could have done a whole day. We were quite heavily packed in and to do the movements you had to be aware of your neighbour. You'd get terribly grubby because you had to lie on the floor and then there was the whole business of being armed with all these instruments and loads of sheets of paper.

In the morning, before the class, there would be all the anxiety as well, the whole success-failure thing. What would come out? Would anything nice come out? Would I be able to do it? Then once you were there, once you started, it was all too fast to get bogged down into that kind of worry. You just got on with it. I remember the frenzy of using all our different instruments. He'd say, 'Position such and such. Take this position. Take that position.' You'd panic and think, what position is that? Everything moved so fast. There wasn't time to think. You were moving from one thing to the next, taking another instrument, one with your foot and one with your hand and then another position on the instrument. I suppose everyone experienced it in a different way, although there was a common factor. It was magical, that first term. I remember being not just high, but vibrant. It was a quality that spread into my everyday life.

Cecil's classes were an entrance back into work. In the 1960s I'd done the foundation years at Colchester and Chelsea. I told myself I'd teach for five years and after that I'd do my painting. I did the first B Ed degree in primary school teaching that had ever been awarded. I came to Cecil in 1985. I was at Central in Cecil's classes the last three years of his life. He died in 1989. I did the summer colour course, just the once, at the City Lit. Colour has always been my main interest, more than drawing. I found it different from the drawing classes, which were so much more opening and freeing.

I always related well to Cecil. I felt that he liked me. I remember talking to him just before he died. He was going into hospital to have his operation and he was very depressed. I tried to tell him to take Rescue Remedy. I knew he wasn't into complementary medicines, but he was telling me all about his physical symptoms. He didn't let on, but I knew he had cancer of the bowel. It must have spread to his liver or kidneys because he was quite yellow. I think he was very fed up with it all. He might have been frightened as well, I don't know; maybe he knew he was more ill than people thought at the time.

Cecil had some inner knowledge or knowing he channelled through his pupils. What made him so special for me was his spiritual approach, his dynamism, the way he used all the different instruments. But the 'nth' thing that made him special, and Mrs Tweedie too, is still an unknown quality. Mrs Tweedie had done a long spiritual training, but I don't know what it was with Cecil. There's no point wondering about it, because the mind can't analyse it. I knew when I first went to his classes it was that special quality that touched my heart so deeply and made it race and do funny things, as well as really helping me to move on in my painting a bit. Cecil and Mrs Tweedie were two very different, but complementary, energies, that hit my heart. There are only very few people who can do that in such depth in one's life.

I really appreciated Tweedie because of her not putting herself on a pedestal. She would always direct you back on yourself and not to the guru. The responsibility for your spiritual life was yours and you had tremendous freedom. That's what I really liked. Cecil was the same. He never put himself on a pedestal. He was freeing us up too, setting up something for us to work with in ourselves, to echo and mirror back to ourselves our inner work. I think it was a particular way of working with the learning. I would have been interested to see how that related to his way of painting. I liked most of his paintings, especially those small paintings of heads. They were little gems. Some of the big ones I wasn't so keen on.

Before I came to Cecil, I did a whole series of paintings of women dissolving into landscapes. In a sense, that was allowing something through and I suppose Cecil's work really strengthened or emphasised that aspect. I still often say, 'Oh God, Cecil, I'm bloody terrified. I don't know how I am going to put anything on this white canvas.' I sort of have a little word with him. I remember taking a couple of paintings in to him, just before he died. One was of Marie-Louise; she was meditating in Mrs Tweedie's room and I felt this angel at the end of her bed. I was very drawn to do a painting of that. Cecil was a bit critical of it, but I can't remember what he said. I know he wasn't as positive as I'd hoped.

Generally, Cecil was very supportive which was encouraging. I remember him being aware of the whole class and it was a huge, cramped class, yet he always knew if someone was doing something that wasn't right because he would suddenly hoot out, 'You're using the wrong instrument', or 'It's the right hand', or when people were moving, 'It's *not* like that', and he'd stop the record and we'd all have to get back down on the floor and start again.

I always wanted to sit near him in class because if you sat on the other side of the room you couldn't hear him and that was very frustrating. What he had to say was, to me, like jewels.

I have long periods of not painting, then I go back to it. About five years ago after my mother died, I re-entered the Christian tradition I was brought up in. I've been re-exploring that in my painting. They've poured out of me, images to do with the Crucifixion and the Holy Spirit, but I have had no feedback. They might be terribly subjective; I don't know. One painting I did was a take-off of Cecil. I used his title *The Wounded Angel* because, since coming back to Christianity, I'm fascinated by angels and things like that.

I feel so much freer with writing. I haven't been doing it that long, only for about a year. Painting becomes such hard graft. When I'm writing, the images tend to come one after the other or if they don't, I'll sit and mull. I really like using words and I mix the senses like hearing the moon or the singing, luminous light of the moon. It just seems to bubble up from me.

After Cecil died, I used to go over to see Elisabeth and give her acupuncture and massage. I gave her about eight sessions. She would always give me tea first. We'd sit and chat. She was such an extraordinary being, so tall and erect, with those wonderful hats. Once, she took me into Cecil's painting room which she was re-arranging at the time. I remember seeing the little gas ring Cecil made his tea on. I saw some of her gouaches and I was knocked out by them. I'd love to have something by her. Her work is wonderful, so spontaneous, an amazing light and energy come through.

Two of the greatest things I remember learning from him were not being concerned about success or failure and not grasping. That played an important role in my life: I like to look at landscapes and such things, but Cecil would say, 'Allow it to come to you. Don't grasp it with your eyes.' It was the same as the allowing of the drawing, allowing the energy of it to develop and come to you. In these last ten years, I've often tried to put the non-grasping into practice, especially when I am looking at beautiful things. I can hear Cecil saying, 'Don't grasp. Allow it, then let it go.' That's hard. If I see a beautiful scene or a flower, I always want more. I want to keep enjoying it more and more. It's hard just to enjoy it and let it go. The grasping and the expectation often come up for me, especially when I'm painting; it's the success-failure thing. I find it difficult not to expect, but just to allow this painting out and not to judge it.

In my work as a healer, I ask for help and healing for my clients and I've had to work a lot at the feeling that I'm not good enough. It's tough when you're dealing with someone else's health and it's a huge responsibility because they expect to feel better. Usually they do feel there's a difference, but it might not be exactly what they expected. It might take a different form. I think Cecil helped me to empty myself of expectations and of the attachment to getting someone well, whatever that is. Indirectly, he nourished something in me.

students

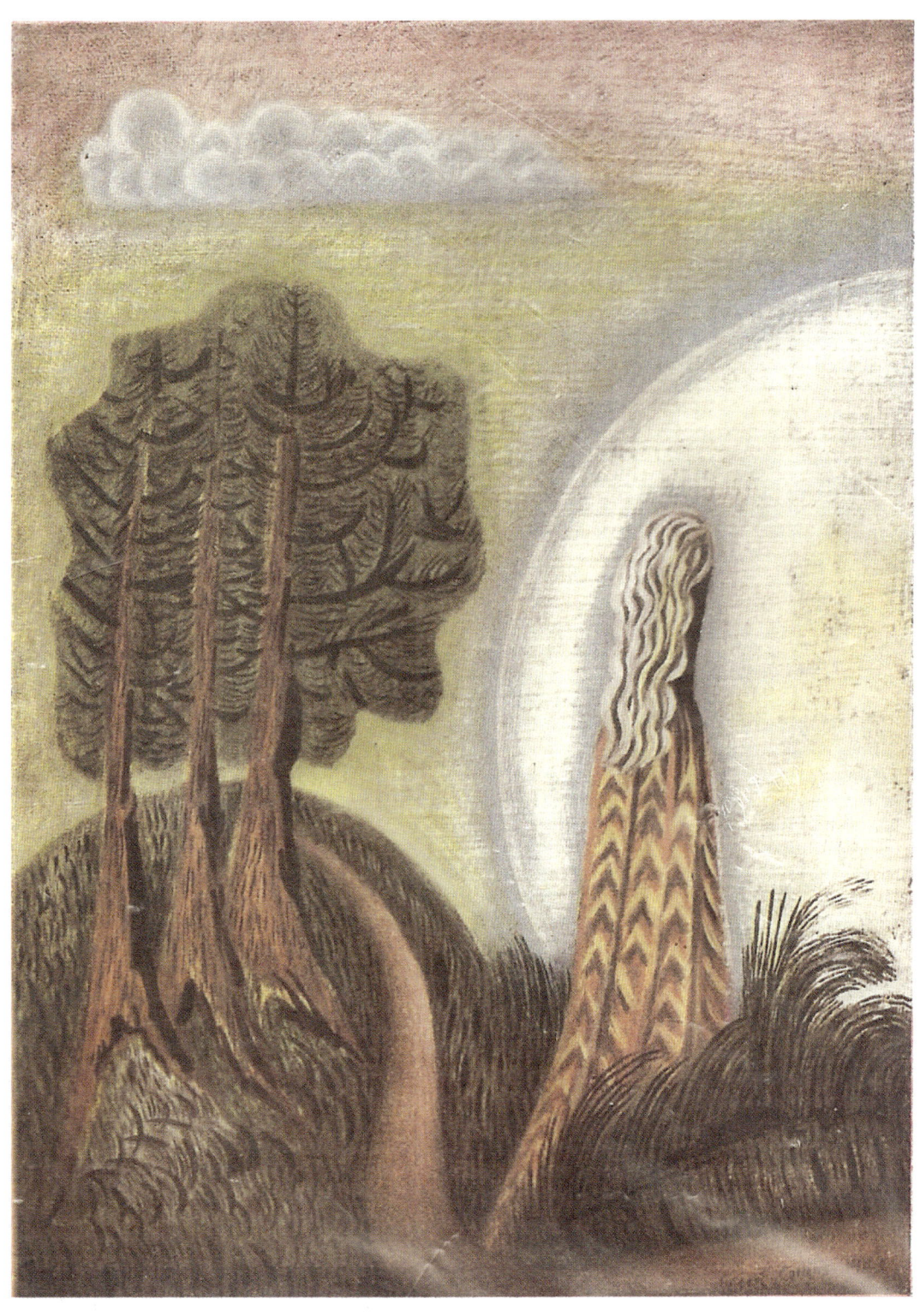

Cecil Collins
The Greeting
1943
Oil on canvas
25.4 x 17.8cm

MARCIA BLAKENHAM

Marica Blakenham is married to Lord Blakenham. While their three children were growing up, she graduated in English from Kings College, London. She attended Cecil's classes at Central St Martins from 1979 to 1989. Since then, she has been one of the principals setting up Maggie's Centres. These extraordinary architectural projects, named after their initiator, Maggie Keswick Jencks, are inspiring and caring places for people facing a cancer diagnosis. It has been Marcia's job to keep the spirit of the centres alive and forward looking. She also continues to paint and make ceramics.

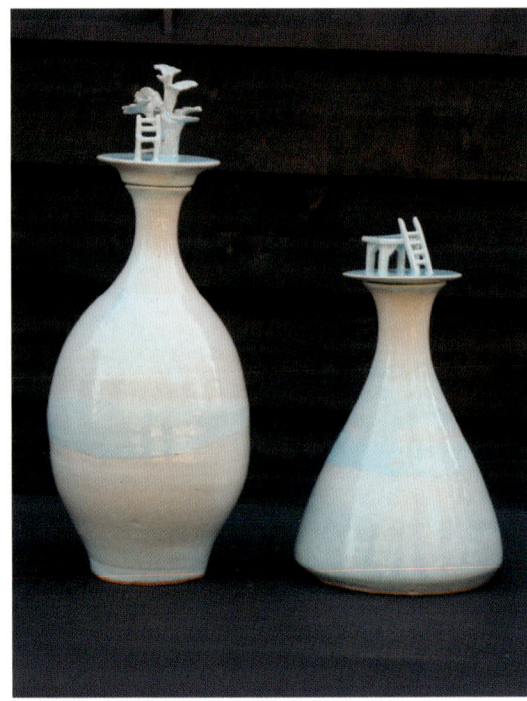

Marcia Blakenham
Landscape pots
2007
Stoneware
46cm

I came to Cecil through a rather nice accident. I was with a friend and we met a friend of hers, Stella Astor, who was one of Cecil's pupils. Stella had come from one of his classes and had a portfolio of drawings with her. She told me about the classes and I thought they sounded amazing. She gave me very good advice: 'Just go and camp outside the door at Central and wait till he comes out, then see whether he'll take you because he's completely booked up and quite idiosyncratic about who he takes or who he doesn't.'

So that's exactly what I did and out came this strange figure and I said, 'I'd like to join your class.' I think he handed me over to Ruth. And I was under her tutelage for a class or two and then after showing some of my work to Cecil I was in. I remember being terribly impressed because what I did was not interesting and yet he looked at it so very carefully. Now, I can scarcely believe that he would have taken such care.

What is interesting is that somebody who was a painter tried to get in and Cecil didn't accept her, although he let in some people, like a nurse who turned up, who'd never drawn in their lives. I think he saw drawing not just as something to be done for its own sake, but as a kind of lifestyle.

Looking back, those classes had all the ingredients for stimulating good drawing, such as rhythm, tone and quality of mark, that sort of thing, although Cecil never talked about it like that. I don't know why he had to make a mystique about the instruments and the seven tones he instructed us to use. Why didn't he just say, 'These are the qualities needed for a good drawing, which is why I'm teaching it like this.' Instead he made it almost into a religion. He could have said, 'We're looking at the quality of the mark,' but he never did. He just said, 'Tone one,' or whatever it was. He gave very precise instructions. It meant that you had no choices and no control. Everything depended on the quality of the different kinds of instrument we were instructed to use and on the rhythms and harmonies.

I don't feel his teaching was letting something from outside come through the drawing or even something from inside. It was much more about making marks, long or slow or stabbing. I've kept a pile of my drawings and, when I look through them, I see they're all exactly the same in a way. There's nothing individual about them. It's just good marks and good tones and good harmonies.

I remember in one of the classes when we were all moving to music. There was a man who Cecil felt wasn't moving in the right way and he said, 'No, get down, get down. Can't you hear? Get down.' This man, who wasn't a regular student, became terribly upset. I got so angry with Cecil, right in the middle of the class. It was a real fight. I said, 'He doesn't hear it like that,' and Cecil said: 'It's not him or what he thinks. It's the music.' Then I remember bursting into tears and being terribly upset myself. I thought Cecil was being very unfair, but maybe he did feel this man was doing it all wrong. At the time, Cecil absolutely cut me off at the knees. You were either a disciple or you were not. Cecil had to win. However, I went back again because I must at some level have rather liked being knocked back into subservience.

In hindsight, maybe Cecil was right. In many ways, he was a

good teacher. His wonderful class always opened something out for you. That's what was great. You made marks that you didn't know you could and which you didn't know about. They didn't perhaps make great art, but as a student you felt absolutely intense about it.

He encouraged a disciple attitude and those who wanted to walked into it quite happily. He wanted you to give in to him, to capitulate completely. He liked that. You felt he knew what you were doing and what you were thinking and what you felt like, which couldn't have been true. It was horribly exciting, but it wasn't very good or healthy for his students that there was such a tremendous guru-disciple thing going on.

I think now that it was quite naughty in a way. His students learnt a kind of religion, but not something that turned them into better painters. How many good painters have come out of Cecil's classes? How many have gone on and found their own voice? In a way it was more like art therapy, although he'd be horrified by me saying that. There was something overtly spiritual in what he was talking about, but I don't think that was what made one feel so intense about the classes. At the time, I was completely bitten, hook, line and sinker. They were seductive. But I'm not sure that being a tremendous admirer brought out the best in you.

I've often wondered at his incredible knack of getting into other people's heads and I feel slightly disturbed about it. There was something unfortunate in the students that liked it, a sort of neediness that he responded to. It made me feel uncomfortable. It was almost as if he got off on that ability to make each student feel special. If you didn't get too hooked on him, that was fine, but I do think it had a real danger. In some ways, it was a kind of addiction and he loved the ability he had to draw people to him. I never felt that he was genuinely interested in people. That's what makes me a little bit suspicious and worried. I don't know why we were so excited about being recognised by somebody who didn't care for you personally and was only interested in what creative energies could come through you.

I think that, looking back, it was particularly true of the most vulnerable students: they liked being penetrated by his sensitivity to them psychologically. He picked up on the way you were feeling or something you wanted. It's one of the things that made you feel special because you felt that it was unique to you. Actually, I think that he was asexual, but that he liked penetrating psychologically. I don't think it was spiritual at all.

Once I remember I was in a quite bad way when I went to his class. I said 'I'm absolutely electric, spangling with nerves. What should I do?' Cecil said, 'Get the hell out of there.' He was laughing, which was a very sensible thing to do. There wasn't any kind of 'dive into the eye of the heart' or whatever. I think the fact that he laughed was rather good.

Cecil used to go round and look at the work you were doing and I remember quite often hoping that he would stop at mine. Whenever he did, you would feel he had some understanding of where you were psychologically. There would be some kind of reference to how your drawing was representing your inner state. I can't remember anything specific he said, but part of the excitement was to feel recognised. It was like he was using his charisma as a way of getting you entranced. I've had other teachers and I feel they weren't as intrusive. It's not for the art teacher to get involved with what the creative part is in the student, but I think that's what Cecil enjoyed. He didn't say anything; he didn't have to. I'm not sure he ever said of a drawing, 'It's good'. He might have said, 'Interesting' or 'This particular aspect is interesting' and he'd probably say something about the quality of the marks or the energy.

He often picked up my work, which is what makes me feel a bit suspicious that I was somebody who wanted to be intruded upon. I was in analysis at the same time and I'm pretty sure that, if anything, it was the analysis that got me through. Funnily enough, I think I would be painting without Cecil. I certainly wasn't a painter before going to Cecil's classes, but you could say I wasn't a painter before analysis too. I did paint before, but I was even worse than now. I had no training.

The awful thing is I can't see whether his paintings are good any more. I'm not sure whether his reputation will last. He talked a lot about painting, and about his paintings, and I can't look at them without remembering all that and the relationship I had with him, which I feel was not quite right. I trust my distrust. I suppose I became disenchanted when I stopped going to his classes and could look at them more objectively and also when I saw what other people were like with him and how they talked about him.

I'm not sure why I became a favoured student. I had a life outside the classes and I'm being a bit mean, but I feel it was maybe a little bit of snobbery on his part as my husband was a big businessman and I've got a title. I think Cecil quite liked all that. The students were in a separate category from the friends' group. Initially, I was a student and enchanted by the excitement and the fun that he brought out in the classes and then it crossed over into friendship.

I don't remember how the friendship began. Perhaps he asked me to go and have tea with him and Elisabeth. In my mind, it became almost like a switch over from Cecil to Elisabeth. It seemed to me there was a longer period after he died when the relationship with Elisabeth became a real friendship, whereas with Cecil it wasn't. I was half student and half somebody with whom he quite liked to mix socially. He didn't act in social situations the way he did in class. You didn't feel in social conversation with him that he had this way

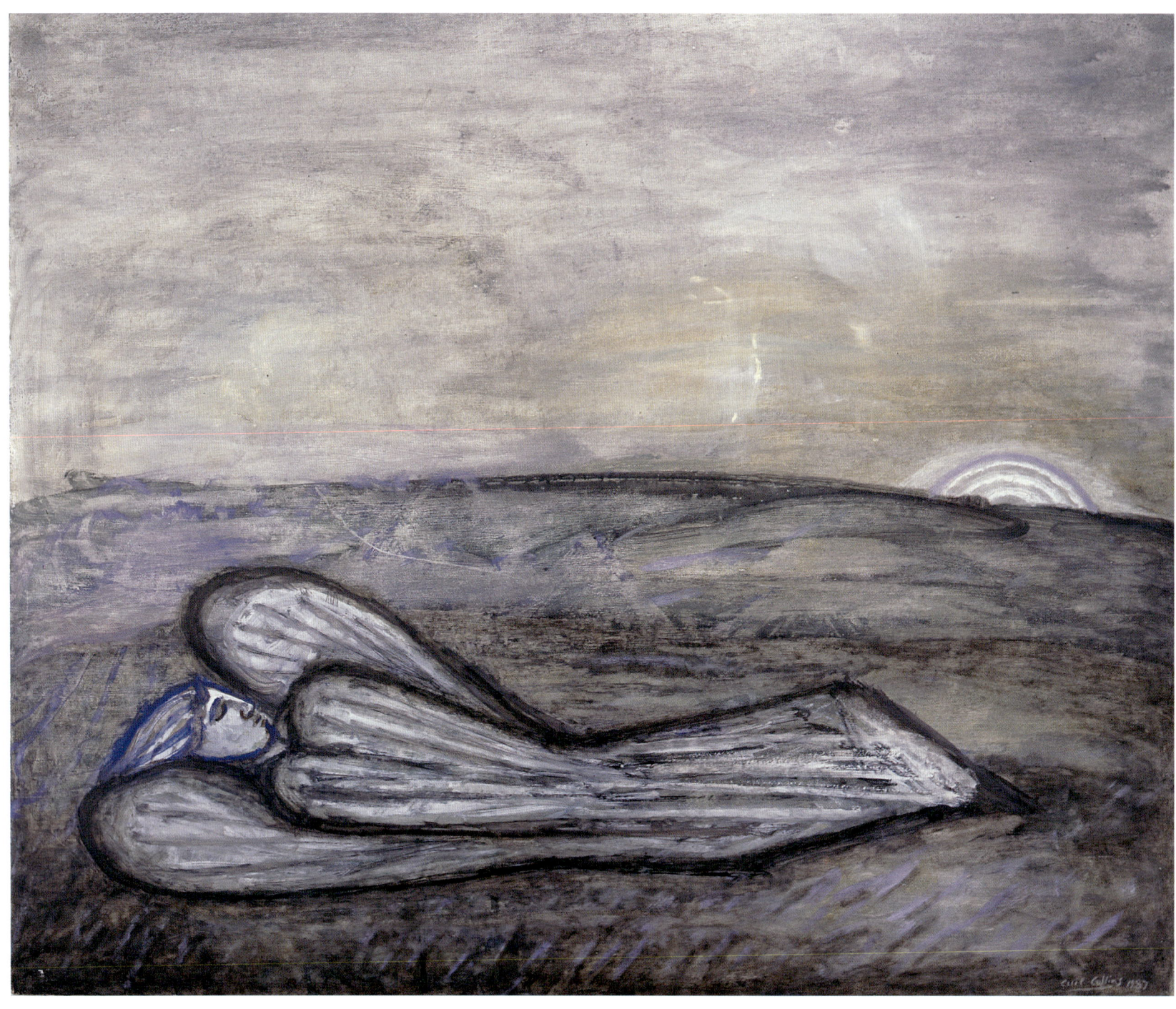

of getting into you and knowing exactly what you were feeling. With Cecil, it wasn't a real friendship because I'm not sure that he was capable of relationships.

When I look back to my visits to Paultons Square, I don't remember Cecil upstairs in the living room. He was always on the floor below in the room he more or less lived in because he slept in it and also used it as a studio.

Cecil hated Francis Bacon. I think he felt threatened by him. Bacon definitely had something that Cecil didn't. Bacon had a muddled life, but a bigger life because there's something more than just looking at the 'eye of the heart'. There's more to life than spirit, there really is.

Elisabeth had almost deliberately given up her very well-off family background when she married Cecil. I wondered whether some of the allure of Cecil was to give her family a bit of a kick in the teeth

Cecil Collins
The Dream of the Angel
1987
Tempera on canvas
71 x 81cm

because I think she would have quite enjoyed that. He was quite awful to them and to his own mother too. Thinking about it, I'm not sure that he wasn't saying to Elisabeth, 'Either me or the rest of the world' and she decided against her family and to stay with him. What was different with Elisabeth was that she was looking after the artist, whereas most women of that generation were looking after the man.

Both Cecil and Elisabeth were in their own way quite innocent. They had perhaps the attitude of 'it's the two of us against the world. This is how to be a creative spirit.' Cecil felt that nobody understood him. Elisabeth was his supporter, his mother and his muse.

I remember Elisabeth telling me about something that had happened much earlier. She'd got frightfully cross with Cecil because she heard him expressing her opinions and passing them off as his own. She decided she wouldn't share her thoughts with him any more. She stopped telling him things, because she got so fed up with him taking her ideas. She'd noticed that he talked all the time when they were with other people so that she couldn't say anything much. I didn't know Elisabeth well enough then, but I know people said, and she herself said, that she never used to speak while Cecil was around.

I think some of her frustrations developed when she felt he'd taken things from her: for instance she had done the first drawing of the Fool. In a way, he'd never let her be herself. She'd always been either an icon of some kind or a muse, but she wasn't cross about that at the time. She often said that she felt she'd had to cook the meat and two veg twice a day when she might have been painting, but she missed him dreadfully when he died. She said, 'You can't imagine what it's like not to have anybody who thinks you are the most important person in the world to them.'

I felt they were rather an embattled pair. They'd lived an extremely impecunious life in the beginning, pumping their own water at their cottage in Buckinghamshire. It must have been a very hard life, but when I knew her, this was all in the past. It was a curious partnership in the sense that she was so idealised and it felt very unphysical. One supposes it was successful between them, but what makes it quite surprising is that I think Elisabeth wouldn't have been uninterested in the physical side of marriage and not to be this kind of idol.

It's interesting that the figures in Cecil's painting don't have bodies, for example in the double portrait of the artist and his wife which is a beautiful painting. Elisabeth didn't have children, but I think Cecil took that over too. They had no affection for or interest in children at all. She did say to me once that she had decided when they first started off that he was the artist and she was going to support him. That was going to be her artistic endeavour. She'd made that decision.

Elisabeth was quite down to earth, not airy-fairy at all. Cecil was much more in the Mrs Tweedie camp; Elisabeth wasn't. I'd once visited Mrs Tweedie, who was a pretty extraordinary character in her own right. She had a strong ego, but she didn't go in for encouraging adulation as Cecil seemed to. I remember walking in and there were all these people sitting in total silence. They were all sitting on the floor and she was the only one on a chair, the only one with her eyes open. She was like a spider with this web of people all around her. After I'd been, I said to Elisabeth, 'I'm not sure about Mrs Tweedie. I don't know whether she's very good.' Then Elisabeth said something fascinating to me, 'Well, I think if there is anybody up there, they probably don't care, as long as the essences that are going up are strong, it doesn't matter whether the essences are good or bad.'

A lot of people with difficulties feel they need a Mrs Tweedie or a Cecil. I went into analysis which is just a different way of dealing with one's problems and, I think, a better way, because it helps you make the most of yourself and not hang on to something which can be like a crutch, rather than helping you stand up on your own.

At this period Cecil was doing beautiful little panels in the medium that only he knew, although he let David Cranswick into the secret of using layers of varnish. He was only doing small panels and Anthony d'Offay said, 'If I'm going to give you another exhibition, you've got to go bigger.' When I think of it, in fact, he had been bigger and then he'd gone back to being small again.

I was at the dinner that Anthony gave for them. I don't remember much about the meal except that Cecil gave a speech which was a bit me-me-me. I was very honoured to be asked. I think it was the first time I'd realised that I wasn't just another student, but a friend. The people who weren't just students, Robin Baring and others, what have we got in common? We're well-off and kind of upper class. I think John Tavener was there and Peter Bowles, the actor, who's a great admirer of Cecil's paintings.

William Anderson was writing a book about Cecil and for some reason Cecil wanted more illustrations. He told me I was to buy one of his paintings so that he could pay for these extra colour pages. Cecil chose the painting. It was a funny little landscape of a rather evil-looking volcano, which I sold later. I didn't really like it. At the time I thought that's not the one I'd have chosen, but I wasn't given any choice; that was the one I was buying. Cecil could be very controlling.

I love Cecil's painting of *The Dream of **the** Angel* that we have, but I don't find it life affirming. I feel it's more of an abstraction. It's a fairytale, a sort of illustration of his message. In art that never works, it becomes propaganda. It sounds like an odd thing to say, but I can't remember what other Cecils I've got, apart from the one that he made me buy.

Cecil used to teach a colour class, but he didn't seem to have absorbed what he could teach. There is a very narrow colour range in *The Dream of the Angel*. He didn't have an emotional feel about colour, nor an instinctive colour sense; he analysed it instead. In class we used to do little whirlpools of colour. There's no question for me that Elisabeth was the better colourist.

If Elisabeth had had a relationship with Cecil like he had with his students, she might have gone on forever thinking that he was this extraordinary human being. Even in the early days she was never sucked into that kind of fascination of being penetrated psychologically. She certainly saw bits that she didn't think highly of. I only know how she talked latterly and it was definitely that she thought Cecil was an extraordinary painter and that this was worth everything.

I had this feeling of Cecil as a very lonely, very buttoned-up character. Those piles of notes to himself on scraps of paper found in his studio after his death were so pathetic. I remember thinking when Elisabeth told me about them, I just can't bear it. There were layers of things like, 'Be nice to Bell'. Funnily enough I think better of him because of the notes because at least he did realise he'd overshadowed Elisabeth. It was almost as if instead of thinking or doing or feeling, he wrote it down. I don't know for how long a period he made these notes. Cecil was interested in sitting, listening to music in his funny little studio, making his piles of paper. Elisabeth did a lot of this making notes to herself too. Their paintings, books, everything is always signed: absolutely every single little teeny-weeny bit of paper is signed.

Towards the end of Cecil's life, I'd asked them both for dinner. It must have been a celebratory dinner at Christmas with Neil MacGregor. It was going to be just the five of us: Cecil and Elisabeth, Neil, and my husband Michael and me. At the last moment, a telephone call came from Elisabeth. Cecil had had the most terrible haemorrhage due to his bowel cancer. 'Can you come to help?' she asked. Elisabeth was an old woman by then and it was too much for her at her age. It was a blood bath. I don't know what had happened, but there she was coping with the whole situation, and by the time I arrived, he was quite chirpy. I remember taking the dinner along to Paultons Square and it was quite a shock to see him emerging out of all this mess and saying, 'Yes, I'd like some dinner please.' Then sitting up and eating it.

Cecil didn't waver in his vision, but there was no room for growth in it either. He'd strangled himself with that mystical idea of the 'eye of the heart'. Mystical experience is supposed to be physical as well. That's why it's described in such physical terms. Mystic writings are about the physical and I suppose that again makes me wonder whether Cecil had had a really deep experience or whether it was merely an idea.

I'm not even sure whether Cecil really believed in his spiritual vision. I think it might have been a torture to him in fact. It's not like Blake who had a real conviction in a mad kind of way. Cecil didn't want to be compared with Blake, however there's a lot that's similar. They're both illustrating an idea, though the way they painted and the images they used are not similar. If you think of the English visionary painters, Samuel Palmer feels more like someone who actually experienced transcendence and painted it without much thinking about it, whereas both Blake and Cecil thought about it.

I think Cecil had to believe in his vision. Like Elisabeth, he'd invested his whole life in it. That's why the retrospective was so important to him. He deferred his operation until after the show. He'd much rather die than not have that retrospective at the Tate. It was totally important and he worked really hard to get it.

Anyone who met Elisabeth was knocked out by her. She was like a queen. She always wore a hat and made these rather astonishing comments. They were often totally waspish, even of people who were supposed to be her friends. She was very sharp indeed about Kathleen. Elisabeth said that Kathleen was a witch and that she cast spells. When she felt a spell coming she laughed and the spell lost its power. Elisabeth thought that Kathleen was slightly making up to Cecil and she was jealous a little I think. She used to refer to Kathleen as 'Downstairs'. They didn't speak if they crossed on the stairs.

Elisabeth got very lonely towards the end. I'd take her out to Thierry's and was glad to because one had the feeling that she hadn't eaten for a long time. She used to say that she hadn't spoken to anybody for a whole weekend. She lived in the two rooms at the top of the house and didn't use Cecil's studio.

I have a painting of Elisabeth's, which I chose. I don't remember what she called it. I love it. I think it was in one of her last exhibitions. She dated it between 1936 and 1982 which she thought was perfectly sensible because it was true, but Jane England said, 'You can't put a date like that.'

Clearing out the place after Elisabeth died was quite extraordinary. It was like a cornucopia, cram packed, but quite neat. The flat was being emptied and I took some of their books because what was going to happen to them otherwise? She was a very serious reader. There is a Maritain with an inscription, given to Cecil by Elisabeth on his twenty-second birthday. They did have interesting books and were both extraordinarily well read. *The Study of the Kabala* was another of their books.

I have very mixed feelings about Cecil now. If I sound cross it's because I feel as if I've been a little conned and I think I was a bit of a fool because I became too enchanted. Aside from this, there's no question that Cecil's teaching was absolutely liberating for learning how to draw. Cecil released something in me.

RAPHAEL BLOCK

Raphael was born in Israel and from the age of nine was brought up in London. He works as a teacher. He moved to California with his family in 1993, where he lives in an old apple orchard writing and presenting poetry.

I joined Cecil's classes at the City Lit in around 1985 through the influence of Mrs Tweedie. There was clearly a backward and forward flow between them. I would hear her telling people to go to Cecil and he would send people to her. I thought, I'll try this. I'd heard an awful lot about him so I was basically terrified.

Art was not my field, but because I'd been to other life drawing classes before, I was very conscious of how drawings reflected inner states. I already knew how valuable these experiences were in terms of work upon oneself. I experienced it as an alchemical work.

I followed whatever movement and painting he asked everyone to do. I knew I wasn't going to become an artist and didn't have half the training a lot of other people had, but I was there because of what he could offer. For me, it was a tool for transformation.

I'd already been with Mrs Tweedie for a number of years so I was centering myself as well as being open. I wasn't following like a sheep. Cecil had a very precise way of instructing us how to use each instrument and the subtleties of whether using the belly, the heel or whatever parts of the brush and the yin-yang balance of each particular instrument.

Cecil's teaching was designed to work on the state we were in and one of the ways he did that was through music. When he played tapes and had us move, it was often done with almost exaggerated solemnity. He was calling us to attention, to that part of us that might have been slumbering. He had us mix the ink with water each time to create the octave of tonalities, seven or eight different shades, again implicitly featuring music.

When he was in his twenties, Cecil had a vision where a bird was singing in the tree and the visual and the auditory became alive and one.

I went to Cecil's classes at City Lit for a year and I did two summers of his colour course. I didn't understand all the complementaries of the colours of which he had such a precise working knowledge. I love the matrix idea that Cecil introduced where one would draw freely with both hands and then some kind of form would emerge, once the matrix was established. I've used that at times when I've needed to get in touch with strong emotions, going a little wild on a piece of paper with some charcoal, then giving it features. It reflects something that's possibly true in the universe, in terms of how matter emerges from what appears to be a lack of form. Matrix, matter, mother are all from the same root word and are obviously related. Things that were seeded during that year developed, grew and began to find their place in my being in a meaningful way.

Cecil detested self-expression; he was more interested in one's higher self. He had an incisive eye and tongue and was so clear and strong in his views. He would refer to Francis Bacon as a butcher. I didn't like Bacon's paintings at the Tate, but there were so many huge canvases on display that, until I heard it put in such an uncompromising way, I thought he must be a great artist.

At that point in my life, when I was allowing more of the feminine to emerge, I found resonance with Cecil's description of the whole spectrum of yin to yang in terms of feminine to masculine, within my being. It was part of an ongoing exploration of vulnerability and openness. It took me many years to come to my own understanding of these words used in the group. For a long time I saw it mostly through my wife Deborah's eyes.

Deborah and I married in 1987. We'd met twenty months previously, at the end of 1985, at a drawing class run by Lynette Howells. I went on a different day from the one on which I normally went and I was overawed when I saw Deborah, together with a friend of hers, Catherine Henderson, these two incredibly tall, Amazonian women.

She enrolled in Cecil's classes early on and he personally helped her to stay in England. Deborah was from San Francisco and every year she had this traumatic thing of having to renew her visa. One year he wrote a letter to Immigration for her. Of Deborah's four years with Cecil at Central, the last one was modelling and they were the hardest of all as she was a self-conscious person. It was also really hard as you're working flat out holding the poses. I think Cecil asked her to model because she was a dancer and she had a beautiful body, so she was beautiful in her movement. I didn't mind her modelling. I had enormous respect for Cecil's work.

I was with Deborah at Cecil's Retrospective at the Tate in 1989 and a friend happened to come in and told us the news that he'd passed away. It was very poignant to be surrounded by his work when we heard that he'd moved on to the very plane that he had delineated so vigorously. I remember having this feeling of awe at being present in this magical moment.

I have never seen an angel, but Cecil opened the door of possibility to that realm in a way that I don't think others have. I do believe in angels in terms of Old and New Testament stories, but Cecil experienced angels as a living, breathing reality, as did one or two other people in Mrs Tweedie's group. Cecil was such a staunch depicter of their powers; in his paintings, they were not meek or mild or ossified Christian archetypes. It added a wonderful dimension to one's life. I could accept the reality of his paintings regardless of the fact that my senses didn't perceive them.

These days I experience the openness relatively often. It's about allowing life to flow through one and that obviously has a bitter sweetness of varying degrees. Having one's heart broken does open one to other people's suffering and understanding their pain. If you haven't suffered yourself, you're not going to be able to relate to other people's plight. Cecil had this wonderful saying, 'God enters through the wound', and that has been true in my experience.

DEBORAH BLOCK'S NOTES FROM CECIL'S CLASSES

Deborah Block, was born in 1951 in San Francisco. She trained in dance and Trager work. In the 1980s she toured Europe and after meeting the Sufi Teacher Irina Tweedie, she settled in London. She also joined Cecil's classes at the City Lit. In 1993 she returned to California with her husband, Raphael and daughter Theadora. She taught dance and movement classes and Traeger work. She died from cancer in 2002.

To have the courage and integrity to give the world what it doesn't know.

One has to be weak sometimes to find the real feeling. You can't find it being clever or strong.

Those caught in appearances, in the superficial are isolated – inner meaning brings you (contact) into wholeness, unity, oneness with all.

Three poems by Raphael Block

SPRING

With a whoop and a fling
blossoms she brings,
it's April, it's April, it's April,
she sings.

Pop out to see
my purple tablecloth billow
waves of songbird
on branches and twigs
pink and white bursts.

Step lively to
Fall's rattling shells,
crows' flap 'n gab,
buzzing wings and legs.

Under the gliding moon
owls beat the meadow
blazing with thirst,
eight stalk silken eyes sip
my million morning tears.

OLD AND DELVED

Dappling, flaking, silvery brown,
cracked, pecked, split, holy, delved trunk,
limbs hanging by a thread.

Thicket of an old, unpruned apple tree,
rich, leafy mold stewing
in your mossy base -
home to thousands.

One hundred years
of hollowing,
to bear everything -
sweet fruit.

FALLEN FRUIT

I have fallen in love again;
I know this because I find myself
resting in a patch on the fallen,
cracked trunk, old, rounded and open,
and following you over the bank
as you slowly sweep across the field.

A cat's mew from her den
away in the blackberry bushes
follows me, as she beds herself
on a mole hill or hayed furrow,
and rolls over into a "You know
what I want you to do," position,

slants her closed eyes
earthy purring, pumping limbs
stretching twice as long
as the day, blisses out
while I scratch her favorite spots.

Pausing under a tree,
picking and sniffing
through the Gravensteins,
yellow skins splashed with magenta
drip, firm formfuls of breathtaking

smells, a dull thud draws me
to the next. Stooping
to pick the prize – darkened
reds on yellow ground,
the promise of a rough, crunchy taste,

a branch stays my shirt.
Caught by the crook of the neck!
I struggle, then break
into a chuckle,
"It's you I want –
snag me over and over again!"

MARTIN BOULD

Born in Leeds, Yorkshire, in 1949, Martin Bould studied Geography at Southampton University and worked as a Town Planner after obtaining a post-graduate diploma from PCL, London. When he was twenty-nine he left to pursue his original desire to become an artist. He joined a Gurdjieff group for three years, and then met Mrs Tweedie. He works as a freelance restorer for the main icon galleries in London. He is married with two children.

A lasting memory I have of Cecil's class was when he looked at a painting I'd just done and said, 'I suggest you put that under the tap for a while.' It was a very helpful comment, because it was painted with thick gouache and naturally under water it blurred, so I could go on working on it afterwards. I understood him to mean that I should be less attached to form, be less tight in the execution and to work in a looser way, more connected to the flow of creativity.

I would sum up my appreciation of Cecil Collins and what he showed me in two sentences. He showed by example that art can come from deep within and can depict another world, the world of the soul. As such, it can be free from the influence of social trends and fashion and can express something eternal in a manner of lasting quality.

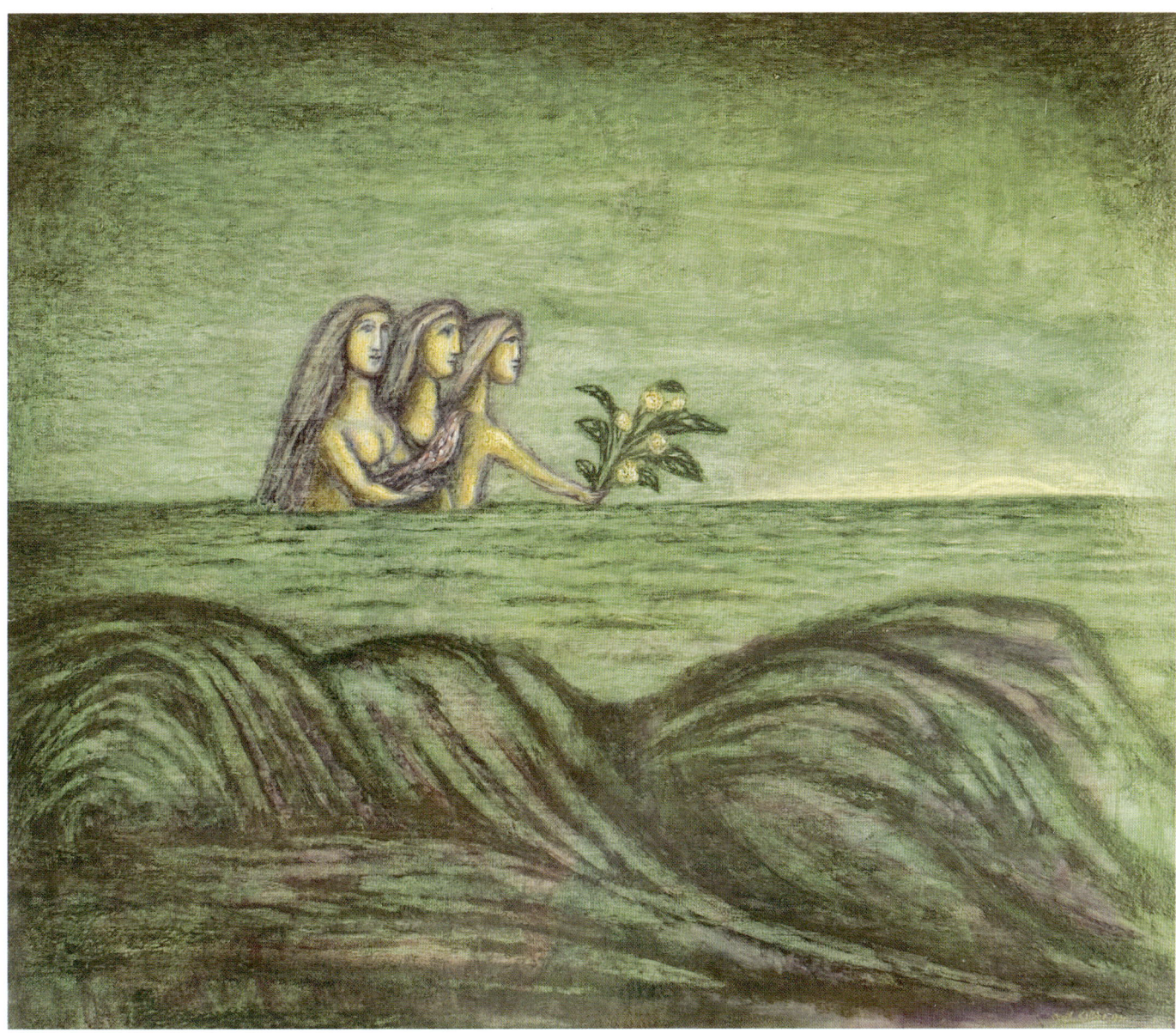

Cecil Collins
Daybreak
1971
Mixed media on board
75 x 85cm

ANN BRUNSKILL

After attending Chelsea School of Art, Ann Brunskill became a printmaker, then under the imprint of Worlds End Press made small editions of hand-printed large-format books, using etchings, wood-cuts and monoprints to compliment the text. During this time she studied with Cecil. Her work is in public and private collections. Currently she is mainly painting.

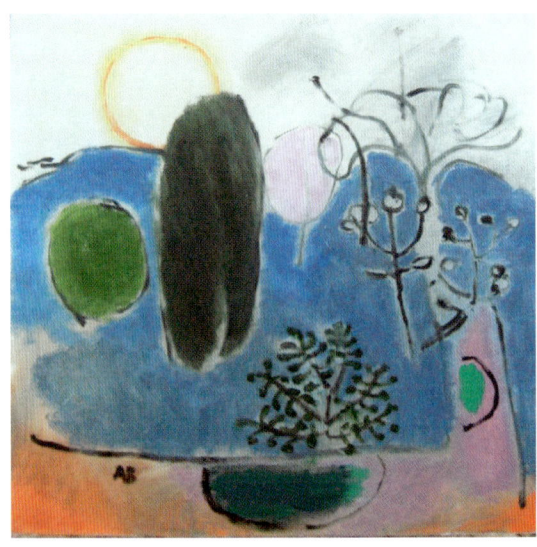

Ann Brunskill
Garden Path
2007
Oil on canvas
40 x 40cm

I first went to Cecil for drawing at City Lit in the 1970s. I was a very bad student. Cecil used to refer to me in a slightly edgy way, making little witticisms about me and I found it very hard to let down my guard. In Cecil's class, we used to be given models for three minutes or less. Most people would just give up and that was what he wanted them to do, but I was desperate to get it down in the three minutes. I didn't surrender; I didn't leave a space which is what he wanted me to do.

I'd been to art school and already had my own way of looking at the world. I was a printmaker and etcher after I left art school. Between 1970 and 1980, I lived on a wharf in Wapping and published very large and elaborate books, hand-printed on a nineteenth-century press. It took me a long time to be convinced about Cecil. I continued with his classes because I knew that what was there was marvellous, but a part of me fought against it. Lots of people fell in love with him immediately. One friend of mine went to Cecil and it was nothing short of a revelation to her; the experience opened her heart. She's an old woman like me now, but she adored that time with Cecil.

He used to make us grind up our ink and I disliked that intensely. It took so long and the result was so pathetic, such a small amount of ink. All this was so that you could really take trouble in what you were doing and care about the state of your mind. Usually there's no room for anything in our heads, except for what we happen to be thinking at that moment, but there should be. There should be a space where a bit of silence connects you with things.

What I loved about Cecil's teaching was the unity of the body and of life. He would involve us physically with dancing and movement. I have always loved dancing and moving and the music he chose was very pure. There was also the unity of the instruments and ourselves as the instrument. Cecil was very taciturn in class. He would tell us what to do, put on the music and nod, then somebody would get up and it gained its own momentum. He was quite Zen in his approach, skilful and disciplined in a very factual, practical way.

He was a very amusing man and sharp in a worldly way. He was profoundly anti the world as it was and as it was being lived. He was tremendously unfashionable in his outlook and in bad odour at Central because this was the 1970s when everybody was drawing things in abstract rectangles.

Cecil was not physically strong, but he was very brave and determined, obstinate one might say. He got cross if people didn't like or appreciate his work. He had long-standing troubles with the Tate when they fell under what you might call a dictatorship. He had good friends there, but they weren't always able to help.

Later on I joined his painting group in City Lit in the summer weeks. That was a complete revelation to me because while I'd done lots of drawings, I'd never done any painting before. We had models and these powder poster colours, which were delicious, all crumbly. I found the act of putting one colour against another totally fascinating. It opened a door. It was heaven.

I remember Cecil had us drawing a little triangle and you had the dominant colour, the second colour and then a teeny weeny little colour that was different. You mixed them together and made a third tone that was always harmonious, but in the crack of the triangle at the bottom there was a little sharp note from another colour that made everything vital. Cecil used to get people to draw one colour outline, then use another colour for everything else. I loved those classes. I went for two years, but they were always oversubscribed and when I wanted to come back again he said, 'No, you know all this now.'

students

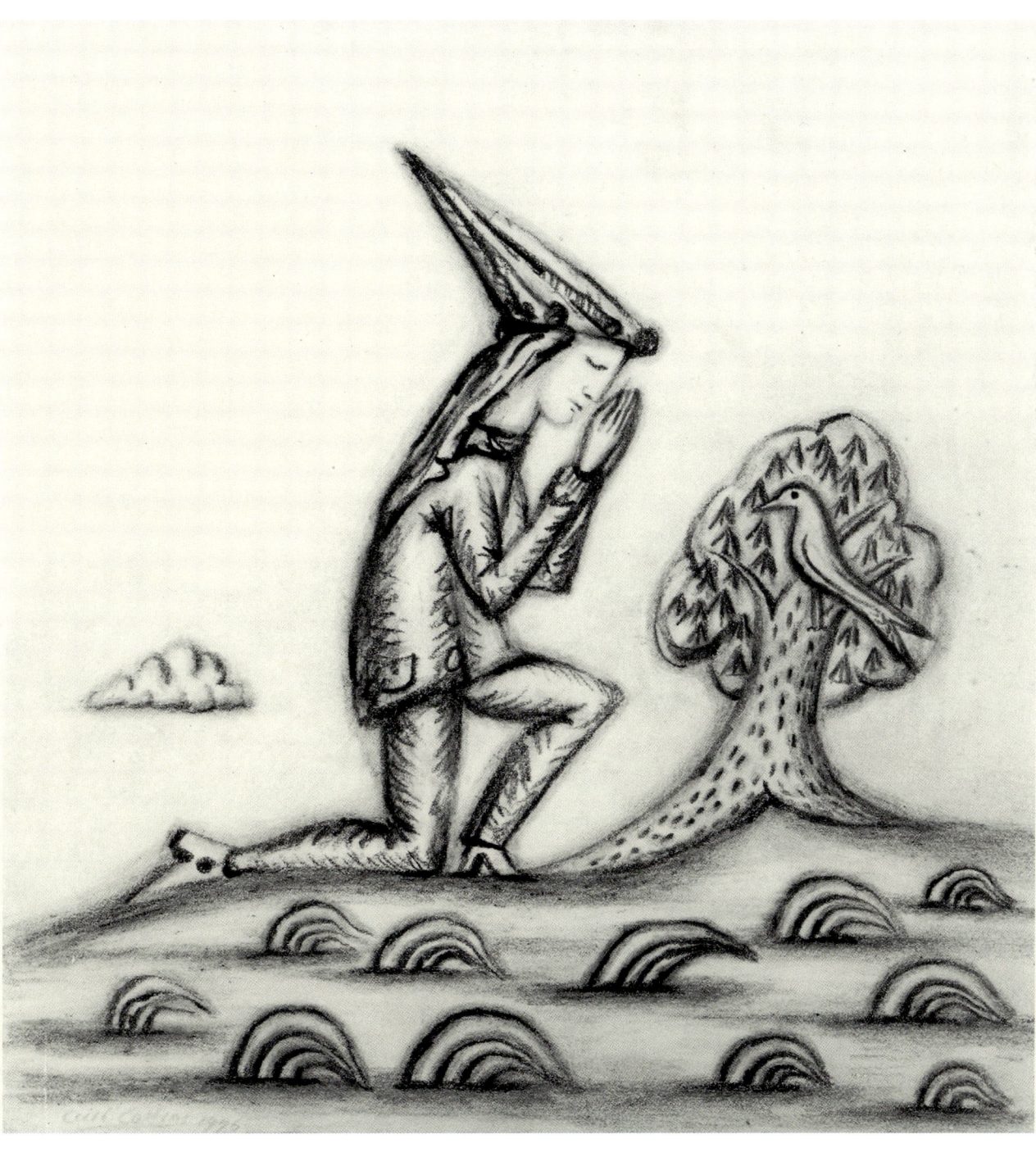

Cecil Collins
A Fool Praying
1976
Pencil on paper
24 x 20cm

One of my wood-block prints was inspired directly by Cecil after coming back from one of his classes. It's the only thing I've done in which I consciously felt Cecil coming through. I was drawing like we used to draw, but with a knife instead. I cut it directly on the wood with a Japanese knife.

Sometimes I draw with two hands or in a way that inhibits the drawing. I go cross-eyed which I do often anyway. If I'm drawing somebody, I won't look at them directly; I'll be looking somewhere else and I find I draw with freedom and it's more accurate. You may go quite wild and the whole thing may go off the page or be miles too big and it's very difficult to get the scale right, but still I use those sort of techniques that I derived from Cecil to try and unsettle myself.

I found in Cecil a great teacher. I was totally in sympathy with the way he saw what was beyond appearances. I felt we were on the same path and shared a particular way of looking at the world and maybe he thought that too.

MICHAEL CHAITOW

Michael Chaitow is a painter and teaches part-time. His paintings share some of the metaphysical and visionary concerns of William Blake. He first worked in advertising agencies as a commercial artist and then studied at Chelsea and Central St Martins Schools of Art. He subsequently won a two-year commonwealth Painting Scholarship to India.

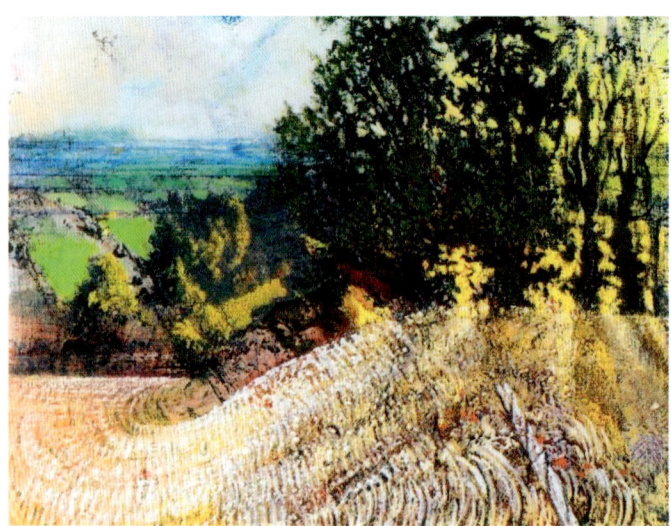

Michael Chaitow
Summer Dawns
2007
Oil on panel
66 x 84cm

I first met Cecil when I went to the Central School of Art. In my first year our tutors would warn us about this strange man, Cecil Collins, who was a second-year tutor and into some quasi-religion or something. When I met him at the beginning of my second year it was like meeting a kindred spirit because some years before I had done my first major painting on the theme of dawn. One of the first things he told me was, 'I'm a painter of the dawn.' The hairs on the back of my neck stood up. I had found my first-year tutors were very cynical and rational. At the time I met Cecil, I was in a 'Dark Night,' searching for my way forward.

I was impressed that Cecil took trouble over students. He was very warm and you felt he was someone of integrity and quality. I spoke to him about Rilke, who is a great love of mine, and the next day, Cecil brought in a Macmillan publication of Rilke's letters. He gave a lot of time outside teaching hours. For example, some years later I remember him taking us all to the V&A on a day he wasn't teaching to see the Berlioz exhibition.

Fortunately, he was allocated to me as my tutor. According to Cecil, it was a group from the student intake from my year who were sympathetic to his approach that enabled him to restart his method of teaching. He hadn't taught that kind of group life drawing class for a decade. There were about ten of us in his class. Cecil always said it was important that we kept in touch with each other because 'You can lose this knowledge and you need each other for strength'. He always stressed that.

At the end of the 1960s and early 70s, everyone was into post-abstract expressionism and life drawing was considered old hat. I had to battle and insist there was a life drawing class at least once a week. Normally, you'd have a model for a whole day and might do two drawings and suddenly Cecil had us doing a hundred drawings a day. It was absolutely shattering. It was so prescriptive and directive:

'Left hand, do that. Right hand, do this.' During the first or second lesson, I walked out because I, or my ego, just couldn't handle it. I felt he was attacking me and left the room. Half an hour later, Cecil followed me out. He always called me Mr Chaitow, never Michael. 'You're a strange bird,' he said laughing, and persuaded me to carry on. Going back into the class I remember thinking, yes, I do accept this, and somewhere there was a sort of surrender. I understood on some level it was necessary and that it wouldn't exclude one's own individuality or one's originality. Before that, I was thinking that this was intrusive; I wanted my own style, my own work, but then I came back and there was a conscious, 'Yes'.

Cecil was the kind of man who really saw inside you which was slightly unnerving, but also consoling, because one both wanted and yet resisted that. Cecil could be quite stern too. At one point, I was doing these large abstract oil paintings in black and white with a lot of grey which I sometimes did with my eyes closed. When I look back on it, these gestural paintings personified some of the things that Cecil was teaching and I think he recognised that in me. I remember I had this huge canvas about the size of a wall. I quite liked those paintings; they were in very thick oil paint with ridges that were built up like a kind of calligraphy. I started talking about this painting analytically for about fifteen minutes. Cecil patiently listened to all this and then said, 'Mr Chaitow, there are only two kinds of painting. Good painting and bad painting,' and he just walked away. I was quite devastated in a way, but I did see the funny side of it and felt that it was a pretty astute observation.

Working with Cecil changed my work utterly, spiritually. I think that psychoanalysts wouldn't agree with this, but I totally believe that your psychological worldview is dependent on your spiritual state. Before I met him, I was doing dark paintings in greys, black and white. Once I'd met him, everything became luminous with translucent colour. It was radiant because he affected the centre of my being. The sun was shining in my heart and the paintings reflected that. Those glazes and the colour transformed me from being in a grey hell. That's what Cecil was doing, affecting people right in their centre and of course you do resist because it's so scary.

After leaving Central School, my relationship with Cecil changed gradually from a tutor-pupil relationship to that of a friendship. It happened after I returned from a two-year scholarship in India. I brought presents for him and and joined his class at the City Lit. That's when he gave me one of his paintings for the first time, which I still have. It's like a sibyl looking out. I see it as a vision, a standing figure looking out.

Cecil could intuit what people needed. Although it was a group class and he treated everyone the same, I found he was extremely specific with different people in the way that he handled them. The kinds of things he would say to me and the sort of promptings he would give were unique to me.

Cecil was always truthful with everybody. I have been rather blocked and cut off in my life and Cecil was very helpful to me.

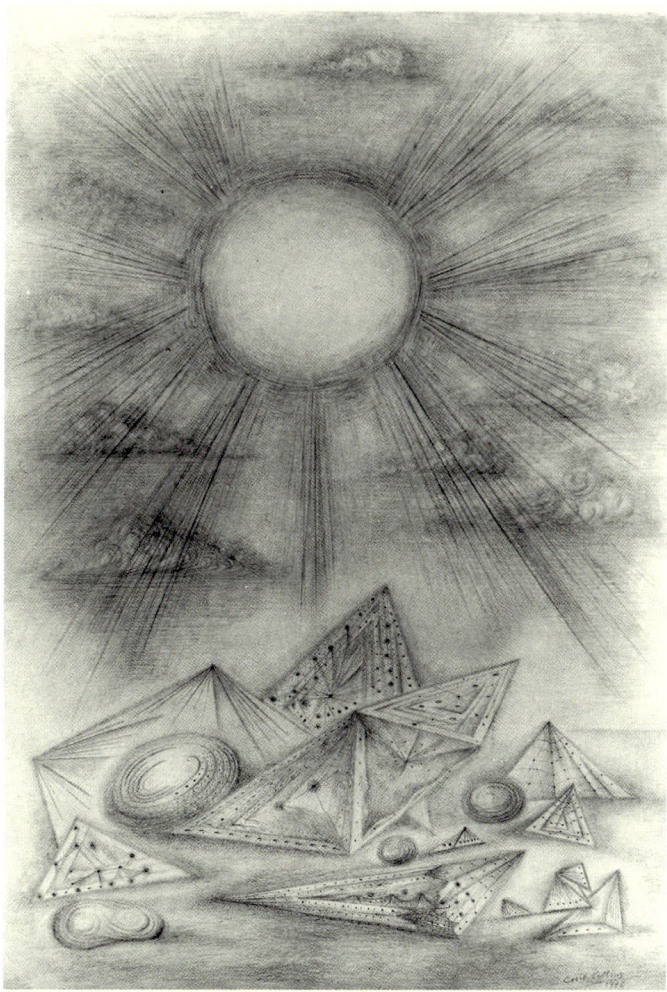

Cecil Collins
The Sun Blessing Stones
1945
Pencil on paper
56 x 38cm

For me, the classes were all to do with letting go and surrendering. I was holding on to this localised identity and personality and then he might give you a bit of a prompting and you'd suddenly reach that point where 'It' draws and you realise what he'd been pushing you towards. When that 'It' takes over, that's really what it's all about, the ego is not involved. Then Cecil became peripheral because he'd done his task like a midwife, but our whole conditioning is against that. *I am this and I want to do this and I'm trying to do this and I'd like to do this.* Our whole personality-ego structure is so endemic and inflexible and with me particularly so. I have to paint because I'm very self-protective; it's a way of letting go of that.

The most signficant moments with Cecil were one-to-one outside the class. I remember a moment when I met him at Central School late in the evening. You can't believe how someone can be so human. He was truly human, able to show his vulnerability, and you felt you could respond in the same way. Tears came to my eyes and we were just together.

I had a dream after he died about a river which seemed be the Thames, but it was like the traditional idea of the Styx and at the same time the Thames. It was terribly grey and misty and I was crossing this river in a boat. I came to the other side and Cecil was there in that old raincoat that he usually wore. Weeping uncontrollably, I went to kiss his breast and as I did so my right eye was opened. I hadn't realised it was closed and it sort of brushed his. Then I kissed his heart.

I had another dream and although he didn't appear in it at first, I knew it was all to do with him. It was as if he'd died and I was grieving. Then suddenly I met him and it was a bit like that meeting with him late evening in Central. I wanted to touch his feet and kiss them, like an Indian. It was a great veneration that I felt.

There was a later dream about the divine sun which is the light behind the light of the sun. Plato talks about this, the non-physical sun, the divine sun. Cecil often spoke of this and it's in some of his late paintings, but I'd never experienced it before. I now understand much more as a result of this dream. I'm in a valley and see this unbelievably beautiful sun which I know is the divine light, the divine sun, but there is a roadblock of red-and-white striped oil drums so I can't get through. I turn to the right and there's a temple which I know is a temple to the divine sun and inside there's a priesthood. I go into a courtyard with black-and-white marble squares and on one of the squares there's a shaped stone. I pick it up and turn it over and my image is on the stone and I know that, on some level, I am connected to it. Then I put it back carefully and leave it there. I know Cecil is present, telling me I'm connected to that.

GARY COOK

Gary Cook studied art and design at East London University and worked as a commercial graphic designer for South Bank University. He obtained an MA in Art and Design Education from London University and has been teaching art for the last twenty-four years, currently at an International School. He has twin daughters and lives in London.

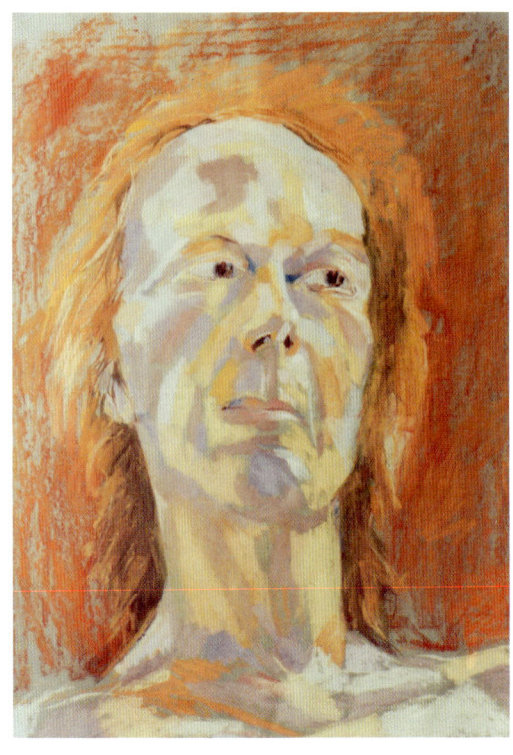

Gary Cook
Portrait
1992
Pastel on paper
90 x 60cm

The first time I ever saw Cecil I was with a friend, Slobodan, in South Kensington and there was this old man in front of a shop window, looking at toy soldiers and Slobodan walked right up behind this chap and put his leg behind him and said, 'Hello Cecil.' Cecil jumped and nearly fell over. I thought he looked like a bit like a old tramp. Cecil's wife, Elisabeth, used to call him 'Parce' because he looked as if he was done up with bits of string. He reminded me of my father because my father used to dress like that too.

At sixteen, I wanted nice clothes, a car and girlfriends so I left school to train as an accountant. I hated it and only lasted two weeks. I scuffled back to school thinking, I'm going to do what I love doing, not what I should be doing. It was at that point I took up art. If I'd left school at eighteen with a couple of A levels in Maths or something, it would have been much harder to change direction. I did Communication Design at what's now called East London University. The course ranged from fresco painting to photography. I went to Cecil's classes at the Central. They told me it was full, but someone told me to speak to Patrick Reyntiens and he just signed the piece of paper and said, 'You can go to the class.'

I was keen so was always the first to arrive. Cecil would make me arrange all the furniture. I felt all right to begin with but, after a bit, I felt like a donkey and I got pissed off with it. I didn't particularly enjoy Cecil's classes. I found them a bit frustrating. He said once that he found it more difficult to teach people who already knew how to paint and draw. He preferred to teach people who didn't know at all. I didn't think I was learning anything when I was doing his classes. I'm not sure that I was good at it, but what I was doing looked good and I knew what I was doing, but I suspect with Cecil it went a lot deeper than that. Cecil's teaching was almost certainly a vehicle for something else.

I remember this business of kissing the brushes and getting down on your knees and the ladies who came well equipped with knee pads already strapped on. Cecil's classes were never fun; they were very hard work. 'Get up. Get down. Get on your knees. Do this. Do that. Get the other chalk.' It was relentless; you were driven. In the end, you had to submit.

My problem was that I could turn out a really good drawing that looked like a Cecil-type drawing. One of my criticisms was that all the drawings looked the same. You could immediately recognise a Cecil-type life drawing. I suspect that there was an element of power going on there. I certainly wasn't about to become one of his clones. I was not going to turn out drawings like everyone else's. He paid absolutely no attention to my work. I don't think he ever commented on it. He never spoke to me except to ask me to move the furniture.

Maybe he wasn't teaching me about art. Maybe he was breaking down my ego which I got a bit fed up with in the end. Maybe I did go there for that. Maybe he just didn't work for me. I wasn't sure why I went there. Perhaps it was partly because I was swayed by how much I'd heard about him. I had wanted to be in the presence of someone like that, to see what came out of it and I felt like nothing happened. I did the whole term and then didn't go again. I never did a colour class with him.

I would have liked a bit more personal attention. I felt completely ignored and when I arrived it was, 'Can you move this and move that and do this and push that around.' But I never felt that it was an abuse of power or that it was destructive or perverse.

I thought I'd learnt nothing and then, without realising it, I started using very similar techniques in my teaching, though not so much in my own drawing and painting. Without knowing it, I'd somehow taken some of it on board. I can't say that I taught the way he did, but up to a point it changed my style. There were a couple of things I learnt: one was the technique and the other was his attitude towards his students. Another thing I got from his classes was this business of shocking people out of their preconceptions. For example, you're going to draw with both your eyes closed or draw with your left hand. It's provocative.

I was doing it in my life drawing classes without even twigging it. Suddenly I thought, 'Hang on, where have I got this from?' It helped with the life drawing; it freed up my students and they found all kinds of different ways of working. It moved blocks and I think they really enjoyed it as well. It was fun because they didn't know what was going to happen in the art class.

Then I had a dream in which I went to Cecil and I asked him if I could join his class. So I followed it up and phoned him. He said, 'Come and see me and bring your portfolio.' He was no longer working at Central because he'd been pushed out of there and I traipsed halfway across London to the City Lit with this dirty, great, heavy portfolio. I told a colleague at work that I'd had this dream and that I was going to do something about it. He thought I was bonkers and I realised that you've got to be careful what you say because half the world wouldn't take a dream seriously. For them it's nonsense that your mind produces when you're asleep.

Cecil didn't seem to recognise me when I got there. I don't think he even knew my name. He said, 'What do you do?' 'I teach.' 'What do you teach?' 'Art,' and he said, 'You don't need this. You get what you need from teaching. You can't come to my class.' He didn't even look at my portfolio. I was hopping mad. I was effing and blinding and it was hilarious because there were always a lot of ladies around Cecil who were saying, 'You mustn't say things like that about him.' They were all in awe of him and put him on a pedestal. I felt I hadn't been given a chance. Obviously, Cecil wasn't interested in the art. He was interested in me or not, as the case may be, but it wasn't personal.

Sometimes with artists, the conversation is terribly boring because all they ever talk about is their art. This was true of Cecil, I think. I think it's true of most artists. I can't imagine they're easy people to live with. That said, Cecil was a very humble man; I don't think he made a big deal of himself. It was the people around him who did that. I don't think it went to his head, although it must have been difficult to avoid, especially when you've got all these lovely ladies adoring you.

Some of the people around Cecil were very possessive of him. Cecil had this inner circle, but I don't think it was his doing. It did irritate me a bit, though not that much. It wasn't as if I was desperate to be part of his inner circle; I had Tweedie's. Everyone wants to be on the inner circle even if they say they're not interested, but I can genuinely say I wasn't too fussed about it with Cecil and I was certainly never part of that circle.

There were people who were close to Cecil. Slobodan and Maria knew him personally. I was the best man at Maria and Slobodan's wedding at the Serbian Orthodox church. The reception was teeming with people and Cecil and Elisabeth were in the thick of it, the centre of attention. Elisabeth was wearing an elegant hat. I overheard her saying that she'd do anything for a cup of tea so I ran off and managed to get one for her. I couldn't get near her so I gave it to Michael Chaitow. I said, 'Can you pass this on?' It went through about six people's hands and by the time it got to Elisabeth, it was half a cup and cold. I had forgotten all about it, but she went to the trouble to find out who had got the tea and to pass on her thanks which was rather sweet.

After he died, people were invited to a house near Queen's Park to choose some of his books. Someone who'd been invited said, 'Gary, why don't you come along?' There were some interesting books there and I don't just mean big, fat, expensive volumes of Rembrandt. They had a load of his books signed by Cecil, as well as books with his comments in the margins.

Cecil Collins
Treading Blind
1940
Photo etched relief block, letterpress printed
21.5 x 14cm

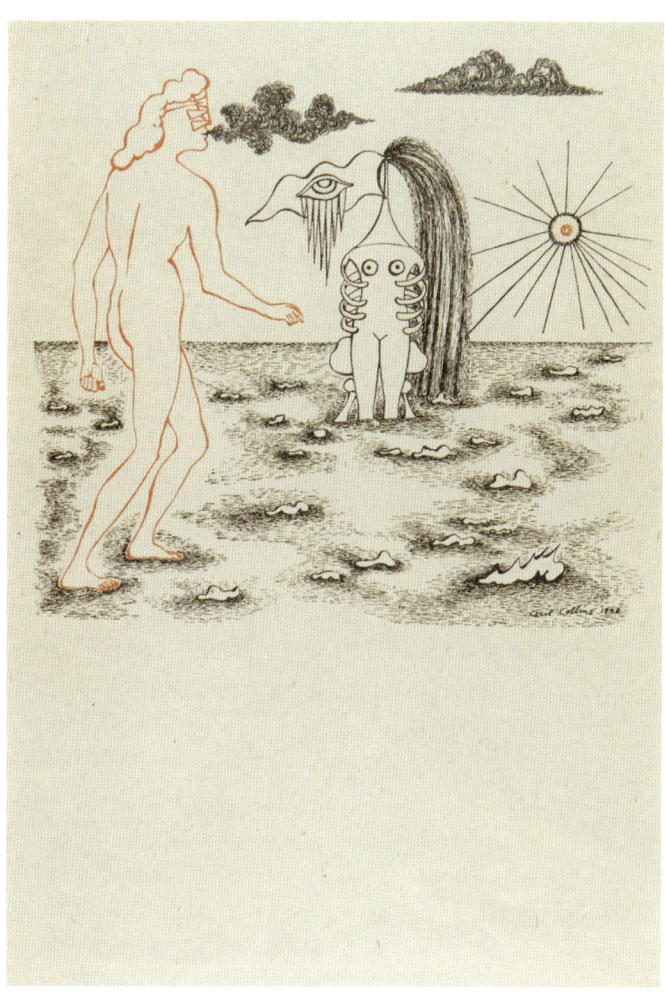

LILY CORBETT

Lily Corbett was born in Hampshire. She is an artist and picture restorer. She has an MA in sacred and traditional art from The Prince's School of Traditional Arts where she now teaches.

Cecil Collins changed my life. I came to know him in 1976 when I was keen to learn how to draw well. I had already held a Cecil Collins painting in my hands, having cleaned a yellow and white angel which is now in a private collection. At the time, it was owned by the art dealers, Abbott and Holder. The actor Peter Bowles had told me about seeking Cecil's book *The Vision of the Fool*, finding it in the British Museum Library, reading it and being incredibly inspired. Hearing of Cecil's vision from such an enthusiast, I discovered Cecil was teaching classes at the City Lit where I already attended several acting classes so I decided to apply for Cecil's class. I took some of my work to the Head of the Art Department, James Burr, and was accepted on the course.

Arriving at the life room on the first day, what immediately caught my attention were the instruments the students were using: Chinese brushes and ink, quill and reed pens, Conté crayons, pencils and charcoal. I was fascinated and inspired by these traditional instruments and I resolved to learn to use them and do justice to their beauty. Only later I became aware of Cecil sitting in the corner by the door, his long body stooped over with very large, punched brown leather lace-up shoes emerging from thin woollen socked ankles below grey trousers. He wore a sensible tweed jacket, with coloured patches on the elbows. Later, I learnt these were beautifully sewn by his wife, Elisabeth. On that day, the model didn't show up and we drew a plant all day. I was plunged in at the deep end, left hand, right hand, feet, brush in the mouth. It was a surprise and a revelation. On other model-less occasions, an ancient tree root would be produced.

Cecil's voice spoke from his corner at the back, quietly, clearly, with full command, 'Reed pen left hand, fourth position, tone four. Quill pen right hand, second position, tone seven.' We drew. 'Change please.' Then, 'Chinese brush left hand, position four, tone seven, on the heel. Right hand Chinese brush, tone one, first position, on the toe.' Working for one minute then, 'Harmonise with quill pen, tone four, first position, by the nib.' Scratch, dip, scratch, becoming aware of the breath of the quill. How often we dipped and splattered and drew. Another series. On we went, both hands at play, holding instrument by instrument in different ways with different tones and different positions on the body. What an all-consuming exercise it was. What a glorious day, being guided by an extraordinary teacher and exploring new ways of drawing. I could not have been more interested, fascinated and inspired. Cecil came up to me at the end of the day and said, 'You drew well today.' He was most encouraging.

I followed his instructions and found it a great relief to work on my creativity in silence as formerly I had focused on speech and acting; to respond to the model with the inspiring instruments, to be centred and make contact with the 'flow'. I found the energy of the class healing as we contacted a central and true part of our creativity together. Cecil never talked too much. He would often begin the class with an orientation to come into the moment and prepare oneself for the class. Then, with an introduction speaking of the techniques and the theme we would study that day, he taught us the 'language of drawing'. His instructions were straightforward. 'Left hand brush, right hand red chalk, little finger tone three of the right hand.' Sometimes you'd write on the bottom of your page a notation of what you were doing to remember the sequence. It may sound complicated, but he was so clear that it was possible. Often we'd work on the highly technical study in the first half of the class, then he'd say, 'Forget all about that,' and we'd work with the creative flow.

The technical part kept the mind happy with something to do so you had a chance of letting go of the issues you brought into the classroom, including the desire to do a good drawing which always holds one back. You concentrated on the model, establishing a communication. In a way, we are always drawing ourselves, but in relation to the model. The whole body is the instrument; it isn't just hand and eye.

The techniques that Cecil taught us we repeated again and again until it was a bodily response in the moment. Among those techniques were tonality, intervals, spaces and the phrases going from a dot to a continuous line. We were also introduced to feminine and masculine energy in drawing represented by curved and straight lines respectively. Realising that everything outside is also inside, the long quest is to realise the masculine and feminine attributes in equilibrium within oneself, as well as in the drawing. Each person has a different balance. It's about understanding when the masculine mode of being articulate, active and direct is required and when the passive, receptive and quiet of the feminine mode is needed. You could say the world of the feminine is lunar, about reflected light. The feminine has empathy. How is someone feeling? How is the model feeling or the whole class? The masculine is solar, about radiating and action. There was a wonderful atmosphere of everyone working together, taking the same positions, working on the technique, but we'd all produce something unique using the same instruments in a slightly different way.

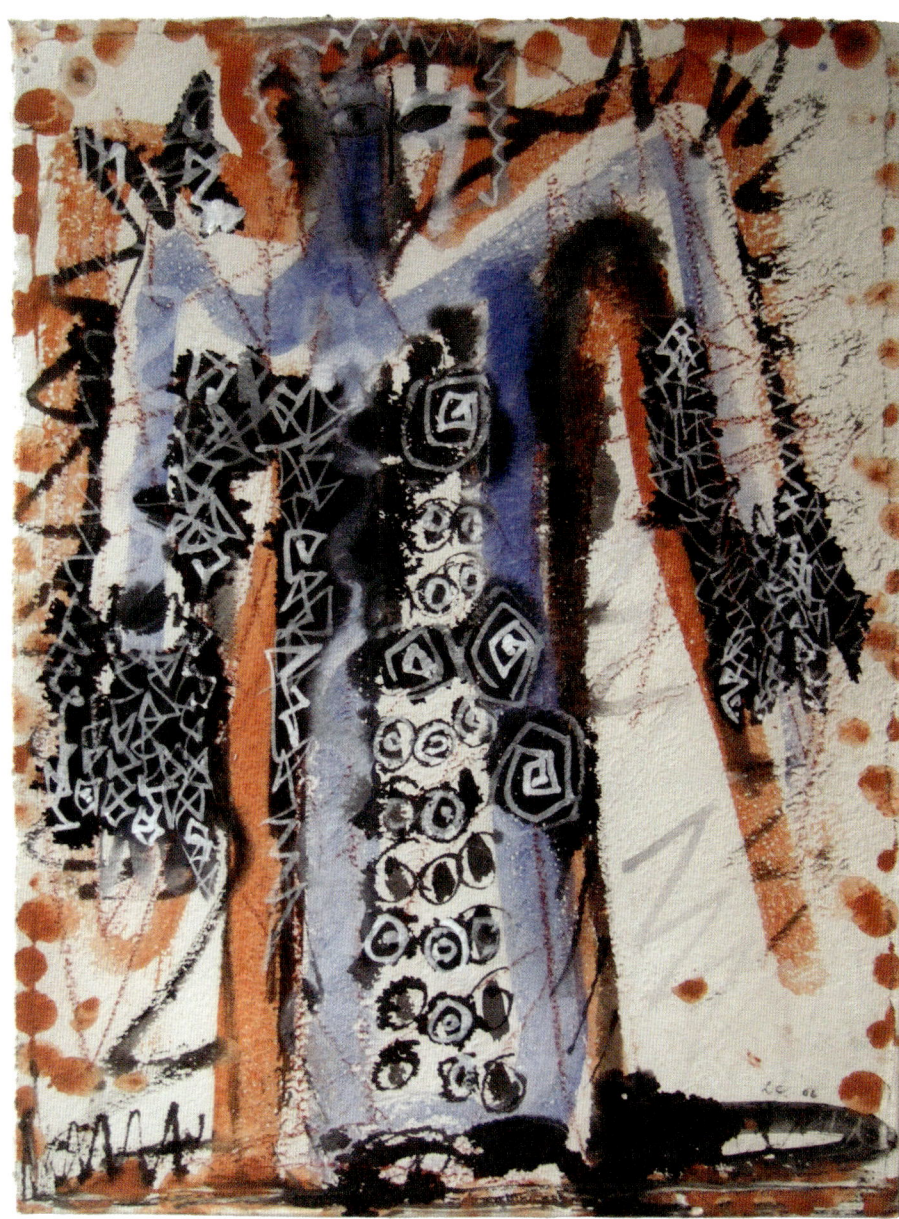

Lily Corbett
Lightening Man
2006
Chinese ink, water colour and gouache on paper
38 x 28cm

things together. Cecil talked about the importance of harmonious relationships. It's very difficult to relate to others in a huge group, but in a small group, you can get to know each other individually and deepen the bond; you can become a family. Drawing is all about relationship: relationship between one line and another, the shortness or the length and the spaces between them.

In one class, we would bow to the model, the paper and instruments and to each other. Cecil made us aware of the courtesy and respect required in relationships. Similarly, in a good drawing, one mark relates to another; there's a respect between the marks. You're not going to scribble away. Although most of the drawings were done at high speed, a Zen quality of connectedness emerged. Sometimes we worked in pairs on the same drawing, watching your partner make their mark before you responded with yours, as in a dialogue. Cecil talked about drawing as a dance. I based one of my recent egg tempera paintings on a fourteenth-century Persian miniature from a series of paintings entitled 'In Homage to Poetry'. In the original, each part and line is in harmony, relating the embrace of vine and tree, the gesture between one plant and another, one leaf and another, between one bird and another. As the miniature was a fine early example of painting that illustrated Cecil's teaching on harmony, I did it as an exercise in relationship. Cecil led us on the path of 'seeing with the eye of the heart' or 'purity of response', as a child sees. Everything is new and wondrous and relates to his theme of the Fool, the Fool as 'purity of consciousness'.

In 1979 Cecil gave me Mrs Tweedie's address and recommended that I visit her. I knew she taught meditation so I went to see her in Chatsworth Road where she was living in a council flat. I walked in through the open door and into her sitting room where she was surrounded by people. I asked her, 'How do you meditate?' That was my first question. She said, 'Darling, think of someone you love and feel love for them. In this way the mind is merged into the heart, the thoughts die down and the mind rests in love and peace.'

This was another beginning for me. I visited Mrs Tweedie for twelve years. I felt that the teaching Cecil and Mrs Tweedie had to offer went hand in hand. They were both on the path of love. Cecil talked about the feminine and the masculine and he made me aware of those two energies in drawing and in myself because each human being has both these qualities. In my understanding, Cecil had introduced me to a teacher who was his feminine counterpart.

Cecil had worked from the model at art school and with Mark Tobey at Dartington Hall. Cecil used to say, 'This is all very difficult, but I've done it.' He also said that once you can draw the human form, you could draw anything. In his summer painting classes we worked from the imagination, the model or nature. Cecil himself always

Cecil was very aware of what was happening in the world, though I don't know if he read newspapers. He and Elisabeth had an ancient TV, a white one. Cecil was one of those people who had a clear overview of what was going on, which brought a certain prophetic quality. He said the future is about working together in small groups. He foretold huge unemployment when people would no longer be needed. Even in the 1970s, he was saying that people would be retiring earlier, that there wouldn't be jobs. Well, there aren't; it seems computers have taken over for the time being. Later on, people came who called him a guru and he made it clear, 'I'm not a guru.' I wanted to learn how to draw and he was a great teacher.

His classes brought a new lease of life to people who were developing their creativity. The class would have fifteen or so students, a small enough group to have a chance to work through

Cecil Collins

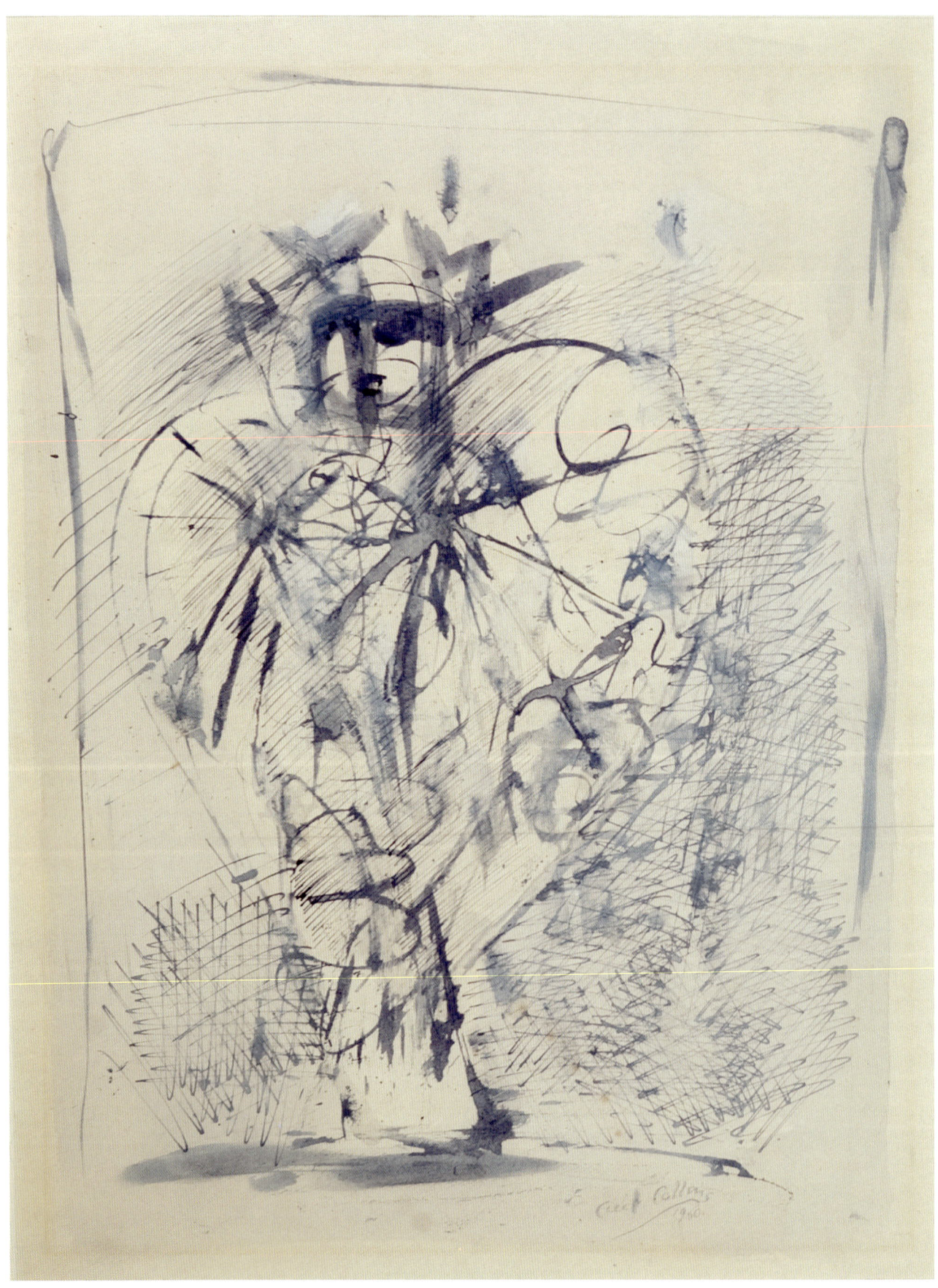

Cecil Collins
Blue Angel
1960
Blue ink and wash
45 x 33cm

worked from the imagination. I don't think he felt the need to work from the external any more. After Elisabeth and Cecil had been to Ireland, I remember Cecil said to me, 'I had to go and leave all that beauty.' He was talking about the beauty he had to leave behind in his studio to look at the external beauty of Ireland, but he would rather have stayed at home working on the internal beauty. He didn't like travelling much. Once, Elisabeth told me, they went to Greece and she and their friends travelled round the islands while he stayed in the hotel.

His classes were an act of giving to people and teaching a technique, but when he was painting at home, he was like a monk working in communion with his own imagination, receiving from within and manifesting it through technique. The two actions were a good balance for Cecil. He loved teaching, having contact with the students, working with them. Together, in class, we created some very special silent atmospheres. Cecil had a great sense of humour and made me smile on many occasions. Sometimes you need a sudden surprise that makes you laugh. Laughter opens up your heart and makes you feed good. As a friend tells her students, 'Laughter is the High Priest of communication.' The Dalai Lama is an adept at this technique and so was Cecil.

Cecil was very intelligent and extremely sensitive and understood people well. He was a very sympathetic teacher and you could not have studied with a better drawing master. He helped me enormously when I had close family bereavements and was still suffering two years later. He stood behind me one day as I was sitting in class and said, 'Your relationship with them is now, not then.' For me, hearing that was a turning point and now, years later, my departed family are in me; they're not somewhere else. Once Cecil said to me in the summer painting class, 'I know every brick of the Temple of Philae.' He was quite serious although I knew he had never been to Egypt. This was a mysterious remark. He said that creativity has nothing to do with therapy. Focus on your creativity. If you've got problems and you work on your creativity, you're going to feel better.

We worked in three rows round the room in a horseshoe. Cecil would sit at the back and sometimes he would come round when you were working if there was room to get behind you or in the break he would look at the drawings. He never said anything critical. Cecil would select a drawing as a good one and you'd wonder why. He'd say, 'Yes, the drawing needs that particular mark there,' because he was seeing the relationship of the marks. He wasn't looking for a copy of the figure because copying would impose a system of measurement and reduce the model to a system. We were taught to interpret form, not to copy it.

A good drawing is a harmonious drawing where all the lines are relating; a drawing that has this quality has a feeling of wholeness. As a restorer, I have examined paintings and their structure in depth. When I was eight years old, my grandmother would take me to Portobello Road market where I developed a fascination for old drawings and watercolours and began to buy them with my pocket money for a penny or tuppence. I later sold some of them for a huge mark-up price of two shillings and sixpence or five shillings at our antique shop in Windsor which enabled me to enlarge my collection. I have spent a lifetime looking at drawings and paintings and realising that beauty is all in the eye of the beholder, but of course, there are rules of harmony that create a work of quality. Cecil would choose the most abstract drawings to pin up and then we'd talk about them. He would say, 'Yes, that mark.' We would look at possibly a large black mark on a drawing. 'Yes, the whole thing is supported by this mark.' He was aware of quality; he'd been teaching it long enough.

When you lose yourself in the work, when you're really in touch and focused, it's as if the drawings are doing themselves, but it's not always easy to reach that state. It's not about getting it right. You could get it so-called 'right' with measured academic drawing, but there's no such thing as getting it right or wrong. It's about connecting with the flow, facilitated by a knowledge of technique that is instilled in the body, that's when a drawing may happen that surprises you.

From time to time, we would have a slideshow of Rembrandt drawings and Cecil would point out the abstract mark making and how Rembrandt harmonised the mistakes from a blot or splatter made by a reed or quill pen. He showed us the whole rhythm and spacing of those Rembrandt drawings.

He admired some of the Italian Renaissance art, but knew that time was when a departure from the sacred to the secular occurred. He related time to breath. There was a breathing out before the Renaissance and then came a breathing in. To explain this, he would draw a diagram of a row of cylinders on the blackboard. The first could be seen as a clear, structured cylinder. The next had fewer lines and was more abstract and so on until the last was composed of a single line. This last, simple, clear cylinder symbolised the pre-Renaissance which did not have perspective as we know it today. The complex cylinder represented the energy of the post-Renaissance which has brought us into the world of copying. He made us aware of the division that was created in art by the Renaissance. In considering religious art, he regarded the crucifix showing a murdered man on a tree as a terrible symbol for a church.

We went to interesting talks recommended by Cecil, for example, one by his friend Glen Schaefer and others arranged by Temenos. Music was high on the agenda, a whole variety, chanting Buddhist monks and music by John Tavener, including his opera, *St Theresa*, at Covent Garden.

I focused as much as I could in the classes. In the early years I had to do a lot of healing. My life gradually transformed and I brought myself into alignment. Where I'd been dispersed or chaotic, going to the class helped me become more earthed and less diffused. Cecil was instrumental in reconnecting me with my creativity. I was caught up and distracted in the circumference as opposed to getting in touch with the centre. I would go to his class and, without really knowing what was going on, be put in touch with my centre. It was only after I'd started teaching myself that I realised much more consciously what happened.

I'd spoken to Cecil a little bit about teaching and then, in 1986, I told him I felt ready to begin. I studied with him in his City Lit class for eleven years. When I moved on to begin my teaching, it was a huge step for me. Instead of all those years of receiving a teaching, I would be giving it. He requested I write my notes into a book so that he could see them. This I did and he then gave me his blessing to start teaching. We would discuss the teaching from time to time. He told me to make the teaching my own and to use music that moved me, not necessarily the music he used, although I do, as many of those pieces are dear to me and remind me of his classes. Music is an important tool in the class for making students aware of rhythm, feeling and harmony in a drawing. I also always remember him saying, 'There is a spiritual element in the class.' Love is the basis of the spiritual and the essence of his teaching was love; learning how to come into a relationship with oneself and everything and everyone. For me, it is a continuing journey of transformation, in tandem with developing drawing. When I began to teach, I realised I had to leave the weekly class. I knew I needed to focus on 'giving out' rather than 'receiving' and there was a huge demand for his class so he said, 'Come twice a term.' So that's what happened until he died.

I approached Ruth to see if she would be prepared to share a class and teach on alternate weeks. She agreed and Cecil supported our collaboration. We began the classes in a studio in my Battersea house. Students found out about the class by word of mouth and came from the Central, where Ruth was based, and I had some students from Chelsea. Later, we went to Nomi Rowe's studio in Covent Garden and taught there until 1989 when the studio was demolished. At that time, I had moved. I had building work going on at home and needed the energy to focus on my house. It was May 1989 and I was drawing in Cecil's Central class, not knowing it would be the last class of his career. I said to Cecil, 'I'm going to stop the classes,' and he said, 'We'll review it in the autumn.' Then he died in the June and I didn't start teaching again in the autumn.

For many years, some of Cecil's students would meet once a month to draw together. One person would take the group and we'd learn from each other. That's how I carried on my teaching in a small way for many years. Then in 2002 I started to step in and take Jeremy Gale's class if he was away. Jeremy's Monday class was in my home for sixteen years and he's become an extraordinary teacher. Although that came to an end, we do give weekend drawing workshops together and have again the opportunity to share and develop the teaching we received from Cecil.

In the late 1970s Elisabeth had a very unfortunate accident. She tripped over some builders' rubble on the streeet and broke her leg. This resulted in her spending weeks in hospital and a nursing home. Cecil was desperate and miserable so I thought I could help him by cooking steak and kidney pies as he loved that sort of old-fashioned English food. This was the beginning of my cooking for them and I continued until 1999. I would take a dish on Saturday afternoon and have tea with Elisabeth. We'd sit and chat while Cecil was downstairs painting in his room. Elisabeth was like a contemporary; you weren't aware that there was a huge age gap. She was such an empathetic person. Cecil loved her deeply and she looked after him. It was an amazing union. They were both extraordinary people. After Cecil died, Elisabeth more or less gave up cooking. Sometimes, she ordered something from the pie man on Chelsea Green and I continued my Saturday visits.

Cecil and Elisabeth were huge readers. Cecil would often recommend various books. After Elisabeth died, Marcia took Cecil and Elisabeth's library to her house in Queen's Park so people could choose books there. This was to avoid people going up and down the stairs and disturbing Kathleen Raine. A very amusing get together and book day was organised by Marcia. The books left over were sold and the proceeds given to the Artists' Benevolent Fund as had happened with the remainder of Elisabeth's own work which was sold through the Jane England Gallery.

Cecil's teaching was an act of sharing what he had cultivated in himself. He told me his class was unique and it was. During all the years I studied with him not one class was the same as another. There were so many ways, themes, combinations of technique and of drawing with different people that it was always fresh. Cecil often used *A Child of Our Time* by Michael Tippett. In this music, there's a climax and then there's another much greater climax, an aural example of the small happiness and the great happiness, the happiness really worth having that Cecil often spoke about. He used to say, 'Learn to enjoy being vulnerable.' When you're vulnerable, you're not charging ahead with the ego, you're more open, more receptive and aware. It's a big process and a journey of a lifetime for me. I am forever grateful that I had the good fortune to have met Cecil and Elisabeth and to have studied with him.

DAVID CRANSWICK

Award winning artist, David Cranswick, trained at Camberwell School of Art, Royal Academy of Arts and with Cecil at Central College of Art and City Lit, before gaining his PhD from the Royal College of Art. He teaches at the Prince of Wales Foundation and is personal tutor to His Highness Prince Michael of Kent. He continues to exhibit internationally.

There was a man in Brighton, where I was living at the time, who used to talk to me about this Cecil Collins who was teaching painting and combining it with meditation. That's the way he described it. I thought, that sounds dangerous to me, steer well clear. When I moved back to London in 1984 to be with Mrs Tweedie, I heard more about Cecil there, but again I got put off because it sounded a little as if it were orientated around people who were not really devoted to art.

It was Mrs Tweedie who, very forcefully, sent me to Cecil. Suddenly, in the middle of the afternoon, when everyone was there, she told me to get out. 'You're wasting your time. I've got nothing to teach you. Go to Cecil, he'll teach you everything you need.' It was quite shocking because I'd been with Mrs Tweedie every day for about eighteen months. I lived just round the corner and my whole life was orientated around going there. I remember as I went out of the door I was still pretty shaken. I said, 'Do you mean don't come back here, you've nothing to teach me?' She said, 'No, of course you can come back, but you go to Cecil.' I did as she told me immediately.

I went to see Cecil at the Central. That was in 1985 at the end of the summer term. I caught someone I knew must be him coming down the stairs and asked, 'Are you Cecil Collins?' and he answered, 'Yes.' I said, 'I'm a painter and I'm interested in joining your classes.' He told me I would have to go along at the beginning of term and enrol. I was also hoping to get into the City Lit because Cecil's class was running there as well, but they told me no chance; it was completely full. So I started going to the Central and, after a short while, Cecil said there was a space for me at the City Lit. I went and queued at four o'clock in the morning to enrol, as everyone did. It was a lovely ritual and quite in keeping with the classes. It was a good test of people's devotion and determination.

The first time I went into his class I was nervous and excited at the same time. Cecil asked me what training I'd had and I told him I'd studied at Camberwell and at the Royal Academy. He said, 'Bring in some examples of your work.' I brought in some sketches and paintings and he had a good look through them, then asked, 'What is it you want to learn from me?' I said, 'Basically I've come to an end with this. It doesn't seem to be going anywhere or have any particular meaning and I've lost the will or the purpose.' He was quite pleased with that, I think, and said, 'You can join the class.'

I had my freshly purchased Chinese ink stick and the stone. People at Tweedie's had told me exactly what I needed: the quill pens, reed pens, Chinese brushes, Conté crayon and charcoal. It was quite exciting. I liked buying all these things, but I really didn't know what they were for.

When Cecil taught, he'd be in his corner usually, with that old gramophone player. The students would be sitting at tables, not standing at easels. There'd be a model in the centre, then he would just start with the instructions, usually with the tones. I remember at the beginning it was three tones and then, gradually as we progressed, we'd go into the seven tones. At the Academy we occasionally had a model that held very short poses, but in Cecil's class the poses were happening so much faster, and we were also working with the left hand, the right hand, with our toes and our nose, and with different positions on the instruments. It was impossible to resort to my old practices of looking carefully and trying to get that line exact or whatever. My drawings were all over the place.

My recollection is that the themes were always repeating themselves, very much in a circular way. We'd go through a whole sequence of different themes. It might be lying on the floor in the archetypal positions; going from horizontal on the floor, up onto the knees, to vertical. We didn't do that every week, but we might do it for two or three weeks in a row and then that would be it for a while. The experiences were always so completely different that for the first year, I had no idea what I was doing. I just knew I had to do it because Mrs Tweedie had said I should and I had trust in Cecil that this wasn't some superficial activity. It had meaning.

I used to feel absolutely exhausted physically. People would say afterwards I looked white. It was nothing to do with the hours I spent there because when I go out painting or drawing for a whole day, I don't come away drained at all. I think what made Cecil so exhausting was the fact that it was going against all my training. I came from a very academic background, especially at the Royal Academy. I was very focused on tight and controlled life drawing, incredibly measured. Cecil's classes were slowly breaking down all the previous understanding and ideas I'd built up around what art was about and all the habits I'd got into, and the sense of security through the technique that I'd developed. All of that was being undermined. I was giving it everything and yet nothing was happening. Everything was crumbling beneath me, but I wasn't thinking, oh my God, my drawing looks terrible. There was none of that going on. It was just a slow breaking down. Cecil wasn't saying that you have to get rid of the mastery of being able to draw. He often said, 'You've got to have a more creative flow of energy. The technical side is only one aspect of it.'

I knew that Cecil's approach was completely different from the normal intellectual one. His was more personal, right from his heart, from a level of understanding that went way beyond anything that I'd been working with before. Mrs Tweedie had once asked me how I felt about my painting and I said I'd like to work more from the unconscious, so there was already a part of me that was wanting to let go of the outer fabric and look more inwards. I sensed that was really where Cecil was coming from, the inner spiritual aspect of the work, rather than superficial entertainment of the ego, which everyone else seemed to be involved with. Learning with Cecil was very much by absorption. Having recently talked to people who have studied with various masters in India and Pakistan, I've understood that his was very much a traditional way of teaching. It's more a matter of training, not the words of instruction themselves.

At the end of each morning or afternoon or during morning breaks, people would have their drawings out and Cecil would go around and talk, briefly, to various students. He would say things like, 'Oh, that's going very well,' or 'You're still holding on too tight,' or 'You're still caught up in this or that.' Then he'd come to another one and say, 'That's wonderful. You're breaking through there, it's starting to flow and you're really getting in touch with your heart.'

I used to love those comments; they intrigued me. I'd go round with Ceil sometimes and look at the drawings. Before he would say anything, I'd try and see for myself: is that going to be entering the flow more or is that going to be stuck? I was trying to understand what he was seeing because I couldn't see it. In a way, it gave me hope because, as far as I was concerned, my drawings were completely chaotic, but he had a few interesting things to say about mine too. 'This area,' he'd say, 'is still a little encrusted with your conditioning and here it's starting to loosen up a bit.' Often drawings which I thought were the worst of the worst, he would give a very positive comment.

Cecil understood the world very well. He understood people and where their problems were and how one can, in one way or another, work with that. Once, somebody spilt all their ink on the floor and he said, 'Quick, put your paper on top of it and then put it on the table. Now work with that.' Looking back, I have the sense that Cecil really lived what he taught. Sometimes, when I watched him wander off after I'd been talking to him for a while, it was like watching one of the figures from his paintings, and it was as if he was now walking back into his own painting again.

I got to know Cecil more personally after Ruth had asked me, at Cecil's request, whether I might be willing to go to his house to collect him and take him to the college. Ruth said, 'We need somebody with a car to do this because he's not really well and he's getting a bit old to catch buses.' I said, 'Yes, of course, I'd be more than happy.'

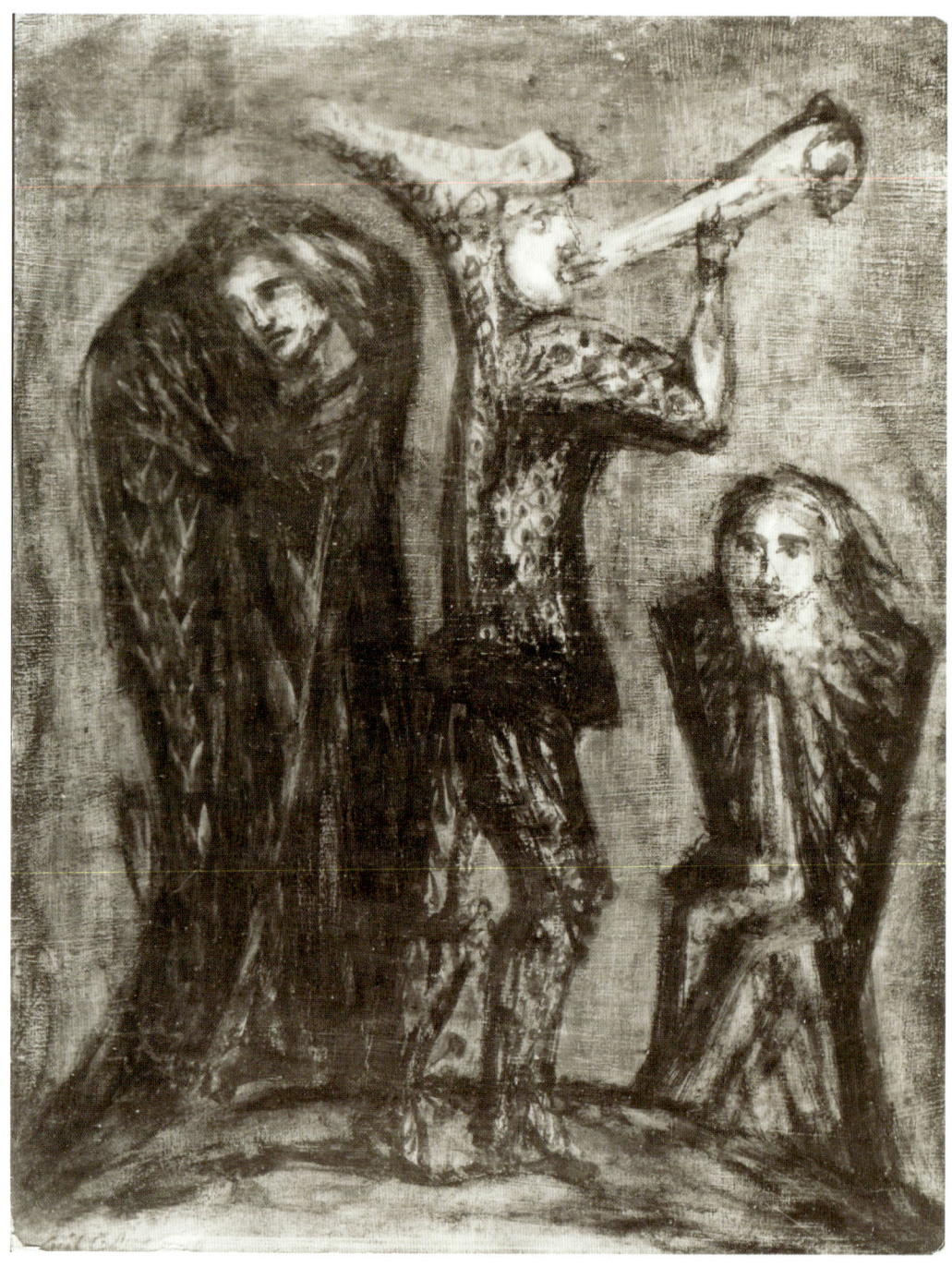

Cecil Collins
Fool and Angels
1969
Oil on board
23 x 17cm

I collected him every week and brought him back home again. I acted as a kind of chauffeur and then I started to help round the house if anything needed sorting out and also in his studio with various things. This was about halfway through the course of the first year. Some days I'd go to the house and he wouldn't be ready, so we'd talk a bit in his studio and he'd show me a few things. Then he started inviting me to lunch, sometimes at his house or we'd go out, but not on teaching days. Sometimes, after we'd been clearing or going through things together in his studio, we would sit down and both nod off. Cecil once said, 'It's a good sign.'

Sometimes, if Cecil wasn't at home, Elisabeth and I would talk about things. I had a good link with her, but it was very different from the relationship with Cecil because he was my teacher and she was the wife of my teacher. She was a wonderful woman, very clever and sharp. Often I'd have tea with both of them at four o'clock. It was very punctual. Elisabeth always had it ready and we had interesting talks up in their lounge on the top floor.

For Cecil, Elisabeth was a manifestation of the feminine principle and that's why he often said she was the real artist because she was, in a sense, part of the vehicle for the whole vision to come through. He'd say that in front of her and she would just smile. I would listen and try to understand.

In a way, Elisabeth sacrificed her own work, her own potential. All the focus was on Cecil, but I don't think she saw it as a sacrifice. It was instinctive for her because what was coming from it was so valuable. I remember one deep conversation I had with Elisabeth. Cecil was downstairs in his studio doing something and we were upstairs for about five or ten minutes and she talked about a time in the past when they were on a picnic in the country. Cecil was resting and she decided to go for a walk. She went over a hill, then along and up another hill and saw a whole other world. It was a kind of paradise and she had the choice of disappearing into it and being incredibly happy, but she knew she couldn't do it; she had to come back because Cecil needed her.

Cecil had that very intuitive aspect of his work, but also the very intellectual side too. I think this ties in very much with his passion for music and its structure. Cecil said that music and art are very closely linked and that he got much of his inspiration from music. He used to spend hours listening to tapes and he recorded a lot from the radio. He loved the music of Stravinsky. I remember, not long before Cecil died, he talked often about how he thought his paintings would really ring a chord with the Russians. He was always very keen to exhibit there, although he never did. Once, when he'd played Arvo Pärt's music in class, Cecil told me that he had been to an Arvo Pärt concert in London and had invited him to lunch at their flat. According to Cecil, because Arvo Pärt could hardly speak any English, he sat there not saying a great deal, but that it was a very good meeting and the language was not really important; it didn't matter.

Cecil also loved humour and jokes and told me about the tricks he used to play on people. In the class, he used to play with words sometimes and make everyone laugh. When Cecil laughed, his whole being would just completely crack up with the humour of the situation.

There was one joke he often told about a Scotsman who, invited by his French friend, goes to France on a shooting trip. They go out shooting for rabbits and after walking for some time they see, suddenly, on the top of a hill this lovely white fluffy rabbit. The Scotsman immediately gets his rifle and is about to shoot, but the Frenchman says, 'No, no, don't shoot, that's Richard. We never shoot Richard.' So they walk on and see this lovely, grey rabbit with white chest and a bit of white on its nose. The Scotsman quickly gets his gun ready again and the Frenchman says, 'No, that's Florence. We never shoot Florence.' This went on for some time and then they come round a corner and there's this scraggy, emaciated rabbit sitting there and the Scotsman thinks there's no point in shooting that, it's such a wretched specimen, but the Frenchman says, 'Shoot, quick, that's Robert. We always shoot Robert!' There was that time when he was at the Royal College and he was painting naked which was an element of his playfulness and he told me about his painting of the nude pregnant woman, which at that time had shocked people. I'm can't be absolutely sure about it, but I always tie the two incidents together somehow.

I remember Cecil talking about some of the old masters. For instance, when he gave me an exercise with tonal and colour perspective, he related that to Claude as being the first one to put that into practice. He asked me once as we were driving to the City Lit, 'If you could choose to be any artist, who would it be?' I said, 'I'd probably be Rembrandt, who would you be?' Cecil said, 'I'd be Vermeer. To me, he is one of the most mystical and mysterious of all the artists. I've already been through the experience of Rembrandt.' I understood him to mean that whole emotional world Rembrandt was painting, as well as the other aspects to do with the deeper levels of his work, such as Rembrandt's ability in some of his portraits to make contact with the spiritual element. It breathes through the paint somehow, you can feel it. Cecil had been through all that.

When Cecil talked about the Renaissance and medieval artists, he stressed the importance of the materials themselves and the importance of the ritual way these were prepared and how today materials are taken for granted, especially with modern technological advances. The whole significance of the craft practices and the ritual of the techniques is all to do with preparing your inward state. People ask me why I spend so much time preparing materials that can be bought in a shop, but it's not about the mechanics. This is very much something I got from Cecil's class and through his talking to me about the old masters and how they worked and what we've lost from that period. Cecil also recommended reading about people like the artist-craftsman, Eric Gill. He was a stone cutter and wrote wonderfully about the sacred aspect of the craft, art as a form of worship.

I remember at the end of his life when Cecil was too ill to walk and I was pushing him in a wheelchair round his big Retrospective at the Tate, someone came up to chat to him and asked if I was his son and Cecil said, 'He's my spiritual son.'

It wasn't until after Cecil died that I felt ready for teaching. Before then, over the years, I'd tried getting teaching jobs at adult education places, but was faced with closed doors. It was very difficult at first, then I put up some notices at the Central, in the cafeteria, and got a call from the Royal College of Art about six weeks later. One of the tutors had seen my poster, taken a photocopy of it, and shown it to the head of department there. They asked me, 'Would you like to come and give a five-day workshop to MA and PhD students?' I thought, crikey, am I out of my depth? But it went very well and I've been teaching there for seventeen years now. The Royal College told me I had to do a PhD and I said, 'Okay, but I haven't got any money.' Then I spoke to the Head of the Visual and Traditional Arts Department who turned out to be Keith Critchlow.

I had first met Keith some time back. I'd been with Cecil in his studio and he'd said, 'Let's go across the road,' because he had his favourite pub in the King's Road. We often used to go along and have a beer. Cecil loved their lunches of bangers and mash and that sort of food. As we were going downstairs, there was a knock at the door and it was Keith Critchlow whom I'd not met before. Cecil said, 'We're just going out to lunch, would you like to join us?' Keith said, 'Yes.'

After we'd had lunch, said goodbye to Keith and come back, Cecil said to me, 'Keith will be a very great influence later in your life.' He predicted that Keith would be an important connection for me. It was strange that I should get phoned up out of the blue to teach at the Royal College. I didn't even know then that it was Keith Critchlow. I thought, okay, I'll teach these students, but what is this department? When I got there I saw Keith and he loved everything I was teaching, the whole alchemical thing. It was something that was lacking in the department there and in art colleges everywhere. The Royal College was where Keith started out, but they didn't quite understand what he was doing so they didn't trust him. Keith said he always tried to keep a fog around his classes because the more they knew, the more they'd have tools to get him out. Finally he was thrown out, just like with Cecil at the Central. They wanted to get rid of him.

Once a year for a week I teach the first year students at the Royal College and also at the Prince of Wales School of Traditional Arts. It really is like an alchemical workshop because I talk about all the pigments from the plants, roots, rocks and berries and relate it back to the alchemical process, and how in earlier periods it was very much part of the practice of alchemy. Making and preparing these colours is an integral part of the creative process and the students love it. They love the magic of the substances, the breaking down, the washing, the precipitating, the cooking and the colours that come from that process. The way the colours appear is quite magical.

You make a dye by extracting the colour out of a plant or maybe its roots, berries or bark. There are also some insects you can use or mineral rocks. Lapis lazuli has a very lengthy and complex recipe that was developed in the twelfth century. You make it by kneading all the blue into a putty till you've got a ball of blue and then you leave it in water overnight. The next day you knead the putty underneath the water, and if you've got the recipe right, the pure colour bleeds out into the water and all the impurities remain in the putty. It's the best recipe. The older recipe was just to separate out little bits of impurity with tweezers, not nearly so effective.

When you use another process, which is precipitation, you use alum salt and get quite a reaction bubbling up. Then this sponge-like stuff precipitates out of the liquid. Often with plants, you don't see what the colour will be. They look very ordinary and uninteresting, but you drain off the liquid and then you dry the pigments out. Visually it's wonderful the way such beautiful colours come out of these materials.

We talk a lot about the earth and the cosmos, the macrocosm and the microcosm, how they're all connected. The whole thing comes together; everything is related. The alchemical side is very much the heart of the whole work which takes what could be just a mechanical, physical process into something much deeper and more spiritual. If it hasn't got that alchemical element, then to me it's pointless.

Teaching for Cecil was a way of lighting the flame in other people's hearts, to keep the vision alive. Not his vision, because he never referred to it as his vision, but the vision that's in all of us. He wanted that vision to be reawakened in others so that the flame could go on, because he was very concerned about what was happening in the world. The vision was an awakening to one's own inner world, the inner world of the imagination which is universal and eternal. That's why it doesn't belong to anyone, it comes from the point in us which is beyond the ego. It's universal and infinite; it speaks to everyone.

ROSALIND CUTHBERT

Rosalind Cuthbert (MA, RCA, RWA) studied Painting at the Central College of Art and the Royal College of Art in the 1970s. In 1981 she moved to Winscombe, North Somerset, where she still lives with her husband David, also a painter. They have one daughter.

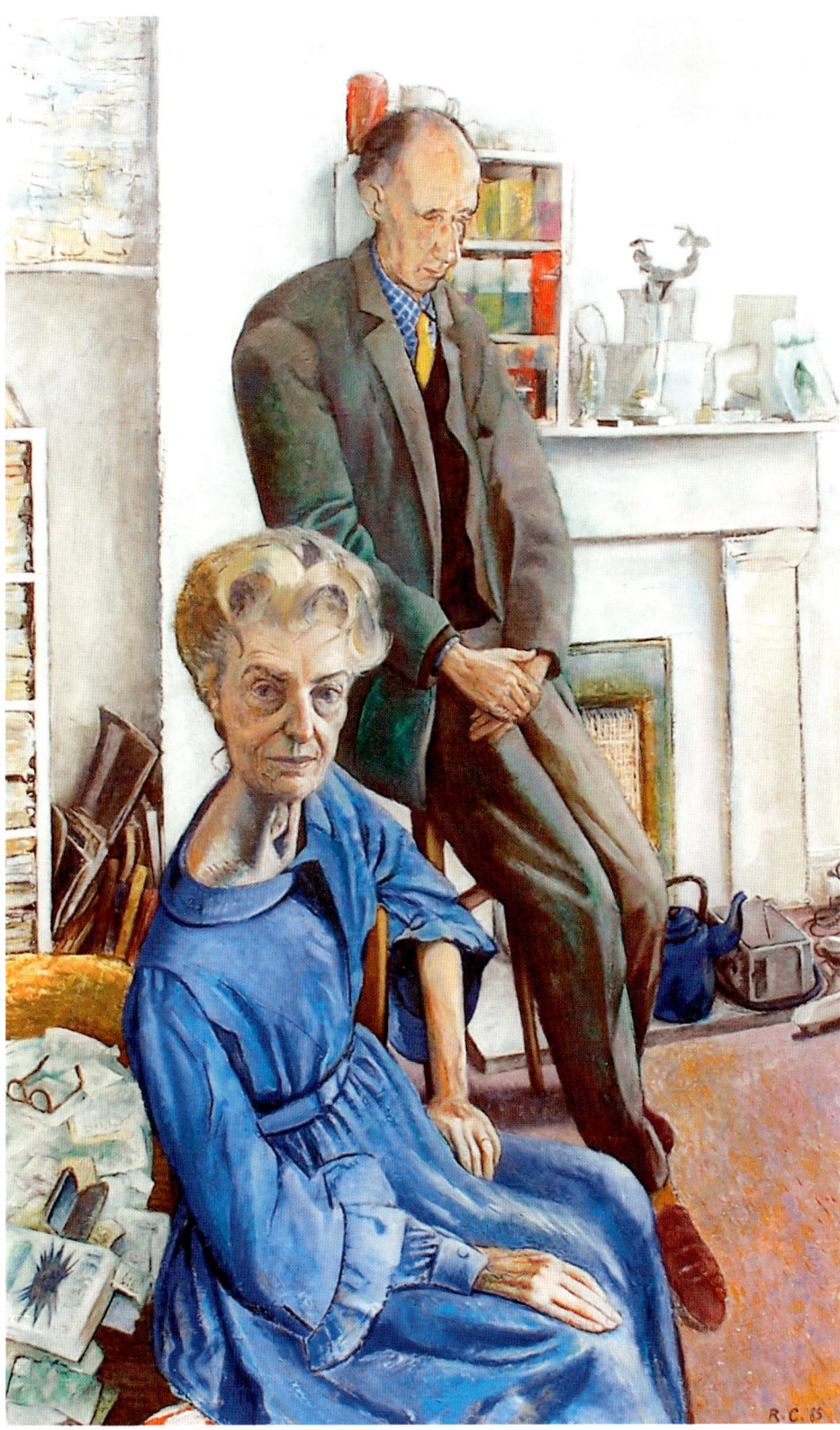

Rosalind Cuthbert
Portrait of Cecil and Elisabeth Collins
1985
Oil on canvas
86 x 51cm

I was a student at the Central College from 1971 to 1974, but I can't remember much about Cecil in my first year except that he gave me a little drawing. This happened because, during that time, one of the images I was working with was a lion. It was originally a caged lion on the back of a lorry that I saw during a hitching adventure, or a misadventure really, that I had in Italy where I fell a foul of a couple of lorry drivers. Then I saw a toy lion at a motorway café so it became a bit of a symbol. The lion took off when I got back to college and became like an emblem and I began collecting drawings of lions. I asked various people if they would give me a lion drawing for my lion scrapbook and Cecil brought in a little drawing, one he'd done quickly on a bit of old paper. That was before he became my personal tutor in the second year so it was really then that I had most to do with him.

In my diary the first mention of Cecil is in October 1972 when he got the whole of the second year together in one of the main studios and talked to us at great length about a higher consciousness. I think there were some exhibitions on at the time which he was referring to. As a result of that talk, some students were suspicious of him. They didn't like the way he would choose certain students and speak to them exclusively. Some people felt a bit left out, I suppose. It was as if Cecil was cultivating just a few students, which indeed he was. He would choose people who were interested in some type of mysticism or who were painting in a way that he thought might point to that. One young student came up to me and asked me what did I think of Cecil Collins? He was obviously suspicious and worried: why had Cecil chosen some students and not others? Cecil was very critical, openly critical, of ways of thinking and of making art that were not his way.

When I was very young, I had a kind of visionary experience. I don't remember much about it now, but the world seemed to stop. Later, when I was on my Foundation course at Somerset College of Art, I started reading Freud and Jung's *Memories, Dreams, Reflections* and looking at books on psychoanalysis and psychology. I was therefore very open to Cecil and mystical, philosophical

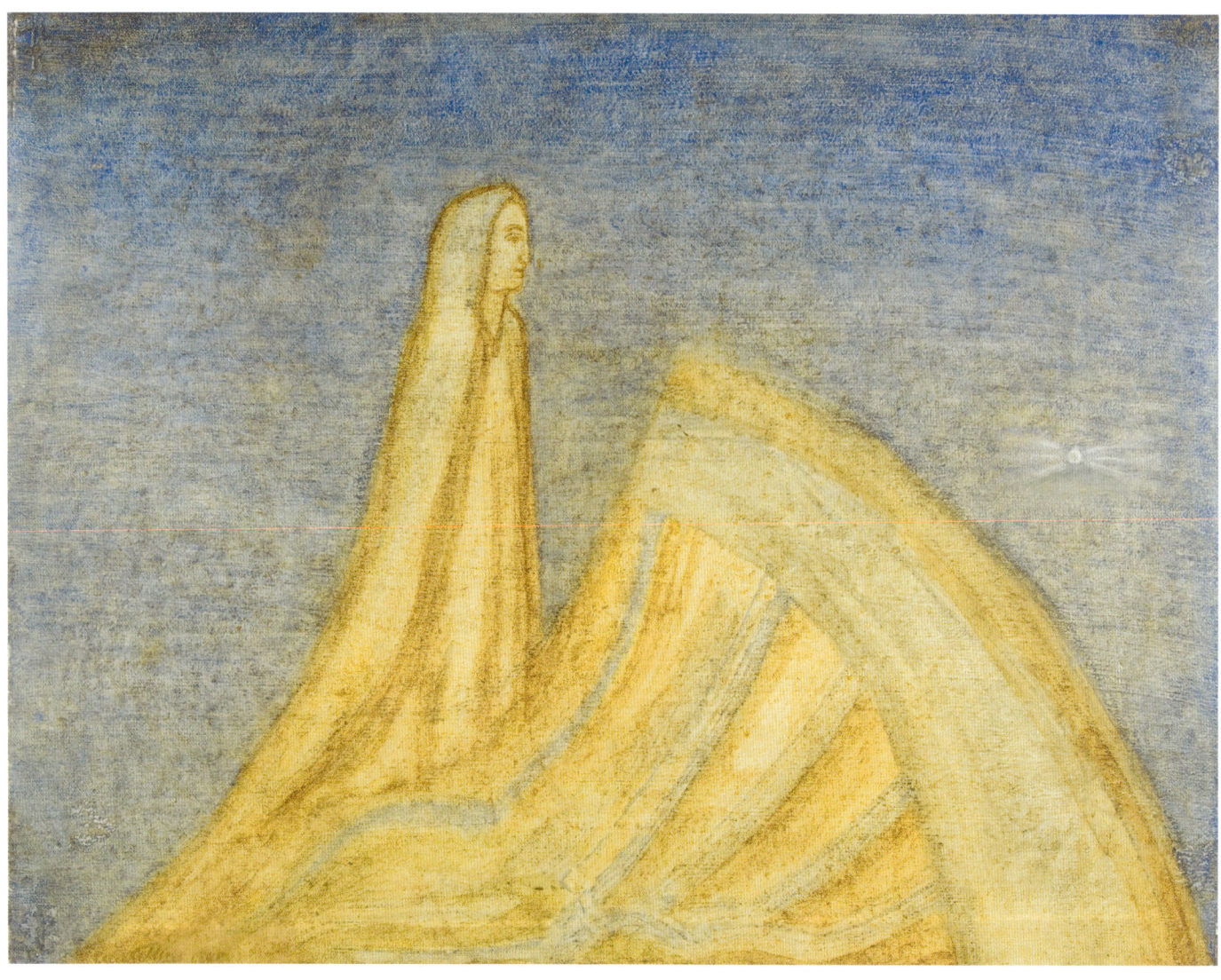

Cecil Collins
Morning Star
1985
Oil on board
30 x 38cm

thinkers like Jacob Boehm and Meister Eckhart. I was interested in them because I'd come across them in Jung. He also lent me a book by Anne Gage, the wife of one of his ex-students, *The One Work*, a sort of spiritual adventure book.

There was a lot of political activity at the Central College. It was a bit schismatic really. In my husband David's first year Morris Kestelman was Head of Fine Art. I never met him because by the time I got there a year later, Bob Clatworthy was head. There was a perception among the students that what Bob and one or two other tutors wanted was to turn the Central College painting department into a kind of nucleus of the New York school of abstraction. It was said that Bob wanted to fire six or seven part-time staff, but not including Cecil as far as I remember at that time. There may have been an attempt to get rid of Cecil before I got there, but, according to my diary, he wasn't among the ones under threat then.

There was a lot of political conniving going on and I'm not sure how big a part Cecil had in it at that stage. My husband was the student representative and had a lot to do with voicing the students' concerns at meetings. At one there was a big kafuffle between Bob Clatworthy and some leading lights among the students and one or two staff. There was an Australian sculptor tutor we called Digger who was one of those they wanted to get rid of. He spoke up at one meeting and was positively rude which resulted in his leaving, though he probably went under his own steam. That was during my first year and David's second. In the end, I think Clatworthy failed to get rid of any of the part-timers because the students successfully prevented it happening. Cecil obviously survived that round, but subsequently he was fighting for his life as a tutor and tempers ran high.

During my second year, the distrust of Cecil was obvious when I was being assessed not by Cecil, but by John Plumb and Mark Vaux who were hard-edge abstractionists. Their remarks to me consisted mainly of hinting at a content in my work which showed the dreaded

Cecil Collins' influence. At least that's what I wrote in my diary so they obviously were very suspicious of Cecil. I asked them where this content showed itself. Apparently it was in the kind of marks and colours I used which John Plumb said he'd seen fifteen other students use in his eight years of teaching at the Central. It was as if they were trying to get me to admit this influence. Certainly their critique was based on this distrust of Cecil. One drawing especially came under fire because it had particular shapes in it. One tutor said he'd seen several students use those spikes in such a circle to which I replied, 'Nobody told me to use those shapes,' but he said, 'It's more subtle than that, Ros,' as if there was a kind of dark force about Cecil's influence.

At that time, I was interested in symbolism and my paintings were semi-abstract, but also symbolic so the shape could have been a halo or a sun or something; I don't remember now. I suppose you have to appreciate that these guys had a whole different approach to painting. They were looking at the superficial: the surface, the colours, the shape itself and they weren't looking beyond that. Maybe they were in one sense, but they certainly weren't looking in a mystical way at colour relationships. They were developing and using a visual language and I think they were probably very nervous of Cecil's influence because it was something they didn't understand.

Cecil was a very astute political manoeuvrerer and very good at getting students to support him in his campaign. In my third year, just when I was about to leave the Central, Cecil confided in me that he'd had a letter from Bob Clatworthy to say that he couldn't come back the next year. The reasons given were his age and also cuts in staffing hours. Cecil said he was very angry so he'd told Bob precisely what he thought and Bob had said, 'Okay, you can stay.'

That was a big year for Cecil because many eminent artists got up a petition in support of him. For Cecil, his work as a teacher was as important to him as his work as an artist. I can't put words in Cecil's mouth, but I've recorded from some conversation we had that his teaching and his painting were dependent on one another and his work as a teacher was immensely important to him.

Cecil was very active as a teacher and did a lot more than just come round the studios and talk to the students. He was always recommending books, exhibitions, performances and taking us to see things. Obviously, he was interested in my painting, but he was also interested in me as a person which I think was fairly unusual as far as tutor-student relationships go. I didn't want to be one of his devotees or be sucked in by him like some students who were very much under his spell. One girl in David's year was completely confused between Cecil's teaching and the kind she was getting from the abstract art tutors and so she did two sorts of painting. She would pull one lot out for Cecil and the other lot out for the others.

I think if you weren't sympathetic to Cecil he would come over as a very strong threat. He could be very dominant, but, more than that, he was secretive. He had, I suppose, experienced criticism in the past from other tutors and was sensitive to criticism of his work, but there was this very secret, mystical side to him which he didn't share with everyone. People and other students could see that there was something they were not party to.

Once, a few days after he'd told me about a lecture Archbishop Bloom was giving at the Overseas League and had showed a film about Carl Jung in the painting department, Cecil invited me and three or four students to a very nice day out. We went first of all to Nadia Boulanger's master class at the Royal College of Music which was fabulous and really fascinating, then we had lunch at the V&A. This was followed by a visit to Baden Powell House to watch Stockhausen rehearsing his musicians for a concert at the Queen Elisabeth Hall. I remember his *Hymnen* was played. Cecil obviously knew Stockhausen and was on friendly terms with him. I thought it absolutely amazing that Cecil would do things like that for us and it made a huge impression. It was something quite unique. It was brilliant for me having Cecil to talk to, but although I loved and admired him and was grateful for his attention and teaching, I wanted to stay a bit separate, especially in my third year. I wanted to develop myself as an individual and I was aware that he was a very influential person and I wanted to move out of that orbit; I could see his effect on other students. There were some who were absolutely like devotees, but whose work wasn't very strong. Although I was always, or almost always, glad and grateful for his teaching, I don't think I was ever overwhelmed by Cecil.

On 14 March 1973 I wrote in my diary a long conversation we had about Stockhausen after the visit to the rehearsal. Cecil asked me could I relate Stockhausen with Madame Boulanger, then with Archbishop Blume, then with Jung? We discussed each combination separately and then I asked him could he relate Stockhausen to Kandinsky? At that time, I was very interested in Kandinsky's writings, *Concerning the Spiritual in Art*, as well as his *Point and Line to Plane*. Cecil took some time considering this and finally said, 'I can, but I wouldn't see the point.' 'Why not?' Cecil said, 'because Stockhausen is dealing with something far more important.' After further thought he added, 'Kandinsky is too small.' I disagreed and said, 'I think Kandinsky is the closest, so far as I know, to saying in paint what Stockhausen is endeavouring to say in music.' Then Cecil said a queer thing, 'Hang onto that; it might be useful.' I'm still not sure what he meant.

It was all very interesting, but I found Cecil was a bit dismissive. He was closed to certain things and certain people. I suppose Kandinsky was then part of abstract art and I don't know whether it

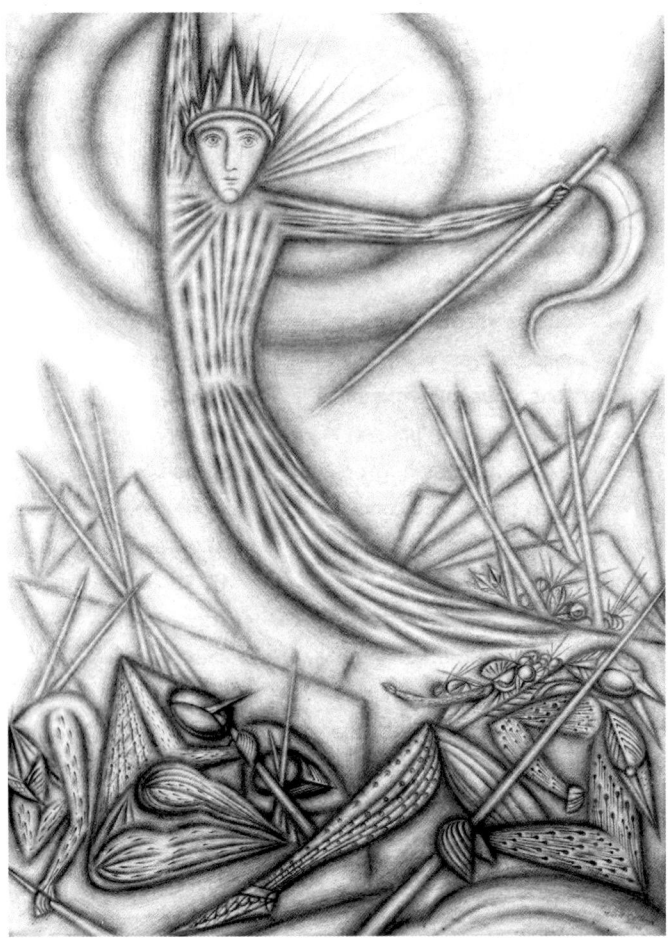

Cecil Collins
The Resurrection
1952
Pencil on paper
76.5 x 52cm

As I was feeling really bad, I didn't want anything to do with it, but it was fun.

Another occasion I remember was my third-year degree show party. David and I went to Moss Bros and hired some suits and dressed up in top hats, tails and moustaches and went to the party. Sadly, Cecil had left early. I said to him afterwards that I was really disappointed to have missed him because I wanted to introduce myself in this disguise to him and he replied, 'I did see you and I said to my friend, "Who could those two be?" What a lovely way to come. It really cheered me up and made me feel good to see that caper.' He must have caught sight of us from across the room.

After college, I went back to teach at the Central College, I taught printmaking for twelve years, one day a week. I used to bump into Cecil and we'd chat. He was still at the Central and Patrick Reyntiens was Head. I think Cecil helped him get the job; that's how powerful he was. Cecil was a very canny man. Everyone was making cuts, but he was still definitely there in 1979 which was when I did the very big painting of him standing in a corridor at Central. I asked him if I could paint him and took photographs of him in the corridor. I made that painting from the photographs and then I asked if he would sit for me. I can't be sure now, but I think I did that painting first and then several smaller portraits of Cecil and then he sat for me.

I went round to his house one morning and he and his wife were both there. On impulse, I asked Elisabeth to sit for me because she was draped in a nice, long blue dress and looked lovely. I did a drawing of both Elisabeth and Cecil and a double portrait of them together. It's really a portrait of her with Cecil. She's in the foreground of the painting. I worked from a drawing I did of both of them like the one I've still got and took photos as well and did the portrait from that. I also did a couple of other little portraits of them, a profile which is on my website, and another one of Cecil, a head, which I sold.

I think Cecil liked the one I did of him in the corridor. He twinkled at me and said, 'You've given me burglar's hands.' That was a very Cecil remark, but I think he was flattered about the portrait. It was bought by the Contemporary Arts Society when it was in an exhibition at the Arnolfini Gallery in Bristol and it's now in a collection at Chelmsford City Gallery. I've never been to see whether it's actually on show there.

I've still got the one with Elisabeth. I experimented with that painting. I drew in charcoal on the canvas before I painted and so in one or two places, especially around Cecil's head, you can still see fragments of the charcoal underdrawing which gives it a more fragile quality perhaps. Cecil was perfectly happy for me to do his portrait; in fact, he enjoyed it.

was to do with that, but Cecil certainly didn't like his work. He also thought Paul Klee was overrated and that he was just someone who was interested in nature spirits. Because I like Klee I didn't accept Cecil's view, but I didn't argue with him over it.

Cecil had told me about his classes at the City Lit in my second year and I attended one weekly all that year. I can't imagine that the powers-that-be, Bob Clatworthy and Co, approved, but the class was very useful because Cecil was teaching something quite new to me. His approach to drawing was innovative and idiosyncratic, something I hadn't come across before, really contemplative drawing. I got a lot from that.

Cecil also had a mischievous side and liked playing the fool. There was one time I remember Cecil literally fooling around which I recorded in my diary. I was feeling ghastly and had just been diagnosed with hepatitis so the college doctor told me to go home and rest. As I was gathering my things together in the studio, Cecil was fooling around with a student, blowing down a long piece of cardboard tube and making amazing sounds come out of it, a bit like a didgeridoo.

SAIED DAI

Saied Dai was born in Iran in 1958. He studied Fine Art at Bournemouth and Poole College of Art and Design, at the Royal Academy of Arts and also with Cecil at the City Lit and Central Schools, London. He taught at the Royal Academy of Arts and the Prince of Wales School of Architecture. He was elected to the Royal Society of Portrait Painters in 2004 and awarded the Ondaatje Prize for Portraiture in 2006.

Saied Dai
Portrait of Cecil Collins
1988
Oil on gesso board
61 x 43cm

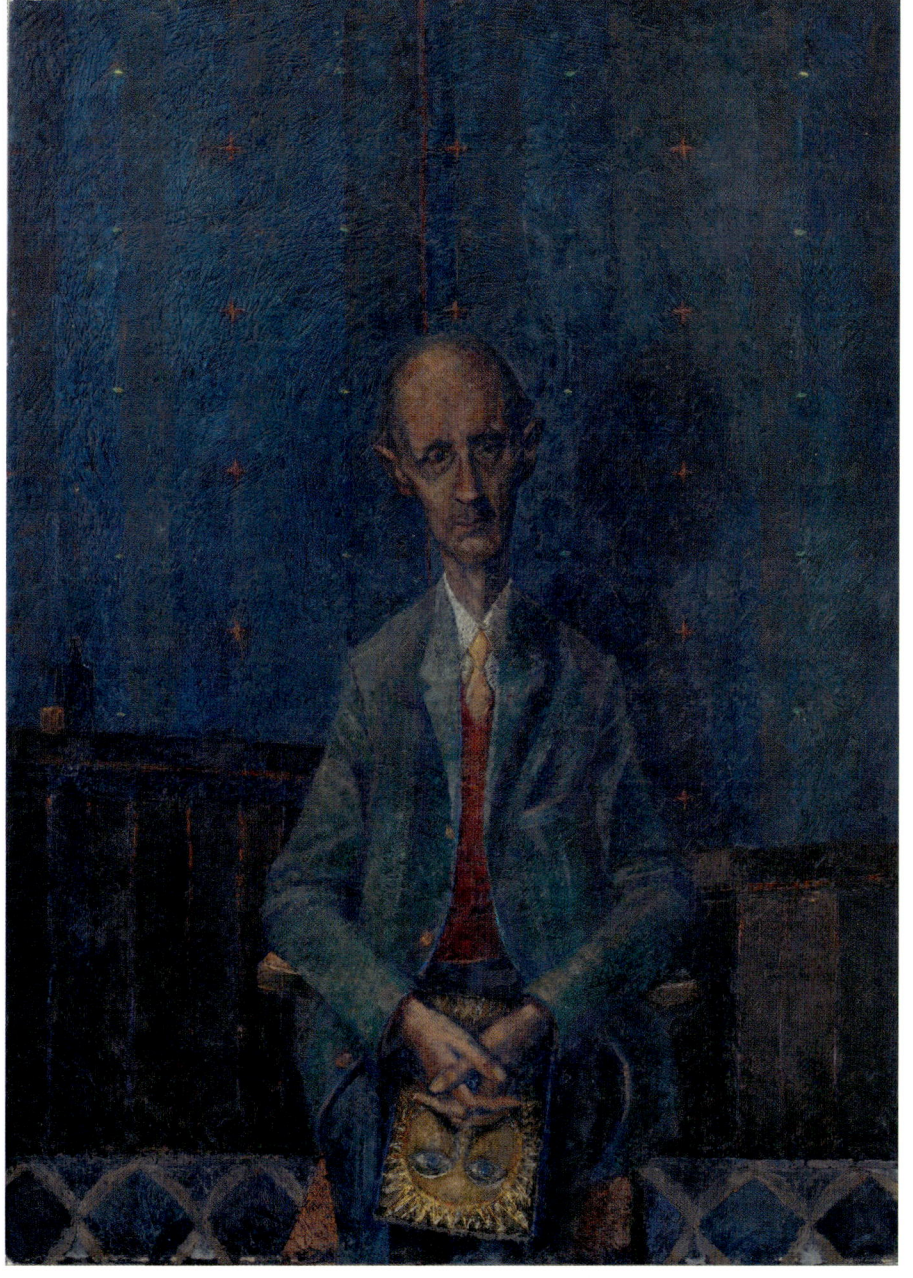

The portrait I made of Cecil was begun when he was quite ill, the year before he died. It was finished posthumously and I struggled with it over a long period of time. Elisabeth had it in her possession for about a year and she said, 'It is a compliment when I tell you that it upsets me.' With her approval it was exhibited at the National Portrait Gallery for the BP Portrait Exhibition. It is not the idealised or romanticised image of Cecil that people may hold. I was attempting to show the humanity and vulnerability of someone who has managed to achieve some equanimity in this complex world.

Whatever the limitations of the painting, the portrait presents him as a real man, fragile and prone to melancholy. It shows a rather frail figure, but with a very powerful presence. I think for a painting to survive repeated scrutiny over a long period of time, one has to err towards silence rather than noise. Silence lasts a lot longer. At the same time, the picture has to be a good likeness.

I had often thought of painting a portrait of Elisabeth as a pendant, but in her lifetime it never seemed right or appropriate, although we discussed the idea. Elisabeth was like the day to Cecil's night. Cecil was definitely in the twilight and Elisabeth in the sunlight. The palette for Elisabeth's portrait would have to be the complement of Cecil's. Many people hold a sentimental and romanticised view of Elisabeth. Such memories can distort the actuality, which is really a disservice to the person.

I had quite a rigorous formal art education. As a student one is brought into contact with the history of art through a chain of teachers, who may not necessarily be well known to the general public, but are famous among artists. I also had the good fortune to benefit from the remarkable people teaching at the Royal Academy Schools. An artist's pedigree can be judged by the people they have been taught by.

I was in my first year at the Royal Academy when I met Cecil. He was not officially one of the tutors there, but it was common practice to invite artists, to introduce students to different approaches and ideas. Our first meeting was as significant as it was comic. Cecil was walking through the studios, he passed my space and then a second later, walked backwards and stopped, as though seeing something in a shop window. I had no knowledge of him at all, but I think he detected some potential. He asked a little about my background and made an enigmatic remark about the work, saying, 'It is as if an Arabian stallion is trying to get out,' referring to my Persian background. Then he suggested I should join his classes. That was my introduction to Cecil. It was an intriguing, almost Sphinx-like comment to a young student.

Cecil's classes were fundamentally based on a very fast, intuitive, gestural response rather than studied, investigative, analytical drawing. I do not think I could have made purposeful use of his teaching without having gone through several years of art school. I came into contact with the right influence at the right time.

After twenty years as a teacher myself, involved in all the problems of education, I have since realised that there was a particular culture around Cecil's classes. Very few people came from any kind of visually formal background. This was not a bad thing in itself but as with music, to get into its profundities, you have to be more conversant with the language. You cannot dabble; it is the same with art. It seems that one of the responsibilities of being a teacher is to ensure that what is being communicated is not distorted by students into what they think you mean, or want it to mean. Perhaps Cecil allowed this to happen unchecked.

Cecil's classes concentrated more on psychological and therapeutic motivations than on the formal language of art. He created an atmosphere that was the antithesis of art school, where constructive criticism is the foundation of learning. In art therapy it is not appropriate or necessary to criticise, because what matters is the emotional connection and release.

Although I did not learn about art in formal, practical terms in his classes, I learnt much about the nature of creativity. His teaching awakened me to the psychology and the motives that underly the making of art. His concerns were predominantly about awareness, perception and relationship. These things are implicit, but are never explicitly talked about in art school.

The idea that there is a 'spiritual art' and then there is 'other art' is misleading. Cecil never made that distinction. There are legions of people who make so-called 'spiritual art' that cannot be taken seriously, because it is based on a fundamental misconception and misapprehension as to what spirituality is. One of the problems with 'spiritual work' is that it ends up using the same clichéd iconography and does not recognise the sacred in things that inherently do not have that symbolism. There is more profundity and spirituality in a Vermeer or a Piero della Francesca or a Georges de la Tour.

Cecil used wonderful colourful language and metaphors when teaching. For instance he would talk about the Four Horsemen of the Apocalypse darkening the sky. He would certainly have raised a few eyebrows if he had been walking around an art school saying such things. His language was sometimes a barrier to communication because it was messianic and biblical, a delight in a way, but not necessarily helpful. I found it more poetic than practical. The process of creativity is more down to earth and not quite so metaphysical. To say that you are a medium and that there are forces acting through you is not very useful, whereas if you just look at a piece of work, you can see what someone is trying to express and how well they are succeeding with the means at their disposal.

What was more important for Cecil was the awakening of something in the person through the process rather than the outcome: the journey was more important than the arriving. In art school, however, the arriving is more important. The best teaching is cathartic in the most positive sense, creating an inward movement. Such a moment of discovery can be emotional and beneficial. I witnessed this reaction many times. It was poignant, because it was unexpected. When the penny has dropped, it brings you to a moment of silence.

Cecil's class predominantly consisted of women. He often talked about the feminine and masculine elements in art, and the necessity for the feminine to become more prevalent, as it had been overlooked. We used to do an exercise where Cecil would get everyone to lie prostrate on the dirty floor. He used to say, 'I am the only man in London who could have so many women at my feet.'

As a broad generalisation, in my experience the psychology of learning tends to be different for women than for men. Women are usually less burdened by ego and more able to listen and co-operate. Teaching men is very different, in that the ego tends to be uppermost and there is more resistance. The advantage women have is often also a drawback, in that they tend not to be so questioning and, in some ways, less critical of the art that is produced. On the other hand, men can intellectualise so much as to miss the essence altogether.

Sometimes, Cecil would make flippant comments dismissing much in the history of art. Privately we had some heated discussions about art in general. I tried to clarify what he meant and on what basis could he dismiss somebody like Piero della Francesca, as he did on one occasion. Teachers have to be cautious in making such unqualified assertions, because students who have a disdain for all education in art and a disposition to trust all to wild chance, will latch on to such a statement to justify their position.

One day coming into Keeley House, Cecil and I ended up in a lift together. He put his arm on my shoulder. It was just a simple token of affection and appreciation, an acknowledgement that, even though I was constantly asking him questions, it was all right. We both entered the class with mysterious grins on our faces. When there is affection, one's questioning becomes more probing, because one is trying to get to the root of things. It is when you are indifferent that you do not ask questions.

Cecil would boast of having avoided art education, despite going through the Royal College of Art. Having an art training and rejecting it through investigation is not quite the same as never having gone through it at all. At his best, he produced some wonderful paintings, which will stand the test of time and what is being expressed is

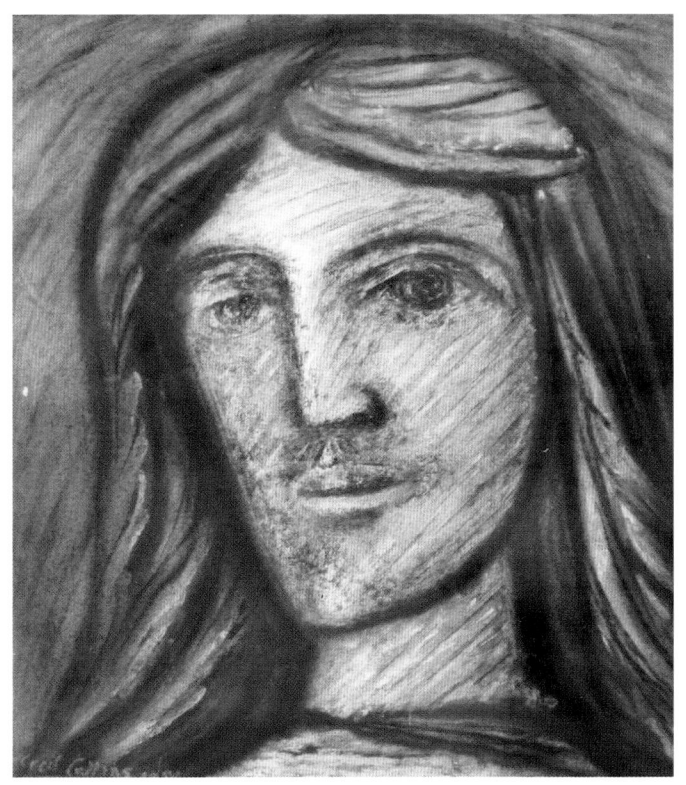

Cecil Collins
Head
1956
Pastel
35.5 x 30.5cm

far more laudable and significant than much of the nonsense that goes for art these days. His concern was that art should make you a better human being. This was the object and the goal, whether you managed to achieve it or not. The degree to which an artist can actually transcend their time is the real test of creativity.

Cecil's drawing is quite linear, hard and spiky, whereas a lot of his teaching tends to emphasise the opposite. It was interesting that Elisabeth said Cecil's approach to his own work was not like how he taught. In some ways, Elisabeth manifested his teaching more obviously. They were both quite intuitive artists; they generally did not set about working something out, although he made an exception in the case of the double portrait. Generally, Cecil's work is very cerebral: it is based on an idea. He did some interesting paintings in the 1960s where he would find the image within the process of accidental marks, which he called a matrix.

Just before he died Cecil was made an RA. It was shameful that recognition from the art establishment came so late. Fame can be a very destructive thing and Elisabeth thought it came to Cecil at exactly the right time, because she believed it would have distorted his path had it come any earlier.

Cecil appeared to be a bit Victorian in his treatment of Elisabeth, in the sense that she was always in the background. It would have been enlightening if Elisabeth had exhibited side by side with Cecil, as she managed to manifest in her painting some of the freedom he taught, and did not necessarily achieve in his own work. She was certainly a better colourist, even though she had started her art training as a sculptor.

I visited Cecil's studio on two or three occasions and afterwards we would all have tea together, sitting round an old-fashioned toaster by the fireplace, a wonderful 1940s contraption with flaps. I got to know Elisabeth better after I started doing the portrait of Cecil and the relationship flowered after Cecil died. Physically, she still had the vestiges of a young girl about her. I always found her very beautiful. She often said, 'I want to be beautiful.'

All the visually appealing arrangements in their home were made by Elisabeth. Cecil's studio was not a particularly aesthetic environment, with his stacks of paintings and mountains of papers. It was a picture of organised chaos, but had its own beauty. It seemed that Elisabeth dealt with most of the practicalities of day to day life; she kept the world at bay, which allowed Cecil to maintain his innocence. I remember a wonderfully eccentric jacket of his on which Elisabeth had sewn dozens of multi-coloured patches.

Elisabeth made tiny notes to herself in spidery red handwriting that contained luminous little quotes. I came across a note on a torn bit of paper stuck on a nail, which read 'Speak to the wall that the door may hear.' There were many enigmatic little comments like that, including Cecil's little drawings or doodles.

In spite of his delicate physical stature, Cecil was quite down to earth in some respects. I remember in the canteen one day seeing this frail, ethereal man, almost transparent, order a huge lorry driver's meal of pie, chips and baked beans. It was like Desperate Dan in the Beano. He was also fond of beer.

In retrospect, I think Cecil was one of the most remarkable teachers I have ever come across. He was always unpredictable and full of surprises. The vast, devoted following he acquired is a testament to the power and the effectiveness of his teaching. Like all remarkable people, Cecil was complex and full of contradictions, but his teaching was born out of love.

I was far too full of concepts and ideas when I first knew Cecil. Elisabeth helped me to absorb and consolidate all the things I had learnt with him. It was a wonderfully complete circle. She was not aiming to teach; she did it by example. Behind every great man, there is an even greater woman.

When I was working on Cecil's portrait, he played Samuel Barber's *Adagio for Strings*, which I will always associate with him. It is a moving and heartrending piece, sad and introspective, but with great tranquillity and beauty. There is a saying of Cecil's that has remained with me, 'I'm the most disenchanted man you will ever meet, but at the same time, the most enchanted.'

ALEXANDRA DRYSDALE

Chelsea College of Art graduate Alexandra Drysdale teaches art and art history and is a NADFAS lecturer. In 2007 she was Artist in Residence at Bundanon, Australia. Her artist in residency at St Mary Magdalene church, Herefordshire, inspired her painting series, *The Journey of Love* which was exhibited in Ely Cathedral. Alexandra lives in Cambridge and continues to paint and exhibit her work.

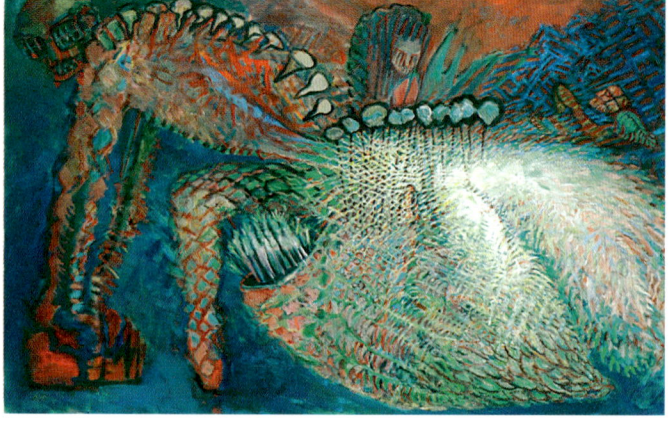

Alexandra Drysdale
Love's Swan Song
2004
Oil on canvas
106 x 167cm

I've known Cecil all my life. My mother had been a student of his before I was born. I can remember him coming to our home in Surrey a couple of times. I remember his hunched back and how there was something strange about him because of that. He had a kind of cheekiness and a childish way about him. I remember him talking about some otherworldly creatures in the woods.

Elisabeth was quite formidable in some ways. She always looked lovely in wonderful hats. My image of Cecil and Elisabeth was that they were very much together. She had a very regal, huge presence and was rather unattainable. Her appearance was very important to her.

When I was a student at Chelsea Art School, I wanted to do life-drawing but I didn't like the way it was taught by Euan Uglow, all measurement and plumb lines. So instead, in 1981, I started going to Cecil's classes at the City Lit because he had completely the opposite attitude.

I found it quite nerve-wracking because I was just eighteen and everyone else in the class was more like forty years old. I would have got a lot more out of it now. I'd turn up with pink stripy hair, a black leather jacket and Doc Martens and I'd go into this room where it was all soft and spiritual and I'd think, 'oh my God'. I was a punky art student and they were all beautiful women with their long, flowing hair. I was sure he could see through this kind of aggressive punk outfit and was probably amused by it. I felt that he had his favourites like Lily and Ginger and Shelley and they always happened to be the most beautiful women in the class. I was rather outside his fan club.

Initially, you felt quite separate from the materials and, in a way, from your feelings, but gradually, through the classes, you got to know the materials and became in tune with your feelings as well. It made me much more aware of how the inner world affected the way I saw the outer world, and how I felt within. I think that was probably the main thing.

When we had to do our movements, I used to dread that he might pick on me to lead. It seemed that I had to do it quite often and I always found it nerve wracking. On a few occasions I found it incredibly emotional. I remember one time dancing, moving and breaking down in sobs. I kept dancing with tears rolling down my face. The other students were all moved by this as well. It was one of those moments. When you were following someone else's movements, sometimes it could be very painful, especially if they were tense. You would feel all the tension and be following them in what was a vulnerable moment. Some people found it quite easy and others found it absolute agony. Because you had the other students moving with you, you had a sense of their support. You weren't completely isolated, but because of the tension, a kind of fear, it did release a lot inside you. The drawings that came out of it were usually very beautiful so I suppose something worked on an emotional level. I don't think his priority was to turn out artists, though I hoped that I'd come away at the end with a few lovely drawings.

I'd go back to Chelsea where it was very different and I'd be looking at the drawings I'd done and, in some ways, it made me feel worse. I didn't know what to do with the drawings, who to show them to. I ended up keeping them hidden because tutors at Chelsea would have thought Cecil was an eccentric sentimentalist and totally out of touch with Modernism. One time, I got Cecil to come and give a lecture about his work at Chelsea. It was such a change to what we heard from our tutors. Luckily, there was a teacher at Chelsea who worked with his imagination, Ken Kiff. He would have been up Cecil's street.

At the time, I thought Cecil had some quite narrow ideas about art. Once I took my tutor, Roger Ackling, to meet Cecil at Paultons Square and I remember having an argument about Francis Bacon whose work Cecil loathed. It was quite an awkward encounter and it brought out how Roger was much more open to different kinds of art than Cecil. It made me realise how isolated Cecil was from contemporary art practice. There were lots of other things going on which Cecil didn't know about; a lot of artists like Roger who were making work in a very authentic and deep way, but whose work was totally abstract. It showed Cecil's limitation. Considering his classes were about using materials and finding the true nature of those instruments, it was surprising that he wasn't interested in the language of art of other people. The only artists that I remember him talking about and whose work he cared about were dead, people like Paul Klee, Rembrandt, Picasso, Miró, though he did like Chagall who was still alive, but very old. It was wonderful when Peter Fuller started writing about Cecil. It enabled younger people like myself to be more assertive about criticising the formalist modernist orthodoxy that had dominated the art school.

It's interesting that while Cecil taught this method of drawing, he rarely ever drew from life himself. It's a shame that he didn't carry on drawing from life because it made him retreat too much into an inner world and to see the outer world in such a negative way. He over-stressed the negative side of society, how the world is so awful now and we're heading for an apocalypse and we couldn't be making these visionary paintings without that negativity. But it seems to me that humanity has always been heading for an apocalypse of one sort or other. But at the time of working with Cecil I was young and I didn't have such a gloomy outlook. His teaching wasn't gloomy at all, it was the opposite. Sometimes I feel his paintings become too sweet and then I don't believe in them. Too much isolation can lead to sentimentality. But maybe it's just my problem rather than the pictures.

There are a few paintings of his that I think are totally wonderful like *The Hymn to Night* that my mother bought and *The Wounded Angel* [1967]. I remember seeing *The Wounded Angel* at his show in Plymouth and sobbing in front of it. It completely got me. To make one painting like that is a huge achievement. If a painting has that effect on you, then it puts Cecil on a par with some of the Giottos or Botticellis. There are a few of Cecil's paintings that I think are masterpieces, but there are quite a lot which don't do anything for me, as if he had lost some of the tension between the vision and life.

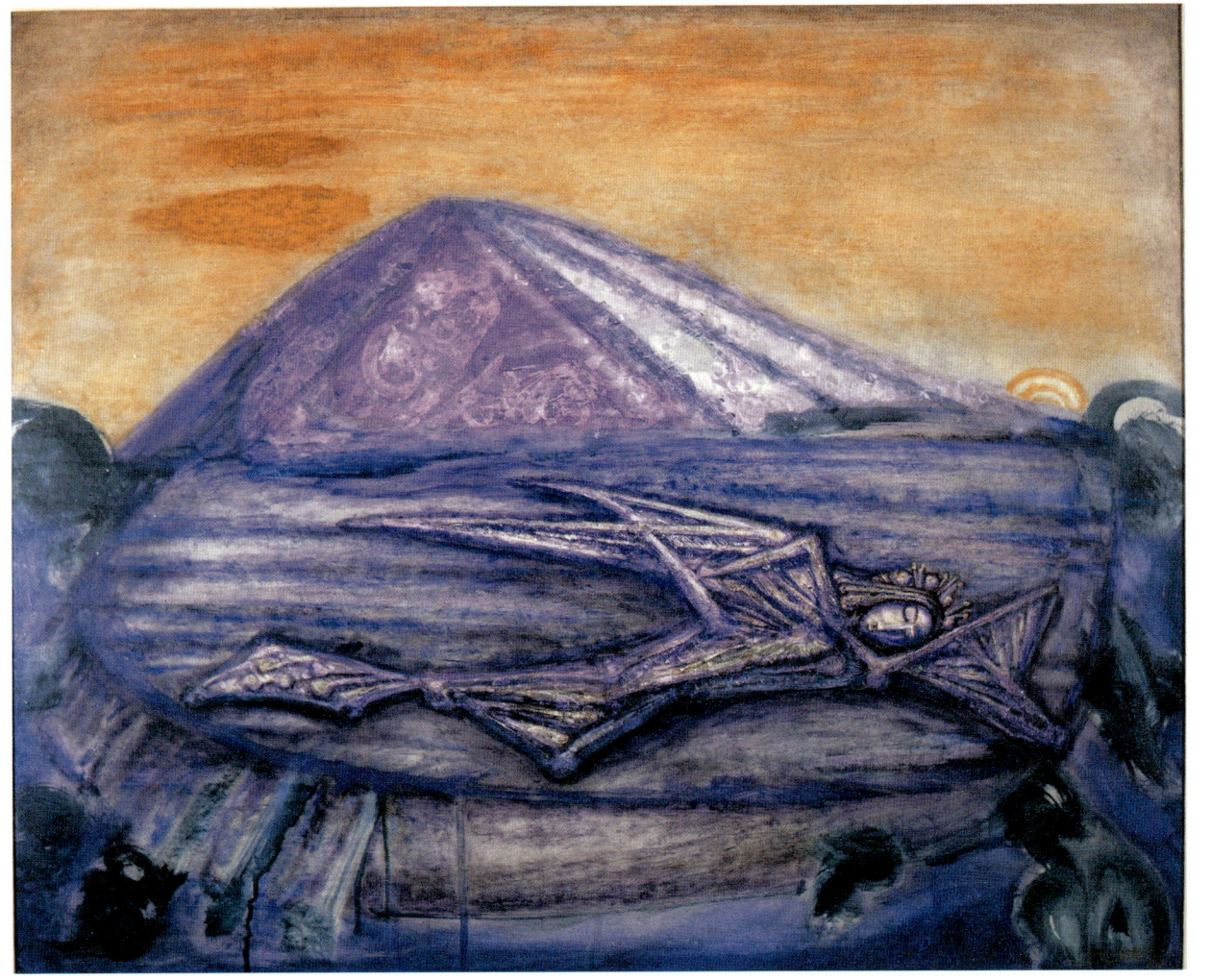

Cecil Collins
Wounded Angel
1967
mixed media on board
75 x 90cm

Because of Cecil and a couple of his pictures that I grew up with, my instinct as regards my own art has always been to work from within. Cecil's classes made me much more aware of how my inner world affected the way I saw the outer world. He broadened my vocabulary with regards to mark-making. How you don't only draw with a 2B pencil; you should use the appropriate medium for whatever it is that you need to express. You shouldn't force a medium to perform against its own nature for your own ends. You should work with it. Cecil was trying to get us to open up to all our potential: to draw, to be creative, to use everything within us. He wanted us to absorb the spirit of his teaching and then to go off and do it in our own way. I haven't taught the Cecil technique for many years, but it affected me all my life in the sense that I've always been trying to find a way to live that enables me to see the world in a deep, open way.

MERIDA DRYSDALE

Educated in Washington DC, then at the Byam Shaw in 1951, Merida Drysdale spent three years at the Central School of Arts and Crafts before training as a calligrapher. For thirty-five years she has been involved with Heritage and Conservation, serving for twenty years as Councillor Emeritus on the Council of the National Trust for Scotland and ten years on the Council of the National Trust.

I was a student of Cecil's at the Central in about 1952. At that time, he shared a life drawing class with Mervyn Peake. Cecil's teaching was an absolute revelation. I was just deciding that I really wasn't good enough and that everybody else was much better and more talented than I was and that I shouldn't be doing it at all. Then I was quite revived by Cecil because I found with him I could draw. It was most extraordinary but, unfortunately, it didn't really last once I was no longer in Cecil's class. I never did painting with him, though I wish I had.

I don't remember anything about Mervyn Peake's teaching, but I can see him and Cecil locked up in the little tutor's room which was walled off with glass from the students' area and they sat in there while we were doing our life drawings. Mervyn and Cecil were a rather droopy, terribly thin, melancholy looking pair. Mervyn tended to sit in a corner drawing and Cecil would emerge to do this brilliant teaching.

I remember lying on the ground, listening to music, then it stopping suddenly, then ten lines of the pencil and that was it. Cecil was already doing a lot of the things which he developed later. It was thrilling to be in his class, though I dare say that other teachers thought it was very peculiar. I don't think I had any contact with Mervyn. He occasionally came round and drew on other people's drawings, but that was as much as I remember. If I'd had any sense, I would have kept them. I don't think Cecil ever did that.

I believe I was responsible for getting Robin Baring into the Central. He's a distant kin by marriage and a social friend and he was learning to draw in a conventional way. I can't remember whether he was actually at an art school. Anyway, he'd decided he wanted to be a painter and, at that time, he wanted to draw like Rex Whistler. Since I was at the Central, I told him about Cecil and he joined Cecil's class and that revolutionised Robin's life. Another person who was in the class at that time was Gwynneth Johnstone, one of Augustus John's daughters. Gwynneth was delightful, rather bohemian in that old-fashioned sense, and she did very fascinating, rather primitive drawings. She had a great cloud of frizzy hair which stood out from her face and she wore flat shoes and great big, full, long skirts. I remember one fascinating painting she did of a huge cat sitting on top of a great green apple tree.

The Principal was William Johnston who was a very good artist when he had the time, a terrific snob and a tremendous character. At that time, my father was commanding the troops in London District so William Johnston got in touch with him and said, 'Merida's drawing needs tightening up,' and suggested that I did calligraphy. I pretty well gave up everything else and went and did calligraphy with Mervyn Oliver and Irene Wellington. I was never brilliant, but I was adequate and did it freelance for many years. It was the time of the Coronation which meant that there was plenty of work for calligraphers, which was wonderful.

Another person who knows a lot about Cecil and his contemporaries is Lucy Rothenstein. My parents knew her father, John, and I met him with them, but I only knew about Lucy because when I passionately wanted to buy Cecil's painting, *Hymn To Night*, and I hadn't got any money, the competitor for it was, or so I understood, John Rothenstein or his daughter, Lucy. Anyway, Cecil made a great thing about this, saying in effect that either he would let it to go to the Tate or that I would have it. I like to think he wanted me to have it. That was probably in 1957 or 1958. I hadn't got any money of my own at all apart from a small allowance from my father. No other picture ever gave me that feeling and I've got one or two nice things that I must have bought when I was pretty young, but I never had anything that I absolutely had to have like Cecil's. I was so determined to have it I trotted off to the National Provincial Bank, as it was then, because it had been used by my mother's family for generations and got a loan. They would only give me £300 and the picture cost £350. I paid Cecil the £300 and gave him an IOU for £50. Ever after when I saw Cecil, although we didn't keep very closely in touch so there were long periods when I didn't see him, we'd always have this great joke. 'I've got your IOU,' he'd say, 'Where's that £50?' He didn't mind really; it was a joke and he never had his £50.

I've got two other Cecils. One was a wedding present from him. It's an enchanting small gouache. It should be called *The Lovers*. I don't think it is, but that's how I've always thought of it. It's of two funny little figures in a landscape. I've also got a fascinating Byzantine head which I bought from him when I was still at art school. I was already involved with Andrew, my husband, who was at Cambridge and I took him to meet Cecil and bought my first Collins. The head is a little painting, beautifully framed by him.

Andrew and I visited Cecil quite often in his top floor living room

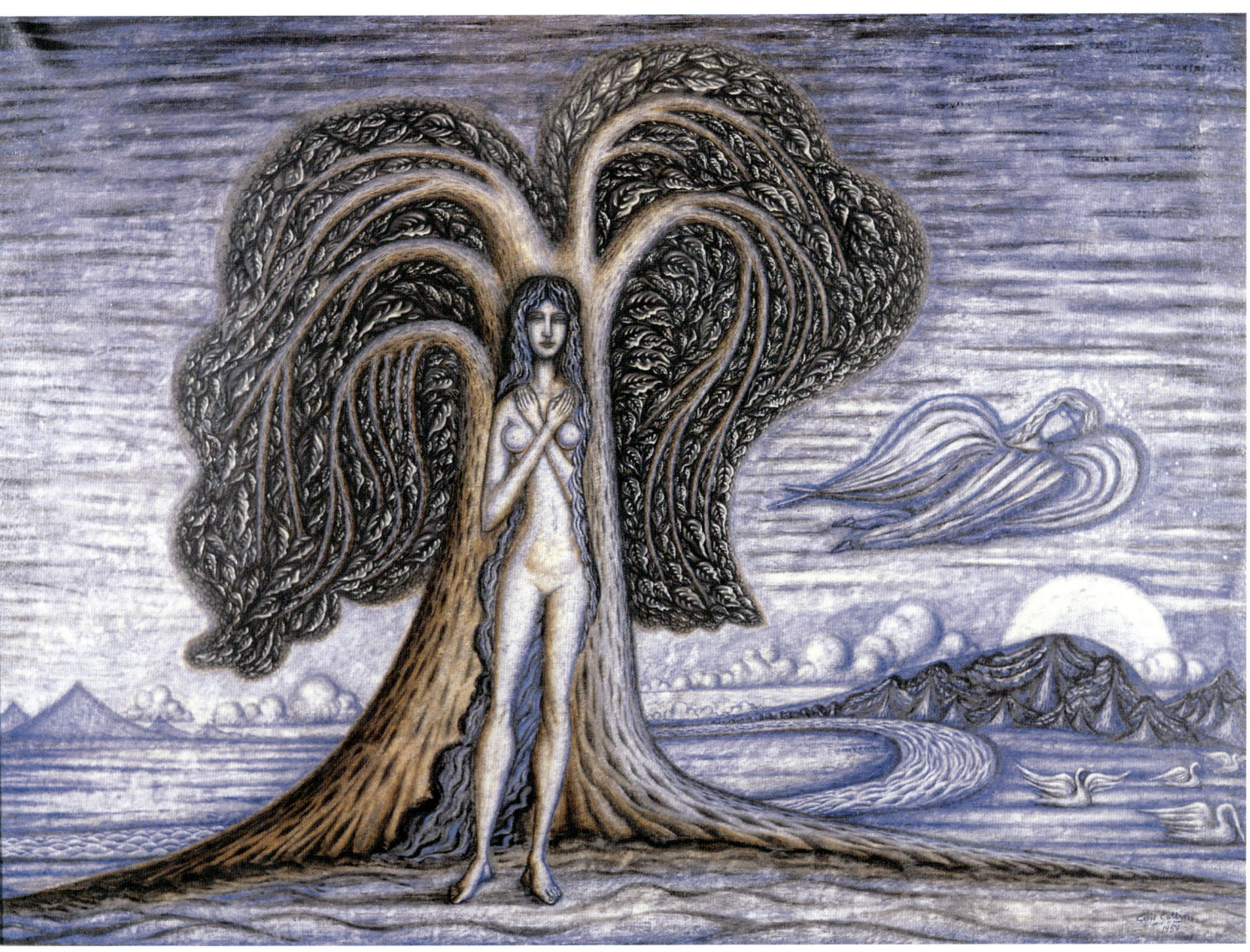

Cecil Collins
Hymn to Night
1951
Oil on canvas
90 x 120cm

in Paultons Square in London. I used to go to a drawing class there too with a few rather socially eminent people. He would squeeze in about six people. I have visions of us sitting in front of a fire and drawing on boards. We didn't have a model; there wouldn't have been room. I can't have done it very often. It was when I was married and probably inundated with babies and all that sort of thing. I remember taking Andrew once and I think he did a bit of drawing. It was completely informal. Probably Cecil just said to a few people he'd met socially, 'Come along and draw.' It was more a sort of social gathering than a class, with lots of Cecil's stories and jokes.

Cecil and Elisabeth came two or three times to our house in Surrey when the children were young. I also remember going to see Elisabeth when she was recovering from a broken hip or something. She was staying at a convalescent place in Kent which was quite near where we lived and I went to see her there. I've got a little painting of hers which I bought at that exhibition in the Jane England Gallery. I met Robin there and we both arrived late and we'd missed all the best ones. My one is a funny little head and I'm not particularly enamoured of it.

I remember going with my daughter, Alexandra, to that big exhibition of Cecil's in Plymouth. She was so moved by one of his pictures that she stood in front of it weeping. I had the same sort of emotional reaction when I stood in front of my Collins, *Hymn to Night* at Cecil's great Retrospective at the Tate.

I continued to go one day a week to the Central for a long time after I was married. I can't remember now how one did it, but it was all very informal. You couldn't do that now, pop in one day a week when it suited you. The only decent drawings I ever did were all, I'm sure, produced under Cecil's tuition. I've got three of them framed, but they are very much student art. I absolutely adored Cecil's class. I thought it was a bit odd at first, but I very quickly realised that it was magical. The extraordinary thing for me was, with him, I could draw.

RUTH EISENHART

Born in South Africa, Ruth Eisenhart lives in London and has practised as a professional artist/sculptor since graduating from the Central School of Art in 1984. She is a part-time tutor at the London University of the Arts and also conducts workshops internationally. She has work in private collections world-wide.

I met Cecil Collins in 1979 in my first year at the Central School of Art and Design where I was studying sculpture. One of the life models told me about an interesting teacher she'd been modelling for and that I should try his class. I was reluctant at first because I'd done so much drawing on the Foundation course and found it rather boring. I guess my curiosity is probably what made me go in the end. I ran into the class as I was late and after I'd skidded to a halt, I saw everybody was already settled and busy drawing. The impression I'd got from the model was that the tutor was dynamic so I was expecting to find a trendy young man. Instead, what I saw was an old man, bent over due to curvature of the spine, sitting very quietly in a corner by himself. I wondered if I was in the wrong class and whether I should retreat slowly and leave. Fortunately, I heard him speak and in that moment knew I'd come home!

When *Fools and Angels* was being filmed in Cecil's life class and it came to doing the movement to music, I never dreamt Cecil would ask me, although he often did at other times. I was sure he was going to ask Shelley Latham as she was very attractive, moved beautifully and would look good on television. I was dressed in my usual T-shirt and dirty jeans so when he asked me and I went to stand out in front of the class and camera, I was so nervous I thought I was going to faint. My legs were trembling in sheer terror as I thought about what all the people I knew would think when they saw the film and what a fool I looked doing strange movements to music. Then suddenly it flashed through my mind that this film was about Cecil and not about me, and from that moment on I lost all self-consciousness and became very calm and at one with the music. It was an extraordinary experience about 'letting go'. Afterwards, I collapsed beside him and said, 'How could you?' He simply smiled his mischievous, knowing smile and put a reassuring arm around me. The irony was that the camera had run out of film so none of that sequence appeared. I had no shattering experiences like that again in his class. When Cecil would ask at the beginning of a lesson, 'Any discoveries?' other students shared their insights, but I never seemed to remember or was too nervous to say anything in case I said the wrong thing. The most important message I got from his teaching was what it meant to be an artist and that it was more about working on myself and the way I related to life as a human being, rather than becoming skilled or clever at what I did.

I was one of the main organisers of the college petition in 1986 to protest on his behalf when he was asked to retire because of his age so I got to know Cecil much better as we had many meetings and discussions. He advised and led from behind and I dealt with the authorities, although I knew I couldn't confront them head on. I felt that they wouldn't understand Cecil's importance as a teacher and that he should only retire when he was ready to do so. After a great deal of letter writing and getting a large number of signatures for the petition, I felt a real sense of achievement when the Central decided to change their minds and, from then on, Cecil was left to teach unhindered until his death in 1989.

Cecil's teaching was very much about the relationship between masculine and feminine energies and how one of these should always be in service to the other. On one occasion when I'd seen a film in which Rodin was seen to treat his models/mistresses rather badly, I was shocked to find that Cecil was inclined to Rodin's point of view that the female should make sacrifices for the male. Perhaps he was a product of his time and was rather more conservative in that respect?

I was hungry for Cecil's teaching and I always tried to sit near him to listen and absorb as much as I could. I often used to walk round the class with him during the break to learn from what he said to each student when looking at their work and the way he encouraged and guided each one. He really cared about his students. His insights into my own work were sometimes unexpected. When he looked at a painting on the theme of *Temenos* that I had done, he said that it was trying to tell me something. I had no idea what he meant and in the end he had to tell me. It was that I should be a painter. I was studying sculpture and, as I'd always had problems working with colour, I decided to follow my heart and continue making sculpture, although I enjoy using colour when I do mono-printing.

When I show my students films on Cecil, someone always comments on how serious and solemn he looks. I tell them that he could be very light-hearted and had a child-like sense of humour, delighting in telling silly jokes like the one about the woman who goes to the psychiatrist. While she lies on the couch, he seduces her, makes passionate love to her, then says, 'That's my problem. Now what's yours?' My favourite joke of his is about a coach load of pilgrims returning to England from a trip to Lourdes. When they go through customs, one man is asked if he has anything to declare, he says 'No.' The officer then asks him, 'What's in all these bottles?' 'Only holy water from Lourdes.' The officer opens one and finds it contains wine. 'What is this then?' The surprised man throws up his hands and exclaims, *'Un miracle!'* Try to imagine Cecil throwing up his hands and looking heavenwards as he exclaims, *'Un miracle!'* in his bad French accent.

Cecil used to tell us, 'Face the sun, with the shadows behind you.' He brought out the idealistic side in us. This was unlike Francis Bacon who was his bête-noire. I understood what Cecil meant about the decadence, despair and lack of hope in Bacon's work, but I still couldn`t help admiring the very seductive way he handled paint.

Cecil had a very clear vision which he was able to convey through his work and teaching. In his last year of teaching, his lessons seemed to be pared down to the bare essentials; it seemed more like a meditation than a drawing lesson. We drew only one or two figurations throughout the whole day. Everything seemed to slow down and become very still. Although at that time he was quite weak physically, his perceptions were sharper than ever.

As I lived near the Central, I was always the first one to arrive and set up the tables and get everything ready for the class to begin on time. Cecil needed this help and relied on my assistance. The time came when I made a conscious decision not to return to his class the next term. I knew I had to break the umbilical cord if I was to find my own voice. It was very difficult to do after studying with him for eight years. I felt I was letting him down. The day when I told him of my decision to leave is forever etched on my mind. I was in the Anthony d'Offay Gallery, walking round with Cecil, looking at his paintings and he gave me a very interesting commentary about them. Afterwards he sat down on a chair and that's when I plucked up my courage and told him. Although I can't remember what his reply was, I could tell that he was surprised and somewhat disappointed. I needn't have worried because another student, David Cranswick, was very capable and happy to carry on where I'd left off. To make sure I wasn't tempted to return, I joined a ceramic class at another college. Cecil would telephone sometimes and ask me to take his class when he wasn't well or had to keep medical appointments. After he died, the Central School asked me to continue his classes. This was difficult at first because I was very conscious of his presence and felt he was looking over my shoulder. I didn't think I could live up to his high standards. There were also problems with some students who thought of me as his successor. I had to make it very clear that Cecil was unique and could never be replaced. In retrospect, I see that I was a very devoted and keen student of his for many years. He said to me that every student gets what they need from his teaching. I will never be able to measure how much I received from Cecil's teaching, but I know that I am eternally grateful for what he gave me as it made a huge difference to the development of my work and the enrichment of my life.

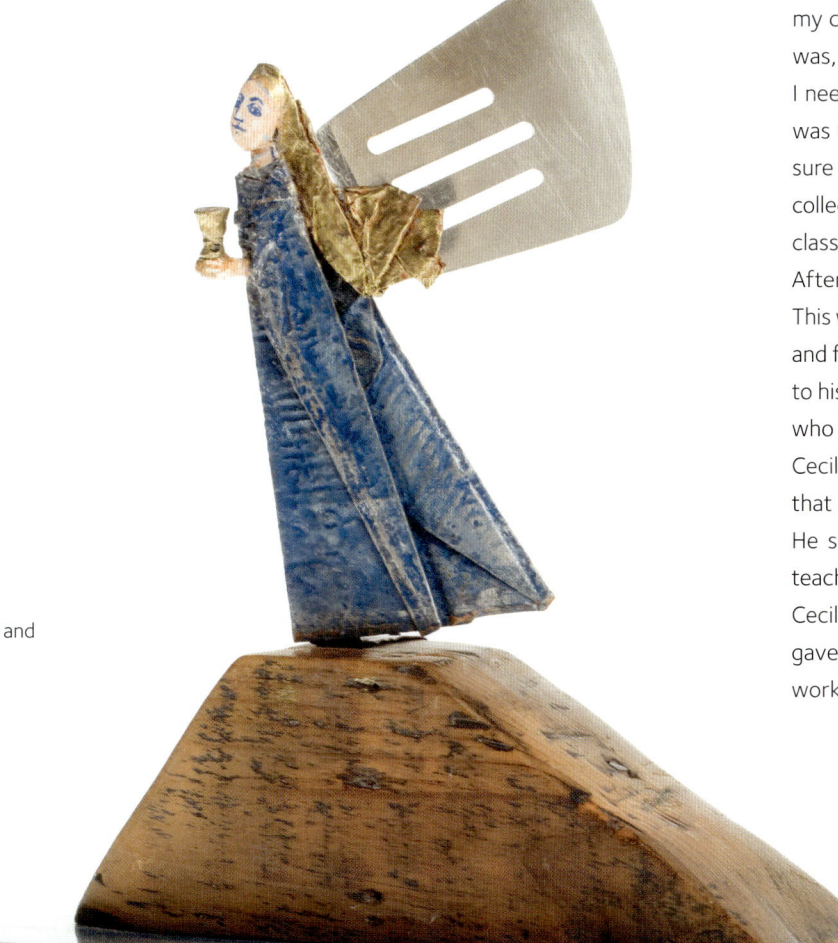

Ruth Eisenhart
Angel with Chalice
(dedicated to Cecil Collins)
2008
Mixed media: found objects, paint, wood and marble
26 x 24 x 10cm

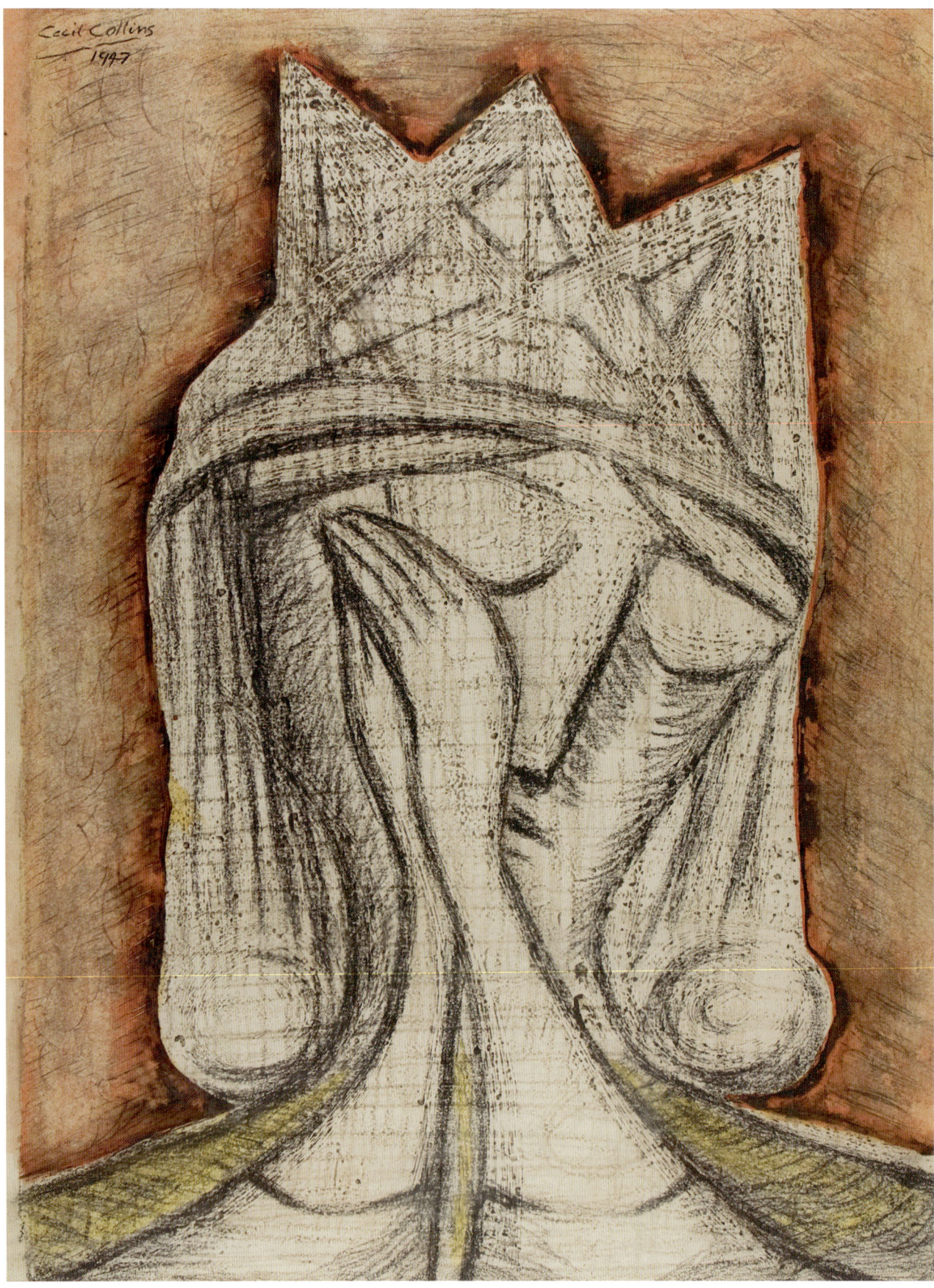

Cecil Collins
A Fool Praying
1947
Chalk and watercolour
26 x 37cm

MIRIAM FREEDMAN

Born in Slovakia, Miriam Freedman emigrated to Israel as a child and then trained as a teacher. In 1958 she came to Britain. She has studied autogenic training, yoga and Tai Chi. She met Mrs Tweedie in 1978 and studied with Cecil from 1982 to 1985. She is married with two children and a grandchild and lives in London.

I came to Israel in 1946 as a child after the war so I was educated there. I was trained as a kindergarten teacher, but I always loved art and I had a wonderful art teacher who used to take us every Saturday to museums. I always got ten out of ten for painting.

I started going to Mrs Tweedie in 1978. Mrs Tweedie and Cecil didn't meet very often, but she used to go to exhibitions of his and people who came to Mrs Tweedie would talk about how Cecil had said this or Cecil had said that. I wanted to have that experience because I thought it was connected to Mrs Tweedie and her group.

One day in 1982, David Cranswick and Sheila Griffin and a few other people said that there was an opportunity to go to the City Lit. We queued all night in our sleeping bags. There were about twenty or thirty people, but that's quite a lot for an art class and I was fortunate that we got there early because I was in the first ten. It was a terrible night. We were freezing and the police came by to ask what was going on and I was wondering myself why I was there. At nine they opened the doors and I walked in. Cecil was interviewing people and they were showing him their work, but I didn't have a portfolio with me. When my turn came I said, 'I misunderstood. I've got some work at home, but I didn't bring it.' He said, 'Everybody has to show me their work. What is your background? Did you study art?' I said, 'Only in school.' He looked at me. I'll never forget his blue, penetrating eyes, and I said, 'I waited all night and I'd be very disappointed not to be able to come to your class for at least a term or two.' He said, 'I'll give you a chance.'

Cecil liked people who didn't have proper academic training. When I joined his class, I noticed there were some people who painted beautifully, but he used to ignore them. He would go around the tables looking at the work and at one point he said, 'I prefer a person who does not know how to paint and who works from intuition and who will actually be inspired by music.'

The classes were for the whole day over two sessions. The first session was from ten until one o'clock. I was quite taken by Cecil's whole system, which was completely alien to me, although I was used to lying on the floor because I had been giving yoga classes since 1966. He talked about the tones and how we were going to make our own ink. He told us to bring a natural piece of chalk, charcoal, Conté crayon, pencils, quill, brushes and so on. It was fascinating not knowing what was going to happen. It was an adventure.

I showed Mrs Tweedie my work, but she was not pleased that I'd gone. She didn't want me to do counselling either, but I did it anyway. I took a three year course in counselling which overlapped my three years with Cecil.

I signed up for a six week class with Cecil in the summer term when he was teaching colours. It was amazing. We covered the spectrum: different shades of green, different shapes, things like that. After spending the summer with colour, I saw Cecil as much more vibrant, more lively. I think it was probably to do with it being the summer season because he was a summer person. The painting class was more structured than the drawing class and very disciplined. I didn't think that part of it was natural to Cecil as he was a visionary or intuitive artist, but I understood why he was doing it. I think he was showing us that we had to develop and find colours that were right for us. He'd start with music, meditation and movement, then he would stop and wander round and then he would do it again. It was both structured and unstructured.

When I first came into the class, he did something terrible to me. It was like Tweedie in a way: shock treatment. He was sitting in a corner of the U-shaped tables. He spoke very quietly, 'Would you like to demonstrate some movements?' He said it two or three times. I thought I heard my name. He said it three times to a woman who did not move. I couldn't get through the closely packed tables and crawled under the table and went and stood in front of everybody. I said, 'What shall I do?' Cecil said, 'I didn't call you, and I can't tell you.' I felt humiliated and embarrassed. My heart was pumping. I wanted to burst out crying, but I didn't walk out. Maybe he wanted me to walk out; I don't know. But I was absolutely devastated and it took me a very long time to get over that.

Cecil made some comments about my work. He kept asking me where did the painting or drawing come from and I said to him, 'I think it came from the model.' He said, 'Are you sure it came from the model?' Then I said, 'It was inspired by the music,' and he said, 'Come on.' I knew that what he wanted me to say was that it came from inside, but I resisted saying that. So he said again, 'Are you sure?' He used to tease me. He would go to this person or that person, leaving me out. Tweedie used to do the same thing. Once she had this big cake and she cut a jolly big piece and gave one piece to Sheila and a piece to herself, but she left me out. I couldn't say anything; Sheila couldn't say anything. I was sitting there and I burst out crying. 'Why are you crying, darling?' she asked. 'Is there anything you want? Is anything wrong?' I said, 'No.' She used to do things like that.

Cecil used to get terrible depressions, usually in winter, especially in February. When he was very low, something inside must have stayed open to creativity because he said, 'That's when I created my best work.' I was studying a lot of alternative therapies at that time to rehabilitate myself. I was studying under someone who usually only accepted medical people for the course, but an exception was made in my case. Cecil said, 'I hear that you're teaching autogenic training.' He wanted to know what it was. I said, 'It's like saying a mantra. It's just a word, but if you don't have the right setting and the right timing, then it doesn't have much power.' I explained to him that it was a form of deep relaxation. You penetrate the unconscious and find out why you've got a migraine or why you've had a sleepless night or why you're depressed. This technique helps you to find the cause of your symptoms. Autogenic technique is a form of auto-suggestion; you suggest something to yourself to work on the consciousness. He asked me to give him a session so I said, 'You'll have to come to me.' The healer should never offer him or herself, you have to seek the healer. He didn't come; he just said, 'Could we not do it here during break time?' I said, 'I've never done it that way,' but I gave Cecil three sessions over the following three weeks. After that, he treated me differently, perhaps because in his eyes I had gained some confidence or because I seemed more important to him.

I met Elisabeth at Ginger Gilmour's fiftieth birthday party which was a fantastic affair and there were a lot of people there. Elisabeth said, 'Let's have a bit of a chat,' so we went to one of the rooms and she kept me there for a few hours. I was very interested in her so she told me how she met Cecil and a bit about her life. We got on very well. Elisabeth said, 'We must meet again,' and I said, 'I would love that.' Very soon afterwards I got a phone call from Lily to say, 'Elisabeth would like to see you'. She was very frail already. She invited me on a particular day to go for tea. We had a lovely tea together and she gave me a book, one of Cecil's, *The Vision of the Fool*. She also gave me a book of poetry. She signed it and her hand was very shaky.

Very late in her life Lily and Jeremy took her to an osteopath in Golders Green. I lived a few minutes away so Elisabeth said, 'I'm coming to see you, but don't prepare anything,' I said I'd make a light lunch. It was just smoked salmon sandwiches and a big bowl of salad because that's what she wanted. My God, was she hungry. She sat in my home and I said, 'I loved Cecil's book, Elisabeth.' She said, 'So many people do and they also loved Cecil.' I said, 'You had your work to do and Cecil had his work and that's the way it is.' Before we could meet again, she died.

I've got two pictures of Cecil's. One is a print and the other one is gouache. He selected the gouache for me specifically; it's called *The Philosopher's Stone*. The print is *The Fool*. I had asked Cecil in a class, 'I would like to have one of my teacher's pictures. Could I buy one?' and he joked, 'I'm very expensive.' Then he said, 'I'll think about it,' but nothing happened. David Cranswick was very friendly with him and I said, 'When you next see him, could you remind him?' Cecil agreed to sell a painting to me. I gave the money to David and Cecil sent me *The Philosopher's Stone* and the clown. He probably realised I wouldn't spend thousands. He sold *The Philosopher's Stone* to me for a reasonable price. Once I asked him to write something down, but he wouldn't sign it. He said, 'No.' He didn't want to do that in case I sold it. That's why artists don't want to sign anything.

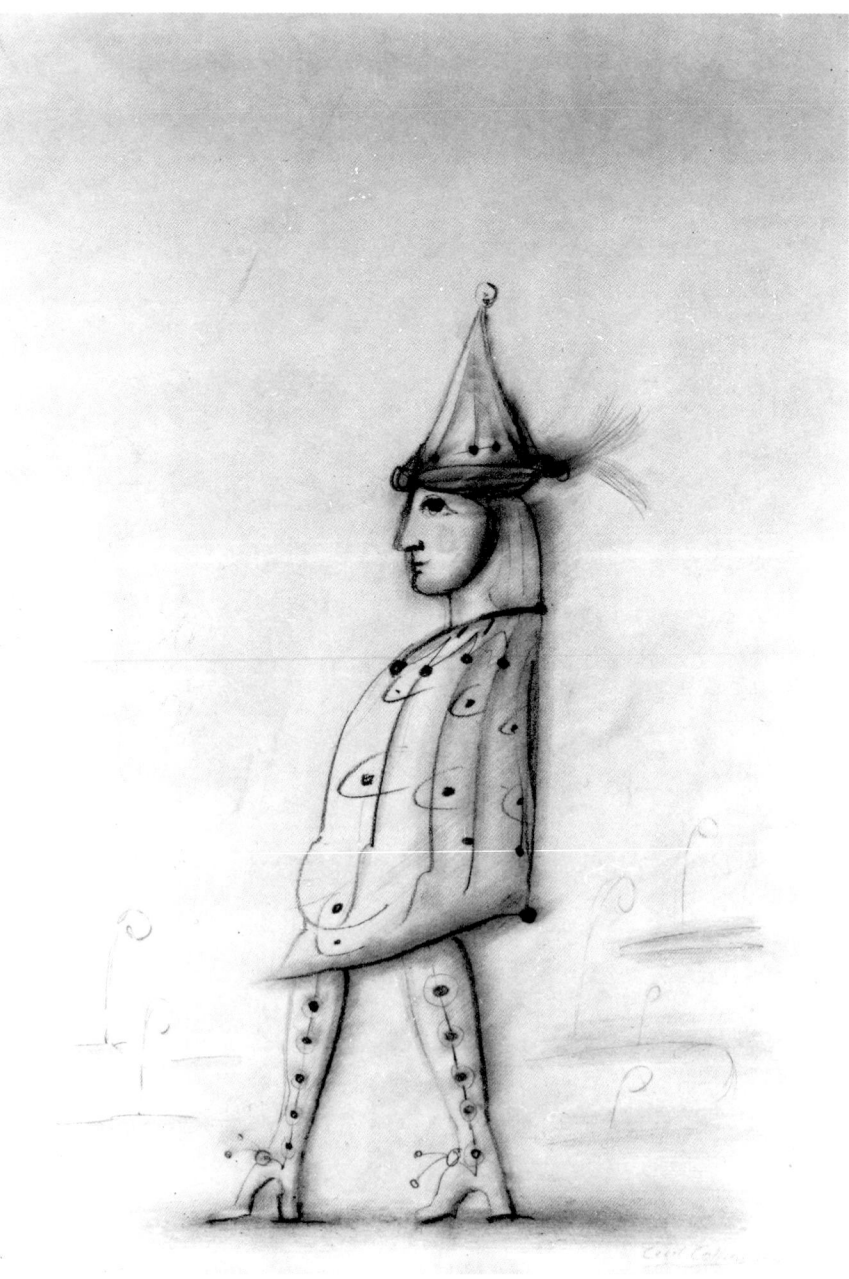

Cecil Collins
A Fool Walking
1976
Pencil on paper

JEREMY GALE

Jeremy Gale was born in Africa in 1961. He graduated from the Central School of Art, London, before studying in Florence on an Italian Government Scholarship. He lives in London and paints in Sussex where he has a studio.

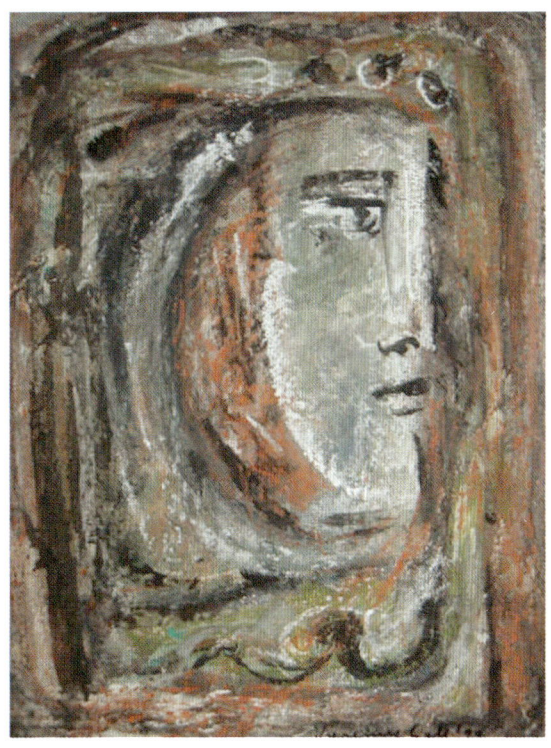

Jeremy Gale
Vision Head
1999
Mixed media on gesso board
14.5 x 19.5cm

During one of John Allitt's history of art lectures at the Central School of Art, he showed slides of various artists and I remember being drawn to several which had a very different quality. I was looking at them, still trying to listen to the lecture, when I found myself absorbed in one particular painting. This was by Cecil Collins. There was something quite mysterious in his work, which was beyond analysis.

Then, in my final year, I remember seeing a sign on the Central's stairway saying, CECIL COLLINS LIFE DRAWING, ALL WELCOME. It was an all-day class and I thought, I'm going to that. I had been to various life drawing classes at the college and in most of them the students were very much left to themselves. On seeing the notice and recalling Cecil's picture I decided to go along, feeling he might have a different approach.

The life drawing room was on the fifth floor and I found my way up, walked in and was immediately struck by a person slumped in a battered old chair in the corner and realised this must be Cecil Collins. He had this incredibly potent presence and I had the strange experience of an inner voice saying, 'This man has something to teach.'

The first class was a revelation. I loved the use of the different instruments: Chinese brushes with bamboo handles, stick ink, reed pens, Conté crayon, charcoal, pencils and quills. We listened to music and moved to it, as well as being silent before drawing the model. Cecil's instructions to kneel or lie on the floor, to use the left hand or both hands together seemed most strange to me and often felt very awkward. The initial term, I was struggling with the classes although I was enjoying them because they were such fun and so different. I hadn't really got the hang or it, but the overriding feeling was longing for the next week's class. With hindsight, I can understand how affected I was; it was as if Cecil was speaking directly to my soul. It was like water to a dried-up river bed.

He often made us go through the experience of centering at the beginning of the class. He talked about silence being our natural state, about getting underneath the surface into this deeper part of our mind where there's stillness and silence and who we really are.

Even though it was a class of about twenty, he could pick up what was happening in each of us. He could tune into the students, into another person, in a very extraordinary way. I've since discovered from my own teaching, that this ability comes from an intuitive sense about people which I've learnt to trust. I can appreciate Cecil's accuracy even more now.

It was so rare for him to look at the students' work, so when the first time he came round remains in my memory. Once, at the end of the class, I was looking at the drawing I'd done. Suddenly, I could feel him behind me. I don't know how he got there so quickly. He seemed to have flown. He pointed to my drawing and said, 'Shakers and Quakers.'

In surprise I said, 'Yes, I went to a Quaker school.' 'Ha!' said Cecil. Now, when I look at that drawing of a figure with arms raised, outstretched like branches waving and shaking in the wind, I understand what he saw when he tuned into me. I hadn't realised that this side of me was coming into the drawing class. I had been at a Quaker boarding school for seven years and their form of worship is silence and in Cecil's classes we orientated in silence before drawing. The tradition of Quakerism I'd been brought up in at school had started to come through and continued to influence and support me in my drawing.

The first term contained the seed experiences of my relationship with Cecil; everything else followed on from that. There was an acknowledgement of the contemplative tradition which was the root of Cecil's own vision, and also of the Quakers, and of the importance silent reflection was to become in my life. Cecil thought the imaginary world, especially in early childhood, was being eroded as a result of formal education starting too young. For me, his teaching was an affirmation of what is real, and indicated, 'This is the direction to go in and if you shake a bit, that's great.' You're in touch with something which happens through that silence.

When Cecil was teaching, he would be aligning the group mind of the class so the stillness and centredness was the place from where you related to everything: the instruments, the paper, each other and to him. In this place of oneness there was a feeling of love towards everything. It allowed you to let go of so much unnecessary mind chatter and conceptualised ideas and gave you the connection with your inner guidance and that was freeing. You had the sensational experience of the flow coming through you and the brush, or whatever you were using, doing what it wanted. You were the instrument for the instrument. That freedom is also a sense of love.

Once, I remember registering at the beginning of the class that Cecil hadn't said anything and at the point when we'd stopped talking, he'd started the lesson. I think his presence had an effect energetically on the group mind. It was both an energetic field and also a conscious awareness of the effect of this energy. Through his attitude and his experience, he was like a tuning fork. We were being pitched up, then suddenly there was a moment where he had a connection with the class and he would begin as soon as we were silent.

I had that experience myself when I began to teach. I walked into a particularly lively group happily chatting away. I didn't want to disrupt their enjoyment of each other. I noticed that as I tuned in and centred myself, they slowly quietened down. It's like the Hawaiian Islands. They're all different islands, but when you drop below the surface of the sea, it's all one land mass. It's rather like that when you teach. You make the choice to go under the surface to where we're all one. At the moment when the students have quietened down and you're centred, there is a moment of intimacy with the group as a whole that is both terrifying and astounding in its possibilities. When you have this contact, teaching can begin.

I wanted to share what I was experiencing with my art-student friends who were not attending his classes, but their reaction was, 'You're kneeling and you're doing what on the floor?' They were a bit challenged by it. Entering Cecil's classroom was like walking through a psychic doorway, opening the student into a whole other world and that can seem daunting. They asked me, 'Is he religious? Is he a religious man?' I hadn't made the connection between what he was doing with us, having us kneel, as being something religious, so I was taken aback by the question. In the next class I asked him point blank, 'Cecil are you religious?' Total silence. No answer whatsoever. I didn't know if I shouldn't have asked or whether I'd asked in the wrong way. Part of me shrivelled up, pretended it hadn't happened so I thought, I'll just get on with my drawing.

He didn't behave according to one's expectations of a teacher. He didn't respond to make you feel comfortable or to fit in socially with you. There was none of that. I was left with this question from my peers which I felt was important. Some months later, he started to talk about what it meant to be religious to the whole class. He made it into a teaching. He'd taken the question in, listened to it, saw where it was coming from and reflected on what was required as an answer. I was so moved by that. No one had considered a question that deeply and with such care and attention before. He would not be pressured into having to give an answer or to play the role of a teacher. Allowing the question to rest, to let it be and to sit with it had a huge effect on me. It was a teaching in itself, not only the answer, but how one can be in relationship to oneself and to each other and have a non-pressured relationship which can be shared. Through this experience with him, I learned that to contemplate something was acceptable and appropriate; a deep question deserves consideration.

All he said was, 'To be religious is to see clearly.' It took me years to begin to understand what he meant by that and I still don't get it completely. Without my being aware of it, clarity was the focus all the time, how to articulate something you often don't see clearly. The ultimate irony is to be a painter of something that's invisible and I believe Cecil and his work create a bridge to that reality.

From my experience with Cecil as a student, I learnt how art can help orientate people to the possibility of change, to open their hearts. The atmosphere created in Cecil's classes helped me become more reflective and contemplative. There was a mixed show at the Tate which included a lightly-drawn painting by Cecil of a golden head. I remember centering myself, then having an experience of going into the painting. It seemed the most natural thing to enter into the world or space he was coming from. His work always invited you to be in that place with him. In front of his painting, contemplating and entering into it, I could feel a shift in my awareness, my consciousness expanding in tune with the image. I discovered that art can actually facilitate such a change.

That shift in consciousness was embodied in the materials of the painting. I felt that the materials held the vibration of his state of consciousness. There is a kind of magic when consciousness and the materials the artist uses become one. Cecil only painted when he felt like it and he would have periods when he didn't, but when he did they were often intense times. His work and his

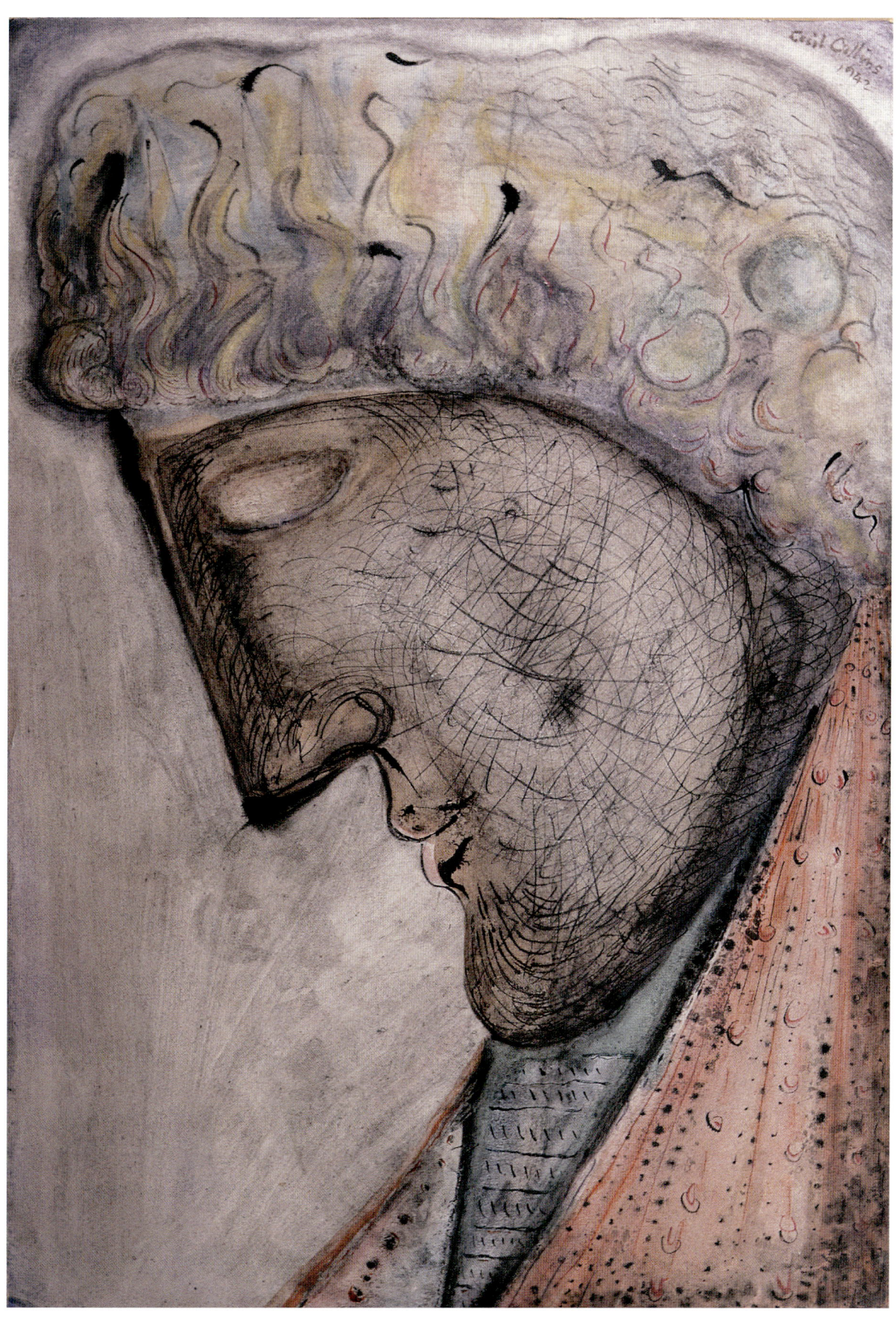

Cecil Collins
Man in Meditation
1942
Ink and watercolour on paper
56 x 39cm

consciousness were one. That's also the magic of icons where the same thing happens: the artists meditate and purify themselves before beginning to paint. Cecil really brought that whole tradition into a more contemporary idiom.

As an artist, he had an absolute inner knowledge of what was required as his special contribution to the world. To paint anything and to bring it to any kind of conclusion, there's an element of organising the line, the colour, the composition and then the framing. I can understand very well how Cecil could apply that to worldly things. He seemed to know exactly what would allow him to operate effectively. Cecil was very discriminating and knew how to interact with people at their own level because he had an inner vision.

I experienced his discrimination when I asked him if I could show him some of my work that I wanted to exhibit in the school where I was teaching. He looked at my series of prints and said, 'What is the level you want to pitch it at?' The prints, which were diffuse and ethereal, wouldn't be understood, he said, 'So probably best not to show those this time.' I learnt it's not about exhibiting just because you want to show your work; it's about understanding your audience and finding the correct level on which to communicate with them.

So many students wanted to be in Cecil's class that he interviewed them personally. At the beginning of the autumn term in 1988, I was the last person to be interviewed and Cecil barely spoke a word; he got up and walked away. I discovered later the reason for this was that Cecil felt the classes were becoming unhelpful for me; I needed grounding. I began to understand the idea was for me to integrate what I'd learnt. This was an important teaching, although very painful at the time.

I remember having tea with Cecil and Elisabeth at Paultons Square and after we'd looked at one of Elisabeth's paintings Cecil took me aside and said, 'You know Elisabeth's the real painter.' I had to digest that idea because for me Cecil was the painter. I certainly understood that she was his muse, but this seemed to go beyond that. She wasn't just his muse; she was like the fountain of life for him. He knew that it's the feminine side that holds the secret. Elisabeth embodied the feminine side of Cecil's vision and he never seemed to lose sight of what we are all here for and what direction we're supposed to be going. He lived through the worst times of the twentieth century and that's an astounding vision to maintain through eighty years.

Elisabeth held the more human level of relationships. It was always so wonderful to meet her. There was this easy and loving relationship that comes from the feminine side. Cecil and Elisabeth had this amazing vision together which was extraordinary.

One time, I collected Elisabeth at Paultons Square. We met downstairs and she stepped into my car as if it were a Rolls Royce. She was so elegant, my driving changed. I felt she was a crystal goblet I could not jar in any way. I didn't want to go round bends too fast because she'd tilt. It was like driving a queen. She lived on the fourth floor and it was as if she was coming down from another level and I felt responsible while driving, not to bring any harm to this exceptional being.

I felt you could talk to Elisabeth about anything. Even when she was ninety-four, there was no age barrier. She was an amazing listener, absolutely open and responsive with an undying curiosity about life. It was very refreshing. At the Jane England Gallery where Elisabeth had an exhibition, I bought one of her gouache paintings called *Greek Woman*, because I was so drawn to it. It's definitely visionary and, for me, this painting has a quality of an archetype, that of a queen. Her sense of colour and her use of brush-mark are quintessentially her own.

When Elisabeth spoke about something significant, it was always in the flow of a conversation so it would be said in passing, but her observations stuck with you. One time when she talked about angels she mentioned, 'They pop in and often at odd times.'

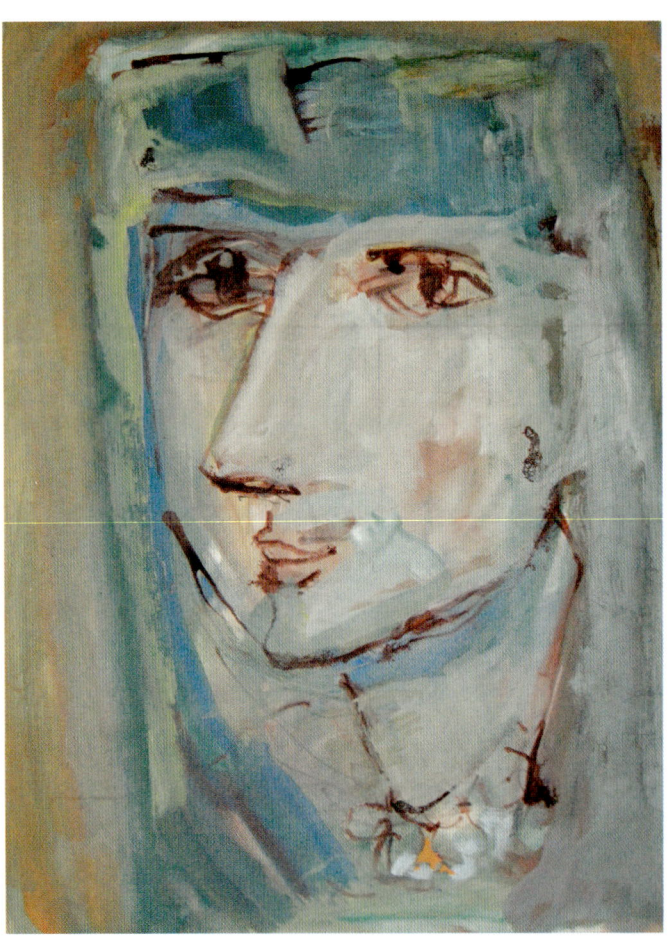

Elisabeth Collins
Greek Woman
1987
Sepia ink and gouache on paper
40.5 x 29cm

I knew Cecil mainly as a student and for a relatively short time, but it felt so intense, as if I knew him through an inner connection. I experienced this symbolically in a dream I had after his last class at the Central School two weeks before he died. In the dream, all his students were gathered round him in the life-room at the Central, but Cecil was there in the middle of the room as a solid shaft of golden light. That's what he was like, a pillar of light. Through his attention on that reality, it became real for him and for everyone in the room. His presence was colossal and so evident during his life and poignantly absent after he died, except for the memories he left with us all and in his paintings such as the large, mainly blue, *Head of an Angel* [1987].

I have a slide of this painting to show my students because, for me, it is the self-portrait of his spiritual being with that total clarity and blue of the eyes. It is the most extraordinary painting. Those late paintings are the fruition of his life's work, everything that he'd learnt, experienced, accomplished and attained. For me, the *Head of an Angel* is the pictorial answer to my question about whether he was a religious man. He described the painting as, 'An icon of a cleansed mirror, which has been wiped free of dust to give a clear image.'

It has been important for me to differentiate between William Blake and Cecil Collins as they are so often considered similar. What they share is that they're both mystics, but certainly their work is utterly different. Blake was rooted in the eighteenth century and the figures were from his imagination, yet they're basically academic forms. Unlike Cecil who always said his work had no object; there's no objective reference point. Cecil's figures grow out of rhythm and energy, nothing to do with the outer form, yet they cascade into a form that looks like a figure.

Where I think people might misunderstand Cecil is that he was unequivocal about what he wanted to paint and what his vision was. His apparent lack of interest in anyone else's vision was because of the need to maintain his own vision. If you ran against the tide as he did, I can see why he had to be totally focused on that. By giving it his whole attention, it exists at a metaphysical level outside the vested interests of the ego. As people began to appreciate what he was doing, then he could relax into that exchange, recognition and influence of like-minded people.

Cecil had two sides. He was as austere as a church father going through the desert of his time and yet he was also incredibly tender. There is a photograph of Cecil with the class and in it his expression, I believe, is that of an enlightened being. Cecil loved those drawing classes; it was his highlight of the week. I know from my own experience that being a painter is very solitary, working alone in a studio, while teaching is an opportunity to serve and connect with people. You teach what you need to know, what you need to learn and it is a way of reinforcing the vision by sharing it, because in sharing it, you open up to it.

I can understand why teaching was so important for Cecil, because it was another way to remember that divine reality he'd experienced from his earliest childhood and a way to share it and awaken other people to it. Lots of people talk about oneness now and I believe that Cecil's vision was of one universality. I can't imagine how hard it must have been for him to go against the stream. For him to paint fools and angels, finding those images to communicate his vision, speaks of his specific task as an artist to bridge the universality of spirit with the symbols which orientate us through a particular dark period in the world. When enormous changes occur in the world, there are usually great teachers around and I think Cecil and Elisabeth were among them. Certainly for me they were and for many other people as well. I'm enormously grateful to them both for shining their light.

Cecil said in one of his essays that Christ was the greatest Fool and I think Cecil was the greatest Fool of the twentieth century. He embodied the Fool: the quick-wittedness, the spontaneity, the playfulness and the wisdom. For me, he was the archetype of the wise old man and you can't be the wise old man without also being the wise child.

I would say that his whole life was focused on the inner life and for him painting was a way of communing with that world. When that other realm is awakened, as it was for me in his classes, it was such a highly-charged experience. All my values were turned upside down and part of my awareness shifted to and remains in that other dimension which is extraordinarily vivid, iridescent and full of magic. This change in my perceptions led to me dressing very colourfully as a student, twenty years ago, and Cecil made a comment to me about dress code, 'Quiet on the outside and colourful on the inside,' he said. I felt this was to help me bring the outer and the inner into balance. I understood that he meant it was important to keep the colour on the inside, that through your attention on the inner life, you give colour to it and keep that alive. It wasn't a big deal, but it expressed his point of view because he did take great care about how he dressed.

His clothes were of a certain quality and tradition and it didn't matter if they were full of holes or patched. Elisabeth gave him the nickname 'Parce,' short for a loosely wrapped up parcel, which was how he appeared sometimes. He really was focused more on the inner world. My most lasting impression of Cecil was his total commitment to and embodiment of the divine reality.

GINGER GILMOUR

Born in the USA, Ginger Gilmour moved to England in the early 1970s. She studied life drawing with Cecil Collins at the City Lit for over ten years, sculpture with Rudolph Steiner Sculpture Studio, West Sussex, and Colour Therapy with Lily Cornford for over fifteen years. She has taught and practised in England, Europe and the USA.

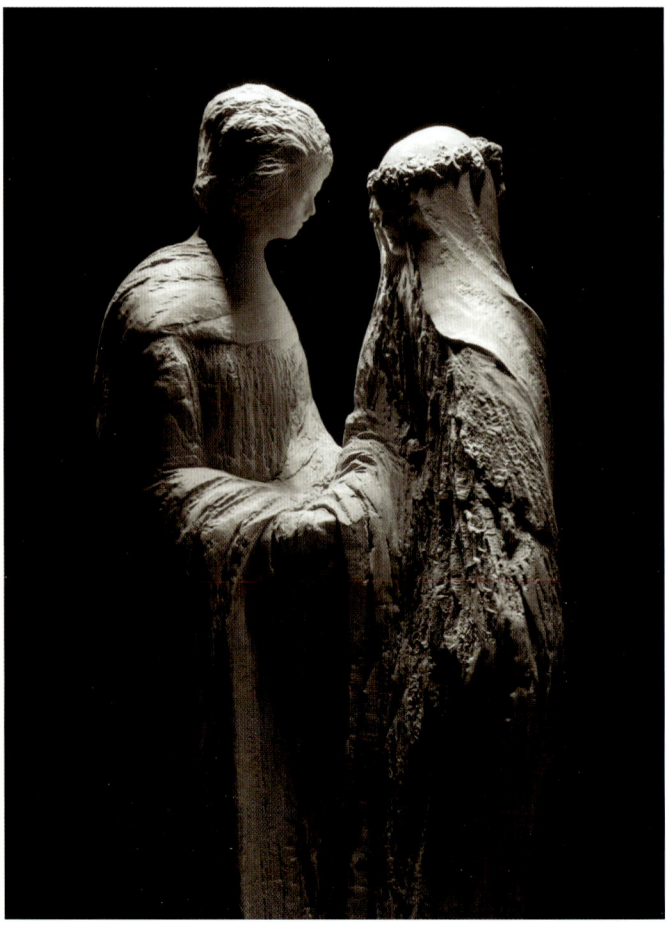

Ginger Gilmour
Sacred Vow: Two hearts merge as One within Sacred Love
2004
Bronze (edition 1:9)
68 x 34 x 23cm

I had been going to Mrs Tweedie and discovered Michael Chaitow's classes and I'd done a few paintings with him. I showed them to Mrs Tweedie and she said, 'You have to go and see the painter and teacher Cecil Collins.' She said that he was a spiritual teacher and that between the two of them, there wouldn't be much left of me but rice paper. 'At least it's edible,' I said and she laughed.

So I went to the City Lit and signed up, but there was no room in Cecil's class so I came back and told Mrs Tweedie. Then I got a card in the post saying that I had a place. Years later, I learnt from Miriam Freedman how it came about that I got in. Miriam had been told by Mrs Tweedie to pass a message to Cecil that she really wanted me in the class.

When I first came to Cecil, I brought him some of my paintings. There was one watercolour in which I painted myself as a figure with wings down on a sandy beach with water, mountains and clouds. It looked like a broken person and he said, 'Next time this person flies, it will not have wings made of wax.' I decided to call that watercolour *My Icarus*. Then he said to me, 'Ginger, if you're going to be in my class, I do not want you to do any of your own work for two years.' So I didn't.

Being an American, you always have a smile on your face and you're very exuberant and I remember one time I came in and Cecil was sitting by the door. He ducked and with his wry smile said, 'Ginger. One day you'll have a real smile on your face.' Boy, did he put me through it that day. Usually, no matter what he did to me I could do the most perfect little drawings, something really cute to look at, but that day he had us working with so many different instruments, with black ink and water-diluted tones, that eventually I had just one big black blob on the paper. You couldn't make anything beautiful out of that at all. Cecil was laughing his head off. I know that he was doing that specifically to throw me. I lost the plot completely.

I feel that, ultimately, he did not want us to be dependent on him. He was showing us the art of being human as spiritual beings. There are inspirational people that you sometimes want to emulate and copy, but I personally do not believe that Tweedie, Cecil or Elisabeth ever wanted us to be carbon copies. They wanted us to be individuals.

After two years' abstinence, I started doing some paintings at home. Cecil gave us a formula for a particular varnish which I still have and he said that the etheric aspect is caught in the glazes. In my paintings I've been playing with transparent and opaque colours with layers of alternating clear glazes. I have found that as the light travels through it creates a doorway between the visible and the invisible. It's as if you're experiencing the colour outside and yet you're being drawn in as well.

My friendship with Cecil and Elisabeth began in this way. Once, when I was going to New York, Mrs Tweedie gave me her book and said, 'Would you please take it to Dr Engel because he's going to do the Foreword.' I hadn't met him, but he was well known in the group. I said, 'I'd be very honoured to do that.' I called him up and he had me come over. He had a very classical New York apartment with a

Victorian feel to it. At first, I was sitting in his long corridor looking at all these books piled everywhere. He said, 'Come in, Ginger,' so I came in and sat down and it was as if time became timeless in that instant. He talked to me about Mrs Tweedie and her book, then he looked at me and asked, 'Do you want to come again tomorrow? I have more things I need to talk to you about.'

On our second meeting Dr Engel said to me, 'Ginger, I'm curious how modern rock-and-roll sounds, what effect it has on the psyche. Do you know anyone who could get me in to hear something like that?' I said, 'I think I might be able to arrange that.' My husband Dave was doing a July the Fourth concert in Madison Square Garden so I got our limousine to pick him up and bring him there. You can take the car straight into the bowels of the arena and that was an experience for him. He came early so I took him around. He was interested in the mixers and all the technical things. He was interested in everything.

Usually I brought stars like Hayley Mills on tours but, on this particular one, the road crew were getting all these spiritual people. In Los Angeles a Lama came who was close to Chogyam Rinpoche and in London Mrs Tweedie came. Now we had Dr Engel coming who was a top Jungian and interested in everything these people were doing in rock-and-roll. At the end of the concert he came up to me and said, 'Ginger, I don't know whether you would agree with me or not, but the place that we seek in meditation, your husband is seeking to give us the same experience of harmony through transforming chaos.' He thanked me and gave me some pamphlets about Madame Blavatsky. I sent those to Elisabeth Collins whom I hadn't yet met, because I knew she was interested. That began the friendship.

I had tea with Elisabeth alone. We talked about the pamphlet, but more about the essence it was concerned with. She was looking deep into my eyes. She had such gentleness, but a direct observational ability. As I was leaving she called, 'Ginger!' I turned around and she said, 'Don't ever forget your angel.' At the time, even the thought that angels really existed was enough for me. Elisabeth had spoken in such an energetic way from a truth I couldn't deny. My personality was questioning what that meant. Over the years, it went very deep inside and eventually what it really meant came to me and I felt very moved. Sometimes the use of a single word can help someone, but it's a great responsibility. I hope I will be able to be as responsible as Elisabeth was when I use that energy that speaks from the truth. If you're pure of heart, it always happens.

When I went to Cecil's exhibition in Aldeburgh, he told me that a man had come to see his work and wanted to tear it all up. Cecil said, 'This happens sometimes.' I was to discover this myself many years later when I was given an exhibition of my own in Westbourne Grove. I came home thrilled and told David, 'This woman said I could have an exhibition!' David was working downstairs with a man called Anthony with whom he wrote lyrics. Anthony said to me, 'I love your Christmas cards. Can I see the work that you're going to exhibit?' I said, 'Sure, come on upstairs.' I had a very small library room, just off our bedroom. In there were six huge canvases with another in the bathroom. Anthony walked in and started spitting and spluttering and swearing at me. I had this one Cecil-type picture of a figure with the hands up, all in ochres, white light coming down, optical colour where the lead white paint had created a bit of violet which is something that happens in your aura when you start getting more in service to the divine. He said, 'That one is like piss.' There was another one of a couple embracing in the water and he said, 'You should slice that one up. It's disgusting.' He sat down on the divan and kept going on and on. I was so surprised. Finally, he said, 'Let me out of here.' I said, 'Anthony, the door's unlocked. You wanted to come. I'm not keeping you here.' He stood up, then sat down again and started telling me about how his wife had left him. My pictures had hit all his buttons and actually it was an exciting compliment, but I didn't know that then because I was still a novice and thrown by his reaction.

When I went to Cecil's class the next day, I was as white as a sheet. Cecil said, 'Ginger, are you all right?' I told him the story of what had happened and he said, 'Give me the date of your exhibition because Elisabeth and I are going to come. If you're getting reactions like that, you're painting the truth.' I had thirty-five paintings in the exhibition, plus drawings from Cecil's classes and they all sold in one day. Everyone from Tweedie and Cecil came. It was an amazing feeling and I felt honoured by the love that everyone came in with because I was really nervous.

Cecil and Elisabeth coming to that exhibition further opened up my relationship with them and I started to be invited to dinners at their house. At one of them Cecil asked me about a particularly difficult time in my life and after I told him the story he said, 'Ginger, you truly must have a lot of angels around you to have got through that one.'

Fifteen years ago, a vision that had come in the night told me, 'You have to do sculptural paintings.' I was a sculptress at the time so I enrolled in some Steiner Anthroposophical painting classes and got completely besotted with that. They emphasised the line and the curve and the space, but they didn't articulate it in the same way that Cecil did. His use of colour, and the way he feels the essence, simply allows the form to come: those moments of allowing it, of waiting, not trying to codify it. So the two trainings are now marrying. I want to inspire people to touch their own creative imagination so the observer becomes aware of how much more we are than mere appearances. I want my work to reflect more than just physical imagery so I play with how things of material substance matter so little. Some faces might be connected to bodies that dissolve into the abstract and in most of my work I play with the line, its relationship to the curve, to an infinite space. We naturally want to finish things, so by having to finish the line, you're relating a straight line which is the masculine, with the curve which is feminine, with the space which is spirit, the triad. You're linking those and in your imagination you're creating harmony and you'll feel harmony, but you might have to pass through some of your 'cat's meat,' as Cecil used to say, in order to reach that harmony.

I have bought several works by Cecil and have sold most of them on so I could finance my own work. I have two drawings of his in the kitchen. Elisabeth said that those two were original ones that he gave to her in testimony of their relationship. One time I was at an exhibition with Elisabeth. We sat down on a window ledge and were talking about relationships. I was having a very difficult time and she said to me, 'I don't know if you agree with me, but this lifetime is very short and looking at my own life and marriage with Cecil, I realised that I had a soul purpose there and it was for humanity. At first it was very difficult, but now it has switched.' She continued, 'I don't know what your destiny is, but this might help you gain a perspective.' Another time Cecil said to me that in his early days he had an analytical sword with which he used to stab his paradisiacal heart until one day his sword became the caretaker and warrior protector of his heart.

I equate the two stories. While Cecil was alive, Elisabeth often talked about how she had less time to do her own work because of the nature of their interrelationship and what she felt her role had to be. They shared a vision and were deeply in love and that's what gets you through. After he died, she was dealing with him not being there by saying, 'Now I have the chance to do my own work.' Theirs was the archetypal man and woman marriage, the woman behind the man. Part of her destiny was not to leave a footprint. Children are a whole other dimension and that wasn't Elisabeth's task so why would she spend energy on it when other people were meant to do that instead? Elisabeth was given a higher bliss. Cecil and Elisabeth never came to a Pink Floyd concert. My fiftieth birthday party was one of Elisabeth's last adventures out. I did a labyrinth fire walk and Elisabeth sat up in my bedroom watching from the window and that was very special.

When Elisabeth passed over, John Tavener organised a funeral in the Greek Orthodox church. I went up to the coffin and looked at her and I remembered how she had said, 'Do not forget your angel.' She and Cecil, Mrs Tweedie, Dr Engel and many more people were my inspiration and my supporters. I began to understand that Mrs Tweedie and Cecil were re-mothering and fathering me on a spiritual level. That was not in my vocabulary at the time but now, looking back, they were the inspirational people who believed in me and touched me deeply which led me to find the being I am. I saw how they all had such courage to live in this physical realm with all its difficulties and kept heaven here. I was so touched by that. They helped me to see it was here and I was so grateful. They showed us that, beyond our limitations, we're profound human beings. Our lives stand for beauty. They brought beauty and harmony out of the chaos. Those moments are so amazing. They showed us that any of us can achieve this. If we remember to look, for instance, at the daffodils and at the rainbow, we don't forget. It's important to remember.

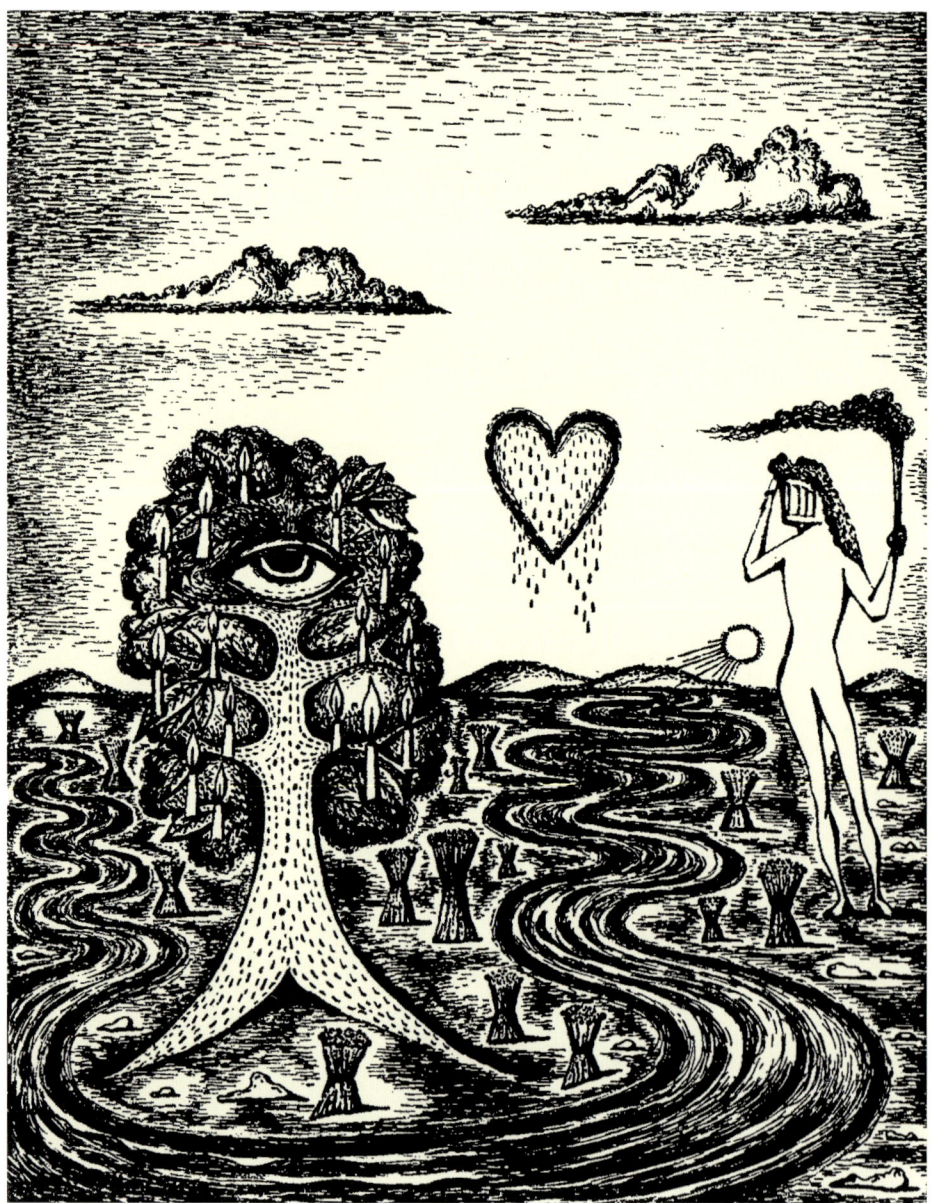

Cecil Collins
The Gates of Silence
1944
Ink on paper
Illustration to a poem by Wrey Gardiner

SHEILA GRIFFIN

Sheila Mary Griffin was born in Yorkshire in 1941 and moved to London in 1966. She studied art with Lynette Howells in 1985, then with Cecil Collins from 1986 until his death in 1989. She has a degree in Fine Arts from Hertfordshire University.

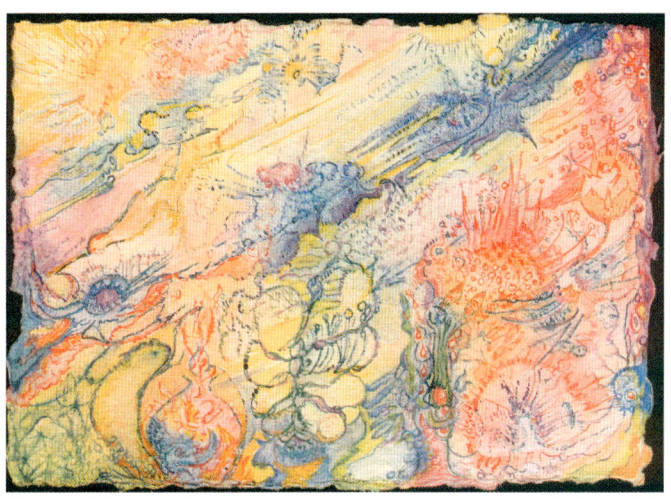

Sheila Griffin
Untitled
2003
Red chalk and Chinese ink

When I started Cecil Collins' drawing classes at the City Lit Institute in September 1986, I was a forty-five year old housewife with four children. I came to Cecil through Miriam Freedman. I hadn't studied art since I was at school. Cecil's classes were so popular we queued overnight to get a place. I felt very privileged to be one of sixteen students in Cecil's morning class. He was a quiet unassuming man in his late seventies. Some students were teachers or artists and had already studied with him. We drew a female nude. We moved with the model to music, held the position of the model and then drew with whichever instruments he told us to. Someone told me that Cecil could tell whether your movements were from the flow of the music or from the mind and I got to the point where I thought I could tell if people were just doing their Tai Chi movements. It's a very interesting experience to be doing these movements and then find that you're not only moved by the music, but also by your own response to the music.

During these lessons, Cecil told us that his teaching was about the study of the real nature of creativity through the use of natural organic instruments. He spoke of making oneself vulnerable as the only way to learn how to be oneself. It's not a surface thing, there's a lot of depth and it has nothing to do with one's needs. In this way, we could enter the creative flow individually or as a group. When this happened, it was an unforgettable experience. The drawing seemed 'to do itself'. Cecil's teaching for me was not just about being creative as an artist, but as a person. It was to do with getting to know oneself, accepting what we are, allowing oneself to be vulnerable. He said, 'Everything creative is to do with relationship.' We had to get rid of the 'success/failure syndrome'. 'It is fear that blocks our contact with the flow.' I found Cecil's teaching an inspiration to live life fully, not to be afraid of making mistakes. An important statement for me was, 'Shyness is self-regarding.' This really shook me and helped me to look at a situation and make a clearer decision. Through his teaching, he reminded me of the magic in life. He gave me the opportunity of studying, among others, Rembrandt's drawings in the British Museum. I had loved his paintings since I was very young so this was a profound experience for me.

Cecil attracted many students because he really cared about them. He wanted to share his own experience and knowledge. He said, 'I teach you to teach yourself. We know everything already; we've just forgotten.' He always advised us to learn the technique of drawing. 'Once you have it, you can throw it behind you, but it's always at your disposal.' He also explained that it was a matter of educating our emotions and attitudes and having the courage to persist and to be aware. Perpetual awareness in drawing is necessary. It was important not to be afraid of failure, but to accept it without depression, as it was inevitable on the path of creativity. He told us that hidden in the unconscious is the image of perfection, and that perfection had to be our aim; we had to accept nothing less, never to compromise in our pursuit to reach it. To be haunted by perfection brings a sense of failure because we are not there yet, but we also get a sense of exhilaration from its beauty. In the first state of consciousness there is no happiness, only wants based on vested interests, subjective desires and fears. To reach the second state, we need ritual meditation to transform the subjectivity of ego into the objective practice of love and compassion. This is the state of great happiness. It can be achieved only by hard work on oneself.

After Cecil's death, I continued my studies. I was eventually accepted on a degree course in fine art that took five years, part time. I also held drawing classes in my home for four years which is something I would never have had the confidence to do without my experience of Cecil Collins' teaching.

MERIEL HOARE

Meriel Hoare studied at the Slade School of Art in London, with Oscar Kokoschka in his School of Seeing in Salzburg and with Cecil Collins at the City Lit.

Cecil changed my life. I first came into contact with his work in an exhibition of drawings at the Tate. There was a perfume, a scent of 'otherness' which went straight to my heart. Then I discovered Cecil was still alive and teaching. I went to the City Lit and enrolled for his weekly classes.

Cecil used music in his classes and would have the model move with the music until he asked her or him to hold their position. Cecil would make the students copy the model's movements, to help empathise with the feelings of the model and the atmosphere of the pose. However as it was a crowded room, I was always concerned about knocking into the other students. It was different if he asked me to lead the movement. Cecil always insisted that I let down my long hair which I used to wear in a bun at the nape of my neck. This was very releasing as I come from a conventional and very formal background. I enjoyed leading as I could go into the music, really move freely and enter a completely different space.

I remember at the end of the first day Cecil looked through my drawings very slowly. Fed up with me and clicking his false teeth, he said acidly, 'What a pity. You haven't seen anything at all.' This to me was a gift; I thought, my God, he's right. I saw the whole picture of my life: I was thirty-five and I'd always betrayed my real feelings for social acceptability. Something in me knew that Cecil's teaching was going to be crucial. I don't know why I thought it was so important, but your heart knows things about which your mind hasn't any knowledge.

Finally, in the last class, after all the years I'd been with him, he picked up a drawing off the floor and said, 'This is a nice drawing.' Then he looked up and saw I was there and said, 'Did you do it?' and I said, 'Yes.' He scrutinised it and said, 'Your marks are full of arrogance.' I saw exactly what he meant. Without realising it I'd found a little prescription that worked and I was just beating the drum with it, the ego drum, hoping for recognition. Cecil was extremely perceptive. From his point of view, I wasn't a great student. To start with I was very left-brained, analytical and not especially sensitive.

Cecil used to say something in class that touched me even though I didn't understand a word of it then, 'Atmosphere is knowledge,' and I have since discovered the absolute truth of that. The atmosphere of the model's pose links us with the mystery of being alive. He taught me to experience the living presence of the model and to allow myself to freely express that experience on paper. Cecil said to me, 'Don't draw like I draw. Don't imitate me. Stick to your own way.' He opened a major door for me; he opened drawing and living and that there was more to life than meets the eye. Cecil said, 'Education is nothing but organised crime.' I thought it was a hilarious joke at the time, but I see now it is completely true.

Once, after a class with Cecil, I was talking about what I was learning with great enthusiasm to a friend in my village and she said, 'Could you do for me what Cecil's done for you?' I said, 'No, of course I couldn't. I'm not particularly good at drawing and I'm definitely not a teacher.' Then I went back to Cecil and said, 'Isn't that a fantastic joke?' He said, 'No. Begin with her.' So I did. At first, I hadn't a clue what I was doing; I was just emulating Cecil verbatim. It took me years to let go of Cecil's way of teaching. Eventually, I integrated what I'd learnt and it was much better because it was truthful to myself and therefore more helpful to my students.

People who think they're only coming to draw at my workshops also find the plain quietness of being. Sometimes they even discover a new intimacy with life, others and themselves, but don't necessarily know what's happening. To me, that's the mystery. It's very low key and can only be alluded to. It opens up for each person over time. It doesn't really matter if they don't understand a word of what I say. They go away with this experience of being and that's what I love about the whole thing.

I wasn't part of the Cecil group; I was on the fringe. Cecil and I were never really close, but I did get very close to Elisabeth. I loved her and she loved me. We went with her once to the Cirque du Soleil at the Albert Hall. She loved it.

Elisabeth was under Cecil's shadow, but that was the typical relationship in their generation; girls served their husbands. I have as much respect for Elisabeth as I have for Cecil and to me she was just as much of a master. Cecil must have realised it because from his paintings you can see she was his muse and much more than that. She was the life of him, I felt. Cecil was quite an inhibited, dry man; I didn't feel much bodily celebration in him. She was the juice of him and he was the mouthpiece of them both. It seemed to me almost as if Cecil and Elisabeth were one person and Cecil couldn't have been what he was without Elisabeth. One could say she was the content and he was the form.

I've come to understand the masculine and feminine as form and formlessness. To me, the content is the feminine and the manifestation is the masculine. In drawing, the feminine is the intuitive touch, the feeling response to what I call the atmosphere, or the being-ness, of the pose. The masculine has to bow to the feminine in order to articulate that on the paper. This is what Cecil taught me. I also learnt about how the masculine didn't have to get it just right. This was the surrender of the masculine to the feminine because the feminine has no boundaries and is the fundamental matrix which can appear as a total mess. When the masculine and feminine, the form and the formless, are plaited together, then there is harmony and beauty.

Cecil planted a seed for me and when I started giving classes myself, it started opening. The amazing thing is that this seed is still growing. He challenged what I thought I knew. His wonderful teaching goes on unfolding in ever more subtle ways. He was truly remarkable and a complete mystery. I'm not sure he realised quite how much he was giving to us, but he helped me to appreciate the sacredness of life and to find my own language with which to express it. He often said, 'You don't see with your eyes; they are merely windows. You see with the heart.'

Cecil Collins
Daybreak: Head and Tree
1971
Oil on board
16 x 21cm

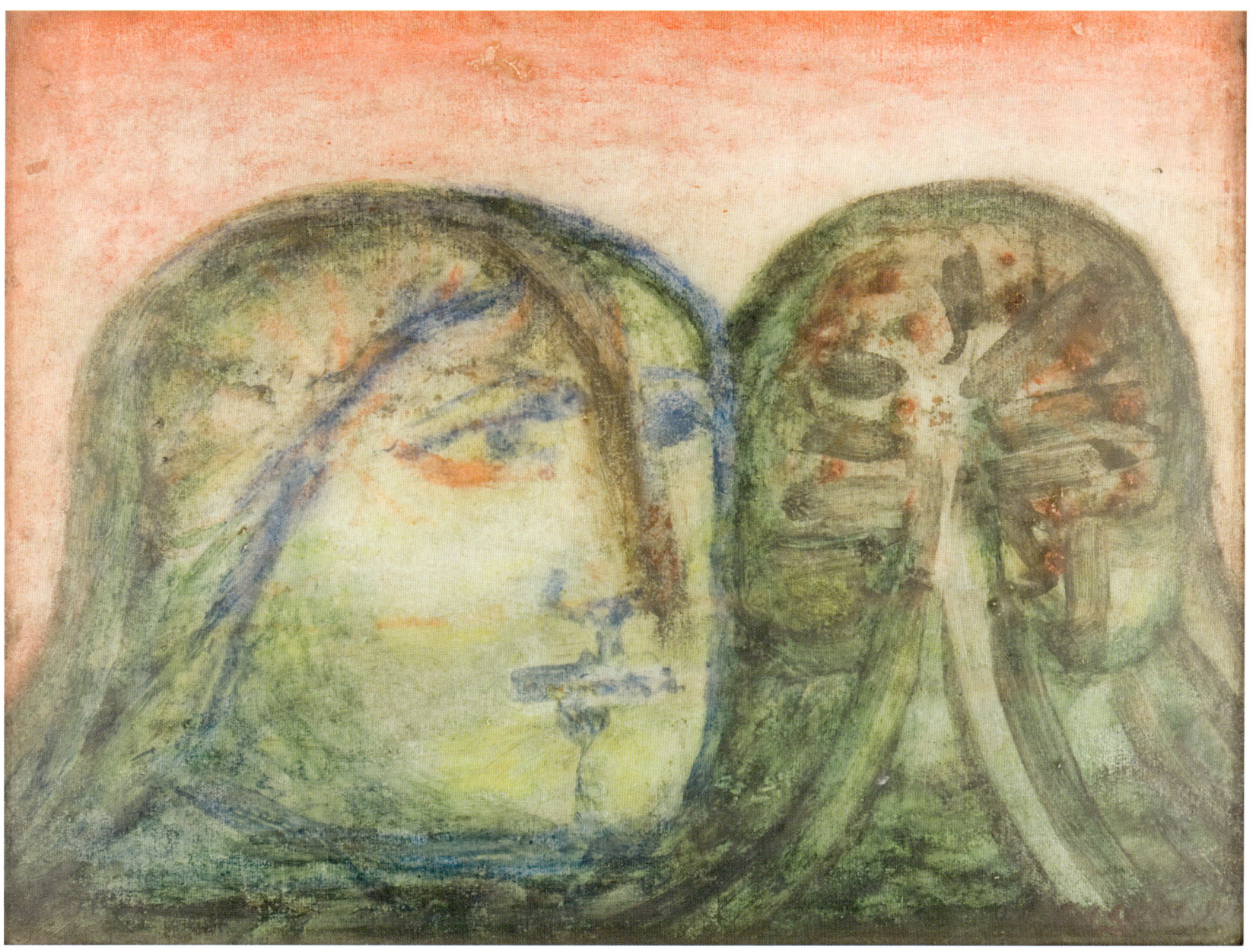

IAN HOPTON

After ten years in the Merchant Navy, Ian Hopton studied Architecture. Having painted since 1965, he became a full-time mature student at West Surrey Art College and attended Cecil Collins' life drawing classes. In 1990 he moved to France where he works as a painter and printmaker.

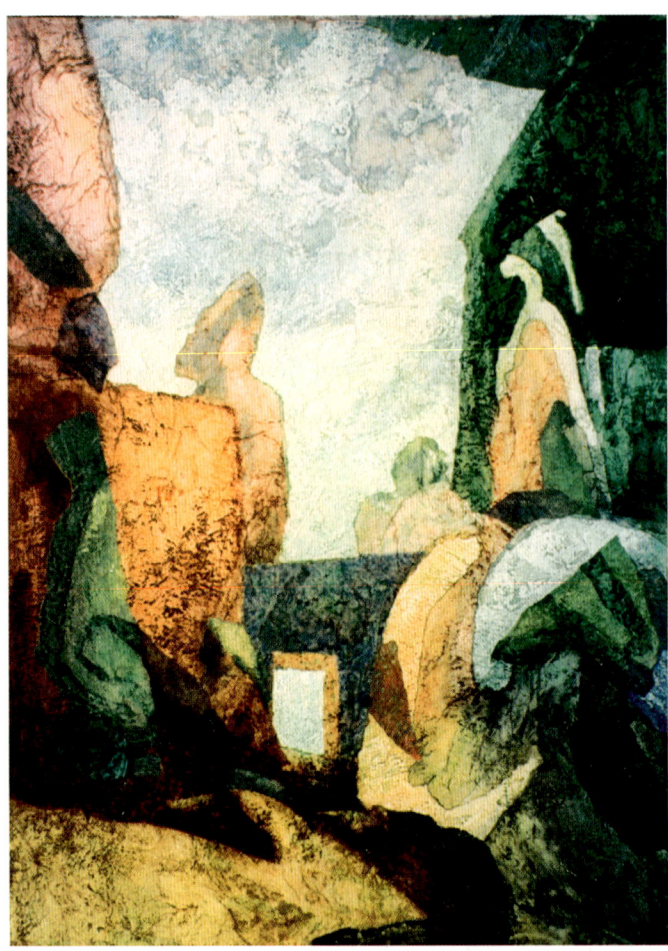

Ian Hopton
Recollection of Egypt 4
2001
Tempera and collaged paper on board
95 x 66cm

I studied architecture at Manchester University for four years, but when I was doing my practical year out I discovered philosophy at the School of Economic Science (SES). I was deeply impressed and decided to stay with that and study in my own way. I didn't get my architecture degree, but I carried on practising with the firm I'd done my year out with, York Rosenberg and Mardall, and I stayed with them for thirteen years. I worked on St Thomas's Hospital and Gatwick Airport and several other big projects and then I went to Hong Kong for six months. At the end of that period, I thought I ought to get qualified so I went to the South Bank Polytechnic, as it was then called, but I just wasn't interested. I thought, why am I doing this and not doing what I want to do, which is painting? I wanted to be an artist.

I did a course at the City Lit on traditional painting techniques: mixing your own paint, encaustic painting, oil painting, things like that. It was very interesting. I was also doing life drawing and life sculpture at the John Cass Art College. While at the City Lit, I met a woman who was a student of Cecil's. She told me there was a life drawing class at the City Lit and suggested I come along and try it. I started and from the outset I was very impressed.

I don't particularly remember the first class of Cecil's I went to. I thought it was just another life drawing class and initially I didn't have any view at all. I didn't have the equipment I needed like Chinese brushes and had to borrow things off people. They were kind to me and I struggled through it, but it was all a bit bewildering. I remember thinking, 'maybe this is a special week and he's doing these funny things. It'll all be different next week', but when next week came, I found out this was how he worked. We had to go through all these movements and so on.

After several months, I thought I'll have to talk to this man because he kept saying things I'd heard at the SES. The teaching there is quite formal; there's a set script that is written at the most senior level and the tutors read it out; they don't interpret it. It's very organised and some people say it's authoritarian, which it is, because there's one author, but I think that's quite a good system providing the person at the top knows what he's talking about.

Cecil's afternoon class started at two and went on till five. Somewhere in the middle there was a break of twenty minutes or so, but, for the first few months, I couldn't get near Cecil because he was surrounded by women admirers. It was quite difficult to fight your way through without being impolite. I managed to collar Cecil after class one day and said, 'Have you heard about SES?' He said, 'Of course.' He'd heard about lots of things long before my time, but he didn't seem to want to talk about it. Cecil wasn't a very forthcoming person, I found. You had to winkle information out of him. I felt a bit as if I was intruding, but I did ask one or two questions and I realised that he had studied with the same group there in the 1940s or perhaps even before the war.

Cecil was always very detached and impersonal. He didn't want to get involved with any particular student, at least that was my impression. His class wasn't a social group. People did their drawing, they finished and then went home. At the end of three hours, you were feeling pretty exhausted anyway. You just wanted to crawl away and lick your wounds. I'm exaggerating, but it was exhausting because of all the strange things you had to do, such as the movements which maybe men are a bit more inhibited about. Also, all the techniques are quite difficult. Cecil deliberately employed them to test people. I think he was trying to get art out of people and that was his way of doing it. I was there for the art, not for the consciousness. I'd given up striving for that by then.

In the SES, which some people called the SAS as it was rather like a spiritual commando course, they had lots of study groups which were extremely interesting: very good Sanskrit, Vedic mathematics, geometry, art. I questioned their lack of interest in modern creativity, contemporary creativity. I was in the art group, but it was all strictly traditional figurative art which seemed terribly limited somehow. This is just my own view, but I was curious to know Cecil's. I asked Cecil why he left the group and he said something to the effect that it was inhibiting his artistic spirit. I felt like that myself.

Cecil could be quite particular about language. That was like the SES where you had to say things very precisely and not be slack about your descriptions or use words unnecessarily. The SES had lots of rules and regulations to assist you with your daily life and one of them was do and say nothing unnecessary. Cecil would gently correct you if you used the wrong word, but he wasn't trying to score points or anything. He was not that sort of person at all. I remember him correcting me one time. It was a trivial little thing. I used the word 'category' in some context or other and he said, 'It's not a category; it's a grouping.' I'd used the wrong word and was put in my place. He was the good shepherd because he was the person who knew how to keep you on track in terms of art and the spiritual aspect of it.

You accepted being bossed around by Cecil because you felt it was for a purpose; it wasn't vanity. It was an act of love, like leading a child. A child doesn't necessarily have to understand exactly why it has to do this in a particular way. The parent who loves the child makes the child do it. The child only understands this later on.

Cecil would comment on the students' work sometimes, but very rarely. He didn't seem to have any particular interest in the final result. It was the process that was important. Now and then, he would walk round the room and have a look and make comments. I remember him saying once about my drawing that it was rather baroque; other people have said something similar.

I think Cecil's technique was practised long before Cecil's time. The Old Masters knew all about how to free up. They just drew their feelings; they weren't trying to draw a horse or anything. It was the feelings about the horse and I think this is what Cecil was trying to get across, draw your feelings, rather than what you see. This is what I try to explain in my booklet.

Cecil was a powerful feminist in my view. He was trying to develop the feminine aspect within everybody, especially artists. Maybe that's why so many women were attracted to him. Once he said, not about any particular student, that a lot of the work was too feminine. He didn't explain what he meant and I assumed he was generalising about the whole group and meant that the work was too unstructured and vague. It's very easy to get into these lovely vague shapes and forms and it needed a bit of structure and definition. He seemed to relate everything to the masculine and feminine.

I don't think anyone queried his comments. You never challenged Cecil. It was amazing. He was such a quiet, diffident man and yet he seemed to have such authority whenever he said something. He kept you on your toes all the time. He knew when to stop the music, for instance, and start the drawing, and then to change the situation so we had to abandon that and start something else. We're not used to being aware, being there consciously, and it's uncomfortable. We want some relief and I was quite glad when the three hours came to an end. Another half hour and I would have been completely exhausted.

One had the sense that Cecil was recharged by the class and so was everyone. It's a curious paradox again. You're exhausted and exhilarated at the same time by some special kind of energy which Cecil knew how to generate. Yet he was very fragile. You looked at him and thought he'd fall over at any time. He always reminded me of an old bird because he was very stooped. You were willing to do whatever he said because you trusted him. His skill as a teacher was that he knew how to establish that.

Cecil had a very disciplined technique. It was a bit like Zen. I've never practised Zen in a direct way, but from what I've read about its spiritual methods, Zen seems quite fierce and difficult to handle for most people. Like some ancient Zen teachers, Cecil would metaphorically 'hit you on the shoulder with a stick' to wake you up. He did that through his technique of cutting things off at a particular moment or by starting something else. Swapping drawings was part of the technique, cutting through attachment. If you were getting too precious about your work, he'd ask us to hand it over to the next student and they'd continue.

Cecil seemed to be able to combine various sources. He put them all into a kind of formula and used art as the medium. In most philosophical or religious groups contemporary art doesn't figure very highly and is not taken very seriously, but for Cecil art was a vehicle for self-realisation.

Architectural work was by comparison a joy, a pleasure, because you knew what you were doing, at least as far as you ever know. The science was important, and there were also certain aesthetic standards. But art is a jungle, a minefield. You don't know where you are, you're bewildered. It's the nature of the problem for artists. You try and try, struggling to find an aesthetic of some kind and failing. You continue failing and you don't know what to do about it. That's par for the course. Then Cecil came along and cut through everything, simply by having us doing it, not thinking about it, eliminating the intellect and going directly at it. Being like a child. Making a truthful painting. What is the truth in art? It's the spontaneous mark and it's so obvious. It's free and it isn't precise and yet it is precise. It's not trying to get it right, but there is a kind of rightness about it. There's a truth to it in a general sense and that's the strange mystery. Prior to Cecil, I didn't know anything about that, not really. I'd been to the British Museum and the National Gallery and seen these wonderful drawings of the Old Masters, but how did they do it? Cecil knew how to do it.

I'd never heard of Cecil Collins when I first started his class and then somebody told me that he had a painting in the Tate Gallery, so I trotted along to see it. In fact, I'd walked past his painting several times, but I had no idea that I'd seen anything Cecil had done. He never showed his work and I wondered where these amazing Cecils were. Then I saw these strange little paintings of clowns or fools rather. They didn't appeal to me immediately. They were highly personal symbolist arrangements with a particular repetitive style of spikiness. I was very unsure about them, but that didn't matter because what mattered to me was his teaching. I thought that's fine, that's the kind of painting he does. Later, I heard about *The Vision of the Fool* and read that. I thought it was very interesting as a philosophical statement and an attitude. It was coming from somewhere that I felt I recognised.

Initially, I put my feelings about Cecil's paintings to one side. Over the years, I've looked at them again. I still don't feel particularly attracted to them, but they grow on you. It's a curious thing, but it's simply a matter of a respect for whatever the man does because you know and love the man and you look at what he was trying to say and respect it. As far as I could understand it, he was bringing out the things that were within him, whatever they were. This is something that I try now to do in my painting: simply make marks. When I'm being egotistical about it, they're my marks, not somebody else's marks. They may be unpleasant or weird, but that's what I have to do. I can't make somebody else's marks. It's like handwriting. Everyone is unique. My own feeling is that we destroy our originality by trying to do art according to a style or an idea. One thing you have to say about a Cecil painting is that it is original and therefore you can't copy it. You can copy his philosophy, not his art. Originality comes from the origin and that's inside everyone.

When I first started with Cecil in 1980 you went along and signed up a week before, but five years later people were queuing up all night just to get a queue ticket. They then had to get back in the queue to sign up. That's how popular Cecil was with the students, not with the authorities of course, nor with his employers or the art world, whatever that is. One year I missed out and didn't get there at four in the morning and I thought, why not let other people have a go? All I'm doing is repeating the same thing. I'd stayed with him for about six years. A time comes when you feel you have to move on and do your own thing. It was pretty well the same curriculum each year which was fine because one assumes there's a turnover of students.

Cecil rarely spoke; sometimes he would stop and talk and then everyone would be scribbling notes down madly. Here was the voice of the oracle and you wanted to remember as much as you could. Those were tremendous moments and then you'd go back to the drawing, trying to get it right. You knew what to do theoretically and you knew the techniques, but you still weren't producing good drawings.

I'm a great believer in the view that it doesn't matter how clever you are, how talented you are, all that matters is the end result. People look at a drawing and say, 'It's not very good is it? You've been doing it for fifteen years. Maybe you should try plumbing.' Nobody ever said anything like that in Cecil's class, but that's the hard truth about art. Art is a ruthless judge of our ability and talent; I think it's unforgiving. Cecil was simply presenting a teaching and you had to make the best of it yourself.

Right from the outset I felt that I was making progress in Cecil's class, but I can't really say that there was a big difference between when I began and when I ended. I just wanted to continue doing it. It was a useful thing to do and I enjoyed it. I was working very hard as an architect in the treadmill of earning a living and this was one period of three hours where you felt that you were involved in a civilised activity that was worthwhile. It was one of the best parts of a week that was often very stressful and taxing. You were in a different world for three hours, a world of art, so it was a valuable period and that's why I kept on. Maybe it was self indulgence, maybe I wasn't really progressing. Maybe I was enjoying it in a masochistic way because it was also quite painful, that's the curious thing. I used to go through the door and take a deep breath and think, I'm going to do the best I can. I would do all these things in this rapid and immediate way and I'd have a great heap of drawings. Then I'd get home and look through them and think maybe one or two of them are okay, but the rest are nothing. I really wanted to be able to do good drawings so there's a kind of ambition or an aim there which is contrary to the philosophy of detachment.

You felt like an instrument in Cecil's classes. That was all part of his technique. You felt like a conductor of these things that were inside you. He knew how to make you bring them out, which you did to the best of your ability by listening very carefully and trying to do everything he said, without trying. It was so contradictory. The more you stopped trying, the better the drawings were somehow.

Cecil managed to open a doorway or a window within oneself. It was like an electric current. It wasn't in the first lesson, but at some point I did a drawing and thought, 'that's remarkable. Where did that come from?' Although I was sitting there holding the instruments, I realised I was a vehicle for something, an instrument myself. It was something quite precious and I couldn't explain it. There was this man who somehow knew how to get you to do it and that was incredible. It was a form of magic.

ARCHETYPAL POSTURES: IN THE PROCESS OF CREATIVITY
by Ian Hopton
La Fontbelle Press, 2005

One of the typical ceremonies that took place during the life drawing classes conducted by Cecil Collins in the 1970s and 1980s. Cecil made comments on each posture and the following account is the best recollection from memory and notes of what he said.

The process of creativity is from the horizontal to the vertical. The movements represent the unfolding of creation. The feelings generated within the space created by the face and the palms of the hands are crucial.

The first posture, prostrate, represents the state of total submission and surrender prior to any creative act. The first response to the creative urge is to overcome the inertia of passivity and raise the body from the ground to a kneeling position. This act in itself is symbolic of Man's capacity to free himself from the earthbound condition of the animal, subject entirely to the laws of nature. Being aware of his boldness he is nevertheless overcome with humility as expressed in the first kneeling posture with the face down and the palms forward.

In the second kneeling posture the head remains down but the arms are raised forward with palms up, and this expresses a condition of appeal, as though for guidance.

This leads to the third kneeling posture in which the head is raised and the gaze is straight forward. This represents a condition of seeking and enquiry and perhaps symbolises the role of the intellect in the creative process.

The fourth kneeling posture is where the arms are outstretched, the palms still upwards. This is a very open gesture of worship and acknowledgement. In this posture one becomes very aware of the relationship between the face and the palms of the hands and of the lines of energy between.

For the fifth kneeling posture the face is raised upwards with the arms remaining outstretched and this symbolises the condition of joy and rejoicing; the natural outcome of creativity.

The man, further emboldened, takes the next step and adopts the half-kneeling posture which represents the critical moment of decision. It represents a state of transition. It cannot be sustained. The man must commit himself to go forward or relapse. But in the process of creativity he must decide to go forward; there is no turning back.

The first half-kneeling posture is again with head down and palms forward, representing humility, and the four succeeding postures follow the same pattern as for the kneeling position, thus completing eleven postures.

With the twelfth posture the man rises to his full stature which is the standing position but he repeats the same sequence of five postures beginning with humility then appeal, seeking, worship and finally rejoicing which in this last standing position also represents exultation.

The students remain in each posture for a minute or so in silence and a state of awareness that naturally increases as the ceremony proceeds.

To describe these postures as archetypes is not an exaggeration. Participating within a group in this ceremony enabled one to experience the meaning of symbolism as an existing reality not as some remote intellectual concept lifted from another age or another culture. One became aware of some connection with an ancient knowledge of Man's fundamental condition and perhaps his capacity to re-discover his own divine nature through the creative process.

GAY HUTCHINGS

Gay studied painting and printmaking and later stained glass at Central School of Art and Design, London, where Cecil Collins was her personal tutor. She continues to practise as a printmaker, exhibiting with the East Anglian group, 12 PM, as a stained glass artist and as a painter.

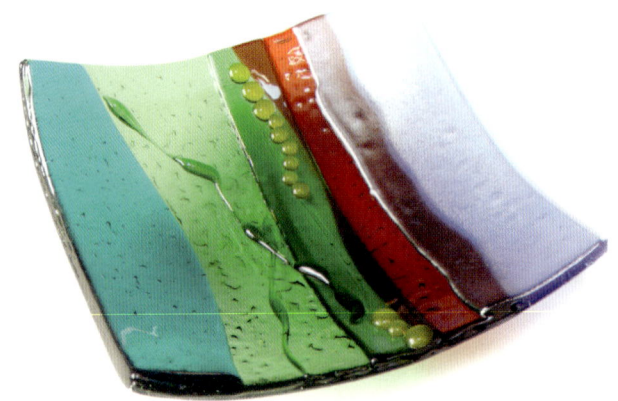

Gay Hutchings
Square Dish
2007
Fused/slumped glass
23 x 23cm

My My first year as a full time painting student at Central was in 1976. I had been working for ten years when I went to art school so I was quite grounded. I found my first year very difficult because there were a lot of unsympathetic tutors at Central. There was a great antipathy to Cecil and to mature students. In fact, we were the last intake of mature students. That year there were seven of us over twenty-five; the next year there were none. At the beginning of our second year, we were able to choose our personal tutors so I chose Cecil and I paid the penalty. Cecil's tutees were a definite group and we were all destined to get a third class degree. Certainly none of us would ever get a first. In fact, most of us got a 2:2, but nobody really cared; it didn't matter because we felt we were getting the benefit of something that, if the tutors didn't understand, they were the ones who were missing out. We were older than some of the tutors and they didn't like that and, in particular, they didn't like Cecil. One of the tutors drew on my drawing. I never forgave him for that. 'This is how it should be done,' he said. I thought, Aargh, get off my drawing.

When I began Cecil's life drawing classes, the slowness annoyed me because I'd been in public relations where everything was frenetic. In Cecil's class, everyone was calm and quiet and I found that difficult to begin with. I kept going for nearly a year. What held me there? I believed there had to be something I hadn't yet understood. He used to sit in the corner and only rarely did he come round, but sometimes when he did he would say, 'One day you'll understand,' and I kept thinking, carry on, I'm sure it'll be fine, but in an impatient way. Then after two or three terms, it happened. The class was the same as usual and this might sound completely silly, but it was like a flash. I suddenly understood. I thought, my God, now I know what it's all about. It may have been written all over my face because Cecil came over to me at the end of the class and said, 'Now you know.' I was astonished at how observant he was.

I remember it as a turning point; a blinding light. It was like Paul on the road to Damascus. It's about getting away from drawing what you see. Spontaneity is not the word; it's what Cecil called 'the eye of the heart.' You're not looking with your eyes, you're seeing through your eyes with 'the eye of the heart'. It's about being able to see differently, being able to put down what is really there without actually having to see it. So that was it. I was hooked. I still tell people about this revelation.

Cecil was extraordinary. He wasn't judgmental; he wasn't stuffing knowledge into us. Cecil would say, 'We'll have a minute of silence now for centring.' He never raised his voice. I still do it when I remember. Sit still, with both feet on the ground and hands on your knees.

I had sympathy with those who didn't understand what Cecil's classes were about because I'd been there too. Cecil, for instance, used to throw out anybody who was chewing gum. He'd see someone chewing gum and he'd say, 'What's that in your mouth? Either get rid of it or leave. It's a waste of energy so don't do it or leave my class.' Some of them never came back, but that was their loss. You were supposed to be concentrating your energy on the class, not wasting it on chewing gum. He was quite firm, but he was also very funny.

Most of the students were women. I think it's because they are more open to that kind of atmosphere and teaching, perhaps more receptive to delving into themselves, while with men, it's the macho thing. They don't want to seem effeminate. I remember Saied. He was very sceptical. He would never take his shoes off. He'd arrive in these beautiful polished black lace-ups and Cecil used to say, 'Everybody take their shoes off and lie on the floor,' amongst all the charcoal; get dirty. Saied hated it and he refused. In the end Cecil just ignored it. He probably saw something in him and must have found it interesting that he wouldn't take his shoes off. Yet now Saied's a great fan of Cecil's. I think Saied found it alien to begin with, but he kept coming.

The main criticism of Cecil's classes is that we all turned out the same kind of drawings, Cecil-type drawings, but you have to start with something. It's like cooking; you have the same utensils and ingredients, but you can cook something completely different with them. If you're all taught to make an apple pie or a beef stew, then that's what you get. So it was with Cecil. We had the same instruments, the same model and the same amount of time, three seconds or whatever it was, so they were bound to look similar. But I ended up doing glass; Willow's making books; Michael Chaitow's painting and Danny Lane is creating glass. For Cecil, it wasn't restricted to painting or drawing; he appreciated every art form, whether it was theatre or music. He thought it was up to the individual to make his or her own decisions. I remember Cecil saying that your drawing is your handwriting because everybody writes differently. We're all taught the alphabet and yet no two people write alike. It's the same for drawing, so it's absurd for somebody to say you should be drawing it one way or another because each person makes their own interpretation.

Cecil was a great observer and many of the things he used to say have stayed with me. 'You have to imagine that you're swimming in a lake and that the more you swim, the closer you are to the other side.' It's terribly obvious really, but in the context of getting through a difficult time, it was very helpful. 'You're one of those people who will never be working in a straight line,' he once said to me. 'You'll have highs and lows like a rollercoaster and you'll have great moments of activity and energy and achievement and then you'll have moments where you can't work at all.' That's been quite comforting over the years.

I got married the same year I graduated and went back to Essex where I set up my own studio. It was some years after that that I came back to his classes at Central. When I had been a full-time student, Cecil's classes were part of the college curriculum, but by this time they had got pushed out and were being run by the external section.

I used to come up to Central one morning a week. The first time I came, he greeted me warmly. He was wonderful. I was doing those classes when my marriage started to fall apart and they had a strange effect on me. I'd find it very emotional. I remember in an earlier year there was a girl who used to come into the class and cry all the time and I thought, why is she doing that? Cecil wasn't worried; he just let her cry. Then I found it was happening to me and I thought, oh dear, this is terrible. I think those classes were so emotional because you were searching into yourself. You were bringing out all sorts of things that you'd perhaps been holding back. He let people have their own experiences in class. I carried on with them for about five or six years, until Cecil died.

He'd never look at what you were drawing and sometimes I'd find that very frustrating. You'd long for him to come and comment, but it wasn't about, 'You've made a beautiful drawing.' That wasn't it. It was much more about your experience of how you were approaching the drawing. It was never about the end product. He would never be specific. He'd say, 'You're beginning to understand,' or something like that which was a bit vague and annoying. He'd never spoon-feed you which happens a lot these days. He used to say, 'Education comes from *exducare*, to draw out, not to shove in,' and that's exactly what he did. The 'drawing out' came through the music and the movement. It's not something you would do spontaneously without being asked to. Cecil could read people. It made you feel very transparent. He was a father figure because he was a lot older and terribly wise. That's what I found so amazing about him. He was a wonderfully wise teacher in the widest sense. I had huge respect for him, but I wasn't frightened of him. His teaching has calmed me down.

Very early on, as with the classes, I was a bit mystified by Cecil's own work, but then I gradually began to understand about the Fool and the Angel. I began to understand how he made them, where they came from in him, that they were imaginative. I think he had a very difficult time because he never fitted into a mould. People couldn't pigeonhole him. I find his paintings wonderful, but some are not terribly well painted. Surprisingly, he didn't pay that much attention to the medium. I've got one, *The Secret Songs of Spring*,

Cecil Collins
Landscape with Young Girl and Unicorn
1940s

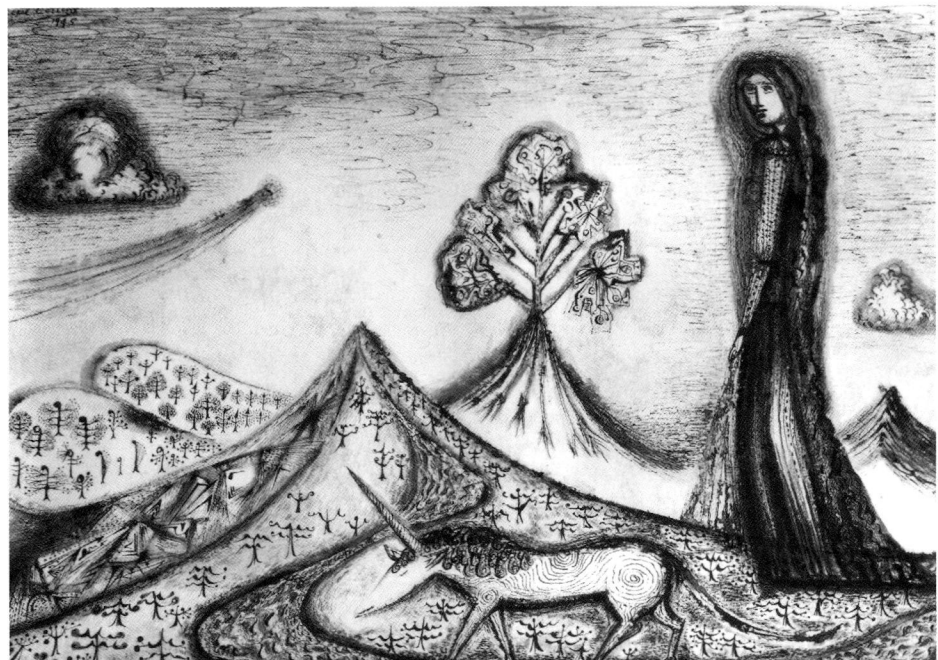

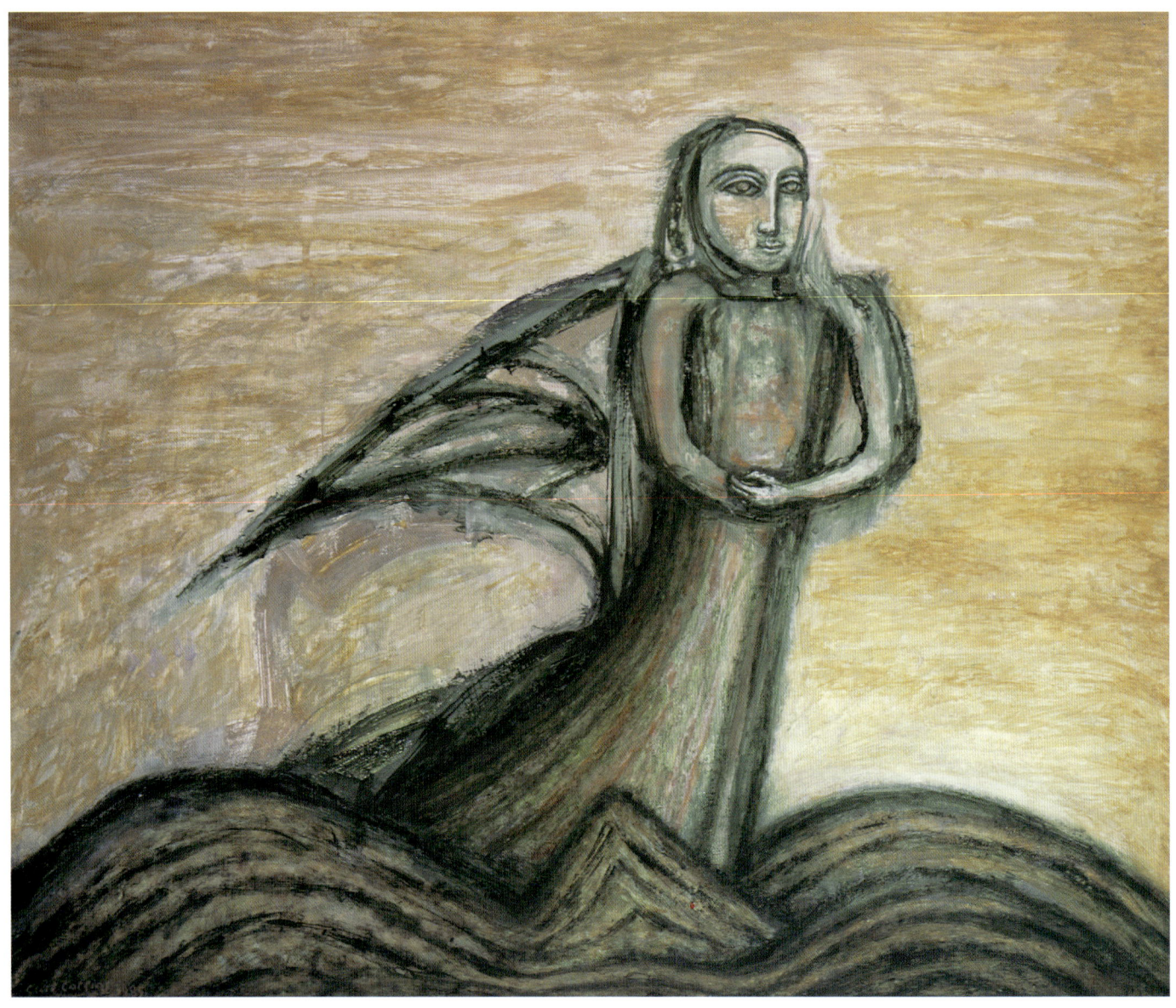

Cecil Collins
Offering of Dawn
1985
Mixed media
51 x 61cm

where the lead white has come through the green. Cecil wouldn't allow it to be included in his Tate show because he said it had changed. Judith Collins, who curated that exhibition took it to an expert at the National Gallery who said, 'This happens with pictures. It's just the way it's metamorphosed; don't touch it.' Of course I was disappointed that my painting had changed. I bought that from Anthony d'Offay in the 1980s. I wish I'd bought more.

Ages after I left Central, when my son, Robert, was born, Cecil had an exhibition in Aldeburgh. I went up there with Robert in a sling and Cecil came over and said, 'This is your greatest creation,' and I thought, 'Am I that bad at art?' It was sort of humorous.

I've stayed in touch with a lot of the ex-students, particularly Ruth Eisenhart and Willow Winston. I shared a studio with Willow along with Nicola Tassie and Danny Lane; there were four of us in the turret at the top of Central. For two years we were hidden away up there and we could escape from all these terrible people who didn't like us. Willow was a year ahead of me. I didn't get to know Ruth till later because she was in sculpture and a year behind me. I met her through Cecil's drawing classes. Anybody who had anything to do with Cecil has an affinity. We're all connected by this thread, so that when we meet after years, it's still there.

In 1990 and 1993 Amal, Ruth, Willow and I organised two big exhibitions of Cecil's students work at Central. Ever since then Ruth, Willow, Amal and I have been judging the Cecil Collins' Memorial Prize for Drawing. This was set up from the bequest Cecil left to Central which was only a couple of thousand pounds, maybe it was a bit more. Originally, the prize was awarded once a year; now it's every other year. Sadly, it has never really got the recognition it should have done, although it's open to all departments, including pottery, jewellery and furniture design, not just fine art. Through the years we have found that the departments have not publicised it. Another problem is that the prize money it's not enough to attract people. Nobody seems interested even though it looks good on a CV and the prize-winning work is exhibited in the college. We're trying to get the college to match the amount of money, or for somebody else to put in some extra funds. It's all been a bit frustrating and difficult. Recently, there was only one entry and we had to say, 'You can't give one person a prize when there isn't any competition.' Theoretically, the heads of departments all know about it and it's supposed to be pinned on the notice board, but they can be very obstructive or lethargic. I don't know whether it's an anti-Cecil sentiment, maybe they're just bureaucratic and difficult. Whatever the reason the prize is biennial now.

Since then, Ruth and I have worked together teaching classes. I haven't taught much. I only share the class with Ruth, partly because I've got so much else on and because I didn't want to tread on her toes. I've taught glass, but that's not the same thing. Ruth used to come out to where I lived and I'd organise the people and the class and the place, but I didn't want to take it over. A lot of the people in the classes were my friends. I noticed how she would go round and look at people's work and I remember that Cecil rarely did that.

Going into stained glass was quite a departure because I have to deal with clients rather than just doing what I want. One of the things that happened when I went back to Cecil's class was that, for the first time, I was able to tie in what I was learning in his classes with what I was actually doing. In the beginning it was completely separate. It was Cecil's classes and the rest, painting, printmaking, whatever, but I never tied the two together. Five or six years later, I suddenly started to be able to use what I'd learnt in the life drawing classes in my own work which was much more landscape based.

Now all those threads have come together. I can make stained glass windows if I need to, but what I'm doing is making landscape paintings in glass, but without lead. Amal used to say, 'Can't you stop being a painter? Remember you can have green sky and blue grass in glass.'

The new work I've been doing is much smaller and much more manageable and abstract than I could do with a paintbrush or printmaking. I've been using the pieces of coloured glass and, as happened in Cecil's classes, without really knowing what I was doing, without intentionally saying, 'I'm going to put this colour here,' it all comes together. I look at it and think, did I make that? The extraordinary thing is that you can have this complete concentration for a couple of hours as we used to in the drawing classes. You're completely focused, but in a way you're not there. You're just in the moment and then it's done. That's what I like about it. These pieces are small; they don't take too long and come from within me. Cecil often used to say, 'Don't stand outside yourself looking down or looking at what you're doing.' For the first time, I've been able to combine everything I ever learnt into these relatively small glass works.

Cecil was a purposeful teacher. His teaching is possibly a greater legacy than his paintings, but I don't know whether or not that will be appreciated. I resisted taking notes in class because I don't think you can take it in and respond if all you're doing is mechanically writing down what he's saying. We were supposed to be in it and with it and learning. I used to watch another student taking notes and think, she's missing the whole point of these classes. It's perfectly natural that if somebody's talking and it's interesting, you make notes for fear of forgetting what they've said. It's like when people are touring and taking photos all the time. I take a small sketchbook and even though I might only do a handful of drawings, I get the essence of what I've seen. Sometimes I even do the drawing afterwards. That's something I learnt from Cecil, to trust your memory, your version of what it was. I only ever work from my own drawings.

Cecil really did free something in me. I've had other teachers who said you must go and draw every day and, religiously, I went out once or twice a week to paint the landscape. With my glass work I'm finding that I don't need to do that any more because I can remember what I've seen. It might not even be something specific, but I'll remember a juxtaposition of colour. What Cecil gave us was the confidence to put it down. Cecil gave me confidence in myself. He made me realise that I actually had something to offer and I've always said I would not be an artist if I hadn't met Cecil. I was twenty-seven when I went to art school. I'd been to evening classes and had a teacher who kept saying, 'You should go to art school,' but I had a very high-powered job and a mortgage, and I thought, give it all up and go to art school? You must be mad, but I did it anyway. Then I met Cecil and he made it worthwhile, whereas before I was thinking, what am I doing here with all these eighteen year olds? He gave my choice meaning because he had confidence in me. That's what is so difficult for other people to understand, because if you've just been an art student with the usual run-of-the-mill tutors, you don't have that. That's why the students marched in the streets to keep Cecil employed. Central wanted to fire him because he was over the age of retirement; I suppose he was seventy then. I remember going on two marches. When we took our banners down to County Hall to protest at Cecil's dismissal, Cecil would sit back and let us all do it for him. He had faith that whatever was going to happen would happen. Cecil wasn't manipulative and he didn't want anything from us. Completely selflessly, he was giving to us everything he knew.

JONATHAN KNIGHT

Born in 1943, Jonathan Knight was educated at Eton and the Architectural Association. He set up one of the first development, design and building companies. Then he worked in Camden and Westminster Councils during which time he studied painting and sculpture. In 1993 he set up St Paul's Steiner Project providing the first permanent home for a Steiner School in London. In 2003 he became a crofter on the Isle of Mull.

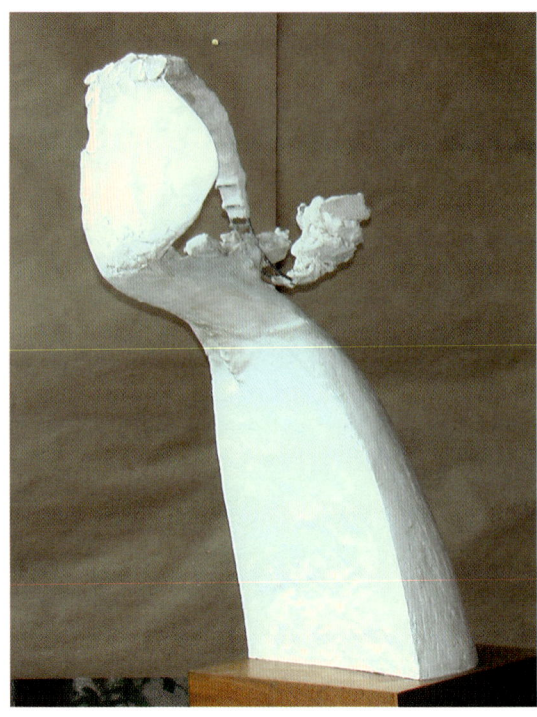

Jonathan Knight
Goddess
Plaster

I was a student of Cecil's right at the end, in 1988 or 1989. Gail Nichol, whom I'd met at Jean Gibson's sculpture class, introduced me to him. Gail asked Cecil if I could come along to one of his classes and I did, even though it was halfway through the year. The following year I enrolled properly, along with everybody else. This was at the Central. I think Cecil had given up the City Lit by then.

My first experience of being in his class was completely terrifying. This was my own personal response, of course. The way his classes worked were that you had a lot of people in the room in a circle and you had a model in the middle and the model would move and everybody around had to copy her movements. Then, at a certain point, Cecil would say 'Right,' and the model would stay in the pose that she'd got herself into. Everybody else would stop moving and sit down to start drawing her very quickly. Cecil would then prescribe very precisely what you would use for your sketches of the model: what instruments and what tone because you had seven tones of ink from practically water to pitch black, which position to use on the instruments because there were seven positions on the instrument itself and then which hand to hold the instrument in because you were drawing with both hands. Then he would decide the length of the pose. A pose wouldn't extend more than one or two minutes and would usually be less than that and sometimes as little as a few seconds. During the course of the lesson, you would turn out twenty or thirty sketches.

One of the reasons I found it all so excruciating was because I was physically lacking in self confidence. The idea of making movements, copying a model, was very difficult because you felt everyone was looking at you and also you were being given very awkward things to work with which you hadn't used before. You were working with your left hand as well as with your right, so you were being exposed to a lot of uncertainties as to what sort of mess you were going to make. I'd trained as an architect, but that wasn't really quite the point. I was just unused to doing something where you weren't able to control what you were doing, especially when you were working with your left hand which is particularly uncontrolled. Cecil would call that your feminine side and your right hand, which was one you were able to control, worked from the masculine side. Cecil said that using the female side was like weaving an endless web of creativity and the male side was working in a more intellectual way, selecting and formulating out of the never-ending female creativity/chaos and the two had to work together. There had to be a sort of conversation between the left and the right.

The idea was that you, too, were in harmony, empathising with the model which is why you had to move with the model and why you had to build a relationship with your instruments as well. You were totally out of your ego and into the room where you were in tune with your instruments, in tune with your paper and with the model. You were creating out of your inner self and you were totally out of control. You thought you were making a terrible mess and it would be highly embarrassing if anyone said, 'What's that you've done?' I was so ashamed of what I was doing I certainly didn't want anyone to see what awful marks I'd made so, at the end of each pose, I immediately turned the piece of paper upside down so nobody could look at it. This pile of paper developed over the lesson: some of them I felt were a little bit better than others, some not too bad.

At the end of the lesson, I took my little pile home and hoped nobody would notice what I'd done. Later that night, I would get them out and put them on the bed and the really fascinating thing was that those that you'd been most uncomfortable with and thought were awful were the best and those that you thought you'd done not too badly were the worst. This happened every single time and I got to realise that it would always be like that. It was extremely intriguing because you realised that you were tapping into a sort of creativity deep inside yourself if you allowed it to happen. Why I found that so amazing was because I realised that what Cecil said about vulnerability is so utterly true: an artist can't be truly creative unless they can work with their vulnerability. I learnt that if you can stay with your vulnerability, however uncomfortable, in there somewhere is your true creativity.

Over the year I did become a little less self-conscious, but I still found I had to summon up the courage to go to the classes. I

Cecil Collins
Composition
1933
Pen, ink and watercolour
20 x 25cm

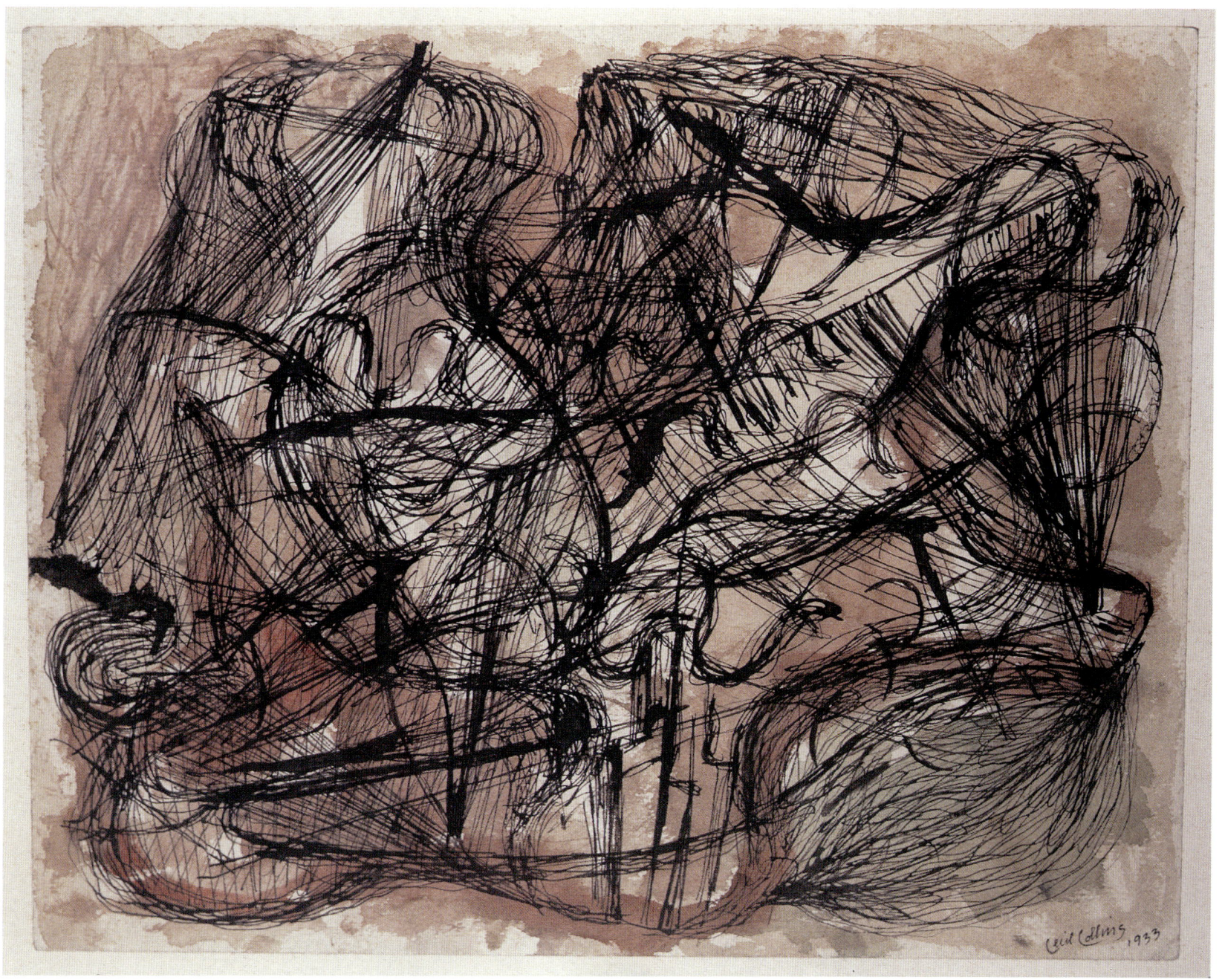

really found it very difficult. I didn't stay away because I knew that they were important and also I did find what Cecil said, though he didn't say very much, was incredibly interesting. He would talk a bit during the lesson, particularly at the beginning, but always very quietly which was also interesting. I thought that he did it on purpose. You had to really listen to hear what he was saying.

There was another excruciating moment in his class and, for me, this was probably the worst. Towards the end of the class he would ask one of his students to go into the middle of the room and initiate the movement. That person would then move, the model would copy that person and so would the whole class. Then Cecil would go round the students, one after the other, saying their name and inviting them to do the movement and then they'd do it. The extraordinary thing was that he went round and when it was my turn, there was a kind of pause and he skipped over me. I was so relieved because, quite honestly, I don't think I'd have been able to do it. I think he sensed this. He had perhaps twenty people in the room, but I felt that he actually was tuned into me at that point.

There would always be more women than men in Cecil's class. That didn't bother me; in fact, I rather liked it. He talked a lot about the feminine and that was attractive to women, but I don't necessarily think that's a particularly good thing because a lot of women there possibly enjoyed it too much. They indulged in their feminine. In one sense, Cecil rather liked having all these women around but, in another sense, he probably also realised that wasn't necessarily very healthy. I wasn't comfortable with it at first, but later I became much more accepting. I started to like women a lot which I hadn't before.

Another experience I remember was when I had to enrol. I had to bring some work along and I took a piece of sculpture. Cecil looked at it and liked it, but the interesting thing is that, although I didn't see him very many times and I didn't talk to him much at all, Cecil remembered me. The last time I saw him was at his retrospective at the Tate when he was obviously quite ill. It was literally a week or so before he died and he was very sparing with what he could say to people. The thing I found very moving was that he actually spoke to me and said that it was important that I concentrated on technique which was a slightly unusual thing for him to say, but he was utterly right because technique was where I was weak. In spite of having very few conversations with him, he knew exactly the right thing to say. I did ask him one question: whether he had a work in his mind before he began or did he work out of the moment and he said it was both. Then he pointed across to one of the paintings on the wall which was of a boat with some people rowing. He said he had had that one in his mind before he did it; he knew exactly what he was painting.

Cecil once said, and I totally agree with him, that painting is not a pleasurable activity. He didn't enjoy it himself; in fact, he hated painting. He found it excruciating, probably in the same way I do. I'm not painting at the moment, but I am thinking of doing sculpture again. Sculpture's my main interest really.

I've always wanted to ask about a period in Cecil's work which seems out of context with the rest of it. If you take the beginning of Cecil's work and the end, they join up. In other words, his earliest work and his latest work are very closely connected, but the 'Matrix' period is slightly outside of that and I wonder how it linked to the theme of his life. It seems to relate to the way he taught in that he could see something coming out of the marks you made, out of the chaos, the female chaos. Perhaps it helped him to renew his faith in his vision.

I think that Cecil said some very profound things. With him, you weren't just doing the art; you were brought into something more than that. In fact, I've rather come to the conclusion that these days especially, when there are no boundaries whatsoever, you can do anything and often there's no context, you can't just look at the work any more; you have to know the person who's done it. It's all conceptual; you have to read what's on the walls. That's why I find Cecil's work so amazing because it's not just the marks on a piece of paper; it's also the whole human being behind that. I also apply this to other artists: when you know a bit more about them, it helps your appreciation of the work. You're getting something through the work which you won't get unless you have understood the person. If you knew nothing about Cecil, you could still enter into that world, but it would be much harder. Knowing Cecil enriches his work because there is more to Cecil than just the paintings. He was a philosopher and his philosophy, his way of life, what he taught us and his painting were all one. I think that's what makes him a great human being and why what he thought and taught and felt and his painting are so important for now, for the future.

Perhaps the one thing that has had the most long-term effect for me, or my art, is that he taught me the importance of vulnerability. Although vulnerability is a horrid thing, within the horrid is your source of creativity which is your source of happiness. We have to move on and you only truly move on through being vulnerable. Let's say you're miserable, you feel uncomfortable, then it's very reassuring to know that if you stay with that vulnerability, you will find the seeds of your happiness. That's a wonderful lesson to have learnt from Cecil. That lesson was re-emphasised when I met my psychoanalyst who's a Jungian. I asked him once what he thought was his greatest attribute. After a long pause, he said, 'My ability to suffer,' but he wasn't somebody who was miserable; it was a reaffirmation of the same thing Cecil had talked about.

MARIA LANCASTER

Maria Lancaster studied painting at Central College of Art and Design. She researched Eastern and Western painting techniques at the University of London Institute of Education. She has taught traditional painting techniques, painting from the imagination and a Zen approach to drawing, in which she has incorporated some of Cecil Collins' drawing methods. She lives in London where she continues to paint, runs workshops and exhibits her work.

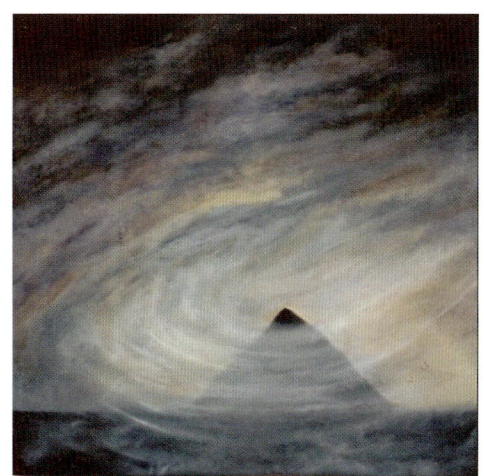

Maria Lancaster
The Mountain
1974
122 x 122cm

It's very strange the whole thing with Cecil Collins because I heard of him long before I met him. I fell in love with a sculptor while I was doing my foundation course at Hammersmith and I wanted to go on to Chelsea School of Art. Chelsea was my first choice because I lived in Chelsea. Central was my second because I had visited it and didn't like the look of it, but this sculptor had been a student there and he said, 'No, no, you must put Central as your first choice.' I said, 'Why? Chelsea is so much nicer.' 'Cecil Collins is there.' 'And who is Cecil Collins?' 'He's a Sufi.' 'How do you know?' 'I don't know how I know. I just know.'

I'd been with the Sufi teacher Mrs Tweedie since I was twenty-one after Slobodan had discovered her so that was one signal. The other signal came during the foundation course. I had done lots of tiny paintings of dreamy subjects and one of the tutors said, 'You must meet Cecil Collins.' Gosh, I thought, here he comes again. Who is this Cecil Collins?

Amazingly, I got into Central and I asked some of the first years there, 'Is there someone called Cecil Collins teaching here?' Nobody knew as he had nothing to do with the first-year students. Then in my second or third term there was a huge political meeting about part-time staff being phased out. The head of the art department and the art tutors were all present and suddenly this old man got up and spoke perfect sense about what art should be and I thought, this must be Cecil Collins. He walked out of the meeting early and I followed him. He went up the back stairs and I followed him up to the top floor. We just looked at each other in silence, then I said, 'Are you Cecil Collins?' He said, 'Yes'. I told him that I was doing painting in the first year and that I loved what he'd said at the meeting and that was it. He told me that he was a tutor for the second- and third-year students.

When I came into my second year, I worked in the room where Cecil spent a lot of his time as part-time tutor and we really got to know each other then. I think he came in one day a week. He would sit down and look at whatever I was doing and we'd talk. He'd tell me all sorts of funny things. I think he thought I needed 'joke therapy' and that I was depressed. He had this wonderful story about the Brontës. 'When I was a very young man,' he said, 'I looked into the eyes of a very old woman who had known the Brontës and asked her, 'What were they like?' and she said, 'Ooh, them young girls in them hats.' He had all sorts of stories. He was always telling me about what he was reading and had I read this, had I read that. He introduced me to Isak Dinesen and he was very taken with a book of psychic discoveries from behind the Iron Curtain. I remember going back to Slobodan saying, 'He's only interested in psychic things.' That was my mistaken impression at first. Of course, Cecil had no idea I was involved with Mrs Tweedie.

There were lots of jokes. I don't know how the edible orchestra began, but Cecil must have said something like, 'I always think musical instruments make such wonderful dishes.' His all-time favourites were the Dumpling Double Bass and the Apple Crumble Horn. Another was Timpani Trifle. We invented a whole orchestra. Every week he'd come and say, 'I've thought of a new one.' Some others were Baked Bassoons, Barbecued Drums, Braised Horns, Candied Clarinets, Chilled Cello, Clavecin en Croute, Contre Basse en Chemise, Curried Castanets, Flute Fricasse, Fried Flutes, Grilled Guitars, Grilled Harpsichord, Horn on the Hob, Hornburgers, Ice Cream Cornets, Marinated Mandolins, Organzola, Piano Pie, Pickled Piccolos, Sackbutt Stew, Soused Bagpipes, Stewed Harps, Stewed Recorders, Tarte à la Trompette, Trumpet Terrine, Trumpets on Toast, Viola Vol-au-Vent, Violins St Jacques, Woodwind Salad. It could have gone on forever. Sometimes Cecil invented more complex musical dishes such as La Mayonnnaise (French National Anthem much loved by fish and salads), Risotto in B Flat, Fugue Brulée, Symphony in F 'Le Soufflé' and Poached Piano with Boiled Bassoons and Creamed Altos.

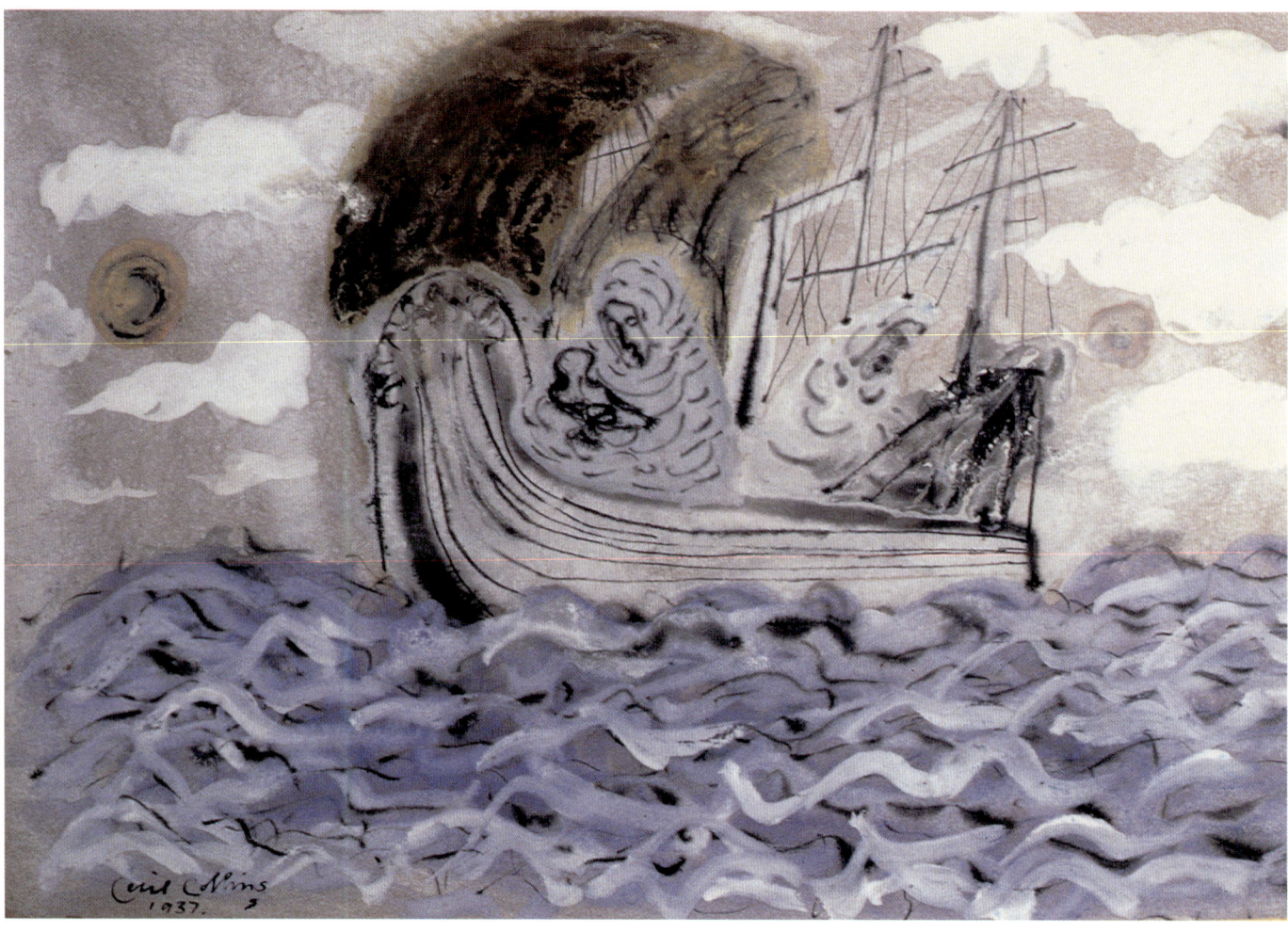

Cecil Collins
The Voyage
1937
Gouache and ink on paper
20.3 x 25.4cm

One day I told Slobodan about Cecil and said, 'You really must meet him,' and Slobodan said, 'Well, ask him round to Tite Street,' which is where we lived, at the top of my grandmother's house. Elisabeth and Cecil came to tea. I think they brought Robert Temple with them, an unusual American scholar who'd written a book about Sirius. They came, they had tea and after they'd left Slobodan said, 'When Mrs Tweedie gives her next lecture, we must tell them.' Eventually, Mrs Tweedie gave a lecture on *The Smile*. It was about the smile as a state of being; as an effect of the state of *samadhi*. Both Cecil and Elisabeth came to it. Mrs Tweedie showed slides of Khmer Buddhas from Angkor Wat and of *L'Inconnue de la Seine* and Leonardo's *Mona Lisa*.

At the end of the lecture Slobodan said, 'Mrs Tweedie, come and meet Maria's teacher.' Mrs Tweedie turned to Elisabeth and said, 'Ah, my dear, you are Maria's teacher. I've heard so much about you.' She completely ignored Cecil. She must have wanted to set something straight or to give Elisabeth the credit that was due her. In fact, Mrs Tweedie was impressed with Cecil and, as time went on, more people from Central, like Michael Chaitow, came to her. When Cecil began to teach at the City Lit, some people from Mrs Tweedie's group went to his classes and reported what went on. She then became very interested in Cecil and began to send people to him. Mrs Tweedie said that Cecil was one of the masters her Sufi teacher had told her she would meet when she came back to the West.

Cecil had a great role in teaching me the techniques of painting. He introduced me to the writings of Max Doerner and to the fan brush and I learned a lot of glazing techniques from him. Cecil used to say, 'Armies march on their stomachs and paintings march on their grounds,' meaning that it was important to prime the painting in the right way. At that time, I was doing oil paintings of landscapes and I'd done one of a mountain. Cecil came into the room and turned it upside down and said, 'Now let's see what's really going on here.' I was disconcerted by him seeing it that way. I did lots of pretty paintings of landscapes and mountains and he said, 'You've got to be careful not to get too busy with the icing on the cake.' It was good advice.

Cecil did two workshops at Central. I think one was to do with colour and the other with imaginative painting. I felt that he had incorporated certain Zen Buddhist techniques and, of course, the diluting of the inks is a Chinese painting technique. In one of the imaginative painting workshops, which lasted all day, he enforced silence throughout, even during the lunch break. At the time, my rebellious streak balked at this, though now I realise it was a very important part of the experience.

Cecil once told me a story about a Chinese painter who'd done an enormous mural in an emperor's palace. The emperor asked the painter where he lived, whereupon the painter walked into a tiny door in his painting and disappeared and was never seen again. I saw a lot of Cecil at that time and became very close to him. Sometimes he would bring in a very small painting, exquisitely painted, and he would pull it out of his pocket and say: 'This is something I've been working on.'

It was during my second year, in 1974, that I got into trouble at Central. The progress committee told me I might not be able to stay on and might not get my degree. I had to show my work to all the heads of department who had to decide whether I should be kept on. They all got into a tremendous argument. Someone said, 'Her paintings are religious,' while others disagreed and complained about their small size. In the end, it was all right and I got my degree, but it was a challenging time and Cecil dropped me. I think it was to protect me, but it was very painful. I felt very alone, but Mrs Tweedie was watching with interest. She said, 'I knew you'd go far when I heard you had trouble.' In Mrs Tweedie's opinion, it was spiritually very good if anyone had trouble. She was trying to help me; she was being kind.

I had a dream in which Cecil called me Pinocchio. I understand why! I obviously gave him a hard time because I was thinking silly things like, you're not spiritual. I know someone better than you. Mrs Tweedie, and, I prefer Slobodan's paintings to yours. Slobodan had initiated me into painting and was my inspiration so there was perhaps a slight clash between the ancient painting tradition as represented by Slobodan and Cecil's modern, innovative way.

Meanwhile, Central was trying to get rid of Cecil who was planning his strategy to take them on. There was so much negativity towards him. It was extraordinary because, in the end, the head of department left, or died, I forget which, and the principal left so there was a clean sweep. They'd thought Cecil was a dotty, airy-fairy old man. They'd no idea. I think they had a shock because Cecil uncovered a lot of corruption in the department. One of the part-time teachers, Colin Cina, undertook to look into why there was so little money for part-time tutors in the budget and discovered the misallocation of funds.

In a way, I think Cecil as a painter was one thing and Cecil as a teacher was something quite different. Cecil was a master at what he was doing. That was his work, pure energy. He could see clearly: when somebody was depressed, when they were hiding something. He said to me, 'You've got things to paint now, but will you have anything to paint about when you're sixty?' It made me think, gosh, that's a thought, I don't know. Then I did stop painting, but I kept in touch with him. One day he said, 'I hear you haven't been painting.' I said, 'I've given it up. I'm really more interested in spiritual life.' He said, 'When I was with Ouspensky, I went though a phase like that. I didn't paint for years. I renounced it.' Cecil told me so many things. Once he said, 'There is the little happiness and the great happiness. In order to reach the little happiness, there are tears that are hot, but there are tears that are cool and these have to do with the joy of the great happiness.' He used to say lots of absurd things too. He loved quoting from *Alice in Wonderland* and *Alice Through the Looking Glass* where 'painting in oils' turned into 'fainting in coils'.

Cecil was very interested in Greece. I think he'd had an exhibition there. At Central, he once showed the film *Electra* with Irene Papas in the title role. It was in Greek. I remember an amazing scene where Electra, on hearing that her brother Orestes has died, lets out this incredible, almost operatic cry. It was an amazing sound. Cecil said that the actors in Greek traditional theatre trained for years. They had to go through voice training because they were working with only the natural acoustics of the amphitheatre. He gave a fantastic talk about catharsis which is really what he was doing in his teaching work. He was very keen on the whole idea of catharsis. Cecil said Spain and Greece were the places where they understood his work. I don't think I heard him talk much about Chinese or Zen things, except once he mentioned how wonderful it was that there was such a word as *suchness* in Zen.

Cecil loved music and he did a lot for us musically at Central. He adored Nadia Boulanger who was a great music teacher. He arranged for some of us to go and hear her, but she was ill so we heard Yehudi Menuhin instead who suddenly stood on his head in front of us all. It was a fantastic moment. Cecil used to talk a lot about Chopin. He liked the minor keys in Chopin's music and their delicate quality. One subject on which we didn't agree was Stockhausen. He insisted we went to this concert and I hated it. The day after I told him, 'Piccadilly Circus was like peace after that concert.' I think he thought that I was a bit of a stick in the mud. Segovia we did agree on. He had this lovely way of describing Segovia: 'He's a genius, but he doesn't show off. He occasionally pulls it out of his sleeve and you see a little flash of it.'

Cecil's imagery was always very vivid. Once in the studio at Central, the student in the cubicle next to me was flicking black and white oil paints at a canvas with a brush. A lot of the time the stuff would fall on the floor and Cecil walked across and imitated skidding, saying, 'It's like bird droppings at the bottom of a cage, isn't it?'

Another funny incident occurred when Slobodan had his first exhibition in Chelsea Town Hall. Slobodan asked the receptionist, 'Did anyone come in?' 'Only an old tramp,' was the reply. Slobodan wondered who this could be and then found that he'd signed his name in the visitors' book; it was Cecil. He was probably in his old mac and with a packet of butterscotch in his pocket. Butterscotch was a great thing with him.

Cecil was instrumental in getting us students to go to lectures at the Royal Overseas League; some of them were absolutely fascinating. He and Elisabeth belonged to the Society for Spiritual and Psychological Studies which was run by a wonderful lady called Alison Barnard. There was a marvellous talk there once by Laurens van der Post on the 'shadow'. It was a one-day seminar and Mrs Tweedie came and was very inspired. In a way, her circle and Cecil's overlapped. After one of these talks, I bumped into Elisabeth at a bus stop in Piccadilly. It was just a little while before Slobodan and I got married so it was rather strange when she suddenly said, 'I must tell you something. Never marry an artist.' 'Why do you say this?' I said, rather cheekily adding, 'You married one,' and she said, 'Yes, but I know there was reason why I married one.' So I said, 'Why shouldn't I marry one?' and she said, 'It will interfere with your work.' However, I did go and marry one. I don't know if it interfered with my work, I don't think it did, but the marriage didn't last.

We got married in February. We had an Eastern Orthodox ceremony at the Serbian Orthodox Church in Lancaster Road and the reception was at my grandmother's house. It was lovely. Elisabeth and Cecil were among the guests. They lived quite near us, in Paultons Square in Chelsea. I think Cecil quite enjoyed my grandmother's house. He found it rather curious and romantic.

One of the last times I saw Cecil was at the Royal College of Art. I'd heard that he was giving a talk there so I went and found him sitting in one of the seats and we had a sort of hug. He gave this extraordinary talk about how one had to be alone as an artist. It was something I was very much going through then and it was very curious, but I felt that I got a lot of help from that talk.

I can't remember if it was after he died or not that I had a dream in which he was talking about the Way of the Warrior and he looked right into my eyes. I could feel his eyes going straight into me and I realised that I was beginning to be much more interested in working with the unconscious and with his teaching. He gave me something in that dream.

CECIL COLLINS

Notes for his talk before the screening at Central School of Art of the award winning film, *Elektra*, 1962, directed, scripted and produced by Cacoyannis, b. 1922, prominent Greek Cypriot film-maker. The film starring Irene Papas in the title role was based on the eponymous play by the Greek tragedian Euripides, (480 BC – 406 BC). Cacoyannis is best known for his 1964 film, *Zorba the Greek*, (Alexis Zorba) based on the eponymous novel by Nikos Kazantzakis, 1946, starring Anthony Quinn in the title role.

We are falling victims to meaninglessness. We have lost the power to identify with life. In the ancient world, Hell was precisely a place like that; a place of empty ghosts, a place of shadows.
It results in a slave state, without inner content.
The younger generation feel a deep hunger, which is unfulfilled by modern education. The young are offered only politics as a solution to life.
We are surrounded by vast quantities of mere information; quantities we cannot possibly assimilate. But our emotional life is left quite uneducated by this system.
What we need to fill this gap is real knowledge: the knowledge that was called Tradition which is universal knowledge.
Art is important precisely because it was not born yesterday.
In the Greek plays we see ourselves. They are ceremonies, rituals, a cleansing or purification. They assist us to become a real, that is, an archetypal man.
Purification leads to freedom, to real culture, to life.
The theme of the plays is Exile and Return.
Man is a sleepwalker. He does not know who he is. He does terrible deeds, and does not know it. The plays are designed to provoke *anemnesis*, reawakening, the remembrance of self-knowledge; 'Know thy self.'
The function of the play is to dis-identify the soul from this unreal life by the shock of purification, *catharsis*. This provokes a judgement (*crisis*), a turning round (*metania*), the birth of a new consciousness.
The purpose of art is Peace; the harmonisation of the soul.
The audience sat in complete silence before the play; a silence which was a gathering together, a concentration. Such a silence forms a threshold to the archetypal world.

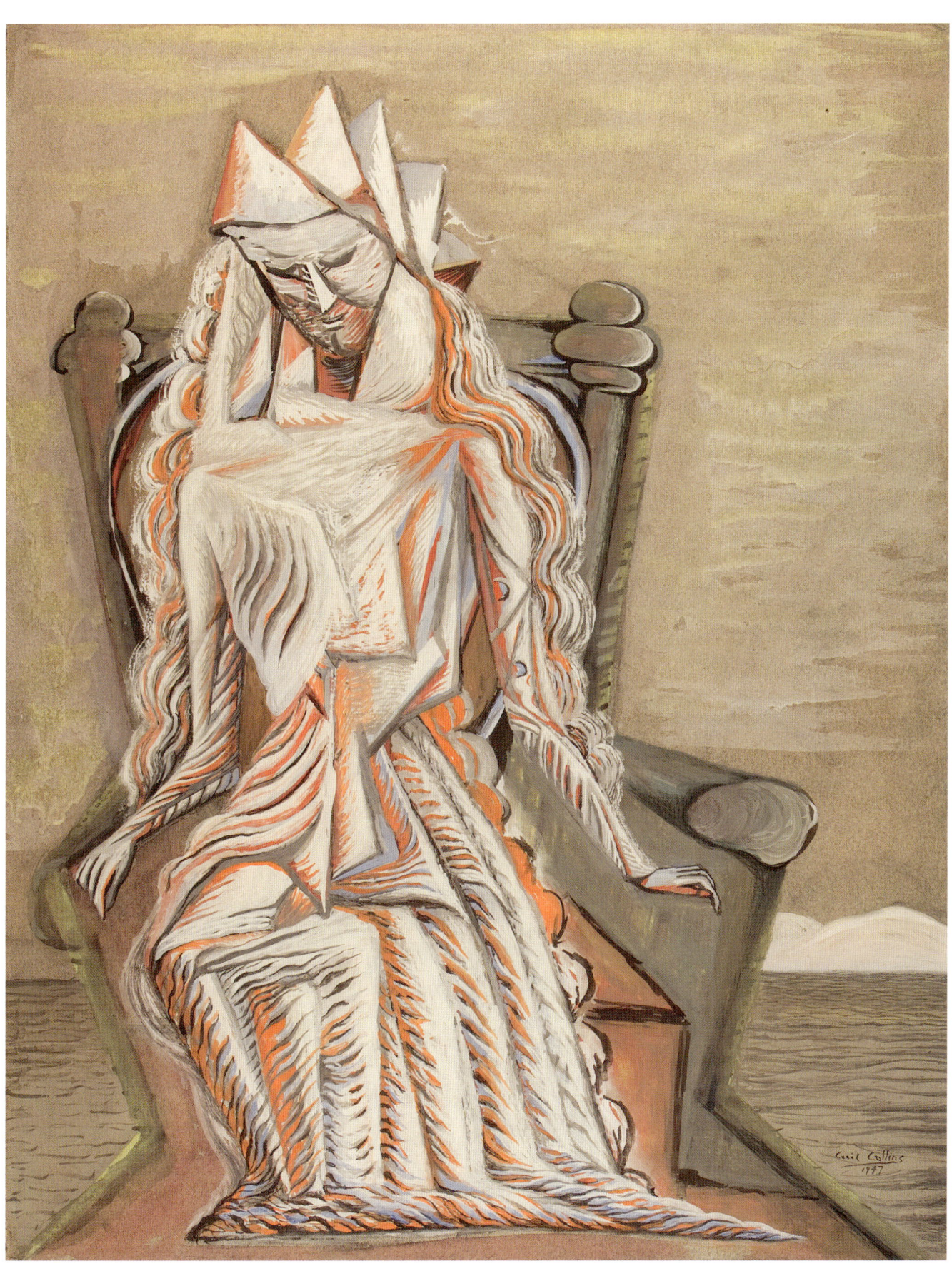

Cecil Collins
Enthroned Figure
1947
Gouache on paper
40 x 31cm

DANNY LANE

Danny Lane lives his art. At his studio, he creates spontaneously on an industrial scale with his team of diversely skilled artisans. For twenty-five years, Lane has continuously created intimate and monumental scale works in steel, glass and wood.

I came to the UK to work with Patrick Reyntiens, the stained glass artist. I'd already been experimenting on a very small craft level in America and I wanted to take it further. I heard about a school called Burleighfield that Patrick had in Beaconsfield, Buckinghamshire, and managed to get there in 1975 when I was twenty. I also did a summer course at the Ruskin School of Art in Oxford. I studied with Patrick for eight months and was going to stay on and work with him, but his school fell apart because of financial difficulties. I moved to London and studied at Byam Shaw for one year, then went to the Central School of Art which is where I connected with Cecil and entered his drawing class. I knew immediately that was it.

I followed Cecil's class intensely for the entire three years I was a student. I attended his City Lit classes at the same time so I did several drawing classes a week, plus I had Cecil as my tutor. We could choose our tutors and I chose him. I was very fortunate. I received so much from Cecil and was deeply involved with him for four or five years. He was the only one of all of my teachers who said anything that rang true for me and made sense. Compared to the art world and its pundits, he was from another planet, a different age. Cecil was from the future. As he said, 'We're primitives of the new age.'

Cecil's training was incredibly disciplined. His drawing course would show you almost every conceivable mark that could be made with the utensils and the equipment that we were using. One of the things which has continued to open up and become richer for me over the decades is that he encouraged an almost playful mentality in his students. Get your hands and fingers busy doing things and your mind becomes totally engaged. Seven tones of ink, or eight, as in an octave, and all of the different marks we would make, the different ways in which we would hold the pen, the different tensions, things like that. When we were struggling so much with the tools, we forgot ourselves, became absorbed and were, therefore, free of ourselves. If you look at any artist or any culture, the most fertile period occurs in the struggle with the materials.

As a teacher, Cecil was unique because outside Eastern schools of teaching, there are very few courses or people able to describe this way of looking at things completely. A lot of traditions have had this very strict structure and process of teaching, such as doing scales in music, for instance. That structure has been completely lost in the West from the visual arts with the lack of focus on the craft of painting. People don't now put a great value on being able to draw something; they're all result driven. In traditional training, students would be encouraged to copy nature. When else does a person sit and look at a tree for a full day? Making art and studying nature are ways of knowing the world, participating in it. Unless you go to somewhere like the National Gallery and copy a painting, you have no idea what the artist went through until you try to recreate it yourself. It's a way of going into something and we have lost all of that. Cecil's drawing class predates the discovery of Mandelbrot's theory of fractal geometry and how we have that in us. It's not just copying nature; when we begin to create, we must be nature. So there is a yogic process in the training of an artist that is the diminishment of self and becoming a vehicle for something that needs to speak and be present in the world, to be seen and made manifest.

It was Cecil who introduced me to Mrs Tweedie. At the Central I was having a very hard time, ending up in tears with the critiques I'd received from the rationalist tutors. In the end Cecil said, 'I can't help you with these things, but here's somebody you might go and see,' and he gave me her address because it was more a life problem than an art one. Mrs Tweedie showed me there are other ways to approach living and life.

I've never felt satisfied with doing things by halves. I like total immersion and to give myself completely to what I'm doing. I'm only discovering now that the day to day, in a sense, is sacred and there are many layers in that. I think Cecil is the person who best described the act of creativity and the meaning of being an artist as a form of worship or meditation. For me, as an artist, that is my true form. It's a way of life and, ultimately, it was Mrs Tweedie who made that very clear to me in the one conversation we had. I always felt shy in her presence and also within the context of the group, but one day she asked me how I was doing, how was meditation going. I said, 'I don't meditate when I'm not here,' and she said, 'You may meditate; you may not. You may progress, but maybe you won't. That's okay.' I felt so relieved and said, 'I make art and I'd really very much like to show you what I do,' and she said, 'Bring me some photographs.' I ran off to get them and raced back because it was so important for me. Mrs Tweedie looked at my photographs and said that she wanted to say something which she'd prefer to say to the whole group because there were a lot of other artists involved and maybe this would cover a few people. She told me that it was in my art that I surrender and that I must do it with complete commitment and conviction. Then she said, 'You may drink; you may smoke; you may

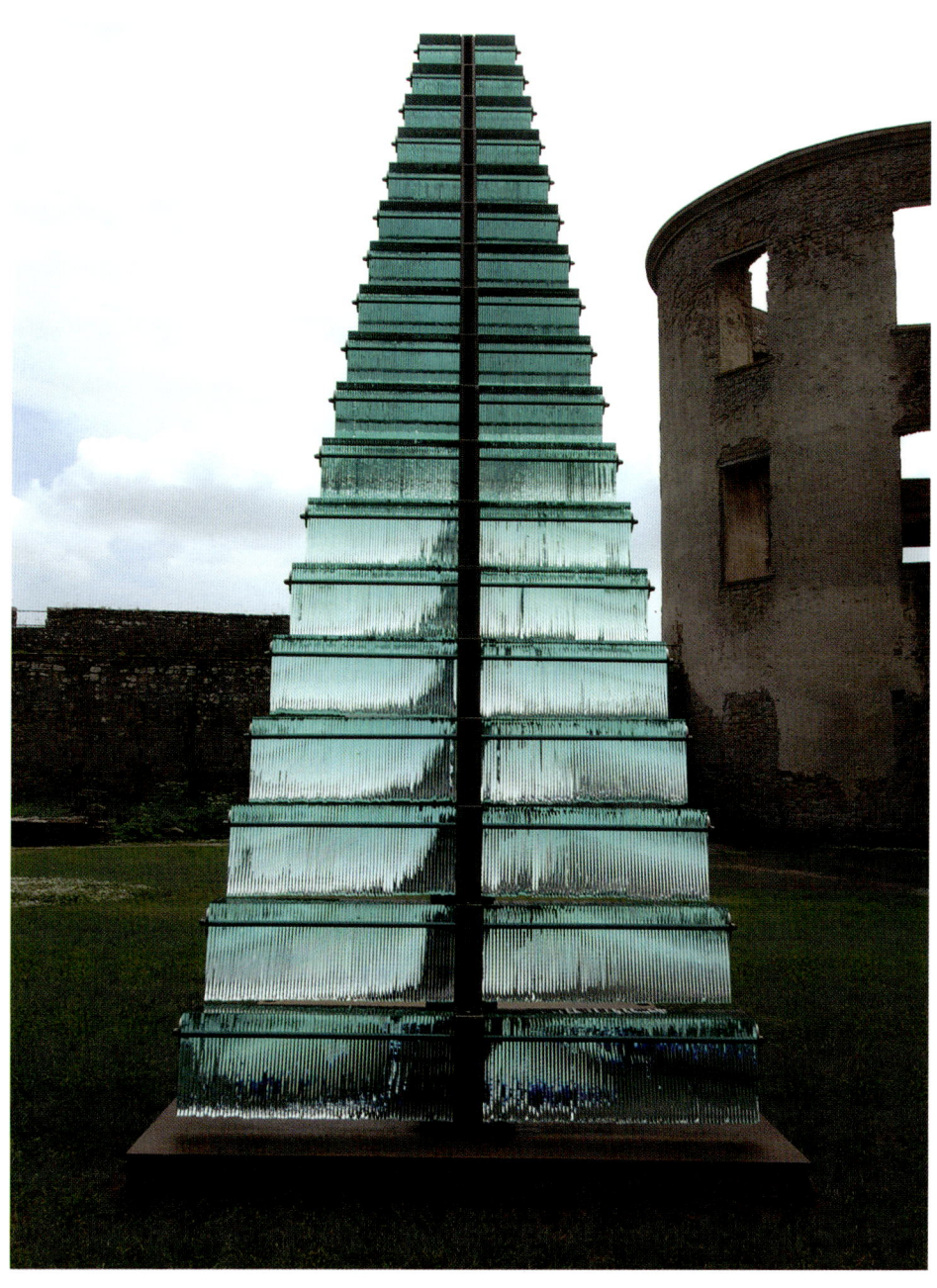

Danny Lane
Stairway
2005
Glass, steel
600 x 190 x 418cm
Borgholm Castle,
Sweden

coax all of these things along in the right direction. Occasionally, you've got to do an almost violent act in opening something up or making something happen, but then there's also the day to day, just keep it moving along in the right direction.

It was mainly young women students who went to Cecil's classes at the Central and he had a very good relationship with them because his process was quite a feminine, intuitive one, though Cecil himself had a balance between his masculine and feminine sides. There were very few male students and none of them stayed long. It was somewhat different at the City Lit because the people there tended to be mature students.

Like any good teacher, Cecil kept things from getting too serious. He had this severity and intensity and yet suddenly he'd flip into a very light sense of humour; he had such a good wit about him. If you value your teacher's input, naturally you sit up straight; that's quite common in any training, but I think it's important not to get too caught up in the role of artist. That's where humour helps. You have to laugh at yourself and see that being an artist is quite a big folly, yet it's terribly serious too. I remember one time at Central a young woman was chewing gum in class and Cecil said to her, 'This may work better for you if you don't chew gum,' and she said, 'I always chew gum.' 'Well, maybe when you're making love to your boyfriend you're chewing gum,' he said and he meant it quite humorously, but she was totally upset and stormed out.

I've been concerned a great deal with, 'Am I running off on my own ego trip with what I'm doing? Is this an issue of self expression or am I being a vehicle of spirit?' Inflation is the biggest threat for any human being who begins to make a little progress, so self-criticism and reality checks are extremely important. The key Cecil gave was in his sense of humour. If your spirit has humour, and is vivacious, if you're faithful and obedient to the subject, then it's going to kick you up the ass, wake you up and remind you it doesn't hurt to fall down occasionally. We're human; we're not divine, although we might have a bit of it in us and that's the Fool.

Another thing I remember is Cecil picking up a drawing and, although his eyes weren't that bad, he'd pull it so close that you would see he was looking, not at the drawing, but at the line. He was reading the energy in the line, the experience of the human being in the trace the line leaves. There is a tentativeness, a willingness to discover what is contained in a drawn line. It's as if the line has an energy that is beyond the basic dumb materials of which it was made. One becomes more developed and layered, but the need to keep that openness and freshness goes on. Other times he'd be sitting in his corner at the back of the class and suddenly he'd say the name of the person he was in touch with or tell them to pay attention. Sometimes he had his students keep silence the whole day. It was quite extraordinary for all of us to go off and have lunch and keep

have women. Things may happen, but you make your work.' That was a very strong imperative for me. I'm quite keen on meditation and I need a bit of stillness outside of this continuous activity. I don't have much quiet time. I used to be able to go to Chartres Cathedral and sit there in the morning and get bathed and cleaned in that light. Now I want to get those feelings into my work.

Cecil had a way of knowing things, but I don't think he would ever have forced an issue on anyone or have said, 'This is the way to look at things.' His teaching was like animal husbandry. It was shepherding. I see it here in my workshop, now that my role is to silent through an entire day, focusing on this containment.

When I was with Cecil, I was trying very hard and took it all quite seriously, but at the same time I smoked dope and enjoyed drinking so in some ways I was also having a lot of fun. I suppose I've always been very earthed in that sense. I talked to Cecil about marijuana and stuff and he said, 'Ah, you mean aiding and abetting.' Then he added, 'Of course artists have done this for centuries.'

Through Cecil, I learnt that the musical connection was extremely important and it has continued to be for me. I also learned a lot from Patrick Reyntiens and from looking at medieval architecture and seeing it as frozen music which tied in with Cecil's discipline of working in controlled tones of ink. If the piano isn't tuned, there's not a clear note and you can't have a muddy note. It's like people mixing colours from different tubes of paint that have nothing to do with one another, whereas the discipline of working with a limited palette of three colours, which we learned with Cecil, that's where one would get the glow, the inner light in the painting.

Cecil's approach to things allowed a certain element of risk. In the process you wouldn't control the image; you would allow it to emerge. Another thing that Cecil spoke about frequently was of meeting the viewer halfway. If you spell everything out and the painting is completely literal, nobody's making any discoveries or connections for themselves so it's a question of how many clues do you give, how hard do you work to finish a piece?

One time we were talking about the injury we can do to ourselves in the life process. Cecil said in the early days it was as though he had a sword and injured himself a great deal with it, then he learned that he had a garden and he used the sword to protect the entrance to his garden. That's something for everyone no matter how old they are, but particularly when you're young and have a lot of aptitude, energy and vitality. You express yourself; you're effervescent and then the world shoots you down or limits you. You can go through a process of self-criticism, injury and doubt, especially when you think of yourself in relationship to what your peers or critics say. One of Cecil's points about self-regarding was that it is remarkable how little other people look at us; we only think they do.

I'm more an admirer of Cecil's drawing than I am of his painting. He knew so much that maybe it affected his ability to be free or intuitive. A big part of his work was as a teacher and what he brought to it and his paintings are part of his teaching.

There were two occasions during my time at the Central when Cecil was supposed to retire and the school was trying to get rid of him. There were, let's say, some 890 students at the Central then and I got 879 signatures in support of Cecil. We flattened them. There was no way that Central could get rid of him then. John Allitt, who taught art history, was a big supporter and, of course,

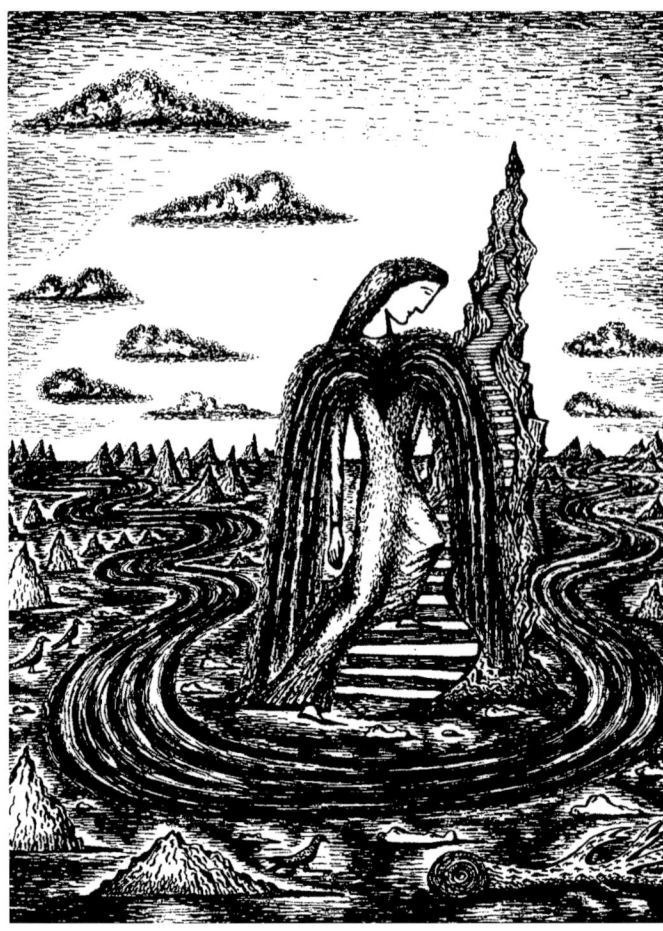

Cecil Collins
The Gates of Silence
1944
Ink on paper
Illustration to a poem by Wrey Gardiner

Patrick Reyntiens who was Head of Fine Art there. They understood Cecil down to the bones. It was Patrick who made the stained glass windows to Cecil's design in Basingstoke.

When I left art college, I had this idea to work with glass again and to make everyday objects. I forgot about being a painter and embarked on a whole different route. Then in the 1980s I fell in with avant-garde furniture where I developed things like the glass chair and then a standard lamp made of glass pieces shish-kebabbed onto a big long screw that had been forged. It's like a column running to heaven that never quite gets there. When I did that piece in 1985, it was bought by museums and was apparently quite radical in design. I was taking the energy, the contradiction of breaking glass, which hadn't been explored before. My work was presented in the design area at the furniture fair in Milan which was a publicity jet stream. Without realising it, I became one of the foremost designers. It just happened that way. My stuff's probably all over the world. It's important to be known in order to get the freedom to do what you want to do.

A coffee table I made for an Indian client was about three metres in length and I basically rendered a ribbon of steel and put a huge plate of glass on top. As the steel heated, you could force it into shape. The twist in steel was like doing one of the gestures from Cecil's class, a line drawing in metal, but taking a month to do. You're drawing in 3D with these materials.

I remember Mrs Tweedie asking me at one point to bring her a piece of the glass that I work with and she said something quite interesting. 'This colour of green is almost on another level of consciousness; it exists with its opposite.' These two colours, orange and green, are very interesting together and are something beyond our comprehension, but we might feel it.

What happens with glass is alchemical. I've been working towards the containment within one studio and within one person of a big field of different materials and understandings that are in opposition and in parallel with one another. There's a whole life's work in this. I'm a painter by nature and with some pieces which are big walls of glass I've brought a drawn element back on that scale, because these pieces are all structural and it's bringing this quality of light into modern architecture.

I think the overall impetus of my work has a lot to do with Cecil and Mrs Tweedie. They opened so many doors for approaching the subject and knowing the subject itself. Cecil always said in order to create art, we need to know our subject, know our materials, our means and know ourselves.

The writer Coomaraswamy talks in one of his essays about aesthetic shock, this incredibly powerful impact which knocks the person's mind out long enough for them to get something else. I think that's a very interesting idea. You felt this seeing and perceiving beauty, this excruciating bliss at Tweedie's and at Cecil's. This seeing something that was so beautiful, you could only cry. It's like grace, something touching you for a moment and then you think, I can get on now with my job.

After leaving the Central, I saw Cecil maybe once in a blue moon, but I did run into him at one of his exhibitions at d'Offay's and I gave him photographs of what I'd done. 'You're not painting any more,' he said, 'You're drawing with light.' Then, years later, I saw him at his Retrospective at the Tate when he was very ill. I approached him and greeted him, and because he was in a wheelchair there was nothing to do but get down on my knees. I held his hand and said, 'Cecil, I want to thank you for everything that you've done for me and for all of us. The doors you have opened have been amazing.'

Cecil Collins
Promised Land
1942
Watercolour
35.5 x 53.3cm

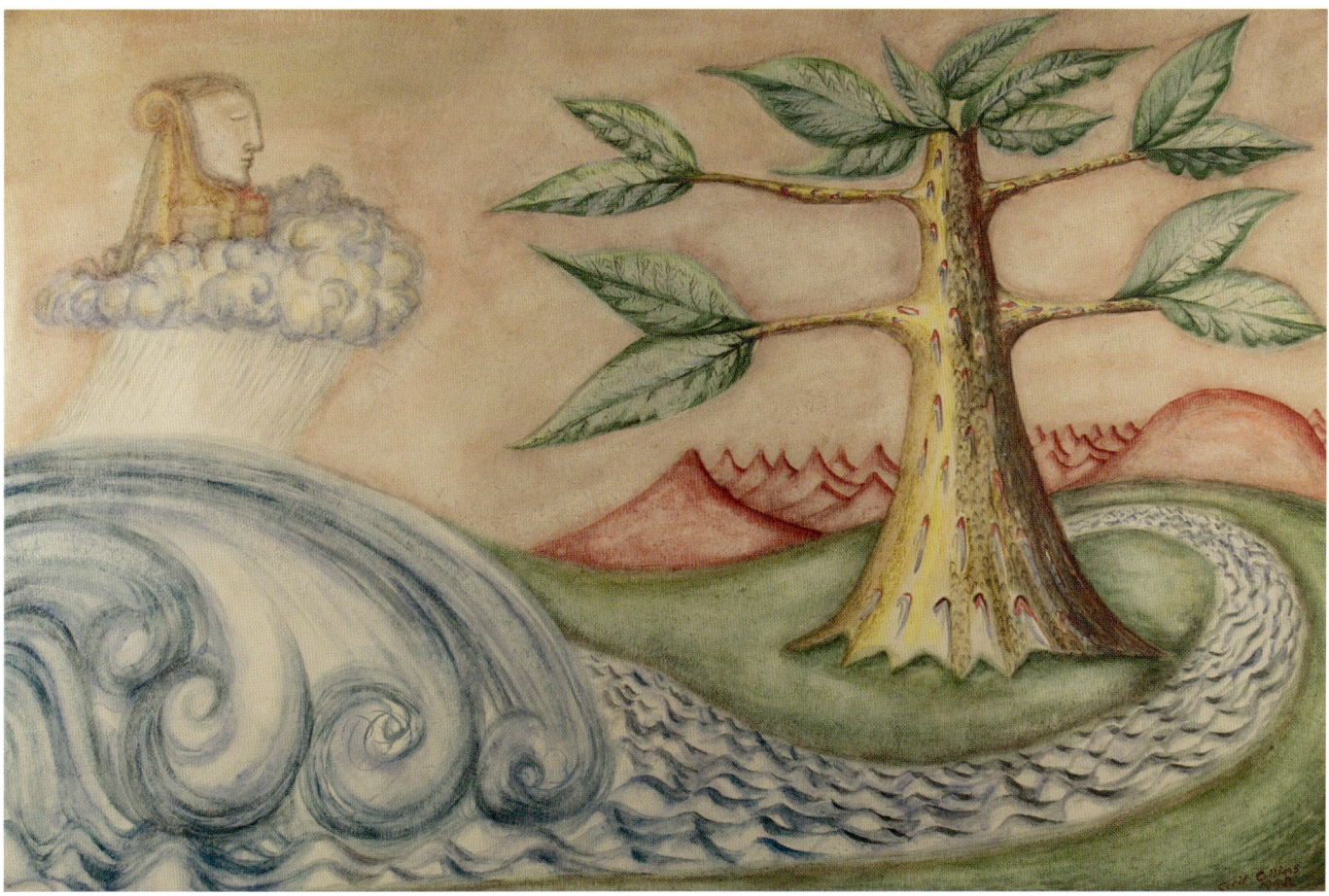

SHELLEY LATHAM

Born in Johannesburg, South Africa in 1950, graduated with distinction from JHB College of Art (1969 – 1971). She arrived in the UK in 1973 and worked as a fashion model until 1983. She studied with Cecil Collins from 1977 at the City Lit and married Andy Barrs in 1988. They have two children, Luke and Tayah, and live on the outskirts of Bath. Shelley sings with an a cappella group and continues to paint. Together she and Andy set up charities as they see a need.

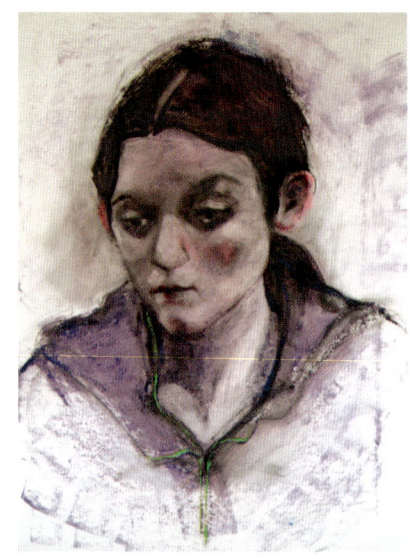

Shelley Latham
Tara
2007
Oil on paper
70 x 102cm

I'd gone to art school in South Africa where I'd done commercial art. I worked in advertising for a year or so and decided it wasn't for me. When somebody comes up with a really good storyline, it can be fantastic, but I didn't like trying to sell a product I didn't believe in. In London I'd been fashion modelling, but lots of things had changed in my life and there was something very big missing. I realised I needed to start doing some drawing again.

I was going out with someone who was at art school and he said, 'There's this person Cecil Collins teaching at the City Lit. Everybody says that he is extraordinary and has a unique method of teaching. You must go to him,' so I went along in 1977 and enrolled. It meant queuing for miles at four in the morning. If you were within the number they allowed at the City Lit, you got in.

I remember coming along to the first class and doing these very slick drawings. Although I hadn't done any for ages, I could still draw or so I thought. Cecil came and looked at my drawings which I thought were in proportion and looked quite stylish. He just flicked through them. 'Mmmm,' he said, 'bit of work you've got to do here. You've got a long way to go.' I was taken aback because I thought my drawing looked better than that of the student next to me, but I was there to learn and to discover so that feeling passed. It was the old story; when the student is ready, the teacher will find him or her. It was absolutely right for me. Cecil was a life teacher to me. I've always felt that he gave me another view on life and allowed me to reach an inner self that I hadn't previously been able to tap into. Although I might have had some inkling, I didn't know where to find what I was seeking.

Cecil was quite fixed in his dismissal of the way the world was going and of what he didn't think was right about it. I dare say he must have wondered what I was doing at the City Lit as I was still a model and in that world. When you arrived in his class, he always asked us to leave our baggage outside. In a way, there was quite a dilemma for me trying to reconcile this inner and outer self. It was very much about the discovery of how to express that inner world.

A lot of Cecil's classes were very ritualistic. In some you'd spend three quarters of the time walking round the classroom lighting candles or performing some other ritual and maybe doing only seven or eight drawings. The atmosphere was such that you felt part of something important that was going on. I don't think I ever stood back and thought, this feels odd. I loved doing the movement to music and then going back and drawing. I always particularly liked the Rachmaninov he played and *The Swan* by Sibelius, also the beginning of Wagner's *Parsifal*. The note that goes up and up is just beautiful.

Cecil was so strict about things and one quaked in his presence. If he raised an eyebrow at your drawing, you thought, Oh God, but I suppose I was looking for praise from the teacher, as one does. He used to say, 'Get the little man off your shoulders; you're not here to try and make a good drawing. The drawing will come as a gift; it will come as a surprise; it will come despite you and it's only through endlessly pushing yourself, challenging yourself, practising, that your craft will be at your fingertips.'

Cecil used music and movement in many sessions and insisted that we should aim for response and empathy with the model and not simply copy. He was 'educating' us and told us that *educare* from the Latin, meant to lead out, to draw out the potential that lay within each of us. In the beginning, I found it really difficult. It was easy for me to move and to respond to the music, but I felt that in my drawing I didn't manage to make the marks which corresponded to my response to the music: a transference of energy onto the paper. That's what it was about, but it was really hard. The discipline was to break you down, not break you down personally, but break your attachment to copying, to an ego or to making a good painting.

I've always loved music and dancing. When I was a child, I wanted to be a dancer, but then I grew too tall. Also I lived on a farm in South Africa and nobody knew about contemporary dance so that idea went out of the window. At City Lit there were a couple of us that Cecil would often choose to interpret the music with movement and, like the child who wants to be the teacher's pet, I always really enjoyed being asked. It gave me confidence that my response to the music was something he felt was an important element that I could offer and which expressed what he was trying to say in the class. I also enjoyed it when he would ask two students to come in the centre and they'd move together as in a gavotte. You'd keep in harmony with each other in a give and take and that was a very powerful experience. Cecil wouldn't call it a dance; he'd talk about response. *Cortesia* was a word he frequently used; relating with courtesy. You were the movement part of the music he'd chosen which was often full of pain and longing. That yearning felt very appropriate with Cecil; the longing for wholeness, for connectedness, for love, for the experience of being loved and giving love. Sometimes I'd be moving and my heart would be aching, especially when music like *Parsifal* was played.

In Cecil's classes you learnt about respect, relationships, dance, sensitivity. For me, one of the most fantastic exercises was the shared painting experience: the learning to respect someone else's space, their marks, the silent conversation that would happen. This produced some of the best drawings which I've kept. It was a great way of learning how to interact with people. Every day I'm bulldozing my way with my own opinions, but I try to remind myself about this huge life lesson.

Cecil instructed us about rhythms and tones: the rhythms would be the length of lines, the tones were tone one to seven according to the density of the colour, tone one being black and tone seven being the lightest. He would create huge difficulty for us by asking us to use tone seven, the lightest, most delicate with position four on the instrument, which was held like a dagger, a strong jabbing position. All those contradictions were to break your resistance, to break your mindset, to open it out. In the timescale of the class you couldn't do a fully developed three-week study so we were much more spontaneous and quick.

We worked on rhythms, tones and also positions on the instruments; your arm, your wrist, your fingers all being an extension of the instrument. The dance was an expression of the music and mark making for a picture is equivalent to dancing to the notes of a piece of music. It has rhythms, breathing spaces; all come from the same source. If the music had rapid flute notes or fingers on the piano, in a dance you'd make rapid movements and in the drawing you'd interpret them as rapid marks. It was all tied together. Cecil would say, 'Hold,' and the model would hold the pose and we'd all draw. He asked lots of students to move to the music because it was a way of connecting everybody, drawing everybody into the music and into relationship. More often than not, he would ask the model to follow the student or sometimes the students followed the model. Everybody would be moving together. This created a sacred atmosphere; it felt inspiring.

We also spent a lot of time taking up the archetypal poses. These consisted of lying face down on the floor, then lying on your back with your arms out and moving through different positions, from the horizontal to the kneeling, to the half kneeling, to standing with arms crossed over your chest and finally with arms stretched open. That was another form of movement and by taking up these

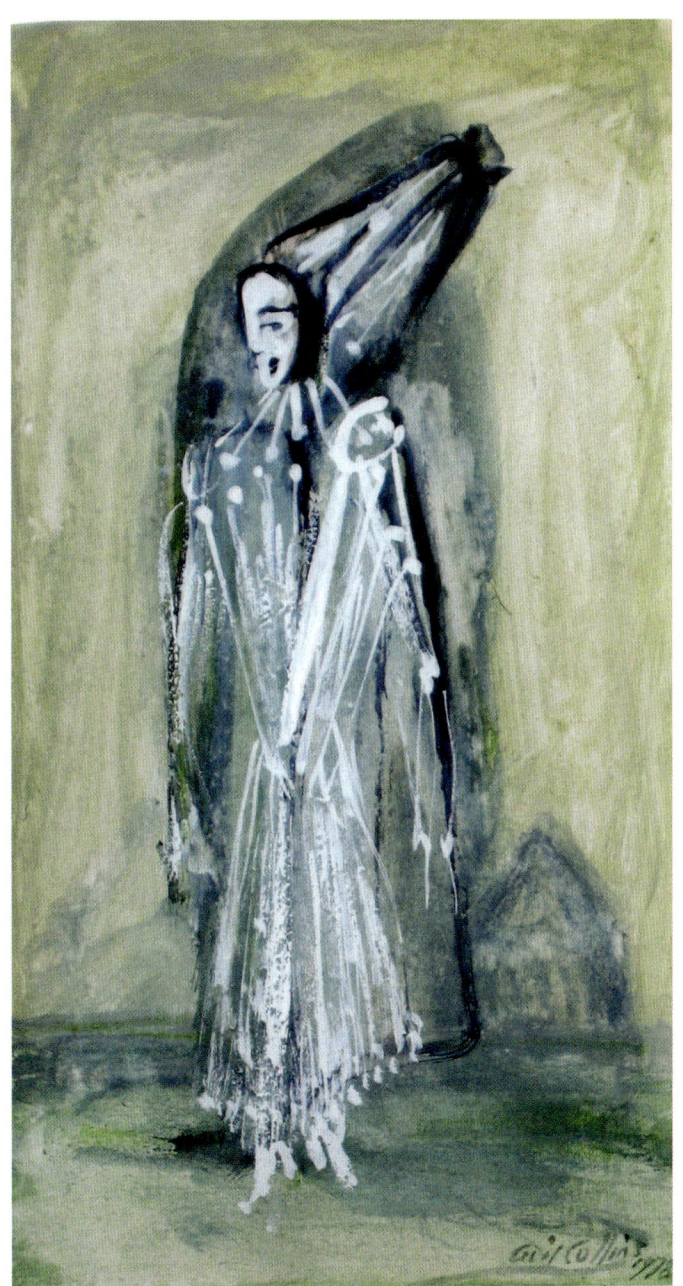

Cecil Collins
The Fool
1978
Gouache on paper
22 x 11.5cm

positions you were also discovering the different emotions, the different senses, the different feelings and the interconnectedness of everything. Depending on the position you were in, you were realising how the feeling in you changed from one of vulnerability to one of openness or of surrender. Those archetypal poses were hard to draw. You never had enough paper; drawings always spilled out over the edge so you ended up with chopped off arms and things like that.

In art school there's generally a lot of tutoring and criticising, but Cecil didn't do much of that. He come round occasionally, mainly at the end of the class, but not often. He would always choose the drawing that, if you'd had the chance, you would have thrown away. He'd say, 'That is a wonderful drawing,' or 'That's the drawing,' and then you'd have to go and pin it up on your wall. As sometimes happens in marriage, you discover that you have to live with something, or someone, for a long time to learn that what you once thought of as not great actually is great and worthwhile.

Cecil is probably the most influential teacher in my life. I feel honoured to have been a beneficiary of his progressive methods. Long ago, there was a clairvoyant lady in South Africa who used to read the crystal ball and I went to her a number of times. Later, when I was living in England, I went back to see her in South Africa and she said, 'I think you're ready to see into the ball.' She turned it around and showed me this man with round glasses, dark hair and a dark beard and said, 'This person is going to be very influential in your life.' I went back to England where I was already attending Cecil's classes and I kept looking for this person.

One evening while I was getting changed before going to see *The Eye of the Heart*, I was wondering who this person was. This was the third time I was going to see the film and I was still looking for this person with the dark beard and dark glasses. Suddenly I registered that in the film there was a photograph of Cecil as a young man standing against a wall with a dark beard and round glasses and this was the person I'd seen in the crystal ball. It had been taken a long time ago and, of course, the person who was teaching me now was an old hunchback with no beard and little hair. The person I was looking for was already in my life and I hadn't recognised it. We often don't see what's right in front of us. That was also, for me, a revelation about the interconnectedness of everything.

I suppose I may never sell many paintings and probably at some point I might just have a great big bonfire and burn everything, but I don't paint for someone else. I know that it's a vehicle through which I can nourish myself internally. The time I spend drawing and painting is actually my meditative time. Doing it enables me be a mother and housewife and look after the horses and walk the dogs and feel sustained. Soul food is what allows me to be more pleasant or more able to function in a good way and to become a nicer person.

Cecil took a sort of wicked delight in the perversity of life. His humour was never destructive, never against anybody. It wasn't a bar room kind of humour. It was affectionate, funny, elfin like. His eyes would twinkle out of his hunched-over form. I think maybe that's how he survived, how he was able to keep going with such courage when he was constantly not accepted by the art establishment. Sadly, for me, none of the books or the films about him show his impishness or what a naughty sprite he was. People seeing the film *The Eye of the Heart* who don't know anything about Cecil might find him very morose, very dark and depressing. These writers and film-makers are very serious about him because he is this spiritual painter of angels objecting to the mechanisation of things, but Cecil was not depressing to be around and his classes were anything but. Cecil's love for his students was not related to the individual, he wanted you to concentrate on yourself and your heart. He was a man of contradictions; there was the humour and the fun, but there was always this sense I had of his sadness as a result of not being accepted by the establishment and of his isolation because of this. It must have given him a feeling of vindication when Tate Britain hosted a retrospective of his work shortly before he died and finally acknowledged his wonderful contribution.

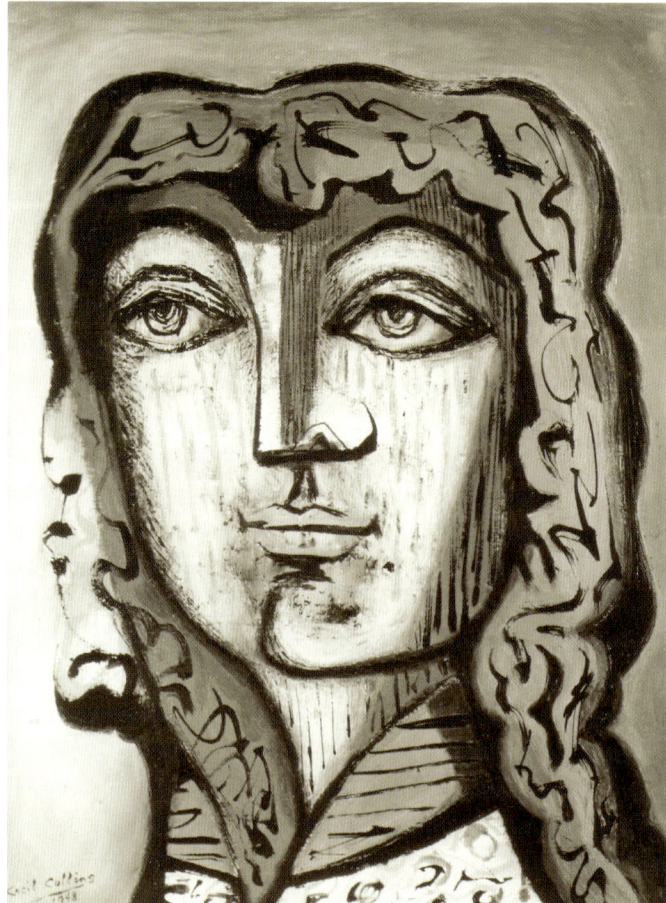

Cecil Collins
Head
1948
Oil on canvas
29 x 37cm

SYLVIE LEBOULANGER

Sylvie Leboulanger was born in France in 1960. She came to England to study art and attended Cecil's classes at the City Lit. She then studied and practised as a psychotherapist. After which she trained at the European School of Osteopathy, and has been practising as a cranial osteopath in north London for the past fifteen years.

At university in France I studied economics and sociology and then took a year's sabbatical working as a shepherd in the south of France. It was a time of being on my own and finding an inner stillness. I feel it was the foundation for my life's quest and meditation. Then I became a social worker and after that I went to England. I decided to stay and go to art college where I did drawing, painting and sculpture as well as pottery, mime and even clowning. I wanted to explore everything. Clowning was quite difficult, but mime was great. After two years I had to be very honest with myself: I knew the world of art was part of the answer, but it wasn't providing it for me at that institution. I had a meeting with the teachers at the art college and I remember they were very judgmental and asked me why I wanted to leave without completing the course. I told them, 'Because there is something that I'm searching for and it's not here.' They said, 'If you worked hard, you would find it. It doesn't happen after two years, it takes a lifetime.' I know this is true, but I was following my heart which was telling me to stop.

Then I met Cecil Collins and Mrs Tweedie within the same week very soon after that. Someone at the art college who'd been modelling for Cecil at the Central School said that she felt he might be the right person for me to connect with. So I went to find out. I went to the City Lit and asked him if I could come to one of his classes and he let me join without going through the formal enrolment. I came to Cecil in my mid-twenties when my life was at a crossroads. Without knowing it, I was a wounded person. I was only aware of having a lot of questions and looking for answers outside myself. Art felt like a good starting point. With hindsight, I realise Cecil was able to see where I was without me knowing myself. At the time I was too naive to understand I was extremely lucky. I just accepted it. The class for me was like a light bulb, like coming home. Cecil showed me that I didn't have to say no to art and creativity. What he was offering was in alignment with my heart's desire

It was the same with Mrs Tweedie, whom I met through a friend who used to do sculpture with me. He said, 'Come and meet this old lady and she will give you a cup of tea.' That was Mrs Tweedie. On my way to see her I was literally dancing in the street, I felt so happy. All this happened without me understanding who I was meeting or where I was being led, but I knew that I had met what I was looking for. I trusted both Cecil and Mrs Tweedie completely and was eager to learn from them. I recognised that they had surrendered to something which was real, that they were both showing the way, through their examples, of what one could do oneself, although it took me years to understand what it was all about. Now I realise that they were constantly telling me in many different ways that it was not about my relationship with them. At first they gave me that information on a subliminal level until gradually, over the years, it started to sink in, that it was a guidance towards my relationship with something else.

When I first came into Cecil's class, it confused my mind completely, but I trusted the fact that I was feeling happy and at home among friends and fellow souls, and Cecil provided a certain level of security from the beginning. He probably also selected people who would have some potential to grow in that space. The structure of Cecil's class and the way he respected and treated the models was an indication for me of where he was coming from. Cecil was reorganising the structure of classes within the art school which was, I think, quite Sufi: he was in the world, but without losing track of doing exactly what was needed. I'd earned my living as a model in my previous college and was aware that they could be treated like objects, like a piece of furniture.

In his class the model became the centre of focus rather than an object. We had to develop the sensitivity to become one with the model and with the course. It was about learning to forget yourself. When he asked us to do some movement, he would observe if you were moving with your ego or not, whether you were aware of making a beautiful movement. He would pick on it and he had a way of conveying to you that he was not interested in that. Through the way we were moving he was able to see if we were really listening, then he would communicate , 'Yes, you've got it.' We had to learn to listen to the music or move with the model or move ourselves without those qualities that belong to the ego. It was the art of listening without grasping, without wanting, without possessing. We became focused on the energy and movement that are at the core of life. He was reprogramming us.

At the beginning of each session Cecil had us prepare the ink we were going to use and then dilute it with water. There were seven levels of tonality from dark to light. We used brush and quill and the drawing had to be very quick. I remember one incident when the model was in a beautiful pose and I started to use a bit of black with my brush, but it spread. I tried to rescue my drawing because

I wanted to evoke the light that I perceived. In the end the whole thing became completely dark grey and with some black lines, but the light wasn't there and I felt terribly depressed. From time to time, Cecil would leave his chair and go behind each student and look at their drawing, sometimes making comments, though most often not. I felt it was his way of checking where they were, not just on the paper, but inside themselves.

It so happened that Cecil was doing his round when I had this black drawing and I thought, please don't let him come now. I'd done beautiful drawings before, which I would have loved him to see, but then he never came. He come instead when I was in grief about my drawing. As he was approaching, my heart was saying, 'No, please,' as if I was revealing the darkness of some deep secret, a fear of the dark, the fear of being seen. I thought he would throw me out of the class for making such a mess.

Cecil came and stared over my shoulder for what seemed like a long time, and then he said to me, 'That's very good,' and moved on. Whatever he saw was beyond my own understanding then, but it touched my heart. It was as if he'd said, 'That's good, you've probably reached the bottom of the pit.' He didn't, of course, say that, but what he said was a gift and the following drawing was probably pure light because I needed to go through that complete acceptance and surrender which I'd been fighting against. I had to face that you couldn't hide or lie in the drawings. What was on the paper was coming from you and not from anybody else, whatever I created was authentic. I wanted a nice drawing, something I could be proud of and share, but I would have hidden this drawing from the world and he'd said it was good.

For me there was a great healing in that moment. You protect yourself because you don't want to see that total darkness, but out of the darkness comes the light. Without the darkness there'd be no creativity. Cecil gave me the tool, literally, and physically through art, to understand. Sometimes we have to go through extremes in order to find the balance. I think probably the black drawing for me was an extreme. A balanced drawing would be a mixture of light and dark, strong and soft line.

Now, years later, I realise the value of the dark, how it contains the light, and how, without the darkness, you can't have the light. Maybe that was what I learnt from Cecil. That was why there was this range of tonalities, from the dark to light and why the black ink was included in the spectrum. I felt that Cecil was working on the soul level and our souls responded to him and this would filter through and register in the personality as joy or vulnerability or sorrow or freedom. Through his teaching, I started to be aware of the restrictions of my ego, to understand more about myself. Like all good teachers, Cecil and Mrs Tweedie gave you the opportunity to experience truth, but it was up to you how open you would be to receive it. They provided the space and the structure for you to discover it for yourself.

My soul was crying out for some sign of the other world and Cecil's art was a sign of it and Mrs Tweedie's meditation was a sign of it and both nourished me for many years. They valued a spiritual world which was not reflected in the world around us. Being in England has been about meeting those teachers and also the fellow students, the fellow travellers treading the same path, following the same teachers so I was not alone. The people that I have met in spiritual groups like Cecil's and Mrs Tweedie's are often outsiders, original artists, thinkers or musicians not fitting any mould. There was a deep mutual respect between Cecil and Mrs Tweedie. I think they met once, but they knew of each other before that: students would report to Cecil about Mrs Tweedie and Mrs Tweedie would hear about Cecil and his work.

Once I was in Cecil's class I then had to re-apply each year and I remember the ritual of queuing to enrol. One year I was in France and I made a mistake about the dates. When I looked in my diary, I realised I needed to be back in London that evening in order to enrol in Cecil's class the next morning. My parents at first said, 'Don't worry, you can do the course another year,' but I said, 'No, I have to be there'. I was in complete distress and they realised how important it was for me so they paid for a flight instead of the boat from Normandy to London. It was lovely that they were so supportive.

There were only twenty or so places available in the class and probably fifty or more people who wanted to join, so it was first come first served. People would come at four o'clock in the morning thinking that they'd be well in advance, but it was already too late. We would queue from seven pm the night before. We would come with candles, sleeping bags and sandwiches and it was all quite joyful. For me, the waiting was like Cecil's painting, *The Dawn*, waiting for the rising of the sun, the new beginning of a new life.

You prepared yourself as you do before going into a temple; it was like an initiation. You had time to reflect on why you were there, why you were so committed to joining Cecil's class, and why you were ready to sleep in the street for it. You were not just saying 'Yes,' to Cecil's class, you were saying 'Yes,' to your own transformation. You were ready to surrender even your own comfort. It's nothing to sleep outside for one night, but it was symbolic of the price of your commitment. You had to queue first to get a number and then you came back in the afternoon and after queuing again, you would have to show Cecil work you'd done. I remember being very nervous because I didn't take it for granted that I would be accepted. He would not automatically say, 'Yes, of course you can join in.' He

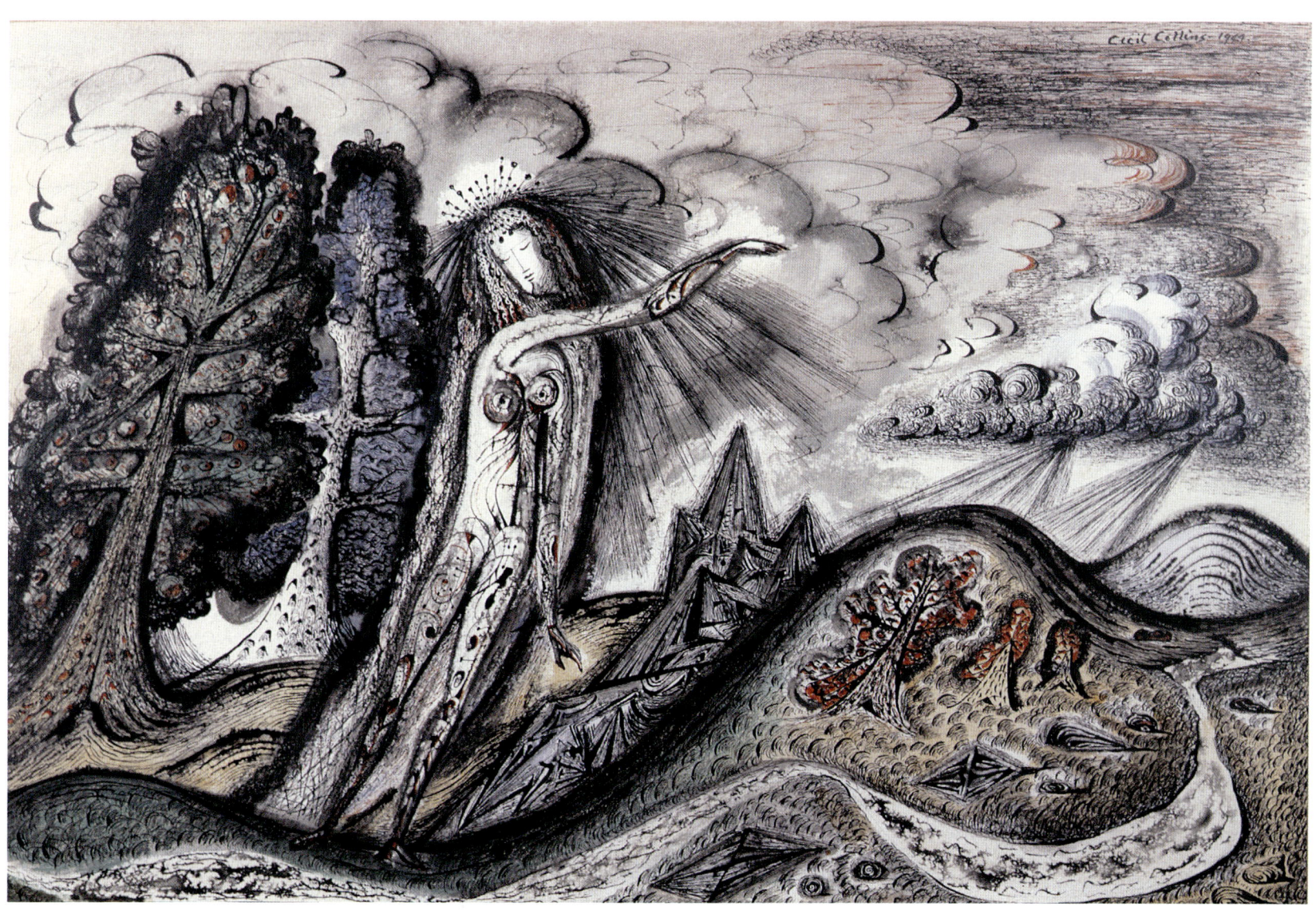

Cecil Collins
The Invocation
1944
Ink and watercolour on paper
38 x 56cm

would pause and take his time. He never made comments about my drawing, but I think he knew how deep my desire was.

I was attracted to being a painter or sculptor, but towards the end of the five years I did with Cecil I became more interested in the parallel path of healing, so I started to be involved with reflexology and psychotherapy. Whatever I learned with Cecil was an important part of my journey and is now part of my process as an osteopath. I needed two references for my application for the osteopathic course and I asked Cecil if he would give me one. I had to tell him that I was making a move towards healing and osteopathy, and I think that unconsciously or consciously I was asking for permission to go away. I felt that he helped me through my development, again on the soul level, but he was not interested in what I was doing as in a sense it didn't matter or was not relevant. He was really saying that I had to take responsibility for my decisions. It's as if a seed was planted in me which was not about how to draw, paint or sculpt, but was about the principle of life: how to live, how to understand, how to see, how to appreciate, how to respect, how to listen, how to love really, how to be open. All that is completely relevant to my work now.

I remember the occasion of going to Basingstoke for the dedication ceremony of his stained glass windows. We had to drive for quite a few hours, but it was a bit like queuing for his class, the journey itself was part of the experience. There was this extraordinary golden light everywhere. The sun was quite low because it was autumn and the leaves were all gold and red. During the ceremony at the church the sun was just hitting the two windows with Cecil's stained glass angels and rays of golden light were going through them to the floor of the church. The memory will stay with me forever. I

Cecil Collins

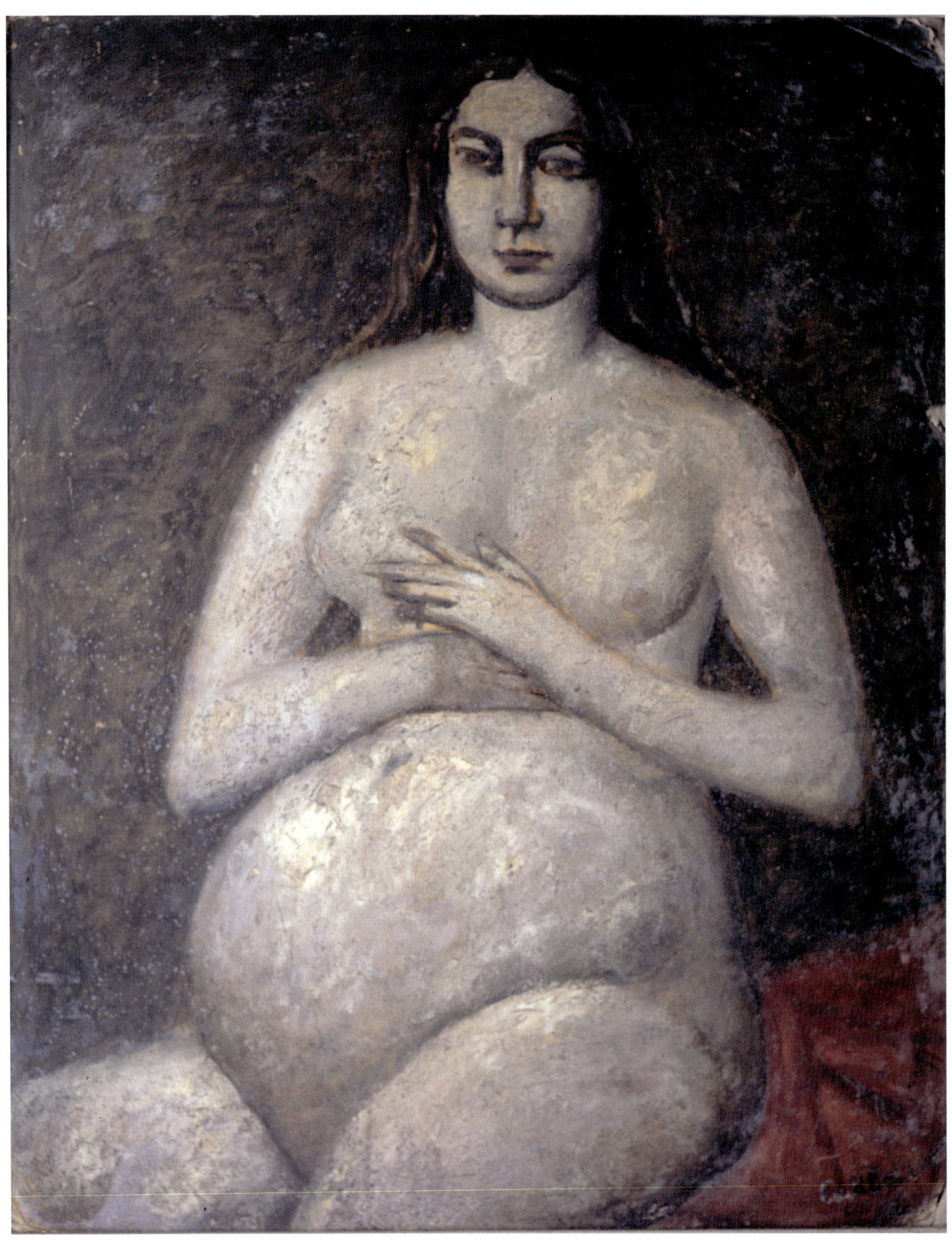

Cecil Collins
Maternity
1929
oil on cardboard
122 x 91.5cm

think Cecil was very proud that within the structure of the Church of England, as he did within the structure of education, he brought his own light and managed to bring in mystical symbols. I think that it was important for him that we could witness the ceremony and share his joy at having accomplished that work.

On the wall of my practice I still have a picture of Cecil's stained glass angel with the eye of the heart open. It's an inspiration for life itself. Patients sometimes look at it and to me, it's very much a symbol of what I'm interested in and what Cecil was conveying: that the whole journey is about the opening of one's heart. I came to Cecil without realising that this was what I was looking for, but now I know. The eye of my heart is slowly opening up, but it will take a lifetime or maybe more. Cecil had that eye very much open. It makes a big difference to be seen by someone who has the eye of the heart open. To be in contact with them makes our hearts start to open, then we have access to our own creativity, our own light.

Cecil talked about the lost paradise and what he made me understand was that the original wound was a separation from the knowledge of paradise, but there was a possibility to reclaim awareness here and now and with our body. Maybe the aim of human beings on earth is to bring heaven on earth through the hearts of people, especially now with all that is going on in the world. Cecil was aware of the dangers of what would happen if we didn't wake up and it was part of his wound to know that we were asleep. He committed his life to try and touch as many of those people who could be open to that and his painting was a message to the world saying, 'Don't forget where we come from. Don't forget what is important.'

It was not just a one-way system. He also acknowledged the support of his students, the support of those who loved him, which give him strength. I've learned from Cecil and Mrs Tweedie, that whatever is given to us is not to be kept at all for ourselves. If your heart is more open it will touch other hearts and hopefully as it spreads more people will be awake. There are stages of evolution: you have the one who knows and you also need the ones who are curious to know and then there are the ones who are not interested. Cecil's words, his painting and teaching are probably becoming less and less at odds with the world which has changed so rapidly since he died. Cecil was a guide. He was ahead of his times and his isolation was due to his awareness which all mystics in the world suffer. They come in advance to show the light, to show the way.

For Cecil's eightieth birthday the students were asked to each make a card, then all the cards were threaded together, and opened out in front of him. I remember spending much time on my card. I painted the eye of the heart with some special things written underneath. I think that was my way of saying good-bye and thank you because it was the last year I studied with him.

Probably the last time I saw him was when he took a group of us students to his exhibition at the Tate. This must have been before the opening because I don't remember other people there. Cecil walked round with us and explained each painting. I have a photo of myself looking at a picture of an Angel and I've got both arms behind me and it's as if my heart was opened to the painting. I remember that I had a feeling of respect, wonder and humility. I knew that I hadn't yet caught the deep meaning of it, but I understood it somewhere and I was hoping that one day I would catch up with this understanding, if possible. I felt like that about the whole exhibition.

I remember a man from the group had one of Cecil's books, an old copy, and he asked Cecil to sign it, which he did. Then Cecil looked at him and said with his witty humour and such a twinkle in his eye, 'Soon that will be worth a few bob.' A few weeks later he died, so he was probably right: this man had something of value from him.

His physical frame was a mystery because there was this huge man, a bit bent over, completely hidden with a hat, a scarf and big raincoat, but what I could always see were his very blue eyes. I remember them as very light blue with twinkles, like two stars in his eyes, and when he was making a joke or being witty the stars shone even more. His light was permanent and his humour was always present.

With increased maturity, my appreciation of what Cecil was trying to teach me, and of how very lucky I was, has grown with time. Thinking of him again like this years later is a pleasure and I realise that in the past he planted a seed and now I'm aware of a flower coming from that seed and I hope it will carry on growing. Indeed, it gets stronger rather than weaker and it's not from the past, it was part of the eternal. It's eternally present.

What Cecil gave me, which is very important and is still guiding me in this period when it's so difficult on the earth, is that we have to respect the balance of the masculine and the feminine as well as the east and the west and focus on the birth of this new energy which is innocent because it's of the soul and as vulnerable as a child. A child is innocent. Innocence has the sense of luminous purity. The child and innocence was very much one of Cecil's themes. If we don't have pure hearts of innocence ourselves we will not recognise it. We will not be able to protect and take care of it, we will probably destroy it. One of Cecil's paintings is of a child being led by the hand, and he spoke often about this subject. It shows that Cecil had a vision of the future, of the child that is to come. I don't think many people would have understood that at the time.

RUTH LUDGATE

After studying with Cecil Collins, Ruth Ludgate taught his method at Westminster Polytechnic and at Bath University. She has exhibited her sculptures and paintings at the Mall Galleries, the Moreton Street Gallery, as well as at private shows. As an educational therapist and counsellor she edited *Transformations*, the journal of Psychotherapists and Counsellors for Social Responsibility and sits on the National Co-ordinating Committee of the Ministry for Peace.

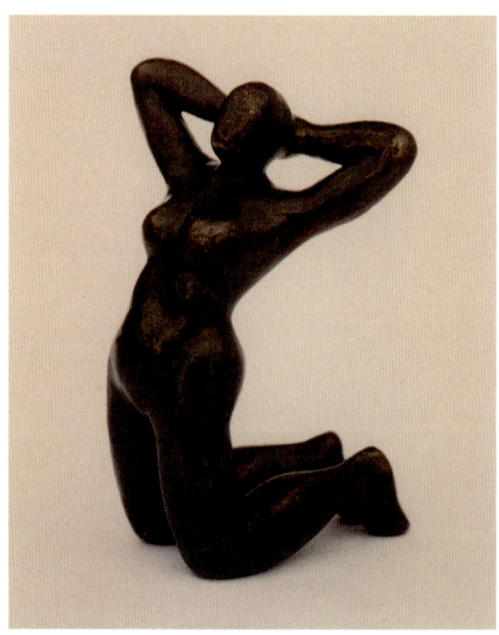

Ruth Ludgate
Free Woman
1990
Bronze
14 x 10 x 8cm

I first met Cecil when I was travelling through my own dark night of the soul. I was a highly educated woman, struggling to engage with my emotional and spiritual needs. By grace, I had found solace in painting; often simply washes of (beautiful) colour, or dark reflections of my psychological state. Eventually, a figure emerged from this darkness, a woman carrying a dove, and a comment from my sister made me consider going to a life class. Through enquiries, I found my way to the City Lit, where a very percipient James Burr, in response to my whispered, 'I am interested in Jung and mysticism,' directed me to Cecil Collins, with the comforting reassurance, 'We aren't concerned about academic drawing here.'

Thus, one autumn day in 1976, I found myself upstairs in the City Lit, surrounded by what seemed to be fearfully confident and experienced artists. People queued up to give their names to the elderly man, who appeared to be the tutor. When I reached him, the last in the queue, he asked me what I had done. I replied, 'Only at home alone.' He said simply, 'You are very lucky.'

The teacher began to speak to the class, and I knew I had come home. There was no model that day, which gave him the chance to make his favourite joke, 'No nudes are good nudes.' So we drew plants in various ways (what did I do for instruments?). I was in the far corner, away from the door, but at the end of the afternoon, Cecil prowled his way round to me, looked at my final drawing, and said, 'That's good. Those plants are really growing.' And I saw that they were.

We learned many lessons along the way. My most poignant lesson came when I had been with Cecil for a couple of years. I had glanced at my neighbour's drawing, and had decidedly judgemental thoughts about it. Cecil wandered past, and commented warmly on the drawing, and its reflection of the student's creativity. I looked again, and learned forever that each person's creativity is special, and what is important is to draw out that individual uniqueness from each student. Although I was unconsciously doing this in my own work with dyslexic children, this made it conscious. I have carried the essence of this lesson into my work as an educational therapist, counsellor and the many years I have spent carrying on Cecil's teaching around England, and abroad, and indeed in my relationships in general.

The City Lit deserves a medal for employing Cecil, so that his gift of teaching and generating creativity could be experienced by people like myself who would never have dared go near an Art School. He coaxed and encouraged each of us to discover our own creative potential. This did not necessarily manifest itself artistically: people were able to go away and pursue widely differing lives, enriched and matured by their experience drawing the 'Cecil' way.

In 1979, just before Easter, I dreamed that Cecil died. In my dream of him it is his seventieth birthday and he is being presented with an endowment. I see him before he goes in and we have a joking exchange. Later, I hear he has died just after being given the endowment. I see Cecil in a doorway looking very pale. I say, 'I love you,' but he goes paler and does not seem to hear except with his eyes. I say it again, he goes white and I know he has heard. There is a sumptuous party to celebrate the endowment, and now Cecil's death.

I was devastated by the dream, both on an inner and outer level, and very upset at the next class. This happened to be the last before Easter and at the end I broke down and wept. When I wished

Cecil a 'Happy Easter,' he simply replied 'Resurrection,' which only made things worse.

A friend had noticed my tears and I told her the dream. Her comments were not only comforting at the time, but relevant for all of us, both then and now. Cecil was bound to die sometime, people can always be with us in spirit, and maybe he has to die for the work to go on. By dying, his spirit and teaching can pervade all of us like coloured dye moving through a piece of material. In this way his spirit can be distilled through us students to carry on the task.

Fortunately, Cecil remained actively alive for another ten years. Then he indeed died as he received the endowment of the Tate Retrospective and membership of the Royal Academy, both of which institutions had ignored him for so long.

On an inner level, of course, dreaming that Cecil died meant that I was on the way to shedding the original childlike projection. Although I went on studying with Cecil until his death, visiting once a term if I wasn't actually part of the class, I was then able to enjoy the relationship as pupil and friend. Without doubt, he gave me and all of us the unconditional love and acceptance of a father. He healed for me the wounds dealt by my biological father, who was himself too raw and vulnerable to give that love.

I was invited to tea with Cecil and Elisabeth one Sunday in December 1979, and as I left, they were standing together at the top of the stairs. She moved closer to him, and in the blink of an eye, I saw them merged into one whole, surrounded by golden-green light. I could feel the rub of my left eyelid on the lower lid for hours afterwards.

Later, in 1986, a friend who worked at the Tate told me, 'It looks as though your friend Cecil Collins is going to get his retrospective at last. It will be in about three years.' In that moment, I saw Cecil walking into an exhibition, held up by two people. My image did not take into account modern technology, but was indeed correct, because Cecil came to his exhibition in 1989 in a wheelchair. He died four weeks later.

There are three qualities in particular that I feel I absorbed from Cecil. First, he put me in touch with my vulnerability. He was always so clear about how we needed to shed our baggage and reach our creativity through being open and vulnerable. He taught me how to let go in my work and allow the drawing and, later, the sculpture to reflect an inner flow, rather than controlled by my mind. This has led to some good and sometimes frighteningly intense experiences in the processes of my creativity. Cecil worked with the archetypes of the Angel and the Fool. I have been particularly involved in working with the Feminine, both in the expression of the female form, and in reflecting the essence of motherhood, goddesses and angels. I want to evoke a feeling of connection between the viewer and the work. Each aspect of the sculpture tells a story, and they cry out to be touched.

Second, his integrity and vision, which together created a wholeness that was inspiring. He lived according to a vision of a new dawn and passed his vision on to numerous students. Perhaps this was the Angel in him. Though it was openly projected onto the wonderful Elisabeth, it was still an aspect of himself. Because of this, he showed an all-embracing acceptance of his students..

His acceptance and faith in our creativity helped us to find an inner and outer potential which we have manifested in many different ways. This was the 'thread' that Cecil offered, a thread to hold on to, and to pass on to those with whom we come into contact, whether through the teaching, work or relationships.

How can I finish without mentioning his sense of humour. He was the embodiment of the Fool in the Tarot stepping out over the cliff full of hope, openness, vulnerability and excitement.

MURIEL MAUFROY

Born and brought up in France, Muriel Maufroy worked as a journalist for the BBC World Service for many years. She has a degree in Persian from the School of Oriental and African Studies and is the author of a book of Rumi's quotations, *Breathing Truth* (Sanyar Press, 1997), and a novel, *Rumi's Daughter* (Rider, 2004). She lives in London and is writing her second novel.

I first heard of Cecil through a Hungarian friend while I was living in the States. This friend had lent me a book of various articles, essays and poetry, some, I must admit, quite above my head. One long interview, however, drew my attention. It was a conversation with a British artist whose thoughts seemed to express some of my own concerns about beauty, art and spirituality. His were more clearly articulated than mine, however, and had an extraordinary impact. They vibrated and had the power to energise.

He talked of the arts as 'a channel of grace' and referred to 'the world of the imagination' as somehow more real than the material world. He talked of the source and the nature of creativity. His words were re-opening the doors of a world I had left behind, both in space and in time: the world of childhood, of enchanted forests, of fairies. Suddenly, there was someone who acknowledged ideas and thoughts which I had almost renounced, failing to find anyone around to value them. But his words were not only offering an entry back into a lost world; they were offering a glimpse of infinite hope.

A few months later, the tide of life took me back to England. I had packed my books, as well as my dreams, and forgot the name of the artist. Only a few weeks after my return to London, I heard of a teacher whose teaching reminded me of the interview I had read. I checked. The name of the teacher and of the interviewed artist were the same: Cecil Collins.

One night at that time I had a dream: I was walking through the streets of London when I was shown a large alley lined with trees in white blossoms. There was a magical quality to the space. White petals were covering the ground, as well as gently floating in the air and I thought, 'How amazing that behind the grey buildings and the grey streets, there are hidden oases such as this.' I woke up with a feeling of elation.

The way I found myself in Cecil's class had the same magical quality as the dream. I was told there was a long waiting list of people wanting to attend Cecil's class, but that he sometimes gave lectures to which everyone was welcome. I took the first opportunity and was there early on the day of the lecture, before the end of his class. He noticed me behind the students and asked me what I wanted. I explained, adding that I would like to take part in his class, and then came the surprising answer, 'But aren't you already in it?'

A few days later, I was in the class: quill, reed pen, charcoal, pencil in hand, struggling with the ink and paper. In fact, as I was soon to discover, I was also struggling with my frustration, anger and self-consciousness. I was shaking with a kind of feverish excitement which I found strange and rather disturbing until I saw a baby who, while crawling, was shaking with excitement at discovering the world around him. I laughed. Here was I, unable to walk yet, but filled with an overwhelming sense of wonder which almost choked me. Never mind the frustration and the anger. There was nothing else to do but go on and stick with the class.

It took me two years before I was able to observe and accept the anger and frustration without either fearing them or indulging in them and then the miracle happened. One day the anger showed itself as strength and power in one of my drawings. That same year in the winter, I found myself with a bad cough left over from a cold. It was, I thought, disturbing the class and made me temporarily unable to draw yet when I tried to leave the room, Cecil told me sternly, 'Coughing is not a problem. Go back to your place.' Red chalk in one hand, brush in the other, out of breath, eyes running, I attempted to draw. My mind was in total confusion. I was desperately attempting to concentrate while trying to contain the cough and hardly knew what I was doing. Then the miracle happened again. There, in front of me, was a drawing of a quality I had never been able to obtain when in so-called control of myself. When Cecil saw the drawing, he simply said, nodding, 'Irritation can be very useful.'

Then there was the day when, for the first time, I had a real feeling for the seventh tone, a wash where the quantity of ink mixed with water is so small that one can hardly see the stroke of the brush on the paper. Looking at my drawing Cecil said, 'Yes, it's like walking on tip-toe,' but then he immediately added, 'You have to bring it back here.' Didn't he know, from his own experience, how difficult that was, how once we have had a glimpse of the world of light and lightness, all we want to do is to leave the heaviness and greyness of our ordinary world?

Cecil was very precise. In those few words he was stating the obligation we have of bringing back into this world the radiance of our discoveries of 'the other world'. Week after week, the lessons came which made his class a place of transformation. Yes, we were learning to draw, but much more than that; we were discovering that creativity was the soul of life. Without it, the world was grey and full of despair and Cecil was giving us the key: there was only one way to live, to give the whole of oneself, with discipline and concentration, to the task of creating. Week after week, he taught us that in order to create, a marriage was necessary, the marriage between skill and technical knowledge, and receptivity to an inner knowledge which we all possess innately, but which we need to re-awaken. His whole teaching was aimed at this re-awakening. That meant that we had to allow creativity to possess us while offering all our skill to it.

I remember the last conversation we had during one of his classes. He talked about the need to have the desire to share, without which, he said, nothing can come to life. The wonder with Cecil was that he always addressed the most real and secret part of yourself, the part we spend so much energy trying to hide or even forget. That day he was telling me that to keep one's knowledge to oneself, whatever the reason – shyness, fear of being thought arrogant, believing that others knew more – was, in fact, selfishness. He actually used that word and he was acknowledging that, at last, I was beginning to come out of my protective shell.

My last memory of Cecil is, as for so many of us, his presence at the Tate Gallery for the Retrospective of his lifework in 1989. It was May and death was near. He was in a wheelchair, his body hardly able to carry him, but the Spirit in him was radiant, the strength emanating from him unequivocal. The last words I heard from him in this life were, 'I have kept faithful to my vision.' A few weeks later, Cecil died, then some dreams came which made me realise how much I loved him and how much I owed him. This man had given me back my own creativity, perhaps the greatest gift a human being can give to another.

BRIGITTE NORLAND

Brigitte Norland (née Hindmarsh) was born in 1954 of Swedish and Anglo-Belgian parents. She studied with Cecil Collins from 1974 to 1979 at the Central School of Art and the City Lit. In 1981 she moved to Devon with her husband, Misha, where they established the School of Homeopathy and brought up four sons. She is a regular contributor to *Resurgence* and continues to teach children, make music, garden and to draw and paint.

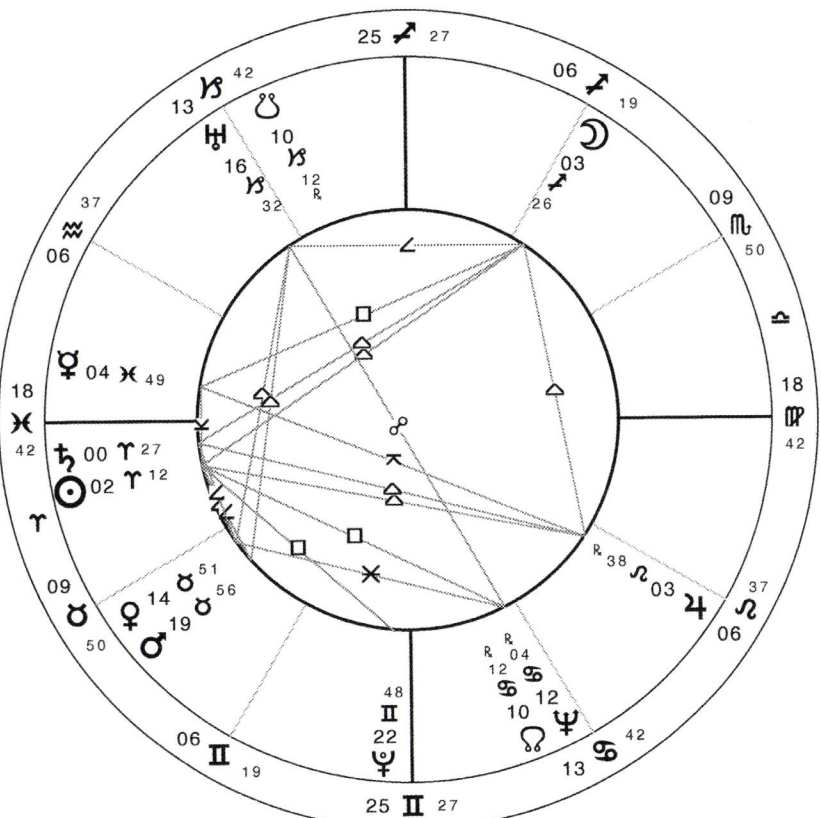

Chart prepared by Brigitte Norland

I met Cecil in 1974 when I applied to join the Fine Art department at the Central School of Art and Design. During the interview, Cecil looked at my controlled drawings and spoke of the flow that comes from contact with the real self. I remember that first meeting with Cecil very clearly because of the way he looked at me. It was a moment of mutual recognition. I knew he could see me as I really was, even if I couldn't. I was desperate because I had so many talents and desires that were all grappling with one another. It was very unusual to find someone who was prepared to communicate with me in that kind of a way. I think what he said was something along the lines of 'Intellect and feeling are not yet connected in you.' It was absolutely true; it was what I was struggling with. I recognised Cecil's stature even though I was a muddle-headed, wilful, intellectually arrogant twenty-year old. Cecil wasn't engaged to do life drawing then, only as a visiting tutor for one, or possibly two, days a week.

The following spring of 1975 he was looking glum one day so I asked him, 'What's the matter?' When he explained the Fine Art department was in the throes of rationalisation and were trying to get rid of all the part-time teachers, I immediately realised there was a service I could do for Cecil. My role as campaigner for their retention brought a closer contact with Cecil. 'Sell cleverness and buy wisdom,' was his advice. 'Live in the great unhappiness, otherwise you have no chance of approaching the Great Happiness.' My background had prepared me for the mentor-pupil relationship. I was ready to listen. There were other people who took an interest in Cecil and got involved with the campaigning but, in the last year, quite a few students stepped back from activism because they didn't want to compromise their degrees. I remember thinking, 'What wimps'.

The tutor I was assigned to initially was a young man who asked me if I went to any galleries. I told him I went to the British Museum nearly every day as it was just round the corner and he said, 'What about contemporary stuff?' I said, 'I'm not relating to that at the moment.' I think I always had an intellectually rebellious streak. In the end, I got so exasperated with him that I swore at him so then I was given to Cecil as his tutee.

Unlike the other tutors, Cecil nurtured the whole student. In his jacket he carried a notebook with details of the books we should read which included T.S. Eliot's *The Wasteland*, the lectures and concerts we should attend, the films we should see, and I tried to do it all. He'd tell me to go and listen to Laurens van der Post, for example. All the concerns of my adult life were touched on and fostered by Cecil: not just painting, but also ecology, music and astrology were embraced with a profound sense of interconnection. Of ecology, Cecil once said that redemption was total, even for the last tin can kicked about on the street. Musically, he opened my ears to the performance and the art of interpretation, sending me to hear Hans Hotter singing, *Winterreise* or listening to master classes with Pierre Bernac and Poulenc who are a sort of French version to Britten and Pears.

Cecil took me under his wing and, although I felt undeserving, I did feel connected to him. He used to come in and spend an hour or so talking to each student. We'd had all these visiting tutors who were allowed to do whatever they liked. There were a few life drawing classes at the Central, but even they were failing because the tutors running the course were conceptual artists. When Cecil started giving his life drawing classes, I remember that although he wasn't really supposed to, he did play us something by Poulenc, but only for one or two classes. He had to be quite careful about how he did things because the authorities at the Central tried to make everyone toe the line.

Cecil used music more in his City Lit classes. Those pieces of Beethoven, Barber's 'Adagio for Strings', Alfred Cortot playing of Chopin, Debussy's *Nocturnes*, Duparc's songs, Elgar, Ravel and Shostakovich remain, like fragrance, a potent key to those realisations arrived at in class.

He also used Tibetan trumpets. When Cecil played a recording of that, it was really good fun because Tibetan ritual music has these big trumpets and some gongs as well. When the trumpets were going, Cecil had us standing up working with brushes which had been lengthened by taping them to a long cane. Then every time the gongs went, you had to kneel down. It had the element of musical chairs when you run round as a child and suddenly have to sit down. I think all that moving around changes what's going on in your body, but it was also to stop us taking ourselves seriously. Laughter undoes you. I remember Cecil saying, 'You're all so stiff today. You're like a load of washerwomen. Take your rags and get down on your floor with your ink pads. You're only allowed to paint with your rag now.' Another time, we had to grind up charcoal and dip our noses in it. That was hilarious. When you get up, you've all got black noses so you laugh at each other. He did that as a way of confronting yourself, like when we had to work on the same drawing with a partner.

One of Cecil's favourite sayings was from the angel in the Book of Revelations: 'I spit thee out because thou art not hot nor cold.' Indifference or disengagement are the greatest sin. One thing that used to make me laugh was his habit of making puns, a little bit like *I'm Sorry I Haven't A Clue*. It was one of his ways of lightening up the atmosphere because the work in the life drawing class would be so intense. We'd have a break and people would go off and get cups of tea and we'd have what Cecil called 'orchestral menus'. The ones I still remember are 'Viola Milanese', 'Cello Kebab' and 'Flute Fool'. He was such fun.

He made us learn to read our bodies in a different way in the different positions he had us take: for example, when we were lying on the floor. That has informed me as an instrumentalist because you need to learn to read your body in what you're playing. In my own teaching of the flute, you're physically involved in making a sound and you can get frustrated and tight so you find something to laugh about and that opens the body for beautiful sound to flow out again. In the Indian spiritual tradition when you're laughing, the little self is not present.

I was very aware of how Cecil could get the right kind of energy out of a group of people; how he turned it one way and then the other. He could orchestrate it like a wonderful concert. As the teacher, you're involved in waking up the inner teacher in all the people that you come into contact with so that they can then find guidance from within themselves and function independently. The implication was that it was up to the pupil to move away, rather than Cecil saying it was time for them to move on. Lots of art teachers say, 'We're going to have thirty-second poses,' and that can be magic but Cecil said, 'If you do it without awareness, it's just a load of monkey tricks.' He was born in the Year of the Monkey so he was a monkey, but he knew about the trickery and he went beyond it. He knew how to use his monkeyness creatively.

I remember talking with him about quite a few students because occasionally we'd share work and evaluate. What I found really interesting in talking to Cecil was how you can read a person from the way they draw. If Cecil looked at a painting, he might think about the balance of masculine and feminine, of dispersal and condensation, for example. He told me to always be aware of the beauty in what people created and how beauty is a moment of grace like the Japanese appreciation of fallen petals. You might do a hundred drawings and no two would be alike. If I remember correctly, one of his favourite little stories was about raking leaves. The Zen master sends his student out to rake up all the leaves and he rakes everything beautifully and the gravel's impeccable and there's not a leaf left and then the master goes out and gives the tree a shake so then there's a fresh fall and that's just perfect.

I remember at the end of my time at Central when we put up our exhibitions I was absolutely exhausted. Cecil made it clear he wasn't available to give me emotional support while I was hanging my work. He had an amazing way, without ever saying no, of making it quite clear that he was unavailable. I said to him once, 'You can switch off or on.' He had a disguise, his invisible cloak as it were. Once when he was apprehended by a policeman in Paultons Square, the policeman thought he was a vagrant. He was wearing his scruffy overcoat and this young policeman was convinced he was up to no good, shuffling

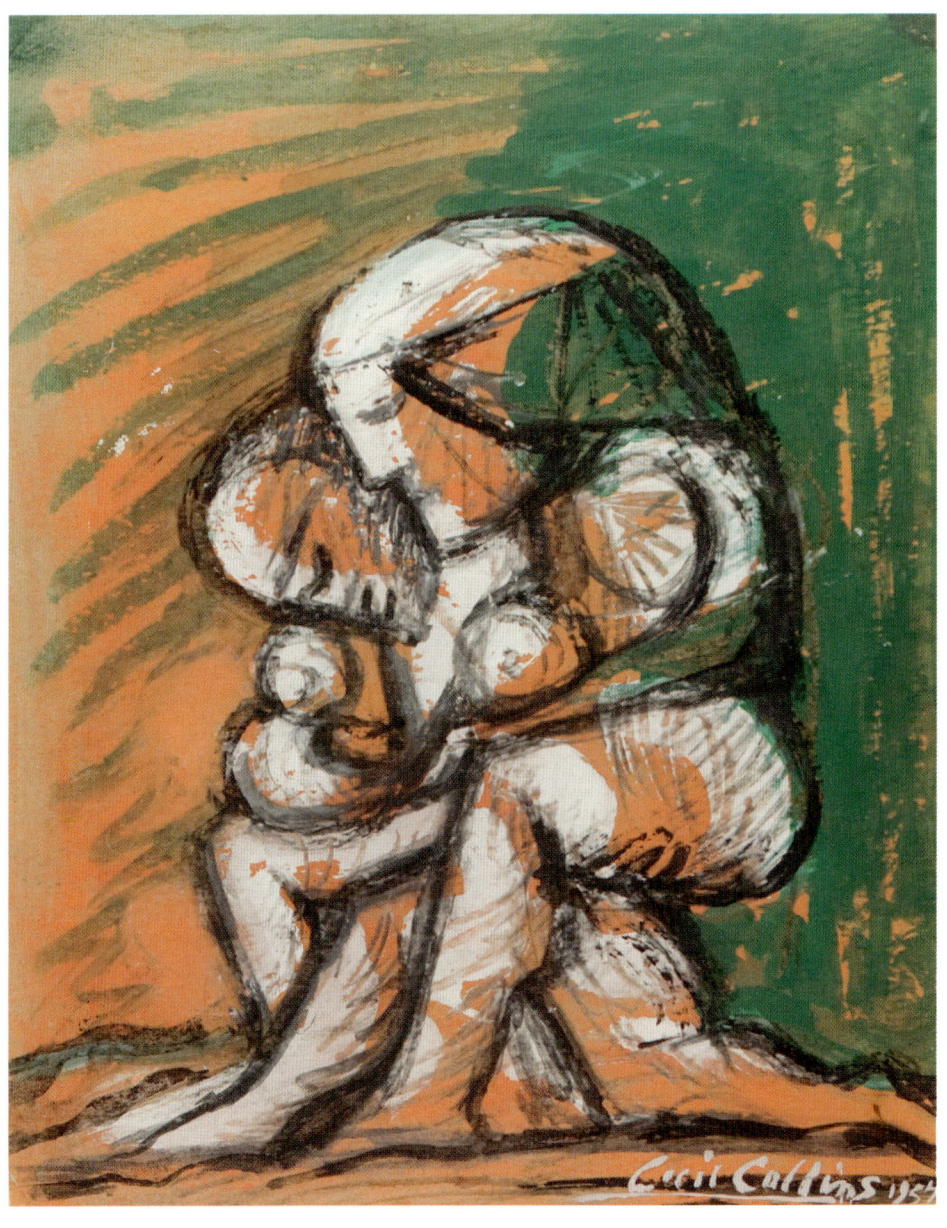

Cecil Collins
The Family
1957
Gouache
18 x 23cm

beside the tree and took up its pose and the twist it had. I imagined that I was the tree, then got up and drew it and I felt something untie at that point. As I understand it, when you want the creative energy to flow, but it hasn't started, you have to put yourself in the position of what you're about to draw; you have to imaginatively become it. If the flow happens, it's great, but you're not attached to whether it does or not. That's the one thing that gets slightly easier as you get older; you know that sometimes it happens and sometimes it doesn't.

He spoke often about *cortesia* which related to the ideals of courtly love and the adoption of certain codes of behaviour in court life where you have an impeccable set of manners. There's a sort of formality which gives space for another energy to come through. In the same way we had to have courtesy in relation to each other, ourselves and the instruments. Cecil taught about the different positions for using the instruments and that each position is a mode of perception and can be related to the position of the whole body. Everyone has his field which may be encompassed by extending the limbs. This gesture, the individuals' field, encompasses a totality of energy, a great archetype which was known to the Greeks as Helios Athanatos. *Cortesia* is the respect for this *helios*, or field, of others, to be left inviolate and the awareness of this space can also be transposed collectively. Where many acknowledge such a space, it becomes sacred, a place of high concentration, a temple, a theatre, a room transformed. Profane actually means outside the temple, not belonging.

I was just so interested and ready to absorb Cecil's teaching and astrologically there were good connections. While I was doing Cecil's life drawing class, which I did over a number of years, my sister Kate Zienko was studying astrology. I asked Cecil about his chart and it was clear that he'd had it done because he knew that the Sun conjuncts with Saturn and his Sun was at the very beginning of Aries and his Saturn was in Pisces, the twelfth house, and had a Pisces ascendant with Saturn close to the ascendant. So he'd got this first moment of Aries which is the pushing upwards and a keynote for Pisces is complete dispersal. It's all the movement of water around the entire earth so such a person is looking to experience the fundamental unity of all phenomena.

I now look at Saturn in Pisces as somebody who takes on the karmic burdens of their family, or their generation, and Cecil literally had it in his body. I think it was due to the malnutrition he'd suffered as a child when his father had been unable to find any work except digging roads.

There's Pisces clowning, but there's also Pisces misery, the victim of the world, and Cecil certainly had an element of that. A transpersonal psychologist who knew Cecil socially once said about

along. He told the young man that he lived in Paultons Square and the policeman didn't believe him and Cecil had to go to the house and get Kathleen Raine to come out and vouch for him. That's a gift of a Pisces ascendant, the ability to swim off in another direction or to just disguise yourself. I also think it's what you project as Cecil did when he was unavailable.

After I joined Cecil's classes, probably in the summer of 1975, and he had us take up the position of the model I could sense how freeing it was, how releasing of the woodenness I felt I still had in my body. It was amazing. Then I went on holiday to Scotland and walked along a river valley. The water was low and there was a shingly beach where a tree had been washed up. I followed what Cecil taught us and lay

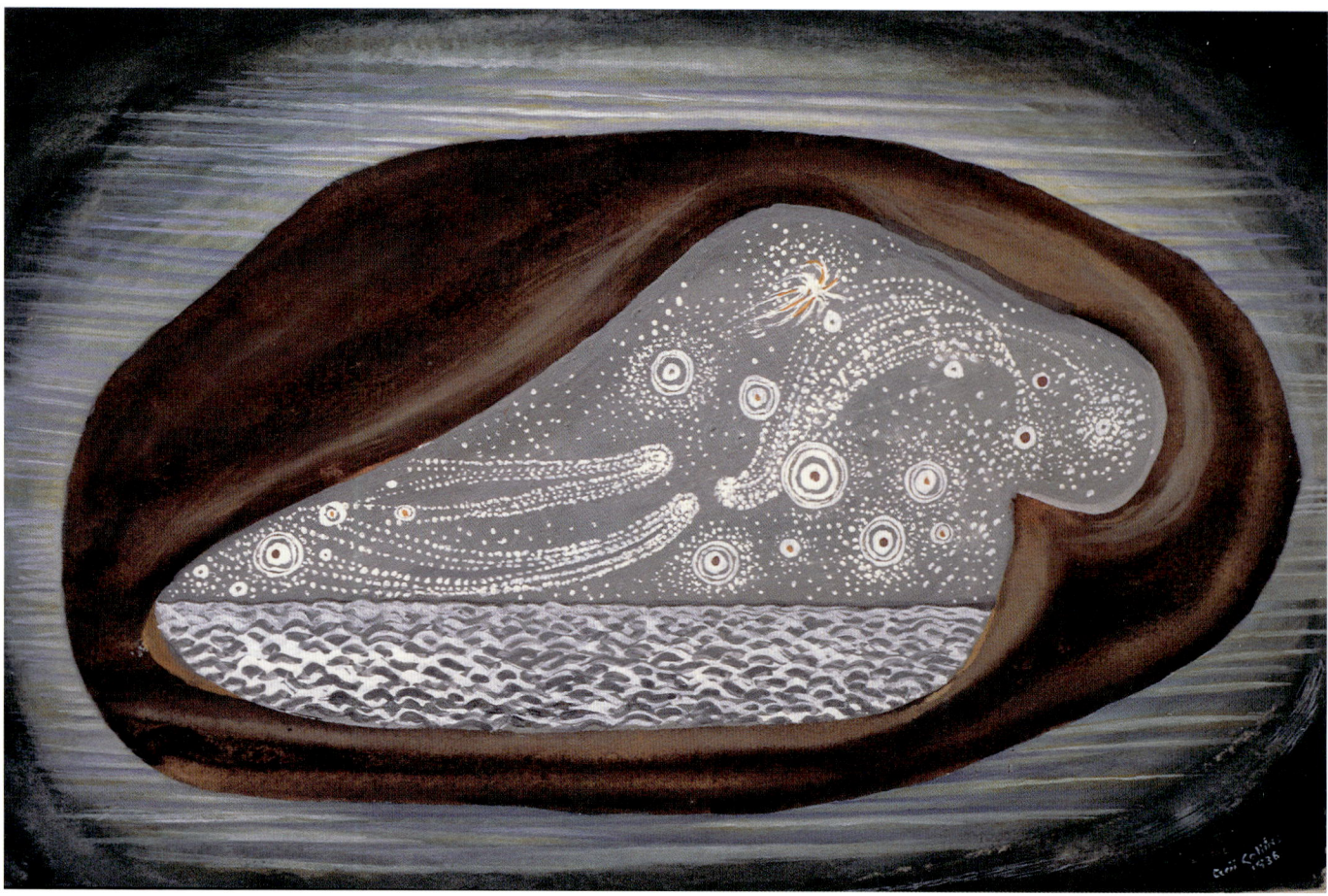

Cecil Collins
Seashell, Mysterious Joy
1936
Gouache on paper
27.5 x 40cm

him, 'Some of us wish he would come down off his cross sometimes.' I think Cecil sometimes used to pretend he had a cold if he didn't feel like going out. It was one of his defences.

He was a bit like Solzhenitsyn or an Old Testament prophet. He needed his position as an outsider to keep his message coming, not with his students, but in the context of the art world. Central had been trying to get rid of Cecil and he was invited by someone at the Tate to come and give a lecture in June 1976 at the beginning of that really hot summer. They were queuing round the block to get in because Cecil had his network. That's the kind of orchestration he was so good at. It was brilliant.

Cecil loved astrological discourse. He resonated with the chart as the theatre of the soul. The planets were, for him, dynamic, elemental forces at play in the human being, embodying the archetypal world that gave him inspiration, as well as celebrating the uniqueness of each human life. Each person is an embodiment of that particular moment in time and space. Each planet and where it sits is like setting up a vibration in music. For example, a Sun conjunct Saturn person has their inner fire weighed down by the lead of Saturn because each planet is associated with a metal. The Sun is gold, the Moon is silver, Saturn is lead and Jupiter is tin, Mars is iron and Mercury is mercury which infiltrates. Saturn is the judge; in the Greek and Roman pantheon he is the ultimate father figure. Jupiter is the impregnating principle, but Saturn is the father energy behind the father, so like the grand or great father, the old man. This represents big issues with fathers or father figures.

My sister who came to Cecil's classes for a short while, drew up the chart, but I've now got a computer and can draw them up for myself. When she gave it to Cecil, we talked about it with him. Cecil was brilliant at tuning in. He would ask questions rather than sit and listen and he would extrapolate out of that. He would have plenty to say about all the different elements as well because, for him, the Sun and Venus were as real as the person next door. Cecil understood astrology because it's another way of placing the archetypes in that circle around you when you are born and the different houses and signs gives them a different setting and affects the way they function in life.

Moon in Sagittarius in a grand trine with Jupiter and the Sun would definitely give you the qualities of leadership or kingliness, not in terms of power, but in terms of brightness and being, like a fiery wheel that keeps turning in the firmament. Cecil had square

Neptune square Pluto so the issues of power and vision were very much needing to be addressed throughout his lifetime, as well as all those aspects of Sun conjunct Saturn which constellate the oppressive nature of the father and hierarchies and social structures. This can take the form of their own very strict codes, or their sense of duty, depending on where the Sun and the Saturn are. If the Sun's in Aries, the impulse is, 'I am', and the Saturn quality is self negation. Cecil talked about himself being Sun conjunct Saturn and for such people credit comes late in life. Their sense of achievement, or what they really have to contribute to society, emerges after their second Saturn return or becomes validated much later because Saturn takes about twenty-nine years to go round the Sun.

Another thing in Cecil's chart is that he'd got Mars conjunct Venus in Taurus and the intensity of this configuration means love and desire are entirely confluent; what you desire to experience and what you desire to do are one and the same. You can't separate them out. Although for him, Venus is in its own sign so Venus has the ascendancy and Mars is in Taurus. If it was just Mars in Taurus, you could say obstinate, perverse. What I've noticed about those with Mars and Venus conjunct, they're extremely attractive; people just love them. It's a quality of being of that conjunction. It brings good fortune in strange ways to people with that configuration, although there may be something really missing from their lives.

One of the things Cecil liked quoting was from Coleridge: 'Beware, beware the flashing eyes, the floating hair... for he on honeydew hath fed and drunk the milk of paradise.' If you asked him what kept him alive, it might have been that.

Cecil's sense of mission appears in the chart because he's got Neptune conjunct with north node and the north node is a point on the Moon's orbit. The Moon has an elliptical orbit and the north and south points of that orbit move as they progress. It's a nineteen-year cycle. According to incarnational astrologers, the south node is where you come from. The north node's where you're going to, but I like to interpret the north node as where meaning unfolds in your life. So if it's conjunct Neptune, then the meaning in your life comes from expanding your vision and researching the nature of illusion and inspiration. Cecil was very good on differentiating fantasy and imagination.

Sun, Moon and Jupiter are very dynamic, very radiant, because they are all at the beginning of their fire signs. They're all in fiery placements with the possible exception of the Moon, so they're incredibly active, but then the initiative is held back by Saturn. Cecil did talk about his own self criticism hampering him in the initial stages of his life. In some ways, the image of St Michael cutting off the serpent's head was one Cecil would relate to. He talked about the dragon in Uccello's painting of *St George* in the National Gallery. We talked about monsters and he told the story about the artist coming to the monastery to paint the *Last Judgement*, or whatever it was, and the abbot warning the monks, 'You must be careful of these artist chaps because they may be doing a very fine and inspiring job, but they enjoy painting the scales on the dragon's tail as much as they enjoy painting the feathers on the angel's wings.' Cecil was not in favour of excluding dark energy, although he was ambivalent about Francis Bacon whom he considered as someone who revelled in the rubbish bin, but said he had an important function which was rubbing people's noses in it. I think if it were Cecil he wouldn't want to stay in the rubbish bin; he'd clean it out.

At one class I went to with Cecil, it was a hot summer afternoon at the City Lit. Somebody was singing in another part of the building and because the windows were open, you could hear absolutely everything. This woman had a ghastly voice and it set everybody on edge that afternoon and Cecil said, 'We'll work with it. Everyone will use red and black, only red and black, and we'll get all those devils out.' He was very good at allowing everything that happened to feed into whatever he was doing. You have to allow the monstrous energy through for the vitality to be expressive. If you learn to see even anger or children screaming as just energy, then it has no quality of being good or bad.

Cecil suggested that I might be able to write a book about his teaching so I did make some notes. I remember feeling that it was a tremendous project to embark on and I couldn't find the words for everything. I felt I was too young at that stage and it was a bit too big for me. Afterwards, William Anderson did a more all-round kind of book, but not specifically about Cecil's way of teaching.

During my studies with him, Cecil said there were seven people who'd really understood his teaching and that I was one of them, but I feel that to be another responsibility which I haven't discharged. I haven't been a painting teacher except when my son Luke was little and I used Cecil's material. I very much felt that, although I could have made a success of it and people drew from what I had to offer, I needed to live out my life in order to embody the teaching.

Though I felt for many years that I had failed Cecil and his generous gift in that he spoke of motherhood and the life of the artist as possibly incompatible, I now realise that what I most learned was to know how to arrive at self-forgetfulness in whatever I was doing, a quality needed as much in mothering as in drawing or playing the flute, and, most of all, in living a life well. I remember Cecil taking us for a tour around the British Museum and there was an AA Service van parked outside attending to someone and he said, 'Ah yes. Service, that's what it's all about.' What I learnt from Cecil informs the way I do everything.

LEI LEI QU

Lei Lei Qu was a founding member of the Stars group, the first contemporary Western influenced art movement to appear in China and challenge the art establishment. He fuses classical Chinese and Western art techniques and has created three major projects, combining paintings with installations: *The First Half of My Life, Here and Now - to Face a New Century* **and** *Everyone's Life is An Epic.* **These have been exhibited at the Venice Biennale, the Beijing Biennale and a one-man show in the Ashmolean Museum, Oxford.**

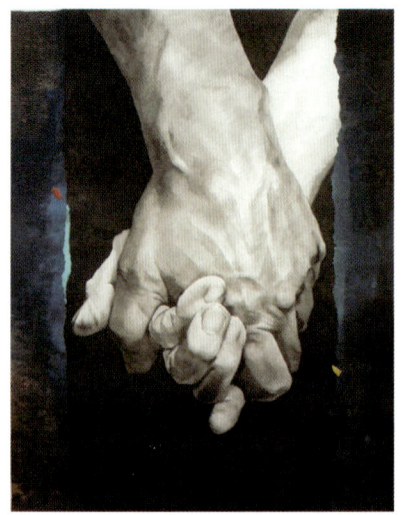

Lei Lei Qu
Journey
2006
Chinese brush, ink and colour on paper with collage
132 x 92cm

The last time I saw Cecil was at his big Retrospective exhibition at the Tate Gallery in 1989. It was a complete view of his life. His students and his students' students, and students' students' students were all there. A couple of weeks after that show he died. Then we were all together again for his beautiful funeral service.

That was the end, but the beginning was when I had a show of my paintings and drawings at a gallery near Holland Park in 1986, not long after I'd arrived in London from Beijing. I met two women there who liked my work. They were from Cecil's class and that was the first time I had heard about him. One was Muriel Maufroy and the other was Ruth Eisenhart. They told me they would like to introduce me to a wonderful man, Cecil Collins. Maybe they liked my work because of my Oriental background and my line drawings. I went to Cecil's classes at Central School and it was fascinating, something I had never experienced before.

In China, we have a purely technical tradition with all brush and ink work following traditional rules. Then I studied twentieth-century Western art and learned about oil painting and later combined the two traditions. Cecil's teaching was quite different. I realised that his idea was to break the way you'd got used to being and discover the potential that's underneath, behind or below the person you thought you were. I learnt a great deal, like on the day I was struggling to break my own rules and felt everything was going wrong. Then he was standing behind me looking at my work very intently and I said to him, 'Everything has gone wrong today.' He looked at me and gave me a such a beautiful smile and simply said, 'Wrong is right, isn't it?' That is the Daoist philosophy. Suddenly I felt so good and when I got home and looked at that day's drawing I thought, It's not that bad! I'd been judging it by my previous standards. Later Cecil told me that Daoist philosophy was a favourite of his, as it is mine.

In class, Cecil sometimes encouraged people to say if they'd discovered or realised anything from what he'd said. Once, he asked me and I spoke about the great eleventh-century intellectual, poet and calligrapher, Su Dong Po, who taught that when you paint, your heart should forget your arm, your arm should forget your hand, your hand should forget your fingers and your fingers should forget your brush. Only then will the artist achieve their best work. I also said that although I'd known this philosophy before, it was only in Cecil's classes I'd felt and had come to realise the truth of this philosophy. I added that Cecil wanted to move from the West towards the East while I was moving from East to West and we were meeting at a cross roads which was very important for me. He only said, 'Good', and the other students said, 'Well done.'

We worked sitting at tables which formed almost a square and spent a lot of time just looking at the model who was usually in the middle. Cecil would sit very quietly in the corner, close his eyes and then give us instructions about what to do. The model moved to the music and he taught us to follow and copy the model's movements. In this way, we came to a better understanding through our own bodies. That was a great help to recreate the pose in a drawing and I continue to use this system in my teaching.

We spent very little time on the actual drawing and a great deal of time on preparation and understanding. This would include physical preparation, as well as meditation and listening to music and, most of all, looking at the model to understand how the pose felt. Sometimes we would lie on the floor, either face up or down. We also spent time touching the instruments and feeling how they ranged from hard, like the reed pens, pencils and charcoal, to the softness of the brushes. We would use our fingers to bring a sense of communication between ourselves, the surface of our hands and the paper so we could discover and understand the relationship of these instruments with the paper. It was that level of detail and depth of communication that led to greater understanding.

He taught us to break our routines and our rules: to paint and draw with the other hand, the 'foreign' hand, the mouth, the feet and the toes. That was great fun because I know how to draw with my right hand too well, but when you use the other hand or your mouth, for example, the drawing is not fully under control and that's sometimes better; instead of making an automatic drawing, something more sincere emerges. It was great to be playful like children and he encouraged us to realise our hidden potential, to increase our understanding of all the relationships. This was much more spiritual than just developing your drawing skills. We forgot the brush, forgot the pen and used our spiritual power to recreate the model in the drawing.

When I'm teaching, I use his techniques and always tell my students that I learnt so much from my master, because Cecil was my master. I find that when I teach, I continue to learn a lot from him. Many of my students have heard of Cecil and are very envious that I had the chance to study with him. I tell them he was such a kind man.

Sometimes he could read your mind. One day, we had a very beautiful young girl called Alex Kingston. She is an actress now. She had beautiful skin, a beautiful shape and made beautiful movements. She was sitting in the centre of the tables before we started and I had a strong urge to touch her skin. At that moment Cecil, who was sitting in the corner as usual, said, 'Take a good look, then put your hand up and imagine your hand is following the body downwards.' I did this and felt that body. It was amazing and probably he got the same feeling as well. Everybody followed her body with their hand and, because she was in the middle of the room, everybody did this from a different angle. From where I was sitting, she had her beautiful back to me and my hand could sense the feeling of her hair, her neck, along her shoulder, down her back to the waist and downwards. It was very, very subtle this sensation as I moved my hand up and down. That feeling was holy; it was a worship of beauty. I drew very well that day and I understood much better my true feelings about beauty. I think Cecil wanted to increase our ability to feel deeply and to realise the sacred nature of our feelings. I learned from him that when we are not painting, we are thinking, but when we start painting, we don't think; we feel. Cecil's own work is, of course, quite philosophical and mysterious. It reflects his person.

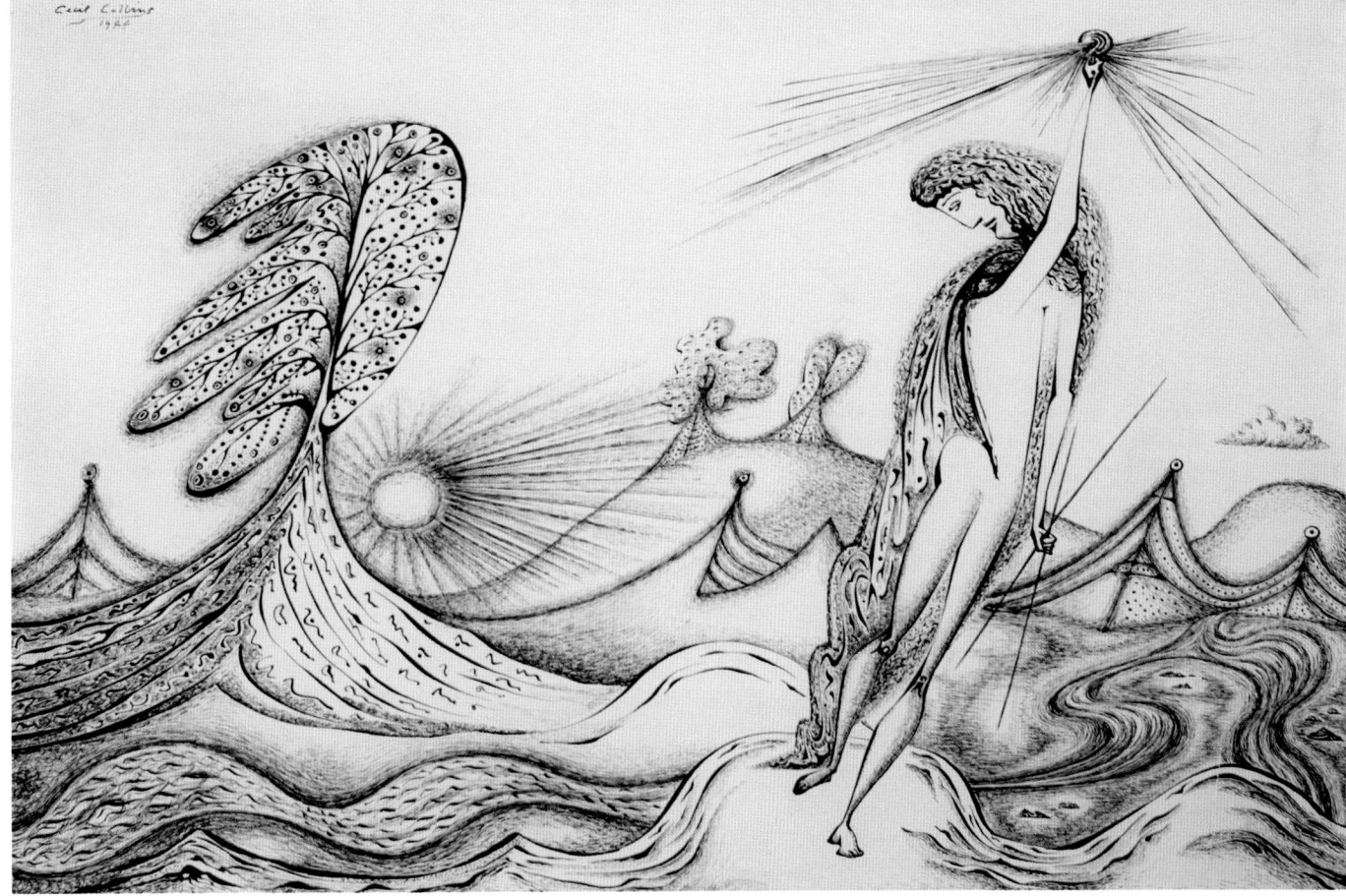

Cecil Collins
Hymn
1944
Pen and ink on paper
39 x 57cm

PHILIP RIDLEY

Philip Ridley was born in 1962 and is an award winning author, artist and film-maker. In 1991, his third children's book, *Krindlekrax*, won the Smarties Prize, and his first feature film as director, *The Reflecting Skin*, won eleven international awards. His artwork has been exhibited in London, Europe and Japan. Ridley has always described himself as a storyteller. His play *Piranha Heights* was recently performed in London and he is completing a film and an opera libretto for the composer Anna Meredith to be performed by young people. He is also working on a sequence of photographic portraits for an exhibition.

I owe so much to Cecil. I adored him and have missed him greatly. I'm evangelical about Cecil wherever I go and in every single interview I do I try to mention him. He's part of the talks I give in schools when I'm invited to talk to the children about my books and how I started writing. Part of my journey towards being an artist was discovering Cecil and how that made me. It affects me every day. I show slides of his work, particularly of *The Sleeping Fool*. Cecil's painting has a figurative symbolism, a fairy-tale quality which features in my own art and writing.

It's not just Cecil's actual artworks themselves, but also how he was as a person and what he had to say about the world has become increasingly relevant, particularly in the past ten years. Cecil always used to say that previously every great culture has believed that what it looks at is what it becomes and so if you present it with ugliness, it will become ugly. Also, there's the whole current debate about religion; where do we find faith and within that, what is the purpose of art? Cecil was talking about all that so many years ago.

When I first met Cecil I didn't even know the difference between an HB and a 3B pencil. I went to school in the East End of London where you were sent to the art room or the library as a punishment. That was marvellous for me. Cecil came along for me at a very particular time when I was thirsting for what he had to offer, although I didn't realise just how confused I was about everything. I came from a background in which there was little interest in the arts and yet I was a child growing up absolutely passionate about visual art, music, writing and ideas.

Although my Mum and Dad were really loving East London parents, they couldn't understand me begging my Dad to drive me to a theatre to see a play as a thirteen year old. They found it strange that I would spend the whole day with a notebook or sketchbook and a pile of pencils and that's all I needed. Like many teenagers, I used to be in emotional turmoil, but unable to talk to anyone. During this period, when I was feeling very down and very bleak, I took myself to the Tate Gallery, as it was then, and saw this absolutely incredible painting *The Sleeping Fool* by Cecil Collins, an artist I'd never heard of. I stood there dumbfounded because it was the first painting that I'd seen, as opposed to reproductions in books.

I saw from the dash against Cecil's date of birth that he was still alive and tracked him down at the library and discovered he was teaching at the Central College of Art, but that you had to be eighteen to enrol. I was determined to join nevertheless. Luckily I was tall and had stubble quite early on so I always looked much older than I was. I was asthmatic so I was excused games at my school and on one of those afternoons I went into Central and asked for the Cecil Collins' drawing class and simply walked in. It was several weeks before Collins asked me my name and whether I'd signed on at the start of term. 'I'm sure I did,' I mumbled and he said, 'Marvellous because I've got one more than is on the register.' I'm sure he realised the situation, but he could see how desperately I needed the tuition.

I used to stay around after the lessons as much as I could, mainly because I needed to get all the other students out of the way. I didn't want to go out and start engaging with them in conversation because obviously I couldn't talk about half the things that they could. They were all these incredibly old people in my eyes, when they must have been between eighteen and twenty-five. So I'd manage to be the last one in and take my place and be the last one out. Cecil knew exactly what was going on and gave me pencils, Chinese ink and everything; he put them on the table for me so they were all there. He knew that I was turning up without all the equipment because I didn't have any of it.

Cecil mentioned so many books and other things during the lessons that you would come away from each class with a notebook full of references to people that you wanted to look up. For example Cecil said about Kathleen Raine's poetry, 'Her words are the purest magic. Go away and read her.' He also mentioned *Le Grand Meaulnes* quite a few times.

Cecil was in his seventies, over six foot tall, but with a very stooped back. He looked like a wizard. He made us do a lot of exercises which I still do today, working with ink and pencil, teaching us how to use

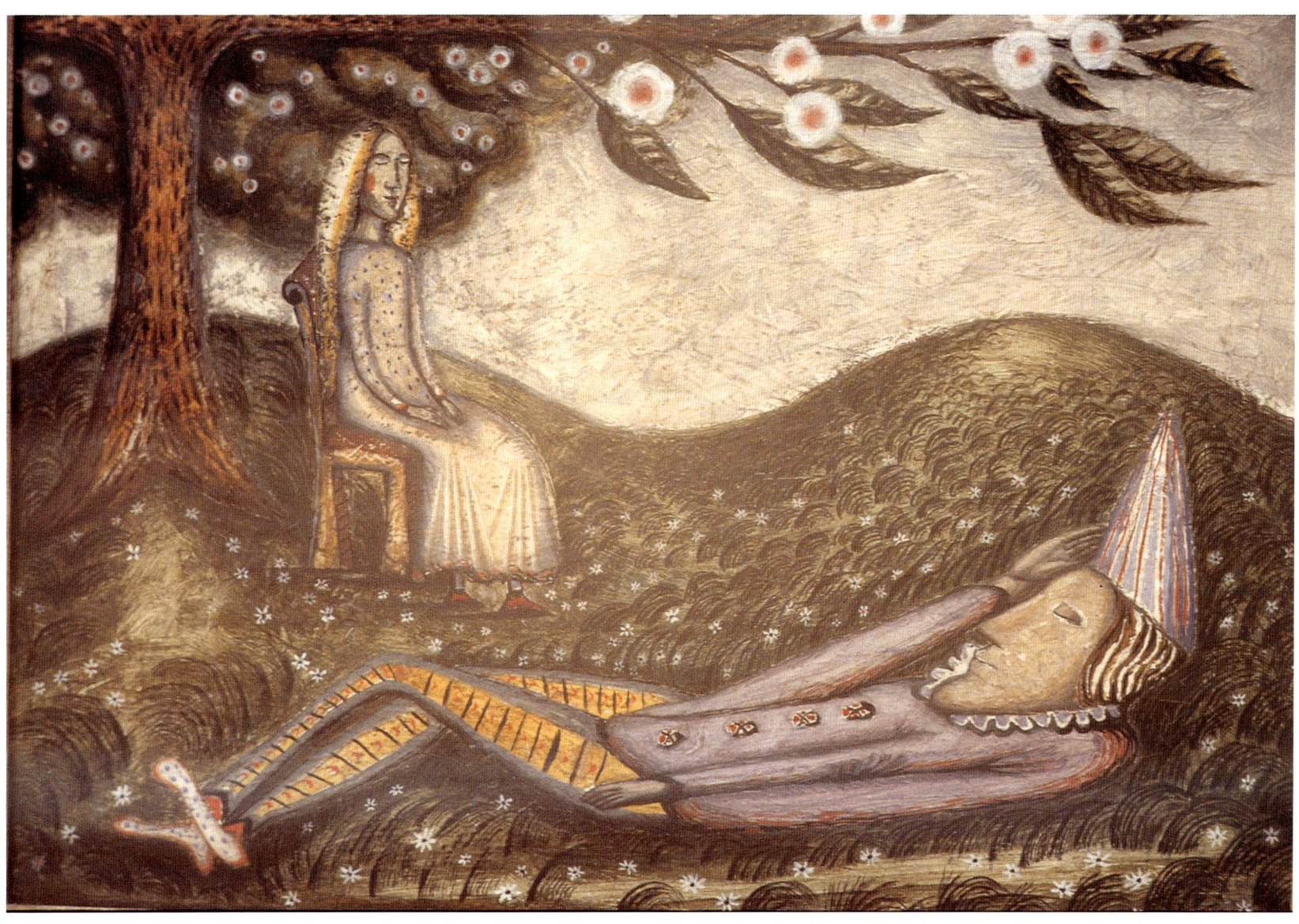

Cecil Collins
The Sleeping Fool
1943
Oil on canvas
29.8 x 40cm

tone. In his classes we'd draw from the model and to have in front of me a naked female form was an absolute revelation. Cecil got us to draw the model for thirty minutes listening, I think, to Wagner and then for thirty minutes listening to Shostakovich. There was a sequence of different pieces of music for us to get into that world. We had to let the music speak to us through our brain, down through our arm, through our hand, out through our fingertips into the pencil and let that become some kind of communion with model, with ourselves and the music. It was a fantastic experience.

One day, one of the pieces of music he'd played was the slow movement of Shostakovich's Fifth Symphony. I hung around afterwards as usual and I said to Cecil, 'I'm so glad you played that because I recently discovered Shostakovich and I love him.' (My Mum and Dad had bought a little radio for me to have in my room and as I was connecting it, the first thing that came on was the opening of that symphony. That was the moment I discovered Shostakovich.) I was talking to Cecil about how sad the music was, how there's a real melancholy behind even its most angry passages, a real yearning, a real despair. He said to me, 'You picked up on that did you? The yearning, the lost voice behind all of that music?' I said, 'Yes.' Cecil looked up at me said, 'That lost voice is very important, it means a lot to artists like us.' It was the most amazing thing he could have said to me at that stage of my life. 'Artists like us.' I'd never even dared think of myself as an artist, let alone thought to hear myself called an artist and then to have him bracket us together. I never ever forgot that and never will.

I was doing three A levels and also Scholarship Level in English because the school wanted me to go to Oxford or Cambridge and I remember we were studying *King Lear*. I came into Cecil's class, obviously completely stressed about all the exams that were coming up and with this pile of books. I'd made thousands of annotations all over this poor Penguin edition of Shakespeare's play with paper markers sticking out. After the lesson he came over and looked at me and said, 'You're doing all of this?' I said, 'Yes, I've got to write an essay tonight on *King Lear* and he said to me, 'Listen, this is all well and good, but it doesn't mean anything unless you cry when Cordelia dies.' Hearing that made me relax and realise that understanding the play was not an intellectual activity. Just because I can write a five-hundred word essay about the use of paternal imagery and animals doesn't mean I've understood anything. I will only understand it when I cry when Cordelia dies.

I couldn't put that into my essay, but in fact, I do remember mentioning it in the next English lesson. Trying it out on the assembled throng, so to speak. I haven't seen looks in faces like that since Sigourney Weaver saw the chest burster in *Alien* for the first time. There was complete shock and disbelief that I was coming out with such irrelevant comments. 'That won't get you an A Level; it won't get you to Oxford, talking sentimental rubbish like that.'

Cecil was picking up very strongly on where education was going. Like nearly everything that he talked about, he understood long before any of us did that education was purely to tick boxes and pass exams to get a good job. For me he was far more avant-garde, more revolutionary than anything else I was experiencing or heard about. What Cecil was saying was so obviously going against the grain of what was acceptable at that point. He had a complete hatred of the state of education and he referred to it as organised crime.

At the end of studying with Cecil I went to Central for the Foundation course interview. They were openly rude about Cecil and dismissed half my portfolio. I had mounted up some of those wonderful fast drawings of the model he got his students to do: for thirty seconds, ten seconds, one second, left hand, right hand, two hands; all of those kinds of drawings. They flipped through the portfolio, wouldn't even look at them and said, 'You've no idea how much of this claptrap we have to sit and look through.' They were utterly dismissive and there was the distinct feeling that they desperately wanted to get Cecil out of that college. It was so bizarre because students would be going into classes given by other teachers and coming out looking totally bored. Whereas Cecil's students would be coming out of his class excited and creatively alive, but that meant nothing at all to those staff members. I've learnt since that such an attitude is not uncommon, sadly, but it was very strange to me at the time. Cecil was the first person who talked to me as if I was an artist and that was an absolute revelation for me. I get quite emotional even now when I talk about it.

While I was at St Martin's in the mid-1980s, I was still going to Cecil's afternoon drawing class at the City Lit. Once, I was talking to Cecil about my work which was a sequence of very stark charcoal drawings. He said to me, 'I know exactly what you're doing here because this is what art is. We try to find an image to capture an emotion, to capture something that cannot be expressed in any other way.' He continued, 'I'll tell you something. Years ago, I was walking down a path one morning and in front of me was a very dark bush. There was a sudden sound, it might have been a distant

Cecil Collins
Fool's Hat
1942
Ink and watercolour on paper
27 x 22cm

clap of thunder, and from this large bush lots of tiny black birds flew out against the beautiful blue sky. It was like the bush exploded into all these tiny birds. In the instant I saw that, I thought, an image of delight and I never forgot that.' There must be a scientific term like synaesthesia for people who see E flat as blue or whatever, for certain images which produce particular kinds of emotion.

While I was at St Martin's, probably during the first year of my painting course, I got very stuck. When I told Cecil that I didn't understand what was going on in my work, he said something which I've never forgotten. 'We create in order to understand. We don't understand and then create.' Don't prejudge what you think it should be, don't write the thesis before you've done the work, was what I understood him to mean. I would say that that was one of the single most important things that anyone has ever said to me and it continues to inform very much the way I work; just let it happen and then afterwards you can shape it or do whatever you want to with it.

When people ask me, 'What are you working on now?' I say, 'I don't know, I'm still doing it so it could become anything, I've got no idea what I'm doing, I'm trusting it to happen.' It's like that whether I'm doing a painting or a piece of writing; I just do what I've always done. I get a pile of paper, some pencils, some paints and I start making marks: I let them begin to speak to me and gradually something either happens or doesn't happen, but each of those journeys is worthwhile. I'm creating and out of that something wonderful might happen.

I work completely without a safety net. I pushed that to a huge extent when I was at St Martin's because part of my performance art phase was to stand up in front of an audience and improvise a story from beginning to end, sometimes for two hours at a time. It was like a jazz riff. Finally that led on to me doing drama. I loved it and I wouldn't mind doing that again for a while. I've always described myself as a storyteller. When anyone says to me, 'You do all these different things: you paint, you write for children, you do stage plays, you do films so what is it that you are?' The answer is that in all of them I'm one thing, which is a storyteller. I think Cecil was a storyteller too. Stories work from image to image really and so it's a sequence and film does that better than almost any other art form. The film I'm finishing at the moment, which I've written and directed, tells a sort of Faustian adult fairy tale. It's the story of a young man who can't make sense of the world. So it's one of my little stories and it's full of the images of my childhood haunts.

I absolutely loved the fact that Cecil could be quite didactic, quite prescriptive; after all, that's what you want from a wizard. You wanted somebody to be completely opinionated. Although within the lessons he was just the opposite, he was completely tolerant and open to everything, but there were certain times if you mentioned particular art movements or the ways art was going or when people said they liked something he obviously thought they shouldn't be liking, there was a kind of irritability, shall we say, that would creep in.

To be fair, a lot that he was dismissive about at the time, he's since been proved right. It's a sign of the high regard I have for him that, ever since he's been gone, nearly every second exhibition I go to I think, I wonder what Cecil would have thought of this? Recently, at the Damien Hirst auction at Sotheby's, I was walking around with some friends and I said aloud, 'What would Cecil have made of this?'

With Cecil it was like energy meeting energy, it was like he was the next evolution in human development: from ape to human to Cecil Collins. His presence was pure energy; it was very kind, warm, very gentle and loving, but it was always about the work, it was about the vitality of creative energy. He used to say, 'We are the primitives of the next age.' It was fantastic to have that around me when I was that young. It opened those doorways of how to think about the world and how to think about yourself within that world. How many people could be saved, genuinely helped, if they were able to experience that? I've often thought that if he'd found a way to have got through to the audience that needed to hear what he was saying, it would have happened in a very big way for him because people are still so hungry for what he offered in his teaching and his art.

I always go around with a postcard of Cecil's *Sleeping Fool*. The effect it had on me was like hearing somebody speak a language that I'd forgotten, but knew that I knew. It made me feel less lonely, that I wasn't going mad, that I could relate to people. It made me feel like singing and dancing and like falling in love. It made me feel courage whereas before I'd been afraid. I remember looking at that painting and understanding things in a strange way not just emotionally, but also painterly technical things of rhyming colours and rhyming shapes. I felt that the roundness of the blossom on the tree was also the curve of the Fool's hat and I understood the way that curve is echoed. I realised for the first time how the effect of an elongated body achieved a particular feeling. It tapped down really deep into a collective subconscious in a way that I had not experienced before. The collective subconscious for me are all those images that are in our DNA, I believe. We create and feel a resonance to these images which answer questions for us at a larger and deeper level than we need to know intellectually.

NICOLA TASSIE

Nicola Tassie trained as a painter at Central School of Art where she studied with Cecil Collins. She is now best known as a ceramicist, making hand-thrown functional ceramic ware and also sculptural still-life groups that interrogate the practices of sculpture, ceramics and painting. She is married and lives in London where she maintains a studio and teaches part-time.

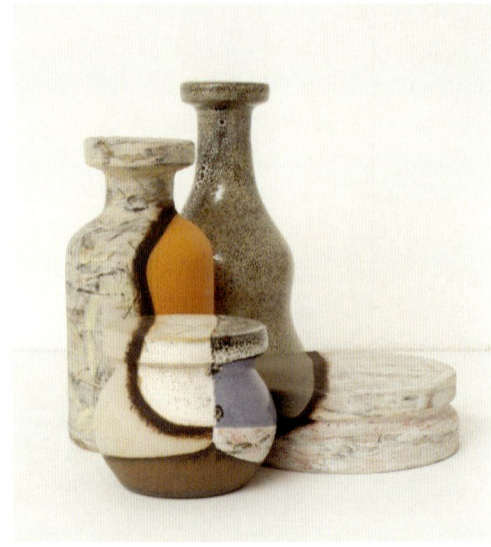

Nicola Tassie
Seaview
2006
Glazed stoneware
18 x 22 x 19cm

I went to Central because I wanted the structure they offered. We had set painting projects and had to do life drawing once a week; it didn't matter which class. If you happened to be free that day, you could elect to go to Cecil's class. A week into the very first term a group of us first years went. We sat down and almost immediately Cecil had the model moving and we had to stand up and follow. After about three poses, Cecil was getting us to go and stand in the middle of the room, we were all terrified. You knew he was going to make each of us take it in turns to do this. We were all deeply self-conscious and I can remember sweating and waiting my turn thinking, I've got to get through this. I've got to just do it. It was one of the most advanced classes he could have given and he did it on purpose, of course he did.

No one refused to do it which I thought was amazing. I think I had my eyes closed and wafted about a bit. Everyone did it and suddenly we all knew each other. The guy next to me was very angular and thought he'd been made fun of. At the end of the class, he was very angry. He didn't say this to Cecil, just to us, and didn't go back.

I think all those movements gave an insight into the people that we were going to be working with for the next three years. I loved it immediately. I loved the fast drawing. I didn't know anything about Cecil. I did mind about standing up and moving, but I felt as if it would be good for me to do that and I also realised that it was a fantastic way to understand the pose in a purely anatomical sense and getting us to use our toes and put brushes in our mouths. He really knew what he was doing, but he was a very cheeky man. He plunged us in.

Cecil always said that you could learn life drawing. You could sit down and study the skeleton and learn to draw that way or you could learn to look and feel and I chose to learn that way. To me, it's a wonderful thing that stodgy old Central which had all kinds of almost ex-army generals teaching there had Cecil as well.

I think Cecil was a wonderful individual. Some people couldn't bear him and others thought it was fantastic to be his student. I was there in 1980 and I think the battle to get rid of Cecil started about then. Patrick was already lobbying to keep him. I don't remember getting too involved in that. I might have signed a petition. Cecil bitched like anything about the system and the bureaucrats and the fact they wanted to get him out, but he didn't criticise anyone personally. I think he rather liked the idea of a student rebellion. I think he orchestrated it in an obvious way: they want to get rid of me, sign a petition to keep me in or something like that. That appealed to our young spirits.

Cecil loved teaching and wanted to carry on. It was important to him to continue at Central because he wanted to stay in touch with what was happening there and be part of modern practice. Although he was very opinionated about the work that was coming out and hated most of it, he was part of that practice. To not care is the worst thing. He definitely had a belief that he wanted to spread to his students. He wanted to give them more than just one choice in how to be. He had a belief that was beyond ego. If you spend your whole life committing yourself to your vision, then you have to carry on. If you stop, then maybe it seems like there's a doubt. I think he knew that he had to be hard sometimes, he wasn't getting at you because he didn't like you; he was impersonal in a funny kind of way.

I didn't do too well at Central. I didn't get on with the other tutors and they were aiming to give me a third. I remember my degree show. We had to put our work up and had to give a talk to Patrick and three other tutors about what we thought we'd learnt the most at the school. I said, 'The thing that I've learnt the most is the life drawing with Cecil Collins. I've done that every single week for three years. I don't think I missed one and I learnt to draw in a way that I had no idea about before. I learnt about philosophy I'd never understood or heard or known about before. If you're talking about learning something real, that was the basis for all my painting and mark making.' I know that that wouldn't have gone down very well because they thought that Cecil was just rubbish and a bit of a dead end for pupils; he was too prescriptive. But Patrick must have said something to Cecil because he came up to me and had a chat about the show. I can't remember everything he said, but it was very much a talk about how to go on from here, about getting a studio and carrying on working and he gave me the name of Mrs Tweedie and said, 'If you have any problems in your life and you need to go and see someone and I'm not here, there's someone to go to.'

I hadn't realised Cecil was noticing so much. I'd thought he was quite casual and maybe that the class was a little bit more about him. Sometimes he seemed a little cruel. I know there were people who absolutely adored him and really wanted his attention and I thought, he's not noticing them. I realise now that was on purpose because they were looking for him rather than thinking about the work. If you're a tutor and you've got lots of people coming in, you don't necessarily clock onto the individual, but Cecil obviously did. He made one of the models cry once, but she was very difficult and he didn't make her cry on purpose. She made a movement and he wasn't pleased with it so he asked her to do it again and maybe again. It was too much for her and she got into a bit of a state. I felt that Cecil was on our side for that because he had to make sure that the model did the right things for us, so there was a nice kind of loyalty to the students.

I realised Cecil was a very anti-authoritarian figure and the complete rebel. I appreciated his sense of humour and his witticisms against people and other tutors; you could joke with him. That was an eye opener because here was an older person on your level and you didn't have to hide anything and that was lovely. I thought it was a shame that the students who were really in love with him, the more sycophantic people, missed that. They couldn't have a joke with him because they were stepping on eggshells a bit. That was a pity because it was definitely the way to go with him. He wanted to find out what young people were like; he didn't want fans. There were a lot of people who took his teaching over to a more mystic, psychic kind of thing and I don't think he wanted that either. He was quite hard with anyone who wanted to push his vision into something that was false.

You need a variety of teachers, but Cecil was definitely the most unusual and interesting person for me at Central. His classes were quite hard work, but they were also amusing and there were lots of funny little incidents. He always wore a huge overcoat and I remember him coming in once and sitting at the back in the corner. 'Psst,' he said, 'come here.' He opened his coat and hanging on the inside were some of his little paintings. They were hanging on a piece of string hooked over a safety pin. They were very small, medallion size, then he closed his coat as if they were fantastic jewels. I realised at that point he had a huge ego. He talked about not having an ego and it was difficult when you realised that he did. It took me a long time to work out that really you have to have an ego to be an individual, but it's about being able to accept that and work through it and not let it dominate.

Cecil taught us the absolute precision of looking at what it is that you're doing. It's like pure concentration which I think is spiritual. That, for me, is the heart of his teaching. You don't go around with a measuring rod, because you aren't doing medical drawings. If you just keep practising, you'll be able to see really clearly with your eyes. You stop worrying about it and do it.

It was wonderful being told what instruments to use because it took away that decision making from you and gave you

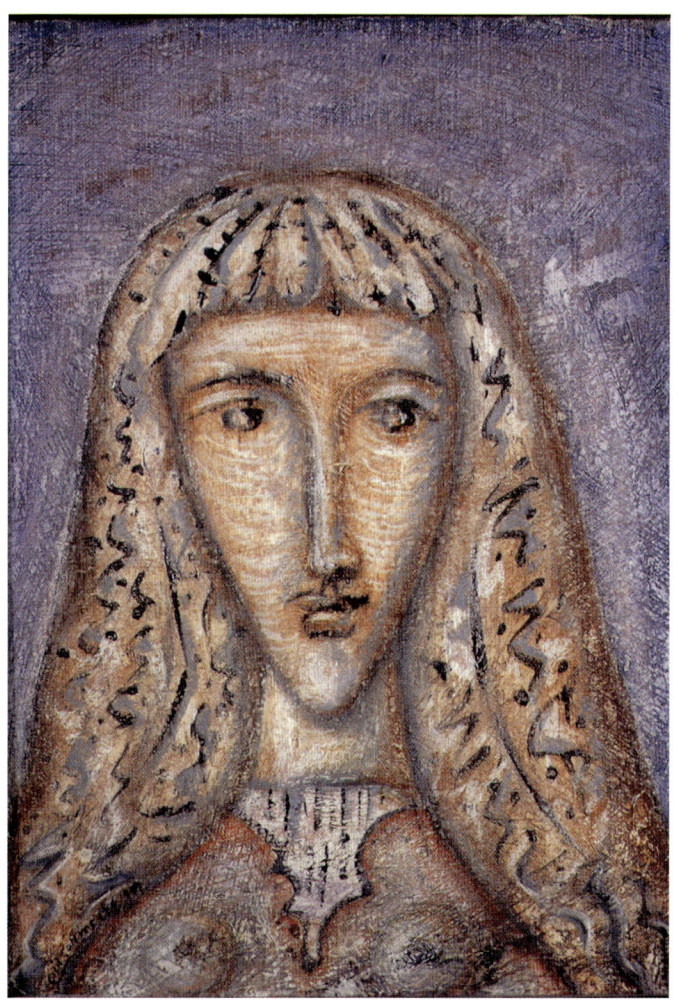

Cecil Collins
Head of a Young Girl
1949
Oil on canvas

freedom to practise. Every now and then, it shovelled up a couple of combinations that you wouldn't have done yourself so that was great. It meant you could concentrate on the form and the materials. If you had picked for yourself, you would have decided in advance how it was going to look.

There was no direction from Cecil about what you were doing. There were a few occasions when he might come round and say, 'Let's have a look at your drawings,' but that didn't happen very often. He would pick out one or two drawings and say, 'This is lovely,' and talk about the balance of the strokes and about the harmonies and the relationship between the instruments and the pose in a quite analytical way. My experience was that often the ones you thought were rather good, the ones your ego was rather pleased with, he would dismiss. Slowly, you began to learn what it was that he was really addressing. You started to appreciate making the chaotic lines and the mess of what Cecil called the 'matrix' and seeing what came out of it a bit more.

When Cecil went round the class, I used to wish he would look at my work, but I didn't feel too put out if he didn't. I think the drawing was so much in the action, that the end product was not what he was interested in; he was concerned with drawing as a great discipline. That's what he was really teaching. The results might not be immediately evident, but they were certainly there for later. Cecil encouraged you to practise letting go and seeing. When Cecil was teaching, it was always about the drawing. He used to say, 'Put your suitcase at the door. Come in and leave your baggage outside.' He would calm you down and create an atmosphere for concentrating. The emphasis was always on that.

I do remember one occasion when Cecil looked at my drawings. We did them on very thin newsprint so it all came through and one was back to front. He took it and said, 'Now that's a lovely drawing.' I was about to say, 'You're looking at the back of it. The paint has seeped through,' but I didn't and I felt like I'd caught him out a bit. I didn't know whether he knew and just carried on anyway. I was a little bit miffed for a while, then I thought it was very funny. He made a particular point of talking about this drawing. Then I realised he was saying it was better back to front because it was looser; that it wasn't just my energy, but that I'd joined with the paper and the material. I began to understand a good drawing is when you are in harmony with the tool and it works.

Sometimes, maybe once or twice, he would talk about a picture that didn't work, but it was always the picture, not the person, that was wrong. It wasn't a personal criticism. If he thought he could see an unbalance or a disharmony, he felt that he could harmonise it by pointing it out. In a way, because they were done so quickly, you couldn't really claim responsibility for the pictures you did.

I remember him talking a lot about the Fool and the Angel in his work. It would be like fairy stories. There'd be the Fool coming to the Angel, someone falling down, things like that. He really believed in them and it was wonderful seeing them come alive. It was a lovely way to explain a painting. If you talk in metaphors about the work, you can understand it. It's not really a princess; it's the idea of everything around that. He spoke in stories, but he wanted you to understood the meaning behind the story.

It was Cecil's vision, but not mine. He had the dreams, he saw the angels, but there was no way that I was able to penetrate that or claim it for myself. It wasn't my practice or my life. I think showing us his little pictures inside his coat was a way of saying they were his and they weren't for you actually. He didn't want you to draw a fool or an angel or something like that. He talked a lot about the Fool, his humility. I saw it through the tools, the materials. His feeling for the instruments was something I completely understood.

I loved his drawings and etchings and loved the little heads that he did. I appreciate them now, but at the beginning I thought some of his drawings were closer to the Surrealists which is where he started. The more icon-like heads were so beautiful: the mark making, the colour, the lightness and everything were absolutely fantastic.

I wish now that I could go back and talk to him more about his earlier paintings. They are much more complex and there's more narrative in them than in his drawings. He only talked about them to me a couple of times, once when I met him outside the school, maybe at his exhibition at Anthony d'Offay's. That was a wonderful show. I thought he had some of his most beautiful things there. They were quite late. For me, those were the pieces I loved the most. His early work can do with quite a bit of help and interpretation because it is so strange. Those sort of pods that are splitting open with things coming out and those chrysalis ideas. They still look incredibly interesting. There's one in Tate Modern hanging with the Surrealists, above Max Ernst. It's difficult to see because it's so high. It's a bit of a jumble that room, but it's interesting seeing Cecil being presented like that. Funnily enough, I think that having gone through a period of anti-painting, people are now very curious about content. They're interested in having more complex paintings that are saying something and they're interested in the technique. I don't think Cecil would be terribly pleased about being in with the Surrealists, but he stands out. There's definitely an individual spirit looking out. He's much more in the heritage of Samuel Palmer and Blake.

I loved the way that Cecil churned up the history of Central. He gave you a better idea of where you came from and where you were going which was much richer and more interesting than what we got from the other tutors. He told you stories, how he

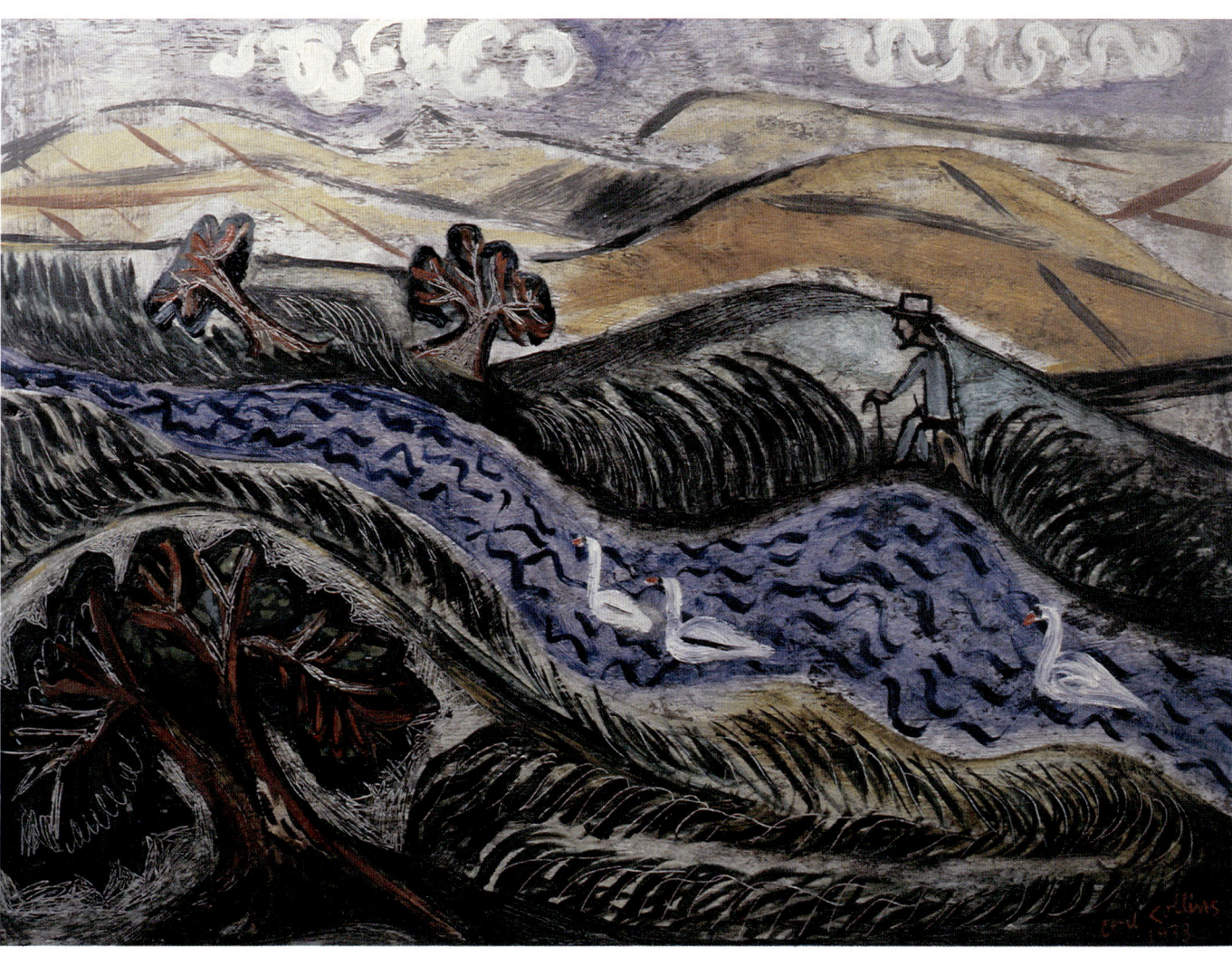

Cecil Collins
Landscape with Artist
1938
mixed media

was taught when he was younger and who he came up against. He talked about when Mervyn Peake taught at Central. I hadn't read *Gormenghast* before and I think I read *Mr Pye* after Cecil talked about it.

I was very interested in Bushman cave art and a few of us students went with Cecil to listen to a talk by Laurens van der Post. We went to quite a few things together: a Steiner talk and one by Glen Schaefer. Cecil would come up and say, 'Have you heard about this person and there's a lecture on that.' He was very friendly with John Allitt who was in the Liberal Studies department at Central and together they introduced us to all sorts of concepts, writers and people we wouldn't otherwise have known about.

I can't remember much about the music he talked about except that he introduced us to Ravel. Sometimes he'd play music, but it didn't happen that often. It was lovely when it did, but mostly we had to move to our own inner music, especially at the beginning when he wanted to find out what we were, and I think that was very important. It was a way of revealing the individual. It's much easier to move to music because that's dancing. You either resolved the movement and ended in a pose or Cecil stopped you when he thought you'd captured a particularly interesting pose. You had to be honest about your movement, which the other students and the model would copy. Then you'd all return to your seats and draw. Perhaps the idea was that you'd end up with a more archetypal kind of drawing because you were doing it so fast. It was a really nice backwards and forwards process: from individual to archetypal, from the general, collective unconscious to single consciousness. The end results were not the most important thing. It was the practice; always the practice.

There were lots of people who said about the sketches, 'It's just fast automatic drawing,' but I had done a lot of that and it's not the same. The inner intention is utterly different. Visually, the brushstroke might be in the wrong place, but it's still come from a different kind of energy; you're not doing a very fast drawing because you're in a hurry. It was more about learning you can't want it; you can't possess it. The drawing might not be arranged in a manner that sings, but every now and then that would happen and was wonderful.

One of Cecil's students, Ruth, was doing sculpture at Central and, if Cecil had to leave the class, she was the person who took over and then I did after she left. I know quite a lot of people in the class found that very difficult because it was Cecil they wanted the attention from. That must have been the time when there was a lot of politics going on at Central because he was often not able to stay for the whole day or had to leave for a while. He was very kind to me and I think he liked me. I was quiet and responsive to his teaching and I was also one of the most regular students. I understood what his approach was about. It really was exactly what I was interested in. I used to enjoy taking over because then I could start using my favourite instruments. I liked red chalk and a brush at that stage and I selected the things I wanted to draw with.

Teaching is quite powerful so you have to be careful about how you use that power. I didn't do too much dancing around or experimenting with the pose or anything like that, but I probably did a bit of everything. I was still interested in all those different instruments that Cecil had introduced me to: reed pens, quill pens, Chinese brushes. I love Chinese brushes; they're still my favourite way of painting. I loved Cecil's idea of the respect for the materials. That's continued to stay with me: the sense before you begin that here are your tools, here are your materials, this is what you are really. I still love and honour that.

After I left college, I went to Lily and Ruth who started a class in Covent Garden. I did some of my best drawings there; it was a lovely time and it was fantastic to have that after leaving the Central. The class lasted all day; there would be Ruth in the morning and Lily in the afternoon. It was great maybe because they were women. They were very different, but there was a wonderful balance between the two, Lily did a lot of matrix work and I felt more comfortable and appreciated it more under her than with Cecil. It took me a while to get something out of it for myself.

I enjoyed doing the drawing and I could have gone on with it, but I stopped and went into clay. I think Lily was surprised, but I needed to get away from the life drawing because it was blocking painting and other ideas. You can't do drawing first and then translate to painting; they're different and I had neglected that side and I've still got a huge urge to get back to painting, but I haven't found a way into it yet.

I went to China a year after I left Central. I bought myself a wonderful collection of brushes and became very interested in Daoism. I found a Daoist temple and sat there and drew all day in the old courtyard with a small gnarled thorn and a huge pine tree in it, very tall and

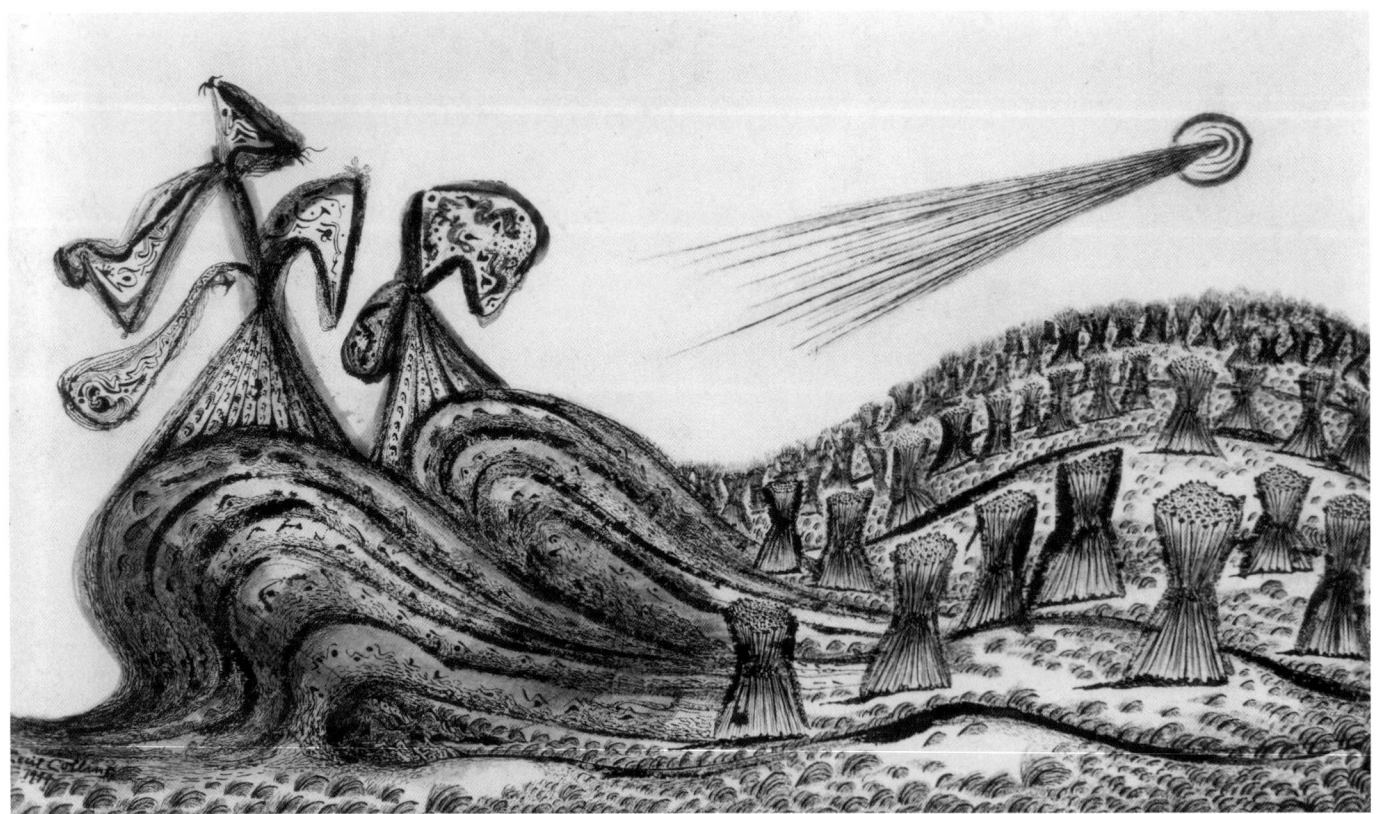

Cecil Collins
Field of Corn
1944
Ink and watercolour on paper
35.5 x 56cm

upright. I stayed in China for about three months, drawing my way around. I had a fantastic time and lots of wonderful conversations about Western art and why it was so ugly and about harmony in the brushstrokes.

I did a lot of paintings of courtyards. Later, I spent some time in Spain in the Alhambra. I liked those open spaces with wind coming in and that atmosphere. I did numerous paintings like that, but got stuck after a while and the pottery took over. A lot of the early pots had dancing figures on them based on the drawings I'd made in Cecil's classes. I'd set up a studio where I was painting for a good five years and doing pottery at evening class and then the pottery took over. I started being able to sell my pots rather than the paintings. The idea was always for the painting to carry on and for the pottery to make my living. I have difficulty with painting, I always have difficulty with subject, but I love the materials, the paint, the colour, the brushes. I still dream about it. Content has been a separate thing. I felt that I had nothing to say, but I remember Cecil's colour exercises. I was very interested in a particular one, working with the very sharp yellows and pinks in this pale high tone. That was fascinating to be affected by that kind of light vibrancy. It's like a high violin string.

Before I got my present studio, I had another one up the road and started taking in children's classes. I used to get groups of girls from Camden High School and I decided to do a Cecil Collins life drawing class with them. I thought, that will churn them all up. It did. It was also terrifying because it was so full of memories for myself and some of the children were so sophisticated. There was one girl who was very good at doing Henry Moore-type drawings. She was very pleased with herself and was annoyed that she wasn't able to show off. Those were heavy responsibilities, to not let someone be like that; I found that quite difficult. You have to believe in the process and not want to be liked and not worry about it. I've always had a bit of a problem with that. I did my classes always as one-offs so there wasn't an opportunity to build up much of a relationship which was hard because students are often quite emotional. They get fed up when they haven't produced anything good and that's quite a lot to cope with at the end of a session, which is always totally exhausting.

If I did a life drawing class in Cecil's way with a load of modern art students, I still think they'd be shocked out of their heads, even though they suppose that they're unshockable by so much art in our society. I would say Cecil's teaching was about you having to put yourself on the line. It's very easy to make a shocking image but, in order for it to be honest, it has to come from an inner truth. Cecil took full responsibility for what he was doing. If it's going to be a stripped down naked truth on the canvas, then do it in the body as well. Taking one hundred per cent responsibility for what you produce, that's one of the hardest things and sometimes I worried whether I believed it enough for myself. It was Cecil's teaching that I was passing on and I felt I wasn't a true enough disciple.

With pottery, you have to be much more patient and definitely have respect for the materials. When I teach, I'm always talking about where clay comes from and trying to use metaphors to give a deeper sense of what it means. I also talk about other potters and other practices.

I met Elisabeth a couple of times. I remember rooms in their flat absolutely crammed full of stuff: books, pictures, everything. She was a wonderfully serene woman and stunningly beautiful and elegant. I liked her show at the Albemarle. I thought what wonderful innocence and spirit her work had. She was very understanding of Cecil's students. She had to deal with all the acolytes around him. Two artists working together is always hard and I wondered what kind of life she must have had with him and what she felt. As a woman, it's always interesting to find out how other women cope with that. I think we have the same problems still. Who's allowed to be obsessed about something outside the home? Am I allowed to be in a dream, thinking about this work the whole time?

There are people whose ego is very big and I think they were attracted to Cecil. It's funny because they were attracted to his ego but, at the same time, the whole teaching was about getting rid of the ego. That created a lot of tension. Many people ended up thinking that perhaps Cecil would wave his magic wand and solve everything for them. They thought that being close to him was sufficient, but it's the working practice that counts. Cecil might be a visionary, but he's not you and being close to him is not going to mean anything. It's always about the work, the drawing, this creativity. I immediately recognised that. I just jumped in the river, found it was swimmable and loved it. I was taken further along a path I wanted to learn about and I got everything out of it.

If I had to say what I've carried through from Cecil's classes, it must be the sense of extending yourself through the materials, through the tools that you use. They become an extension of your fingers and your hands so there's no separation. You're truly concentrated which means you're not thinking of yourself and of what you want. It's always when you don't think about what you want, that you allow something to come through. Throwing clay is like that. If you pre-decide what shape you want, you just can't make it. If you desire it, it won't happen. You have to be absolutely present in the moment and concentrate on it completely. I love that humility in relation to the tools. I always used to bow to the materials, as Cecil had us do, to pay respect to them before I started my drawing. Mentally I still do.

HOWARD VIE

Howard Vie was born in Stockton on Tees, County Durham and studied with Cecil Collins at the City Lit from 1980 to 1987. His recent work as architectural illustrator includes over two hundred and fifty freehand drawings for the Conservation Area Studies published by the London Borough of Richmond upon Thames.

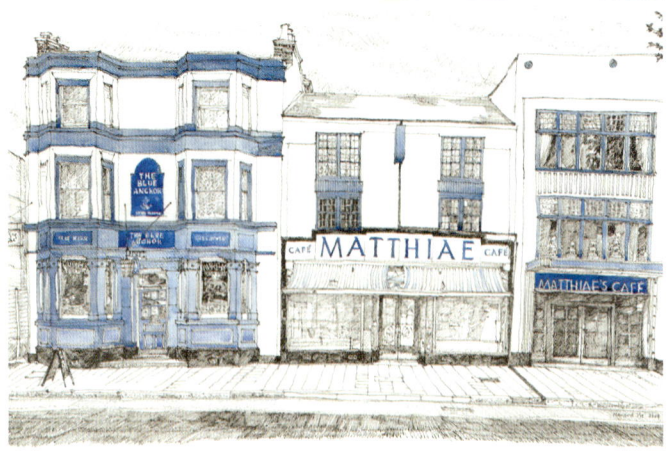

Howard Vie
Matthiae's Bakery, Kew Road, Richmond
2004
Ink drawing and blue watercolour wash
76 x 56cm

I've done a lot of different things. After studying engineering at Cambridge and then architecture at the Architectural Association, I became an electronics technician and worked in California for three years. When I returned to England and was working as a technician at the Royal College of Art, I decided I'd like to do art so that's how I got started. There used to be lots of art classes at the City Lit and I got wind of the amazing things that were going on in the life room: painting with your feet and such like. That sparked off my interest and I went to see if I could join.

In Cecil's classes it was a long, hard road of practise, practise and more practise until eventually you got to the point where you might be able to draw. I've done quite a lot of yoga where you take up positions or move in a certain way and practise over and over again. Cecil's classes were very similar to that. You do the same thing week in, week out and nothing seems to happen, but actually something is happening.

It's amazing the way he could teach people how to draw. He used to start the class with movements and often set these to music. He would get us to move our hands to get a gestural relationship with the brush stroke. I think the richness of the movements and gestures gets built into you. There are things you can learn to do in a mechanical way, but you can't learn to draw mechanically. It's something you get into slowly. Maybe it was all those movements; eventually it became engrained.

I heard a Rachmaninov piano concerto on the radio the other day and it seemed desperately familiar. I'm sure we did movements to it. We were tuning our movements to the different rhythms of drawings; we'd start doing dots, then short strokes, longer lines and then extend into a long continuous line. There were so many things which really enriched the marks we made. When I do my architectural drawings and draw a line, that's still in me. In the last five years, I've done about two hundred drawings of buildings for Richmond Council and, if they're any good, it's down to Cecil. I wouldn't be able to draw at all if it wasn't for him.

He used to do a summer course in which he would make us do colour exercises at the beginning of the class, using a triad of colours in circles or triangles and I'd do them again at home very neatly with nice gouache. His colour theory was absolutely fascinating; it didn't follow the normal optical colour theory that we're all familiar with. It was more like musical notation. I would call it a musical colour theory because it had major and minor colours that corresponded with the major and minor modes in music and he used to refer to colour as vibrations. I think he wanted to get the emotional power of music into paintings, its modes, moods and chords. We studied rhythms with drawings and rhythms with colour and structure where you have a dominant, a sub-dominant and a bass or background. I really liked doing those classes and I've kept all my Cecil material because it's interesting to see the progression from start to finish.

You set the tone of a painting so that a blue-black painting with a few little white highlights sets up a very different mood to a yellow, red and white painting. Sometimes Cecil brought some of his small paintings into class. I remember in particular one of his lovely little blue icon paintings which was of an angel, a hill and a sunrise. It's absolutely exquisite and a fantastic blue and is shown in the film, *The Eye of the Heart*. He used to bring them in the pocket of his suit and show us. The one he did near the end of his life has a yellow face and doesn't have the same depth of painting. It's much bolder and, in a way, cruder than the very different, slightly hidden, mysterious blue one.

He put a lot of effort into organising his classes. It wasn't just him turning up and saying do this, do that. There was music to choose. There might even be films or slide shows he would have selected the images for. He was a multi-faceted person and his teaching was part of that. He said that teaching was an important part of his work as an artist. I suppose it was another way of transmitting his vision.

Cecil had an amazing agenda for what art is. He was a visionary dreamer. I've always been interested in how medieval cathedrals got built, how these fantastic things were created. We don't seem to be able to do anything like that now. I think Cecil gives us a clue as to how and why it was done. He had a sense of the history of art and a reality beyond history. They were constructed for the glory of God. He had a real vision for what art was as part of what it could be and, in a way, he was fulfilling that happening. Cecil taught that there was something else out there. He was communicating some kind of truth and said that he was a Neo-Platonist. Plato describes the cave where people are watching the shadows, but there's light outside and that's the reality. Cecil saw himself and his art as a conduit to bring that light into the world. He wasn't just painting like a classical painter. He was an innovator, but not merely thinking up new ideas.

Cecil had a strong sense of his own importance. He said you needed the egoistic drive as an artist in order to bring visions out into the world. He was successful, a bright spark, hero of the RCA, winner of prizes, bright new kid on the block, exhibitor at the Whitechapel Gallery, but then he turned his back on all that although he desperately wanted recognition. He wanted that exhibition at the Tate Gallery. They did make him a Royal Academician in the end, but very late.

He was fun. He used to play funny games with his false teeth. He'd poke them out and make funny faces. He wasn't a particularly robust person but, in a strange way, it seemed fairly irrelevant because his presence was so powerful.

I was quite attracted by Cecil and wanted to get to know him. He used to have me round to his house to help him tidy up or do DIY jobs. He asked me to help clear his room and I rolled up the ten-foot painting *The Fall of Lucifer* that's now in the Tate. Unfortunately, it was damaged by being stored in this way, but has been restored.

There's a book to be written about the relationship between Cecil and Elizabeth. She used to say, 'I have to keep him in order,' and 'He's being silly again.' She was the practical one and he was the visionary dreamer. They obviously had their *modus operandi* and I remember the pleasure of having tea with them. They lived very modestly at the top of the house. What I remember from being there is the painting behind the sofa, the crockery, the white table and the gas fire in the studio. I remember rummaging around, helping Cecil, and finding old £10 and £20 notes in his studio.

I went to Cecil's private view at the Tate Gallery just before he died. I said I was sorry he'd been ill and he said, 'When you're creative, it doesn't matter,' or something like that. Cecil used to say, 'We're in the midst of a great mystery.' He wanted to share this with other people and he wanted his paintings to have an impact, to transmit his great vision full of depth, breadth and space.

ANNE WALKER

Anne Walker studied at Dartington College of Arts, Devon, Rolle College of Education, Devon, and the Royal College of Art where she obtained an MA in Design in Education. Her work has frequently been shown in group exhibitions. She lives in Worcestershire, teaches occasionally and continues to work in water-based mixed media.

I was introduced to Cecil Collins in the autumn of 1976 by a friend whose life drawings were completely different from much of the impressive, analytical figure drawings I had aspired to at art college. Cecil's classes at the City Lit were already full, but through my friend's intervention, I was asked to attend a class so that Cecil could assess whether one more person could be squeezed in.

My first impressions were of a tall, Victorian room with no easels, only numerous battered tables, and Cecil sitting in the corner, acutely observant, a ringmaster and choreographer. He directed the class, stern and humorous at once. We, the students, listened and then responded to a piece of music, exploring the rhythms with as little self-consciousness as possible: graphite traces, sinuous lines and percussive Conté marks capturing the model's pose and the atmosphere of the moment. 'Left hand, brush, point to belly.' 'Hold pencil in mouth.' I was in awe.

Cecil agreed to let me join and so began three years of unexpectedly intense experiences. Far from learning new techniques, I embarked on the painful breakdown of every preconceived idea I had embraced about figure drawing and many of the approaches I had worked so hard to develop. I found it difficult to allow myself to draw on impulse, to give up the control of mediums and marks. I often enjoyed responding to music and could interpret mood and rhythm through physical movement, but once the drawing activity started, I reverted to old patterns.

I resented being told what drawing implement or medium to use and I resented Cecil's dictatorial teaching style. Left and right hands simultaneously; two different mediums; wrist, elbow and shoulder movements, mouth, even feet. Extreme frustration gave way to deep, muffled anger. I wanted the freedom to draw in ways I felt used to and yet I couldn't leave the class.

The class was crowded, often hot and stuffy, and I found it particularly difficult when, occasionally, Cecil would ask us to lie face down on the floor. I resented the indignity of such a request, not to mention the smell of another student's feet that happened to be near the place I was lying. Every week I turned up and each week I simmered, seemingly getting nowhere. My anger was so deep that I don't think I knew I was angry. I hated Cecil at times.

One term, two incidents occurred during separate classes that served to reflect to me the reality of my condition. During one lesson, Cecil asked each of us to put a drawing on the wall. The class looked and listened while Cecil commented on each anonymous piece of work. I don't remember much of what he said, but it was largely concerned with aspects of visual language shown in various drawings. As he came to my drawing he casually said, 'That drawing is full of anger.' I was shocked. How could he say such a thing? This was supposed to be an art class. I felt like walking out.

On another occasion, a man sitting near me spoke to Cecil about the difficulties of working in such conditions. I empathised with him because he was articulating what I myself felt and would like to have said, but didn't have the courage. To me, the man's words seemed reasonable and politely expressed. At once, Cecil pounced on him with an intellectual emotional power that I had not witnessed before. Cecil finished his response by telling the student to leave the class.

I saw myself in the student. His words were also mine and yet I had not been asked to leave. On the contrary, Cecil had squeezed me into the already-overcrowded class and hadn't responded to any of my previous grumbles in such a way. He could also, apparently, read extreme anger just by looking at my drawing. I felt he hadn't known the drawing was mine and this made his comment all the more penetrative because it was made impersonally. I felt naked.

I realised I needed to face the fact that not only was I very angry, but also this anger, or energy, was beginning to motivate my drawing, even though it was not the sort of motivation I would care to own up to. I wanted to draw beautiful and profound pictures of the human figure, using all the marks I had discovered during the classes.

My drawings, in my opinion, were a mess. I had to accept that, in order to truly draw, I had to work with what I truly was. In other words, I needed to use the anger, as well as other impulses, to make art and not section off parts of myself in order to make the art I aspired to.

Even though my work seemed a mess and nothing seemed to be working the way I wanted it to, I was beginning to truly draw. I also realised that perhaps I wanted, or even needed, to leave the classes. In another situation, it could have been me that Cecil had asked to leave. He didn't and I hadn't, but maybe the time had come to go.

A few months later I did leave, and this time away from the intensity of the weekly classes proved to be important. I was able to start a slow, on-going process of making what I had experienced in Cecil's classes my own, not just a series of techniques which I adopted and applied to every drawing or painting. I aspired to make art from the guts, as well as the intellect: art that had light and darkness, preferably in combination. I began to accept that artwork cannot always be designed, that it will not always go the way I want it to and that all this would take time and hard work.

At the preview of Cecil's Print Exhibition at the Tate Gallery it was crowded, hot and airless. Cecil was surrounded by many of us who wanted to speak to him. I had not seen him since I left the City Lit and during these years my acknowledgement of the value of his classes had given way to a deeper awareness of his brilliance as a teacher. I didn't necessarily understand or share his analysis of art or spirituality in art, but he had been a superb catalyst for change. Whatever creativity is, it had been evident in his classes. I wanted to thank him personally for what he had given me. There was a problem, though; he was completely ring-fenced. A situation then arose which I cannot explain. He was suddenly alone. It was as if all those around him had backed away a few feet. In the centre of his prestigious Tate Gallery exhibition, he was alone.

Momentarily, I felt as if there was no one else in the hall. I caught his eye. He smiled that mischievous smile that always made me wonder what was coming next. I was able to approach him freely, full of gratitude, intent on saying something or other, but he pre-empted me. 'You've changed a lot,' he chuckled. My deep feeling was expressed without words. Nice one, Cecil!

Anne Walker
Infinity Marmalade
2007
Watercolour, ink and gold leaf
15 x 10.5cm

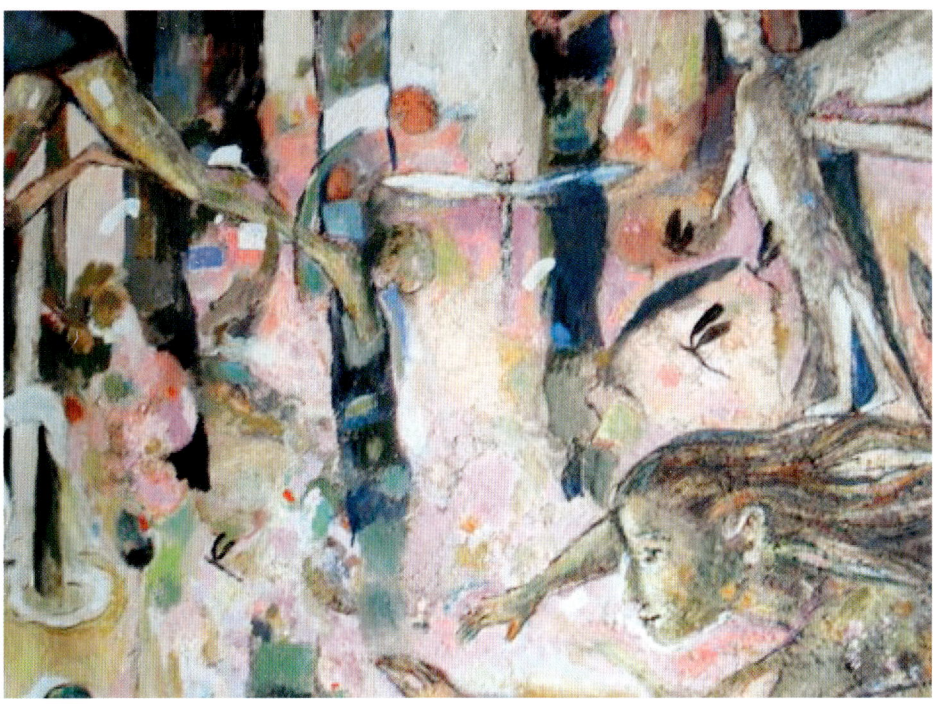

Jaqueline Warner
Demoiselles - Hampstead Pond
2002-2007
Oil on canvas
140 x 125cm

JACQUELINE WARNER

Born in Switzerland in 1945, Jacqueline Warner studied art history at Geneva University before coming to London where she still lives. She studied art with Cecil at the City Lit and continues to paint, make prints and have occasional shows. She is married with two children.

I became interested in Cecil because he'd been called a teacher of genius by a friend who'd gone to his classes. When I heard that, I knew I too would go. At the time, and for years, I felt inadequate and that I was not ready to study with him. Then one day I was looking in my old diary and in it I'd written, 'I want this year to be the year of the transformative vision.'

I was already at Central to do printmaking and had heard of Cecil Collins, but I didn't contact him, probably because my feelings of inadequacy were augmented by the admiration of the people in the department for him, and I also saw the results of his own printmaking. One of the young girls there went to his summer course at the City Lit and I thought the drawing she brought back was wonderful even though she was not doing very good work at Central. I knew then that I must go to his classes.

That summer course was a revelation of colour. I wrote in my diary about a red poppy that had opened up in my garden just then which, for me, was like a symbol, a confirmation that I had done the right thing. I had studied art theory and always assumed that colour is instinctual and some people are devoid of it. Suddenly, after Cecil explained a few things, I had a completely different understanding. When he first told us about colour opposites and their resolution in a third, the harmony became immediately apparent. We had to paint working with these colour opposites. You started with one colour, painting one of the plants available in the wonderfully light studio at the top of the City Lit building. Then you had to do it all in the opposite colour and then, on top, you put the mixture of those two or a third colour. The harmonies were so wonderful.

I did history of art in Geneva and it was only in England that I did a foundation course where the tutors were bringing in all the new ideas introduced by Itten who taught colour theory at the Bauhaus. With Cecil, there was much more of an integrated system than a theory and he included black and white, unlike Itten. Cecil also linked colour with music. That was another revelation. It was very powerful and I still haven't finished exploring the relationship of colour and music. I remember Cecil played us the Schumann *Kinderscenen*. When I hear that music, my body still responds, my hands go up and I move and remember the inspiring time with Cecil. In my diary I wrote, 'Impossibility of becoming unselfconscious, impossibility of moving', but I still feel very moved. To be moved into ourselves, that was very important, especially when you really felt blocked as I noted in my diary.

I put Cecil on a pedestal and there was the feeling of respectful distance that exists between a teacher and a student. Sometimes Cecil would come over and say something very astute like, 'Your energy is dynamic so you can't do melancholy,' or 'You can't do everything.' I had melancholic feelings so I thought I should be able to paint this. Another of the important things he said to me was, 'You have a long way to go till you can drop all the mental and intellectual things.' That was rather awful and discouraging, but it was true and I also felt encouraged by him to go on along the path, however long. He was right as I'm still in the middle of that process. He said that after several sessions when we were becoming a bit more friendly. He understood a lot, but I felt there was always this distance. My father was very distant too and, in a way, Cecil was a bit of a father figure. He was always very formally attired with several jackets. He was like Proust so maybe it was also an image he chose to create. He would dress in layers and layers of material and although he would ask us to move, he would hardly move, but his beautiful hands would gesture to make a point.

During the time I was at the City Lit, there was what I call a star pupil. It wasn't just a feeling on my part; it was self-evident. I think Cecil admired her work although he rarely said anything about anyone else's. The nearest I got to a compliment from him was the first time he saw my work. When he saw what I'd done he said, 'I can see you've been working a lot of years already.' He didn't say, 'You're lost,' but that I'd done a lot of work and therefore I was pleased. I felt good that I had been recognised and what I'd achieved was not nothing. He was very good at being able to understand your inner self through every aspect of what you did, how you behaved and probably how you moved. I think that was one of the things that nourished him: the way we were, the way we moved and worked. In a way, we were all doing art as a process of healing ourselves because one day the star pupil came to the class with her husband who was a young homeopath and he said, 'What I wanted to get from this class is the energy of healing and understanding.' I thought that was very interesting.

I was rereading Winnicott and he also says something like 'being comes before doing'. That was really what you learned in Cecil's classes. Being. The doing grew out of that. He also taught us the meaning of surrendering through the physical body. We had to get down onto the ground, the final position of surrender, and we accepted it. This was also connected to how he introduced us to what he called the instruments. The phrase he used was, 'You will make friends with the instruments: the quill, the paper.' We had to make a lot of the instruments ourselves, the quills, the reed pens, and grind the ink-sticks with water for our drawings. In a way, we made instruments of ourselves. I liked all that. After what we had been taught by other tutors, that nothing mattered, just pick up anything. That's similar to what Picasso said: 'If I don't have blue, then I do it in red.' In a way, that's very good too, but I loved the way Cecil introduced us to the idea of the instrument. It went back into a very ancient idea of the power of materials. If one picked up a stick as a burst of consciousness, then something could happen.

What was interesting was that Cecil didn't have a repertoire. Some themes would return, but how they would appear was always different. That was what was so marvellous. Somebody got one story and others were given a totally different story to make the same point. I remember Cecil's ideas of conviviality. He always said, 'The important thing is the company you keep.' He told many stories and one was about Machiavelli. In the evening Machiavelli went to his study, put on his best robes and hat and conversed with angel philosophers. That was Cecil's story about the importance of the company you keep. Everyone in class said, 'But it didn't do Machiavelli any good.' Cecil was quite provocative and often very ironic.

At the time I was doing Cecil's classes, I was making little carvings with bits and pieces I had found. I made one with a bone for him. On it I carved and painted a face and then stuck a couple of feathers on it so it was sort of like an angel. I felt I had been given so much by him and I wanted to give him something. I remember he said, 'That's nice.' I don't think he liked it at all, but he said, 'I'll put it on as a headdress when we walk in the street.' That was lovely. He liked the idea of the fool and dressing up. I was just re-reading *The Vision of the Fool* and it is so pertinent for now. He was a visionary who also had a bitter sense of irony about the world.

I felt Cecil was a real teacher who maintained a certain distance because people projected so many things onto him as a result of what the exercises and the energy of the classes opened in them. I was someone who had not conceived for years and suddenly the ultimate creative thing happened to me: I became pregnant. Afterwards, Cecil used to say, 'I remember you almost gave birth in the class.' Although when I first went I wasn't pregnant, I certainly felt it was due to going to his classes and partly also because I had taken up yoga a few years before. Then when the baby was born, I stopped going to Cecil's class and felt that I couldn't take up art again for some years.

Just before I became pregnant, an image came to me in a dream and I made a painting on the theme of the Annunciation of a woman and a bird-like figure with a ring. I remember telling Cecil about the dream source of my painting which, at the time, I thought had to do with me being creative. Then shortly afterwards when I discovered I was pregnant, I realised that all those things were so connected: the personal creative and Cecil. I can't remember what he said, if anything. There was nothing to say or maybe because I felt he had something to do with it, he thought perhaps it was too personal to comment. I felt that his teaching about the creative and the union of masculine and feminine energies had been like an expansion within me, a discovery of what being creative is, what the creative act is. The classes were not about a mechanical repetition or examination of something. All his classes were about finding out more and more about the creative. For me, that was very important, especially at that time. He used to say self-expression was nothing. That was another revelation because one always assumed it was about the individual artist, revealing one's own originality.

One of the criticisms of his classes was that, after a while, everybody produced the same sort of work, but there's an element of that happening with all teachers, not just Cecil. Sometimes people had to leave his class to integrate his teaching into their own being and work. I don't know if some people felt they'd understood what he taught, and mistakenly thought it meant they had to do something specific, which was just the opposite of what he was teaching. It was as if they had to conform to something he'd never prescribed. I think he couldn't prevent it happening and perhaps he had to allow it. Then if real understanding was going to develop, they would have to come through that stage. Their misunderstanding was also connected to this false idea that one had to be feeling terribly spiritual. I've seen how sharply Cecil could deflate *that* because the purpose was wholeness, not goal orientated or a separation of everyday life and spirit.

Music was so important to Cecil and in the classes. He wouldn't listen to any interpretation or any piece of music, he always selected what he considered the finest. He would choose music which would provide an opening for us into that inner dimension he was focused on. Of course, the music was linked with silence. In his classes, at the beginning and at the end, there was a period of silence. Maybe he played the music to make you listen to the silence. The movement, too, I found very important. There was an attunement of the body and the hands. Although I still follow a lot of what he taught, I've lost that practice now working on my own, but I wonder if maybe I should start doing it again. I do listen to music that I've selected, that has meaning for me, and it often has the same effect, to loosen and open one up and refine one's senses. When I go down into my studio, to open that creative flow, I often start by doing my meditation. Going into the silence. I feel it's a kind of prayer as well. That's what Cecil was showing us: how it happened and how it could be. It isn't about self-expression because creative energy is universal and our own individual expression of it happens automatically if we can enter the silence.

Cecil Collins
By the Waters
1980
Gouache
46 x 59cm

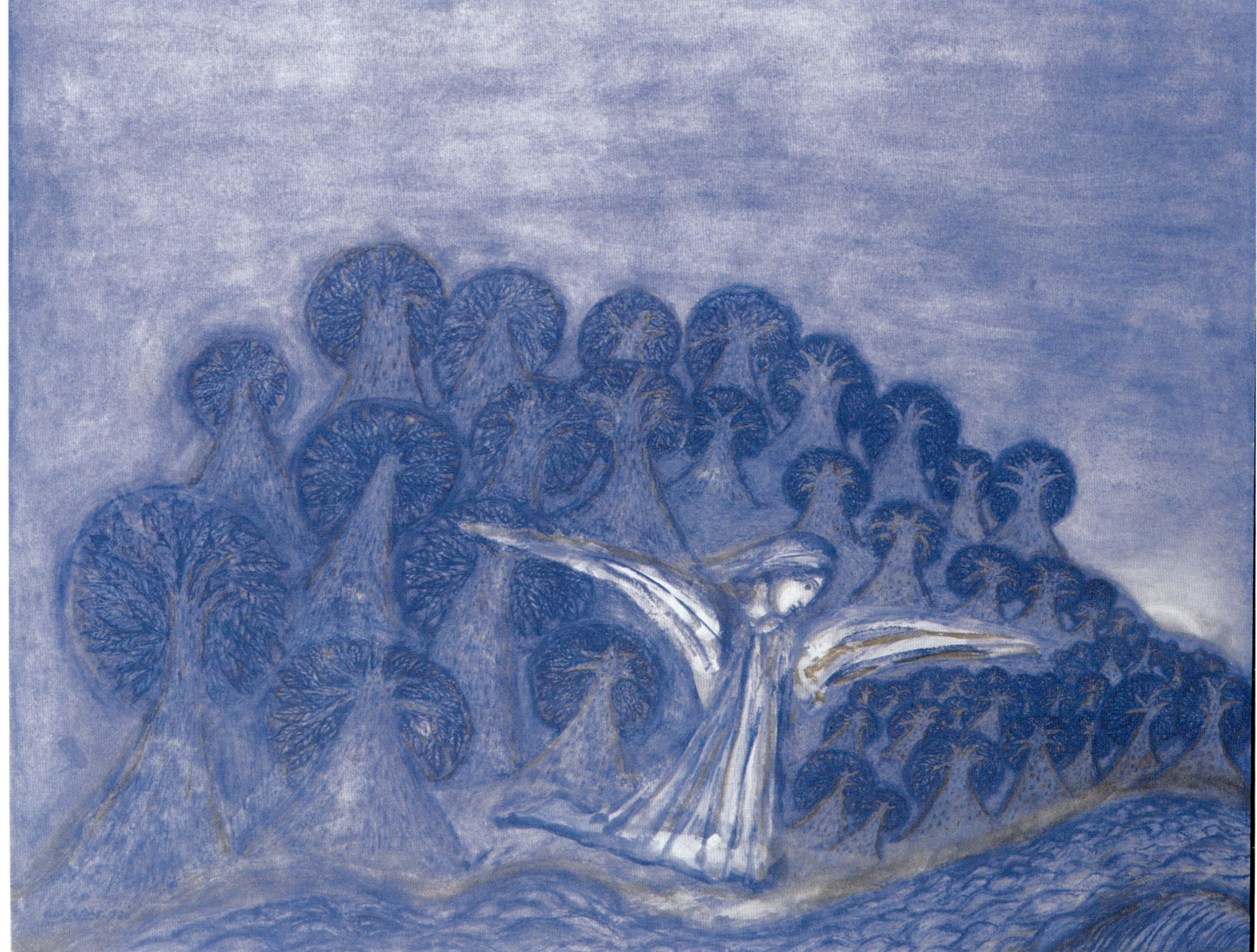

WILLOW WINSTON

Willow Winston has degrees in Painting and Printmaking from the Central College of Art and Design, winning the Stowells Trophy for printmaking while there. Her art is in major museums and collections in the UK and the US. She has taught at colleges in both countries. She continues to explore the common ground between science, visual art and music in work which ranges from book-art to large-scale sculpture.

Cecil was such a great example to us. I first met him in the spring of 1974 when I started at Central College of Art. Two years before that, I had taken my vows as an artist and I'd largely worked by myself, completely isolated. I was very inspired by William Blake and knew that I had to engrave, but I didn't really want to go to art school because I thought it would fiddle with my brain. However, Central was just right. It was totally open and fine art oriented. I'd met up with Leonard Marchant who taught in the etching studio and was a specialist in mezzotint. Leonard said, 'I think you'll have to apply to come here.' He convened an interview for me and I pitched up a week or two later. On the panel interviewing me was Cecil and two or three other people. Cecil sat there looking interestingly eccentric and kind. I had a whole portfolio of drawings with me, some of which were very extraordinary and some more ordinary. At some point Cecil said to me, 'I see you have a very rich inner life,' and I thought, oh no. They'll never let me in now. They've found me out. So I said, 'Yes, but I do all sorts of drawings of landscape and from life. Look.' I started to pull out all these ordinary drawings from my portfolio and Cecil said, 'It's perfectly all right to have a rich inner life.'

After the interview was over and it was settled that I was going to join the postgraduate department, Cecil came up to me and said that any time I wanted to speak to him or had a problem, he'd be very pleased to meet me. He explained that he was in the school two or three days a week and then he showed me where I could find him. He'd found for himself a small space round the back where he'd created his own little kingdom. It was very special. He used to come up by the lift to the fourth floor. If you turned left out of the lift, there was a narrow passageway that didn't seem to go anywhere, but a door led into the back of a studio that Cecil reckoned was the best studio of all as it had north-facing light and very tall windows. There was a screen which I think Cecil must have erected himself. It cut off a weeny corner, but didn't take anything away from the students' painting space. This extraordinary cubbyhole was where I would find him if I wanted him.

I worked very hard at Central. I produced one image after another in etching and in engraving. I would go most weeks to see Cecil to show him my new work. The printmaking department was

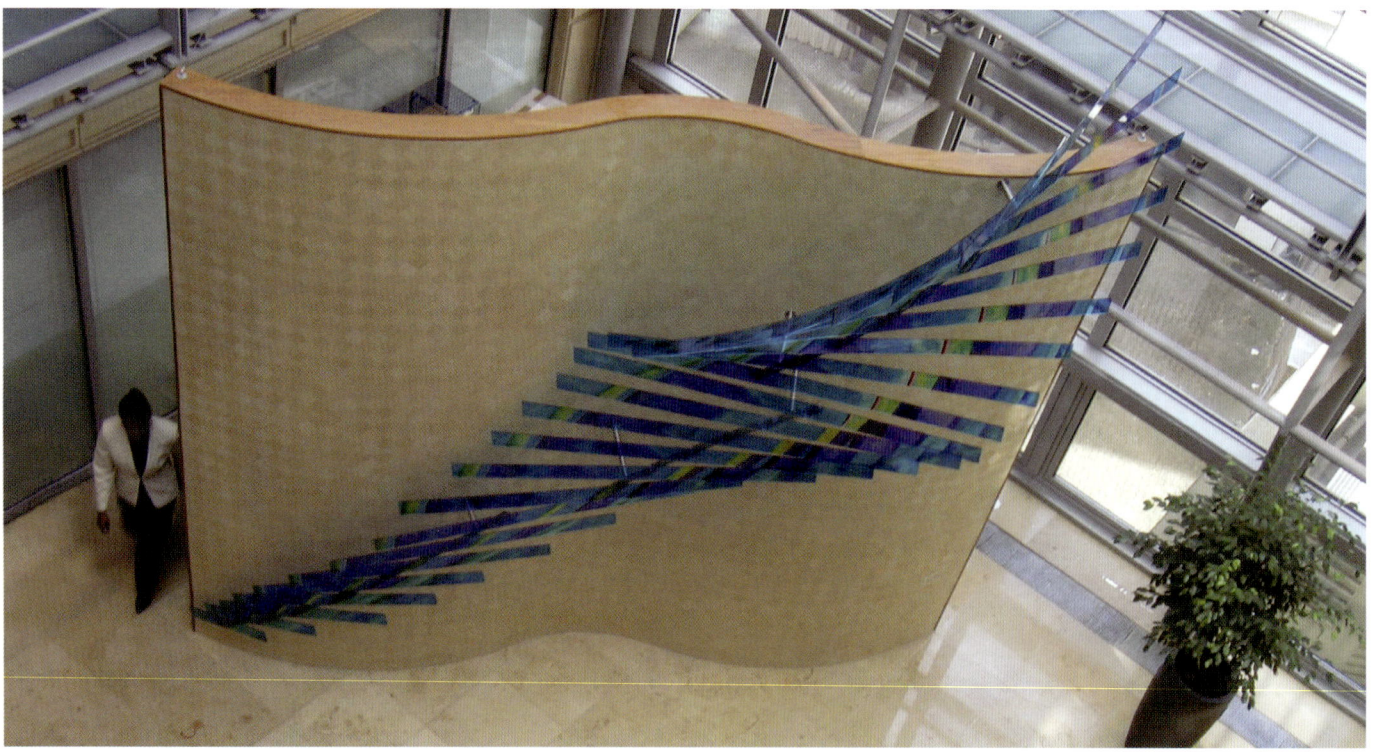

Willow Winston
Thames Tide Rising
2005
Cast acrylic/stainless steel/glass paint
450 x 530 x 180cm
commissioned by John Laing plc for their London Head Office

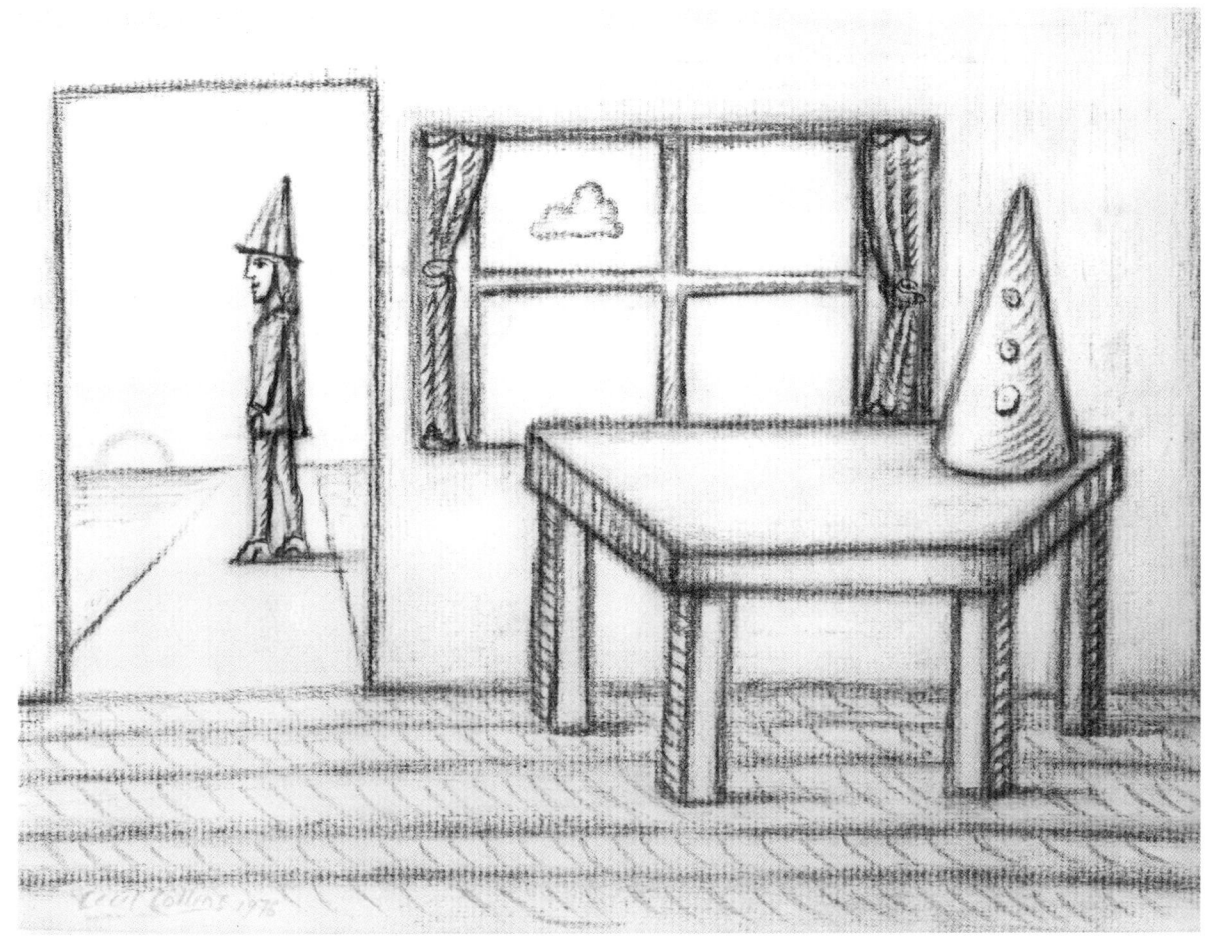

Cecil Collins
The Afternoon of the Fools II
1976
Pencil on paper
20.3 x 24.2cm

very sympathetic and supportive, but Cecil talked about what lay behind the image, not just about the image-making. The inner life of the work wasn't about technique or how I'd made the image. Technique can be quite deceptive; it can interfere. In a way, I almost had to destroy my technique in order to really achieve my artistry and that's what Cecil was so wonderful about. Cecil's understanding was so deep that he wasn't deceived by my technique. He was interested in my vision, but he knew that I could go much further if I left behind my ability, my natural inclination, which was a bit too virtuosic. One day I remember him saying to me something like, 'You need to go to the other side of the cloud. You need to get into the mist, away from your masculine principle which is dominating you so much.' I listened to him; I still listen to him. He encouraged me to think of going beyond being a printmaker. I was very committed to being a printmaker because it's a very democratic art form, but Cecil felt that I needed to expand the energies physically, to the full body. When you're an engraver you tend to be hunched over; it's quite constrained.

On a number of occasions Cecil said that I should paint, but all my work was in black and white and I couldn't bear the thought of using colour. I'd drawn all my life, but I wasn't interested in colour. It was the graphic, the etching that attracted me. I resisted Cecil initially and then a friend of mine gave me some new acrylic paints he'd discovered, Liquitex. Acrylic is normally to be despised, but these were very beautiful colours. I made some images and Cecil said that I should apply to the painting school for a BA. I told Cecil, and this was really weird because I didn't know it myself, 'Well okay. I'll apply for painting here, but actually I want to do sculpture.' I applied to Exeter for sculpture and to Central for painting.

I didn't think that Central would want me because I was one of the people who'd helped to organise sit-ins when Central started the process of wanting to get rid of Cecil, using the excuse that he was over sixty-five. I remember hearing the Beatles' song 'When I'm Sixty-four' blaring out of one of the painting studios. This was played in Cecil's honour, although by then he was sixty-six, but I was so focused on my work I hadn't realised till then that they were trying to get rid of him. Of course I joined in the chorus.

Loads of us went down to County Hall. We sat, filling the whole floor of the ILEA's Education Department there and brought the place to a standstill. I was one of the spokesmen as I could put an argument well. They didn't sack him that time. The following year we marched into the Principal's office in the Central School and we did the equivalent of a sit-in again. There was great rejoicing when a letter in support of Cecil written by Henry Moore and other eminent people appeared in *The Guardian*. It was a major moment. Henry Moore was also a teacher and aware of the world and how art was going down the drain. Cecil was accused of creating a coterie, a kind of a cult, because his students loved him so, but he was the one teacher in the painting department who actually had a technique to impart.

When I got into the painting school, I asked for Cecil as my tutor, obviously. He would pop into my studio most weeks to see what was on the boil. I was working mostly with watercolour as I had not yet fallen in love with oil paint. That put the other tutors out. I remember one of them saying, 'There are only two sorts of painting that are any good and that's French or Italian.' He was implying that those are the only people you have to emulate. Cecil was technical in his advice. He was also very aware of the vibration of a composition. For example, he said of a composition I was working on, 'Be careful there. You might be moving into a visual squeak.' That means when a very important movement of the composition, let's say an angle, comes very close to the edge of the canvas or whatever you're painting on, it literally squeaks because it's so close. 'Watch your intervals,' he'd say. 'You're getting too close to the edge. It's going to squeak.'

The other tutors didn't understand what the students were getting from Cecil. When he spoke of seeing with the 'eye of the heart', he was speaking of himself as a teacher. When he looked at your work, even a scribble, or a tossed away piece of paper, he could tell from the vibrations when you were troubled and would offer some advice, often not directly technical, more spiritual in a way. I remember one occasion when I was in deep despair about the work I was doing he said, 'You're swimming in the middle of this lake and it just seems you're never going to get to the other side. Don't worry. Don't struggle too hard. You will get to the other side.' It was like a lifeline because he understood. You could then move on from unnecessary worry into the work itself. That's what he gave to the students.

His life drawing class was technically amazing. It still works for me. It's not the precision of the technique so much as the precision of the exact experiences of making of a mark, the nature of the feeling, the energy that is contained within the mark and expressed by it. Each type of mark, each type of movement, contains its own living spirit, its own energy. Cecil pinpointed this. He made it quantifiable. The second position entailed the use of the wrist and only the wrist; it's a continually flowing mark. In the first couple of years when he said position two, I struggled. I hated it. For weeks and months, there was little that you would recognise as a drawing and it was the most important lesson of all, the letting go of the ego. Each time you had to overcome whatever resistance you might have. You were almost like a blind person feeling your way towards the real meaning of the mark. Not what it looked like, but what energy it conveyed. In a way, it equates with music: with the scales and the chords, the arpeggios of music. He used a fair amount of music in his life-drawing class for the model to dance to or the students. You'd find yourself lying on the floor with a stick of charcoal or something utterly impossible, drawing the model whose dance we had to follow. It was quite funny though nobody laughed; we were all so stretched. You were much more likely to cry than laugh with all those bits of paper covered with scribble. It was the world of complete dedication to the unknown. There were days when we weren't allowed to talk. He would warn us that it was going to be a whole day of silence, lunchtime as well, no breaks. It turned out to be surprisingly hard.

Cecil was the one teacher who brought in the humanity of the model within the life class. No one else ever mentioned this, it was only about volumes and shadows and such things, but in Cecil's class there was a human being, the model, contributing all his or her energy into this circle of students. Cecil sat on the side giving out his quiet commands, telling us which hand, which instrument to use, which position, whether we lie down, stand up or whatever. The model was at the centre pinning it all together and radiating energy. That's what we had to connect with. We had to find who he or she was in ourselves through these very specific and precise movements. That is something that you carry with you throughout your life as an artist because there is always this need to create a reality, a relationship which can then be communicated to the viewer. Within the life class, it's model, instruments and positions and artist; outside it's artist, toolmaker and viewer. The created image is what connects all three, there's a trinity.

Cecil always spoke of the eternal fight between the angels and the devils with the score being fifty-one to the angels and forty-nine to the devils. That was also a theme within his teaching. Human beings are wonderful and the flame is born and reborn in each generation. That's why I loved Cecil because he was a man with a stronger and bigger flame. We always used to end tutorials on a joke. It felt like a warm moment in the sun when we would both laugh. I'm sure it happened with everyone else. That's another reason why he was loved.

One of my favourite Cecil drawings is *The Healing of the Sanctuary* from 1976. It was one of the first drawings of his I ever saw. The angel stands guard, but every now and then he can draw aside the veil that hides the truth lying behind things and we're allowed glimpses into that eternity. The drawing somehow implies that there is a horizonless, wonderful space lying beyond that curtain.

The Afternoon of the Fool is another drawing I love. It's so jolly and expresses Cecil's humour, the unexpected perspective. The drawing is very simple. There's a fool's hat on the table that could be the dunce's cap or the wizard's hat. I love the nonchalance, the throwaway line. There's the Fool, just sunning himself outside and perfectly content. There's his little house where he's got his spare hat; he's just gone outside to have a breath of air. He's very happy out there.

Cecil sometimes spoke of how he hated painting. I didn't agree with him, but now I understand better. Painting demands the utmost of you and you have to be absolutely honest; you do it without thought of yourself. That emptying, that getting rid of one's ego, is a fearful process. For Cecil, getting to that point might take months.

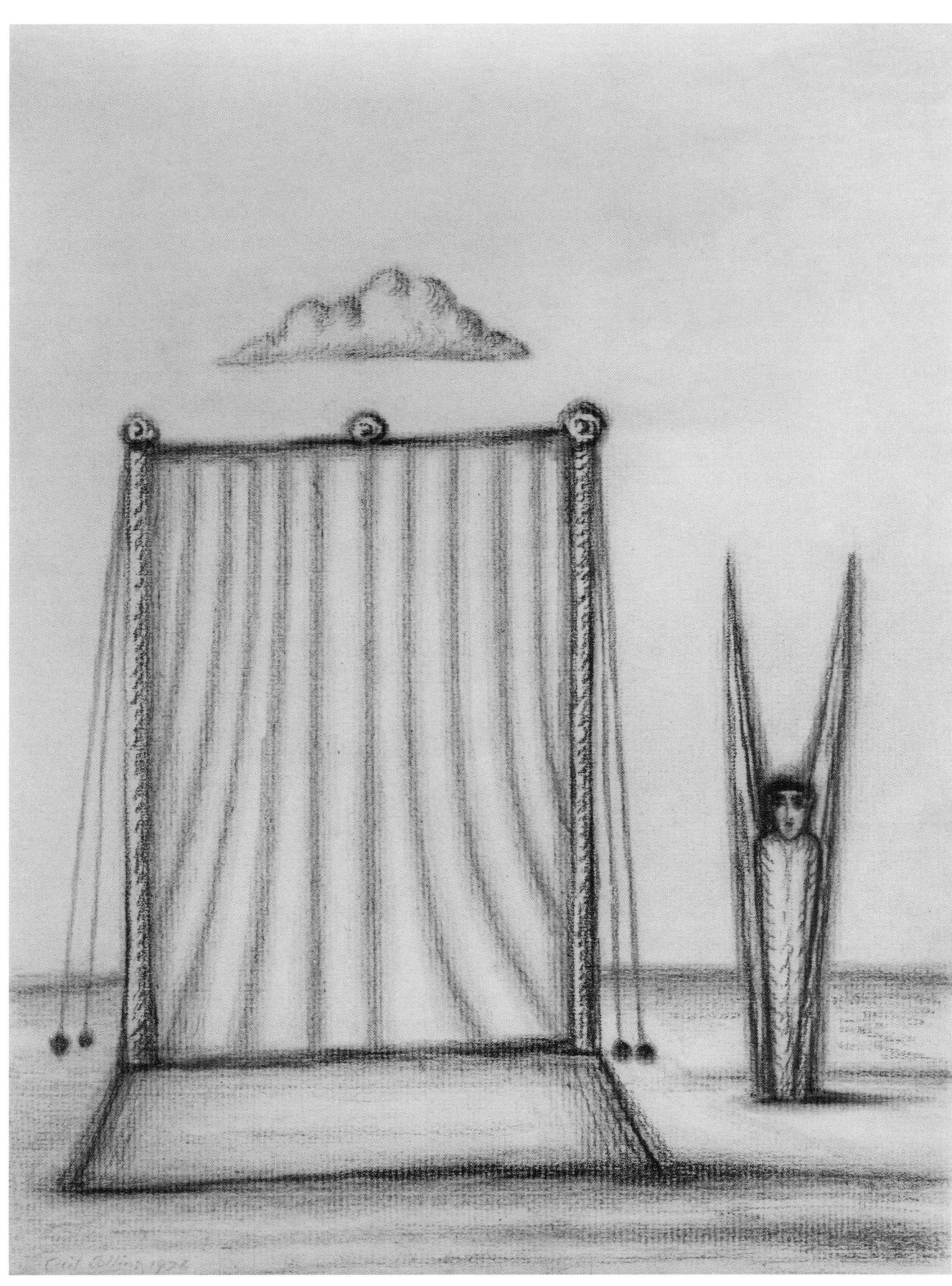

Cecil Collins
The Healing of the Sanctuary
1976
Pencil on paper
31 x 23cm

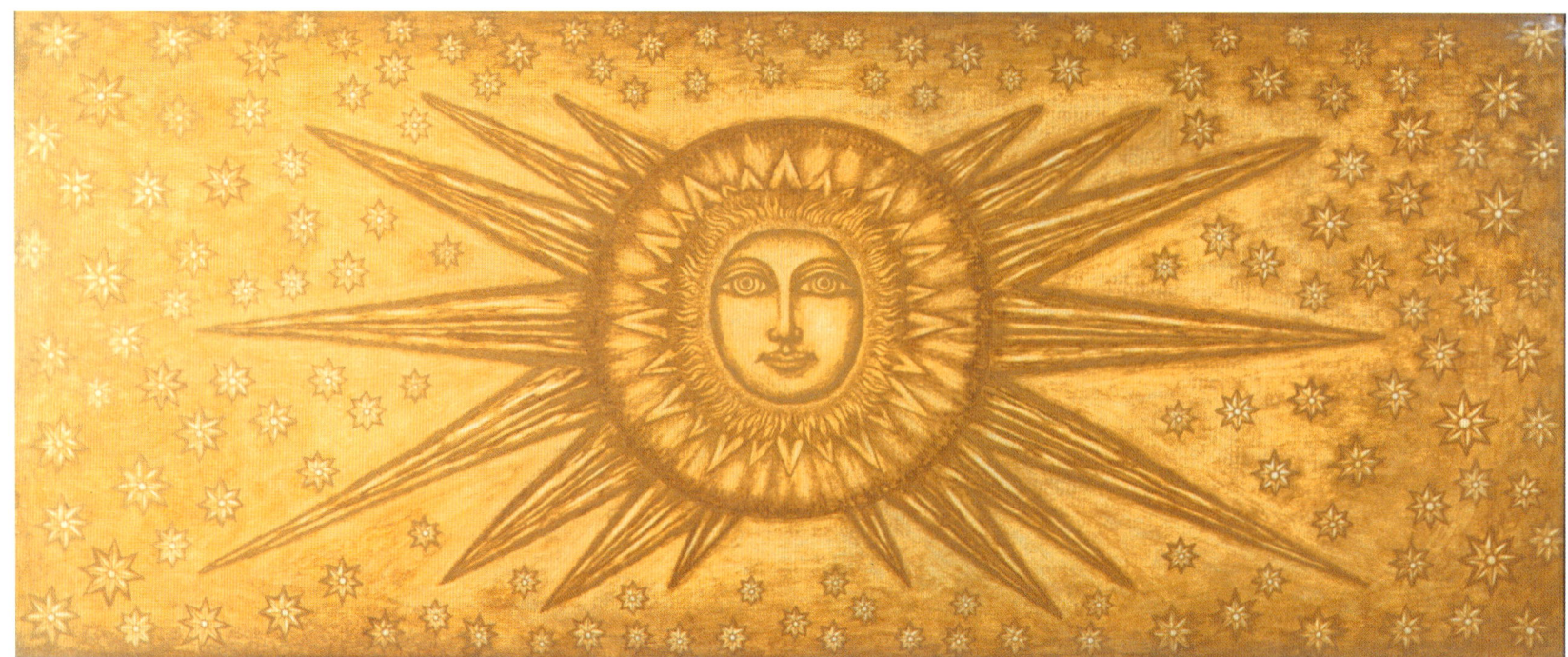

Cecil Collins
Icon of Divine Light
1973
Altar frontal,
Chapel of St Clement,
Chichester Cathedral
Oil on wood panel
168 x 70cm

You connect to the questions, 'What am I?' 'Where am I?' and the deepest question of all, 'Why am I?' It nags at you and it hurts.

Cecil was the first person with whom I could have an honest conversation about the most meaningful aspects of life. As much as a tutor can be one's friend, I felt that we had a real friendship. I had enormous respect for him because he was my master; I was his disciple. I've had other great teachers here and there and great dead teachers like Blake and Poussin and Rembrandt. Cecil knew the world to be beautiful and that was also something he conveyed: joy, the gift of life. The marvellous relationship he had with Elisabeth was also inspiring.

I was thrilled to be able to get one of Elisabeth's lovely paintings, *The Flower in the Hair*. It shows a lion-like person which I'm sure is Cecil in spirit, although not slender like him, but broad with a big head, sitting on a throne maybe. There's also this slim person who is Elisabeth, with her long dress and a foot showing. She's playing with the hair of this big lion person who has a flower wreath around the head. The colours are beautiful desert colours, yellows and ochres. The gouache, pen and ink come wonderfully together in this image. It's very touching. I bought it because I loved it.

Elisabeth was once quite strict with me. It was at the private view of Cecil's Tate Retrospective. She asked me what work I was doing and I said, 'At the moment, I'm designing an opera.' It was an important commission for me. The libretto was essentially the *Lamentations of Thel* by William Blake. The composer was a Russian, Dimitri Smirnov. It was put on at the Almeida and was a world première. This was in 1989, just before *Glasnost* proper. I was doing it with Théâtre de Complicité and it was a very special experience. Elisabeth said, 'Don't you think you should be getting on with your painting?' I was very conscious that she meant something like, 'You've got to be careful. Don't get waylaid. Don't get distracted.'

When I stopped being a painter, there was a part of me that was surprised and dismayed because I was leaving the holy pursuit of painting. For me, painting is the greatest of the arts. Painting is more transcendental than sculpture. It doesn't exist; it's on a flat plane and yet it takes you into its own world and space.

Cecil's work goes beyond time and space. The spaces are definitely there, but they're not exactly of this world although they take a lot of inspiration from this world. What he experienced went into his work, but became transformed into a visual music. Those beautiful rhythms of the Devon hills are transformed into the weaving rhythms of his paintings and drawings. The space that he describes takes you into an experience of that inner identification.

Anything that I know about teaching very largely comes from my contact with Cecil and I know that my teaching gives freedom to the students and that's what Cecil gave to us. He taught us to be self reliant, to experiment, to observe, to calibrate, if you like. It's a science. Cecil knew by your drawing or painting where you were spiritually and psychologically in relation to your work and in relation to the world, physically too, for that matter, because technically he was a master. But he didn't give away his secrets; he wanted you to go through the processes. He taught me about the physicality of painting, what it really means. The conversation that your brush has with the surface, nobody ever told me about that. Cecil did. That's practical; that's not flimsy whimsy. That's him saying get a grip, go and find out about it. This is what you have to do as a painter.

In my teaching, I'm not telling people what to experience. I'm not telling them what to find in themselves. I'm just saying, 'Be open to this experiment and, you never know, perhaps something interesting, amusing or exciting will come out of it.'

All work is directed towards that end and when you are making your own work as an artist, you're trying to create something to give another human being an experience which will open up that inner eye so that they look out at the world and into themselves in another way. It's not to do with anybody going in and fiddling with your brain which is what I feared about going to art school. It is about someone helping you to open your own doors and to come out. When the doors of perceptions are cleansed, then everything will appear as it really is: infinite. Cecil helped you to open your own doors of perception.

JANE WISNER

Jane Wisner, 1944 – 2006, loved painting from early childhood. She studied at the Royal College of Art and in the late 1960s and early 1970s she lived in Tanzania which had a lasting effect on her life and vision. In the early 1980s she attended Cecil's classes which profoundly influenced her art.

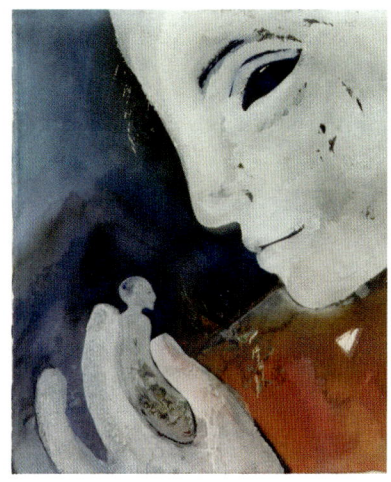

Jane Wisner
Love Speaks with Wisdom
1999
Watercolour on paper

Most of Cecil's students have dreamt about him. The first dream I ever had was simply of him and me standing in grass which was spangled with the small flowers that appear in his painting *The Sleeping Fool*. We were in the realm of his pictures, the Lost Paradise, and the importance was that we were the ones who were to manifest it in this world. He was showing me how, by stepping into it and holding a focus, a purity of consciousness, and clearing away all interference of the ego, we could make room for it. Learning how to become and then to create.

For years and years, I had been striving for peace, strength and inner harmony in my pictures, but I'd not been able to put my belief into words. I had felt so lonely, as if I were the only being on the planet trying to do things in a different way. When I met Cecil, it was as if the loneliness was over. Here was a kind, gentle, perceptive man, full of humour and mischief, erudite, expressing with ease and integrity those truths I'd believed couldn't be expressed. The recognition was so strong that I would be in tears every time we spoke together.

Cecil could never remember my name. To others he'd refer to me as, 'The one who can draw.' I was extremely shy in those days and he would quietly support my self-esteem. At the end of one class, he asked me to take my drawings and spread them out on the podium so everyone could see them. I had been working in a particularly intense way that day and every line was imbued with distilled energy. There was a shift in the way he and I worked after that.

Each class was a precious gift. All boundaries were dispelled in the joy of drawing. I loved the rituals Cecil used and the times he used to talk about mythology and symbols. He would sit in a corner, his eyes lowered, and as he talked the energy would build and change, shift and shimmer. It would pour into us and into the drawings. It often carried an element of great joy and was sometimes very moving. Sometimes a great peace would descend.

I sit writing this in Chichester Cathedral before the *Icon of Divine Light*, which Cecil painted for the altar of St Clement's Chapel. Whenever I am in Chichester, I spend time with this wonderful image. I jump the rope and kneel as close as I can get in order to look into the eyes which gaze back into my soul. I feel the energy change. 'Behold I make all things new.' It is only when one goes beyond the surface of this image that it becomes active. It is only when we allow the divine to enter us that we can create on its behalf; then, if one allows oneself to become receptive and focused, one's whole being is blessed. This is what Cecil's teaching meant to me.

LYNDIE WRIGHT

Designer and puppeteer Lyndie Wright co-founded The Little Angel Theatre in Islington with her husband John in 1961. It is the oldest purpose-built puppet theatre in London. The theatre has established itself as 'the home of British puppetry'. The Little Angel exists to celebrate, explore and develop diverse forms of puppetry and live animation and creates about six productions a year which play in house and on tour.

I wanted to do either puppets or painting. I'd been at art school in South Africa and I remember saving every penny and going to a tourist travel agent one day and booking the cheapest ticket on the *Union Castle* boat to come to England and paint. I arrived in 1958 expecting that art schools would be crying out for students. First I went to Goldsmiths, but I wanted to be in London so I tried the Central School. 'We've taken all the students we can accommodate. You're too late.' 'But I've come all the way from South Africa,' I pleaded and this wonderful man who was Head of the Art Department said, 'Well, if you want it that badly, then obviously you'll have to be one of our students.'

He looked at my paintings and said, 'I think you need quite a lot of drawing,' so I signed up with everyone giving drawing classes. As the year went on, I became aware that Cecil was there and in my last year I got into his class. He was still discovering his teaching. Quite a lot of it was straight life drawing and slowly his ideas were being formulated. It was so exciting even though we only had half a day a week. We started the theatre around that time and there was so much work to do.

Cecil's paintings grew on me more and more. I think the more I discovered, the more important they were to me. When I first went to the Central, people were throwing paint at canvases and I remember going to a class on mural painting and being told by the lecturer, 'There's the dustbin. Throw all your paints away.' As students, we'd agonised over being able to afford them, but we knew we'd be able to get them out of the bin afterwards. I realised that Cecil had also gone through that time when things were being hurled around and canvases were being slashed. It must have had some influence on him. A lot of his paintings that I'm not sure about now were from that period. A little bit of that destructive side came through, but Cecil said there always had to be a dark side because the light side needed the dark side. Somehow that's always been important to me. You can't see the light unless there's the night.

The years passed and I got to thinking that I must start drawing and painting again and, of all the teachers I'd had, it was Cecil I remembered. I thought, He can't possibly still be alive. I went to the Central and they said that he should have retired, but his students had marched down to County Hall to get him reinstated and he was still there. My husband John said, 'Come on. You can draw. You don't need to go back. This could be dangerous, this could be mucking up what you're doing.' John loved my landscape work and didn't want me to get too influenced by all this scribbling that we did in Cecil's class. I'd come back and share with the family what I'd done and you could see him being a bit sceptical at first but, in the end, he realised how important it was to me which was lovely.

I remember the first class after I went back to Cecil. He said in this very soft voice, 'I want you to lie face down on the floor,' and no one took any notice at all. There were a whole lot of new students and they went on sharpening their pencils and doing various things and he never said another word. Slowly, we became aware that this class wasn't going to start until we lay down on the floor so we all got face down on this terribly dirty floor. Then Cecil said, 'Creativity is total submission,' and I thought, That's amazing. It was just wonderful. Putting your face on the floor and your forehead on the paper and getting on with the drawing became so important. Some of the things Cecil said didn't always make sense and you couldn't take them in. Then, years later, you would hear them again and you'd think, I've been hearing this for years and it hasn't meant anything to me until now.

I did drawing with Lily Corbett and Jeremy Gale and it was really interesting because we'd take turns in running the class. It was lovely because the same teaching had gone on for all of us and yet we heard it in our own way, then you'd hear it from someone else's point of view and receive another insight which I found very thrilling. I also went to Ruth Eisenhart's classes after Cecil died which provided a wonderful continuity. I sometimes wished I'd listened more intently and that I'd written down everything, but I don't think Cecil wanted us to do that. He didn't want one to imitate what was going on; he wanted you to feel it. I think Cecil was going into a deeper level and, if one was going to do anything with one's work, one had to find that level. I had been thinking, Shall I be a painter or shall I be a puppeteer? I think Cecil helped me to realise that it didn't matter what you did. When you were actually into that level, it didn't matter whether you were painting or drawing or writing or selling flowers.

Once, I went to a really interesting workshop on myths and legends with Arlene Audergon. By the end of the weekend, although

Lyndie Wright
Venus
2007
Designed and made by Lyndie Wright and Jan Zalud for the RSC and Little Angel Theatre production of Venus and Adonis
Carved wood head, glass eyes, carved reticulated foam body, leather joints and covered in fine gloving leather
c. 1m high
based on Alex Kingston

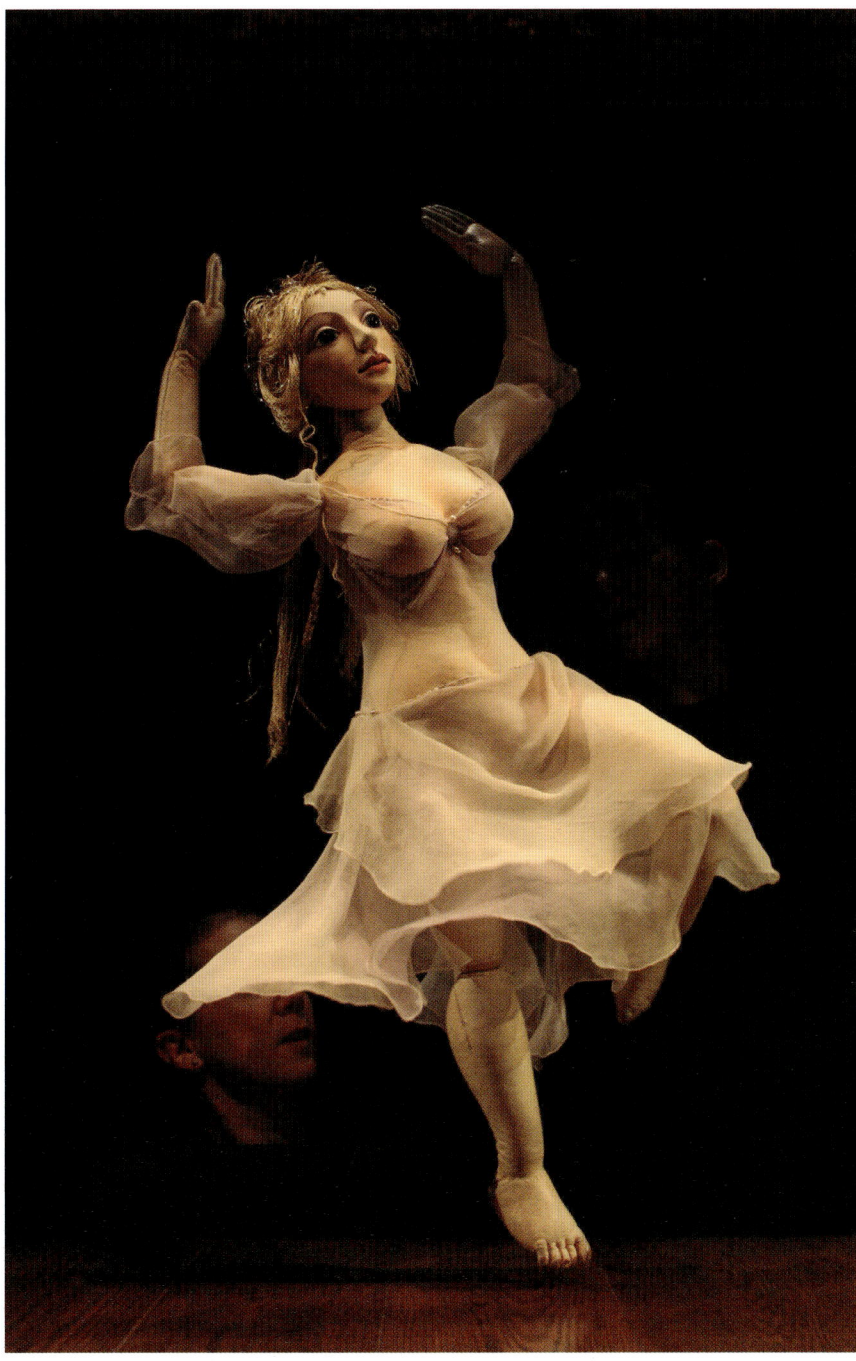

I'd thought, I can't write, suddenly we were writing. I realised this is exactly what Cecil was saying; it doesn't matter how you express it. If you're deeply in something it's going to come out, whether it's words or singing or any of the things one thinks, 'I can't.' It comes from the same place. Cecil's teaching was to live in the moment. I think that was so important because if you do then you're not judging yourself by things that you've done in the past; you're not judging which direction you're going in. You're simply there and creation happens. It made me far less afraid of tackling things. Maybe that also happens with increased age: you tackle things you wouldn't have earlier.

I remember one day Cecil coming round and saying to me, 'That's a wonderful drawing,' and I said, 'Thank you,' and he said, 'It's nothing to do with you.' Hang on, I thought, I worked very hard on this, and then I realised he was right. You learnt as much from him about what hadn't gone right as when you did something that he thought was amazing. One often learns more from going wrong than from doing it right. Those moments were so important: to change things and make things go wrong and not be afraid. There were times when you got into what you thought was a lovely drawing to find you'd actually failed. When I went back to Central the second time, Cecil said that my problem was going to be that I knew too much and had to unlearn things. It seemed such a strange thing to say. Then after a time he said, 'I think you're going to get through this,' and that was a wonderful thing to hear.

I think Cecil inspired obedience. I think he expected it too. My life was very busy at that time. I had the children and the theatre and I would rush in from rehearsals and Cecil would say, 'Until you relax, you're never going to fit everything in.' I remember saying to him, 'It's the only way I'm going to do it. I've got a lot to do. I've got to do this and that.' He didn't argue; he just left you thinking about what he'd said, that it's only when you relax into something that you can get the most out of it. Maybe you weren't ready to take it in then, but maybe the next year you'd be ready.

One of Cecil's models was Alex Kingston, the actress. I don't think she would model for anyone else. I think she chose Cecil because of the way he worked and the way he taught, but it's interesting that Alex has done some wonderful acting. Alex is the most beautiful girl you could ever imagine and I remember one of the male students found it really difficult to draw her, even though he usually drew well and Cecil said, 'It's difficult when someone's as beautiful as this.' That was so lovely. He could see this wonderful looking girl and understand how distracting that was.

I often wonder now whether some of the movements that Cecil made us go through were influenced by the Ballet Jooss which he got very involved with at Dartington. Being a puppeteer, the idea of performing oneself and leading the class was embarrassing at first, then when he chose me to head the class I was surprised that I enjoyed it. He had this ability to know when one was ready. In the end it was such a joy.

Cecil was so certain of himself that you can see why people felt that he had a personal vanity, but it wasn't ego at all. Some people felt that certainty was quite threatening. I remember students walking out when he told them to put their face in the dirt. One woman was so angry that she argued with him and wouldn't accept what he was saying. She said, 'I don't want to be told exactly what to do.' Cecil didn't react; he didn't rise to her at all. He just smiled. In the end, she just grabbed everything and walked out of this class that she'd been so anxious to be in and for which she'd queued a long time. I'd loved to have met her later and asked her whether she regretted leaving. I think she felt we were all being clones or something because she was saying surely part of creativity was to be an individual. Cecil just let it wash over him. He was almost saying, 'In time you'll discover this for yourself. Just stick around.' The whole incident was disturbing because you felt for her and you felt for him being threatened by this woman. He didn't say anything and that was the way he taught too: that these are discoveries you have to make for yourself. There was nothing to say.

I had a friend, Michael, who was Lord Marks of Marks and Spencers. He's dead now, but he was a wonderful chap and a great help to us with the theatre. I introduced him to Cecil and after that Michael became more and more interested in Cecil. He didn't go to his classes, but he bought a lot of Cecil's paintings at Anthony d'Offay's gallery. I went with him to Cecil's last exhibition at the Tate and I remember Cecil going out of his way to have a long talk with Michael. Cecil told him to have faith in himself because he was a wonderful man and he was going along the right way. It was so touching because Cecil must have been very ill and died, I think, two weeks later, but he knew that Michael needed to hear this. I thought how fantastic it was that Cecil, with all those people there, had recognised Michael's need. Michael glowed afterwards and always remembered that talk.

Cecil told me at that exhibition, 'It's wonderful work that you're doing. Keep going.' It was lovely to hear that as I'd often wondered whether I should be doing puppets or painting: was I wasting my time making shows for children. After Cecil died, I was quite keen to look at some of the paintings Cecil had done to see whether there was something that could be used for puppets. I asked Elisabeth what she thought and she said she'd like to talk to people about it. She came back and said she didn't think his work should be performed. It was a shame and I wondered who had put her off the idea. Sometimes people hate puppets and it might have been someone who didn't know about Cecil's interest. It could have been an amazing thing. We'd thrown a party for him at the theatre on his eightieth birthday and put on a performance specially for him. He was very thrilled. I think Elisabeth was very protective of Cecil's image and didn't want to put a foot wrong.

After such a long time, one forgets that some of the things that are so much part of one's life now came from Cecil. Respect for the left hand is something he taught us and it's very important for puppeteers who need to work with both hands. I was quite resistant at first and then it was like a release. It was wonderful and I think that was probably because, having done a lot of drawing, you could let go of the skill of the right hand and the mind telling you which way to go.

We organised a drawing class for the puppeteers and it allowed them to become aware of the left hand. Most puppeteers have a hand they prefer, that's more dextrous, but the fact is that the left hand also has to work and you can't do the puppet without that second hand; it has to be equal. If we're only using one hand, we aren't using the whole of ourselves. We're directing all our intention on one hand; it is straightaway in control. The amazing thing about drawing with an instrument in your mouth is that you were glad to be back with the chalk in your hand again. All those exercises seemed so difficult at first. Cecil got you to draw on your forehead and on your hands and to become aware of what kind of mark would be on the paper. With each of your instruments you'd feel it on your forehead and on your hands and on your lips and then you'd do it with a pencil. It was quite a revelation to me. You'd rest your forehead on the paper, just feeling the paper; it was almost paying homage to the paper as well as feeling it. It was so amazing because you'd go through the same things, year after year, and there were always new things; you'd never actually done everything. I studied with Cecil for many, many years and I never had the sense that I was simply marking time or repeating. You always hoped that this time you'd break through, but it never was like that. It was like nothing was ever completed because you were different so everything would be different each year. Even now I think, gosh, if I just had another year with Cecil, it might be all right. I'm sure he was a Master and in the teaching sense too. There aren't masters like that any longer to teach us. We were very fortunate.

I studied at the Central, but I used to do City Lit colour courses with Cecil during the summer holidays. I've done productions where I've used his colour and built the whole thing choosing my colours, then making everything in that production work within those three colours. That was really interesting. Sometimes you'd work with the harmony and then in would come the witch and you'd bring in the disharmony. You'd break the mould and that always worked. It was very exciting to use his ideas. I don't think anyone was ever aware that there was any kind of pattern behind what one was doing but, for me, it was important.

My son, Joe, also went to a couple of classes with Ruth. It was a difficult time for him then because John had just died and Joe was leaving school and wanted to go into art school. He had to get a portfolio together and I said, 'Go to Ruth and get some life drawing.' I don't know how long he went for, but it helped get him into art school. I think what really impressed him was this thing of living in the present and he knows that that comes from Cecil.

I remember Joe telling me that when he was making *Bodily*

Harm, a TV film for Channel 4, the character played by Timothy Spall received quite a serious letter from his father. They had planned a lovely day filming this scene in Green Park. It turned out to be the most terrible windy, rainy day and Joe thought, 'This is awful. We'll have to change the programme.' He was so disappointed, then he remembered what Cecil Collins had said: that you live in the present. So they went off to Green Park to film anyway. Joe said the wind blowing made all the difference because as Timothy was reading the letter it blew out of his hand and somehow took all the sentimentality away from the scene. In the end they didn't use it; with editing you lose some things if they get in the way of the story. This 'living in the moment' also changed a scene completely during the shooting of *Pride and Prejudice*. It was due to be shot inside the house, but the day turned excessively hot so Joe decided to move the whole thing outside, much to the technicians' consternation, but it made a much more memorable scene. Joe takes this right through his work; being flexible all the time. His technicians and cameramen have had to learn to be as just as flexible. I don't know whether they realise that they're absorbing Cecil's teaching from Joe.

One of the things that I've observed from Cecil's teaching is that in the theatre the audience put their own emotional reactions into the puppets' faces so they gain more, not less, from the experience. They have to imagine the whole story in their head. It's close to story telling, peeling away anything that isn't important. After a show, people often say, 'How did you change the expressions?' But what they are using is their imagination which is why it's so marvellous, challenging them to use their own vision. This is what Cecil taught, the importance of the imagination. I think his legacy will continue to come out in future generations. These things are passed on.

Cecil Collins
Hymn
1946
Gouache on paper
47 x 60.6cm

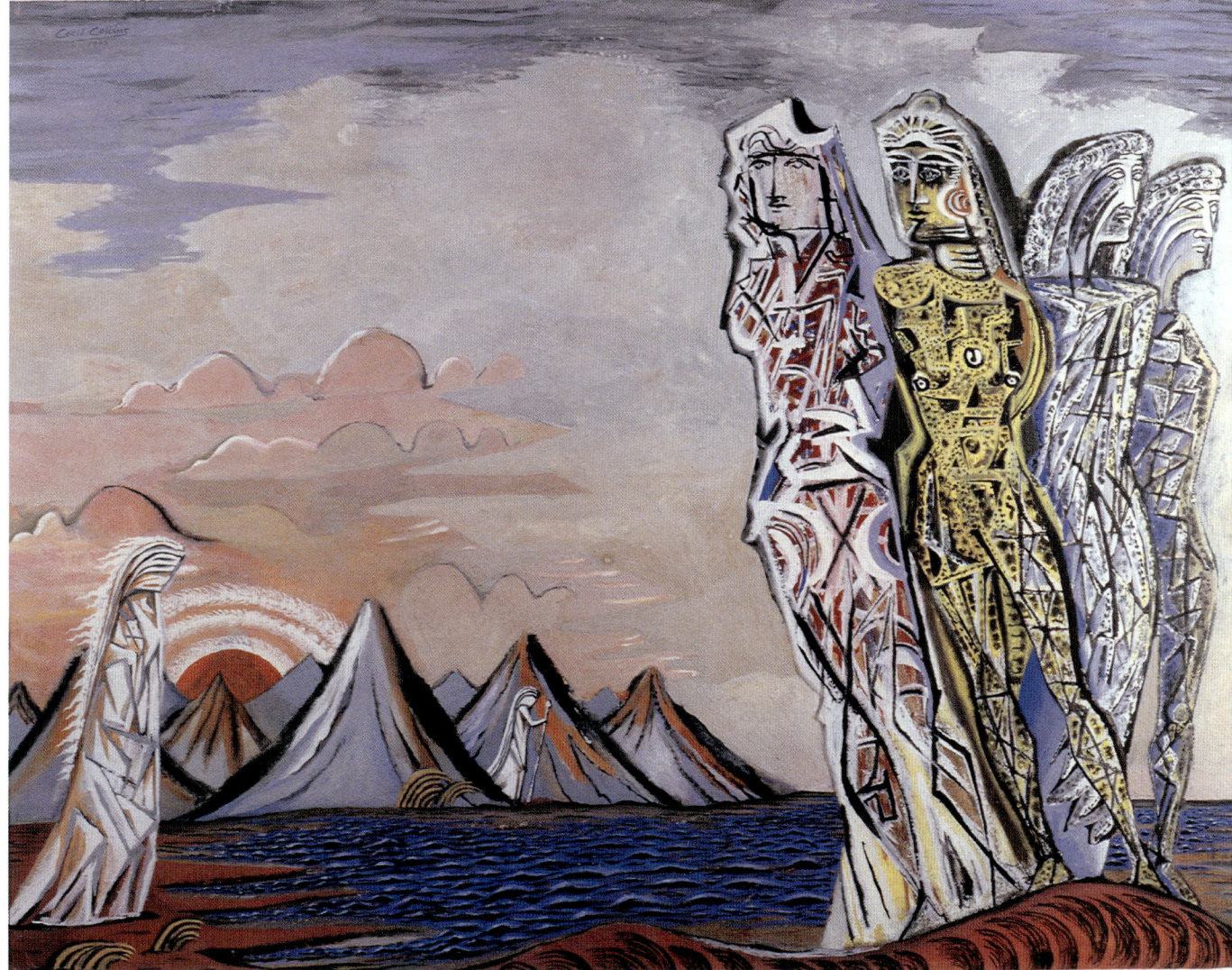

MODELS

MARIGOLD HUTTON

Marigold Hutton, born in 1931, modelled for life classes at various art colleges, including Central School of Art and Design (1952-1954). She then worked as a secretary, until marrying the artist John Hutton. After his death in 1978, she trained as a counsellor, becoming manager of The Listening Centre, Oxford (1993-2000). Since 1995, she has been co-organiser of the travel programme for the Jupiter Trust, based in Oxford.

In the early 1950s I was one of the life models employed by the Central School for the drawing teachers and sat for Cecil Collins and Mervyn Peake when they did a class together. They were memorable because they were so witty; it was quite something to be in the class. I think they were very inspirational as teachers. I was only twenty-one at the time and felt rather dazzled by their presence. I thought I was very privileged to be able to listen to them. Sometimes I did chat with them a bit during breaks as I was very interested in art history. Usually the models were considered a lower order and in the Slade school we were not allowed to mix with the students at all.

I had enormous admiration for Mervyn. I'd been given the first Gormenghast book by Diana Lodge who was a friend of my mother's when I was about eighteen. It made such an impact. Cecil was more distant, frightening actually, whereas Mervyn would tease and joke with you and once took me out for tea between the day and evening classes. Cecil was always a little more aloof although always pleasant. At the same period, I met John Hutton, who much later became my husband, through modelling for him first at Goldsmith's where he was teaching and then privately for the angels which he engraved on the Great West Window of Coventry Cathedral. John had been commissioned by the architect Basil Spence who'd been his second in command at the end of the second world war.

I'd got into modelling through Diana's husband, Oliver, who was an artist and poet suggesting it to me when I was fed up with trying not very successfully to be an actress. Oliver had met Diana when she modelled for him. My parents got to know the Lodges when they rented a cottage from Julian Trevelyan's mother in the same Surrey village that we lived in. Julian and my husband, John, knew each other independently because they'd met in Africa somewhere. Curiously enough Diana was filmed by Jonathan Stedall when she was in her eighties after she'd became a Catholic. It's all rather incestuous and goes on and on.

I remember that once I was taken by John and his first wife, Nell, who was also an artist, to see the Collinses in Cambridge where they were living then. We were looking at Cecil's work and he had that wild-eyed wonderment about things which was delightful. In front of one painting, [*The Eternal Bride*, 1963] he said to us, 'Do you know I was painting this picture and I suddenly looked at the bottom right-hand corner and saw I had painted the cosmic egg.' Of course, it was very difficult not to giggle and I think we managed to be quite polite. He did some beautiful work. I bracket him together with David Jones whose style is a bit similar. Now I'm much more interested in Cecil's symbolism and the interpretation of his pictures than I was at that time.

Strangely enough, Diana Lodge got to know Elisabeth Collins very well in Cambridge. Elisabeth was involved with the mystic Subud movement and Diana was interested in it too. They used to go together to the meetings where they did a particular kind of meditation which included movement.

Another thing I remember is seeing Cecil taking the train from Cambridge to London. I never sat with him on the journey. He was a towering figure because he was very tall and I had a lot of respect for him which he certainly deserved. He had that kind of presence. He used to stand on the platform wearing an incredibly long coat and looking exactly like one those anarchist people who threw bombs in the early 1900s. It was really funny

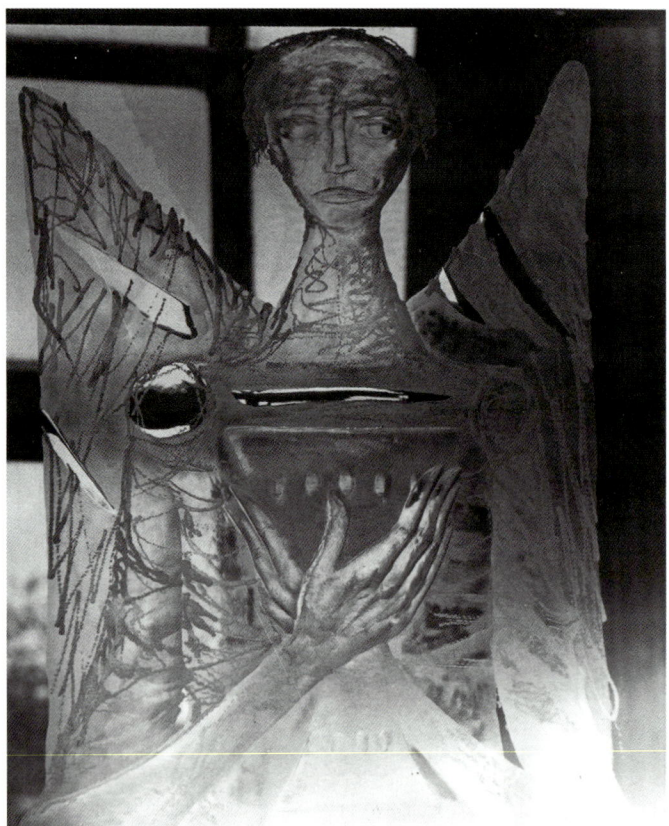

John Hutton
Angel of Gethsemane
Coventry Cathedral
West Window
Consecrated 1962
based on Marigold Hutton

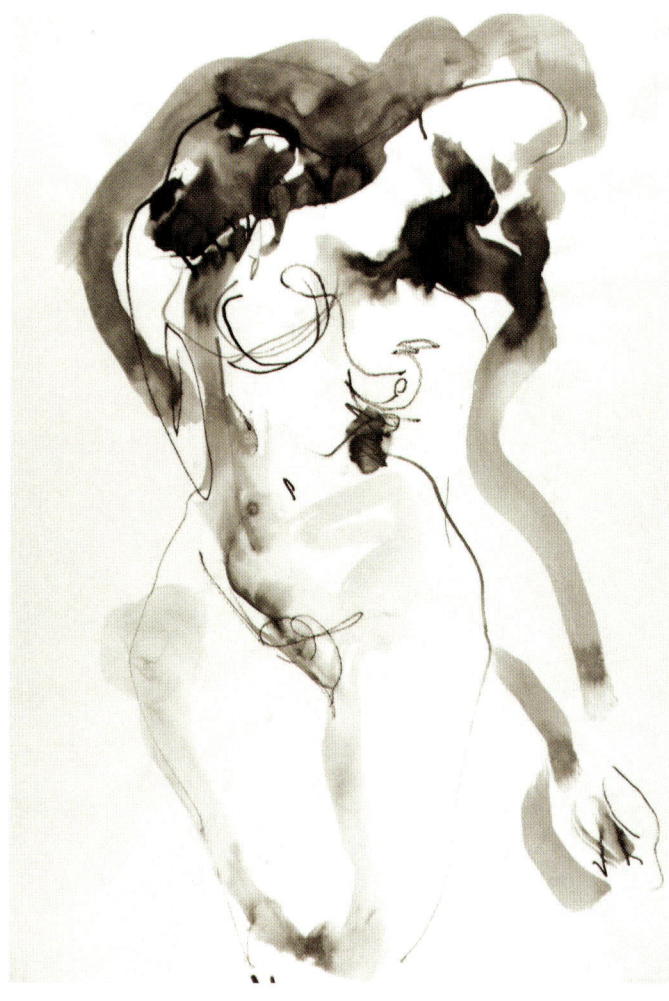

Melissa Alley
drawing of Alex Kingston
late 1980s

ALEX KINGSTON

Born 1963, of mixed English and German parentage, Alex (Alexandra) Kingston is a British actress, best known for her role in the American television medical drama, ER. She now lives in Los Angeles and is married with two daughters and continues her successful career in America and Britain.

I came to model for Cecil because I got to know Lyndie Wright one summer on a drawing and painting holiday. At the time, I was considering whether to go to art rather than drama school. A girlfriend of mine wanted to go to art school and build up her portfolio and so I went on this summer course in France with her. That's where I met Lyndie and her children and we used to hang out with them. Afterwards, back in London, Lyndie attended some art classes in which I modelled. My mother paints and from about the age of fourteen, I would go along with her to model at adult education classes. Instead of receiving a fee, because I like painting, I would be paid in kind so I could paint in a class myself. Later, when Lyndie was going to Cecil's open classes at Central School, she asked whether I would like to model for him as well. That's how it began.

I almost lived at Central and absolutely loved it. Cecil was this wonderfully eccentric man with his furry leopard-skin waistcoat. He wore this dark greyish-greenish suit. He'd always wear a suit, but then on top of his suit jacket, he would also wear this fake fur leopard zip-up waistcoat. I think it was something that would keep him warm because he was so frail. I used to find it really amusing because he always wore this thing and the fake fur had become matted because it had been washed a few times, but it was very funny with these yellow and brown spots.

He would sit in the middle at one of the tables with his record player or tape machine. He was absolutely the master, totally in control. The first time I went it was a totally different way of modelling. I'd been used to sitting for forty minutes, having a break, then doing another forty minutes. The first time when he said, 'I'm going to play a piece of music and you can move to it and when the music stops, just hold that position.' It was like playing musical statues; like being a child. To actually stand in the middle and then for him to say, 'You can move to the music' was something I loved because it was like playing games the whole time. As a model, I felt so involved. It was like an organic process and I was totally part of it. I enjoy modelling and even being still for forty minutes, but I felt more connected to the process in Cecil's classes.

I immediately knew what he meant because I'm an actress so I was in tune with what it was he was wanting. I loved it. I just completely let rip. I felt totally free. I was not embarrassed or scared or anything about being naked. I just loved the fact that I could move and dance naked. Also, the choice of music or sounds he used was amazingly freeing. Sometimes it would be the sound of wind through the trees and leaves rustling or ocean sounds. Another time there'd be a stream trickling. I can't remember the music Cecil used except the sounds of nature, but it was always quite passionate music. I've got a very strong feeling that I moved, or danced to, Mahler. My mind then would be racing because I knew, at some point, he'd stop the music. As much as I was fully present and in the music, I was also observing and wanting to be in a shape that would be really interesting to draw, when he pressed the button, not just be caught standing completely rigid.

In fact, in our kitchen I've got three pictures that one of Cecil's students, Melissa, gave to me. Every time I'm in the kitchen chopping vegetables, I look at them and have wonderful memories of that time in my life. The energy that comes from those drawings is so positive that there is something very uplifting about them. A lot of times people who come to the house, look at them, but don't connect the model with me because they don't know that part of my history. What I love about them is that there's so much life in the images. You can see that it's a figure who's been caught in the moment and there's an energy in each of the shapes. I love them and I even remember what fun it was when I was doing that session. They were thirty second poses and that's what I loved because in that short amount of time an amazing energy was created and the figures seem to have an interior life. That's something you can't do if you're given an hour. Cecil would say things like, 'Have a brush in the left hand and another brush in your mouth,' then he'd tell the students what they were going to do and this is going to be so many minutes. It was wonderful.

One of his students was a woman I got to know, Ruth Eisenhart, who was giving classes in Covent Garden before it became so trendy and while Cecil was still alive. The studio was down a little alley. It was a fantastic place with such character. I loved that. Ruth's classes were pretty much copying what Cecil did. She had the same music, but the amount of time she allowed for the pose would, on the whole, be longer than Cecil's. Sarah, Lyndie Wright's daughter, would also come along to draw and I would be sitting in and drawing in Ruth's class too when my friend was modelling. I got rid of a pile of drawings I had, but I've still kept my favourites that I love looking through. Sometimes I'll say to myself, 'That's really good.' It surprises me, but it could be hanging in a gallery somewhere and people would think, gosh, that's something amazing.

I think people were in awe of Cecil. There was a sort of a reverence towards him because people wanted what he had to teach. He absolutely embodied in his life what he was trying to teach. When you came into his life-drawing room, everything was directed towards him, all attention was given to him and people were sensitive to his condition because he was so old and looked so frail. In his classes everyone was totally absorbed.

I would get really excited and I think that everybody sitting there would be as well because they didn't know what was going to come next. You're not thinking; you can't think. All you're doing is waiting for the instructions, then you just have to follow them with full attention, but you have to leave your brain outside, so to speak. On the whole in normal life, one's constantly trying to control life and one's surroundings, whereas there, it was about having no control at all and letting your subconscious take over. In a way Cecil was giving you the tools which could be thought of him being in control, telling you what to do, but it was more a suggestion, 'This is what I'd like you to try this time. Put your bamboo between your toes and have your brush in your mouth.'

He was in control of the music or whatever sounds he brought to open people's minds and also when he'd stop the music, but he wasn't controlling about what then appeared on the paper or what movement I would have achieved or how I was going to be standing when the button was pressed. I think it's such a shame that there's no one in art schools now teaching like him.

There was such appreciation in Cecil's classes, both towards me and of the students towards each other. During the breaks, I could walk around quite freely and look because people wanted to show what they had done. Each mark on the paper was something they were really excited about and I could understand because I had felt so involved myself. When I'd been modelling for students who'd just come out of school and gone straight into an art school, there wasn't that connection. It was always them and me. I don't know whether it was embarrassment or whether it was because they were part of a more conventional education system. There wasn't that appreciation. You can't put life into the drawing of that person if there's such a distance between you.

Funnily enough, at the same time I was modelling for an artist called Susanna Fiennes. She would hold art classes in the studio of Westminster Boys' School in the evenings for adults who were all professionals; city high-flyers and journalists and things like that, although again these people were enthusiastic and I very much felt part of the group. A lot of them had never put pen to paper before and she was teaching them in a very traditional way. After a couple of years, I told her about Cecil and said, 'Why don't we try a class where maybe we do some short poses for the first half of the class and think of it as a kind of a warm-up to get them to free themselves so they're not measuring in millimeters.' We did it and Susanna joined in because it was such good fun and everyone enjoyed it.

We didn't have music and I would then be taking the classes as the model. I'd be the one saying, 'This is what we'll do. I'm going to move and then I'm going to stop.' I'd say 'You've got thirty seconds to do this,' or 'You've got a minute and a half.' I said, 'I'm going to be dancing around and I'll stop. I'll start moving again, but you have to be ready.' I wasn't wearing a watch so I couldn't time myself properly. It was exciting. It wasn't difficult; it was just about taking leap of faith and letting go. I modelled for this particular class for a long time, pretty much until I came over to the States.

I started modelling for Cecil in 1980 or '81, then from 1983 I was at RADA and didn't model. After I left drama school in 1985, I was really working a lot because that was how I made my living.

Cecil talked to me very little. I didn't have many conversations with him at all. I think the only one was when he asked me, 'Do you want to go to art school?' and I said, ' Well, I'm not sure, I might go to drama school.' He didn't make any comment that I can remember.

One day he came back after he'd been away ill and I remember Ruth coming up to me. She was quite excited and said, 'Cecil's started drawing. His creative juices are starting to flow again.' There were periods when he wasn't active at all and I don't know whether she was telling me because she felt it was through me having had a really positive experience and the atmosphere I'd created in the classes, but it was so nice that Ruth came up to me and said he was drawing again.

I had closer relationships to his students, to the women who would come every week. There were always more women than men. He didn't have that much personal contact with his students, except maybe for Ruth and also Lyndie who would chat with him at breaks. There wasn't that much contact, but there was absolute, quiet veneration.

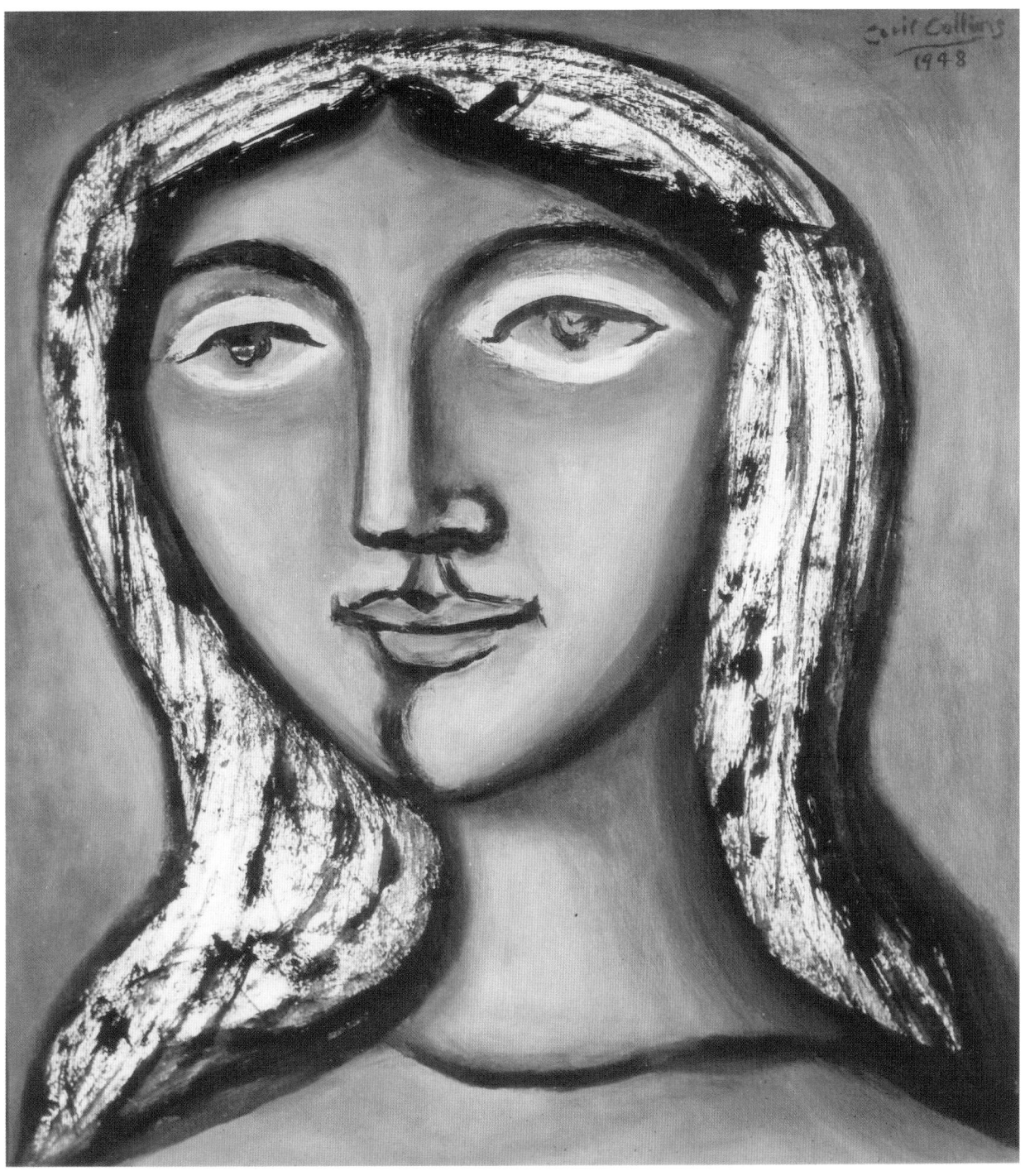

Cecil Collins
Head of a Woman
1948
Oil on paper
32 x 35.5cm

ISOBEL MORRIS

Born in Yorkshire, Isobel Morris built herself a reputation as a pop-rock singer, songwriter and guitarist of rare distinction initially travelling throughout America before returning to Britain and joining up with drummer Jim Kimberley to form the group Bruise. They have toured nationally and internationally to great acclaim, most recently at the Out of the Ordinary Festival in Sussex in September 2008.

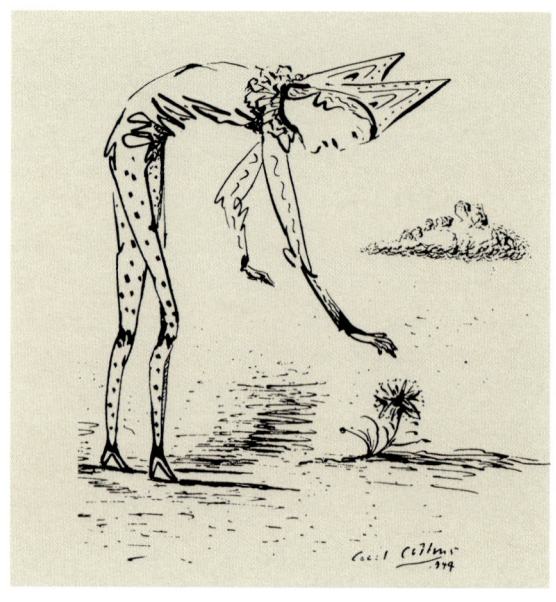

Cecil Collins
Fool and Flower
1944
Ink on Paper
28 x 19cm

Jeremy and Lily were looking for a new female model and I was recommended by a model who'd been working for them for some time and who thought I might be the kind of person who would suit the classes they gave. I sat for Jeremy's Monday evening classes and it was very different from any other life modelling I'd done. I'd modelled for seventeen years and when I started working for Jeremy four years ago I found it disconcerting at first. I was being asked to be so mobile, so physical while being naked. I felt a little self conscious about moving.

Everything that I had done before then, as a model or even when I was drawing from the model had been very much based on being static. For me, a good model is someone who can appear natural and relaxed in a very unnatural setting. You find yourself in a pose which in real life you might glimpse in a movement; you would move through it to get somewhere else. In a life drawing class, you can be asked to stay in that specific position for seven or eight hours at a time. What I endeavour to do is to keep the transient nature of the pose, keep the looseness, the naturalness of the position that I'm in for however long I'm asked to sit there. In that situation you've got a great deal of time to think about lots of things and I like to stay very present in the room. I don't like to daydream, but to concentrate hard on what is happening there. I like to understand what the artists are going through around me.

When you have a teacher who talks clearly in a conventional class, it's really nice to be able to hear what they're saying about colour, the mood of a pose or the nature of the light that's coming through the window and how all these beautiful, tiny things are changing and how, even though a moment is being frozen in time, it depends on a million details put together. I think it's important for the atmosphere of the room as a whole for me to identify that, even though a pose is stationery and unnatural, it's not static or heavy. It's not a still life. My intention to stay consciously present is, I find, very meditative, even though it's impossible not to drift off occasionally during such a long pose.

The way that I was introduced to Jeremy's class was very respectful and understanding. I hadn't been warned that it would involve movement and I'd never done that sort of thing before, but they were very sensitive to the fact that I was a little taken aback and didn't know what was being asked of me. I'm not self-conscious about being naked; that's not a problem. I just wanted to understand what was going on in the class and reassess what was acceptable. When everyone is following the model's movements, it's as if you're leading a roomful of people. In order to be comfortable I stayed dressed for the first fifteen or twenty minutes while I got a feeling for what the class was about and the people who worked in it.

Jeremy made me feel that my comfort was of absolute importance to him and to the group as a whole and he got one of the students to lead the movement so I could get a feeling for how things went. He took care to integrate me rather than letting me feel like an object outside the group. I can't remember if there was music involved or not at the very start, but it was super to have somebody lead the room, almost in a Tai Chi way, and lovely to see that a movement can be so sculptural and how that can be reflected in the work that was done from the pose.

As a model you are usually concerned with the question as to whether you are the object or the subject in a life drawing class, but in a Cecil Collins' style group, I think the division is more blurred. The group as a whole addresses that question, not just the model. So these questions and the one about what the artist is going through as an individual are almost irrelevant because the focus is about the feeling generated by everybody in the room. It's also about the way that whoever is taking the class is leading. You're influenced by any music that might be played and not only as an individual, but by following movements made by each member of the class, you're sharing each other's interpretation of the music.

From the point of view of those drawing or painting, their personal ego is removed from that process because they're given the language in which to express themselves. They're told what to pick up: charcoal, chalk, a pen and then they're told the expressiveness of the marks: whether to use the angular, assertive masculine or more fluid receptive feminine. It doesn't feel like a group of individuals pursuing their own ideal or identity, feeding off the same visual stimulus. Rather, it's a roomful of people creating or tuning in as a group experience to an atmosphere that is potentially already there. There was absolute clarity in the group that that was why they were there and that was the purpose of the class as a whole.

As an artists' model, you find yourself naked in a room full of strangers and, in a situation like that, you have to be very certain of what is and isn't appropriate behaviour. It's perfectly possible to really enjoy this work and I do. I feel that way because I know what a professional model is expected to do and what is overstepping the limits. Not that I am self-conscious in a life drawing class, but in a traditional school or group environment, you're not usually asked to move. You have a certain degree of vulnerability being naked, but there's an extra dimension to that when you are also moving. For example, historically it was considered perfectly decent to have an immobile naked woman on a public stage, but it was against the law for her to move which was thought too erotic.

When you're being a stationary, conventional life model, your personal space is set in stone. No one comes closer than a certain distance, except for the teacher, and the teacher always has the good manners to ask. For a Cecil Collins' class, it is slightly different. The concern isn't that you stay very still and retain your pose for eight hours. It's so different that it's almost not like a life drawing class; it's more like an experience of unity or a meditation in action. I had to prepare myself to be consciously more receptive because your own personal space is moving all the time in order to respond from the heart to the musical stimulus. Sometimes in summer we'd listen to the blackbirds singing in the trees outside and move to that. In order to respond honestly to that, you do have to open up; it's not an academic thing. It's not about the power of the brain, but about the perceptiveness of the heart.

It was quite an easy transition for me to slip into. I could see almost straight away where the style of teaching and drawing was coming from. I feel like I headed in the right direction from quite early on, but I do think that there is always more to be understood about being in that situation. It's endlessly unfolding. Everyone in those classes was there for absolutely the right reason and I never felt I was being taken advantage of. Everyone had the same aim and attitude so it was easy for me to become part of that group and participate in an appropriate way.

It was reflected so much in the drawings that came out of those classes, the life in them and the movement. People were unconcerned with results or goals and details that are distracting in one way, but insignificant, in another. These classes focused on a part of life drawing which is quite often neglected: it was a real joy to see such vitality in the drawings. It's a little sad that when people are focusing on measurement and perspective and lots of technical things, it can be easily overlooked that there's a life force, a live being, right there in front of you. I feel very lucky to have worked with Jeremy and Lily.

Very occasionally I'm a little over-sensitive about my vulnerability as model. When you work naked, you have to be aware that there are some people who are there not to make art and not to grow as human beings, but to get a different sort of pleasure out of the experience.

There was one time when I was feeling a little vulnerable and for no reason, it had nothing to do with the class, I suspected there might be somebody who was not there for the right reasons. This guy was asking questions about my personal life which felt like a bit of an intrusion and I snapped at him. It was the first time he'd been in a class when I had been modelling there, though he was a long term and trusted member of the group. I put up a very definite wall and he immediately backed off and, for a couple of classes, didn't attempt to speak to me again, not resentfully, but in a respectful sort of way. I was able to observe him interacting with the rest of the group and see how they felt about him. I was able to understand that he'd merely been making conversation. I'd made my feelings clear and it was handled extremely diplomatically and I came to realise that I'd absolutely misjudged the chap and there was no problem at all.

For me, the intensity in the classes is created through a coming together of all the people in the room, their concentration, their focusing on the tasks that are being asked of them. Cecil Collins' style classes are different from any other class because in them, there can be some conversation and it doesn't interfere with the mood of a room, it doesn't break an atmosphere. Every part of life is integrated into the class. If somebody thinks of something funny that happened to them and they're in the middle of a drawing and they can't help themselves, they will make a comment and there might be a giggle and this will spill into the room, into the art, into the mood.

Cecil Collins

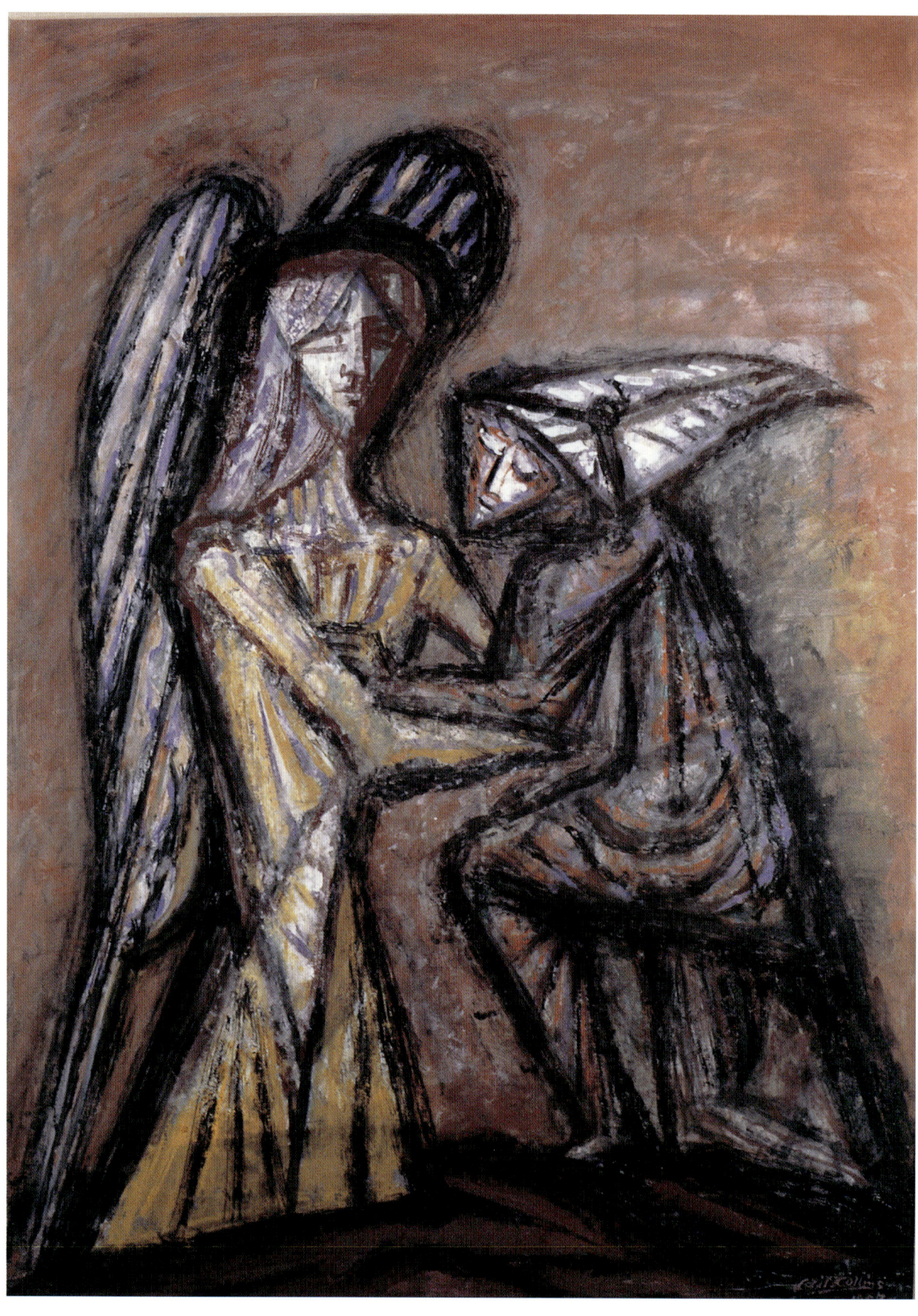

Cecil Collins
Angel Comforting a Fool
1957
Gouache on paper
54 x 39cm

Generally the environment of the class is like a sanctuary. It's a place away from people's troubles: you don't have to think about the minor domestic things or major things pressing on you. From time to time, people will find themselves in a situation where they can't forget about what is weighing on their heart or preying on their mind and it comes into the room with them. It is amazing to see how somebody who is upset can be nurtured by a roomful of people when all you're doing is moving and drawing.

You can't help but observe if somebody is sad or has a cloud over them. In a room full of sensitive people with an atmosphere of positive nurturing intent, then it can be such a healing experience to move to music and to express yourself within a sympathetic group and then to have everybody following you, feeling your pain. Similarly, if there is somebody there who's absolutely filled with joy, something wonderful has happened to them then there's a real lightness and the whole room benefits. I think finding a balance on the whole is something that happens in those classes often.

In a conventional life drawing situation, you're taught to see what is there, not what you believe is there. Everybody knows what a hand looks like and so consequently people can draw what they believe a hand should look like, but in a certain position that model's hand might look like the head of a cat, or have a really different, not hand-like quality. It's forming a different shape and it's such an important part of making art, to be able to allow yourself to see exactly what is there and not let preconceived ideas about what a hand should look like. Preconceived ideas get in the way of what is there.

It's the same thing in music. I'm a singer and songwriter and there are a lot of people who can listen to a piece of music and hear a pretty melody. They are drawn to melody, but don't necessarily hear what is it is that is making them feel a particular mood. Or again, if it's melancholy and the notes are descending, they're taken along with that piece of music, but they're not necessarily conscious of the instruments being used. Music hangs in space just as objects do and music moves in space and attracts you and repels you just like objects do. You could compare it to the way a dark tone recedes and a light tone comes forward in a drawing.

Art and music have so much in common. Just before you go on stage, you get this feeling of nervousness, a combination of dread and excitement, and it can build for days before an actual performance, depending on the size of the gig I suppose, or how important it is to you personally, and this build-up of tension finally stops when you get to release the pressure which is either with the drawing or the performance.

Recently, I joined a life class to draw, not model, and I was feeling incredibly nervous because it had been a long time since I'd been taught or that I'd done any drawing in an academic setting. I was trembling, with a shallow heartbeat and palpating heart. I spoke to one of the other students there about how nervous I felt and he said, 'I feel nervous every time before I pick up a pencil. Any time I'm going to draw, I get this incredible rush of nerves.'

It was amazing to me to discover that similarity, but of course that's the way it feels because art and music are from the same place. It's from life through experience, through your heart. It's what you see and experience of the world, how it impacts on you and how you feel about it in your heart. So before a drawing or a performance there is dread and excitement at the same time and it's possible to recognise it for what it is. I don't feel that is particularly negative. It is more that there is a need to bring out or access a deeper part of yourself to create a drawing or when you're performing. I would say that deeper part is the most important thing. It's your reason for being; it's the way that you communicate most fundamentally, most honestly and most effectively. It's the way you can show the world how it feels to you. It's about our common experience of feeling absolutely alone. No one can know exactly what it's like to be somebody else, but having the ability to communicate feelings in a non-verbal and non-mental way from the heart is a way of bringing people together.

I've always known that I love singing and also that I love drawing and to have been born with that is an incredibly precious thing. For somebody who has never had that knowledge of why they were here or what they were meant to do can be a terrible gap in a human being. It can also be kind of desperate if you're searching for your purpose in life so hard, there is every chance one might overlook the thing that is there for you and you may miss an opportunity. It's such a blessing to have an outlet like drawing, painting, singing or whatever. There must be a million ways, maybe even sport or anything you are completely absorbed in. What an enormous relief that is as well for the brain and for the body. A human being needs to have that, to be able to go there and it happens for everyone in the Cecil style classes.

In the academic classes it's only static if you allow it to be static. I don't think it's just the model's responsibility, it's also the artists', there can be a tendency to seek to make a good drawing that will be acknowledged by others. In a Cecil Collins' class, that doesn't happen and it's not each person relying on himself or herself; it's a group dynamic. At the end of the class, or in a break, particularly in Lily's classes, people will put out their paintings to dry and there'll be laughter, enjoying certain aspects, appreciating the sweep of a line, all sorts of positive responses to drawings as a whole. People don't seem to take personal credit for their drawings. It's not an ego massaging exercise, it's looking back at what everyone's just been through. It's a wonderful thing.

TIM MAYNE

Born in Cambridge in 1953, Tim Mayne is a self-taught artist, musician, songwriter and poet. He has been a lorry and taxi driver, telephone engineer, shop assistant, decorator and a model for life classes. He has exhibited his artwork in London galleries and has two children.

I'd read Quentin Crisp's autobiography. He had been a professional model in London for twenty-five years so I knew about modelling from his perspective. I was flattered and charmed to accept an invitation from Nomi Rowe to model at Hampstead School of Art because I like doing a range of different jobs, especially things I've never done before. Also, I had drawn models so I knew what was expected of them in the traditional sense. Hampstead School of Art is a very intimate college and there were about sixteen people in Nomi's class. They were all very nice people and I felt completely at ease, even my first time, not at all fussed about being naked in front of strangers.

Part of modelling is the teamwork set up between the teacher and the model and the working relationship which brings out the best in the students when both get it right. I had read that Quentin Crisp would often be put in difficult poses and he would stay in them rather than asking for breaks every few minutes. I wanted to do the same if I could. To my surprise with Nomi the poses were often very short, sometimes only a few seconds. Even when the poses were a bit difficult and would make me ache, Nomi was always very aware of my needs and she would give me breaks when needed without me having to ask. We would do three-hour sessions and I thought it was a shame that they weren't longer. In other art colleges, you worked through the entire day and I realised this made a huge difference.

Nomi's method was quite different from anything I'd seen before or from anything I have experienced subsequently working in twelve different London art colleges. Nomi would bring in tapes of music, often a classical piece, and ask me to move or dance, interpreting the music with my movements, instead of standing still in a pose. I would move around naked in front of everyone and she would ask the students to copy my movements and to move in the same way that I was moving which I found amusing. It was almost like a children's game, like musical chairs. Nomi would stop the music and I would hold whatever pose I was in at that moment. All the students would stop at the same moment, copying my pose so they could identify and empathise with me: where my weight was, what strains there were on me, what tension it would cause if I had my arms stretched out and so on. It helped bring out aspects that weren't necessarily visible. I was happy to go along with what was, for me, quite a novel method.

I would stay in the pose and the students would sit down and start to paint or draw me. In Nomi's classes everybody sat down with drawing boards on tables. They had to work in different ways, perhaps to paint or draw with their left hand if they were right-handed or with their right hand if they were left-handed or use the brush or pencil between their teeth and draw that way. It would mean that the lines would go everywhere; you couldn't control them even if you wanted to. It seemed to me part of Nomi's methodology was that, to some degree, you shouldn't control it.

This was fabulous to watch even though, in most cases, the drawings would turn out to be scribbles and scrawls that bemused the students, but this was part of the method Nomi used to loosen them up. Sometimes the results were surprising and very successful. Loosening up knocked away any preconceptions of how the students should draw a model that, in other art colleges, was still the traditional aim of trying to make a photographic likeness.

I was interested in the experience of modelling and worked in other art schools and saw how they operated now which was very different from when I was young. Certain teachers I was working for who had been teaching since the 1950s had become deeply disillusioned. Sometimes they would just set up the class and then walk out. I came across elements of this apathy even in top colleges like St Martins. I had the feeling that students, teachers and art colleges had all lost their way.

In contrast there was a great feeling amongst the students in Nomi's classes. They were happy, regardless of not having produced an ordinary drawing. They knew what they were letting themselves in for and kept coming back week after week. Sometimes at the end of the day there would be spontaneous applause for me, as if I'd taken part in a theatre performance and I would very much like that. It was almost like performance art. That happened on quite a few occasions because everybody could see how well it had gone.

There was the rare occasion where I could see a student's frustration and then they wouldn't cooperate. Nomi would allow for the fact that was so and would improvise too. Classes weren't a set thing for her. She wouldn't necessarily know how I was going to interpret the music in my movement or how the students would respond. She'd bring different types of music and play some pieces longer or shorter. There was an intuitive side to what we were doing and a trust was developed in the students to work in a more intuitive, spontaneous way. There was also a trust of Nomi and her method and all the sessions felt harmonious. I always felt that everybody was happy to take part in that energy and go with the flow. We were all participating in a sort of surreal theatre. That was an aspect I really enjoyed, the fact that it was slightly nutty and there were smiles on people's faces. There was humour in our sessions that wasn't necessarily part of ordinary art lessons that I was involved in elsewhere.

Cecil Collins
Head
1944
Gouache on paper
18 x 18cm

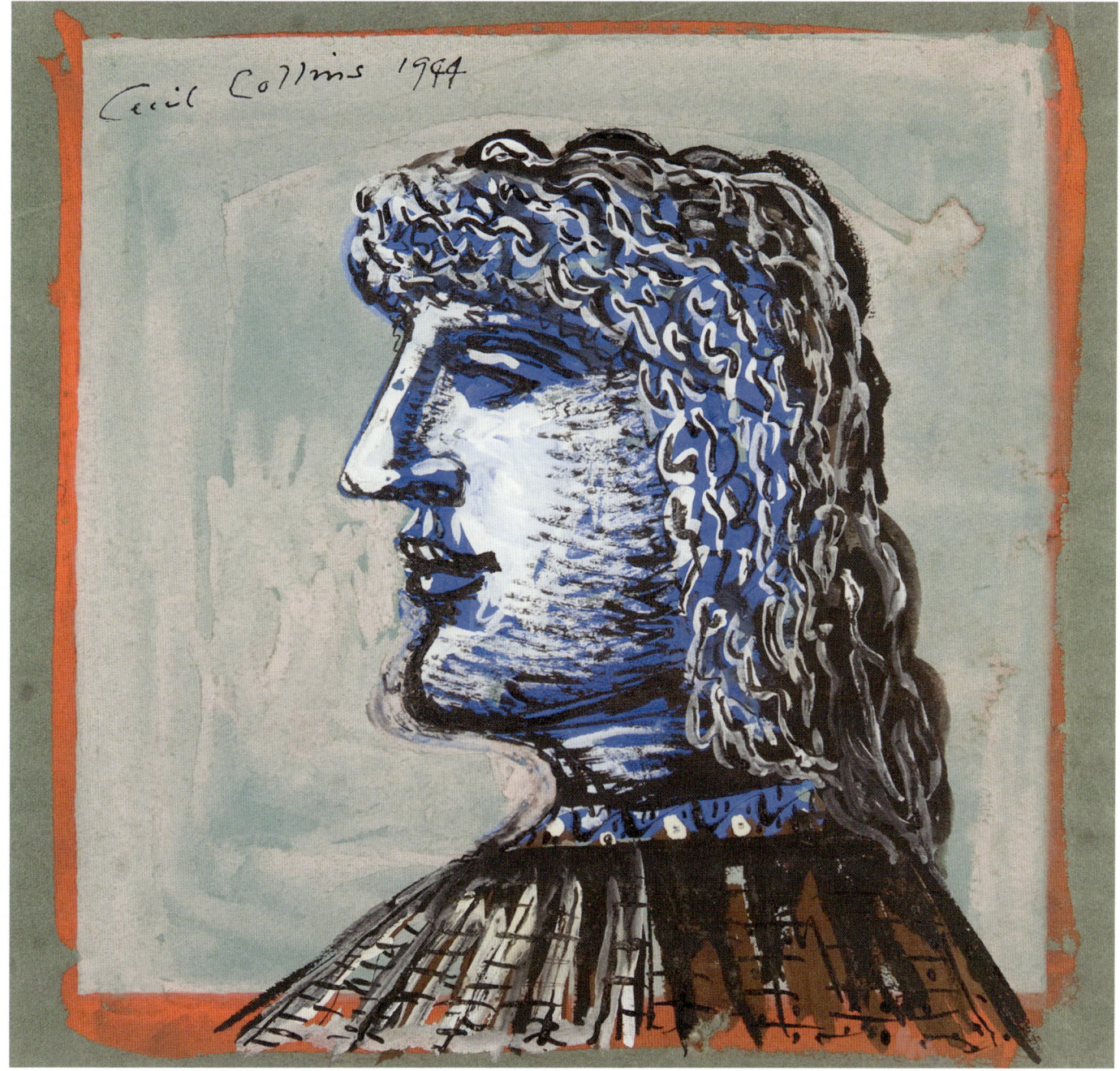

Later, Nomi put me in touch with Elisabeth Collins a couple of years before she died so that I could do some decorating work in her flat. Meeting Elisabeth made quite a strong impression on me. I loved her flat, which was funky and bohemian, just off the Kings Road in Chelsea. I remember going up some stairs with paintings on all the walls, into her flat and immediately I thought, this is just the sort of place that I would like to live in. There was art and art books everywhere, higgledy-piggledy papers and things all over the place. It felt very much like an artist's space.

I did two or three days' work. I had to paint the stairwell and the main room which was an attic. One of the sloping ceilings there was damaged so I did some repair on the ceiling as well. I got the impression that Elisabeth was pleased with my work. I was very respectful of all the paintings. She obviously trusted me and the job went well. There was a lot of her and Cecil's artwork on the walls, including a large mural. Elizabeth had said, 'You must be very careful.' I remember being very concerned that I was going to have to paint around it and that not the slightest drip should go on it. I took the rest of the paintings off the wall and stacked them up but, before I took them down, I looked at them and realised they were all paintings involving man/woman relationships, paintings of couples in love and that the theme was Cecil and Elisabeth's love. Elisabeth confirmed this. She said that they were sort of love letters between her and Cecil, paintings that Cecil had given to her and paintings she'd given to him, perhaps for birthday presents.

I didn't know either of them as artists, but I could see similarities between their two styles. They were very personal paintings and quite touching. What I've seen of Cecil Collins' work isn't really on my wavelength. I appreciate them as they are very well painted and I can see why both Cecil and Elisabeth got their reputations, but they don't affect me, other than the idea of those hanging on their walls being love letters which was moving.

One of the things that struck me was that, for a woman in her nineties, she had an inordinate amount of energy. Over the two or three days that I was there, she was in and out and constantly busy: writing, making and receiving telephone calls, setting up appointments, going out to meetings, but she wasn't flustered. She had a list in front of her, a full diary that she referred to, organising this and that, but her energy level didn't seem to flag. She was physically frail, but mentally completely on top of the situation. At the time she was working towards putting on an exhibition of her own work. I hadn't seen before in anyone of her age the sort of intense social and work calendar that someone in their twenties might have been able to handle.

She had a social life that included a group of people who appeared rich and powerful. I got the impression that she had admirers. Distinguished men were coming round to take her out for lunch, things like that. She was obviously greatly respected as an artist and as a person. She'd had a long life as a professional artist and had lived with a well-known professional artist, was well travelled and had art books all round her. There were all sorts of aspects that I would have talked to her about had I been given the chance, but when I took breaks and had a cup of tea, we barely got to say anything to each other because she was so busy. I regretted that. Although I didn't talk to her for very long, I got the impression that she wouldn't have tolerated fools gladly. She was sharp and seemed so astute. I didn't feel that small talk was her thing. It was her strength of character that came across, but I didn't feel intimidated because I like strong women. She seemed very organised, very bright and on the ball. There was no dodderiness about her at all.

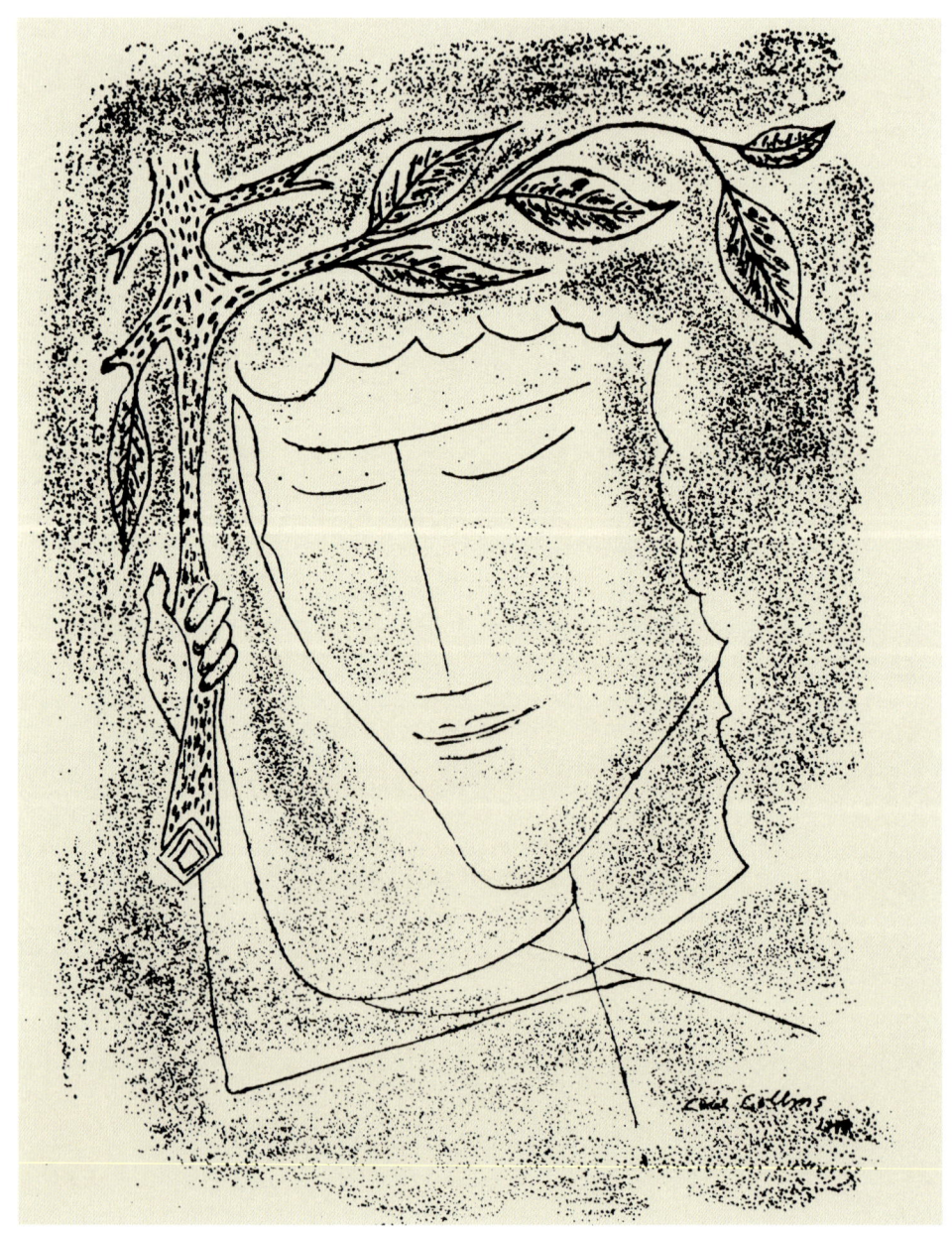

Cecil Collins
Head
1944
Roneo stencil on paper
38.7 x 28.5cm

COLLEAGUES

AMAL GHOSH

Born in 1933 in Calcutta, India, Amal Ghosh moved to Britain in the 1960s to complete his art studies at the Central School of Art. His painting reflects the need for a union of world religions. He was Head of Transparent Imagery for many years at Central Saint Martins College of Art and Design and his work is in many private and pubic collections, including the Victoria and Albert Museum, London, the Musée Municipal in Limoges, France, the Decorative Art Museum in Palanga, Lithuania, the Art Council of Great Britain and the British Council in India. He set up an enamel section at the Visa Bharati University, Santiniketan, India, where he is visiting professor. He divides his time between London and India.

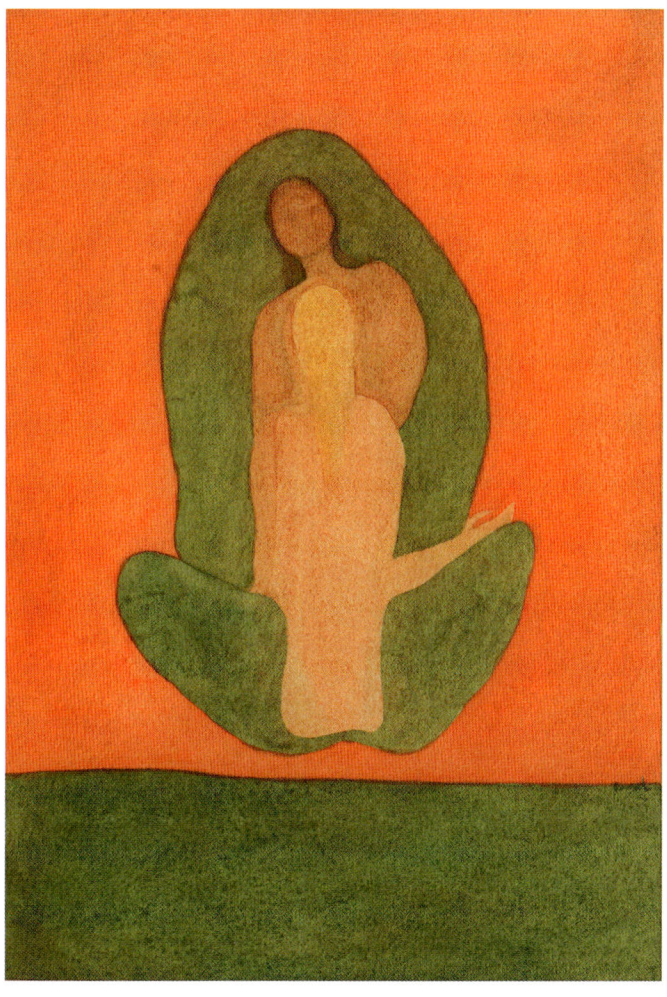

Amal Ghosh
Devotee
2008
Watercolour on handmade paper
60 x 40cm

I came to the Central in 1959 to study stained glass and painting. I'd already done five years painting in Calcutta so it was more of a post-graduate course for me. I met Cecil on my second day there. He was having tea downstairs in the canteen with Morris Kestelman, the Head of Fine Art, who introduced me to Cecil. I joined his class for composition painting and took a portfolio to show him my work. He had already given everybody an exercise to do about rhythm and form, I think. He talked about persona, which didn't mean much to me then and was something I only really understood later. Art school in India at that time was like the Slade in the 1930s. You'd do drawing from the cast, still life, life drawing and life painting. I was good at it and quite proud of my work. Cecil looked at my drawing. 'We'll talk about it in the lunch hour.' I thought he was going to say how good it was, but what he said was, 'Don't come to the class. Go to the British Museum. Go to the ground floor because there's a frieze of Egyptian drawing there. Draw something from that and bring that to me.' I thought, Okay, I'll do that. It wasn't very difficult.

I did the drawing and brought it in the next day. Cecil looked at it and said, 'Now go back and look at Indian sculpture.' The strange thing is that I'd drawn some Indian sculpture, but never spent a day just drawing it. I think I did four days of that, drawing from different areas that Cecil specified each day. I was getting a bit frustrated because I wanted to do painting. I thought it was very odd that Cecil wasn't saying anything. He wasn't discouraging me. He just said, 'Do this, do that,' but nobody else was sent to the British Museum.

After a week he said, 'Do you understand what is happening? Compare the drawings you've done before and these drawings.' I did and the drawings at the British Museum had much more rhythm. Then he said, 'Try again and try to understand the new drawing in relation to the work you were doing before.' Every second day I had to go to the British Museum to do a drawing from India or the Middle East and bring it to him, but there was never any criticism. 'You have to learn how to be you. You are Indian and no work of yours says that you are Indian.' That was incredible. I'd never questioned that I was Indian and it was quite new to me to realise that the patterns of your mind and habitual behaviour could be different fundamentally from what you had assimilated superficially and yet assumed was intrinsically part of yourself.

I'd brought quite a lot of my work from India because I wanted an exhibition. One gallery was very interested in my work and I'd sold two paintings. I told Cecil that and he said, 'Don't have an exhibition and don't sell your work yet.' There was a kind of ethos at Central that students should wait till they left college before they sold their work. I accepted that because, by this time, I'd started looking at Cecil's work. Before I came to England I hadn't known who he was,

193

Cecil Collins

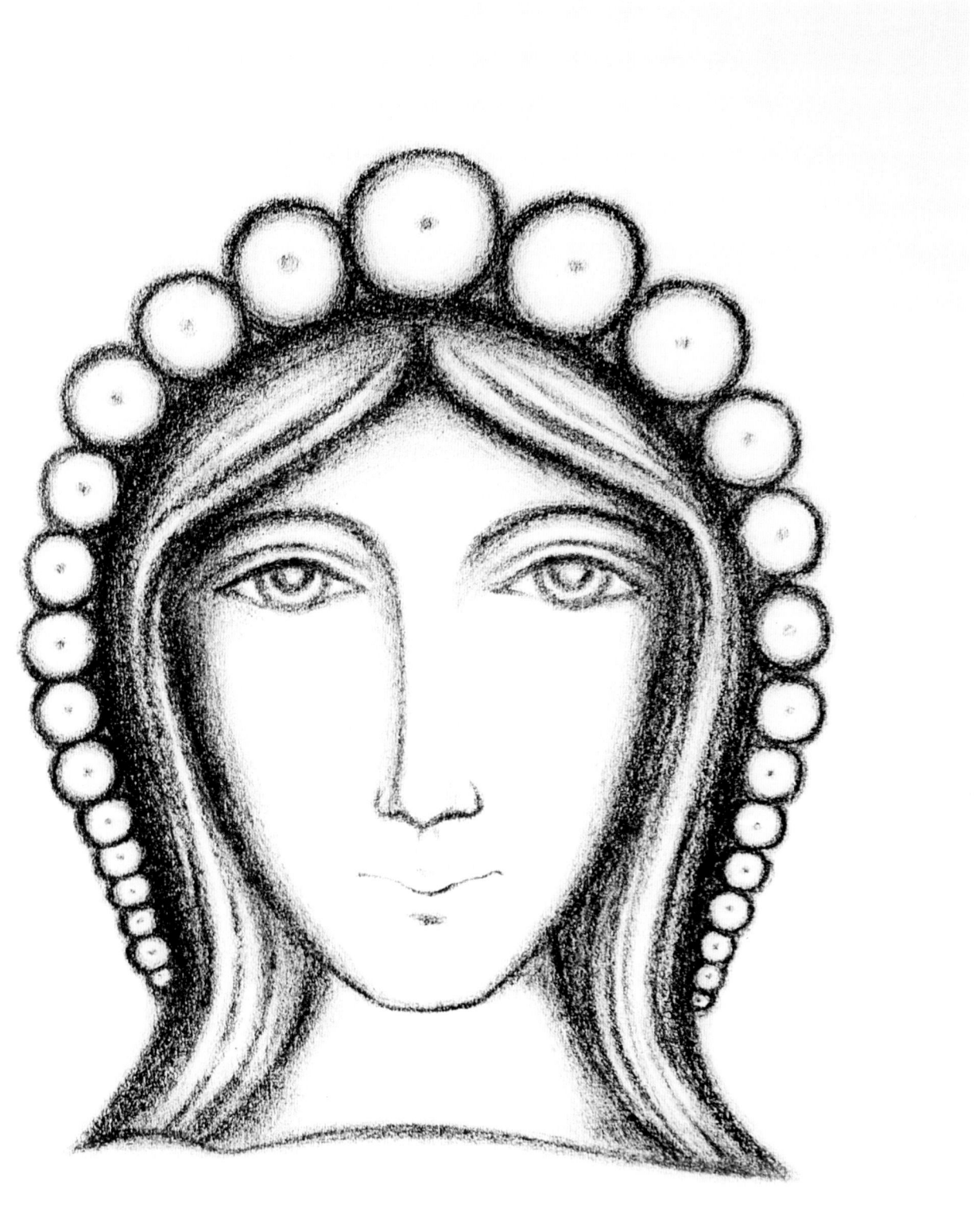

Cecil Collins
Head
1974
Lihograph on paper
40.3 x 32.4cm

then I saw some of his paintings at the Lefevre Gallery.

Cecil asked me one day what did I think of painting, not his painting: he wanted to know what painting I liked and what painter. I knew quite a lot of Western art, but he said I should make a point of going every day to the National Gallery and gave me a list of painters I should see. I wish I still had that list.

He also suggested things to listen to. Bach was the main composer he recommended. Later on, when I started really liking Western music, he suggested Schumann. He's a beautiful composer, but I still don't know why Cecil wanted me to listen to him. Bach I got a lot from and that was the beginning of my understanding of European music.

Cecil talked to me about Indian music and sometimes asked my opinion of something he had heard. He had quite a bit of Indian music. Once or twice he asked if I had some he could borrow for his class, but I had no money then so I had no way of getting the music transferred onto tape. Later, I used Indian music in my teaching at the V&A as well as some of the music Cecil played us in his classes. It worked, but by then I had a feeling for what I should do.

I had another tutor at the Central, Alan Davie, a Scottish painter. Alan used to talk about the dynamics of painting which I'd heard about, but never understood. The whole Indian idea of painting was craft based. I was very skilled at reproducing images, but why you painted was another matter. With both my tutors, Alan and Cecil, and another outstanding artist and tutor at the Central, William Turnbull, the question 'why' was an important issue, although they all approached it in different ways. In fact, Cecil was imposing in a subtle way I did not understand. He never said anything critical about my work, but I understood that I had to learn to come to terms with this 'why' aspect of painting.

Cecil told me to read Jung and then gave me Sylvia Plath's *The Bell Jar*. I started reading and slowly began to understand what Cecil was after. Quite a few of us were interested in Blake and we went with Cecil to look at his work. Cecil didn't say anything, which was quite interesting because he had a lot to say when we did exercises, but when he took us to see anything, he would just say, 'Go and look.' Then when we came back, the exercise would have something to do with what we'd seen, but nothing explicit; it was all implied. It's very difficult to describe how he did it. Later on, when I started reading Mark Tobey, I realised how diffused things have to be to become part of something which could become you. Cecil seemed to be saying this is how it should be and you either reject it or you adopt it.

If you disagreed with Cecil, he never looked angry, but he did look disappointed that you hadn't understood. I don't think he was ever angry with me, but he was disappointed. Then he would give me something to read or tell me to go somewhere or to do something. It took me some time to understand why, because it was never ever straightforward. Something he said has become almost like a mantra: 'Every now and then everything works and that is when you are in a state of grace.' That is so true. You don't have to think, everything comes naturally, while at other times you're struggling and struggling. According to Cecil, that is also very good because that's when you evolve something which is a kind of churning up. In the sense of the Indian creation myth in which through the churning round and round in the sea of knowledge by the snake, symbolising Kundalini energy and power, creation happens. Cecil never talked very much about Indian mythology, but he knew about it. He once spoke to me about Kali, the goddess of destruction and creation. Kali is always shown as quite a vicious looking lady, but he thought the way she was represented was not true. For Cecil, it wasn't a question of ugly or not ugly, he thought that Kali's whole energy had been misinterpreted. I was quite shocked and I think he saw that. Sometimes Cecil was shocking and provocative to make you rethink something you had accepted as a given. Other times, he was reasserting something about himself because quite often he bounced things back to see what I would do and then he talked about it later.

I got to know Cecil better at City Lit after we were both teaching there. James Burr was head of department and the staff used to have tea quite often in his room so Cecil and I would meet there and that's how we started talking about things. I was always a bit shy because I'd come from a tradition where teachers are held in high respect and I never thought Cecil would talk so openly with me. He was never chatty, but he was very much a gossiper. He was curious about everything. I was surprised at how much he knew about everyone and nobody knew that he knew. Cecil had much more freedom at City Lit; I think they gave him a completely free hand and all the people from Central just flocked in. I think he taught maybe eight or nine years at the City Lit and his classes were full almost from the moment they were offered.

In 1964, just after I started teaching at Central, everybody was plotting against Bob Clatworthy who had succeeded Kestelman as Head of Fine Art. Bob came into Central with a lot of power as an ILEA man and it was thought impossible to get rid of him. I had met him earlier at Buckingham Palace when, as a Commonwealth student, I'd been invited to meet the Queen. Bob was also there in some capacity and I got to know him very well. He was a difficult person to deal with, but he was alright with me. Somehow Cecil knew that, although how he did I don't know. It took me quite some time to understand that Cecil wasn't as innocent as he behaved. There were two camps at that time: a drinking crowd and a tea crowd. Cecil, of course, was in the tea crowd. He may well have been behind the students' agitation against Clatworthy. The atmosphere was not good. Cecil would organise meetings with the other tutors and you knew it would be yet another complicated issue, but Cecil had a very precise grasp of what was going on and what was needed. His work was so otherworldly, but he was not a fool at all and always said, 'You have to be planted first and then grow.' He would edit the very explicit letters that he somehow got a group of younger tutors to write to the Governors of the School.

In the end, Clatworthy was given financial encouragement to resign, however there were still conflicting politics and it was difficult to cope with the continuous unrest. Cecil would have a meeting with one group of tutors, then go and have a cup of tea with another. He was a very good politician. He knew what he was doing and he orchestrated things. I always think of him as a system man. When Clatworthy went, Patrick Reyntiens was appointed Head of Fine Art, but Mark Vaux became Head of Painting, around 1968, I think. Mark had trained in America and came from the Hard Edge group of painters and found Cecil, who was in his department, totally unacceptable and wanted him out completely. So Cecil started collecting students who would support and agitate for him.

In class when I started to get the feel of what Cecil was going to say, I realised that it was all very systematic. It was very worked out, not spontaneous at all. He was a very conscious person. In that sense, he was like an Indian master such as Tagore. Both Tagore and Cecil had very strong personalities which couldn't be ignored. Cecil was never intrusive in class and never forced anything. Most of the other tutors would go round and look at your work and talk about it, but Cecil never did. Only if you asked him what he thought, would he make some comments. I absorbed tuition easily and understood what the tutors were after. At the same time, quite a lot of people, including Cecil, told me that I've been influenced too much by certain things, such as the traditional way I was taught the skills of art in India, but sometimes one needs to go through that process. Cecil believed that skill had to become part of your whole psyche. If it is imposed, as it was in my case, then it's not true and Cecil was concerned with truth all the time. That is another thing I learnt from him. Painting was part of the process to understand yourself. It was about you. It's not just about painting; you have to have worked on yourself to create something meaningful.

It took me a long time to free my work from Cecil's influence. It was so strong and he gave me such a lot. Cecil was what he was, but he wanted you to be what you were. He always said that to be an artist is the most important thing. You have to believe in something emotionally, intellectually and with your whole heart to be creative. That is what he was saying in the class too, in a slightly different way. It was not about style, or that he imposed his style on me, but I realised that he was always addressing the soul and that this had became the focus of my work too.

I felt that it was important for me to leave Central and I did one year at St Albans College of Art. That was a very good thing to do. Everything fell into place. Before that, my work was not intellectual; it was all emotional. Now I began to understand what I wanted to do and to stand on my own two feet. By this time, Cecil was getting quite fragile so whenever I saw him it was more social and I was glad about that. I felt I didn't need his mentoring any longer. What was very important for me was that he taught me to be Indian; that was his main gift. He gave me back my identity and my cultural background. He also gave me a lot of strength and encouraged me in my work.

Cecil definitely changed my perception and my way at looking at myself. He gave me the courage to overcome obstacles. I think that strength came from Cecil. He got me to look at myself, to be myself. 'Don't parrot,' he said. It took me a while to understand what he meant. He was after truth all the time. Cecil never ever said no about anything. When I think of my four years with him, I never heard him say no. He would say, 'Look at this,' and you knew that what he meant was look at it again and understand why you'd done it.

Later, when we were part of the same Painting Diploma assessment panel, he would not grade, but would ask the other staff, 'Why did you give eighty per cent to this?' He didn't think that art has anything to do with marking. He reacted very strongly against it. Each student does what they can, but marking had to be done for exams at Central so Cecil's attitude was problematic. At meetings he could be very provocative and mischievous. He would say something very sharp sometimes and he would smile because it took you some time to realise what he'd said, then you smiled.

He wrote forewords to the catalogues of two of my exhibitions. He was very precise in what he said. He dictated the last foreword because he said his hand was not steady. I wrote it down and he said, 'Type it before I sign it.' So I did and he changed two words he had used. He didn't like them and I realised that he wouldn't let the foreword go until the words expressed exactly what he meant. That is the greatness of a person; even a small thing matters. Everything mattered.

There is something slightly repetitive about some of Cecil's paintings, but knowing the kind of person he was, knowing his strength and dignity, I feel this is because of the system he followed. There was a particular way he had to go about things and he wasn't going to deviate from it. He had a vision and if you have that, there is no choice. You can't move away from it. A lot of people have criticised him for being a fanatic, but it was not fanaticism; it was something quite different. He believed in something and that belief was total, as it has to be, and he had the strength and also the ability to conduct his own life the way he wanted. Strength comes from understanding, from believing, from going on and from sharpening your perception. He used to say that everybody has ability; you just have to find how that ability could be put to use in the highest sense of the word and for Cecil it was put to the service of creativity.

MAXWELL PROCTOR

Maxwell Proctor was librarian at Central St Martins College of Art and Design for many years and a devoted admirer of Cecil Collins.

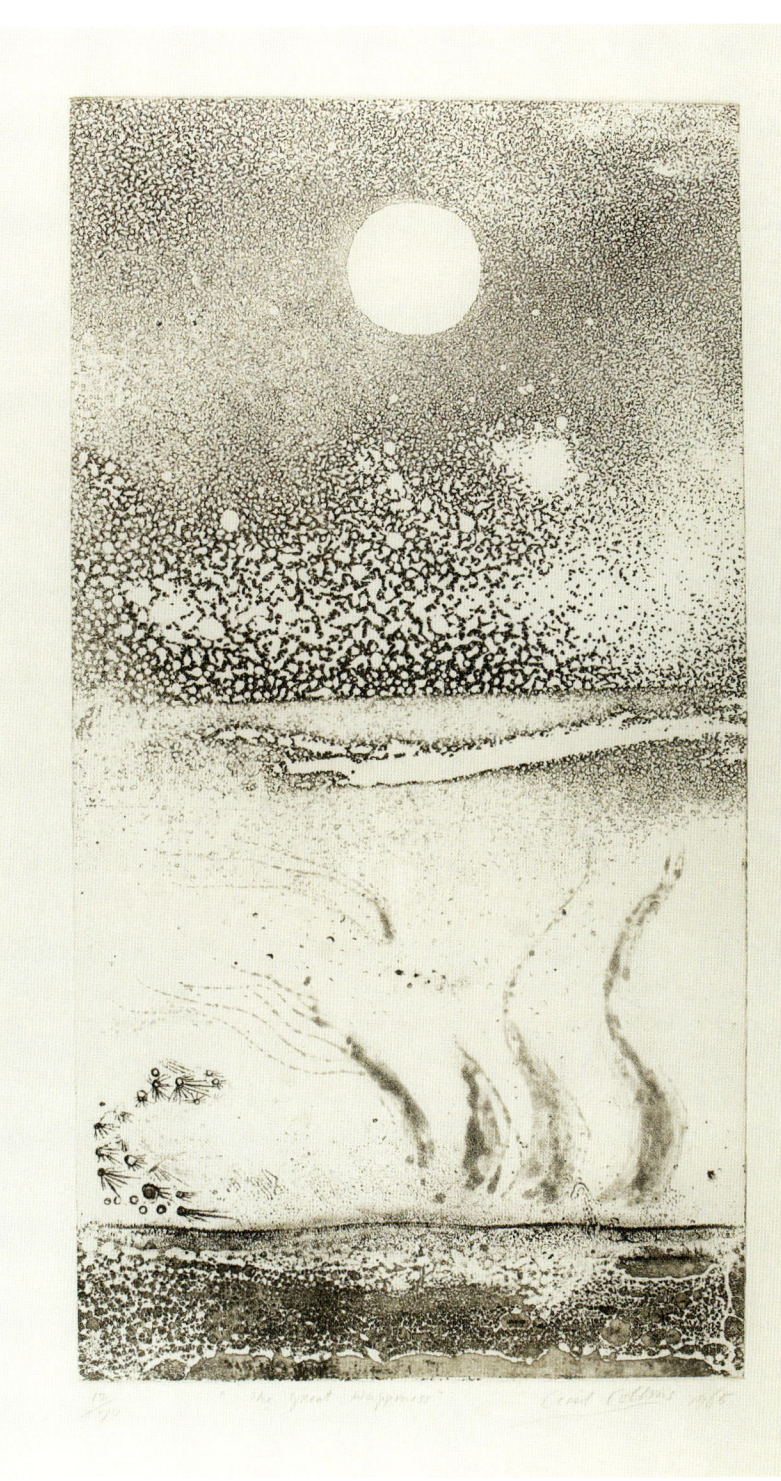

Cecil Collins
The Great Happiness
1963
Etching, aquatint and soft-ground on paper
47.5 x 25.2cm

CECIL COLLINS

for you
the Dawn has come,
the Voyage ended,
the Quest fulfilled,
the Great Happiness attained

at Daybreak
a Golden Angel waited,
greeted you with love,
led you into the Divine Land,
the Lost Paradise,
you were dressed in
the Robes of Life

Music of Dawn,
Mysterious Rejoicing,
Mysterious Joy,
joy of joys,
Joy of the Worlds,
with one Voice
all the angels sang,
sang a glorious Song,
the World's Rejoice,
the Pilgrim-Fool,
the Artist-Poet
had Returned
to Paradise

out of the Sacred Mirror
a butterfly emerged
in light,
dancing, dancing
the Dance of the Worlds
until it became
an Angel of the Sun...

... the Sun Blessing Stones
By the Waters
brought the Peace of the Fool,
the Music of the Worlds,
the Music of the Kingdom

... on earth
sea-shells echoed
the divine music,
the homecoming.

*Written on the occasion of the death of Cecil Collins
4th June, 1989*

DAVID GLUCK

David Gluck, 1939 – 2007, born in Yorkshire, studied at Wakefield School of Art, Leeds College of Art (where he met his future wife, the artist, Sally Hallam) and Royal College of Art, London. He then taught at various colleges of art and at the Central School of Art and Design (1974 – 1994) where he was appointed Head of Printmaking, later becoming Director of Studies of Fine Art. He came to prefer working in watercolour and in 1985 was elected to the Royal Watercolour Society, serving as Vice-President (1999 – 2002). He won several prestigious awards, including first prize in the Singer and Friedlander/Sunday Times competition, 2006, for his landscape *The Evening Sunlight, Petrognano*. He exhibited extensively and his work is held in many private and public collections including Leeds City Art Gallery, the British Museum and the Palace of Westminster.

It must have been about two or three weeks after Cecil's death when it was suggested that I should write an obituary for the Guardian. A few weeks later I got a cheque, I think for £50, so I gave the money to Ruth for her to organise a tea party with great cakes for Cecil's students past and present.

I started teaching printmaking at the Central in 1974 when Michael Patrick was Principal. Cecil had, by then, been teaching there quite a long time. I can only give a college perspective on Cecil because I didn't see him outside that setting. He was a very well known artist and I knew his work before I got to know him when he would bring plates into the etching room, asking technical questions. He was very good and innovative technically. He might do a bit of work in the studio and then take it back home to work on. He always used to come in and nose around to see what was going on and what other people were doing.

He was a very lively character and I liked his dry humour. One funny incident that stands out in my memory happened in the big first year studio. Patrick Reyntiens, then Head of Fine Art, came in with his dog one day and it left a great turd on the floor. Cecil was just walking past and said, 'That dog made a good comment.' He was always so quick-witted and very funny. Unlike a lot of artists who tend to take the easy way out, Cecil never did. He was very tenacious, a bit like a Yorkshire terrier. He would hold on to something and push it through.

In those days, the college gave extra teaching hours on an a priori allocation to certain subjects such as stained glass, printmaking and life drawing to keep them going. Then came the cuts and that's when they tried to reduce Cecil's teaching hours and in 1975, when he reached the age of sixty-five, the ILEA tried to retire him. It's very important to remember that he always taught drawing to the whole college, students from the painting, print-making, ceramics, design and sculpture departments.

After Patrick Reyntiens left in 1984, I became Acting Head for about five years and I got permission to open Cecil's drawing classes on his teaching day to part-time students as we'd already done in the print-making and stained glass departments. We called them 'advanced students'. On enrolment day, people were actually queueing in Southampton Row to get into his class. I made a ruling there was to be a maximum of twenty students for his class and ten to fifteen of his advanced students could come which left five places open for students from the college. That was how we kept them going.

Ruth and a few other students used to come every year and ask, 'Is Cecil alright for next year?' When I was in charge, I just said to the college we want Cecil and that was it, so there was no problem. Then the manoeuvrings started to join Central and St Martin's together as one college which is why they didn't appoint another Head, so I became Course Director in charge of all the students which was effectively Head of Fine Art. I got very fed up with all the politicking and the terrible administration duties so I retired in 1994, although I continued for two or three years part-time. Afterwards I taught at the Royal Academy and the Prince's Trust School of Drawing for three years.

In those days, we had a wide nucleus of staff with different attitudes. Some of the staff were obviously geared towards abstract art, but there were still a lot of others who had different opinions. Even though the general thrust was a certain way, students who veered off a bit out of the straight and narrow could be dealt with. What was marvellous was that Cecil had his ways of dealing with people who had a hostile attitude which was very effective. Some staff could only see what they were interested in, which was basically themselves. So certain sections of people didn't like Cecil's type of work and he didn't like theirs, but it wasn't that they didn't like Cecil. That was the lively part of art school then, whereas today it tends to be all one group thinking the same and if a staff member or a student doesn't toe the line, they're out or don't get a good degree.

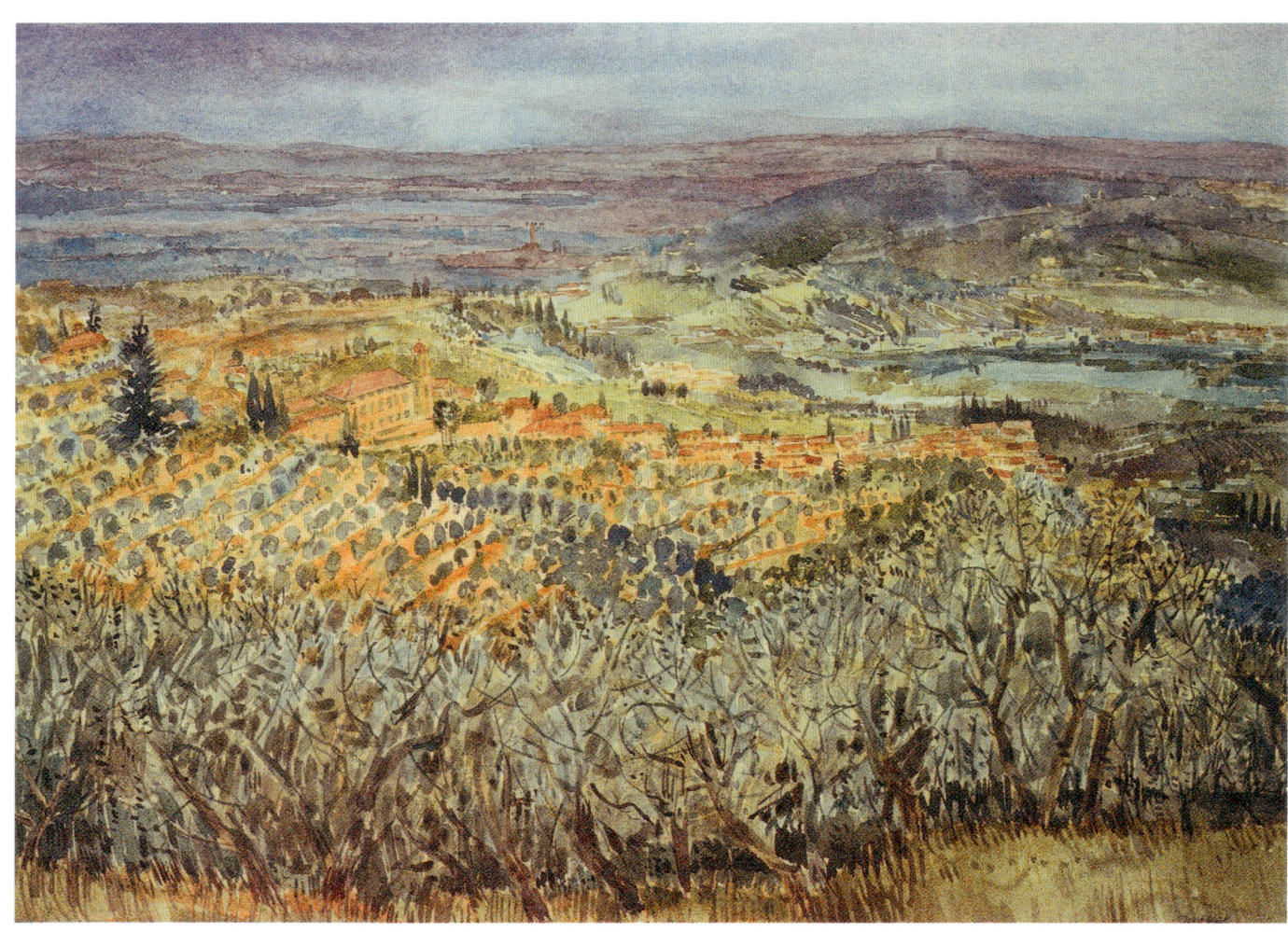

David Gluck
The Evening Sunlight, Petrognano, near Lucca, Italy
2006
Watercolour
52 x 75cm

I knew straight away that Cecil was a special teacher. He was also special in the way he stood up very strongly for what he believed in. He wasn't a shrinking violet and didn't sit in an ivory tower. He was very aware of all that was going on in the world, as well as in the art world and in the college. Cecil obviously taught on a broader base than most tutors and would educate painting students about all sorts of other things as well as drawing. He had a particular vision he wanted to transmit and for other people to be truthful to themselves.

I thought his teaching methods were quite innovative because sometimes in life drawing, the corrections can be mundane and very unimaginative, no more sophisticated than, 'The legs are too long.' Cecil was completely the opposite and I thought he not only got some very good work out of the students, but also got them thinking. That's what art teaching should be about. I'd go in now and again and students would tell me about his classes so I was well aware of what was going on in them. You wouldn't expect all the staff and all the students to think that Cecil was marvellous, but he appealed to a much wider cross section than one might think which is why I made the effort to keep his classes going for the whole college.

During the last ten years or so, when he was doing this specialist drawing class. The students made sure Cecil had his old chair, which was an easy chair, and one of the college portable gramophones so when Cecil waltzed in, it was all ready for him. Somebody like me had to go around searching for material, but for Cecil, the students were so devoted, it was all prepared for him. The only problem Cecil had was the awful old lift which broke down now and then and towards the end, poor old Cecil could hardly get up the five flights of stairs to the life room and would be something like a quarter of an hour late for his class.

We used to go for lunch sometimes or have a coffee together. Cecil always wore that old coat with the elbow patches, winter or summer, and he had a hat that looked as if it had been kicked around. He was always very interested in what was going on and would question me about all the gossip. He wanted to know about everyone.

Cecil's students at Central organised his eightieth birthday party at the college and two hundred ex-students and staff attended. The tributes were so overwhelming and genuine that no one present could doubt that Cecil had achieved the ultimate teacher's accolade, the veneration of his students.

PATRICK REYNTIENS AND ANNE BRUCE

Patrick Reytiens, OBE, b. 1925, was a stained glass artist whose commissioned work is in many public buildings including Coventry Cathedral, the Roman Catholic Cathedral, Liverpool, and the V&A Museum, London. In 1960 he set up an arts educational centre at Burleighfield House, Buckinghamshire, with his wife, Anne.

Anne Bruce, 1927 - 2006, was an artist and teacher who trained at the Slade, University of London and Edinburgh College of Art where she met Patrick Reyntiens. They were married in 1953 and had four children. She exhibited regularly in London, Edinburgh and Paris and in 1962 she was a prize-winner at the John Moore's open Exhibition of Painting and Sculpture

I was Head of Fine Art at the Central from 1976 to 1986. Cecil was already teaching there when I arrived. He was over seventy by then and should have retired. Every year beginning in December and ending with his reappointment in March, I had to write letters putting the case that a man of genius should not be kicked out because of his age. Each January I remember saying, 'The Cecil season has come,' rather like the shooting season in Scotland. It was a bore, but it was a loving chore because I loved Cecil very much.

Cecil and Elisabeth were always very poor which was worrying for him. Before I was at the Central, I had tried to get Lord Goodman to give him a government pension because of the speciality of his art. He was one of the greatest draughtsman of his day with the delicacy of his handling of a line. I'm glad I did the window to his design in Basingstoke which is much underrated. Cecil was a kind of a saint. No fool, he understood everything that was going on and had his own philosophy, but a lot of it was made up from Eastern sources like Baha'i and Sufi. Cecil used to say, 'We've never had a civilisation before that hasn't had some kind of metaphysical base. This is the way towards death.' I believe he was right.

Cecil and I got to know each other in the 1930s when we met at Piggotts, Eric Gill's place near High Wycombe. We became closer because he was friends with Paul Bird, Vice-Principal of the Central, and Paul's younger brother was a friend of mine from Burleighfield House, the art school my wife and I set up and ran. We both came from landed, quasi-aristocratic families and didn't have much money, but we had lots of antique furniture, paintings and carpets. Country houses were going under the hammer for nothing after the war so we bought Burleighfield House, did it up and opened an international school of art. We gave the students a quality of life they wouldn't have known otherwise, but it was the inspiration that mattered, the meeting of souls, hearts and minds. It was not dissimilar to Dartington and this was something Cecil recognised. Some of the students, like Danny Lane, are now world famous.

All careers have tragedies and when I took the job at Central, the trustees felt betrayed and wound up Burleighfield. It was dreadful for my wife who was the main administrator. We had to return £25,000 worth of advance fees. The trustees bought the mortgage and sold the place and we didn't get a penny back.

The Collinses chose their friends carefully. Elisabeth could sum up anybody pretty accurately. She was enormously loyal to Cecil who was almost childlike in his innocence. Once I said to her, 'You've never had children?' and she said, 'No, Cecil was the child.' He was extremely intuitive because of his simplicity. He had this subtle, sharp sense of humour that simple people have because they're not deluding themselves and therefore look upon life with unvarnished eyes. He was the most truthful man I've ever met. I never heard him tell a lie.

It was probably thanks to Richard Morphet that Cecil got his Tate Retrospective, but some people there had reservations. When Sir John Rothenstein was Director, the Tate was a sanctuary for English art, hence the emphasis on people like Stanley Spencer and Ivon Hitchens. Cecil was one of the last people who benefited from that. He was very much bracketed in the English category and that's why it was difficult to show Cecil in 1989 as a master in his own right.

He died only a few days after his exhibition opening. He got into a car, went to the London clinic and died.

ANNE BRUCE REYNTIENS

I had a difficult time trying to learn to paint: becoming an artist wasn't acceptable to my family and too expensive. When I was twenty-three, I paid for myself to go to Edinburgh College of Art which is where I met Patrick. It was a joy to study painting properly.

After I married and had a family, I used to paint in a shed in the garden after breakfast on Saturday mornings. Patrick would look after the children, cook lunch and bring mine out to me. After lunch, I went home and washed up. I won the Jerwood prize while I was doing that. I didn't wait till I had time because you never do. When someone asked why I only did a run of seven prints, I said it was all I could fit in after lunch and before fetching the children from school.

We were having a bad time at Burleighfield and it was very upsetting. Cecil told me to come and join his classes to give me a change. From 1976 to 1978, I would escape for one day a week and go up to London with Patrick and attend Cecil's class.

He was an extraordinary teacher and individual. I used to have lunch with him in the City Lit canteen. He would put his hat on the chair and his coat over the back, lay his tray with his plate, glass, knife and fork, everything very precise. I remember saying, 'You're incredibly organised for somebody who has such a chaotic studio.' He said, 'Anne, you must remember that life is full of contradictions.'

Cecil was very witty and could be very cynical. He was also very sensitive to people and used to have students in tears because he got to the core of their problems just by quietly listening.

Sometimes at about four o'clock, when you were tired, you would bring off something. You had to work with both hands, fast with your right hand, slow with a brush held by the toes of your left foot. We did so many drawings we had to buy the cheapest paper. It was like having played scales.

A lot of people copied him, became little Cecils, but I feel I developed my own way of doing things through him. After I'd finished drawing with him, I could paint a nude figure in any position from my mind without the model and with no effort at all.

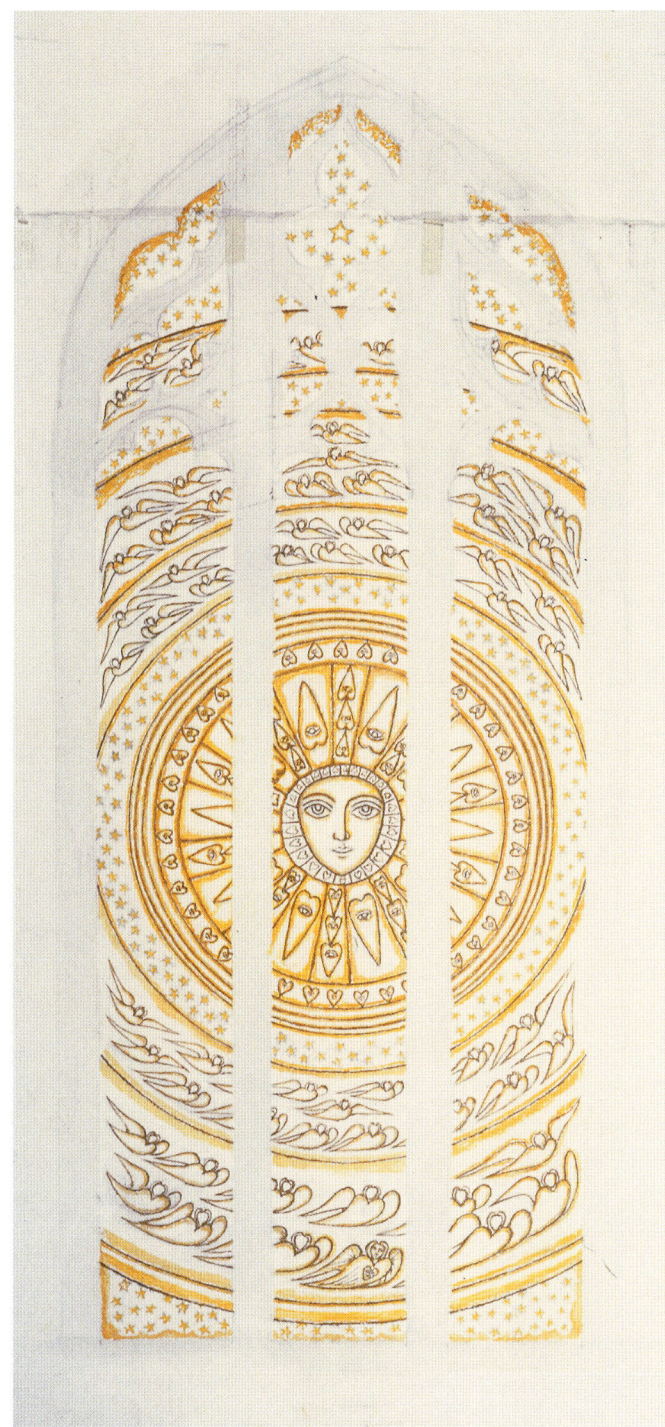

Cecil Collins
The Mystery of the Holy Spirit
1987
Cartoon for stained glass window (30 x 15ft) of All Saints Church, Basingstoke
Gouache and pencil
76 x 30cm
(Glass Artist: Patrick Reyntiens)

Elisabeth was a down-to-earth Yorkshire girl, quite tough. We went to an anniversary celebration of their marriage, their fiftieth perhaps. I remember Cecil going down on his knees to her on that occasion, but he must have given her a hard life.

Cecil was one of the most beautiful people I ever met, with beautiful hands. He was fragile and wouldn't take his coat off for fear of catching cold. He was terribly shocked when I said that I never dried my hair after I washed it. He said, 'Oh God, to go out with wet hair. How crazy.'

He used to tell very funny stories. For example, long ago, a couple of brothers wanted a portrait of their father who'd died. They described him to the artist and a portrait was eventually produced. The two brothers who looked at it and said, 'That's our father, but hasn't he changed?' That's a very Cecilish story.

Once in class he said, 'Last night I floated out of the window and over the square and over the garden. I was just lying there and then somehow I came back again.' When his church windows that Patrick did were finished, Cecil gave a speech about angels. He was so convincing. You really believed him.

Cecil was very demanding and expected a lot of his friends. He issued those royal commands whenever he'd have some pictures in an exhibition. We were all expected to be there and, afterwards, we would have supper at the Chelsea Arts Club. 'It's a very important occasion,' he'd say. 'You must come.' He was very firm about it and you daren't not go.

At his Tate exhibition, Cecil was being wheeled around saying goodbye. It was all so beautiful. That was the last time many of us saw him. Elisabeth told us the last thing he did was to look at her and say, 'We've had a lovely life together.'

JOHN ALLITT

John Stewart Allitt born in France, 1934, was educated in Switzerland, Italy and England. He was senior lecturer in Art history at the Central School of Art (1965 – 1986). He founded the Donizetti Society and promoted performances of little known music by Donizetti and his teacher Mayr. In 1984 John was honoured by the Italian State for his contribution to Italian culture. He had a lifelong enthusiasm for, and led a seminar group through, Dante's Divine Comedy, *at the Temenos Academy and also taught many other Christian based subjects there. The author of numerous books including one on Cecil Collins to be published posthumously by Temenos. He died in England, 2007.*

There's so much I ought to be able to tell you about Cecil, for example the painters he admired: Samuel Palmer, of course, and Blake. Bacon was anathema. I'm sure Cecil and I must have discussed Michelangelo. He would have had more time for Michelangelo than Leonardo because of his poems and, as William Blake did, he would have seen Michelangelo as a visionary.

We spoke a lot about romanticism. For Cecil, romanticism was the last protest against science which made a lot of sense to me. Since then, I've realised that the origins of romanticism lie in Protestantism, particularly in Puritanism. My theory is that if you completely repress music as Cromwell did, it either goes to the rather decayed world of Charles II or it forces visionary experience. You can trace it through Shaftesbury and Thomas Traherne, one of the greatest British theologians and poets.

Cecil got the idea of the great happiness and the little happiness from Traherne. It comes somewhere in the first or the second *Centuries of Meditation.* By the time Traherne died in the early 1670s, the scientists were getting prominence, but at the beginning of the 1700s you get the rich wanting to travel to Italy on the Grand Tour to bring back paintings and anything they could. Then you have what is called the Trahernean side of the English tradition; painting the beauty of British landscape and you have the birth of British watercolours. Constable and Turner come out of that world. It was a protest against the scientific world, but its roots are right back in Puritanism.

Cecil used to say he was a classicist, not a romantic. He may have thought that, but he was inadvertently a romantic as, on the whole, he only painted his own inner visions, his own dreams. He didn't paint landscape and neither did Blake. The visual world is only a mirror of the inner world.

When I arrived at the Central, there were skips in the car park and they were throwing things from the fifth floor into the skips and burning things from the bookbinding department. They were breaking up Albion presses with sledgehammers. If you think something is out of date, break it up. If you don't understand it, get rid of it. You could buy the presses for £20. If only I could have bought one. Now they're worth a fortune.

Two memories: one is of Cecil in his room and the other is of Cecil teaching and my colleague telling me that he was a dangerous man. He rubbished people like Cecil who went on painting figuratively. A valid criticism that was made about Cecil was that there were some students who emulated his style, but it's natural for students, who grow up, suffer and discover their own way of doing things. I imagine Cecil thought the students would all be regarded one day as the Collins' School. In that particular year when I was hauled over the coals about Cecil, there were three girls with huge Cecilish paintings in their diploma exhibition.

Cecil would come to the Central and from his pocket he would take out and show me a little painting of an Angel and say, 'That's Paradise.' In fact, there are a couple of very weak paintings that he did. One he loved and that I thought was atrocious was the Angel with the stream. He would go on and on explaining it and its mythical meanings and I hated it more and more as he went on. I didn't tell him because I wouldn't have wanted to hurt him for anything. The other painting I couldn't stand is the one of the three Angels. He would go on about this one too and it drove me up the wall. When he thought he'd painted a great painting and started interpreting it, he killed it dead, but I think it was his way of handing on what he called his vision. There's another painting about an Angel and a tripod which was inspired by Goethe's *Faust*, Part Two, where Mephistopheles says to Faust, 'Stamp your foot,' and that made a great impression on me. I don't particularly like the painting; it was the idea more than the painting itself that I liked. I think Cecil's greater paintings are the lovely little paintings of Angels rather than the bigger canvases and, of course, there is the wonderful period of the Fool and the pre-war paintings. Cecil wasn't an even painter and the things he signed as great were not for me as moving as some of the others.

Cecil used to bring films into the Central; we had some very interesting ones. He brought in the Laurens van der Post film interviewing Jung. He brought in Stephen Cross' four films on Islam. He brought in a Greek film on the classical myth of Electra, but if you

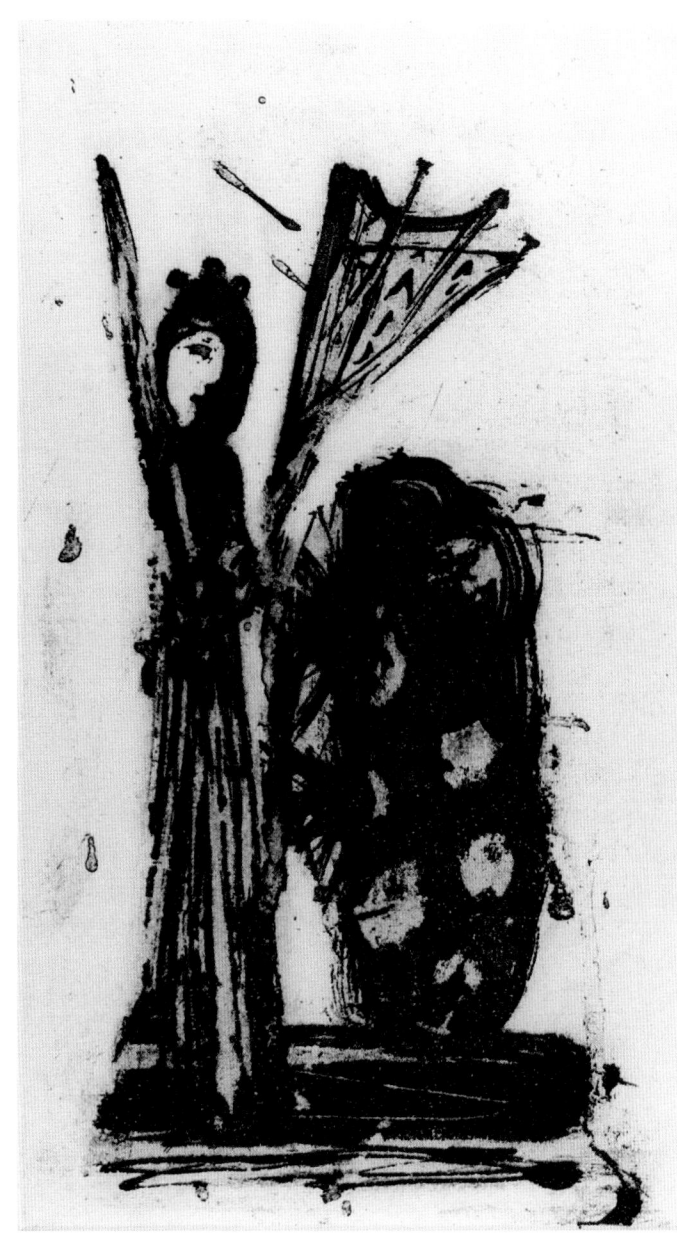

Cecil Collins
Angel
1977
Etching and aquatint on paper
38 x 28.3cm

My wife, Eleanor, and I founded a centre for similar studies in Sussex , but it only lasted two years because our sponsors went bankrupt. Kathleen and Cecil and others came and taught there and Kathleen told me that her inspiration for Temenos came from the centre. I was very enthusiastic about Temenos initially, but I wasn't happy with it in the end. The foundations were wrong somehow. I was rather lucky because I didn't do all that much lecturing there. I took weekly seminars reading Dante and Thomas Traherne. Those were great experiences because you yourself are being taught as you're teaching. Eventually, I stopped lecturing. I was fed up with my own voice. I'm writing now and haven't got time to teach.

Cecil got me through the Central. If he hadn't had been there, I wouldn't have survived. I always believed it would get better and it got worse and worse. Eleanor said, 'You ought to be an optimist,' and I said, 'I was an optimist, but I'm not an optimist about anything now.' Cecil and I spoke every day on the telephone. I used to ring him up in the department and we would talk for about half an hour. I wouldn't have got through the day otherwise. When he was at home painting I'd say, 'I'm sorry to interrupt you,' and he'd say, 'Don't worry!' I'd say what had happened that day and we used to have long conversations about music and on Haydn in particular. He used to do extraordinary things like put his microphone for his recording machine on the window ledge during a thunderstorm and play back the tape of the storm. Another funny thing he used to do was to take a musician or an artist and say, 'He's the Michelangelo of modern art' or 'He's the Puccini of music' or something like that. He was exaggerating, but hitting the nail on the head at the same time.

Another person that we talked about was Charles Williams who I knew from Leeds. He wrote what I think is the best book on Dante ever written. I had started reading Dante with a group of students at the Central in about 1967. I did it during the lunch hour. I had a wonderful group of students nearly all from Fine Art; they'd all broken with hard edge painting. Cecil and I had a terrible influence on them. I got to know Eleanor roughly about this time and we used to meet at her flat nearby. I remember how once the students laid out this wonderful meal for us all and, as we were eating, the head of department came in and I knew my goose had been cooked.

I was at Central for about twenty-two years. I left it for my beloved Camberwell, but things were changing there too as they'd already closed the textile department. Most important for me, when I got out of Central and went to Camberwell, was the realisation that I wasn't mad or insane. It was wonderful because I could talk about Blake to my colleagues. We could have conversations. I said, 'They'll never close the art history department at Camberwell because it's the finest art history department in any art school in the country. It's better than a multitude of art history departments at universities.'

did anything extra at the Central, you were immediately suspect. What I could never understand was how the rest of the staff could despise this, rather than be happy for their students to look at the films and try to understand who Jung was or what a Greek myth is about. Luckily, there were some special friends of Cecil's at Central like Rafael Nadal who used to come and eat with Cecil and me in that ghastly refectory and other members of staff like Paul Bird and Patrick Reyntiens who fought to have Cecil reinstated each time the Central tried to get rid of him. Paul and Cecil used to get people in to talk to a small group. He got Archbishop Anthony Bloom in, for example. They also brought in a Tibetan monk. For Cecil, Tibet was a country where the vision was kept, as it were.

But they did. My head of department called me and said, 'John, we won't be here in a year's time, you know. They're going to close the department and get rid of all us fifty-five-year olds.' I was made redundant, which was traumatic, but also one of the best things that ever happened because then I started writing.

My theory is that the likes of Maggie Thatcher realised that art schools were the last bastion of humanist education and they had to go because they would produce people who would question her and her detestable policies and that's why people like Cecil and myself were not wanted. A good saying of Cecil's was, 'Education is a crime against humanity.' The point is that someone like Cecil couldn't survive in the modern educational world. They'd be inspecting his classes and he'd be having to fill in dreaded forms galore.

Cecil had a lot of very definite views about women. He said women are like cobwebs. They attract all these men into their trap, their cobweb, and they just suck their blood. What women need is either a great devil or a great angel that comes in with a sword and smashes the cobweb of illusions; then they suffer and all the blood that they have sucked from the male falls out. I said, 'What do you make of someone like Michelangelo? He had this extraordinary friendship with Vittoria Colonna who was a brilliant poet?' Cecil would say that, the real function of the male is to provide vision and the role of the feminine is vital in that. Dante's *Beatrice* is perhaps the finest example, but behind every really creative person, there is a wonderful woman.

Cecil had some extraordinary tales. One of them was about this chap who goes and sits with a wise man for three years and keeps on battering him with questions. 'Why don't you give me any answers?' 'I think you'd better go and see my friend, Abba Enoch, who lives on the other side of the Nile. Here are two plates. You've got to hold them together like this. Don't separate them. Take them to Abba Enoch and give them to him like that.' So the man goes off on this five-mile walk to see Abba Enoch and he hears something rattling inside the plates, but he goes on. Eventually, his curiosity is too much and he opens them and there's a dried pea inside. He storms back to the wise old man. 'What do you mean, making me carry a dried pea all that way in an uncomfortable position?' 'If I couldn't trust you with a dried pea,' says the wise man, 'I couldn't trust you with truth.' This is a Cecil story. As with many of his stories, he didn't always acknowledge his sources.

Another comes from a Buddhist tale about an abbot and a monk walking along the river. They come across a woman who's desperate to cross to the other side. The abbot picks her up, takes her to the other side and comes back. A little bit later the monk says, 'What do you mean, picking up a woman when you're an abbot?' 'I put her down twenty minutes ago,' replied the abbot, 'but you're still carrying her.'

For my book on Cecil I took themes: Angels, Fools and so on. I showed it to William Anderson who was very condescending about it. I don't think my Cecil book was very good, but it might have been a starting point. It's a strange business, this creativity thing. I wrote two books in English which my publisher translated and after that he said, 'I'm not translating any more of your books. You've got to write them in Italian if you want them published.' So I wrote a book on British music which is the first book on British music in Italian which I'm rather pleased about. I don't write in English now; I write in Italian.

I must find all those things that I have from Cecil: papers, the play he wrote for the children, paintings, all sorts of things. Cecil gave me a picture once because I made slides of his paintings; we call it the Angel and the plum pudding. My daughter, Nicky, has a wonderful Cecil of the Angel blowing his trumpet over the city, which she was given after Elisabeth's death. I've told her she's really lucky to have that.

I came across some hitherto unknown music by Simon Mayr and, for the first time for a hundred years or more, we put on an opera by him in St John's Smith Square. Cecil and Elizabeth came. I was rather disappointed because the church wasn't completely full, but Cecil said, 'Don't worry. The sound has gone out.' At the time, I thought that he was just being Cecilish when he said that but, in fact, the opera was recorded and broadcast on radio, so the sound did go out. The following year we did another wonderful opera by Mayr and again the place wasn't completely full, but it was broadcast, not in this country but in France, Germany and Italy. Mayr's music has now been revived and recorded and there have been international conferences on him.

I really feel bad that I didn't go to the opening of Cecil's last exhibition, but it was something I just couldn't do. During those last few years, I didn't see much of Cecil and Elisabeth. I felt that I didn't want to go back to the Central. Somehow a door had shut in my life. He was very ill then and I didn't want to see him in that condition. He died soon after. I did go to the show and it was marvellous. It was then I realised that Cecil was a very special artist. I always knew he was, but you have to have eyes to see. I bet some people would see Cecil's work and say, 'Rubbish' and be quite happy looking at the kind of art Cecil called prison bars. I said to him in my imagination, 'Cecil, you are absolutely right,' and it was as if the bars were pushed on one side and life took off. It was one of those moving experiences.

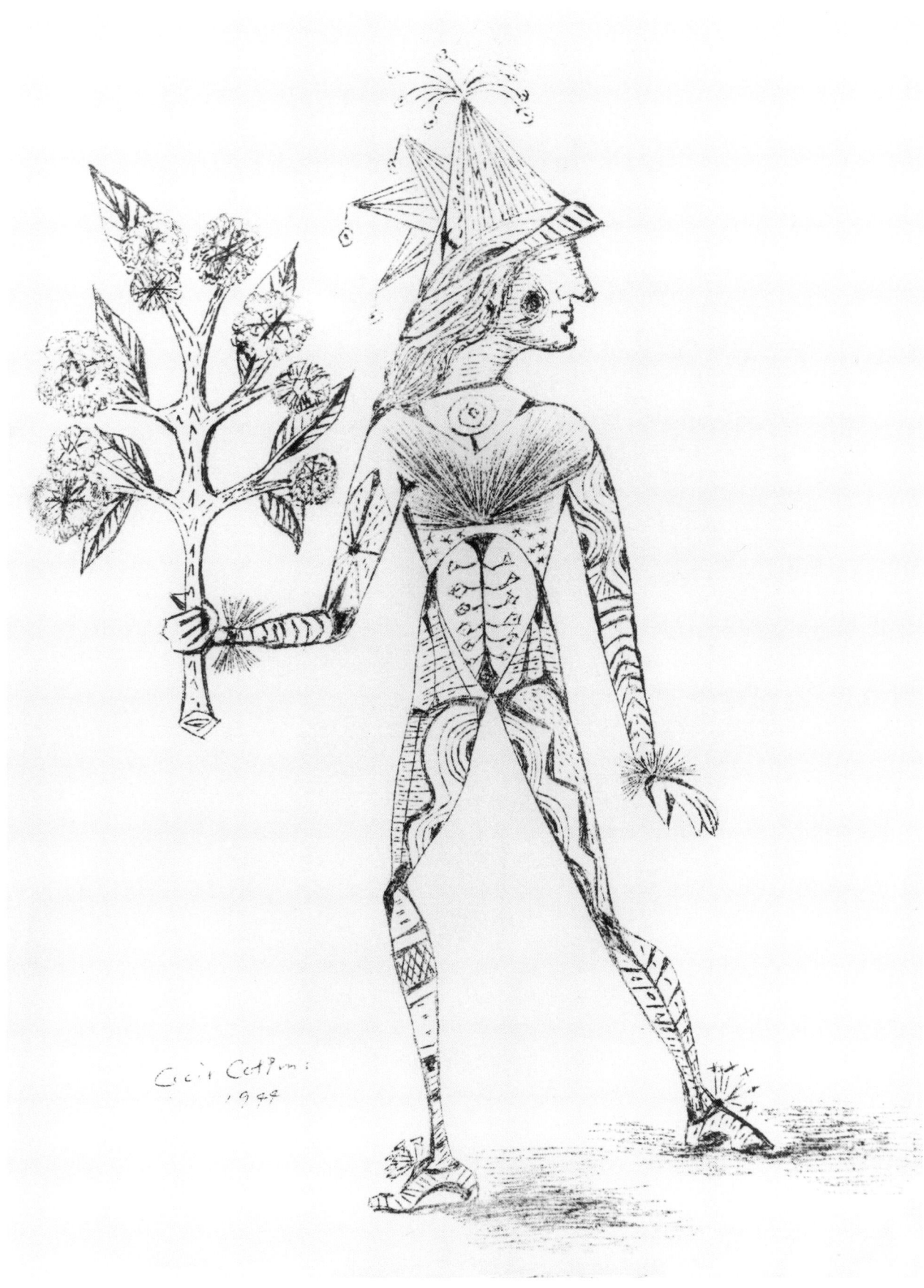

Cecil Collins
The Voice of the Fool
1944
Roneo print on paper
38.2 x 28.2cm

There is something more important than being wise, and that is to love freely and unendingly, letting everything grow and flow in its own nature, not trying to impose our nature, but by being alive oneself in such a way as to bring others alive to it.
Cecil Collins

Cecil and Elisabeth Collins
(with John Allitt, his mother and mother-in-law)
Amsterdam
1974

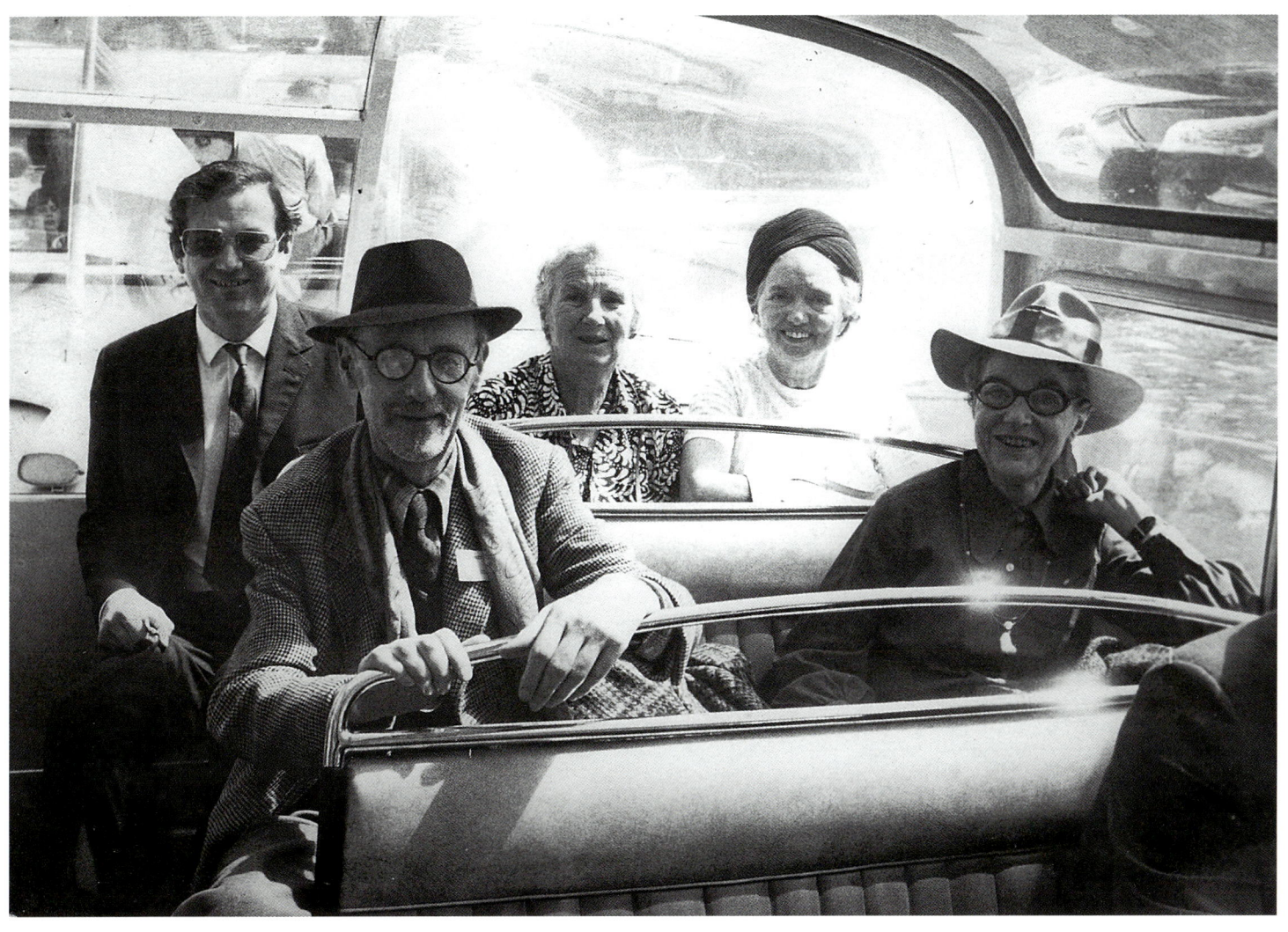

FRIENDS & OTHER RELATIONSHIPS

ELEANOR ALLITT

Born in Cambridge, Eleanor Allitt studied textile design at Central School of Art (Central St Martins). Work with quilting, hand-block printed silk and stenciled interiors followed. Over the last ten years painting has developed, which have been exhibited and are in many private collections. Storytelling has inspired recent work which includes an illustrated book on the Russian story of Babayaga and currently illustrations for the ancient Sumerian myth of Inanna.

My mother was at the Central School. She did silver-smithing and my uncle was there too; he taught bookbinding. It runs in the family. I studied textiles there in the 1960s. After the course finished, I was very busy with the children. I had quite a long break, but then I came back to textiles, doing stencilling and hand-block printed scarves. I used to design and make my own.

John came to the Central about 1967. He tells this story about how after a year there he met Cecil on the stairs. Everybody had told him, 'You don't want to have anything to do with Cecil. He's trouble. We don't want any of that sort of energy around.' Of course, he became John's only and best friend at the Central where he found everybody else so miserable. John and Cecil kept each other going. They used to escape for cups of tea and have long conversations, especially about music.

John left the Central in about 1986. After that he didn't see Cecil so much. He was working in Camberwell which meant driving all the way from West Hampstead, where we were living, to Camberwell and back every day so life got a bit complicated.

I remember going to have meals at Elisabeth and Cecil's flat. First of all, we'd go straight up to the top to Elisabeth. They had a little kitchen on the landing and halfway down the stairs was the big picture that's now in the Tate Modern, the wonderful *Artist and His Wife* with the swans in the background. As you progressed up the stairs, you became aware that you were coming into something really exciting. There'd be interesting bits and pieces of art all over the place. Elisabeth would welcome us. She had a great sense of style and loved to dress up and look spectacular. Cecil would probably be in his studio and I'd be admiring all the lovely things in her sitting room. I loved the crockery because each plate was beautiful and different. There was this nice couch with a fur rug on it, a sheepskin I think. You could sit on it and look out of the window. Elisabeth would make us tea and then the maestro would come upstairs when he'd heard that we'd arrived.

Cecil's studio was crammed full of canvases. There was a narrow passageway to the fireplace with beer bottles on the mantelpiece and that's where his easel was. There was his armchair where he sat and read. His low bed was in the corner. He must have breathed and slept his art, occasionally going upstairs for meals. I don't think he and Elisabeth slept together. There was an incident where John and I went to Cecil's studio and there was a big, staring-eyed Angel with flowing light coming out of it. We hated it; the eyes were like very hard diamonds. Cecil was so proud of it that we had to be very careful what we said. It meant a great deal to him.

Cecil loved to have a good chuckle. I remember one of his favourite stories, which illustrates his love of the absurd or perhaps of the unexpected.

'An old lady lives with her parrot at the top of a high block of flats in Paris. One day her toilet breaks down so she phones for the plumber to come and fix it. Then off she goes with her bag, down all the long winding stairs to do her shopping. She is old and a bit forgetful and after she has been to the *patisserie* and the *épicerie*, she goes to a café to have a coffee, forgetting that the plumber is due to arrive. The time comes for the plumber to visit. It is early afternoon and the sun is hot. After his substantial midday repast of *steak avec pommes frites, tarte au citron, café* and cognac the plumber sets out to visit the old lady and repair her toilet. He trudges up the long winding stairs to the top floor with his heavy plumber's bag and knocks at the door. *'Qu'est que c'est?'* replies the parrot from within, *'C'est le plombier.'* Nothing happens so he knocks a little louder, *'Qu'est que c'est?'* replies the parrot again. *'C'est le plombier.'* Again nothing happens. The plumber, already sweating from his hard trek up all those stairs with his heavy load, mops his brow and knocks again, this time with great and impatient force. *'Qu'est que c'est?'* replies the parrot. *'C'est le plombier,'* Yet again nothing happens, this time the plumber is seized with impatience, his face grows red, his breathing, already laboured, escalates to a level of extreme stress. He falls down and suffers a severe heart attack and dies. Meanwhile the little old lady has suddenly remembered her appointment with the plumber. *'Ah, mon Dieu!'* she exclaims, and trots back to her flat as fast as she can with her shopping in her plaited straw bag. At last she gets to her front door and you can imagine her consternation when she sees the plumber lying flat on the floor. *'Qu'est que c'est?'* she gasps. *'C'est le plombier'* squawks the parrot from inside the appartment.' I love this story and John adored it too because it reminded him of his beloved France.

Eleanor Allitt
Harmony of Love
2008
Acrylic
28 x 18cm

It whispers in every Gale of Wind, and speaks aloud in thunder. It is trampled on the Earth and Crowns us in the Heavens. It burns in the Sun, and Shines in the Stars. It is Constant in the Moon, and guides her changes to Wonderful Ends.

From The Kingdom of God by Thomas Traherne

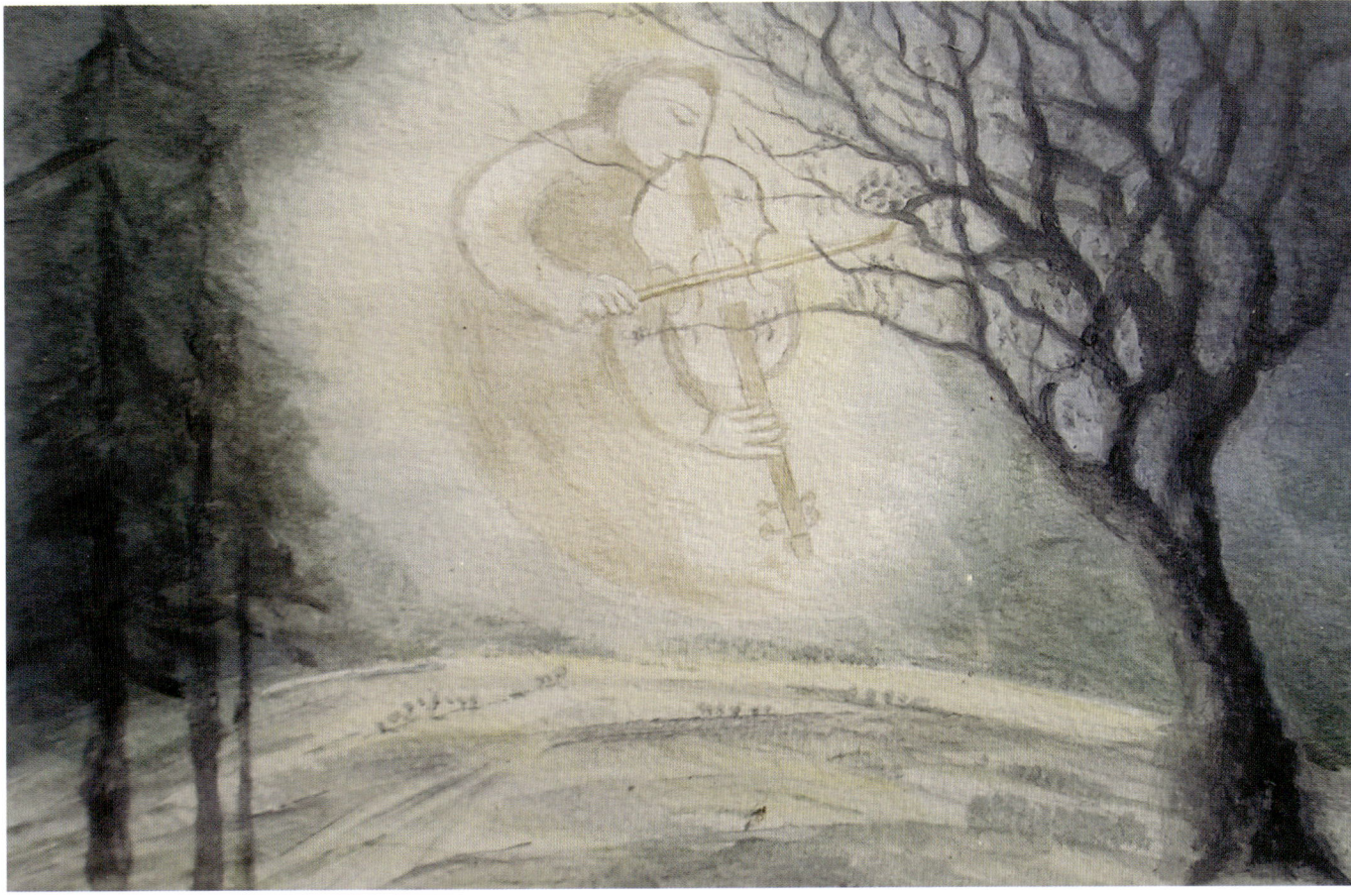

There was always a lot of talk about music because that was one of the big threads that John had in common with Cecil. Elisabeth and I would listen to the men which was always fascinating. John went on his own to see Cecil far more than I did because the twins were little, but I remember having a conversation with Cecil about Stockhausen. Cecil was very intrigued with his music. He also joked about where it goes up and down the scale being a bit like a police siren. This was after they'd been to a Stockhausen concert and, on the way home, they'd heard a police siren going along the street. Elisabeth had said, 'This police siren, if you listen to it, is quite musical. It's like the music we've been hearing.'

Cecil had heard a lot about Donizetti from John. In Amsterdam in 1974 they were producing a very rare Donizetti opera called Il Borgomastro di Saardam (composed 1837). It was the first performance for more than a hundred years so John, his mother and my mother and Cecil and Elisabeth thought that it would be fun to go for a long weekend while I was left holding the babies who were only two years old.

My mother had come across Elisabeth and Cecil in Cambridge and used to say, 'Cecil is a funny old stick. You don't really want to talk to him.' When the weather was mild, Cecil would go round all wrapped up and wearing a hat. He was a bit of a hypochondriac. Elisabeth also used to moan that every day he had to have his meat and two veg.

Cecil and Elisabeth put a lot of energy into seeking out visionary people. Maybe that was partly because they didn't have children. His paintings and his visionary work were his children. He talked a lot about his paintings which was, I think, because he wanted to talk about himself. He could also listen very intently and absorb. He was always searching, but although he went around to all these false teachers, he was really quite discriminating.

In about 1974, I went to his class at the City Lit. I don't remember an awful lot about it, but I was completely captivated by Cecil. I didn't really have a studio then because I was looking after the girls. I wasn't doing any of my quilting work and I thought it would be a nice thing to go to his drawing classes. I had a few precious hours free in the mornings while the twins were at nursery group so I used to go then. Cecil did a whole day, but the mornings were more than enough for me. Cecil wasn't interested in helping people with their work, except through the medium of his teaching. It was a more disconnected way of helping.

I remember having these lovely simple tools. Cecil was very precise in what he wanted us to use: a quill pen, a reed pen, some Chinese ink and brushes, crayon, charcoal. He didn't take the slightest interest in looking at anybody's work and this was very liberating. He would sit there in his corner like a conductor with his orchestra of ladies. He would say something like, 'This pose is for five minutes and do it with your quill pen,' and 'This one is for one minute; this one is for thirty seconds, this one is for twenty seconds; five seconds,' and, 'This one's for one second.' It was quite remarkable and very much up to you to take it or leave it. It was very different from the classes at Central because at the City Lit we just did drawing and the students were adults who Cecil met only one day a week. It wasn't such an intense relationship as at the art school, but I could sense that he liked the adulation.

I found it quite bewildering all the things he used to ask us to do. He loved to shock the class. He would say, 'Mix up some Chinese ink in your dish and then use your rag to swirl around in it and then draw with your rag,' which was brilliant. He would push this even further saying, 'Pour all your ink onto the floor. Mop it around with your rag and then draw.' Fortunately, it was a scruffy art school floor. He would also make you change position a lot, and draw with your right or left hand, your unaccustomed hand or with both hands together. It was very freeing, though I did find myself questioning whether this was the right thing to be doing. I felt inadequate on the academic side, but Cecil wasn't concerned about that. He gave you something different. I'd done textiles before so I'd been drawing plants and flowers and things, but not very much life drawing. Cecil really spurred me on to carry on learning to draw and the classes were a great incentive.

There was a sense of magic about him, not in the class, but when he came to visit us. He liked to shock people and see how far he could go. The twins, when they were about three years old, were rather scared of him, but absolutely fascinated. He was a bit like Dr Drosselmeier in *The Nutcracker*, full of mystery and magic and love, but you didn't want to get too close to him because you never knew what he was going to come out with next. Cecil loved to make the children feel a bit frightened of him and then show them that it was okay. He was like a magician. He gave them a thrill. Cecil adored children and our children were always very excited when Cecil came to visit. He liked to play and entertain them. He certainly wouldn't ignore them. He might tell them a story or produce paper beasts.

The children were especially excited when he came to do a party for Nicky who was Cecil's goddaughter. It must have been her tenth birthday and Cecil said he would invent something. Her birthday is on 29th March and it was sunny enough to be in the garden. He arrived with his mackintosh and hat on. Out from under his coat he brought this beautiful golden goose cut out of white cartridge paper, about fifteen inches across, covered in little felt tip strokes of gold and yellow and orange. Then he narrated a story he had written for her while the children mimed the actions. I remember the children dancing around in the garden, being golden geese, Nicky putting on her flowing princess garments and the twins following along behind. The children have all got different memories of that golden goose story. Cecil enjoyed every moment of it.

Elisabeth didn't take part. She just sat and drank tea. Elisabeth wasn't sure how to relate to children. I think she felt ill at ease with them. Maybe it was because she would have liked to have had her own and that was a sadness she had to deal with. She was a little bit aloof in some ways. I wasn't particularly close to her and, unfortunately, we lost touch with her after Cecil died.

There was another occasion when Cecil came and spent an afternoon painting a mural on Nicky's bedroom wall as a birthday present. It was mythical in lovely clear colours. Mary says she can remember giraffes and Lucy says she can remember a phoenix. Stupidly, we painted over it with emulsion. A friend of mine said, 'You must get the Tate to come and remove it and take it to the gallery,' but that was a bit impractical. Regrettably, we didn't take any photographs of it.

Cecil came every now and then and we took the children to their place several times. There's a photograph of all of us standing in the sitting room with the mural behind us on the wall, the one by the dining table. The children would be welcomed and they were always very intrigued to go and see Cecil. He loved to enter their imaginative world. It was very important to him. It influenced me too and must have gone inside me on a deep level. That's where it came from, this great delight in being completely batty.

LUCY ALLITT

Lucy Allitt, born 1972, has always been closely involved with healing. After working in a gym, she studied anatomy and massage in Birmingham. She now works as a pilates instructor and as a cranio-sacral therapist, with a special interest in somato-emotional release. She is married with one son.

I was very young when I met Cecil, just a small child really. I remember his green tweedy overcoat and his hat and that he had a hairy nose. Looking back now, he seems a sort of Quentin Blake character. I remember him being slightly hunched and I don't know that he really engaged with us as children, but I was slightly fascinated by him. If I think about it, there was something very steady about him behind his eyes which had a clearness to them; there was an intent. That's the only way I can describe it. There was a look behind Cecil's eyes that I could see in my father's: a kind of extraordinary focus on their work. There was something slightly otherworldly about him, I think.

Dad and Cecil must have been very good friends. I think they spoke almost every day at college. I remember going to his house and meeting Elisabeth and having tea there one day. All the cups and saucers were different and they were all very pretty. The house had a very particular smell, a slight mustiness, I think, but not disagreeable. They were, of course, quite old when I knew them. Elisabeth was lovely. She was very gentle and she made us feel part of the occasion.

I remember Cecil coming to paint the mural on the wall of our bedroom. I have this recollection of an incredibly sunny day and pulling the bunk beds away from the wall and him painting. Again, he had that extraordinary look in his eyes, that absolute focus on what he was doing. I remember a phoenix he drew, this beautiful firebird, a phoenix with a crown and pointy beak reaching up into the air, rising up with its wings outstretched. I remember there was a sun and all the lovely golds and yellows and oranges of the birds and the blue he chose for the sky.

I also have a memory of his drawings of clowns and I used to do pictures of clowns in his style in my notebooks at school, quite geometric, with the triangular hat. I imagine that, because he was an artist, I would have wanted to do what he did. It obviously made quite an impression on me because I went on drawing lots of pictures of clowns and little trees and things. I was good at drawing when I was little, about six, I suppose.

One of the things I loved as I got older was being at the table with my mum and dad, listening to my dad talking to friends such as Cecil. I could listen to them and think, yes, I understand and I agree with that. I loved the sound of their voices and I think that goes way back to the pleasure of listening to adult conversations as a child and not maybe understanding it, but enjoying it anyway.

I went to Cecil's Retrospective exhibition at the Tate after he died and I thought it was absolutely exquisite. I hadn't appreciated what he did when I was so tiny.

THE CROWNS OF HAPPINESS

Written by Cecil for his god-daughter Nicoletta Allitt on her tenth birthday and performed with her and her two year old twin sisters in their garden.

SCENE 1
Four princesses gather in a circle outside their palace and dance. The eldest princess tells her younger sisters to go and play, but not to wander far from the palace.

SCENE 2
But the young princesses start wandering and find a strange looking old gate. What fun! They open the gate and enter.

SCENE 3
They find themselves in a garden overgrown with wild flowers. They are lost. They approach a large and cavernous stone house. Around the house the wilderness of flowers gives way to a beautiful garden of roses. 'What beautiful flowers,' they say and can't resist touching them. Suddenly a terrible voice comes from the house, 'Who ah, who ah! Who is touching my flowers?'

The door of the house springs open and out flies a terrible dragon. 'Who ah, who ah!' he says. 'Because you have tried to pick my magic flowers I will turn you all into swans and you will be my prisoners.' He waves his arms. 'Who ah, who ah!' and walks around them three times. They are all turned into swans.

The dragon tells them, 'You can fly about during the day, but at sunset you must return.' The swans hide in the bushes as the dragon returns to his house and shuts the door with a bang.

The swans hear the dragon singing, 'Who ah, ah, ah! Nobody knows that I have stolen the golden Goose of Happiness and she is my prisoner in this house. Ha, ha, ha! Nobody knows because I am a terrible, awful, frightful, craggy-saggy, saggy-aggy dragon. Nobody knows that there is only one way to catch me and that is to get a glass of water from the magic fountain of life that is in the middle of my garden and to sprinkle it on my house and on me. Then I would disappear in a cloud of smoke! Ha, ha, ha! Nobody knows my secret.'

SCENE 4
The swans fly back to the palace. They sit in the palace garden under their sister's window. She is sitting in her room and sees them. They come there every day and she starts to feed them. She doesn't know they are her sisters and they can't tell her as they only speak swan language. Every day at sunset they fly away weeping.

SCENE 5

A little bird in the tree tells the princess that the swans are her sisters being held under a magic spell by the dragon. The only way to break the spell is for her to make a shirt for each swan and each shirt must be made from stinging nettles. The nettles will sting her, but she must finish the job. When she has made them all, she must put them on the swans. She must then circle around each swan three times saying, 'Golden, golden, golden, golden.' They will then turn back into her sisters.

The princess picks some stinging nettles and she cries out because they do hurt her. She works the nettles on a spinning wheel and then she sews three shirts with needle and thread.

SCENE 6

The swans arrive while she is sewing and she hurries up because she wants to finish before sunset. Just in time she completes her task, puts a shirt on each swan and then, one by one, performs the magic circle around them saying, 'Golden, golden, golden, golden.' The swans turn back into her sisters and they all embrace her.

They tell her about the dragon and how he is keeping the golden Goose of Happiness prisoner in his house, but that they know the secret of how to make him disappear. The little bird in the tree tells them that he will lead them a secret way to the magic fountain so that the dragon will not know that they are in his garden.

SCENE 7

The princesses find the old gate in the wall. The little bird tells them to walk on tiptoe so that the dragon will not know that they are in his garden. He leads them to the fountain where they find a golden cup which one of them dips into the fountain.

SCENE 8

Outside the dragon's house the little bird reminds them not to touch the beautiful flowers, continue to walk on tiptoe and put their fingers to their lips and keep very silent.

They can hear the dragon snoring. One of the princesses forgets and cries out, 'Look what a beautiful rose. I must kiss it.' She stops tiptoeing and bends down to kiss the rose. There is a roar from the dragon, 'Who ah, who ah! Who is touching my flowers?'

The door of the house suddenly opens and the terrible dragon emerges, his eyes as big as saucers. 'Quick,' says the bird. 'Sprinkle the water from the fountain of life on the dragon and on his house.' The princesses throw all the water on the dragon and the house and, with a final roar of 'Who ah, who ah, who ah!', he vanishes in a cloud of smoke. The house has also gone and the princesses see the golden goose fast asleep in the middle of the beautiful garden. 'Now,' says the little bird. 'Each of you must kiss the golden goose to awaken the bird.'

As each princess is kissing the golden goose, a beautiful bell is heard and the goose vanishes. In its place stands a handsome prince dressed in shining gold. 'Thank you, princesses. You have made the dragon disappear and you have freed me. I will give each of you a present.' He takes them to the fountain of life and tells them that they must walk around the fountain seven times. They must then kneel and bow seven times to the fountain. Then they must stand up and say, 'Golden, golden, golden, golden,' seven times.

The prince kneels down, opens a door at the bottom of the fountain and takes out four golden crowns, one for each princess. He places these on their heads and kisses each one as he does so.

Now you are all wearing the Crowns of Happiness and that happiness will always be in your hearts.'

The princesses and the prince join hands and dance in a circle singing, 'Golden, golden, golden, golden.' They gradually move off stage and out of the room still singing, 'Golden, golden, golden.'

The Crowns of Happiness, Facsimile

friends & other relationships

Cecil Collins
Fool with Small Girl
1970s
Ink on Paper

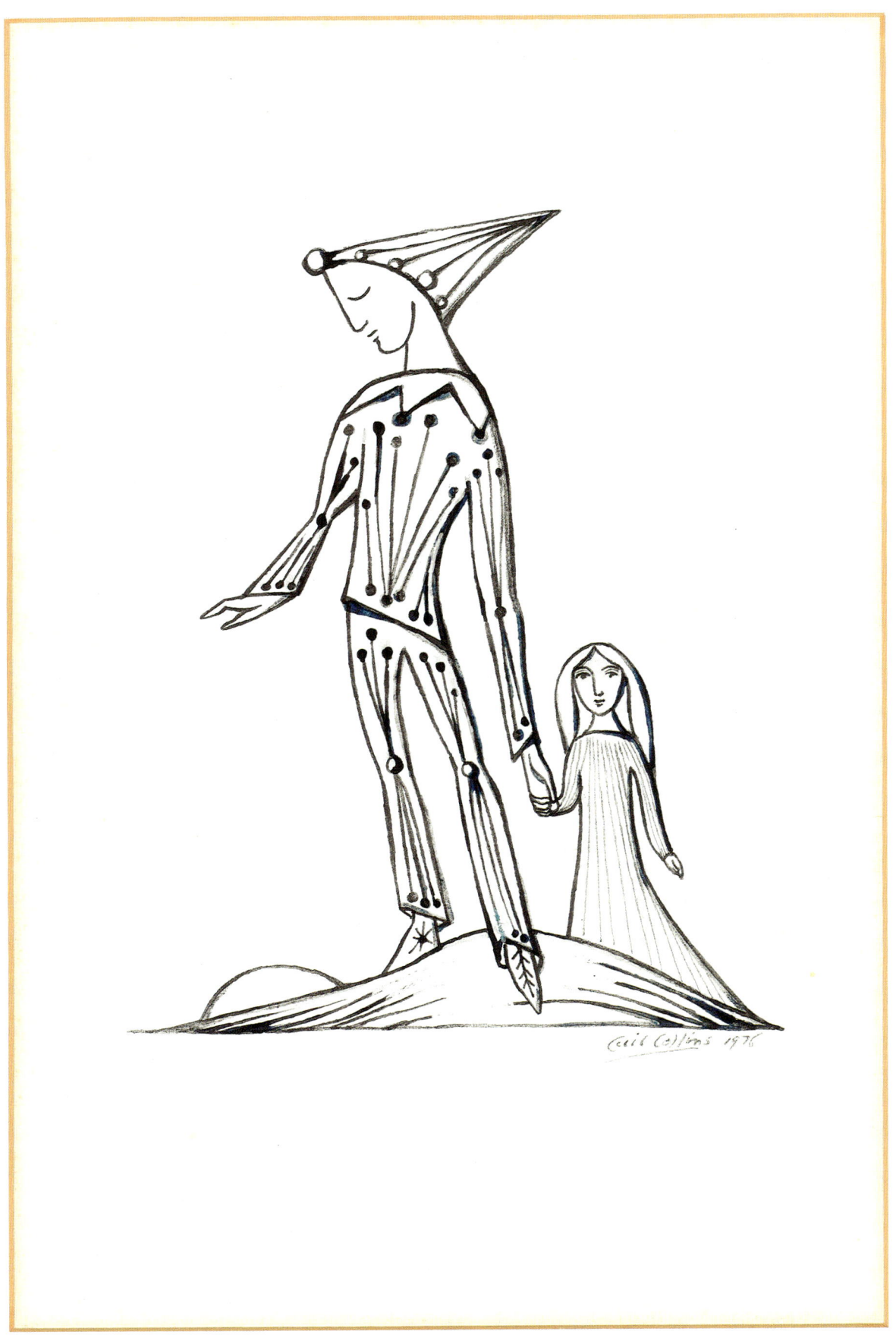

213

NICOLETTA ALLITT

Nicky works with the local hospital trust to improve the environments of people with reduced mobility. She lives in the north of England and has one daughter.

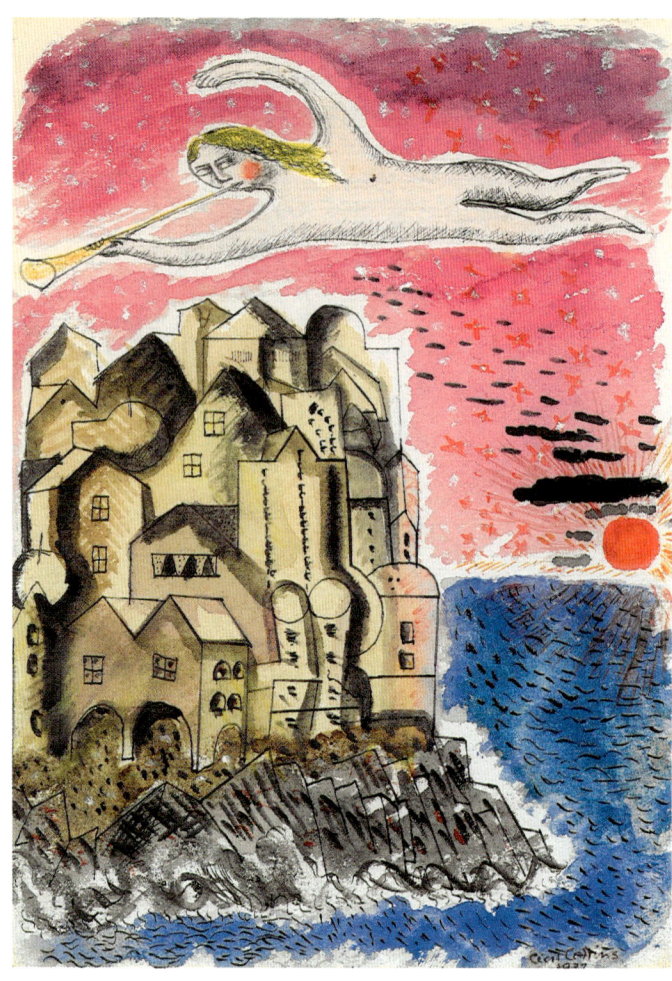

Cecil Collins
Evening
1932
Watercolour and pen on paper
12 x 17.5cm

Cecil was my godfather. I can vaguely remember him becoming my godfather so I guess I was about six or seven at the time. He was a genial uncle-like sort of person, but he wasn't a huge part of our family life. I really related most to him at that time of childhood when I was still playing imaginary games; that was when I remember interacting with him. He was a bit daunting because he was very tall and thin and had a very deep voice. He wasn't somebody you'd rush up to and hug. He was a bit detached so you felt you couldn't go barging in and jump on his knee, but if you were around him, he would be very kind and thoughtful and respectful. You felt he was giving you his considered attention in quite a serious way.

When he brought the fairy story for us to act, we were still in our house in London so I must have been about ten and the twins about two. The play was called *The Crowns of Happiness* and he wrote it for my birthday. He also painted a picture on the wall in my sisters' bedroom. I remember the colours as being sort of gold, not metallic gold, but yellow and orange, colours like that. I might be muddling it up with the cardboard goose he brought us which was definitely those golden colours. We also had a turtle-shell costume which was made out of a big piece of cardboard like a shield with string or elastic underneath and painted to look like a turtle's back. Cecil had made these things for my birthday. The golden goose survived a long time because it was quite a nice thing in itself. It had a base so it was supposed to stand up, but it never really did and it kind of bent over on its legs. It was then stuck on the wall with blu-tack. The golden goose is very big in my imagination and I mix it up with the mural, but I think the mural was a landscape with a sun. It was there for a long time before it got painted over. Everybody was a bit sad to see it go. 'Oh, we don't want to paint over Cecil's picture,' but you have to in the end.

I've got some quite strong memories of Cecil and Elisabeth and their flat in Chelsea. It was a lovely flat, full of interesting curios and a nice place to go and visit as a child. Elisabeth once gave me a little book of oriental fans. Another time she gave me a little beaded handbag which I had until recently. It was like a pouch bag with a little tassel at the bottom and a drawstring at the top, a lovely thing. Another little handbag she gave me that I loved dearly had a tapestry of a lady in a crinoline and a castle or something on it. It had a metal-embossed clasp with a little chain for a handle.

Elisabeth was very striking looking; she always wore hats and big glasses. What I remember about Cecil is that he used to wear these fascinating jackets that had been mended and re-mended with lots of patches and bindings. I absolutely loved those jackets. They were works of art really. I think it was Elisabeth who mended them. Both Cecil and Elisabeth looked very elegant, certainly to me. Elisabeth was sweet, always welcoming if you went to their house. She made tea and buns for my Mum and Dad and I liked looking at her things.

Cecil liked playing games with us. He was good at that kind of thing. I remember one time him coming to the house in London when I was running around pretending to be Lucy in the Narnia books. Lucy had a little bottle of potion with which she could mend wounds and things and I must have had a little bottle too and I said to Cecil, 'This is my magic potion and I can make wounds heal up,' and Cecil said something like, 'Do you think you could mend a broken heart? That's very difficult.' I thought, what's he on about and said, 'Oh, I don't know,' and rushed off. As a child, there are things that puzzle you slightly and stay in your mind, that was one of those things. I also had a strange conversation with him one day about nettles growing in the garden. He said you should have nettles so that the butterflies could come to them, but if you wanted to get rid of them, you had to cut them down seven times a year for seven years.

There must have been some contact with Cecil in my early years of secondary school, but I became quite a disaffected teenager around that time so we wouldn't have had much to say to each other. I would still have had a lot of respect for him, though, because he was quite a big figure, respect-wise, in the family, but I was not fantastic company.

I do remember talking to Cecil about drawing. He said it wasn't the end result that mattered; it was the experience of drawing. I also remember, but now I don't know if this was with Cecil or Eleanor, but it was definitely Cecil's influence, doing pictures that take one second. He used to reduce the time you had to draw for you to get the essence of something.

I went to one of his classes either at the Central School or possibly at Hastings. I wish I'd still got the drawings that I did then because some of them were quite nice. I used to love drawing animals with very swooshy lines, with that kind of movement you get in Chinese brush paintings. I used to do them in all sorts of different mediums like scratchy twigs or biros. Cecil was a big influence in my using things that were not designed for painting. I used to make bamboo pens and used them not only to apply ink in a conventional sort of way, but to scratch the surface of the paper and rough it up a bit. If you do that, it absorbs more paint.

The interesting thing now for me is how influential Cecil was. I've never fully realised that before. He taught me to think about things in a different way from school. At the time, I just thought it was normal. I hadn't realised how lucky I was to have that; you just take it for granted. In fact, all that instant drawing and trying to feel what you were doing and taking on the pose of the model before you began to draw had an enormous influence. I used to think that everybody knows that, but probably they don't. To go for the essence, rather than worry about the details, is absolutely the most important thing. That is reflected a little bit in my work in that sometimes the details are a bit rough, but the essence of it is exactly where it should be. I would say that Cecil's influence has affected my life in everything I did really.

MARY ALLITT

Mary Wells (née Allitt) was born in 1972 and is married with two children. She studied stage management at Bristol Old Vic theatre school and worked as a cameraman. Mary is now a teaching assistant and at home looking after the family. She makes stained glass windows, sews and bakes great cakes.

I remember going to Cecil and Elisabeth's flat in Chelsea when I was about six or seven. We had tea and cakes. My sister, Lucy, and I found it quite boring because it was an adult environment and there wasn't much to do. When we moved to Hastings, we didn't see so much of them, but Cecil came and visited us. He did a painting class there, life modelling I think it was, and I was allowed to do some drawing as well which was a treat. I must have been about eight then. I can't draw to save my life and I dread to think what I produced, probably stick people, but I remember feeling terribly grown up being allowed in.

Cecil was often around at our house when I was a child. I remember Mum and Dad chatting and laughing with him. There was lots of deep conversation too, mostly between Dad and Cecil and Elisabeth to some degree. Cecil was quite earnest while Elisabeth had a lighter, more feminine side. Cecil wasn't particularly friendly with us, but he was a likeable person. Of course he was quite an old man by then.

I wish I could remember the painting Cecil did for Lucy and me. It was on the wall in our bedroom. We had bunk beds and I slept on the bottom bunk and Lucy on the top. I can remember looking at the picture and seeing these animals walk along. It was a bit like them coming off the Ark, two by two. I remember a giraffe's long neck in yellows and browns.

I went with Dad to the Anthony d'Offay exhibition of Cecil's work after Cecil died. I can remember a picture of a Fool under a tree, very purple in colour. I loved it; it was fantastic.

I've got one of Cecil's pictures; it's the artist's proof. I've had it for years. It's a lady's face; she hasn't got a name. Tate Modern have got a copy. She has huge, beautiful almond eyes. It's in my children's room and I've framed lots of their pictures around it. I think Cecil would enjoy that.

Cecil Collins

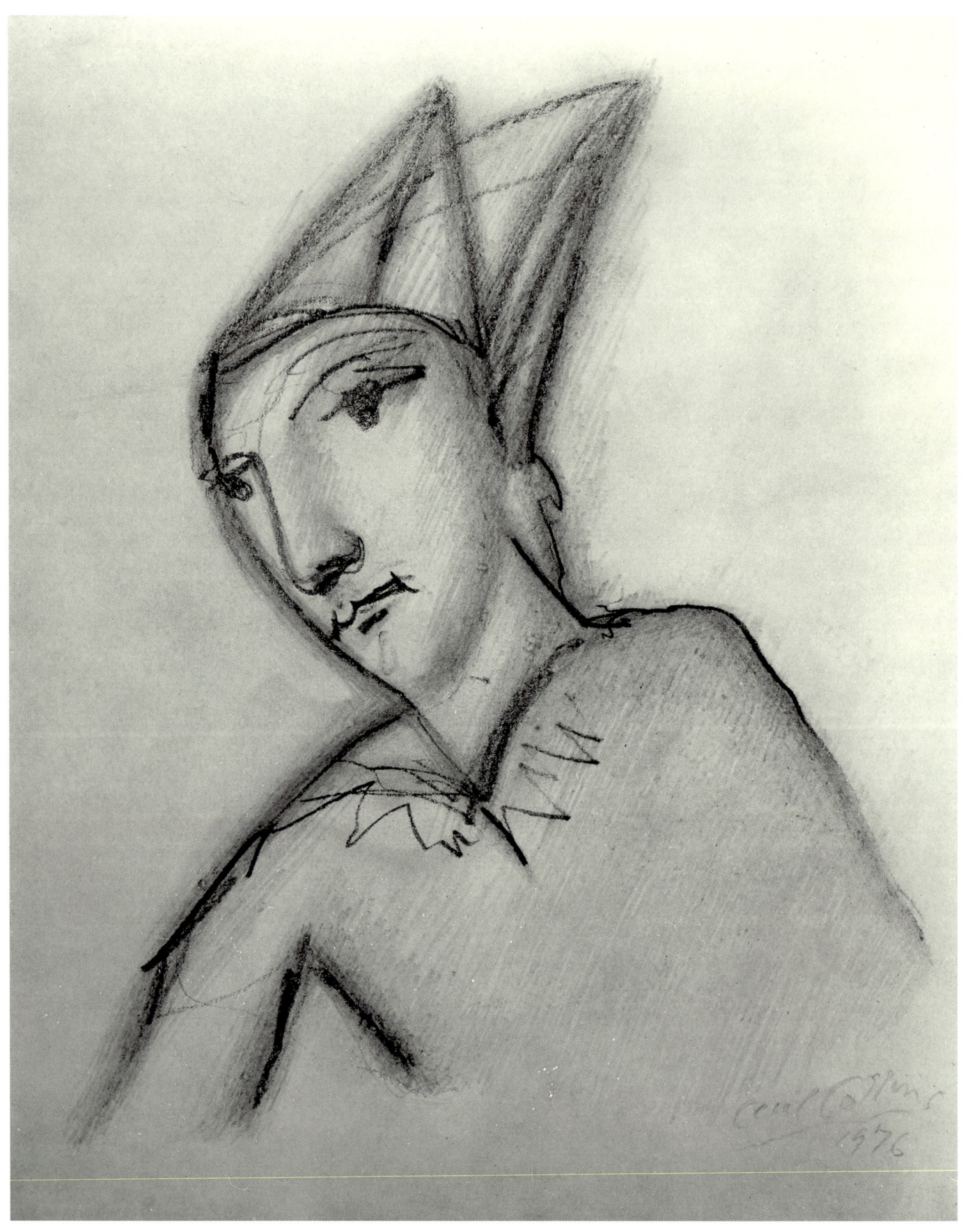

Cecil Collins
Fool
1976
Pencil on paper
29.2 x 24.7cm

JENNIFER ANDERSON

Born in 1934, Jennifer Anderson read French and Italian at Girton, Cambridge, (1953 – 1956). She worked in the Ministry of Education and later, after having three children, as a teacher. She obtained an MA in French from King's College, London, in 1974 and became Headmistress of Frances Holland School, Chelsea in 1982, retiring in 1997.

I married Bill in 1981 and very rapidly after that I became a headmistress. We moved to Chelsea in 1984 and I would think it was then that Bill got to know Cecil. I don't feel that I can contribute a great deal because Bill worked on his book about Cecil very much on his own. Although I met Cecil and his wife, I would not say that I was in the inner circle of their friends. I don't know if they came to our little flat in London, but we went to theirs. Bill saw Cecil almost every day at one point.

I didn't get very close to Elisabeth. I liked her but, at that stage, I think she held herself back because Cecil was the main focus of interest. There's no doubt at all that Elisabeth gave up her own career for Cecil. When she had her exhibition, it was a great success. Her paintings weren't like Cecil's; they didn't have a message. She was a different kind of painter. Bill's book is dedicated to Elisabeth and he says some very nice things about her.

Of course I remember their flat; you could never forget it. What made it so memorable was the way it was decorated. Everything in it had a lot of meaning and beauty. In their flat it always appeared as if they had kept the feeling of being art students. They were not exactly playful, but not quite grown up. It was very personal and it seemed to me that I would have found it extremely small and difficult to live in, but somehow it all fitted. In fact, what one would have thought was quite limiting in space even for a couple of students, somehow was all very beautiful and it suited them or they'd made it suit them. But the relationship with Kathleen Raine who lived below was awful. Elisabeth and Kathleen wouldn't speak to each other. I don't know any more about it than the little I heard from them, but it seemed so uncomfortable. If I'd been Cecil, I would certainly have found it a pretty difficult situation. I've known people who were very friendly with Kathleen and, from them, I've heard nothing but good of her.

One of the things that used to worry me about Cecil, though worry is perhaps too strong a word, was the way his pupils were influenced by him. They were what you could call groupies. They were passionate about his teaching and obviously his teaching was marvellous and he was a great artist, but they didn't have what Cecil had. People could learn from him and paint in his style, but it wasn't their vision. He expected his students to develop their own, but he was such a terribly strong influence.

Bill went to some of his classes just to know what they were like and he was absolutely fascinated by the idea of the matrix and doing things with your eyes shut and all those other things Cecil did. Obviously, it's drawing on the unconscious and I suppose modern critics wouldn't have too much difficulty with that, but Cecil went much further.

When Bill was doing the book, he and I went and visited some of the people who had Cecil's work and you could feel how important these paintings were to the people who owned them. Cecil sent us to a lot of people because of the book. Of course, it was Bill who was sent, but I tended to go with him.

In my headmistress's study I had an artist's proof of the head of the woman with the circles round her head. Cecil selected it for me and I paid for it. I took it to be something like the eternal feminine principle. I'm sure some people thought it was the Virgin Mary, but it wasn't. I lived with that picture all my working life and it was hung very prominently in my study. I didn't try and put it into a mystical category; I didn't feel things had to be promulgated in that way. I felt Cecil kept his childhood vision intact. There were some images that were menacing in his pictures and other things which have a story quality. What I found very interesting was the fact that there was something about the 'spirituality' of his vision, though I'm a bit hesitant about using that word, even with inverted commas, something that made a lot of modern secular critics extremely uncomfortable. Once something has been expressed visually, it's doing something else. It's not only ideas.

I have one other picture by Cecil which is in pencil and watercolour or gouache. It's the head of a Fool and it's extraordinary because it is very like a portrait of Bill. I think Elisabeth gave it to me when Bill died. It was actually dedicated to Bill by Cecil. He should have had it much sooner. The head is in pencil on a very pale yellow background and is titled Head of a Fool. It's dated 1986 so that would have been when Bill and he were getting to know each other.

There was an exhibition at the Tate quite early on in the time that Bill got to know Cecil with several painters. The critics mentioned the others, but not Cecil. It was quite extraordinary. They had gone completely blank about him. Some of the paintings did seem to have a very explicit message and they felt, perhaps, that this wasn't what art should be about. I think the new display at the Tate will be very interesting. Cecil is bound to be re-evaluated because the critics have ignored him so pointedly for so long, almost as if there's a conspiracy of silence.

LAWRENCE BALL

As a composer and pianist, Lawrence Ball has dedicated much of his life to exploring the relationship between sound and silence, between meditation and music. He plays piano, Turkish saz and synthesizer. He founded the Planet Tree Music Festival (London) and performs and organises concerts in Europe and America.

I first met Cecil at a recital I gave at Central School and I think he must have been quite impressed with what he heard. After the concert, he said there was an incredible energy in the room. He insisted that Stephen Cross use my music in the film about him, *The Eye of the Heart*. Stephen made sure I had a fee and I put the money towards a new piano. For about thirty years, that was the only time anyone ever paid me anything for writing music.

Cecil was very keen on a special kind of sound I used to make, like a kind of everlasting sound. I play a chord on the piano with a sustained pedal depressed, then in the recording I fade in the chord so you don't hear the hammers. The sustained harmonies sound like a stream of light coming from eternity and he adored that. He thought it was really very beautiful. My composition, *Breath of Bells* was used in a sequence showing Fools in the film by Stephen Cross. I think it has two improvised piano parts and then an electronic sound part so you have three layers.

It was Brigitte's idea that I ought to give a recital at Central and she also suggested I come to Mrs Tweedie's meditation group where I met a whole host of people who had a big influence in my life. Mrs Tweedie and Cecil Collins were the twin stars of mystical spirituality for many and a lot of people went from one to the other. I visited Mrs Tweedie from 1975 to 1977, but then I decided that I'd absorbed everything I felt I wanted to from there.

I remember going to Paultons Square a couple of times where Cecil and Elisabeth lived on the top floors. I also met Cecil at a gathering at Tite Street at the home of Slobodan and Maria. On that occasion, we had a longer chat and he said he thought my music was liturgical. I didn't really agree with him, but I knew he was trying to find a way to appreciate what I was doing. We'd sometimes chat on the phone and he'd rail against what he called the whizz-kiddery, people being flashy or clever. He hated that, in contrast to his appreciative friendship with John Tavener. Cecil also thought very highly of Arvo Pärt. I think because Cecil focused more on classical music, anything that had jazz or rock elements in it were hard for him to pursue; he tended to be a bit precious about what he would like. He knew Stravinsky and liked what he called the coolness of Stravinsky. He also mentioned Stockhausen and Messiaen, both composers who interested him.

Cecil even got me a ticket to hear a Stockhausen concert in London. The ticket was meant for his friend, Herbert Whone, but as he couldn't make it from Yorkshire where he lived, Cecil gave me the ticket. Whone was interested in the deeper implications of music and I was fascinated by his insights into the symbolism of gongs and bells. He wrote an excellent book, called *The Hidden Face of Music*. Cecil also talked a bit about Satie who was the only twentieth century composer we both held in high esteem. Even Stravinsky hadn't informed what I had done very much at that point. Cecil was very enthusiastic about Gagaku; the first time I ever heard this ancient ceremonial court music of Japan was at the Albert Hall on Cecil's recommendation. It's very beautiful and I discovered later was also a big influence on Hovhaness.

Cecil was an unusual man. I don't think there's anyone in the arts in Britain who held the spiritual flag so high as he did in an artistic field and as a teacher he was unique. Our conversations were not so much an open discussion about how we each saw what was going on in the world, more towards what we each needed to be getting on with. I think he felt that I was way out on a limb somewhere and needed a bit of encouragement which, to some extent, was true. Whenever we spoke, he always took it upon himself to be fatherly and come out with an interpretation about what I was doing and tell me what principles were important. He was very much wearing the teacher's hat. He was quite ferocious in his own spirited way. I think I had a very mild personality compared to him. It wasn't an easy dialogue, but I think we both knew that we were quite unique so we made the best of what there was.

Mostly we talked about what it means to be an artist. I must confess I wasn't able to make as much of what he had to say then, being even more immature than I am now. It was unusual for him to take an interest in someone like me because I wasn't trying to paint or draw. He actually said to me that in his next life he wanted to be a musician, a composer, so I think I must have represented something to him.

The fact he was there and was willing to spend time talking to me and used my music to play to his students was a great thing. There was a sense of being supported by a commonality of vision. Every time I sit down to play the piano, I meet a certain inner resistance and I have to stay with whatever's going on. The fact that Cecil showed kinship towards me has helped me to overcome or transcend that process. The fact that Cecil took me into his confidence and talked to me about what he thought was important in art and music is, in itself, a testimony to his great trust of my receptivity to those principles.

Cecil was a spiritual teacher though I think he didn't have a specific teaching to give; his teaching was in how to be, when you were there with your brush or pencil or whatever. I'm not a visual artist, but I think that any good teacher of art, music or science with something worthwhile to offer will be a spiritual teacher whether it's covert or overt. A lot of people who come to spirituality through a specific teaching, tend to take on the same thought forms as the teacher and often get attached to the teacher. For instance, Messiaen was asked by his student George Benjamin, later a prominent British composer, to find a chord for him on which he could base all his own work. I think Messiaen must have been very embarrassed and to his credit was mature enough not to give him a chord. Fortunately Benjamin came up with one of his own.

Mrs Tweedie was different because she was coming from the heart so she was really getting people to be in touch with their own experience which is unusual. For someone like me, and I think for Cecil too, the whole point of art is that you learn to live through your individual take on reality. You can't take on the thought forms of a teaching no matter how spiritual. That was another way in which Cecil helped me maintain my sense of trying to deal with the world in an original way. It is very difficult to be a spiritual artist and follow your instincts at the same time because you take on the world at point-blank range. People don't respond when you borrow something and act as a sort of mouthpiece for some spiritual teaching; that doesn't work in art. The public are looking for something that isn't second-hand and which transcends the level of thought. Ultimately, when you create art, it's about changing the energy.

It sounds bleak, but I think there's more darkness than light in the world, though it is changing. Cecil was one of those people who are sensitive to the light and had the uphill task of moving the world forward.

Lawrence Ball
Breath of Bells
Improvised for film (*Eye of the Heart*, 1978) about Cecil Collins, later scored for solo piano

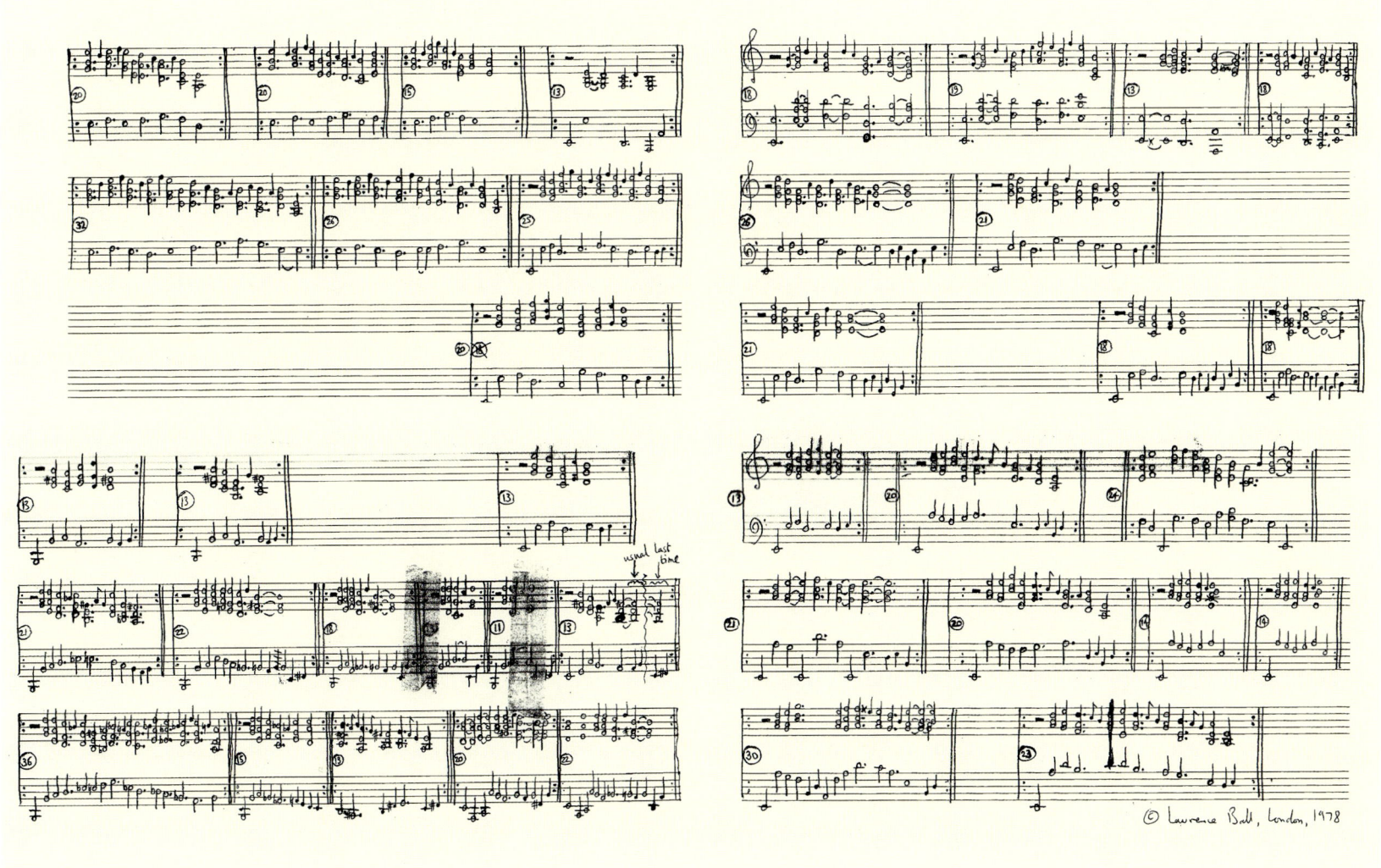

ROBIN & ANNE BARING

Born in 1931, Robin Baring trained as a farmer before serving in the Royal Navy. Later, he worked for Christie's the auctioneers, before studying with Cecil Collins at the Central School of Art, London (1955-1958) He has exhibited at the Crane Kalman Gallery, London and continues to explore the poetic and iconic vocabulary of symbols in his slowly meditated works, producing only three or four canvasses a year. He believes that archetypal imagery can never be owned by an individual since it belongs to the Collective and comes from deep places in the psyche. He likes to let his paintings open like flowers: mysterious and evocative images that work on the soul of the viewer. He was the executor of Cecil and Elisabeth's estate and closely involved, assisted by the Art Fund, with distributing his paintings and drawings to many museums in Britain, including the Tate which holds the Collins archive.

Anne Baring (née Gage) travelled widely in India and the Far East during the 1950's before training and practicing as a Jungian analyst. She is a member of the Scientific and Medical Network and has lectured in both the United Kingdom and the United States. She is the author and co-author of five books including The Myth of the Goddess: Evolution of an Image (with Jules Cashford). She is currently working to promote the affirmation of a new vision of reality and an exploration of the issues facing us at this crucial time of choice.

RB: I met Cecil first in 1955 as a student at the Central. I had knocked on the door of the Fine Art department and the head, Morris Kestelman, came out and said, 'What do you want?' I said that I wanted to learn to paint and he said, 'I've got several people you could study with: Patrick Heron, Keith Vaughan, Cecil Collins and Merlyn Evans if you want to learn etching and printing. Why don't you try Collins for life drawing and composition and Keith Vaughan for still life? You will find them interesting.' In those days, nobody asked whether I had touched a brush.

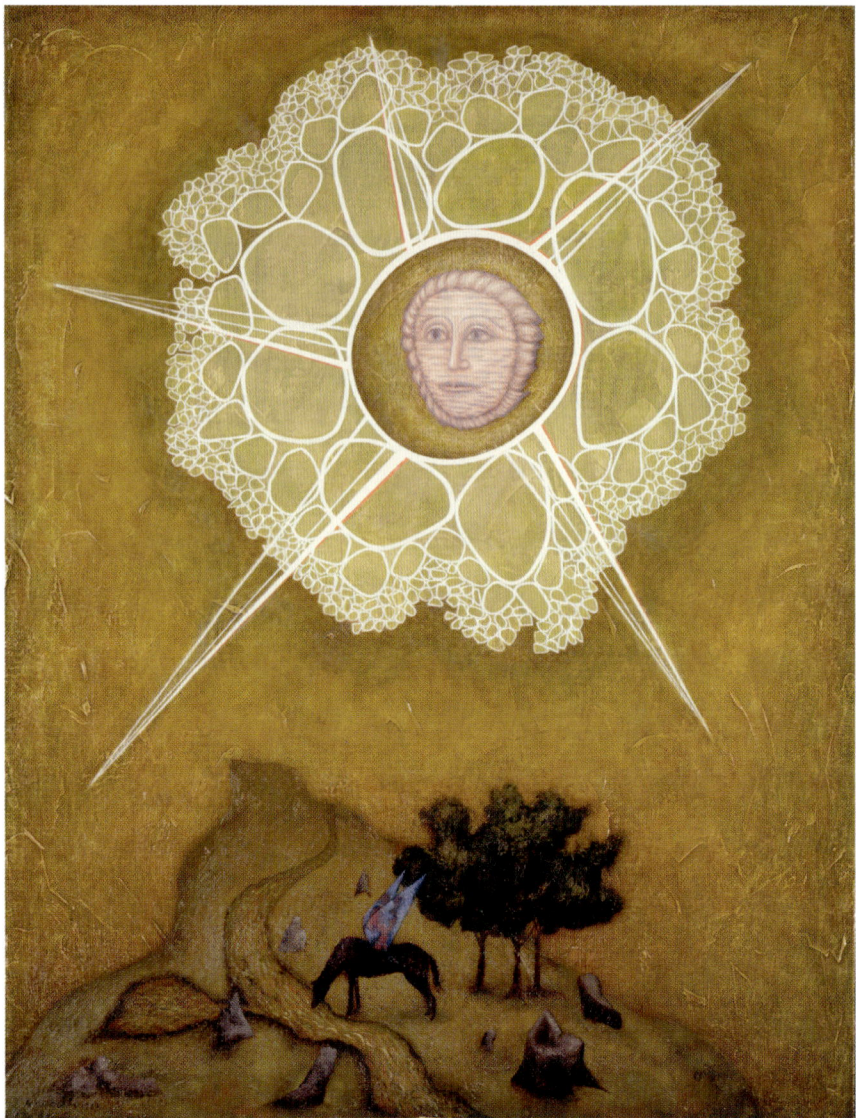

Cecil had only started teaching at the Central about two years before I arrived. His teaching was in its infancy compared to his later years when it became even more innovative. I thought it was quite way out when I joined his classes because he taught drawing with your eyes shut, drawing with two hands at once, sometimes pencil in one hand and pen in the other. He would also sometimes ask us to move one place to left or right, completing our neighbour's drawing which produced horrifying results for most of us. Some people got up and left the class saying, 'I'm not going to have this sort of rubbish. I start my drawing and before I know it, my next door neighbour's mucked it up.' I think this exercise was designed to free you from trying to do a good drawing so that the creativity could flow. Cecil was unmoved by these temporary tantrums. When I joined his class, I found I could draw and paint much better than I expected. It gave me rather a high and probably made me think I was better than I actually was.

Robin Baring
Landscape
oil on board
101.5 x 76cm

Sometimes Cecil walked round behind us as we drew, but there were days when he just sat at his table in the corner and added to the voluminous notes he got out from his jacket pocket. He always used a red ball-point pen. He appeared to take very little interest in what was going on although, in reality, he was fully aware and was very intuitive about every aspect of the class. However hot it was, he always wore his old tweed overcoat and, in winter, put a mackintosh on top of it and held a handkerchief over his nose and wore a brown homburg hat whenever he was outside.

He related very well with all his students, especially the girls, who thought he was the cat's whiskers. He was extremely good at charming them and telling funny stories which were often outrageous. One day he was explaining to us about transforming the basic artist's material of paint, ink, pencil, etcetera into something marvellous and magical, but there was always the risk we might end up creating a mess. He illustrated the perils of transformation with this story. A girl had just broken with her boyfriend and was going home over Westminster Bridge. She had a beautiful red rose in her décolletage which, in despair, she threw over the parapet into the Thames which, in those days, was particularly nasty, greasy and brown. The rose swirled off downstream and suddenly an enormous turd gurgled up from below the surface right alongside it. 'Get away from me, you disgusting thing,' said the rose. 'I've spent the evening in a beautiful lady's décolletage and here you are trying to get close to me.' The turd said, 'Ah yes, but last night I was a Peach Melba.'

Cecil could be very funny, witty and light hearted, but sometimes he was depressed. He told me once, 'I'm in the middle of a very deep depression.' Then he couldn't paint and everything went black. His teaching at the Central School was an outlet which validated him and the admiration of his students encouraged him.

AB: Cecil probably had these depressions all his life.

RB Yes. His pattern was to create a number of paintings over a short period and then have long fallow periods. His depressions were perhaps exacerbated by the constant struggle to gain the recognition he deserved for his work, in spite of exhibiting continuously.

I can remember Henry Moore once asked me who I had studied with and I said, 'Cecil Collins; a remarkable teacher.' Henry Moore looked puzzled for a moment and said, 'Is that the chap who paints Fools?' Cecil wasn't rated by the modern movement. Visionary painting was not seen as mainstream, but Cecil once said to me that he considered his own work to be mainstream and the modern movement just a temporary aberration. Similarly, the work of Gustave Moreau, Odilon Redon and James Ensor, for instance, were never given the recognition they merited.

I became close to Cecil slowly. I think there were not many students who were on his wavelength at the Central at that early stage. Later, as he became well known, his classes were much sought after. Sometimes we used to go for tea after the life class, he and I and Alan Reynolds who was also teaching at the school at that time. We went to the hotel that existed in those days in Bloomsbury Square across from Southampton Row. Alan and Cecil would get through an enormous heap of hot, buttered toast and copious amounts of tea. I was amazed at the quantity. The waitress was always enchanted when they came in and she'd say, 'I'll make extra portions of hot, buttered toast.'

Some time later Cecil invited me up to Cambridge. It was a ground floor flat in Selwyn Gardens. That was where I first met Elisabeth. We had lunch together and I remember them saying, 'You must come out into the garden because it is looking absolutely wonderful.' I thought it odd because what I could see out of the window seemed to be a wilderness. Cecil opened the door which I think gave on to a verandah and said, 'You must come and see the apple tree. It's in full blossom and the flowers are wonderful.' They'd trodden a path through the brambles which were thriving. I couldn't see any flowers except for the apple blossom which was spectacular and I remember thinking, 'If these two think this is a garden, I'm not sure that I'm at the right address.'

Afterwards, Cecil showed me his paintings. He had a big room for a studio much larger than his later one in London. There were wonderful paintings and drawings everywhere and he pulled out more from various stacks. I remember the early painting, *The Fall of Lucifer*, 1933, which is now in Tate Britain, was leaning against one wall. This shows the size of the room because it's almost ten foot high. I was amazed and excited by what he showed me.

From what they said, I had the impression that they were terribly bored living in Cambridge. They found the academic life quite dull. Cecil said that all the academics were sound asleep. I think they both desperately wanted to get back to London, Elisabeth especially, because while Cecil was in London teaching she was sitting there with nothing to do.

Through Cecil I later met Mark Tobey who used to come over from Switzerland where he was living at the time. He was very nice, slightly withdrawn and, I felt, a bit guarded. He was immensely cultured and sensitive, immersed in the civilisation and the philosophies of the Far East. It was through Tobey that Cecil became interested in the Baha'i faith. Tobey came to tea with Cecil and Elisabeth on several occasions when they were installed in Paultons Square. Tobey was quite famous, much more so than Cecil. They used to talk together about old times at Dartington and discuss their ideas which coincided at many levels. Tobey was a wonderful painter. There should be another retrospective exhibition of his work. I believe he is undervalued. I think Tobey, in many ways, is just as good as Pollock, possibly even better, but on a much more intimate scale.

Cecil was passionately interested in music. He admired Karlheinz Stockhausen who I met at Cecil's studio in Cambridge and who, in turn, was an admirer of Cecil's work. Cecil loved Stravinsky's music and we once went to listen to Stravinsky conducting his own music at the Festival Hall. By then, Stravinsky was elderly and only conducted one piece. When we sat down, there were three empty seats in the row in front of us. As the lights went down, three figures took their places in them. Much to our delight, it was Stravinsky, accompanied by Isaiah Berlin and someone we didn't recognise. During the interval, they remained in their seats and a crowd soon gathered in the aisles, gazing in awe at this icon of twentieth century music.

While Cecil was teaching at the Central School, a new Head of Fine Art, Robert Clatworthy who was installed by the Inner London Education Authority tried to get rid of Cecil.

AB: Robin had to write letters and Cecil's students rose up in his defence.

RB: Cecil got me going. He used to ring up in the middle of the night and say, 'Cecil here. I think a letter to Mrs Thatcher wouldn't be out of place. Do you think you could write one?' After a few further calls I said, 'Why don't we talk to your MP?' I rang up the MP for Kensington and Chelsea and said, 'Look, we've got this problem. A distinguished member of your constituency, Cecil Collins, is being sacked from the Central School for no good reason and we believe the ILEA are behind it.' His MP said, 'Unfortunately, I'm not allowed to do anything to help in such a case because I'm a Junior Minister, but I suggest you telephone the office of Sir Keith Joseph who is the Minister of Education. So I talked to Keith Joseph's private secretary and explained the problem. He said, 'Please come round to the Minister's office and we can talk more about this.'

I thought I would take someone else along to add weight so I rang Bill Anderson who had published a book on Cecil and his work and he agreed to come. We went round and were introduced to Keith Joseph who said, 'My private secretary has told me what the problem is and I suggest that you talk further with him and we will see what we can do to help.' His private secretary said that Cecil's problem tied in very well with Mrs Thatcher's wish to get rid of the ILEA. He would arrange for a private motion to be put forward in the House of Commons, saying that at the Central School, an eminent member of the staff was facing dismissal for no good reason which was producing student unrest.

Somehow the ILEA got wind of what was going on and, some days after our approach to Keith Joseph, a letter came from the ILEA to Cecil saying that he could work for as long as he liked and retire at his own discretion. Not long after that, the ILEA was closed down.

AB: Cecil was very focused and he had an extraordinary insight into human nature.

RB: Cecil could be quite manipulative.

AB: And quite rightly. He was fighting for what he believed in and his position.

RB: Cecil also persuaded me to write a letter to the Arts Council suggesting it was high time they put on an exhibition of his work. When I heard, 'Cecil here,' on the telephone I'd think, 'Oh no, not another letter!' That said, I thought it was a disgrace that he had never been offered an exhibition by the Arts Council or the Tate. The Arts Council replied that it wasn't up to them to give Cecil an exhibition; it was up to the Tate. Cecil was now some age, so I wrote to the Tate suggesting they put on a retrospective exhibition fairly soon otherwise it might turn out to be a posthumous one. The exhibition finally happened in 1989 and Cecil died about three weeks after it opened.

Over the years, I have bought many of Cecil's works. I helped him assemble his paintings and drawings for his Retrospective at the Whitechapel Gallery in 1959 so I was familiar with almost everything in his studio from an early stage. Some of his work appealed less to me, but there were many I really loved and wanted to have.

He never offered them to me. I'd see them and say, 'Cecil, is that for sale?' Sometimes he'd say, 'Yes,' but usually he said, 'No, it belongs to Elisabeth,' which was always his answer if he didn't want to sell. In the end, I assembled quite a collection.

Figure and Landscape, 1933 (Pen and ink)
Cecil's studio was absolute chaos, you could hardly get into it. He used to pretend that he knew where everything was. He slept on a mattress on the floor in one corner. In Cambridge he had his own bedroom. Once I was in his studio and he said, 'Can you help me undo some old portfolios underneath that chair?' We pulled out one and there were about twenty early drawings in it and I bought one, the *Figure and Landscape*. It is a stunning drawing. It could be a Greek god and there is such a wonderful light on the sea. I don't think Cecil remembered it because he'd done it very early on. He hadn't even written the title on the back. That was unlike him as he usually titled everything and documented exactly what it was.

friends & other relationships

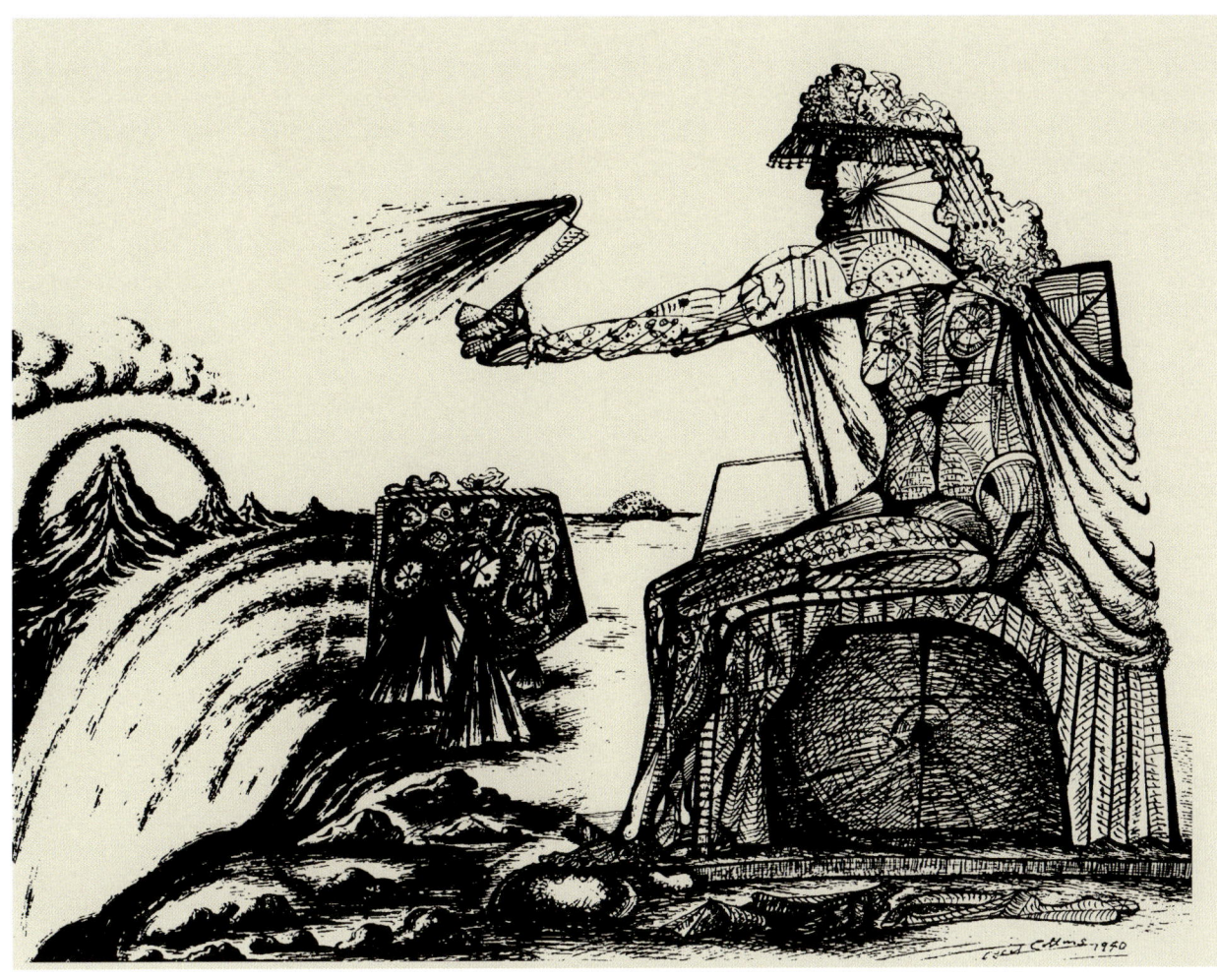

Cecil Collins
The Oracle
1940
Ink on paper
36.5 x 55cm

The Green Pilgrim, 1937 (Pen and green ink and watercolour)
This has faded slightly despite being kept in the shadows. Cecil was looking at it one day when he and Elisabeth were staying with us. He pointed to an area below the feet of the Pilgrim where there is a lyrical passage, partly geometric in form drawn in white and said, 'That's Mark Tobey' I asked him, 'Why do you say that?' He replied, 'Tobey got his *White Writing* from me.' I don't know whether this is true, but Cecil certainly produced a number of very linear drawings around this date in white ink on green paper. *A Song the Worlds Rejoice* (1935) in the British Museum is a very good example..

The Oracle, 1940 (Pen and ink)
Cecil always put the titles and dates of his pictures on the back. He was obviously dissatisfied with part of this drawing because there is a collaged addition.

Christ before the Judge, 1954 (Oil on board)
It's a painting of Byzantine magnificence. It had its Green & Stone frame around it and someone advised me to take it to Pollack in St James's Street said to be one of the best framers in London at that time. I rang Cecil and he came with me. Mr Pollack looked at the painting and said, 'I know exactly what this painting needs. You must trust me absolutely.' A few weeks later, Cecil and I went back and there was *Christ before the Judge* in a magnificent, simple timber frame on which the hand planed marks had been left. It was finished in antiqued grey painted gesso decorated with little stars in antiqued black and gold leaf. We were both delighted with the result.

Landscape of the God, 1961 (Pen and ink and watercolour)
A very fine work. I had another landscape by Cecil in a similar style and, I suppose, part of the same series of watercolours. I liked it less than *Landscape of the God* and needed some money and thought I would thin out my collection. I put it in for sale at Christie's and went to the auction to see what would happen. Sitting not far from me was a man who looked like a young version of Cecil. He had a woolly beard like Cecil had when I first knew him. I thought what a strange character to find in the auction room, especially as he seemed to be taking no interest in what was going on. When my Cecil came up, he suddenly leapt to his feet, bid and bought it. He disappeared before I had time to ask him who he was and why he was interested in Cecil's work.

Woman and Red Landscape, 1962 (Oil and tempera)
I wanted to buy *Woman and Red Landscape* when I saw it in Cecil's studio. He exhibited it, I think, at Tooths Gallery and someone else bought it. One day, I walked into Sotheby's and there it was hanging on the wall for sale so I left a bid for it and got it after all.

Woman and Landscape: Invocation, 1962 (Oil and tempera)
I'm never quite sure whether I like *Woman and Landscape: Invocation*. I find his technique tends to be a bit too shiny. The glazing makes it look more like a tile. Cecil was very keen on it and talked me into it. He was enormously confident in the importance of his work. He once told me that his work was not created for criticism.

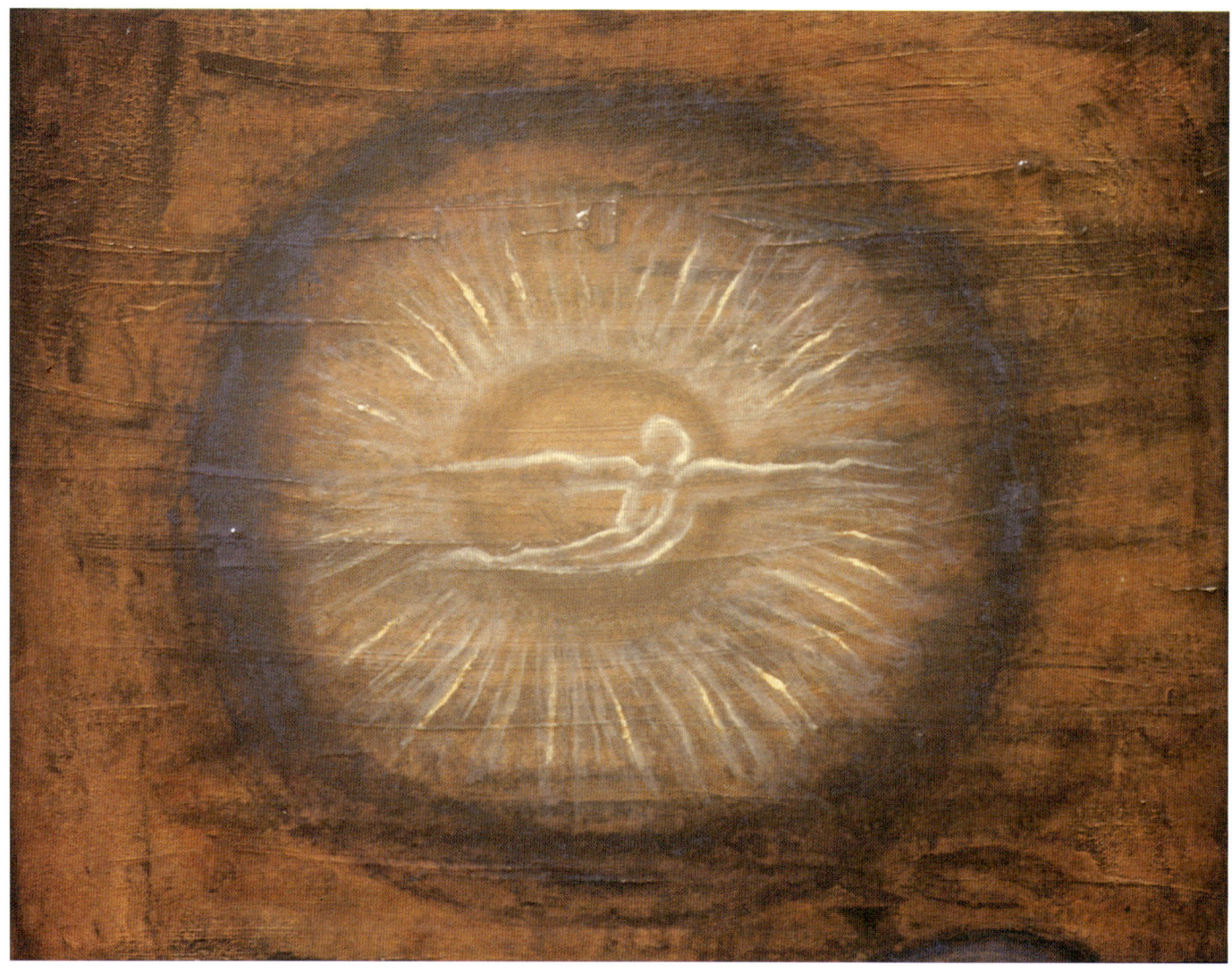

Cecil Collins
Angel of the Sun
1964
Mixed media on board
33 x 30cm
(detail)

The Guardian of Paradise, 1963 (Oil and tempera)
I find this a difficult painting. It's so dark. When we first saw it Anne said, 'That's marvellous.' So we bought it. Cecil was not good at choosing frames and he didn't have the money available so his paintings ended up in standard Green & Stone frames of the period. The gold frame on this painting is much too bright and distracts from the picture. It needs to be reframed. It's another of the glazed ones which show their colours best when they are well lit. The technique involved layers of water-based tempera between the glazes. These were sometimes applied as thinly as watercolour and carried the same risks of fading.

Purple Figure, 1964 (Oil and tempera)
In the 60s Cecil's painting technique consisted of many layers of glazing, but one of the problems with his glazed works is that he often used violet and violet fades. When we bought it, this one was an absolutely wonderful violet and it's completely gone. The funny thing is I've got a Graham Sutherland which had a marvellous violet sky, but that's gone too. Its now grey even though it has always been kept in shady corners.

The Angel of the Apocalypse, 1969 (Oil and tempera)
This is a wonderful painting with an amazingly free technique. I saw it on his easel for ages and every time I saw it the background was different until he used gold paint on it, then glazed and varnished it. It has been lent to several exhibitions.

AB: Robin was already friends with Cecil when we married in 1960. Cecil didn't want us to get married at all. He thought that I would ruin Robin's artistic life and said so in no uncertain terms which made me very grumpy. Cecil could be very arrogant and quite sure that he was right about everything, but he came round in the end when he saw that our marriage worked out all right.

RB: Really you became even closer to Cecil than I was. Anne's interest in mythology, the history of religion and the psyche coincided with Cecil's interests.

AB: I became very fond of him.

RB: Around 1958, I found a copy of *Modern Man in Search of a Soul* by Jung in a Charing Cross Road bookshop and this opened new worlds to me. When I mentioned Jung to Cecil, to my surprise, he didn't seem interested. I'm fairly sure he had read Freud and this had probably put him off psychology. Later, he became very interested and I think it was Kathleen Raine's enthusiasm for Jung's work which persuaded him.

AB: Cecil thought that psychology might take away his Angels.

RB: He once quoted Rilke to me who'd said of psychotherapy, 'I don't want to get rid of my devils for fear of offending my angels.' Elisabeth told me much later that they had once considered consulting a psychiatrist, but had decided against it.

AB: Cecil got on very well with my mother, Thalia Gage, and so did Elisabeth. They became great friends.

RB: Elisabeth said to me once that your mother was the most remarkable woman she had ever met. Thalia and Anne's father owned Cecil's painting, *The Angel of the Flowing Light* (1968), now in Tate Britain. They lived in France and it hung in their sitting room. Thalia was a poet who had won several French prizes for poetry, including the Louise Labbé one. She was also a fine painter.

AB: Cecil and Elisabeth went to stay with my parents once while we were there with our daughter Francesca, who was Cecil's goddaughter, and her cousins. Cecil was a genius with children and devised a treasure hunt for them. The treasure was a head which he had painted on a stone and then hidden in the garden. The children searched everywhere and eventually Francesca found it and has it to this day.

When Elisabeth and Cecil came to supper with us in London and Francesca was very small, Cecil would always go upstairs to see her in bed to say goodnight. He told her that he always flew up from Chelsea on the back of a swan. Francesca believed this absolutely and still claims that she could see the swan when they leaned out of the nursery window to look at the tree where Cecil said the swan had landed.

RB: Elisabeth found it very difficult to get Cecil to go anywhere. He was a very nervous traveller.

AB: I remember they once went to Annecy and to the south of France where they visited the Picasso Museum in Antibes. They also went to Athens where Cecil had an exhibition and gave a lecture.

RB: Cecil once told me that he didn't want any of his paintings to go abroad, 'My paintings belong in England.' Benjamin Britten and Peter Pears, who owned the 1952 pencil drawing, *The Ressurection*, invited Cecil to mount the Aldeburgh Festival exhibition of his work in 1984. Anne and I went up for the private view and I was introduced to Anne d'Offay who was there with her husband, Anthony. The first thing she said to me was, 'This is an important painter who has been overlooked.' Later, after joining the Anthony d'Offay Gallery, Cecil at last began to feel that he was financially secure. I think it was a great relief after so long. Several of Cecil's very good paintings were sold to an American collector. Cecil accepted that because he liked the collector who had visited his studio in Paultons Square.

AB: Cecil and Elisabeth had lived frugally all their lives from the years at Dartington onwards.

Elisabeth must have been very beautiful with her great mass of hair. I think, in some ways, she did throw herself away by marrying Cecil, but she was surrounded by interesting people which enriched her life. After his death she told Robin that, soon after they met at the Royal College of Art, she realised that her role in life was to look after Cecil which she did with great devotion.

RB: Although she was very talented, her family hadn't wanted her to go to art college and she said they were horrified when she announced that she wanted to marry Cecil. I think the relationship with her family broke down at that point. I suspect that she was quite a fire-brand at that time.

AB: She came from a strong-minded Yorkshire family, quite fierce, all of them. Elisabeth had a strong American mother, as well as a strong Yorkshire father.

RB: As a result of a business transaction to do with her family's business in Yorkshire, Elisabeth suddenly became well off after Cecil died. For the first time, she could live comfortably and without financial worries. She said to me, 'I do wish I'd had this money while Cecil was still alive. It would have solved so many of the problems of our life.'

Elisabeth found the paying of bills and general accountancy difficult after Cecil's death so I used to help her. I had looked after the affairs of my father and my aunt and their affairs during their final years so I knew what was necessary. She asked me how much money she had and I said, 'You've got plenty of money now and you can live just however you want.' She asked, 'What do you think I should do?' I said, 'Why don't you take your friends out to good restaurants and start off with champagne and you could buy some more clothes.' She must have liked this idea because, some time later, one of her friends rang me to say that they were concerned about Elisabeth taking her friends out to lunch and spending money like water. I reassured her friend it was all right and I hoped that the good lunches would continue.

AB: She had no idea about money and, of course, had never needed to because Cecil looked after that side of their life.

RB: Elisabeth said she had never learned arithmetic. In fact, I'm not sure she ever went to school. Bank statements and invoices were a mystery to her. She was enchantingly naïve about figures and, on one occasion, very unusually, her balance showed an amazing £50,000. She said with much laughter, 'Is that £50 or £500?' When I said it was £50,000 she said, 'Is that a lot?' It was a real pleasure seeing her enjoying herself, free from the anxieties which she had felt about her future on her own.

AB: While Cecil was alive, Elisabeth used to have lovely dinner parties. We would eat round the table in the enchanting living room Elisabeth had created at the top of the house. There were wonderful books everywhere. Her bedroom was upstairs next to it. Cecil's studio was next to the bathroom on the floor below. Cecil used to come up from his studio after the guests had all arrived and make a grand entrance. He loved to be king-pin.

RB: If they came to dinner with us in London, Anne would chat away with Cecil the whole time and I would talk to Elisabeth. Cecil used to cut his food up into very small pieces. He took ages and when we had all finished, he would still be on his main course.

Once, long after I'd stopped being Cecil's student, he came to dinner with us and was in one of his ascetic humourless moods. In an unguarded moment I said to him, 'Cecil, why don't you take off your hair shirt?' As I said it, I knew it was a mistake. He became very angry in a way that I had never seen before. I believe that although I was no longer studying with him, he saw me still as a student who was criticising the master.

AB: Elisabeth's life must have been very difficult domestically, but somehow she produced delicious simple meals for any number of friends on that dreadful cooker on the landing outside the living room. I got our plumber once to come and see if he could do something with it. He took one look and said, 'This is not only illegal, it's dangerous,' and fled.

RB: Instead of the flame coming out of the burner, it came out of a pipe a good inch below it. It didn't worry Elisabeth at all.

AB: The fridge they had was also totally inadequate. Why they didn't die of food poisoning or a gas explosion, I don't know.

We met many friends there: Jonathan and Jackie Stedall, Glen Schaefer, Rafael and Jacinta Nadal, John and Eleanor Allitt, John and Maryanna Tavener and Philip Sherrard when he was over from Greece.

RB: Rafael had known Lorca and one day he brought some of Lorca's letters from his collection, some of them illustrated with his drawings. He didn't need much encouragement to recite Lorca's poems in Spanish with great passion, which was an amazing experience. Thetis Blacker was also often there. Cecil and Elisabeth and Thetis were a little group around Kathleen Raine. Thetis told me that Kathleen had taught her everything she knew.

As I understood it, Kathleen wanted to live in London and she approached Cecil and Elisabeth who were still stuck in Cambridge and asked if they would take the lease of the top two floors in Paultons Square. This would enable Kathleen to purchase the house. They started on a good footing and I think they were very happy. It solved all their problems and Kathleen let off the basement to Winifred Nicholson. It seemed to work very well.

Sadly, they fell out after some years and even at the time of her death, Elisabeth was still not on speaking terms with Kathleen. The cause of the rupture is something of a mystery. I used to act as a go-between and managed to maintain my neutrality. When I was visiting Elisabeth, Kathleen often used to see me in the front hall and beckon me in to have tea. To the end, Kathleen was a tremendous and faithful admirer of Cecil and his work.

Although Elisabeth made some very good paintings in the early years of their marriage, her work seems to have petered out after she married Cecil. I think that she must have felt rather in the shadow of Cecil's talent, also there were the daily chores and I'm sure Cecil was not very good at helping. After Cecil's death, Elisabeth took up her painting again. When her first show at the Jane England Gallery was a sell out, I remember Elisabeth saying to me, 'If I'd known my paintings would sell like that and people liked them so much, why did I ever give up?'

I admired Elisabeth's paintings very much. They have enormous poetry and, luckily, I have a number of them too. Everything she touched in life, she turned into poetry.

AB: Elisabeth told us that when she and Cecil went off on their honeymoon, Cecil's mother came too. Elisabeth took a dim view of this, but I think Cecil thought it was quite nice. Cecil's mother was an amazing lady and Cecil was in awe of her.

RB: Cecil and Elisabeth had a very close relationship in spite of the difficulties. Elisabeth once broke her leg and had to have a hip replacement. She tripped over a fire hose in Oxford Street and was taken off to hospital. Cecil went to see her and her report to me was that Cecil came in and said 'Who's going to cook my dinner?' We said, 'Cecil come and have dinner with us.' He came round and we asked if he'd seen Elisabeth and he said, 'Yes, she went for me so much I've come out like a bald parrot.'

I think Elisabeth put her creativity into caring for Cecil although the daily round was a burden to her. I believe that in the early days she even moulded Cecil as a human being, but she must have done this with enormous tact. Towards the end of his life, Cecil was full of praise for her and often if he was making a speech, he would say how much he owed everything to her.

AB: I remember going to see Cecil in hospital once.

RB: Yes, you're quite right. He went in because he was in pain.

AB: It was a stone in the urinary tract.

Cecil Collins
The Guardian of Paradise
1963
Oil on board
104 x 110cm

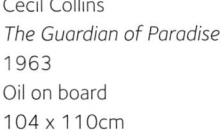

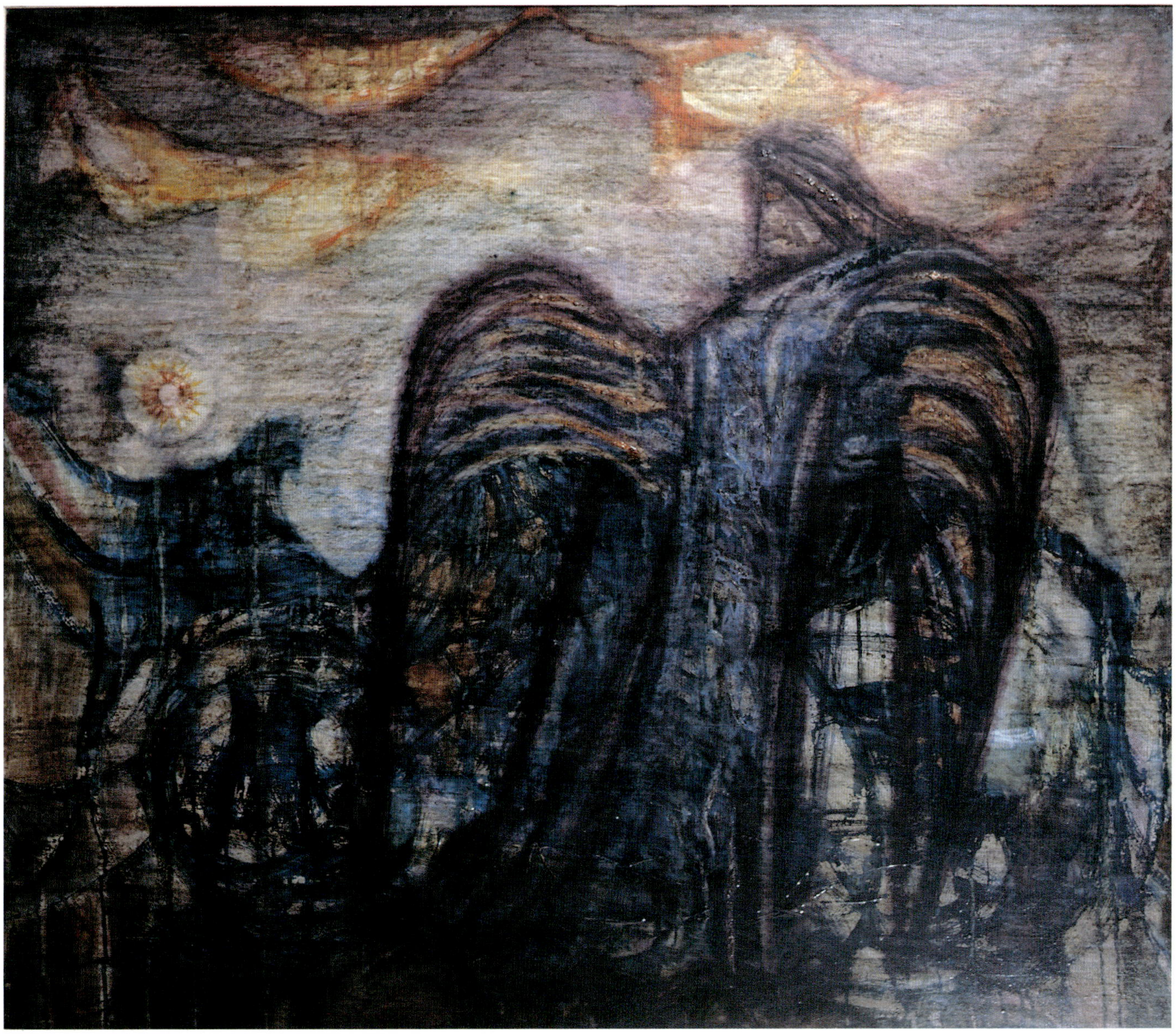

RB: After the stone was removed, he brought it home. He was very proud of it and kept it on the mantelpiece. I remember it as being surprisingly large and perfectly cylindrical and beautifully rounded at both ends like some sort of projectile. It was quite a mysterious object because it didn't look natural, nor man-made. I said to Cecil, 'It may be the Philosopher's Stone.' He was delighted with this idea, especially because he had managed to make it himself. When he died, I thought I must find the stone; it must go to the Tate Archive but, sadly, it was nowhere to be found.

AB: Cecil and Elisabeth had a very difficult time in the months before his Retrospective Exhibition at the Tate. I don't know how Elisabeth coped with his final illness, but close friends were a tremendous support and came round nearly every day to help her. The most grievous aspect of the last weeks was the fact that they coincided with the opening of the long-awaited Retrospective.

Cecil was thrilled to be acknowledged at last and at the private view, I proudly pushed him round the room in a wheelchair as he was too weak to walk. It was very moving to watch him greet his many friends and supporters and feel the warmth flowing towards him.

The end came fairly quickly, three weeks after the opening. Fortunately, he was able to have a room in the London Clinic and was made as comfortable as possible. I went to see him just before he died, taking with me a posy of flowers as a small token. I told him of the deep affection I felt for him and the gratitude for our long friendship.

RB: After Elisabeth's death, the Art Fund handled the distribution to museums of the remaining work in Cecil's studio. As one of Elisabeth's Executors, the other being her nephew, Edward Wood, I was overwhelmed by the problem of how to deal with the mass of material in Cecil's studio and telephoned Richard Morphet who advised me to approach the Art Fund and at once our problem was resolved. Three of Elisabeth's friends helped me to sort out the flat and catalogue the studio contents: Marcia Blakenham, Lily Corbett and Jeremy Gale. For me, it was the final act of a long saga which had started when I was twenty-four.

AB: Its amazing to think that Cecil and Elisabeth were very much in our lives for nearly thirty years. Cecil certainly was a big influence, not so much on my writing, but he was a focus for ideas and people who were interested in the same things as us, perhaps me even more than Robin.

RB: Cecil had a huge influence on me when I first met him. At the time, I was becoming interested in the sort of ideas which took me away from my conventional background and upbringing. Suddenly I found myself in the presence of a man who confirmed for me those ideas and helped me to understand them. From the start, I felt I was on a similar wavelength with Cecil; about the inner world, the world of transcendental realities. He reinforced my belief that archetypal imagery and the poetic vocabulary of symbols can never be owned by an individual since they belong to the Collective and come from deep places in the psyche. Painting as a form of meditation; then the mysterious and evocative images can open like flowers that work on the soul of the viewer.

AB: He really did set the course of your life to painting, I think.

RB: I think he did. That would be correct and that's why I am so grateful to him.

Cecil Collins
The Pilgrim Fool
1936
Watercolour with pen and ink
25.5 x 20.5cm

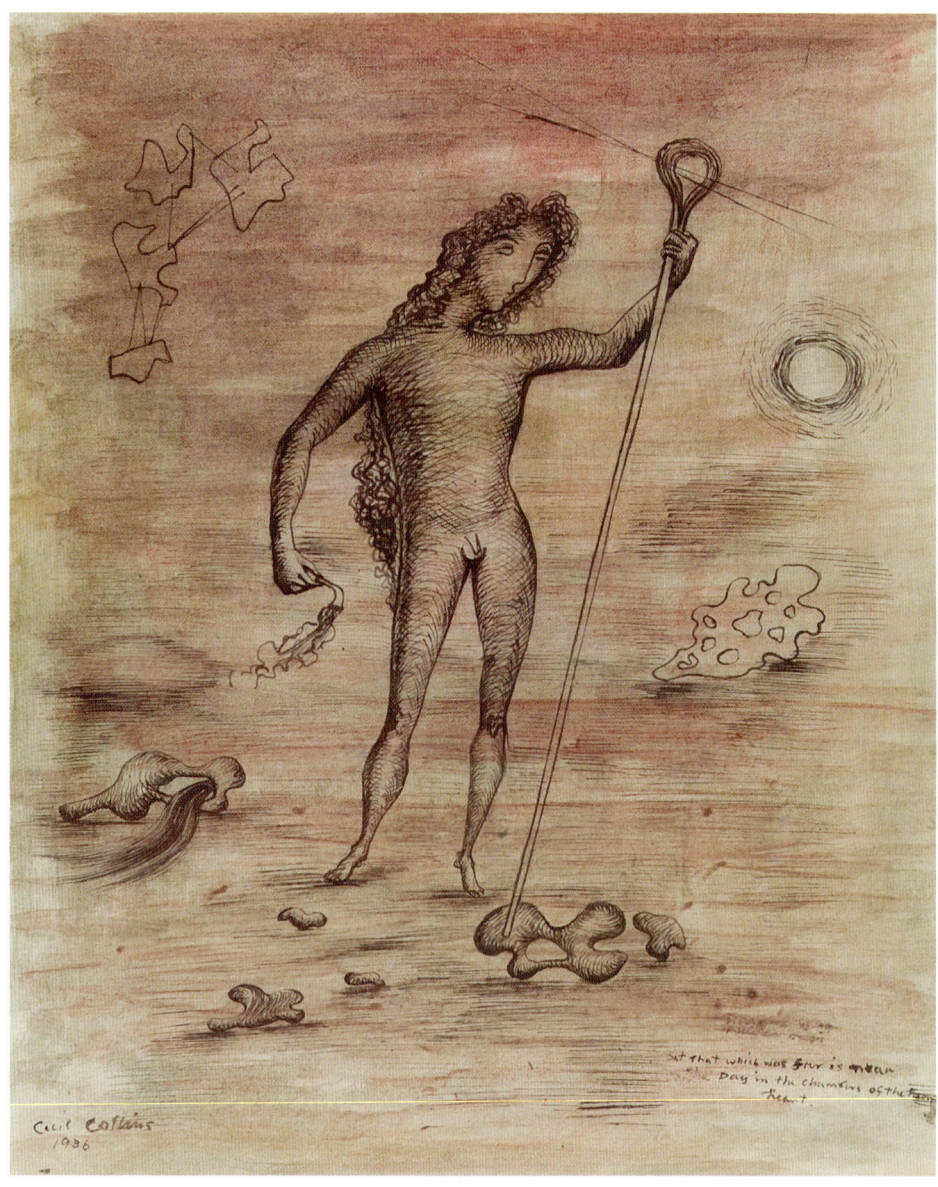

JULIAN BARNARD

Julian Barnard is the founder of Healing Herbs, a Bach Flower Remedies business which has been running for eighteen years. He trained in herbal medicine in Australia with Dorothy Hall and is the author of books about Dr Bach and the Flower Remedies.

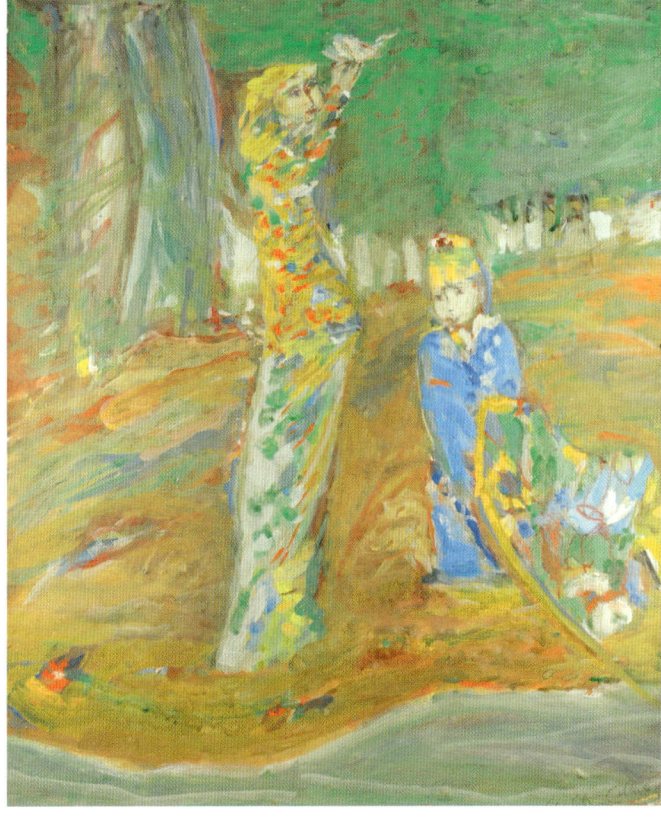

Elisabeth Collins
People in a Wood
1987
Gouache
63.5 x 50.8cm

In 1967 or '68 I was studying at the A.A. I came to know about Cecil through friends who met with students who were at Central at that time. I never took a class with him, but I knew people who did, like Michael Chaitow. We used to be involved with the Sufis and those kinds of interests that you float into when you're in your twenties, when you come into contact with great people without being aware of it.

I remember Irina Tweedie and Kathleen Raine who I knew of as a poet and RILKO, the Research Into Lost Knowledge Organisation. I attended their meetings because Warren Kenton and Keith Critchlow were my tutors at the A. A. I didn't end up as an architect. Instead, I earned a living doing building, decorating and carpentry. For some time, another friend had been working for Cecil in that sort of a role, but he got married and moved to Yorkshire so I inherited his role. I worked for Cecil and Elisabeth whenever they wanted anything done and also for Kathleen. There were always lots of things. Sometimes up in the roof fixing the water tank and sometimes mending the chairs, doing whatever needed to be done. This was a terrific opportunity for me because I got to know them as people. I lived in Shepherd's Bush and used to drive over to Paultons Square with a yellow Post Office van.

Cecil used to pay me partly with money and partly with prints and that's how I started to collect his pictures. I was a photographer as well so I took photographs of many of Cecil's and Elisabeth's work. There was a very interesting dynamic between the two of them insofar as they were both painters. I think Elisabeth stopped painting simply in order to support Cecil. One day he was saying to her, 'No, you should be painting.' I think it was about the time that I was making a photographic record of all of Cecil's pictures. He said that I should take photographs of Elisabeth's work as well. She had a portfolio of pictures done in the 1940s under the bed in her studio, which was in the back room on the very top floor.

In later years, his studio had racks for paintings. I built those for him along one wall, but he hated them because he didn't like to be organised. I think it was probably Elisabeth's idea. It had come to a point where Cecil wasn't quite sure what he had and you could hardly get in the room which wasn't very big anyway. It was just impossible. You couldn't move and you could only just get to the desk. I don't remember exactly the size, but the impression you had was that it was like in the Ionesco play, The New Tenant, where the stage gradually fills with furniture. I built him all these shelving units for his books, but he put them in back to front in piles so that you couldn't read the titles.

Cecil must count for me as one of the great influences on my thinking and my view of life, although I never was a student of his and didn't always go along with what he thought. There were two sides to Cecil: there were the causes he was espousing at the time, but there was also this inner vision. It was the inner vision that I felt most a deep and strong link with. I didn't always find Cecil an easy person to talk to. He was a bit of a one-way street. If you were travelling the way he was walking, you would follow his ideas, but it was not two-way traffic if you tried to introduce and relate these ideas to something else. I remember I had been studying Goethe's colour theory, only in a very superficial way, but Cecil would have nothing to do with this. I thought, okay so it doesn't square with Cecil's colour theory. I suppose his mind may have been closed, but I always felt it was more defensive than real. When Stephen Cross was filming Cecil for *The Eye of the Heart* we went up to Biddulph Grange. I can be seen in the film too as the pilgrim Fool in a pointed hat by the lake. In those days I had a beard.

Cecil would always enjoy a good beer and we used to go out for lunch together, usually at the King's Head opposite the square in the King's Road. I always thought he was rather serious and it took me a long time to realise that there was this twinkle in him and to recognise his dry humour. He didn't have a repertoire of jokes, but there were particular things for which he had a funny phrase. When you sat at a table with Cecil and Elisabeth, she would never say very much, but the way Cecil led the conversation, was fairly humorous.

I was studying astrology and I said to the Collinses, 'I'll do your charts for you.' They were both very intrigued by this and I did Cecil's chart first. His birthday was 25th March so he was just into Aries on the cusp between Aries and Pisces. In the chart, you could see the inner life and the inner world, which was most apparent in Cecil when you felt that he had withdrawn. One image I have of Cecil is in the studio with his back to the door (most people don't sit with their backs to the door), slightly hunched over his music equipment. He had good quality sound equipment, not that I knew much about these things then, but it was quite elaborate. He had very large headphones, probably Sennheiser. I remember him with these great headphones on, listening to music. He was not really in that room at all. You never heard the music, but it was as if he'd gone into a different space, a different world.

Sitting upstairs with Elisabeth at the white painted table they had, I drew up her chart. I remember saying, 'When I look at these two charts together, there's something I can't reconcile. I don't quite know how to say this to you, Elisabeth, but it's as though there's a whole part of you that Cecil doesn't know about,' and she said, 'Yes, but don't tell him.' This is an interesting reflection on astrology. You could see in their charts where they related and then there was this other area in Elisabeth that was completely hidden from him. I don't mean this unkindly, but I think Cecil was always more interested in himself.

In Bach Flower Remedies, Cecil was a Clematis type which can't self-structure, can't stand independently, but the positive aspect of the clematis is that it brings a vision and makes real the dream and the light in this level of reality. He used to wear these very heavy brogue shoes. They had a thick sole and each one weighed a couple of pounds and he would say, 'I have to wear these to keep me down on the earth otherwise I'll float away.' That's typical of the Clematis archetype in Bach Remedies.

Elisabeth was one of the few people I've met who, right until the last, was still consciously looking to discover something new and was always inquisitive about life and, for that reason, I have an enormous admiration and respect for her. In terms of Bach Flower Remedies, she was what I would describe as a Water Violet, a very private person who doesn't want to mix very much with the world. Sometimes if I'm teaching Bach Remedies, I'll describe Elisabeth as this archetype. Water Violet people live alone and are very content to be withdrawn from the world and live within their own space; they don't need things from other people. I think she had a very strong inner life, but you didn't always see it.

I think Elisabeth would have liked to have children. Although one might say Cecil had children in his students, he couldn't actually have dealt with having another child apart from himself in the house. I wanted my son to meet them. When I introduced him to them, he was fifteen and Elisabeth was much more tolerant and indulgent of him than Cecil.

They were very loving towards me, not in any intimate or personal way, but they gave me space in their life. It was wonderful to share the way they saw the world and the way that life was for them. There are a lot of things that I absorbed from Cecil without really being conscious of it at the time, especially his way of looking at things. With flower remedies, instead of telling you a plant's Latin name or its chemical composition or even what virtue or value it might have as a herb, all of which is book knowledge, if instead you look with the eyes of the Fool, then you see what the plant actually is in its own terms. You don't try to dictate to it what you think about it. That's what Cecil would have understood in relation to the Fool.

Cecil was not wildly generous about money, but then I think he didn't have a lot. When you work for somebody, it's difficult to get the money out of some customers, but I never had that feeling with Cecil. He'd always pay up on the nail. On occasion I would have up to half the money due in prints, at whatever price Cecil set upon them. Then, having made that transaction, Cecil said, 'And now I'm going to give you this.' He was pretty generous in that way.

Then I decided I was going to train as a Steiner teacher at about the same time I got married and I don't think that sat at all well with Cecil. It changed my relationship with him and Elisabeth. I stopped working for the Collinses after I moved to Herefordshire. For a while, I was going up to London to make furniture and cupboards and all kinds of things for them, but I think it became apparent that I couldn't come up to London to do all this work and they probably found somebody else. After Cecil died, I occasionally saw Elisabeth and we had a meal together at various restaurants and the Chelsea Arts Club.

When he talked about painting, Cecil would describe how he would go to a different place in order to see something and bring it back, but it was in the act of bringing it back that he created it; brought it into being in the painting. There's that famous comment in one of the films where he said, 'Some pictures are in my mind and they're so complete that they don't need to be painted.' It was in the process of discovering and in the process of creation that he realised and recognised what it was.

That's the act of a Clematis, bringing a vision of a better future, of a different world into this reality. I don't know of anybody who did that more successfully than Cecil. In some of his pictures, you can see that it was as though he was intoxicated by what he'd experienced. I've got a couple of those pictures. One of them includes words something like 'blissful hours in the afternoon of the heart.' In this 1936 pen and ink drawing of a figure holding a staff, light is coming through the staff and water is springing from dry bones. It's as though he went from a sterile and hostile world, which is our ordinary reality, into this other space. It's not a world of the imagination; it is another space. It's a reality in which he saw things differently. Not that I'd make the link with C S Lewis and Cecil, but it's the place where Aslan sings things into being.

It's very hard to choose but, in my view, *Joy of the Worlds* (1937) is among Cecil's best work. There's another very powerful picture of an Angel with a spring of water flowing out from the side. I went to a lecture with slideshow and this picture was on a 35mm transparency that was projected onto a screen. The eye was about two foot across and there was this depth in the eye which appeared, to me, like a whole landscape. It's as if the background of the whole picture was in the eye. I asked Cecil, 'Is that possible?' He chuckled and said, 'Of course.'

Cecil used to say, not to me, but to other students who I heard it from, that he alone had recreated Rembrandt's wonderful techniques with glazing. I think it's a fair point because he coloured into the glaze and then repeatedly glazed and then painted on the glaze. These very complex layers gave a wonderful luminous quality. The fact that Cecil painted into the paint as much as he did meant that all kinds of things were in there, but weren't necessarily visible unless the light changed. If the light changed, or one's perception of the picture changed, then you would see things that might not be what he had consciously put in, but nonetheless were there.

There's a print of a head with coils all around it; a very powerful picture of the anima. I have a copy of this. It was part of a trade-off of work for photographs I had done. I said, 'I want one of these,' and he said, 'Are you sure? Not everybody can live with this picture. People have been known to think they like it and then bring it back because they couldn't live with it.' But I'm very happy. My kitchen is a very tall living space, and the print is in a very strong position. I love it. Blake says, 'To see the world in a grain of sand, and to see heaven in a wild flower,' I think that's what I received and understood from Cecil. What could be more important than for that message to be spread through the world? As the light darkens every day, one longs for anything that is like a message from home.

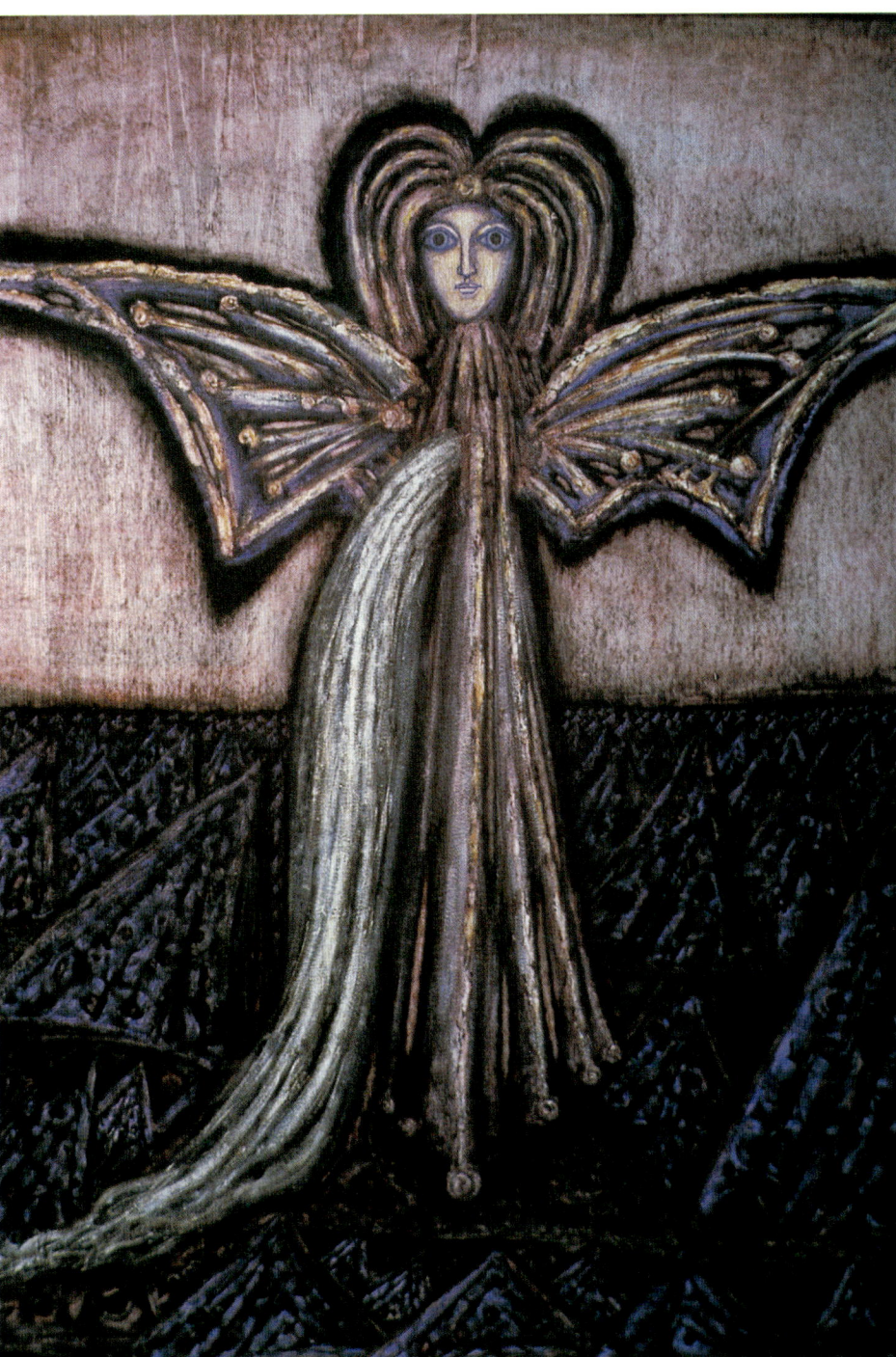

Cecil Collins
The Angel of the Flowing Light
1968
Oil on board
122 x 106cm

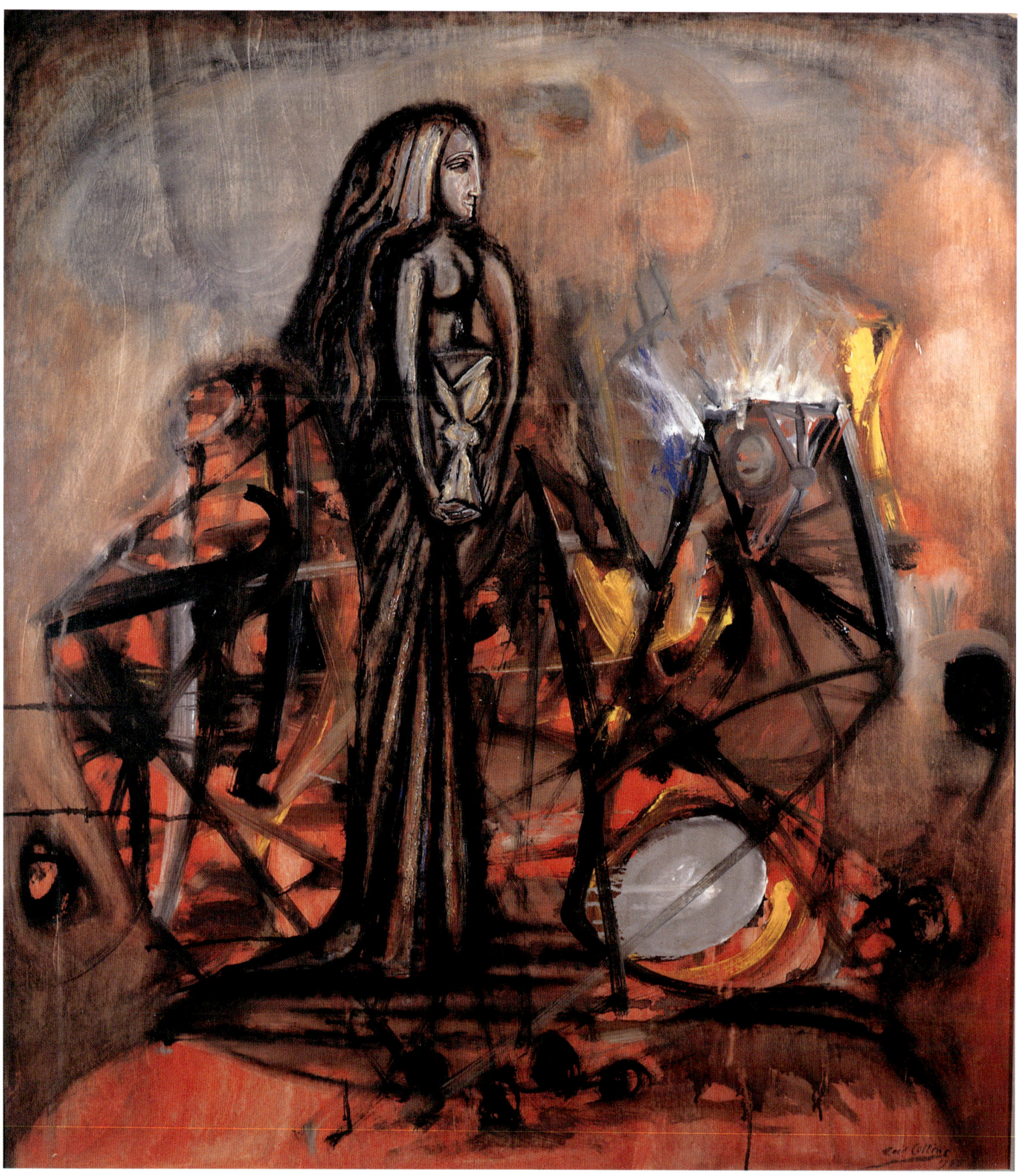

THETIS BLACKER

Born in 1927 and originally trained as a singer, Thetis Blacker appeared at Glyndebourne before retraining as an artist at Chelsea College of Art. She specialised in batik work which she learnt during Asian travels as a Churchill Fellow. Her flamboyant symbolic work was commissioned by cathedrals in the Britain, Europe and America, including Winchester, Durham Cathderal and St George's Chapel, Windsor. The University of Durham gave her an honorary D.Litt and she was an active Fellow of the Temenos Academy, founded in 1992 by her close friends, Kathleen Raine, Brian Keeble, Keith Critchlow and Philip Sherrard. She died in 2007.

For fifty years I was both a singer and a painter. I'd painted from the age of twelve and had some very good teachers. In the 1960s I began to paint more and it took over from the singing. I was earning more as a painter and also, as a painter anything you think is no good can be thrown into the wastepaper basket. That's a great luxury singers don't have.

I was introduced to Cecil Collins and David Jones by Kathleen Raine at a memorable dinner she gave in the summer of 1960. A year earlier I had been enchanted by Cecil's work at his Retrospective in the Whitechapel Gallery. I had felt that I recognized the figures of Angel, Fool and Woman in his magical, dream-like paintings. It was as if they were known in my heart, but forgotten ages ago and I was profoundly moved. I had longed to meet the artist so it was wonderful for me that it happened. At that time, Cecil was staying in Kathleen's house for his teaching days at the Central and returning each week to Cambridge where he lived with his wife, Elisabeth. Eventually, they bought a long lease from Kathleen, who owned the freehold, and moved into the top two floors of her house.

Cecil began to teach me privately when I moved to Glebe Place, not far from Kathleen's house in Paultons Square. I was surprised to find that he did not impose his art-style on his student, but on the other hand, he didn't bring out one's intrinsic voice as it were. He opened his own world and said, 'You can come in if you like,' but he never entered one's own imaginative world. In fact, he was not the least bit interested in anybody else's world.

We spent a lot of time together talking about painting, about the technique and the vision which manifested in a picture. He would bring records round to play on my gramophone and we would listen to them together and he would then go on a kind of imaginative journey. He gave me the palette of paints I should use and I've still got the list which included raw umber. He showed me how to mix colours with his secret methods, then we painted a picture together. He started and did five minutes, then I continued for another five, then he did and so on. We timed each other. He said that if we didn't like what the other one had done, we could paint it out. By the end of the picture, he'd painted out everything I'd done except two little knobs on a fool's head.

When I first met Cecil, I was amazed and intoxicated by his glorious, romantic, beautiful vision. After a while, I found that I was painting Fools and Women and Angels all the time. Maurice Collis came to see me and said, 'Your friendship with Cecil Collins is not doing your career as a painter any good. It's time you broke away from his influence.' I listened to what Maurice said because he was a good friend and a wise man. I looked at what I'd done and realised that it wasn't good.

In those days, I was young and good looking. I was in my early thirties; he was coming up to sixty. Cecil and I saw a lot of each other, but Cecil became terribly possessive and so demanding that, in the end, I felt I just couldn't stand it. He would come in the morning at nine o'clock and sometimes stay till midnight. I would have to feed him and pay for everything.

There is a great big, flaming oil painting of a woman called *The Eternal Bride*, from 1963, which was on the cover of his Tooth Gallery exhibition catalogue. For him, it was one of his best. He took me round the show and said, 'This is a portrait. This is an image of your immortal soul.' I looked at it and didn't think it worked as a picture. It was partly abstract, partly figurative, and the woman had an awful sterility about her. She had the profile of Elisabeth who, at that time, I wrongly thought was terribly hard and cold. I said to him, 'That is not a portrait of my immortal soul. My immortal soul does not look like that.' The whole of the middle looked like a female vulva. For me, it was not a product of a purely spiritual vision. I admired his paintings enormously, but I felt that he had no right telling me what my soul looked like. After that, I didn't see him for a couple of months during the summer holidays.

Then one day, I went to dinner with Kathleen and he was there, just him and Kathleen and me. He said he'd walk me back home afterwards. No sooner had we got out of Kathleen's when he turned on me and said I was a traitor; I had betrayed the great gift of vision he'd given me. At first, I couldn't think what he was talking about and then I realised it must be because I had had the temerity

Cecil Collins
The Eternal Bride
1963
Oil on board
120 x 114cm

to criticise his painting. We walked via the little back streets to Glebe Place where I lived and he kept stopping and shouting at me about me being a Judas. People opened their windows and said, 'Shut up. Go away. You're disturbing us.' It was quite phenomenal. I didn't apologise. I had nothing to apologise for. I was amazed, but also thought it was completely insane. Even though I was thoroughly fed up with him and his demands on my time, I was very sad because, after that, he cut me out of his life. He treated me as if I was an amiable acquaintance. He loved admiring one from afar. For him, a woman was either a cook and somebody who paid for everything or she sat on a pedestal. He liked to look upon one's body as an artist. He never would have wanted to do anything, but I think he liked to think he could have. In fact there were other people in my life, handsome young men for whom I had genuine feelings. At that age, one's got dozens of friends. Some of them were admirers and some just plain friends and one would go out to dinner with them or go to exhibitions or the cinema or the opera.

When I first knew Cecil, he'd been through a very productive time in the run-up to the 1959 exhibition at the Whitechapel Gallery. Some of his best paintings were in that exhibition, his huge, wonderful abstracts. After that, I don't think he ever did anything that equalled them. What he didn't realise was that these paintings were the finest he'd ever done. Bryan Robertson who ran the gallery and who, I think, was the best assessor of Cecil's work, agreed and thought they were extremely good. Later, Cecil went back to the more figurative work which wasn't quite so successful. When he had that huge Retrospective at the Tate, Judy Collins and Richard Morphet went along with his choice; he didn't want any of his abstracts there. That's why the Tate exhibition wasn't as powerful as the one at the Whitechapel. I think where Cecil is concerned, his energy went into his Vision and in those great abstract paintings, there was real power. He then did the mixed abstract and figurative ones like the woman in the fiery furnace he called *The Eternal Bride* which he thought was absolutely marvellous and managed to persuade a lot of other people to accept his view.

He was very persuasive because his vision was so pure and wonderful. He had such a lot of contradictions, but everything was knitted together with his terrific sense of fun and humour. He could be, at the same time, both witty and profound. He could transform a situation and startle or delight one with a flash of insight or a quip. Once when I was singing at Glyndebourne, Cecil was taken for a tramp because he'd come on his own to the opera and his picnic consisted of a ham sandwich out of a brown paper bag and a bottle of beer. There he sat, huddled inside his shabby and musty old coat, amidst the elegant guests in their black ties, dinner jackets and evening dresses and, of course, he caused consternation. A flustered usher rushed in to alert the front-of-house manager with whom I'd been talking and I followed out when he went to deal with this intruder. Luckily, I was able to forestall any unpleasantness by giving Cecil a hug and introducing him as one of Britain's greatest living painters.

During the 1960s, when Cecil really was not being appreciated, I went round making out that I was a kind of connoisseur. I would say to a number of people, 'I'm an art adviser and I'm thinking of suggesting Cecil Collins. Do you stock his work?' They would say, 'Yes, one or two,' and then I would chat them up. I'd say, 'He's now got some marvellous stuff and one of my clients might be interested, but it would be better if we bought through you.' Then I got a friend to dress up and pretend to be a very rich client. What we did was just make the galleries aware of him. I thoroughly enjoyed doing it. I managed to get him an exhibition at Tooth's as a result, I'm sure.

One day he was sitting in my flat when my mother and her sisters came to call. I must say they did look like three crows, upper middle class ladies all wearing black hats and coats with very prim accents and prim clothes. When they came into the room, he was sitting in the best armchair and he never even got up. He just looked over his shoulder and talked to them as if they were intruders. I was so under his spell, this was fairly early on, that I thought how amazing that he can treat my mother in this way. They were absolutely horrified and left very soon afterwards. They hadn't got a good word for him because he had been frightfully rude.

Later, Cecil and my mother met at a conference and got on like a house on fire because they talked about the efficacy of prunes for breakfast. After that, my mother was always very amused by Cecil and disregarded his ill manners as just being part of his artistic eccentricity. His rudeness had no long-lasting effect, but he must have behaved in exactly the same way to Elisabeth's family. Elisabeth also came from an upper middle class well-to-do family in the north and Cecil came from an absolutely humble background. She told me he was foul to her parents. In the end, she had to decide, them or him, and she chose Cecil. She renounced all her cultured background and all her beautiful furniture.

The faces of all Cecil's women always looked like Elisabeth. From Cecil's paintings it was obvious that he saw her as very beautiful but, for me, Elisabeth never equated in any way with my idea of beauty. I thought she looked bizarre with this head that wobbled all the time and those enormous hats and those protruding eyes and long nose and deep voice and sallow, leathery skin and extremely thin body. Also, I never thought she looked feminine. I always thought she looked extremely infertile.

I always liked Elisabeth's work and thought she was a much better painter than people gave her credit for. When I was signed

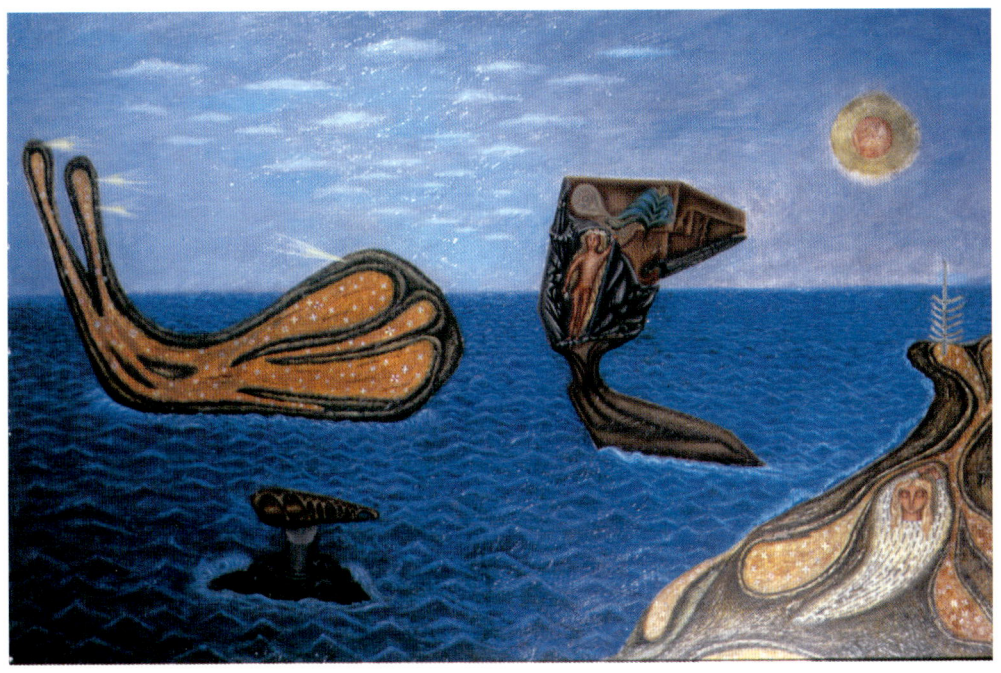

Cecil Collins
Virgin Images in the Magical Process of Time,
1935
Oil on Wood
74 x 114cm

up to show at the Fortescue Swan Gallery just by the Brompton Oratory, I introduced Oliver Swan, who ran the gallery, to Elisabeth and got him to sign her up. She showed there months before I did and those paintings were the best she ever did. They were done on newsprint so they've gone very brown. I've got a couple of them and I think they're really lovely, but neither Cecil nor Elisabeth ever acknowledged I'd done anything to help. When people denigrated Elisabeth's work, I always stood up for her because I thought she drew frightfully well so I think she stored that up in her memory. I got one after she died which was my inheritance, as it were. It's some kind of lovely animal. I like the simplicity of it and the muted colours. Elisabeth had a much better sense of colour than Cecil. His were sometimes apt to go to rather lurid purples. That show of Elisabeth's was almost completely sold out. Her prices were reasonable which, of course, Cecil's weren't apt to be. I also introduced her to Jane England of the England Gallery. I was awfully glad that Elisabeth had that final flowering of her work and that the England Gallery showed her, but I thought the pictures chosen for her posthumous show there were not good ones.

It was a doomed project for the Collinses to be living in the same house as Kathleen. I loved Kathleen and I loved Cecil and Elisabeth, but I could never have shared a house with any of them, They were far too strong and demanding. I got so fed up with the ridiculous feud between Kathleen and Elisabeth which was prolonged entirely by Elisabeth. Kathleen never appreciated Elisabeth's work and did make very dismissive remarks about it which were unfortunately repeated by someone to Elisabeth. I thought Kathleen was very silly and naughty not to appreciate it more, but she adored and worshipped Cecil because he knew exactly how to talk to her. He was good with her parents too when they spent their last years in her house. Every day he talked to them comfortingly and amusingly. He was always kind and helpful with anyone who was unhappy or in pain. What was interesting was that there was Kathleen in that house with Cecil above and Winifred Nicholson in the basement. Winifred and Cecil were so unalike and yet I don't think they ever crossed swords.

I think they all respected one another's work, but what Kathleen didn't realise was this phenomenal parsimony which both Collinses suffered from. Cecil never paid for anything, not even his own beer, and never got a round. He once bought me a ham salad at a pub in the King's Road. That was the only time he ever gave me a return for the dozens, if not hundreds, of meals he had off me. He was very generous in other ways, though, as he gave me the painting lessons also poems, drawings, lithographs, as well as paintings.

I often used to have Elisabeth to lunch. She was one of those lovely friends to whom you could say, 'If you have nothing else to do, come and have lunch.' She'd always come and she would occasionally say, 'I've been to you so often, I must ask you back,' so she'd take me to Thierry's restaurant in the King's Road. We'd sit there and have a nice meal, but she'd never ask for the bill until one had to get going. 'Let me help,' I'd say and she'd say, 'How kind of you,' and pass the bill to me. This happened again and again until I never wanted to have a meal with her because it meant I paid. Finally I thought, I'm jolly well not going to pay this time. As I've got nothing to do all afternoon, I'll sit it out. Anyway, the bill came. They brought it because we were the last in the restaurant and I made no attempt to pay. Eventually I thought, we're going to be here all afternoon so I gave her a kiss and said, 'Elisabeth, how sweet of you to take me out to lunch. So sorry I've got to go. Will you be able to get home?' She did have to pay that time, but the next time I saw her, there was the most frightful hullaballoo about how she was nearly knocked over crossing the road and I'd left her there all alone.

Elisabeth was mean but, after she died, to our amazement, we found she'd left her various friends, more or less the same kind of thing, apart from Jonathan Stedall who, of course, got everything. She left me one of Cecil's pictures which I was allowed to select, a legacy of money and a piece of her beautiful jewellery. We were able, I and her other friends, to choose from her jewel box. I was astounded because apparently I was third on the list. There was a hierarchy which I had never realised.

I do feel that Cecil's work is much more variable in quality than he would admit. He believed that the world of the imagination was more real than the material tangible world and he guarded this sacred kingdom of the heart unexpectedly fiercely for such a gentle and charming man. For him, every line he drew, whether on a napkin or a scrap of paper was, as it were, drawn by the hand of God. His pictures at their best were icons, channels of divine grace, but I don't think he was at all critical of his own work. Looking back, I feel sorry for him because I know the agony that one goes through when the imagination isn't working. It isn't just that you do bad work; you can't work at all. I was astounded that Brian Keeble considered the drawings in Cecil's notebook were so wonderful. I would have put them on the bonfire if they'd been mine and yet when Cecil thought he'd lost that notebook, he was beside himself. To my mind, I felt those drawings were poor and did his reputation no good at all when they were reproduced in the book Brian Keeble published, whereas the writings, the aphorisms and other things in it are charming and delightful and full of wisdom.

I was always sad that Cecil behaved as if Stanley Spencer didn't exist 'Oh, he goes his way,' I think is what Cecil said about him. When Spencer, who was even more eccentric than Cecil and a superb painter and an amazing visionary, had an enormous exhibition at the Royal Academy and then another one at the Tate, Cecil didn't want to know about it. He thought that his world was the world and that is why he couldn't accept somebody like Stanley Spencer whose angels and figures of resurrection were so beefy and round and there were these great, huge, fleshy women.

Everyone, of course, compared Cecil with Blake which always annoyed him because he said Blake wasn't a patch on him. The painter whose vision I think really did have something in common with his was Samuel Palmer. The person he really felt threatened by was Picasso. Cecil felt perhaps that he should have been more feted than Picasso. Cecil couldn't understand why he was so famous and so prolific. His view of Francis Bacon was, I always thought, rather funny. He used to tell me that Bacon had said of one of Cecil's paintings, 'If only I could have painted that picture.'

It has to be faced that Cecil was physically deformed; therefore he knew that he couldn't compete with other men. That's why he was so jealous of all those charming Guards officers who used to take me out in the old days because they were proper men. Cecil had this awful hunched back and pigeon chest, as well as a cleft palette. He had to compensate for this by having a realm that was his alone in which he-men didn't compete. They didn't exist; they didn't figure, but beautiful women who inspired him did. He created holy Fools who were completely unthreatening to himself and to everybody else. There was, therefore, a whole element that was compensatory in Cecil's work and that is why he couldn't bear to have it threatened. If his visionary world was exploded, he would have felt that he had

nothing left at all. Of course, it wasn't quite that simple because his realm of the imagination did become a reality in which we could participate. He saw everything in his own way.

I loved to go for walks with him. He'd look up at the clouds and say, 'Oh look at the angel. Look at that trumpet there,' and that angel's trumpet would be an aeroplane stream. Then there'd be a chugging boat going along the Thames and we'd look down over the bridge and he'd say, 'Look at that boat of fools taking them to where they hopefully want to go.' You'd look down and see these round faces looking up and they all looked like Cecil's paintings. It was like when you went to Cookham and looked at Stanley Spencer's pictures. When you came out, everybody looked like the people in his paintings. That was exactly how Cecil made one see everything in his terms. It really awakened an awareness of this other dimension in the natural world. His imaginary landscapes were enchanting: his trees, his hills, his rivers. He could so easily have done pictures of Albert Bridge and the ship of fools. I found it so curious that he didn't do anything from nature and yet I feel he could have if had he wanted.

I introduced Cecil to the Centre for Spiritual and Psychological Studies, a society run by Alison Barnard. I said to her, 'He'd give such marvellous lectures, very spiritual.' I asked Kathleen, who was involved with the Centre, to persuade him because he was very reluctant. He said to me that he didn't really want to go back to speaking because his rational mind was so much at war with his visionary mind and he had reached the point in life when he didn't really want to use words any more. I said, 'Poo-bah! You're so good with words,' He said, 'No, I don't think you realise what my dilemma is,' but Kathleen and I persuaded him to give a lecture and he was so good; everybody loved him. Afterwards, it became a major thing in his life, especially as the society not only paid for him and Elisabeth, but he also got them to pay for many of his students too. At that time, I was earning terribly little myself so when they had these foreign jaunts I was a little miffed because I couldn't always afford to go.

Once, we did go to France together for a conference the Centre organized at the Benoît Prieuré, which was a very old monastery on the outskirts of Paris. It was like a little sanctuary in the suburbs. It was quite amazing. There were about fifteen of us, I suppose, including all my family and Cecil and Elisabeth. We spent about a week there. Cecil was terribly funny because he couldn't speak proper French, but he could imitate it and pick up words. It became completely surreal. He would talk about his *corsage sauvage* and *des corsages sauvages des lapins bicyclettes* or *des bicyclettes lapins* and all of these wonderful corsets being worn by rabbit bicyclists. He was in very good form and everybody adored it. It had me in stitches the whole time

PETER BOWLES

London born, Peter Bowles has had a long and distinguished career as an actor for stage, film and television and as a film producer. Among his many memorable roles were Richard DeVere in *To the Manor Born* and as Sir Guthrie Featherstone in *Rumpole of the Bailey*. He is married with three children and lives in London.

I have a great love of art and started to collect it in the early Sixties. This was because when our children were small and began to go to nursery school, my wife, Susan, became friends with another mother there, Lucy Rothenstein who invited us both over for tea. Lucy is the daughter of Sir John Rothenstein who was Director of the Tate Gallery. It was in her home that I saw my first paintings; my first Stanley Spencer which she had on her wall. Then I read about him and of course he's another visionary like Cecil, but his style of painting and everything is different. Spencer's vision is based on finding good and in his case also finding God in every aspect of ordinary life and in his local street too.

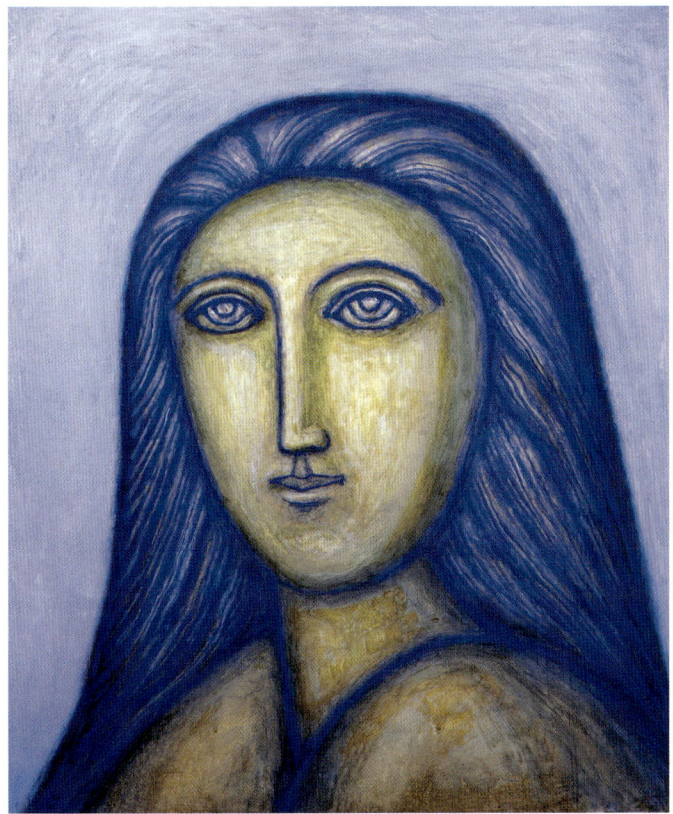

Cecil Collins
Head of an Angel
1987
Tempera
61 x 51cm

I first came into contact with Cecil's work on a visit to the Tate in the early Seventies and was very taken with *The Sleeping Fool*. I enquired about Cecil and discovered that he'd written *The Vision of the Fool*. It was out of print so I went to the Victoria and Albert Museum where they had a copy. I read it and was very taken by that as well.

I think I looked him up in the telephone book and phoned him and he invited me round to Paultons Square where he was living. He welcomed me in and we got on immediately. He had a nice sense of humour and it was very like mine. I was very poor in those days, but I was very keen to buy something of his and he showed me a selection of works. There was a painting, of the Angel Gabriel and Adam, a large oil, that I liked very much and he said it would be £800. I said, 'Can I pay you £50 pounds a month?' and he said, 'Yes.'

In the painting Gabriel has got his arms outstretched and it has a big tree in it. I had it in my home and it was wonderful. When I got up in the morning, the first thing I did was to go and look at it. It was quite a presence in my house. I paid Cecil fifty pounds a month for about eight months, but then I couldn't afford it any more so I told him and he said, 'That's all right. I've still got the money.' I was paying him in cash so he gave me back the cash and took the painting. It was sold about eight years ago for £28,000.

Then I met Peter Nahum who was a great fan of Cecil's; I used to see Cecil at Peter's sometimes. I became friends with Cecil and Elisabeth and used to go to their home, or more often, meet Cecil for a drink at the Chelsea Arts Club. I used to see him as often as I could.

I saw a side of Cecil which I don't know whether other people did, but I was very pleased to see it and that's why our friendship was so good. The main thing in our relationship was joking. We laughed a lot together and were unphilosophical companions. His outlook on life, I discovered, was rather like mine. He believed in goodness and the human spirit. He also believed that there was evil. We shared this belief as I've met both. We were similar in terms of how we looked at the goodness around us and how we believed in love and the spiritual side of life, though I wouldn't like to compare myself to Cecil. He was a great artist. That's why I think more people should know of Cecil's work and be affected by it, in the same way Samuel Palmer's paintings offer comfort and an inner peace. I've never compared Cecil to William Blake, but if people do, it's only a question of the word visionary, that's all. Cecil was a visionary painter. He painted from his vision of the world.

I was in my forties before I made a proper breakthrough and became well known. It was *To the Manor Born* that made me into a household name. When I met Cecil, I was a struggling actor. I felt frustrated and unrecognised and possibly he felt that too, but we didn't talk about it because he wasn't a moaner. If anything, he was a fighter. Even when he was really quite ill, he didn't complain. It was wonderful to be at the big Tate Retrospective. It was Cecil's moment of recognition, along with the MBE he was awarded towards the end of his life.

I acquired three of his paintings and was left a wonderful painting by Elisabeth when she died. One of Cecil's pictures that I have is a late work, *Head of an Angel*. All the knowledge and all the love of the world are within that painting. There's nothing like it. It's most moving and everybody who comes here is taken by it and says so, although to my frustration people who come to visit never say anything about my art collection. It's as if they don't see it, but everyone mentions how moved they are by that one. I've seen a great deal of Cecil's work and as that's one of the very last things he painted, he must have known he was ill while he was working on it. There's something extraordinary distilled within that painting.

LUCY CARTER

Daughter of Sir John Rothenstein, Director of the Tate Gallery (1937-1964), Lucy Carter studied painting at the Ruskin School of Drawing and Fine Art, University of Oxford. She is married to Simon Carter and they live in Somerset where she is a keen gardener and continues to paint. She was previously married to Lord Dynevor and has four children.

I studied fine art at the Ruskin in Oxford where I met Alexander Antrim with whom I set up picture restoring. We apprenticed with Helmut Ruhemann at the National Gallery who had been Chief Restorer at the National Gallery in Berlin. My father and Kenneth Clark managed to get Ruhemann out of Germany. Ruhemann set up this marvellous conservation studio at the National Gallery using chemical and photographic analysis. I would have liked to work in the Gallery, but if you've got four children, you can't. I worked from my studio home so I was there for my children while they were growing up and it's been lovely for me to do it like that.

My father loved painting when he was younger, but my grandfather rather put my father off from doing anything about it. My grandfather said, 'No, John. Don't think of being a painter. Michael's the one with talent.' My father was rather crushed by this. He went to Oxford instead, then did a degree in history of art at London University. There were very few places that did history of art in those days.

My father was a tremendous admirer of Cecil Collins. We used to go and see the Collinses when they lived in Selwyn Gardens in Cambridge. I've got a lovely picture I inherited from my father called *Wavell Trees* of a magical landscape. He would have bought more of Cecil's work, but if he wanted to purchase things, he always had to give the Tate first option so very often the things he liked were snapped up by the Tate.

When I visited the Collinses in Cambridge, there was a wonderful feeling of an art that was created and lived. I remember the calmness of their way of life and the beautiful things around them and a very serene atmosphere. It felt as if you were going into a lovely, spiritual place.

I was the Secretary of the Oxford Art Club when I was at the Ruskin. We were allowed to have a room at the Ashmolean and two of us could choose the artists we wanted to show. I organised an exhibition there of Cecil's work in 1953. I'd borrowed most of the show so there were only a few for sale. The sad thing is that he didn't sell anything. Cecil was fairly hard up at that time and I think it was a disappointment. Oxford was, in many ways, not very active about the visual arts. The Ashmolean was so grubby and dreary then.

I fell in love with this wonderful picture he painted in 1951 called *Hymn to Night*. I said to Cecil, 'When I have some money, I want to buy that.' When I got married and had some money, I rang Cecil up and said, 'Have you still got that painting?' and he said, 'No, I sold it yesterday.' By chance, I found out that Merida owned it. I went to see it recently and it was just as wonderful as I'd remembered.

When I couldn't buy *Hymn to Night*, I went to Cecil's studio in the early 1960s with my then husband, Richard. There were all sorts of marvellous things I would have loved to have bought, but Cecil wouldn't sell any of the pictures we wanted. They were his children and he didn't want to let them out of his sight. He was so wrapped up in his own world and I know other people have had the same problem, having to go and visit him often to get anything out of him. The result is that we both bought gouaches of seated Fools that neither of us deeply loved. We had them for about fifteen years before I sold mine and then Richard sold his in order to buy something else. We rather regret it now.

I also regret that we don't have any of Elisabeth's paintings. When I lived in London, I became good friends with some neighbours, Peter Bowles the actor and his wife, Susan, who are great admirers of Cecil and Elisabeth's work. In fact, I think it was coming to our house that opened Peter's eye to art. He's become a very clever collector with a very good eye.

I went to some of Cecil's exhibitions at Anthony d'Offay and it's good that he saw the excellence of Cecil's work, but I didn't think he had the best ones. Probably d'Offay's taste was different from mine, though I think it was very important for Cecil's career at that point.

STEPHEN CROSS

Stephen Cross writes and lectures on Indian and European thought and serves on the Academic Board of the Temenos Academy. A former documentary film-maker, in 1978 he produced for the Arts Council, *The Eye of the Heart*, the first film to explore the painting and ideas of Cecil Collins.

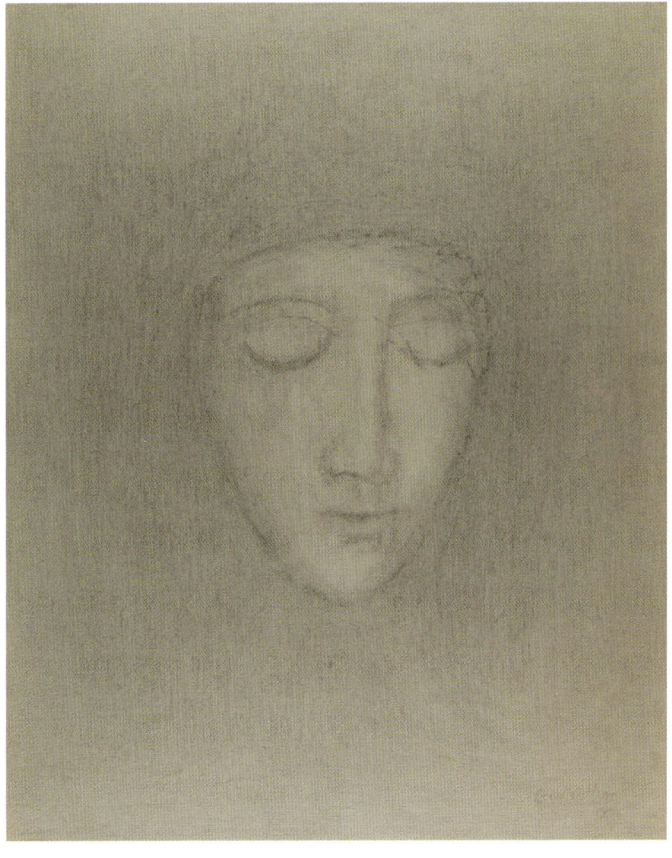

Cecil Collins
Head
1967
Pencil
30.5 x 23.8cm

I met my wife, Gay, through Cecil and Elisabeth and, as a wedding present, they gave us a copy of the *Kneeling Fool* which Cecil had etched the previous year, 1977. It is a very lovely and thoughtful image. I also particularly like some of the paintings he did in oil using thick glazes which hardly anyone does nowadays.

It was Kathleen Raine who suggested I should make a film on Cecil's work. I'd got in touch with her in 1972 after reading her book, *Defending Ancient Springs*, and I remember we were in her drawing room talking about Yeats. Somehow we got onto the subject of Cecil's paintings. Kathleen looked hard at me and said, 'You ought to think of doing a film about him.' This was a bit of a shock as I already had more than enough on my plate so I said something like, 'Yes, but there's plenty of time. I'll try to do it sometime in the future.' She replied, 'Don't leave it too long. People don't last forever.' She was a great support to Cecil for many years. They were comrades; they had a lot in common and fought for the same values.

I'd already been attracted to Cecil's paintings before meeting Kathleen when I saw his exhibition at Tooth's gallery in 1965; I've kept the catalogue with that splendid Sybil he'd painted two years before on the cover, *The Eternal Bride*. It's still one of my favourite paintings by Cecil. What I find extraordinary about it is that, perhaps unconsciously, it represents the force which in India is called *Shakti*, the great sacred feminine power or goddess which drives the world and keeps it going. Cecil painted the figure intuitively, as it came to him. She stands in her splendour, surrounded by those tremendous glowing creative energies swirling round her; it's a magnificent and profound painting.

I got to know Cecil and Elisabeth at a dinner given by Kathleen. They all lived in the same house in Paultons Square. Kathleen was downstairs and they were upstairs. I was making a film on Odilon Redon at the time and Kathleen had told me that Cecil loved Redon's work so there was plenty of common ground between us and we hit it off right away. I found Cecil was very easy to get to know. He had this attractive sense of humour which would break through now and then. It's one of my regrets that I wasn't able to capture more of this side of him on film.

The film about Cecil was made about five years later. Like the Redon film, it was produced for the Arts Council of Great Britain. Initially, they weren't too keen on a film about Cecil. No film, television presentation or major book had appeared on him previously and I think they regarded him as a bit of a romantic, not the latest thing in British painting. It was similar to the BBC; there is a tendency to wait until an artist is almost a household name before doing a programme on them. What they should be doing, of course, is helping to discover him. I remember asking Alan Bowness about Cecil while I was researching Redon at the Warburg Institute. He is very perceptive and I thought he might back the idea of a film, but his answer was a surprising one. Although he thought that Cecil had created some good paintings, he said, 'Basically he doesn't produce enough.'

Then quite out of the blue, I had a letter from Kenneth Clark who had seen my series, *The Traditional World of Islam*, on the BBC and had understood that it was trying to do for the Islamic world what his own series, *Civilisation*, had done for Europe a little earlier. His letter was very kind and generous and came just at the moment I needed to get some backing for the film so I wrote to ask him what he thought of Cecil's work. He replied that Cecil Collins was the most neglected British artist of his generation and that some of his paintings can be compared to those of Rouault which was a very acute observation as you would expect of Clark. I was able to pass his letter on to the Arts Council and I think that this, together with the fact that the film on Redon had been having some success at festivals, finally tipped the balance and they financed the film.

I tried to get some of Cecil's own ideas and creativity into *The Eye of the Heart* and to make it as much as possible Cecil's own film, as if he were making the film, with me as an instrument. I found him very easy to work with, not controlling at all, so I felt free to make the film any way I wanted. When you're making a film about an artist, you're very fortunate if you have him or her still alive and willing to work with you.

For example, we had a short sequence in which figures from Cecil's paintings appear briefly, as if they'd come to life. It was done in the setting of the gardens at Biddulph Grange, with their almost surrealist Egyptian topiary pyramid. The theatre designer, Claire Lyth, did the costumes for this, but the imagery for them came from Cecil's work. Near the start of the film there's a great open book lying on ground on the pages of which living eyes appear. Gay reminded me they were my eyes which I'd forgotten. This mysterious image was Cecil's idea. Similarly, the music used in the film reflects Cecil's sensibility. Music was very important to him. His taste was very wide, ranging from Stockhausen, with whom he had some personal acquaintance, to Lili Boulanger and the deeply romantic music of Humperdinck's *Hänsel and Gretel*. The music of Lawrence Ball used for parts of the film was suggested by Cecil.

While I was preparing for the film, I had the wonderful experience of Cecil showing me the paintings he still had in his possession. I went up to his extraordinary room at the top of the house. He had several big wooden racks at the back of the room with dozens and dozens of paintings. I suppose he was hanging on to them for the big exhibition that every artist hopes for and which, fortunately, Cecil eventually had at his Tate Retrospective in 1989.

We were up there for hours as he brought out one after the other to show me. He talked brilliantly about his paintings because behind them lay a coherent world of ideas. As with poetry, good painting grows out of insight and profound thought which was obviously underlying Cecil's work. It was fascinating because he would talk about the paintings in a quite objective way, as if he hadn't done them at all. He certainly thought the paintings were of importance and that this should be recognised, but there wasn't any personal vanity in Cecil or any attempt to present himself as a great man or interesting personality. The very ordinary and even shabby way in which he dressed reflected this. I felt that what Cecil had to say helped to open up and enrich the paintings he showed me. I didn't find it limiting at all. You could still put your own interpretation on each painting; in fact, they had layers of meaning and could be seen in several different ways.

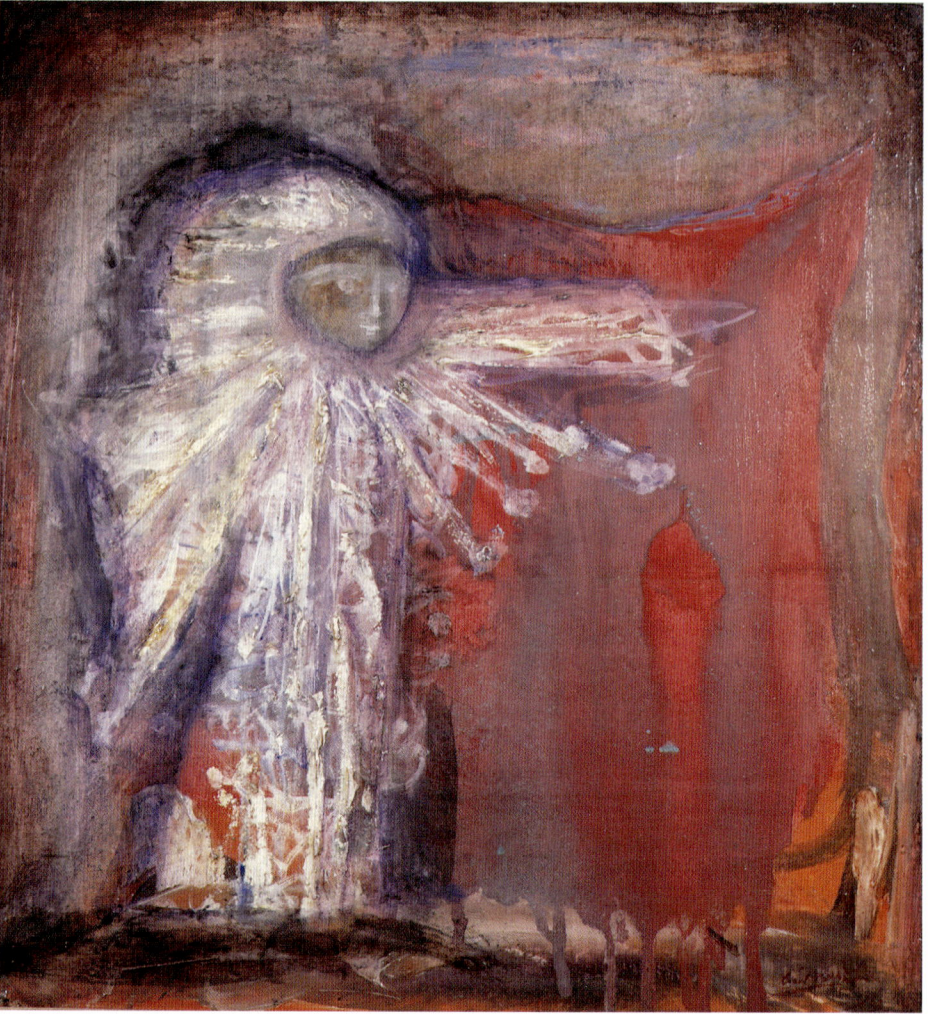

Cecil Collins
Angel and Fiery Landscape
1964
Mixed media on board
33 x 30.5cm

Later on, we were able to film Cecil as he was painting and I was also able to watch him doing so beforehand. Although he was aware of our presence, it didn't seem to bother him at all. He was absorbed by the way in which the emerging images had a life of their own as if they had an objective reality quite apart from him; he was only the medium through which they appeared. It wasn't a preconception he was now turning into a painting. It was something that he would allow to grow out of the actual motions of putting the paint on the canvas.

In preparation for the filming I drove down to Devon with Cecil and Elisabeth. We visited Dartington, which Cecil often used to talk about. They had stayed there for several years during the war and this had certainly been a good and creative time for them both. It is where Cecil had his vision of the blackbird singing in a tree which meant so much to him. It must have been a very interesting society. The Ballet Jooss Company was at Dartington for some of the time which, no doubt, kept things fairly lively. The American painter, Mark Tobey, was also there. Cecil regarded him as a very creative influence on his own work, but I never succeeded in getting him to tell me as much as I'd have liked about Tobey. Another person who came to Dartington was Arthur Waley, famous for his books about Chinese thought and for his marvellous translation of *Monkey*. Elisabeth had an amusing story about him. In spite of his knowledge of the civilisation, he had never actually been to China. Someone asked him if he wouldn't like to do so. 'Oh, no!' Waley replied at once. 'That would spoil it all.'

Cecil had some good stories too. One was about Herbert Read, the great authority on modern art during the post-war years. It was said of Read, Cecil told me, that he was present at the birth of every new movement, but absent at the funeral!

Dartington held happy memories and on the way back Cecil's rather mischievous sense of humour made its appearance. We were passing through Dorset and a series of impressive double-barreled place names were coming up: Grimstone Stratton, Alton Pancras, Melbury Osmond and others. 'Ah,' said Cecil with a twinkle in his eye, 'what splendid names for a successful career as a painter.' He was well aware of the little tricks that painters use to promote themselves and of their shortcomings too.

There were periods when Cecil didn't paint much, but I think this was more out of laziness than depression. In fact, I never saw him in deep depression though he may have suffered from such periods earlier in life. I once sent him a postcard of a drawing by Daumier entitled *Artists at Work*. It shows an open landscape with four or five painters and their easels scattered around. No one is working. The artist in the foreground is fast asleep on the ground and the others are lazing around in various ways. Cecil, with a faintly rueful smile, admitted that it was spot on.

On another occasion we went to Buckinghamshire to see the little cottage where Cecil and Elisabeth once lived; there's a photo of them there in the film. It was only a few miles from the property which Eric Gill had at that time when he was at the height of his success and surrounded by disciples and students. Cecil made a few visits to him, but was a much younger, relatively unknown and very poor artist. One has the impression he was treated pretty much as an outsider. I'm sure Cecil would have appreciated Gill's art and the metaphysical ideas behind it, but probably not the personality and life-style. I think Cecil had reservations about him. When we visited the place for the film, it looked like a deserted farm. There were stone cuttings lying around in heaps and you could still pick up fragments with Gill's splendid lettering on them. Cecil stood there and gazed around him and said rather sadly, 'Look, it's all come to this.'

Cecil told me that if he walked in the evening past the cottage near his own in which Edmund Rubbra, the composer, lived he would hear Rubbra tapping away at the typewriter. Cecil said, 'Writing letters to important people'. One sensed that this sort of self-promotion was not something Cecil was very good at and that he suffered as a result. He told me how he traipsed round London once with a suitcase full of paintings to try and get a gallery show, but with no success. There are photos of Cecil where he looks as if he's trying to be the serious artist, complete with beard, but he was much more interesting than this adopted persona.

I think, at times, he desperately needed Elisabeth's support. Without her, I'm not too sure what would have happened to him. He seems to have had a bad time in the 1950s and 60s when they lived in Cambridge. He told me once, 'If I'd stayed in Cambridge, I'd have died as an artist.' I think when they moved to London and came into contact with Kathleen and other like-minded people, it was a kind of return to life for him.

While I was making the film, Elisabeth was always there, but in the background. She was supportive, but she didn't contribute ideas; she left it all to Cecil. She was very discreet and very much her own person. She wasn't humble; on the contrary, I think she was rather proud. She was a talented artist in her own right and there is no doubt she sacrificed her career for Cecil after they met at the Royal College. In a way, he was her work of art. I once asked her why she hadn't painted more herself and she simply said, 'Two artists in the same family? It would never do!' Yet in spite of this she never ceased to be an artist in a private sort of way. There was some sharing of the imagery too and it's possible that the figure of the Fool originated with Elisabeth, although it's hard to be sure. After Cecil's death, she did some lovely paintings and had several successful shows.

When I first knew Cecil, he'd been teaching at Central School for quite a few years. His one reliable friend and ally among the staff was the late John Allitt, otherwise the place was in the hands of Modernists and Minimalists. Cecil was very much the odd person out with quite a different set of values. *The Vision of the Fool* isn't exactly a Minimalist manifesto! I think a number of the students valued him for that very reason. They were interested in representational art again and in the life of the soul. He used to say the Modernists were in deep trouble because suddenly they were not modern any more. There were several attempts to get rid of Cecil by retiring him and he relished the fact that every time the students would rebel in his favour and save the situation. It was encouraging for him to find this support among the young. They seemed to be undercutting the very people who'd dominated the arts during most of his lifetime. 'What's their favourite word?' I remember him asking me about the emerging generation. 'What is their buzz word?'

At the City Lit it was a different situation. There Cecil's ideas and teaching methods were always appreciated. By and large, I think at the time *The Eye of the Heart* was made, it helped Cecil to have a documentary supported by the Arts Council. He was certainly not unknown before, but the film helped because, soon after, Anthony d'Offay appeared on the scene. Having a powerful dealer behind him at last really put Cecil on the map. That was followed by William Anderson's excellent monograph on Cecil and the books published by Brian Keeble so it was a very positive period for him.

EYE OF THE HEART:
THE PAINTINGS OF CECIL COLLINS

Transcript of Film Commentary

My painting is a quest. My painting really is a theatre of the soul in which the life of the soul is re-enacted, the mystery of the soul is re-enacted, and the quest of the soul is re-enacted.

I think that the difference is that my face is turned towards the dawn, towards the rising sun. A great deal of the art of our time is dealing with negative things and merely mechanically reflecting the world as it is. I believe that there are two main groups of artists: the ones who are painting the decay, the end of civilisation, and these are the most popular of all because that is the line of least resistance, everybody can recognise it. There are perhaps very few whose face is turned towards the rising of the sun, who sense the beginnings of a new civilisation.

We are caught in a transitional period as I see it and that is why we feel so strange. Something old and dying is in us and something new is being born in us and we're stretched between the two. We have in us the Old Man, known under the zodiac sign of Saturn and we have in us also the Child; and this child is Vision.

I'm not really a teacher. I'm really an artist that comes and endeavours to share my creative experience with the students. That's very important. I find the climate now far more sympathetic and more real to me. I'm grateful to it and more happy now. When I was young, for example, one would be laughed at for mentioning the word God. One, in fact, was laughed at, but now young people understand this. Things that I've written thirty years ago are now things which they can read and understand and respond to. The whole climate of the world has changed. I believe my painting is understood by them more than by anyone and what they understand is this quest for the unknown.

After I left college I came in contact with Surrealism. I was immediately attracted to it because they had at least refused the status quo. They didn't accept this inhuman technological civilisation. They were the only people I knew who had rejected it as a whole. They were a movement, not just one of two individuals. There was an excitement about them and also the excitement of discovering some who at least shared one's rejection.

It was only later on that I saw their rejection was negative and not positive in the sense that they had nothing to offer in its place. When I discovered in my own art this presence of another world, which was always with me, it became clearer to me as it showed me that this world was absent from theirs. When I discovered, for example, that they believed, naively in my opinion, in an ideal society made politically and economically and also that they believed in modern psychology, Freud in particular, that they didn't have any sense of a reality transcending man or any real purpose, then I realised the truth about them and the difference between us. The difference between them and my own art was entirely in the question of a metaphysical reality, a reality which transcends man. Surrealism is really the Romantic Movement gone to seed and, in a strange way, they belonged to the nineteenth century. I mean Marx's optimism and Freud's pessimism is very much of the nineteenth century.

You see, in our age which has no form to its culture and no collective agreement, the best painters are idiosyncratic, individual. There are very good painters whom I admire, but I still feel lonely. I feel lonely with every kind of being that doesn't share this reality. I seek in my art to evoke in the human heart the mystery, which is life itself, so that one can realise the nature of life without definition because anyway there's no explanation for it.

There are roughly two ways I work. One way, I work with the pictures in my mind, inwardly, and I work every detail out beforehand. Sometimes, sitting in the bus or sitting in a train when I'm relaxed, I bring these pictures up as in a library and work on all the details. Now some of these pictures are so complete I know I'll never paint them; they are not necessary to paint any more. That's the danger of it.

What is interesting about it, of course, is when you have a picture in your mind, in your imagination, it is infinite and perhaps anyone can do that. It's when you come to manifest it in the world of limitations that the real problem comes. You're then up against what denies you, and what denies you is very important in creativity. If you have nothing to deny you, you can't create: it must resist you. I think that is the difference between a professional and an amateur artist, the amateur perhaps is the only one who enjoys painting; all the time, I mean. Because painting is beyond enjoyment. It's a strange process of birth, painful, often without any feeling whatsoever, yet at the

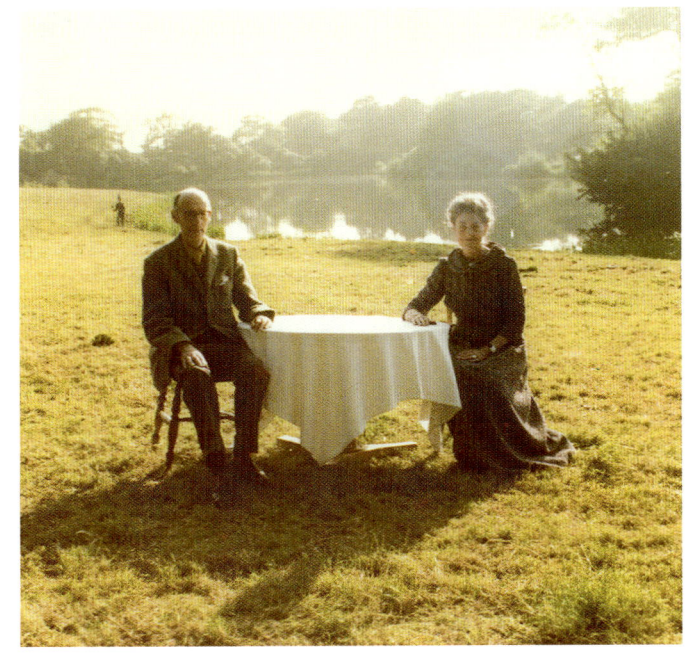

Cecil and Elisabeth,
Biddulph Grange Park,
Staffordshire,
from the film
The Eye of the Heart
Directed by
Stephen Cross
1978
(Arts Council of Great Britain)

end, it reveals itself. The child is born, as it were, and this miracle reveals itself. Sometimes, I only have feeling and joy after it's done, months after it's done, but certainly never when I'm doing it.

The other way I have of working is that I have no idea what I'm going to paint at all. I take the materials and I work the colours and the colours excite me; something starts to move inside of me, something starts to flow. I realise that all these pictures are already inside of me in the form of seeds, as in a garden, and the action of moving the paint, or some circumstances that's conducive, will make these seeds open inside of me and reveal themselves to me. The whole of the picture is a mystery to me, it unfolds under my very fingers, it surprises me. I must have that surprise; that surprise is to me the authentic note of a vision. Then I know that I didn't invent it, that it was born.

If we're dealing with the indescribable, it is quite obvious that we cannot define this reality, therefore it would be a waste of time to try and explain it. It's not necessary to understand in order to create, but it's necessary to create in order to understand. That is the way round it works. In other words, everything creative is this leap into the unknown and into the darkness. The stimulus that we have for the unknown is mirrored in certain images, very old images, very constant images, that come and go in the various cycles of history. For example, the Angel is not only a very old image, but it's very universal, you find it in every culture. And the Fool is the symbol of primal innocence, virginity of consciousness, which we've got to re-win again. I see all education that is real as a re-winning of this fundamental creative innocence, this virginity of spirit, this way of seeing directly as we did once as a child. The Fool is purity of consciousness, like the old Taoist saints, you know, that wandered through the world. It needs pure perception; it's what education should be about, but isn't.

The fundamental view of man, according to the great cultures, was that there existed a metaphysical reality from which everything had an origin and that this reality was reflected in an intermediary world of archetypal images, so that man, in his relative mind, could make contact with that which was absolute. If these archetypal images die away from man's consciousness he is left in the prison of the ego. The result will be fragmentation and lack of unity and madness.

Our civilisation is the only one not to be based on a metaphysical basis. It, therefore, could be considered abnormal. This, I think, is the root of the whole question. We have as a consequence a one-dimensional civilisation: one mode of thinking, linear and one mode of education, leaving out the metaphysical dimension in man. Look at modern architecture, it is merely a mental diagram, it doesn't come from the life of the psyche. That is why people feel so alone in modern cities; they are empty diagrams, merely rational. Modern architecture has no secrets. You cannot live with something which has no secrets.

The old idea that man had an archetype to live by and to live towards, as it were, is basic to all traditional art, of course, and it's basic to my art too. I believe that my art in its own lyrical way is fulfilling the same kind of function as traditional art. It is concerned with the transformation of man's consciousness. It's not self-expression: that, I think, belongs to a sentimental age which has lost a transcendental goal to live by and I think that the creative person is someone who is haunted by a perfection. The reflection of perfection in my painting takes the form of the anima, the soul, the psyche, which is in the form of a woman and this is, of course, an archetype which is very ancient.

The other archetype which has haunted me all my life is the Angel which represents an entirely different dimension of consciousness. It's the relationship of all these images, one with the other, that constitutes my painting in the context of things growing: flowers and trees, all images concerned with the giving of life.

I believe that the kind of art we shall need in the future is one that actualises the life of the soul. Man is never happy when the soul is latent and merely in a state of potential, but I have great hopes in the new generation. There is something different about them in that they realised we are becoming more and more ruled by vast mechanical, statistical bureaucracy, all dressed up as the public good. They see, some of them at least, that ultimately this must lead to the concentration camp.

I'm particularly interested in adult education and I think the kind of knowledge that we have today is unbalanced and lacking in equilibrium. There's another kind of knowledge: the knowledge of the education of the inner life, the emotions, the imagination and this is totally neglected. It seems to me that the real education of the human being today is the education of the emotions and of the imagination.

Cecil is shown teaching in class and addresses the students after they have listened and moved to music

It's like having lived through a whole lifetime; and that's what it should be. Remember what poised attention is; it's really being able to be present in one's being. To be present, really, is to be free, because this inner silence is something very fruitful.

We are all over-stimulated by mass triviality. All the time being stimulated, but what is not stimulated by us is the soul. It lies asleep and the psyche, like the body, needs food. Without food, this dimension dies. Here we come to the problem of beauty. Beauty is a knowledge, a gnosis, which feeds the psyche. It is not sensation. It is an actual knowledge that feeds the psyche. We need that food. Our civilisation needs that food.

You are pulled out of your habitual responses by doing this and in consequence the consciousness opens. Immediately it's un crystalised, it opens and there's an increase of sensibility. But if you are very much conditioned with all sorts of training and what not, you pre-judge experience, you decide beforehand what people are like, what drawing should be like. These people here don't decide beforehand. They are therefore virginal and, therefore, creative because to be creative

is to be vulnerable. That's what people never understand: if you're not willing to be vulnerable, you should give up the whole idea of creativity. There is one thing that we're certain about and that is that we're all surrounded by a profound mystery and in some strange way we are asked to participate in this mystery and to collaborate with it. It's the same with painting.

You see, the old legend about loss of paradise is correct, but we have to re-win this paradise and the second paradise is greater and richer than the first paradise. We know the reality of things when we lose them. It is the absence of the paradise that is the stimulus of all creation because that absence stimulates us to return to that paradise. All creation and all real art is the return to the paradise.

If one looks at the last seventy years, modern art has been working on revolt stimulus. Now that modern art has won its victory, and there is nothing more to revolt against, the energy has gone out of it and we have reached bankruptcy. This is a very important point to reach because now it's got to be the real thing; it's got to be life-giving. I believe that we are at the end of a cycle of civilisation and the beginning of a new one. There are some artists who are primitives of a new time whose faces are turned towards the dawn, towards the rising sun. I believe my art is that which faces the sun.

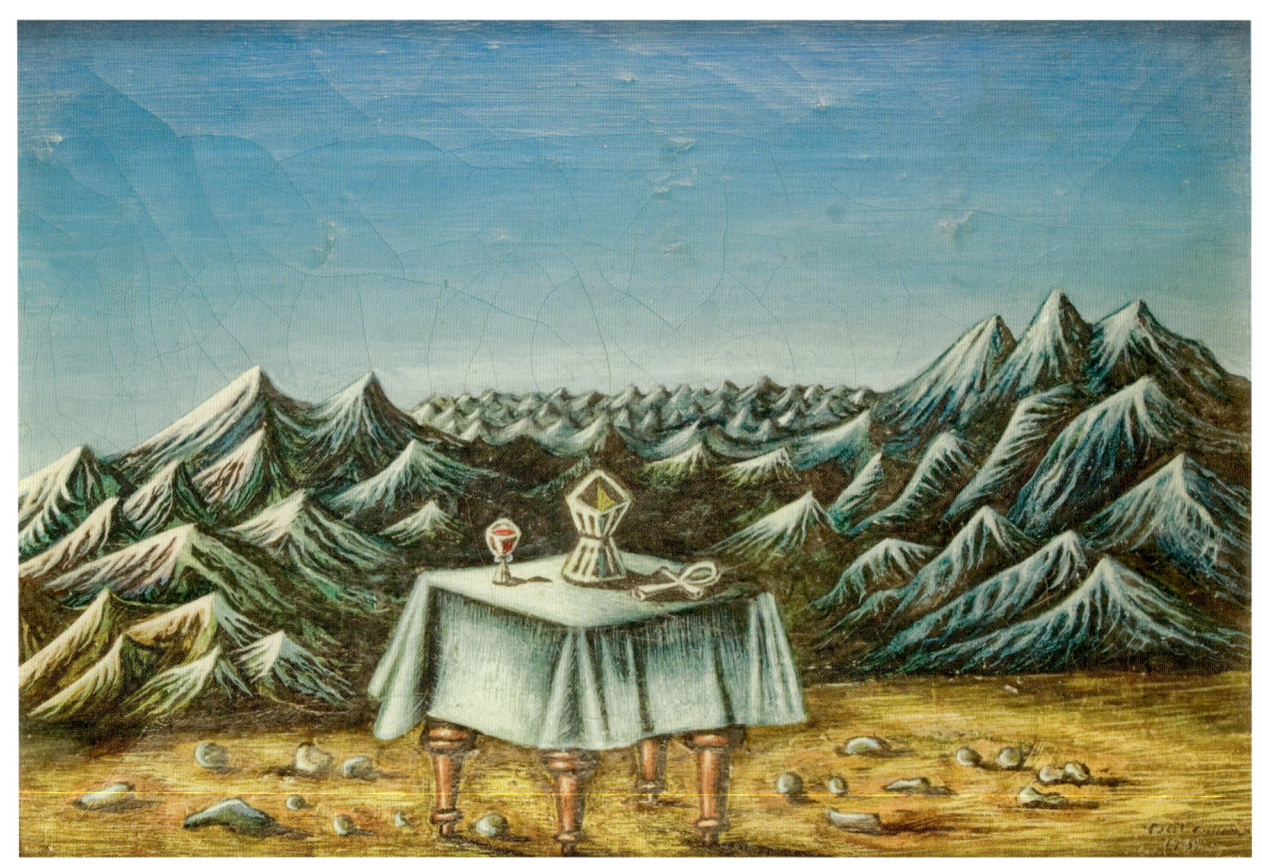

Cecil Collins
Dawn
1939
Oil on canvas
17.5 x 25cm

HELENA DRYSDALE

Helena Drysdale is the author of award winning travel and history books and family memoirs. She wrote and presented the TV documentary, *Dancing with the Dead*. She tutors for the Arvon Foundation and reviews non-fiction for The New Statesman and The Spectator and is currently a Fellow at Exeter University.

My parents were friends of Cecil and Elisabeth and I remember Cecil coming to visit us when I was a child. Once, when I was about eight, we sat on the front lawn and he taught me and my sisters, 'the dance of the fool' as he called it. It was just two steps back, one step forward so it was just a kind of jigging about. It wasn't important or interesting; it was just fun and very sweet that he did it. He used to prance around with us, his funny little feet dancing underneath his big shabby old coat. I remember also his rather badly shaven chin. He had this childlike quality so we loved him. We didn't see him a lot, only a couple of times perhaps, but as my mother had built him up we knew he was going to be somebody special and it was very exciting when he came.

In about 1981 when I was a student at Cambridge, Cecil came and gave a talk for the history of art faculty at Kettle's Yard which I'd organised. He stayed in Trinity College and made a huge fuss because there wasn't a decent heater in this rather gloomy guest room. By then he was quite old and it was all rather tricky. It had been a huge thing getting Cecil to come and then publicising it, getting people to turn up.

I remember going to see the administrator of Kettle's Yard to talk about arrangements for the event. He was very unhelpful and clearly didn't like Cecil's work. As I got to Kettle's Yard, the sky opened and there was a deluge of snow. Throughout the conversation he kept me standing outside in the snow with him looking out through a crack in the door. He never thought to say, 'Would you like to come in?' He soured the whole experience. I was very young and hadn't really organised it properly. Luckily, enough people came and it did work out in the end.

I wrote my dissertation on Cecil. I was only twenty at the time, so I was no expert, but I'd always loved his paintings, especially his *Hymn to Night* which my parents owned. We always used to think it was a portrait of my mother. It wasn't, but the woman in the centre of the picture looks quite like her. When I was doing my thesis, I went and saw Cecil at his flat in London and interviewed him and had tea with him and Elisabeth. Cecil took me down to his studio and we had a lovely time.

I went to his classes at the City Lit, but only four or five times. I found the whole thing absolutely fascinating. I'm not a practising artist, but found it quite liberating because there was no worry that my pictures would be awful compared with everybody else's. We were made to work with the brush between our teeth and our toes and that sort of thing so you can't be skilful. We were all on a level. That was the joy of Cecil really. Although he looked rather melancholy with his very long dangly, slightly jowly face, everything around him and with him was fun.

Later, I went back to see Cecil with Richard, my husband who also paints and also loves Cecil's work and we bought a little 1983 gouache on board from him. It's a little group of angels called *Blue Landscape Dawn* and certainly not a major work, but it's lovely. He must have left it lying around and you can see a trace of some newsprint or something that's been pressed onto it. Cecil got on very well with Richard who had a gallery at that time. I remember Cecil and Elisabeth coming to dinner with us in London and Cecil protested about sitting at the head of the table which had French windows behind him. They were double glazed and firmly shut, but he was really worried about the draught coming through. We kept reassuring him, but he wasn't convinced so we had to move him to another seat. He was frail and had been very poorly as a child, I believe, and was always anxious about catching cold.

I have a painting of Elisabeth's too. It's from her show in Albemarle Street which was a big success and everything was sold. It's called *Tiger in a Mountain Pool* from 1988. We were all so excited for her having thought, poor Elisabeth, she's going to fade away without Cecil, but she had this sort of resurgence after Cecil died. In fact, it was probably Cecil who wouldn't have survived without Elisabeth.

Elisabeth used to come to visit us wearing her wonderful hats and we thought she was very beautiful, but she was a more distant figure. She turned up unexpectedly once down in Devon where my mother has a lovely secluded house by the sea near Dartington. My parents were out. It was rather awful because we stared at her in a who-are-you sort of way, as children do. When my parents returned, I explained that a woman with a big hat had come and my mother thought it might have been Elisabeth and was horrified that we hadn't said 'please stay'. We were too young to realise and we hadn't remembered her. Cecil and Elisabeth had stayed there on an earlier occasion and had absolutely loved the beauty of the location.

Cecil had an enchanting story about staying there: he was standing in the woods above the sea and he looked down and saw a hare at his feet and suddenly realised that he was the hare and the hare was him. It was a very intense moment for him. He felt that had he been an animal, he would have been a hare.

MARY FEDDEN

Born in 1915, Mary Fedden, OBE, RA, studied at the Slade School of Fine Art (1932-1936). She married Julian Trevelyan (1910-1988) in 1951 and became the first woman to teach painting at the Royal College of Art (1958-1964). Since 1950, she has exhibited annually and received several mural commissions. Her work is in numerous public and private collections and she continues to paint every day.

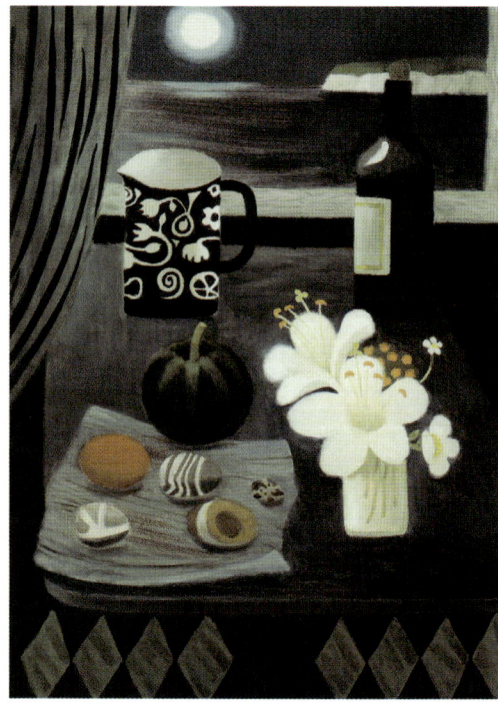

Mary Fedden
Irish Lillies
2006
Oil on canvas
90 x 69 cm

I was looking out of a window upstairs at the Slade and I said to a friend, 'Who's that man?' He said, 'He's called Julian Trevelyan,' and I said, 'I'm going to marry him,' and eventually I did. Julian and I set up in 1949 and we were married in 1951. I met Cecil through Julian. He was Julian's friend very early on, before Julian and I were together. They both exhibited in the Great British Surrealist Exhibition in 1936.

I liked Cecil, he was a sweet man and also an eccentric old thing. He was an incredibly nervous fellow and terribly fussy about his health and worried all the time about himself. I remember he wouldn't go out into the garden without putting on his hat and his overcoat and his muffler in case he got a cold draught, even on a nice day. We'd wander out into the garden and he'd say, 'I must just get my coat.'

Cecil was also very funny and quite giggly. He loved jokes. We both loved seeing him. He used to come to lunch and supper, that sort of thing. He used to tell us the most extraordinarily funny stories and yet they didn't seem to fit in with his character. Julian found him particularly amusing because of these wonderful dotty stories which came pouring out.

Cecil was a very egocentric man. He was really only interested in his own work. The Fool was his sort of standard. He was a very interesting painter because he was the only one of his kind. Julian loved his work. I liked his painting because it was so bizarre. What fascinated me about him was that he was quite religious and he used to pray before he started painting and yet he used to tell these naughty stories.

I remember going to Paultons Square. Kathleen Raine lived on the ground floor and she had a terrible quarrel with Elisabeth. She had the ground floor rooms and Cecil and Elisabeth lived upstairs; we had to creep past her door to go and visit them. I don't know how they could all live in the same house; it must have been misery to have people on the ground floor and upstairs who were not on speaking terms.

Elisabeth became Cecil's slave. She hardly painted at all. She was a good painter and she would have liked to have painted all the time. I remember her saying to me, 'Cecil doesn't let me paint,' or, 'He's very demanding and he thinks I'm wasting his time if I paint,' or something quite unkind.

Julian and I had a studio each. At lunchtime we used to look at each other's work and see what we'd done, but we never worked in the same room. I had a much smaller room than Julian's, with an etching press, but it was quite big enough to work in. We interested each other. He quite liked my painting, but if I'd painted something that he thought was wrong or not very good, he made it quite clear. It was very helpful. I used to say, 'But that's exactly what I meant to do,' rather crossly, but then I usually did what he said and he was always right. He was a very good critic.

I also made comments about his work. He used to say, 'That's ridiculous,' but then I found he'd done it in the end. We helped each other a lot.

It always amazed me that Cecil and Elisabeth were married because they were so different. I thought they were the most ill-assorted pair. Elisabeth was charming, but she was quite formal, upper crust, a rather classy, conventional lady and Cecil was so much the opposite, so bizarre and dotty. She was an unsuitable partner for him, yet somehow they seemed to get on well and obviously they loved each other.

KITTY HAUSER

Kitty Hauser is a historian of visual and material culture who has written for publications including the New Left Review, the Burlington Magazine, and the London Review of Books. Previously a research fellowship at Clare Hall, Cambridge University, she has also taught at the London College of Fashion and the Ruskin School of Drawing and Fine Art, Oxford. She is currently Research Fellow at the University of Sydney.

I was involved with the big Retrospective Stanley Spencer exhibition at the Tate in 2001. I was the Curator of Interpretation and wrote a little book about Stanley Spencer for the Tate series, *British Artists*. I'm still really interested in that whole period and those more anthropological details which art historians often disregard.

While I was at the Courtauld, I was also doing stained glass classes, one with Ruth Adams and another at the City Lit, run by Peter Young. These tutors had both been taught by Cecil Collins and were very enthusiastic about him. He recommended Cecil Collins' *The Vision of the Fool* so I read it. This eventually led me to make Cecil the subject of my MA thesis.

I enjoyed doing the research on fools and folly for the dissertation. I was sharing a flat with a friend who was considering doing a PhD on fools in Shakespearean drama. We had very interesting conversations about folly and fools. His idea was that folly was a rhetorical device, a way of writing, as well as being a theatrical figure which appears on the stage. This can be traced back to Erasmus and the Praise of Folly, but it's almost like satire. It's acting the fool in order to tell the truth. It's not just a person or an idiot; it's a whole way of being. That proved to be a rich seam which was fascinating for me to explore.

I studied Marxist literary theory for my first degree and was still carrying all that Marxist baggage and not quite sure what to do with it. Applying all that hardcore leftwing theory to Cecil Collins was an intellectual experiment and a funny thing to do to, I suppose. Sometimes I thought it was a bit like taking a pickaxe to a peanut, not the right tool for the job, but I wanted to understand the

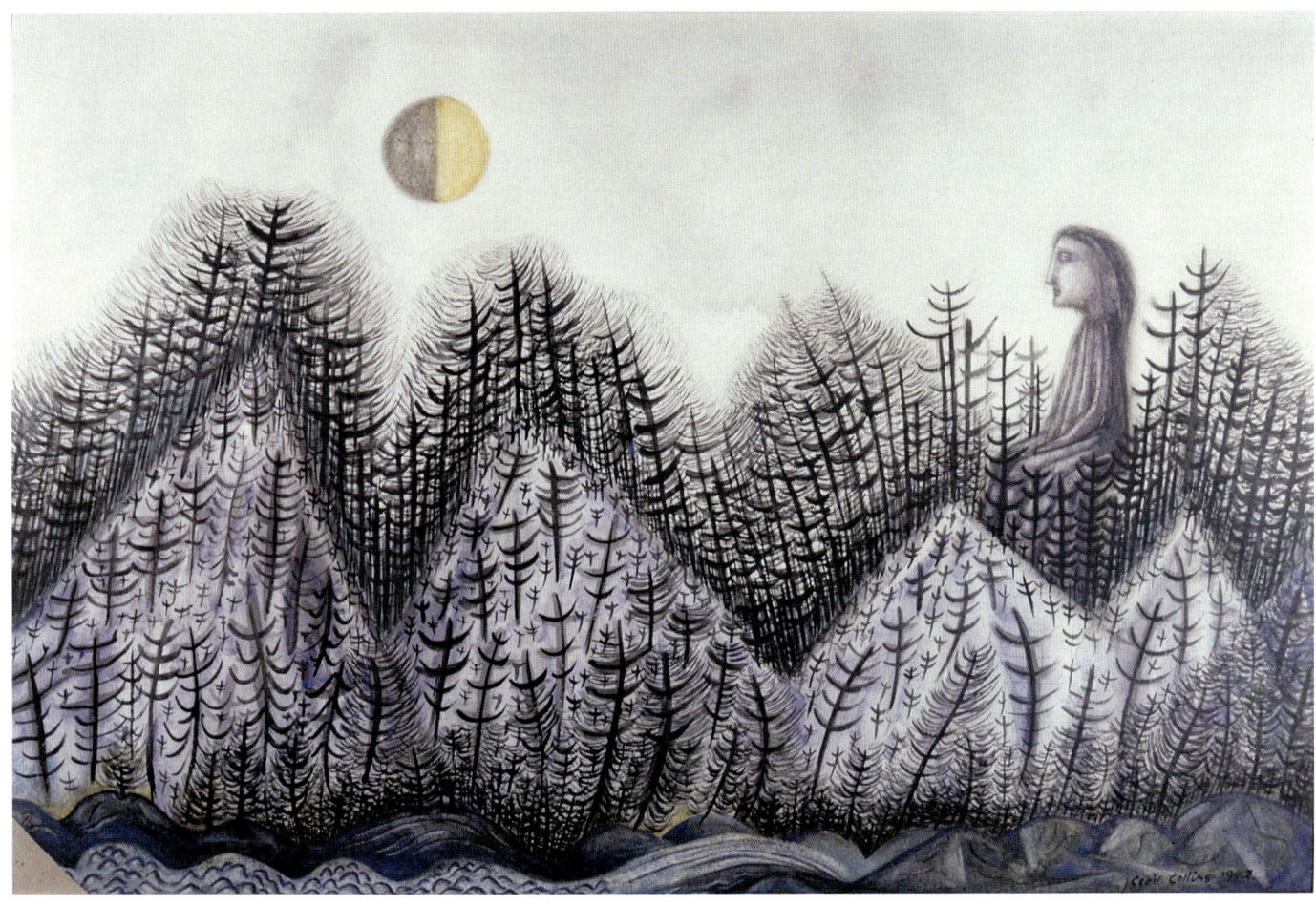

Cecil Collins
The Forest
1942
Watercolour
36.5 x 55cm

extremes of reaction to Collins' work. There were people like Peter Young and others who were taught by Cecil who had those devoted feelings like the attitude of a fan towards him. Other artists have had that, like Stanley Spencer. Most people who write about these artists think they have to take up one position or the other; either he was a godlike human being or he was tiresome and vain. It's a dialectical thing. You have to take a step back and consider what it is that provokes those sorts of reactions to the artist. It's really interesting why that happens. One of the qualities that Stanley Spencer and Cecil share is the right to be creative and to express their vision of the world. People either get completely enchanted by that or find it incredibly irritating. I can empathise with both those opposing viewpoints.

The life that Cecil Collins and his wife led, particularly during the Second World War, was very privileged. Maybe describing it that way is a bit harsh. I didn't mean in terms of financial privilege, though they had the luxury of living on Elisabeth's allowance. They did have the luxury of a lot of time to pursue their own interests, it seemed to me, whereas most other people didn't. They were unusual and they knew it. Certainly, when I spoke to Elisabeth Collins she was very aware of it; she described Dartington as a Shangri-la and what a wonderful environment it was for Cecil. She seemed to have made it her business to make life comfortable so that he could get on with pursuing his vision.

I think one of the things that Cecil Collins contemplated about modern society was precisely that it didn't allow people to have that free time and that it ought to. This is a kind of Marxist idea as well, that modern life ought to free people for leisure. Marx hardly says anything about what life might be like after the Revolution except that people would be free and have the time to hunt in the morning, do something else in the afternoon and read in the evening. The paradox is that it hasn't worked out like that.

During the war years, there was also this feeling that everything had to be mobilised for the war effort and Collins, it seemed to me, was desperately trying to keep open that space of freedom. The other thing was, I think, that the nature of the war and the nature of the enemy meant that artists were co-opted into the war effort themselves so that idealism in art came to serve a purpose for the state because it provided useful ammunition as propaganda against fascism and totalitarianism.

When I was researching my MA on Cecil, I had tea with Elisabeth just once when I went to interview her. I don't think I taped her, which was odd; I'm not sure I even made notes. I liked her very much. Incredibly gracious doesn't cover it: she was very elegant and serene. I remember thinking she was mysterious.

One of the things Elisabeth told me that I thought was interesting, was how drawings were just piled up on the table and then they put a board on top of them, then more drawings went on and then another board. It's a little insight into their domestic life. Instead of clearing up the drawings, they just put a board on top of all the drawings and then more drawings were piled up on top. This pile was in the studio or the living room, I can't remember. She also told me was that Cecil had closely supervised Judith Collins for the Tate catalogue.

I asked her about the Fools and the figures of the Fools in Cecil's work. 'Are they supposed to be funny?' She said, 'Well, yes,' and I said, 'I don't find them exactly rib tickling.' She said, 'Then you must be a very serious young person.' It was quite charming, but they still don't exactly inspire great laughs for me. I got the feeling that perhaps within their little private world, there were probably things about them that they found funny.

Another thing she said that really struck and stayed with me from that interview was when I asked her what the figure of the Fool meant. She said something and then added, 'It was Cecil's thing.' I don't know why I was so struck by it, but I think so often wives or partners of well-known male artists take it upon themselves to explain the work. I thought it was very nice of her just saying it wasn't her thing; it was his thing. That showed, I thought, a healthy separation even though, clearly, they did work very closely together and she did the first picture of the Fool. In fact the only thing I'd seen of hers was a reproduction of that first Fool image in one of the catalogues. I thought it was so mysterious and promising and different to Cecil's. I wanted to know what had happened to her creativity and was pleased to see that she'd started painting again when I read an obituary after she died. Reading it brought back to me that meeting with her and the feeling I had carried away with me of her quality of serenity.

Later, when I was teaching at the Ruskin Art School in Oxford on a casual basis and went for a job interview for a part-time post, it was clearly a source of amusement I'd done my MA thesis on Cecil Collins. I got the impression that he was considered an oddity from some people on the panel.

After my Masters, I'd gone back to Oxford to do a PhD and David Mellor was my external examiner. I returned to that whole world of Cecil Collins, in a way, through the fantastic catalogue of the 1987 show, *A Paradise Lost*, curated by David Mellor at the Barbican in London. I didn't see the exhibition, but the catalogue, which has an interesting section on Cecil, made me feel like I'd been and spoke to me powerfully about the visual aspects of that historical period.

The book based on my PhD is called *Shadow Sites* and, although it's not really about Cecil Collins, it's picking up on my interest in him because it's about neo-romantic art, particularly archaeological photography between the wars. It's about an image of the British landscape because in that picture essay in the *Paradise Lost* catalogue which is called, I think, the 'Origins of the Land,' there's some very evocative juxtapositions of the British landscape images. Really, I've always thought my whole PhD was like an extended footnote to that catalogue.

I believe that an art education doesn't merely train artists, it trains you to see and you can use that for anything in life. I dread to think how Cecil would fare in contemporary education having to write out teaching outcomes. I remember when I looked at the Collins' archive at the Tate in which there are lots of his notes on drawing, I thought it would be nice to publish them. I think this biography of Cecil through people's memories is a really good idea because of the sort of person that I understand he was. It seems very appropriate.

JACK HERBERT

Jack Herbert studied William Blake at Cambridge under Kathleen Raine and, after lecturing in Japan and Germany, returned to become Staff Tutor in literature with the Cambridge University Board of Extra-Mural Studies. He is now a Fellow of the Temenos Academy, London.

I was doing an M. Litt. on Blake in Cambridge in the mid 1950s. Desirée Hirst, a lecturer at Swansea University College, used to come back and forth to Cambridge and she stayed with us on one or two occasions. She had written a very interesting book about traditional symbolism and English thought. Desirée knew Cecil well enough to bring me along to see him when he was living in Selwyn Gardens in Cambridge.

Desirée and I spent about an hour with Cecil. At that time, he was working on the *Angel of the Flowing Light*, and we saw that painting on its easel. It was, as far as I could see, more or less finished, but he was adding layer after layer of glazing to it, like an icon. It was dazzling and had several layers of paint with layers of glazing in between. It shone with a powerful inner glow. I remember he told us that it took him a particularly long time because he was rather physically weak. I had the feeling that Cecil told you directly what he was feeling.

The painting made a deep impression on me, along with Cecil's dedication in spite of his physical frailness. I do think it's one of his best paintings. It was very compelling with those stunning eyes and this light coming out of the side of the Angel.

I got to know Kathleen Raine in my first term as a postgraduate. It was at a dinner in celebration of William Blake in London. Kathleen came in a little late. She must have been in her forties then and she was dressed to the nines with huge black elbow-length gloves. I spent Christmas with my mother in Wales and a card arrived from Kathleen to say that she'd been awarded a research fellowship at her old college, Girton, and that we'd be seeing something of each other because she would be coming up to Cambridge. I was then transferred to Kathleen for supervision for the rest of my time in Cambridge.

I hardly ever met the Collinses when I went to see Kathleen at 47 Paultons Square in London. I believe Elisabeth and Kathleen didn't talk for thirty years. They were two very powerful women.

I used to see Kathleen alone and then take her out to lunch. We used to spend most of the day together talking about this and that and I introduced her to the German romantics. Kathleen was a fascinating person and if she felt that you were on her wavelength or she had some kind of connection with you, she was extremely generous and would do all kinds of things to help you. Otherwise, you could face a blank wall. We got along very well.

The first time that I went to Paultons Square, Kathleen was in the middle of an intense and, from her point of view, misguided relationship with Gavin Maxwell. I never actually met Gavin, only heard about him from Kathleen. He was away and had got Kathleen to look after his otter, Mijbil. I remember most vividly how I rang the bell at Kathleen's and the door opened and this rather large otter with his little harness came to the door and nipped at my trouser leg. Then I went with Kathleen and the otter to her bathroom because it was his feeding time. She'd filled the bath up to the top so that it was deep enough for him to swim and then she put a live eel into the bathwater. Mijbil went straight into the bathwater after the eel, and all you could see was an oval shadow where they were tearing around after each other. It was the kind of experience that you don't forget.

Kathleen used to go every summer to Gavin's cottage on one of the Hebridean islands, and she would look after Mij. When she was there on one occasion she said, 'Wouldn't it be awful if Mij got tangled up in his harness in a branch and couldn't free himself?' Gavin had told her not to remove the harness because, with the harness on, any gamekeeper would realise that it was a pet otter, but very sadly on this occasion Kathleen took off the harness, the gamekeeper saw him, didn't realise that it was Gavin's otter and shot him.

CLIVE HICKS

Clive Hicks is a noted photographer of architecture, sculpture and landscape. He is also a practicing architect with special expertise in designing for the Hospice movement. Apart from the books on which he collaborated, as photographer, with William Anderson, he is also the author of *The Green Man: a Field Guide*, Compass Books, 2000.

Bill Anderson and I did a number of books together about cathedrals and the spiritual quality of places. While we were working on the *Green Man*, we also did the one about Cecil. Bill and I met through the Study Society which discusses spiritual matters. Its proper name, which dates from 1947, is the Society for the Study of Normal Consciousness. Cecil came and spoke there twice, I think. In the Study Society we believe in the idea of living in the present moment, not being angry about anything and not worrying about what hasn't happened. Bill and I were part of the same discussion group and I knew he'd written a book about castles. When he was invited to write a book on British cathedrals, he asked me whether I could do the photographs for it. He saw some samples of my work and that was the beginning of our working together and our friendship. Then we gave a talk together at the annual conference in Hove for the Centre for Spiritual and Psychological Studies on the spiritual basis of medieval architecture. Cecil was on the Centre's Council.

Later Bill said, 'I'm going to be writing the life story of Cecil Collins. Would you care to do the pictures?' At that time, I'd never heard of Cecil Collins. It was an interesting learning experience because I prefer to think of myself as an artistic rather than a technical photographer. I found the difficulty of getting the camera rectilinear with the picture intriguing. When you look in the camera's viewfinder, the picture is rectangular. It's deceptive. You've got to be exactly equidistant from the four corners.

It was a joy to be in Cecil's studio. I recall much laughter and joking. He had a student getting these rolls down from near the ceiling. One was a ten-foot painting of a large biblical scene, *The Fall of Lucifer*, which was being unrolled, as Cecil said, for the first time in thirty years.

Cecil told a story about how somebody was with Picasso when a visitor came with one of Picasso's paintings and he said, 'Maestro, I've just bought this painting of yours from twenty years ago. Would you care to see it?' When it was taken out, Picasso said, 'I'm very sorry, but that's a fake.' When the visitor had gone, the other chap said to Picasso, 'But I was here with you when you painted that,' and Picasso said, 'I painted lots of fakes.' I just loved that.

Another of Cecil's stories was about a man with whom Cecil had been at art college a long time previously. When he met this chap many years afterwards, the man said he had been in Italy in some lesser town and in a gallery he saw a three-quarter life size bronze of a naked young man attributed to Donatello. He went to the gallery owner and said, 'That statue is one I made when I was a student.' The gallery owner pooh-poohed this and the man said, 'I'll tell you what's cut into the underneath of the statue,' which he wouldn't have known if he hadn't done it himself. What intrigues me in the art world is how the statue then became valueless, whereas previously people had enjoyed it.

I photographed two of Cecil's little paintings, eight inches by six inches, which were in the gallery for £4,000 or £6,000 each. I had them made into colour photocopies and glazed then I had them framed so they were exactly the same size as the originals. I took them to Cecil and said, 'If these were in a gallery where you couldn't come closer than three feet away and if the originals were in the same gallery in another room, could anyone tell the difference?' He said, 'Elisabeth and I would know. The colours are slightly different, but basically no one else would.' Of course, they wouldn't stand up to scrutiny as forgeries because they're printed on paper.

On one of the days I was photographing, Cecil, his student and I went out to an Italian place for lunch. While we were eating, I said to Cecil, 'My wife and I both feel we've never grown up and I don't plan to get grown up, ever.' Cecil turned to the student and said, 'There you are. That's the secret. Just don't get grown up.' I recognised how in that respect, although not in many others, Cecil was a kindred spirit. He was certainly not stuffy. I only knew him for a little while, but I don't think he would have agreed to the idea that he was a genius. I got the impression that he had been unrecognised. It had probably tempered him, whereas somebody who gets recognised as a star can be quite spoilt. This lack of recognition was obviously turning round at the time I got to know him. Cecil was a very sharp critic and commentator of everything.

Money was never really mentioned, but Cecil gave me a cheque for the photographing, not related to anything in particular and the amount was of his choosing. He also gave me a print of an etching, *Kneeling Fool*.

I didn't like all of Cecil's work. I prefer his pictures of Angels or other figures. Some of his paintings are more formless and have wild splashes. He said that he would sit in front of the painting with a brush in each hand and try to empty his mind, be without any

friends & other relationships

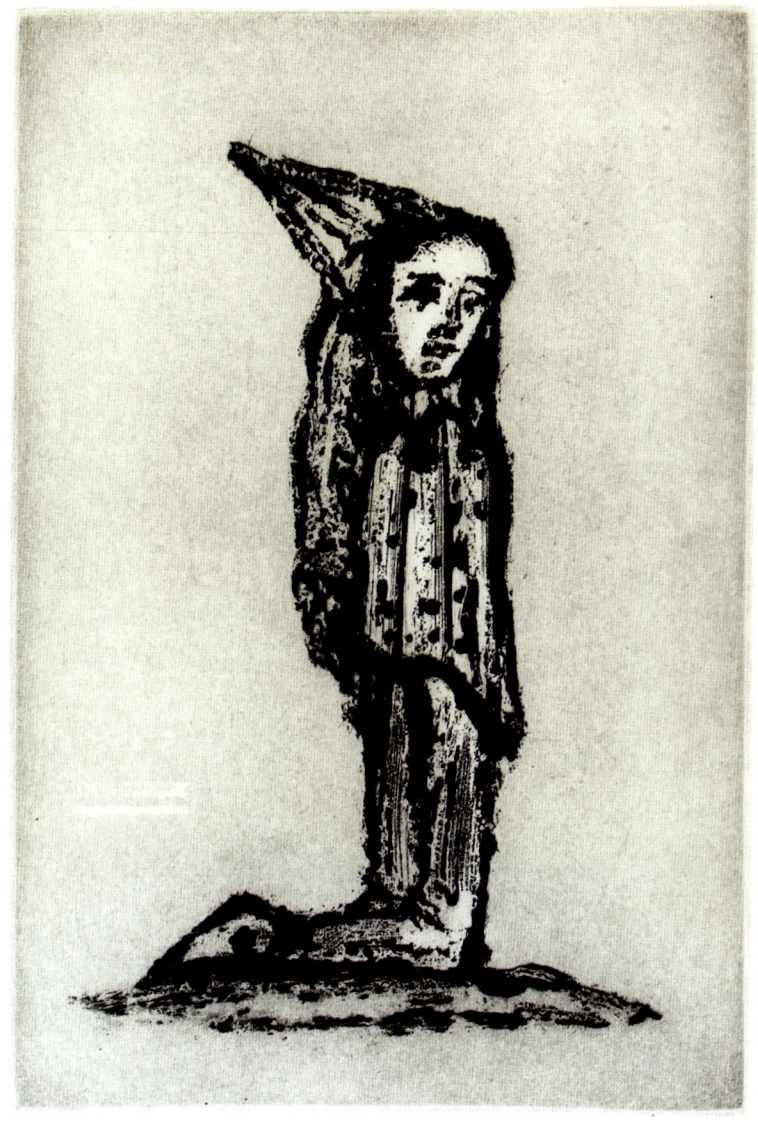

Cecil Collins
The Kneeling Fool
1977
Etching
20 x 13.5cm

start off by drawing lines on the paper or canvas, it's not necessarily obstructive, but it needs more than that.

I also photographed some of Elisabeth's paintings for one of Bill's talks. Bill had a slightly negative attitude to Elisabeth. He thought that she resented the attention given to Cecil and felt that a bit more recognition for herself might have been fitting. When Cecil died, Elisabeth was pretty short with Bill.

I'm still a professional architect. Bill always used to say about being a writer, 'We do our own books as a vocation.' I used to joke back, 'I could actually earn more as a jobbing gardener,' but it was doing something that was fun. This was apart from the *Green Man* book for which Bill's widow, Jennifer, and I, until recently, were each getting a fair sum in royalties and spin-offs. The *Green Man* was entirely different from the other books we did; I would have had to do a lot more jobbing gardening to earn what we got out of that.

Bill and I would do these talks about the spiritual quality of architecture and mention things like numerology, the zodiac, sacred geometry and the cult of the Virgin. The Green Man would come into it as well and we found that people picked on that. In an hour and a half lecture with two hundred photographs, there'd be only about eight pictures of Green Men, but that's what people would pick up on. There was something in the air when we wrote our book on it.

It gave me an insight into the archetype. Jung wrote about archetypes as patterns in everybody's mind. The *Green Man* was our pattern for living in harmony with the world. Jung sometimes referred to the archetypes as if they were external entities acting on us and that's what it felt like writing that book. We felt impelled, but the astonishing thing was that, just as we were working on the book, quite unknown to us, a number of people all over Britain were reviving Green Man folk customs which had died out at the time of the First World War. Something was propelling them; you can't revive a folk custom unless there are a whole lot of people who are going to parade through the streets with you on May Bank Holiday, which they certainly do in Rochester and Hastings. There was a sense of the archetype being re-animated which allowed our book to become so successful. It came out at the right time.

intention. It was not, 'I am going to paint an Angel.' He said he would let his hands move, putting the paint on with both hands at once and, after a while, he would look at it and see what was emerging, then he would give it conscious guidance. He wanted it to happen not automatically, but from an inner part of his being.

Bill and I felt that if a person were in contact with himself and had a skill, whether it be an artist, a poet or a photographer, stonemason or an architect, then the work would emerge. If you're in harmony, your work will be too and a golden section occurs naturally in our bodies and in our brains. Whereas if you

TIMOTHY HYMAN

Born in 1946, Timothy Hyman is a painter and writer on art. He curated the Tate Gallery's Stanley Spencer Retrospective in 2001. His book on Bonnard appeared in 1998 and another on Sienese Painting in 2003. He exhibits at Austin/Desmond, London. In 2007 he won the National Portrait Gallery's Travel Award. His work is in many public and private collections.

For years, I heard about Cecil and Elisabeth from people who were either positive or negative about them. I had a friend called Christopher Couch who'd been in a monastery, but had become an interesting painter and for a while showed at the Marlborough. I think, from a religious perspective, he felt Cecil was peddling an illusion about art and spirituality.

John Allitt once got me in to lecture on Beckmann and I was very struck that nobody in the Cecil world seemed to have looked at German paintings. Afterwards, it was conceded that Beckmann was interesting, but of course Cecil was infinitely better! There was a sense of a hidebound, blinkered provincial art-sect.

I liked the Fool archetype, but there's an awful lot of Cecil's work I don't respond to. I was down in Chichester recently and I don't really like what they've got there of his. Probably the ones I've felt most for are the early ones. Although I'd met Cecil and Elisabeth on some occasion, I hardly got to know him and really only became friends with Elisabeth after his death.

Even before I met Elisabeth, I'd seen some of her work at the Albemarle in that first show she had and thought she was really terrific. She was a great talent. Robin Leanse, a poet who wrote an interesting poem called *The Stone*, arranged for us to meet by inviting my wife, Judith, and me up to have lunch because he knew Elisabeth and I were both passionately interested in Powys. I think Cecil was too; eventually I inherited Cecil's copy of *A Glastonbury Romance*. Elisabeth was wearing her hat and she behaved badly because we were talking immediately, quite deeply, about Powys, excluding everyone else.

That was our first meeting and then it developed that I would meet her and take her to dinner. (She would take me to dinner, actually. This was after Cecil died and she always used to say she'd got pots of money and insisted on paying.) Chelsea Arts Club was important to her as a resource for lunch or dinner and she definitely liked being squired. What she was really looking for, she told me, was a homosexual squire.

Elisabeth and I had a very good literary rapport. I introduced her to Robert Musil whom she adored. She'd never heard of him before and when she went into the nursing home, she took his book with her. After her death, when Marcia organised the distribution of their books, I discovered that Elisabeth had made some really interesting annotations in the Musil.

I saw Elisabeth usually on my own. She was so game and very youthful, (the hat she always wore helped) so that I had no idea she was so old. She used to get the number nineteen bus from Chelsea to Islington and she always came to my shows and things like that.

For me, the friendship with her became especially important; she was a gift to me. At the time I met her, both my parents were dying in very humiliating ways. My father had Alzheimer's and was just hollowing out and my mother had a combination of illnesses and had to go into hospital. I was having to visit both of them a lot and it was awful. So what I set up very often was that after seeing them I'd visit Elisabeth. She gave me hope.

There was one very poignant occasion when Elisabeth told me rather eloquently that she looked out of her window and watched this person whom she described as looking like King Lear, clearly totally lost, talking to people who didn't want to be talked to. She knew from my description that it was my father. He was around eighty-eight and she was probably ninety so it was a fascinating, almost novelistic moment. He was in a nursing home only about a hundred yards away, but he would stray; he would lose himself.

Elisabeth could have been a writer herself; she had a very good mind. Another time I'd lent her an excellent book on the Bible that she'd also annotated in a rather good way. It was The Book of God by Gabriel Josipovici. I can't help thinking there would have been a lot of very fascinating archive material somewhere in her books.

She was completely herself, more or less, until she went into a nursing home when she started to slip a bit, but it wasn't the most humiliating of deaths somehow. There was a second flowering at the end of her life and then this release.

Elisabeth always made it quite clear that she wouldn't have had the relationship with Cecil any other way and that she'd basically given up her own art for him, but she never regretted or resented it. When one looks at her paintings from the early Thirties it's a different genre from Cecil's. We didn't talk much about him at all and she never, as it were, sold Cecil to me. She said, 'It's a great relief to meet someone who isn't interested in Cecil.'

I feel there's an affinity between Elisabeth's late work and Tagore's paintings. I don't know if Elisabeth's late works are of the same quality as the 1930s, but it's those early ones that I love most of all. John Lane and I did an interview together with her for *Resurgence*. It catches a little of the quality of her voice, certainly the way, when asked if she had ever been a Christian, she said 'Never!'

There's a record of Elisabeth and Cecil visiting John Cowper Powys and I got her to talk about it which is entertaining because you've got Powys' own diary entries to compare. Elisabeth said, 'We visited him because I think he's a great master, ... unrecognised and I think everything about the Powys family is so peculiar, so unusual and wonderful ... Somehow or other we found ourselves at the bottom of the lane [in Dorchester] and we went in ...There were shelves all round with books behind and bottles of milk in various stages from green to new; bottles all around. ...John Cowper was in one of his Being-Very-Courteous moods; so whatever you said, he agreed profusely. This was very disconcerting, but Cecil just went on talking ... far too much, all about himself as usual.' That was indeed the case because Powys' still fuming entry for the day after they visited on 1st April, 1935, reads, *They artists with their photos of Mr Cecil Collins' approaches to life, going one further on Picasso, took all my afternoon...'*

Elisabeth once referred to Mark Tobey as a great influence on Cecil. I don't know that Tobey's a terribly interesting artist, but he might have been a great teacher. I've had quite different responses to different paintings by Cecil. Some of the ones with a lot of black lines, don't convince me stylistically, they seem too much like 'Designs' with a sort of forced stylisation. The truth is I don't feel that I've looked at him hard enough. It hasn't meant an awful lot to me except for *The Vision of the Fool*, both the text and his drawings and little paintings on that theme. But the painting in the Tate of the *Sleeping Fool* [1943] is the one that I think of.

Somehow the figure of the Fool is the key to his work; everyone's always recognised that and it's also that he himself had a whole mythology about it which is such a significant part of his work. It might even be that his story of British art is quite close to mine, but he wasn't actually one of the channels through whom I got my inspiration. For instance, in my case it was Beckmann, Sienese painting, Bonnard, Stanley Spencer or someone contemporary like Peter de Francia, who were my mentors. I had a friend who published in Temenos, David Maclagan, and when I asked him, 'Don't you have some doubts about Temenos,' he said, 'Tim, you mean they dock a little too easily in the Great Harbour of the Mysterious?' I feel about lots of art that there's some way in which I want to back off and I felt that slightly with Cecil.

There's an interesting story about Cecil and a childhood friend of mine, Maria Bjornson. He had a very big effect on her. She went to see him when she was a teenager and showed him a drawing and he said, 'You need to study theatre design.' Maria's mother, Mia, was a very remarkable woman, (who became a wise elder for me) and they both felt that they owed Cecil something. For years Maria was extremely badly paid, but then the magical thing happened with her designs for *Phantom of the Opera* and she became a millionairess almost overnight. She was very obsessive, but also a profound and stimulating person. Tragically, she died at fifty-three of a petit mal in the bath.

There isn't a clear-cut division between my painting and writing; it's sort of merged. I would say that writing unblocked my painting. Although I was painting every day as a young man I really wasn't ready. I think a lot of things were unclogged by my writing about painting. In some odd way, one seems to renew the other. On the whole, I feel having a double energy is good, but it isn't altogether trouble-free because when one or the other has a deadline then I start getting in a muddle or panicking. In painting, I think the intellectual part for me needs to be slightly short-circuited and the writing takes care of that. I don't think I'm very disciplined. Quite honestly, I think anyone watching me would wonder how I ever got anything done. But, as one gets older, I think one can get an awful lot done in two or three hours.

Ken Kiff used to say to me, 'It only takes half an hour to paint a picture, but it just has to be the right half hour!' I think there's a lot of truth in that. I put things aside and then take them up months later. You have to see it freshly and if you just go on and on day after day, you often can't see what you're doing.

I've been told that life drawing was the basis of Cecil's teaching and I can't understand why. I could never relate to it at all as it was practiced in the life room at the Slade; I hated it. The model just sat there and I couldn't infuse it with any meaning, I didn't know what my relationship was to this anonymous, unmoving figure. I always felt that there should be a way of posing the model so that her position would have some archetypal meaning. To say something really obvious about Cecil, what I don't understand is that his teaching was so much about drawing from the motif, but he never does that in his art at all. Blake virtually forbade working from Nature. I think Cecil would subscribe to this idea that the imagination and observation are not entirely friends. The idea of the Visionary Artist is my dream, not that we very often make the grade, any of us. I'm a Blakean, but I'm not interested in the neo-classical side. I respond especially to his wonderful sensuousness and also his rhythmic energy, his sense of everything being a cycle. Sometimes there's a natural fluency in Cecil's work, but on the whole it seems very static, hieratical and icon-like. For me, in Blake there is the creation of a world where everything's on the move...

JOHN & TRUDA LANE

John Lane is a painter, writer and educationalist. He has been a promoter and critic of Cecil Collins work. Lane contributes regularly to the journal, Resurgence, for which he is a Trustee and the Art Editor. He was the founder Director of the Beaford Centre for the arts in North Devon and was Chairman of the Dartington Hall Trust. Truda Lane, John's wife, is an artist whose drawings often appear in Resurgence. They met as students at the Slade and have four sons.

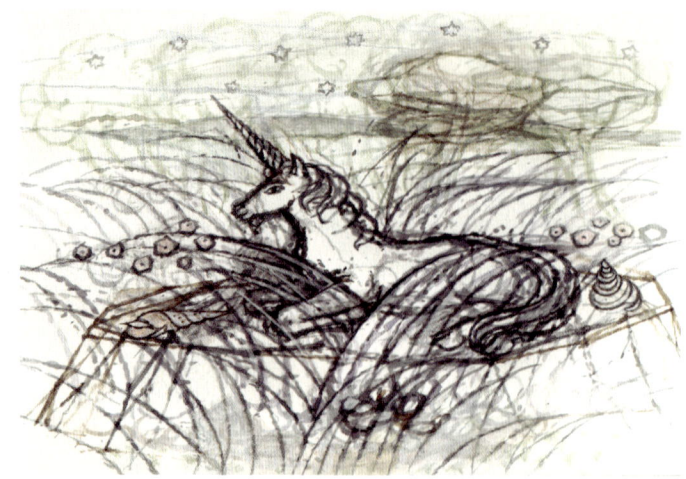

Truda Lane
Unicorn
2002
Watercolour
20 x 11cm

JL: I first met the Collinses at Dartington in the 1970s when they were staying with Mark Kidel and his wife. Mark is a friend of mine who has made several documentary films. I was interested to meet Cecil who'd been at Dartington in the 1940s. We had Dartington in common, painting and a rejection of materialism, so there was never any shortage of discussion and I also knew Kathleen quite well. I liked his humour and his brutal wit. I liked Cecil very much. I consolidated the relationship by visiting him whenever I was in London. He used to ring up quite a lot because I didn't get to London that often. I can remember the feeling I had with Cecil; the feel of his humour, the mood. Sometimes he told jokes. He could be funny, caustic. He'd spend hours talking about how awful the world was, in particular the art world. He could be very sarcastic about contemporary paintings.

At that time, I felt I needed Cecil's art. It was part of my development, whereas now I can see it in greater perspective. Coming across Kathleen, and particularly Cecil, at that time was important and revelatory for me because they were saying or painting or writing about things which I'd always had personal intimations of, but never seen celebrated in print or painting. Although I never went to his classes, Cecil was a brilliant teacher for me, but never influenced my own style. He reaffirmed ideas and thoughts and feelings that one had had, but that were infrequently expressed in the contemporary art scene. But I've moved on and it's all part of my history. Now there isn't the sense of discovery and exploration that there was at that time.

On my visits to the Collinses in London I always used to call on Kathleen downstairs which could be difficult and embarrassing because of their feud. When I'd go to tea there, Elisabeth was lovely and chatty, but I didn't really get to know her until after Cecil's death. He was the grand VIP.

TL: Elisabeth came to stay with us after Cecil died. She was in her eighties then.

JL: Elisabeth could be a bit difficult. Do you remember that restaurant?

TL: That was a bit embarrassing. We were in an excellent restaurant but Elisabeth reacted as if we were in India and wondered where the ice was coming from. We had tumblers of water packed with ice and she seemed to be suspicious about it. She was all right here, but not in the restaurant. I liked Elisabeth enormously and never understood the rift with Kathleen who was far more charitable about Elisabeth. Kathleen said she didn't know what on earth the feud was about. The only thing she could think of was that she'd written something or other about Cecil and never mentioned Elisabeth and wondered whether that was the trouble. Elisabeth grumbled about Kathleen's cat and the fact that she always had a fire downstairs.

JL: There must have been something quite deep that caused the break. It's very sad that they were rattling around in that property and didn't reach a reconciliation at the end of their lives. They must have been quite close at one period because they bought the house together.

TL: After Cecil died, Kathleen said how much she missed him. He used to stop and have a word with her on his way upstairs from shopping which he carried in a string bag.

JL: The two of them must have had a strong intellectual, emotional and spiritual relationship. It's extraordinary that these three people lived in that house and although we're talking about the negative side of that relationship, they must have had a very fruitful one.

TL: Three visionaries together.

JL: At that time I was very keen on Cecil's work. I wrote about it for the little catalogue for the Plymouth exhibition. The problem was I had to do it with limited knowledge because in those days little was known about Cecil. There were no books and I'd seen few paintings, just some reproductions. I knew Bernard Samuels who ran the arts centre in Plymouth and, as it was Cecil's birthplace, I had quite a bit to do with suggesting Cecil's exhibition there. Cecil came down for the opening and afterwards we went to a restaurant.

TL: Someone came round selling red roses and Cecil bought one and gave it to Elisabeth. She said, 'What am I supposed to do with this?' She was very down to earth.

JL: On another occasion I looked at the house where Cecil was born. It was difficult to see because there were alleyways behind with a high wall round the back yard. I think there was an outhouse.

TL: Cecil mentions a child in the back yard looking at the stars and seeing great bowed figures. It must have been himself as a child.

JL: His father was a mechanic, some sort of an engineer in a laundry in Plymouth, then he lost his job and became a road digger. It was a tough childhood for Cecil.

TL: But his mother adored him. He was an only child. I think it's very significant that he didn't go to school. John and I have sometime discussed the fact that Samuel Palmer hardly went to school. Neither did Stanley Spencer. Blake also went to school very little. These visionaries didn't go to school.

JL: It's not just visionaries. A lot of people who don't go to school are very talented in different ways, but are not necessarily visionaries.

I remember John Tavener came down to that exhibition. We were filmed for a TV documentary before the exhibition opened, walking round in a most artificial way, making inane comments about the work. I was very committed to Cecil's work and did what I could within the limits of my powers to write about it and promote it. Cecil was profoundly self-important about his work. He was not a modest man because of his awareness of his vision.

Cecil would phone up about eight or nine o'clock in the evening and say, 'Would you write to the Tate?' or 'Would you write to the Principal of the Central School of Arts and Crafts?' I was one of many who were asked to do this. He didn't dictate what you had to say, but you knew enough context to be able to write and say he was the greatest painter since Rembrandt, probably greater than Rembrandt.

Richard Morphet at the Tate was always pro his work, but I think he was alone in a crowd. One of the letters I wrote was to ask for a retrospective on a smaller scale than the big one he had at the end of his life. It was to ask for a show to give Cecil the recognition he deserved. He himself believed he was a significant artist which, of course, he was.

Sociologically, he came from a lower middle class background and had a big chip on his shoulder. He found that recognition for his art came with difficulty, like a young working-class soldier with officers who had been at public school. I don't know if that's a good analogy. Cecil felt he was the medium of spiritual and other energies. I also think he had a personal desire for fame. It was both, his personal vanity and his vision.

I knew I was being milked, but I didn't mind because I thought it was important that his work should become more widely known. He was out of vogue. It was the time of abstraction and painting for its own sake, so ideologically his work wasn't acceptable. One was pleased to give some support. What is so interesting is that during that time of abstraction you were knocking your head against a brick wall as far as the Tate was concerned. Cecil's work was seen as illustrational with a lot of ideas, but then, for example, the windows at Chartres are illustrational.

The other day, when I was in Chartres, I was looking at an angel with a trumpet at the top of a window and I thought, my God, that's so wonderful, and it was just a fragment, just a spark. The problem for people like Cecil is that they have had to invent their

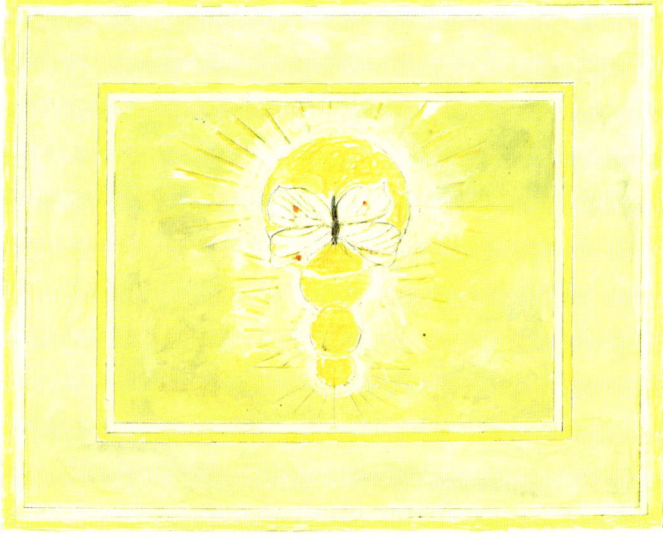

John Lane
The Yellow Butterfly
2004
Watercolour
26 x 30cm

whole vocabulary. They know what they want to say, but they've no means of saying it, whereas the artists or stained-glass makers of Chartres had a total vocabulary understood not only by themselves but their patrons and to some extent the body of worshippers. They had this massive iconography and stylistic knowledge. There isn't anything like that nowadays. That's why I think Cecil's work can look forced because he had to force it out of himself.

TL: He used angels a lot and they weren't forced in any way.

JL: He had a commitment to an idea or to an important and significant aspect of what was missing from British art, but I do think his views about his own art have somehow suffocated independent criticism. I think it's a loss because other people might have had an opportunity to enrich the critical aspect of his work. We're all vehicles of his own self-belief. He was controlling, but that's terribly male. I don't think Winifred Nicholson or Elisabeth, for that matter, were like that. Control isn't necessarily a bad thing; I feel that it's necessary sometimes. It's a huge subject.

TL: Perhaps men see things in a grid, whereas women see in curves. It was a terrible pity Cecil had that controlling effect on Elisabeth. She was a free spirit.

JL: I found some of Cecil's work marvellous and some of it uneven: strained, prickly, derivative and gothic in the wrong sense. During the 1970s, his work was sometimes pretty poor. I think some of the best is the very early work which he did in Dartington and before, and the late work is very lovely, very tender. I don't like the Christ ones.

TL: I don't like the paintings of Christ either. There is a phase of his work I don't like at all. Perhaps it was done in the 50s: blacks and reds, as if he was making a concession to abstraction which I don't think came off. The first Cecil painting I was conscious of was of someone lying in the grass and there was a flower. I didn't know anything about Cecil at that time, but I felt that here was obviously something very interesting. Something new as well. It brought a breath of health. Something imaginative when that sort of thing seemed to have been crushed. One of my favourite paintings of Cecil's is the fool holding a child by the hand. In the background are burning buildings. It's a dark picture. That's perhaps my favourite painting by him.

JL: You have these two innocent figures and destruction in the background. It was done during the 1940s, from Dartington where he was living at that time, you could see the glow in the sky from the bombing of Plymouth. It's a very tender picture. I think the tenderness was again very prominent in the last years.

TL: The drawing of the *Fool Praying*, that's got that tenderness, I'm sure many others have too.

JL: The little painting of a blue angel that we own; that's quite tender.

TL: I find it cloying. I much prefer the lithograph called *Sun Head* that we have, which dates from 1960, I'm keen on that.

JL: Although I understand Cecil's Dartington connections reasonably well, probably better than anyone, I know nothing about his teaching except what I've read and what I've heard from some of the groupies, if you'll excuse the term. On different occasions, various people would come to Dartington, goggle-eyed at the very word Cecil.

I didn't know much about the groupies. I can't even remember their names, but I know they exist and in a way I've never heard of in relation to any other artist. I think Cecil encouraged the adulation; he didn't reject it. I found that side of Cecil unattractive. I think it's obvious that the adulation which they gave him made up for the complete lack of it in the art world, the one complemented the other, but it was a cheap alternative.

Bryan Robertson, who I met in the studio at the BBC when we did a recorded piece on Cecil, told me it was Mark Tobey who taught Cecil everything about teaching and about a lot of the techniques which I know very little about.

I talked to Robin Baring once and the interview was published in *Images of Earth and Spirit*. Robin said, 'You have Giotto and the school of Giotto and you have Collins and you have the school of Collins,' and he was unabashed about the imitative nature of his own work. He thought it was a significant, reasonable thing to do and I can understand that, but most people are committed to the idea of individualism.

TL: We express ourselves as individuals because we are just individuals. Because people were a bit infatuated with Cecil, it made me rather withdraw. I liked Elisabeth enormously. The Fool was Elisabeth's idea and Cecil didn't really admit it.

JL: But it was only an idea; he brought it to fruition. I could forgive him for most things because of his humour. Some of it was self-derogatory, but not self-congratulatory although, paradoxically, he was infatuated and, I believe, in love with himself, but when he let go of that he was delightful. There are tremendous parallels, I think,

Cecil Collins
The Blue Angel
1982
Mixed media on card
29 x 16.5cm

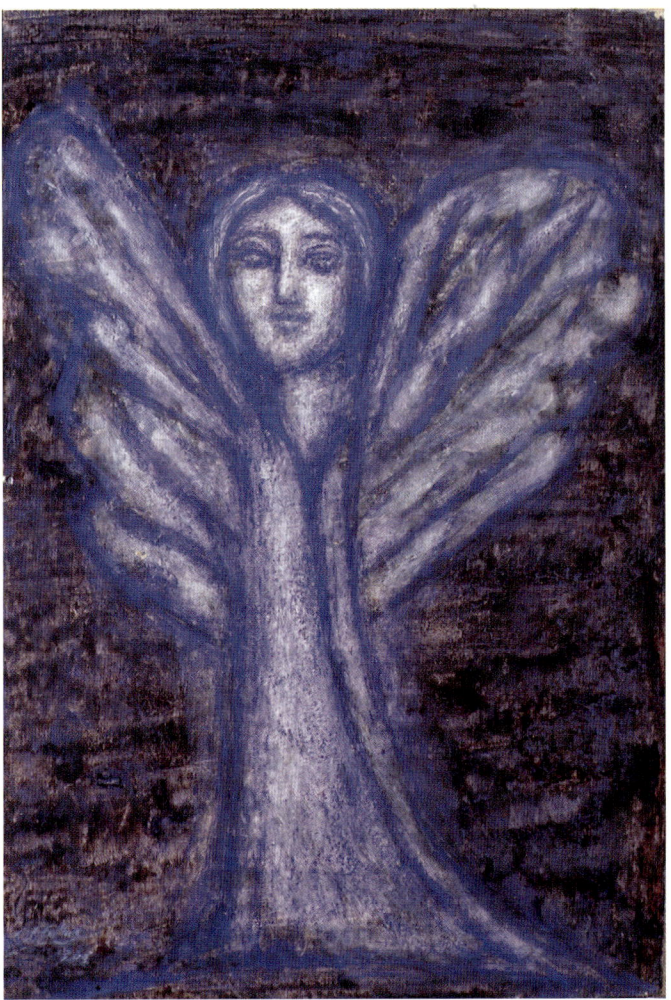

between Morris Graves and Cecil.

They were both committed to an expression of what might be called the spiritual. I don't use that word much because I don't know what it means. Graves has a niche in the American art world, whereas Cecil wasn't always easy to get on with. He wasn't smooth. I'm not criticising Cecil, but I think he could have antagonised a lot of people, partly because of his eccentric determination to develop his own work, partly for personal reasons. I'm not convinced it was simply, intrinsically, because of his message.

In the past, some of my work was that of an administrator. The great skill in administration is not to be hemmed in by determined people who want their own way. I think you could smell it coming off Cecil. This is speculation, but administrators at the Tate would have tried to get that kind of pressure off their back.

Cecil could be an absolute wretch and that made one close down. I don't think that was necessarily because of what he was preaching; I think that was him. There is a distinction between the two. I was mildly irritated by it, but it was alleviated by his humour and self-deprecation and also because I was very sympathetic to

what he was saying. I was absolutely in tune with it. If you want to have exhibitions at the Tate or elsewhere, the art of success, whatever that means, is not to alienate the people whose support you require. I think he did alienate people at the Tate and that's why they took so long to give him an exhibition.

TL: But the Tate always tried to keep people out.

JL: They didn't keep everybody out or there wouldn't have been anything on show, though they do tend always to have only the same kinds of paintings.

Nevertheless, Cecil did jolly well for himself. I mean, for what it's worth, he became a Royal Academician, he got an MBE and several books have been written about him. What happened to Blake? A much greater figure than Cecil. Absolutely nothing. It's even possible that Cecil did much better than David Jones. A lot of other people never achieved anything like that. It's awfully difficult to make a judgement yet about Cecil's importance. I think he's intrinsically English, which is both a strength and a limitation.

I feel that the very late paintings by Paul Nash with sunsets and sunflowers are profoundly spiritual, I worry about that word, but I never got the feeling that Paul Nash walked round with a label, 'I am a spiritual artist,' which was in contrast to Cecil. Do we know what Cecil's religious views were? Did he believe in a concept called God? He talked about the spiritual, but I don't actually know what that meant for him.

There's a very interesting book by Theodore Roszak called *Unfinished Animal*. In it he looks at all pioneers like Steiner and Madame Blavatsky. There's a whole stream of them. I'm not trying to diminish the contribution Cecil made, but he wasn't unique in any sense. Cecil felt uniquely alone, but was he so isolated? What about David Jones and Winifred Nicholson?

TL: Winifred Nicholson, I think, is marvellous. Kathleen was full of admiration for Winifred too. They were great friends. There was a healthiness about Winifred Nicholson's attitude.

JL: The work itself is healthy. Both Elisabeth and Winifred had a wonderful feminine capacity. Winifred's work flows like a river or the rain. Cecil's work is intellectually wrought to a greater extent and this overrides the healthy spontaneity those two had. That's why Cecil's colour is often uninteresting. In him there is an absence of the sensual and, of course, the complexities explored by Stanley Spencer who said, 'I am on the side of angels and dirt.'

TL: Cecil was envious of the feminine and it's something you can't do if you're not a woman. You can't do it. I much prefer the kind of imagination that women have.

JL: Why do you think Elisabeth didn't paint? Was it because she had to look after Cecil?

TL: I had four children. I painted in the evening. I might start painting at nine at night. I don't do that so much now but, when the children were here, I couldn't begin before nine o'clock.

JL: Why didn't Elisabeth do something? Was it a lack of commitment? I mean, what did she have to do? When I was there, I never had elaborate meals. You cooked elaborate meals and had four children. I can't understand why Elisabeth couldn't do her work.

TL: It must be something to do with the weight of Cecil's demands. Elisabeth once said, 'How could I have had any children when I've got Cecil?' She rather implied that she'd got a child, she'd got Cecil and looking after him was enough. Or it was some other thing. Kathleen said to me once that women can't really start their creative work until they've done certain jobs, set things in order in the house.

JL: I can see that psychologically Cecil was very big in one sense, but he didn't need much physical attention surely. His socks were filthy. Cecil must have gone into his funny old room and scurried around in his great pile of papers. Elisabeth didn't need a studio. Even after his death, she didn't really have one.

TL: Well, I don't have a studio.

JL: You don't need a studio unless you're a sculptor. She poked around and did little paintings on scraps of paper.

TL: Sometimes I wish I had a studio so I could walk in and just get on with it and not have to get out all of my materials. That's the advantage of a studio.

JL: Winifred Nicholson had three children and she painted.

TL: She was very involved with them.

JL: And she ran a farm and all the rest. She was active. Elisabeth was quite passive. I don't think she had a lot of energy. She wasn't exactly a sparkling or vital person.

TL: She may have been, in a dreamy way. She might not have wanted to live the kind of life where you organise yourself or say you're definitely going to paint this evening no matter what and nobody's going to stop you. She might not have been like that.

JL: I wondered whether the Tate would have bought Elisabeth's work if it hadn't been for her relationship with Cecil. Although I doubt they would have bought the paintings if they'd been rubbish.

TL: Cecil used to say about Francis Bacon, whose art the Tate were very keen on, 'There's something terribly sick about that sort of brutality.' He saw it as a negative force that had taken over and was very worried about it.

JL: His criticism, maybe, was appropriate for the times, but his critique of the modern world and his understanding of it was neither as rich or as deep as other people's of that time. Cecil wasn't really an intellectual in that sense. For example, Eric Gill was much more penetrating about the problems in the modern world. I mention him because Cecil and Elisabeth knew him when they were living near him in Buckinghamshire. I don't think that Cecil's grasp of anything intellectually or spiritually was out of the ordinary. What was out of the ordinary was his charisma. He could make things sound almost magical, but they weren't actually. I think it was very difficult to pull away from him because of his magnetism. Charisma is like a bright light which needs, or pulls, the dark. One is impelled to explore the shadow because of the charisma. Cecil said what a lot of other people have said, but somehow he could make it special.

When I read Cecil's work now, I find it a bit preachy. I feel resistant to being overpowered. One of the problems, for me, is that I've found it difficult to look at his work freshly, to take off his spectacles while looking at it because I'm always reading it through his own interpretation. I want to get rid of all that and see it for its own sake. For example, I remember going round one of his exhibitions in London; it was in 1981. He'd stand in front of his paintings and whisper with complete detachment, 'Isn't that beautiful. Oh, it's so beautiful,' as if we were looking at a picture that had nothing to do with him. I couldn't believe my ears when we looked at *The Feast of Fools* in this exhibition, he talked about it for a long time; a complex metaphysical interpretation. You could hardly see the painting in the end.

There was such a mixture of the personal and the archetype and, of course, one can be a camouflage, as it were, for the other. It was adulterated with ambition. It's terribly dangerous ground, like missionaries in Africa and makes me queasy, though at one point I was thirsty for what he had to say. Later I felt more critical and wanting to break free from it. Cecil was a great influence at one time, but I grew beyond it, not out of it because it remains an important influence for me.

RICHARD LANNOY

Author, international journalist, photographer, traveller, artist, educator, Richard Lannoy was one of the founding staff of the ICA, London and initiator of the celebrated forum, the Independent Group. His books include *The Speaking Tree: Continuity and Change in Indian Culture*, 1971, *Anandamayi: Her Life and Wisdom*, 1996, *Benares Seen from Within*, 1999. Editor of Lewis Thompson's papers, *Mirror to the Light*, 1984 and *Lewis Thompson; Journals of an Integral Poet*, 2006.

CECIL COLLINS AND LEWIS THOMPSON

After a good deal of memory-scanning, I am uncertain as to exactly when I first saw Cecil Collins' work in reproduction. I thought I'd read something on him by Stephen Spender, but I may be confusing two books: Alex Comfort's in 1946, and Cecil's *Vision of the Fool* the year after. I was definitely acquainted with Cecil's Fool drawings before *Vision of the Fool* was published. Being hard up when Cecil's book came out, I must have decided that the Comfort book was enough, as it would have been a luxury to get a second. Comfort's text, if I remember rightly, was helpful to me. There's a lot of Cecil's work that I don't like at all, but that is quite usual for me with artists' oeuvres, including the greatest! I liked Cecil in phases.

I can see now that I first liked his work when I was not more than sixteen and was alternating between eroticised mystico-spiritual artists and asexual visionary innocent ones. Thus there were periods when I loved Blake, Palmer, David Jones, Cecil Collins and medieval art, then went off them completely and preferred Indian art where the prevalent erotic temperature was more to my liking. As an adolescent, the asexuality of Cecil's work was my chief impediment to fully enjoying his work. What did interest me greatly was the calligraphic penmanship of drawings and watercolours from 1942-47.

Technically, I see Cecil as having got from Surrealism not subjects, but the idea of being faithful to one's imaginative inner imagery, and achieving formal depiction using calligraphy in the way André Masson did in his human figures and landscapes. I believe this to have been a primary influence, although nobody appears to have noticed it, largely because Masson is not well known in Britain. The difference between the two is that one is highly erotic and the other markedly asexual although, curiously, I see a strong Tantric stream in Cecil's work from 1942 onwards.

In 1946, though, it was Cecil's innocent Palmeresque delicacy and visionary intensity that I went for, but it created terrible problems for me as a diligent student. Cecil broke all the rules I'd made for myself, partly from my teachers and partly in dissent from them. He wasn't plastically robust enough to help combat my weaknesses in that area which I was trying, unsuccessfully, to overcome in my life drawing and figure compositions. He seemed to me to take the easy way out in a lot of his draughtsmanship. He was tempting me along paths I considered very dangerous. I often stepped into visionary terrain, but was wary as I did so. Then I'd swing and become soft-hearted, tender, lyrical and eager, so Cecil was back in favour once again. What seesaws I went bumpily through in my four art school years.

As a young art student, I liked to look at Cecil's work, but resisted his stylistic characteristics. For a period in the mid-Forties he seemed to me technically flimsy: all vision and extreme delicacy and not a mix that one could model oneself on. Cecil was a great rarity, an ultra-etherealised Neo-Romantic descendant of the Blake-Palmer visionaries. I had not yet had any exposure to mysticism, either Western or Eastern, which I would alight upon after the reproduction of Cecil's 1942-44 work was published.

I linked Cecil's work from 1944 to the mystical orientation I moved towards when I discovered Indian culture in early 1947, by which time I was ending my art school training. Cecil was an extremely isolated figure and it was too early in his career for me to be able to see where his work was heading. I saw him as a lone figure who, only years later did I realise belonged to a minuscule and nearly invisible strand within the cultural scene which would not produce any visual expression other than the Christian mysticism of David Jones and Stanley Spencer. Cecil, like Lewis Thompson, turns out to have been a forerunner of a trend which, even now, has not produced much work of illuminated vision.

I was acquainted with the Fool archetype through Shakespeare, but not until I discovered the Commedia dell'Arte and the stunningly lyrical mime performance of Jean-Louis Barrault as Baptiste in *Les Enfants du Paradis*, the most influential film in my formative years, did the stylistic delicacy of Cecil begin to crystallise in my mind's eye as a significant visionary enterprise.

While I was at the ICA, we held an ambitious show called *Twentieth Century Poets* which contained a fabulous archive of library manuscripts by all the major modernists. Kathleen Raine figured in this exhibition and so I became acquainted with her two years before I discovered Lewis Thompson.

Cecil went into eclipse for me, while I was preoccupied by my involvement in the first two years of the ICA, only to resurface again when I discovered the literary archive of Lewis Thompson in Benares in 1954.

After I returned from my first India trip, quietly bursting with the immense thrill of having alighted upon this mystical poet of genius who had lived in Benares for six years, I phoned Kathleen and asked if I might come and tell her who and what I'd found. She invited me over to Paultons Square and we met alone for a couple of hours during which I mentioned Thompson without going into details about his life in India. It was a purely literary discussion. She was only faintly interested and at a later date invited me to dinner. The other guest was Philip Sherrard, then in a very Greek Orthodox mood and, as far as I could judge, erudite in the mystical corpus of literature. We left near midnight and walked from her flat to Gloucester Road where I caught the last train home.

On that walk, I decided I would spill the beans about my discovery: not of Lewis Thompson, but of Tantric cosmology and Tantric yoga. I was still several feet off the ground and soaring into the Indian stratosphere at the drop of a hat. I got carried away and for at least half the trek from Chelsea, I expounded the system in some detail, in freshly assimilated, but accurate, factual exposition. Up to that moment, Philip had said nothing, but the sympathetic dinner-time guest suddenly delivered, in ineffably lofty tones, a cold and damning dismissal of everything I had said. He pooh-poohed my claims for the profundity and subtlety of this system and said, like all such phenomena, it was a vast catalogue of superstitions utterly without the least metaphysical or philosophical coherence.

As we reached Gloucester Road, in even colder and now scornful tones, he pronounced his total and completely contemptuous dismissal of all Indians as people who had nothing with which to counter the gross materialism or Western affirmations of spirituality. 'They had,' he said, 'a pathetic desire to copy wholesale all the most trivial appurtenances of Western rule: language, clothing, the technical tricks of a mechanical sort, and try to become nothing more than miserable and impoverished copies of those who knew better, missing all the profound essentials that the West had so generously offered them, including a poorly-assimilated education system.' I never met him again.

Only in 1984 could I, for the first time in my adult life, have all my possessions under one roof. Once I'd edited the Thompson *Aphorisms as Mirror to the Light*, I was for the first time able to face sending the six Fool poems to Cecil at Paultons Square.

I wrote Cecil a very respectful homage and gave him a vividly graphic impression of Thompson's discovery of The Fool Book as I called it. I described to him Thompson's relationships with what he called *avadhutas* which Thompson thought Holy Fools were called in India. I have been told the word doesn't mean that at all, but I am fairly certain it is the word for them in South India. Thompson was particularly attracted to these men and treated them with great affection and respect, especially one that he befriended in Benares during the last year of his life. I wrote to Cecil about this, quoting extracts from Thompson's journal. Then I described to Cecil how his pictures had become a very important influence on Thompson and how a new note of joyous innocence and 'street wisdom' had flowed into his verse, reaching a climax with the Fool series.

In my letter to Cecil, my account was vivid enough to melt the heart of any sceptic. Of course, I had to tell the pathetic story of Thompson's death. On 21 June he wrote the last Fool poem with allusions to a marble head in the Bombay Museum and a journal note describing a dead naked *sadhu* on a *ghat*. In his corrugated tin shack on the roof of a house overlooking the Ganges his thermometer read forty-seven degrees centigrade. He collapsed, half starved, and fell into a coma and died on 23 June 1949, only a few *annas* left, completely alone save for a servant who had brought him his food.

I received no reply to my letter, written to someone whose work I trusted and who was of cardinal significance to Lewis Thompson. It was a shattering moment for me. I was living in obscurity in Norfolk, on the dole and without a phone. Hardly anyone knew my address. Cecil definitely knew it because about a year later I received a slip of paper from an art gallery announcing either an exhibition or a lecture by Cecil. It must have been sent at his suggestion, for they couldn't possibly have known my address by any other means. It is an enigma. There was nobody who might have thought ill of Thompson, or of me, who might have persuaded Cecil to have nothing to do with me. I informed nobody else that I had written to Cecil.

Among Thompson's very few belongings was his copy of Cecil's *Vision of the Fool*. Not only had Thompson been sufficiently attracted to that book when he saw it in an Indian bookshop, but on his tiny scholarship he was able to purchase it and grow to love the drawings reproduced in it, absorbing into his innermost being something of the essence Cecil had distilled.

Right at the end of his tragically curtailed life, he managed to write an extraordinary set of poems which he dedicated to Cecil Collins. Through Thompson I perceived Cecil afresh, suffused with rich and complex multiple associations that spread into many areas of my life. Then Cecil came to personify for me true sincerity and goodness.

Cecil Collins
Three Fools in a Storm
1943
Oil on canvas
29.5 x 39.5cm

ROBIN LEANSE

Born 1951 in Nassau, Bahamas. His poems were first published in 1979 (Bananas magazine). He won the Special Second Prize (judges Ted Hughes and Seamus Heaney) in the Arvon International Poetry Competition 1987. Robin has anthologised and published in various literary magazines. He has five sons and lives in London.

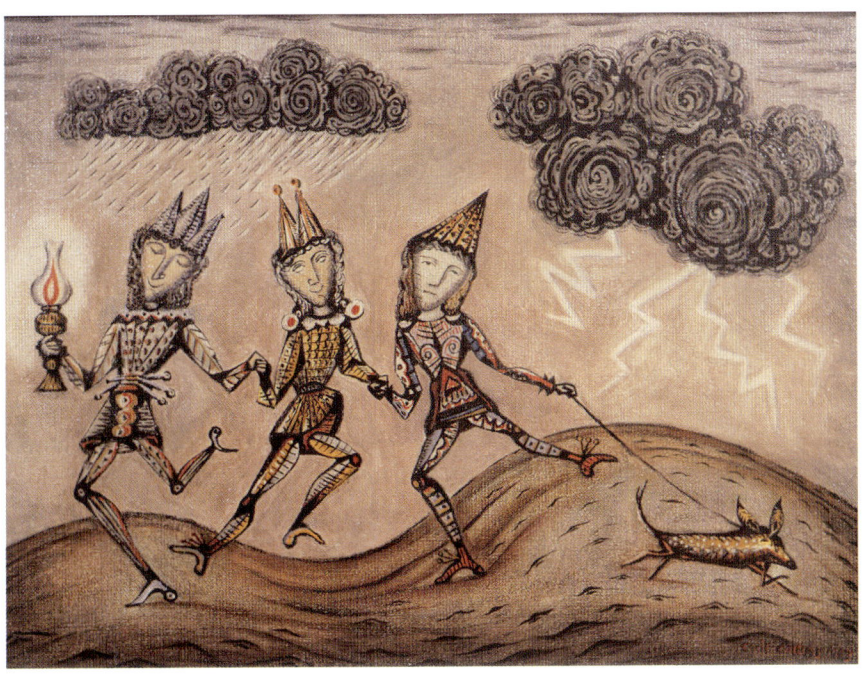

THE FOOL

To Cecil Collins in gratitude for his pictures
Lewis Thompson

THE FOOL IN THE FOREST

The Fool lay down
Under the waving tree,
All on a summer's day –
Oh all the birds
That laugh and cry
In a summer morning,
And leaves and flowers of the tree,
Plucking to dance them free –
A music from the spray!

Lie down, lid down beside
The wending water,
That nets in riddling tears
Clouds of a summer sky.
And so do you lay by
The riddling mind – wild honey, cool
Wild juices of the fruit
Bursting the rind.

THE FOOL AT MORNING

Little child
I greet at dawn
The dawn of your flowering eyes;
You have caught in a net of flowers
The pride of morning.

In your eyes breaking like foam
At every moment blossom
A thousand buds,
Miracle of flowers, O honey of laughing light!
My heart will drown.

Papers of L.Thompson: page 569. By kind permission of Washington State University Libraries. Pullman, WA. USA

I saw Cecil's exhibition at the Tate Gallery in 1981. There was a wonderful drawing of a pilgrim which I wrote about. I very much took to him from that point, but I didn't meet him until just before he died when he came to an exhibition of Ken Kiff's pictures at a gallery in Jermyn Street. He looked frail, but was friendly and asked me to his show opening the following week at Anthony d'Offay's gallery. I never saw him again.

I didn't meet Elisabeth properly until late 1993 or early 1994 at a dinner given by Stephanie and John Macdonald's in Highgate. I liked Elisabeth enormously. I sat next to her. She was very erect and her hat added to her stature, as did her conversation. I could see she was still a beauty though she must have been in her late eighties. She talked about her early life quite a bit and how her people were in newspapers. She told me how she had crossed the Atlantic during the First World War with her mother at the age of six to see her grandmother's estates in Virginia. She said that she was bound by the strictures of her upbringing and wanted to escape that. Art had been the way. When she met and ran away, as it were, with Cecil, that was a really difficult time for her parents and family who disapproved of Cecil. Then and on later occasions she stressed how basic the conditions of life were with Cecil, first in Chelsea then out of London. But it was clearly what she wanted.

The really memorable thing I recall her saying about Cecil had to do with the way in which she felt marginalised. They'd moved to a cottage in Buckinghamshire. Elisabeth said she'd never been able to reconcile herself to one little omission that Cecil had made in his first reaction to this place. He'd said, 'You could make a paradise of this garden,' and she always felt that the whole tenor of their relationship could have been transformed if he'd only said, '*We* could make a paradise of this garden.'

Another thing that she said at our first meeting was that she had reinvented herself. She said, 'I have a completely new life now. My life is transformed.' She said that I should come to see her so I

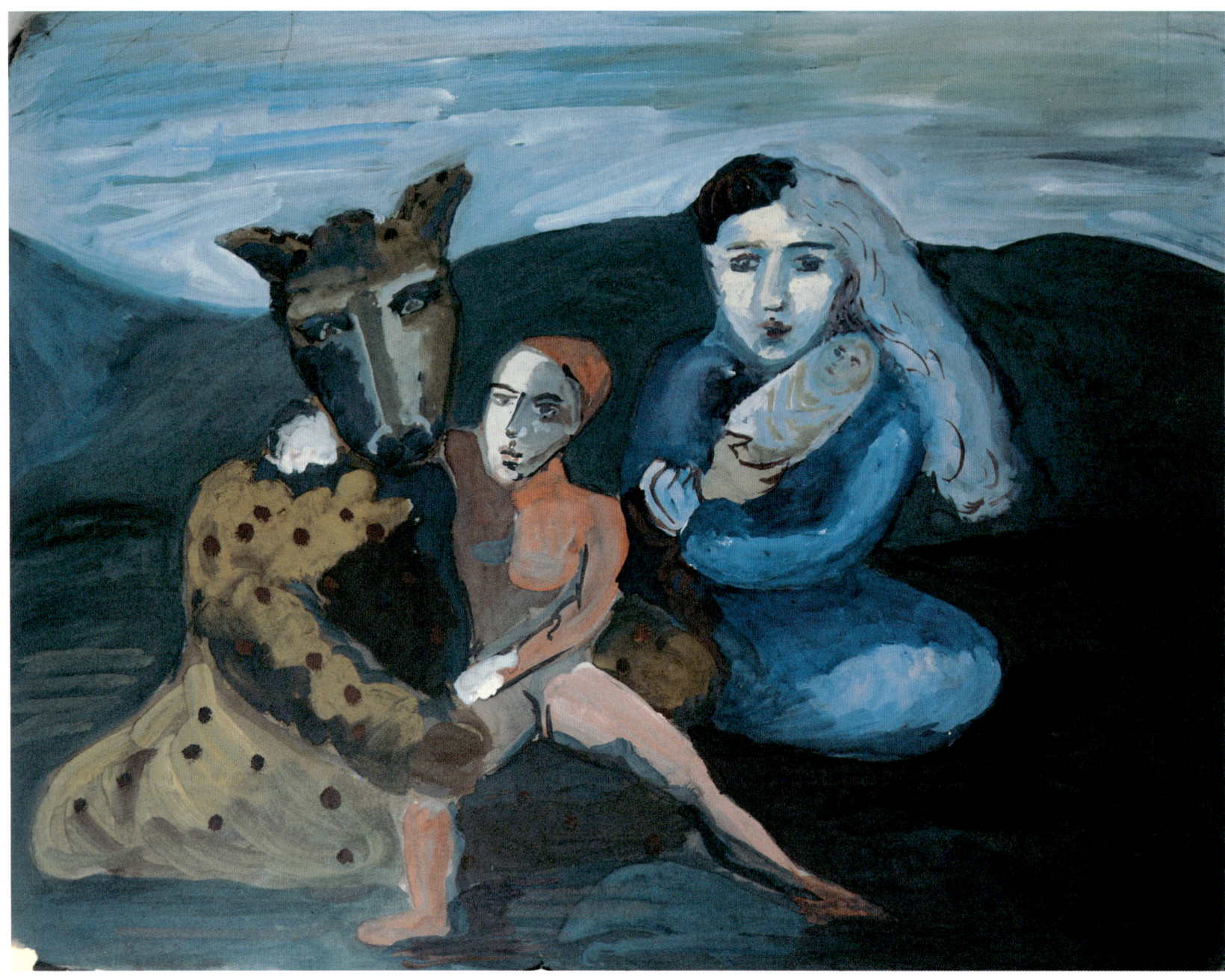

did. We used to go to the Chelsea Arts Club a lot for lunch or supper. She would talk about the Dartington artistic community and how that was nourishing and that St John Perse's poetry became very important for them. I recall her saying how dominant Cecil was in conversations at mealtimes at Dartington, she did not contribute much to these, as that was trespassing on his territory. It was shocking to think of her energy suppressed, presumably for years, all Cecil's life, but she was happy to have the freedom to talk now. She also wrote letters, always in red ink, which I've kept. They were vivid and contained precise images, such as my wife, Kate's, destiny to have twins, because 'she is a comet with two tails'.

I felt very close to her and was so happy to have that friendship and to spend times in her place in Paultons Square. We used to go and talk in her wide top floor room with a sofa on the right by the door on which she put what she was reading and her easel at the other end. She showed me how she had cooked on the landing on a ridiculous stove and you wondered how they hadn't blown themselves up. She used to have to cook a hot meal for Cecil every day and managed to do that. I was able to grasp the delicate trickiness of Kathleen who had the lower half of the house, and who Elisabeth used to call 'Downstairs'. The cat was an anarchic bridge between them over which they had to deal with each other. I understood that it was over

Elisabeth Collins
Actors on a Wild Hill
1940
Gouache
28 x 48.6cm

the matter of how Cecil's legacy was respected. Clearly, Kathleen was very much bound up emotionally and artistically with Cecil. It seemed to me that they were warring women.

At about the time of an exhibition of Cecil's in 1994, I showed Elisabeth a collection of poems I'd just produced that were influenced by some extraordinary times I'd had with a guru, an avatar I should say, called Mother Meera. I wasn't sure that Elisabeth was really interested in that sort of path; in fact she found it indulgent and thought that there were places closer to home to find the truth. Perhaps because Kathleen Raine was so bonkers about India, as part of the antagonism between them, Elisabeth felt Indian spiritual culture was not for her.

Elisabeth was a complete original and she had a wonderful face. She would come out sometimes in a Mary Quant-type wig meant for a much younger woman, a superb coiffure which was stuck on top of her hair. It was a very distinguished pepper-and-salt grey and she looked wonderful. There were two wigs. The other one was brown, a pre-grey colour. I found Elisabeth very enabling of conversation. One felt one wanted to talk to her and she would respond with real understanding and a take of her own and made you feel that there was more to discuss on another occasion. She knew she was a link between the present and the past. She recalled how T. S. Eliot had invited her and Cecil to tea in his flat. They had a formal tea at a decorous table in a room under dustsheets; the image of his poetry in a vignette. Elisabeth also relished telling the story of the friend, who lived downstairs in their house in Cambridge, Karlheinz Stockhausen, taking her to listen to him crashing a dustbin lid repeatedly on its dustbin. 'It's beautiful,' he kept saying. 'Listen.' Her curiosity about people and life were undiminished by age, whether it was a Pink Floyd party with fireworks, the novelty of psychotherapy or the music of another of their friends, John Tavener.

What my wife, Kate, and I both loved about Elisabeth was her honesty. We live in Barnet and one time she came for supper by taxi all the way from Chelsea. This wasn't long before she died and it was a real strain on her health because of her bad back and the cold night air. She was so game and ready to do these things. I think she judged conversations by the very high standards of Dartington or Cecil. She always said how overshadowed she felt by Cecil and how conversations were, on the whole, under Cecil's thumb, but it wasn't a one-sided relationship. For instance she told me that the image of the Fool in Cecil's work had been her idea, and he had adopted it as a real revelation. It must have been mutually beneficial because he would have needed a strong woman.

Elisabeth was not only beautiful and good; she was also very critical of herself. She suggested that Cecil's paintings of her were not the whole truth; they were an idealisation of her. She once told me that she felt we all had our angels and she tried to paint for hers.

In some way, the approval coming over her shoulder was important. When a painting wasn't going well, she would talk about how it affected her very badly, while there were other days when she'd do three things straight off. She seemed to be saying that she was developing as a painter, that painting was a very hard act to get right and she was always afraid of losing the balance required to keep alive the sense of the image without over-conveying it. I said to her that I thought it was like Orpheus' journey back from Hades, where Eurydice is behind you, but if you look back she'll disappear, and when you're painting or writing, if you look back you lose the love that is informing your work. So you have to trust that it's there.

I was always intrigued by the contrast of styles in Cecil's work. In the 1960s, there was a totally new way of interpreting the meaning of images in his drawing. Cecil's real centre of interest became the spikiness and the angularity and relations between things, with lines and angles and rapid changes of direction. What he was producing then lost that spiral fluidity which one associated with his earlier work.

Elisabeth left me Cecil's *Head* which was in the Tate exhibition. It's blue and dreamy. She also left me a very beautiful one of hers called *The Bride*. It was implicit that she wanted Cecil's work to live on and be properly recognised, but I think she also needed to feel that there was enough energy to support her own work after he died. She referred to Cecil a lot. She was devoted to his work, but always conscious, I felt, of the price she had had to pay for it. We talked about how the vision of the unity of everything could be expressed in art. There would be times when she talked about Cecil's need to round on others who were expressing what he believed to be inauthentic views of art and that he would chastise those who he felt were, as she put it, betraying themselves by falling into wrong thinking.

THE PILGRIM

Give me a staff as thin as a pin
and as strong as a pin is strong
and I will drive it through earth's skin
and inject it with my song.

a song that tilts the ear, a nest
built sideways on the tree –
will anchor my path to my quest
and keep earth under me!

Robin Leanse, 1977

RUPERT LOYDELL

Rupert Loydell is Senior Lecturer in English with Creative Writing at University College Falmouth and a widely exhibited abstract artist. He was Managing Editor of Stride Publications (1982 – 2008) and remains the editor. His many poetry publications include *An Experiment in Navigation* and *Home All Along,* containing the *Songs for Cecil.*

FROM SEVEN SONGS FOR CECIL

HYMNS

Where words won't do
then colour must

Intensity rings out
across alien skies

Let all creation sing
itself to wholeness

It is a great happiness
this worship of impulse

a wounded palette
healed and renewed

as daybreak stretches
its new found wings

in a spectacular
spectrum of noise

the wounded angel
flying high

FROM MORE SONGS FOR CECIL COLLINS

THE MUSIC OF DAWN

Alchemy has been worked here.
The land itself is gold,
The hills made precious overnight.

On the beach an angel
Strolls the sand
Conducting this magic.

The sea sings
as the sun warms
the morning swell.

Sky and sea, sun and sand,
angel's robes; the world
as far as can be imagined or seen

is shining with reflected glory,
shimmering as angels
play with paint and light.

DAWN MUSIC

The Angel of Morning
sings sweeter than the sea,
plays with the very light itself
paints anew the day for me.

DAYBREAK

Three women
give flowers
to the sun,

offer themselves
to the sun,

to each other
to the depths
of the land.

They wade into
this green picture
you painted.

The sun's
a smudge of yellow
on a faint horizon

waiting
to spread itself wide
across the night.

In light
the women
will become flesh,

their mystery
revealed as
thin disguise,

their features changed.
Day and secrets
are now broken.

THE ANGEL OF THE FLOWING LIGHT

pours pure sun into shapes
that cannot be imagined,

puts the sparkle in the sea
and pulls rainbows from the storm.

She is the light in lovers' eyes,
the smouldering heat of passion,

the winter warmth in the greenhouse.
and the candle flickering by the bath.

She is the diamond
that cuts the soul apart,

the blazing fire
that burns then heals.

BY THE WATERS

The blue angel
watches the day fade
away each dusk.

Her wings shimmer
purple and gold
in the cool light,

and the trees
sing of wind
in the shadow.

These waters
heal and cleanse,
wash false hope away.

HARRY & LAURA MARSHALL

Directors of Icon Films, Harry and Laura Marshall founded, in 1990, this national and international award winning UK documentary production company. In 1989 the television series, *Art, Faith and Vision* for Channel Four, was produced by them which included a programme on Cecil Collins.

HM: We were interested in making a series about art and creativity for Channel Four as a result of meeting Peter Levi, the Professor of Poetry at Oxford. His publisher was Laura's father, Adrian House, who had introduced him to me because he thought that Peter would be a good person to present it. We had several meetings with him and talked about various artists we might include, Iris Murdoch being one. She'd been my tutor at one stage when I was reading English at Oxford.

I think it was through Elisabeth Frink that we came to Cecil. We'd contacted her and she put us in touch with Canon Keith Walker who had commissioned her to do a head of Christ. Canon Walker also wanted a window to be made by Cecil Collins. That was how I met Cecil and through him, Patrick Reyntiens. Then we met John Tavener who was going to write the music and the piece he wrote for me was wonderful. It was performed by the choir of Christchurch and that brought it full circle for me because the choir-master was a man called Steven Darlington who I'd known and subsequently made a film with in Prague on the first anniversary of the Revolution. We took the Christchurch choir out to Prague with Placido Domingo to perform various pieces, including an *Ave Maria* by Bartok which Steven had found in the Bodleian Library and which had never ever been performed. It was very interesting how everything spun round.

The one big thing that Cecil said that I took away was, 'Everything is in us, with us now,' and that became apparent in the making of the series. It was rather like one of those spider's webs you can't see until you change the direction of the light and then it's very apparent. All the elements were always there. It was just discovering them and putting a light on them.

I know Cecil's lessons were famous. Robin Baring is one of those artists who one immediately sees was tutored by Cecil. I think that was always a bit of a danger with Cecil. After he died, Elisabeth, his widow told me that Cecil had manifested himself, but there wasn't room for two artists in one marriage. Elisabeth not only coped, she blossomed after he died. I think she rather enjoyed the sort of space she got after his death because Cecil was very pungent. I say pungent rather than powerful because it's not a word I associate with Cecil. He wasn't physically impressive. He was quite frail so I didn't think of him as powerful, but thought of him as pungent. If you saw a painting by Cecil, it had a lingering quality about it. I think it was like an incense or an Indian spice, something very definitive.

I remember after Cecil died, Elisabeth went out and bought a pair of shoes that cost £200. She said, 'I'm ninety. I'm going to die soon and I'm probably going to wear them three times. Isn't it an extravagance?' She was ecstatic. She had chosen this ascetic life with Cecil and they had had to live as poor as church mice, although she came from this grand wealthy Yorkshire family.

LM: I remember bringing her lots of ready meals after Cecil died, because she didn't seem to cook for herself at all.

HM: Cecil carried the ego and she carried the anima. He had quite a lot of ego, but Cecil wasn't the slightest bit interested in money. When you saw their flat in Paultons Square, his studio was this extraordinary chaos in a very cramped space. He could have done with a bit of recognition. He hated Frances Bacon with an absolute passion because, compared to him, Bacon had got so much acknowledgement and it bothered Cecil that Bacon's paintings were promoting something pathological, Cecil said that his own work was

Cecil Collins
Tree and Hills
1944
Roneo print
20.3 x 29.5cm

all about life and Bacon's was all about death and. In many ways, they were mirror opposites. I visited Frances Bacon in his studio which was very similar to Cecil's in terms of its absolute chaos. I think that they were twins of that era in the sense that both had been working with archetypes and icons. One was convex and the other was concave. One was light and one was dark.

I remember having lunch with Elisabeth once at that restaurant opposite Paultons Square and she was talking about Eric Gill's incest with his daughters. There was this ninety year old lady and I suddenly realised the entire restaurant was listening to Elisabeth talking about him sodomising his daughters. She didn't judge it. She simply said, 'This is what happened.' I remember her telling me that Eric Gill was once carving this statue outside the BBC. He'd been up a ladder carving it and he never wore any underwear. He wore an artist's smock.

LM: And no trousers.

HM: She just thought it was very funny, but sexuality and romantic physicality wasn't something that Elisabeth ever talked about in relation to Cecil.

Sometimes we had a radio mike on Cecil and Elisabeth while we were filming and they would wander off and you could hear what they were saying. You didn't want to eavesdrop and it tended to happen by accident, but they were often bickering.

LM: Quarrelling gently all the time.

HM: We'd say to them, 'Will you go to the end of the field and walk back towards us,' and they'd be walking along arguing over trivial things. Elisabeth would be saying things like, 'Cecil, stop,' or 'You shouldn't talk so much.' I think that he needed her to keep him in check. If she hadn't been there, this very grounded, matter-of-fact Yorkshire woman, he might have just floated away.

All the letters she ever wrote to me were always in red ink and there's something very unromantic about it. Red is the colour of correction and that's interesting, isn't it? She was a corrective to Cecil and that I think was important in their relationship. Alexander the Great had a fool who used to walk behind him saying, 'You are only human. You are only human.' That was the fool's job. I think she was that person and also the muse. She was multi-tasking. I remember she didn't much care for people who came along and fawned on Cecil. He wasn't immune to flattery; he quite liked that and Elisabeth couldn't bear it.

LM: Elisabeth may have been frustrated in her life. I think she had

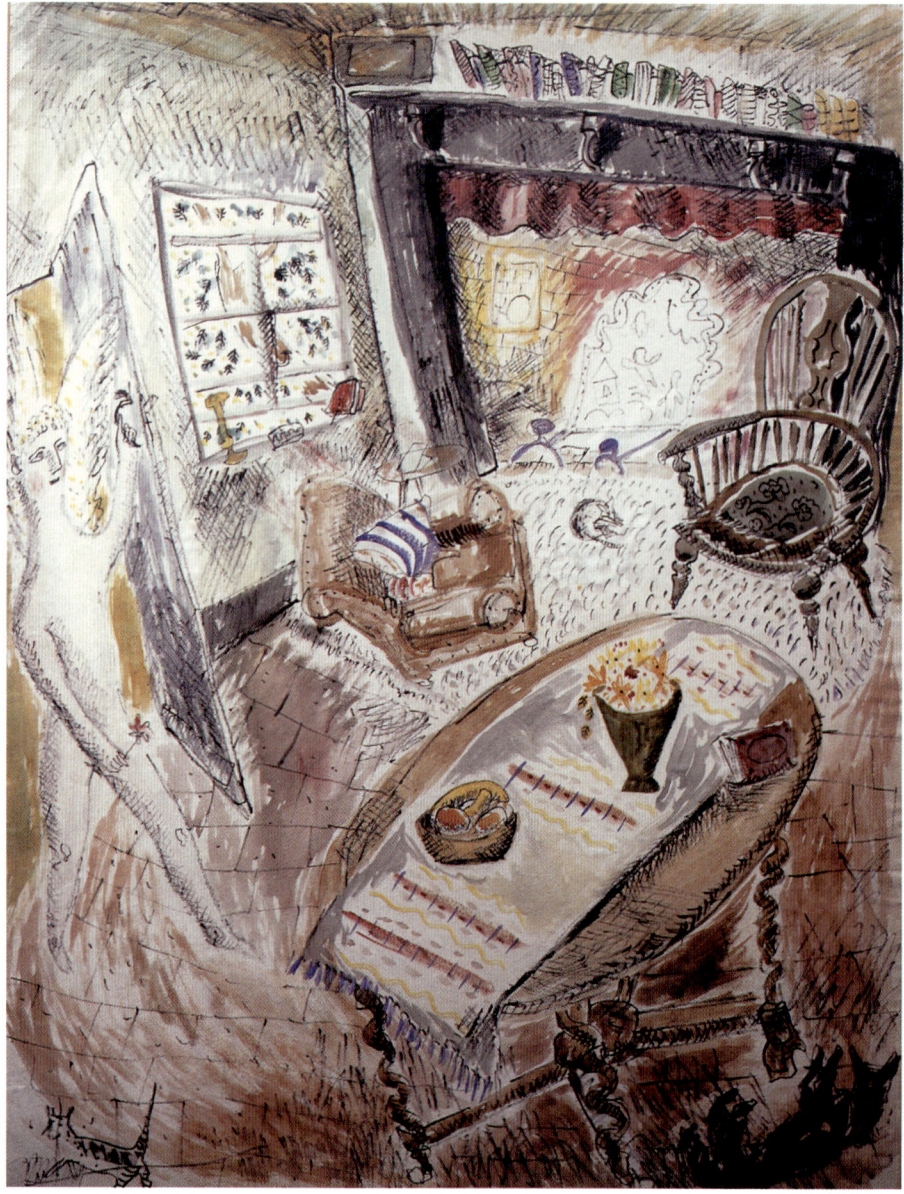

Cecil Collins
The Sitting Room at Monk's Cottage
1932
Ink and watercolour
75 x 55cm

quite interesting relationships, but there was frustration there, an irritation.

HM: I don't think she was frustrated. I think she'd lived the life she'd chosen. She didn't have to marry Cecil. She was financially independent and she told me that her family disapproved intensely. Elisabeth was rebellious and extremely contra-suggestible.

LM: She liked to have private women conversations. Not that she didn't want to see Harry, but she liked having a *tête à tête* with a woman as well.

HM: I remember one occasion Laura and I came down to see them from Carlisle. I buzzed the buzzer and she answered and said, 'You sound like you've got a cold.' I said, 'Yes, I do,' and she said, 'You'd better not come up then. Come back when you're feeling better.' We'd come three hundred miles. Cecil was quite obsessed about not getting colds.

LM: We were quite young then. We didn't know about old people.

HM: Well, that was when we were making the film. It was the first television series that we made when I was twenty-six.

LM: He was the youngest producer working for Channel Four.

HM: It was our first film, our first series in the days when the whole process took a lot longer. Today, if I were to make a film about Cecil and Elisabeth, we'd probably have ten minutes and the edit would be over in four or five weeks. Then it was much more leisurely. I don't know how many days of filming we did with Cecil and Elisabeth. We spent a lot of time with them. I think it was probably a twelve-week edit.

I do remember having a conversation with Cecil, while filming, to try and get him to alter his position because the way he was sitting made his hunchback very prominent. If I could get him to shift slightly the emphasis wouldn't be so much on his hunch, and he just didn't seem to understand at all. It was a bit like Elisabeth's nickname for him, 'Parc,' because he looked like a badly tied up parcel; he had a sort of body dysmorphia. It was paradoxical this physical nature at odds with his higher ideals. That is the very nature of art; it's the interface between the base, corrupt human being who is still able to produce something transcendental and I think that was something quite interesting. It's the sort of junction between the poetic vision which is able to create these extraordinary images and then this shambolic, crumpled heap with a bogey hanging out of his nose.
I think Cecil understood all of that as well although he did see himself as this sort of Gilgamesh at a certain level or a kind of Jesus figure. He had a wonderful confidence. Cecil did have that sense of his destiny and place in the pantheon of British artists and how he fitted in.

He was prescriptive. For example, he was very keen that we should film with Patrick Reyntiens.

LM: Elisabeth was prescriptive too.

HM: Cecil also wanted us to use the music of John Tavener, but they were never intrusive.

LM: I remember it very much as them saying, 'Wouldn't it be lovely if John Tavener wrote the music for the film. There was the enjoyable time when we went to the Chelsea Arts Club for Elisabeth's birthday with John Tavener and he'd written a 'Happy Birthday' song to Elisabeth which we all had to sing.

HM: I remember on one occasion we bought some paintings Elisabeth was exhibiting in the Albermarle gallery. When we got them back, I had them reframed, as I always did on such occasions, and behind the paintings were other paintings. I remember ringing her up and telling her about them, but she didn't want them back.

LM: She let us choose them before they went to the gallery. They were all stacked up in her sitting-room upstairs.

HM: I think they are wonderful. That's what I feel. I remember there was a picture she did that she thought was enormously important of a figure carrying a man across the river. I thought it was a very fine painting. We also bought these lovely pictures by Elisabeth done in 1989. They were on Arthurian themes; one is called *Merlin meets Guinevere at the Edge of the Wood*. The other one's title is *Guinevere Goes to Meet Lancelot* who's rather a Fool like character with lots of dots on his clothes. Then there's Merlin disguised as a raven. The raven is the shape-shifter.

Elisabeth had asked me if there were any of her paintings that I particularly liked and she left me the one I'd indicated in her will. It's titled *A Meeting*, dated Christmas 1988 and has my name on it. She also left me a large watercolour by Cecil which has a sort of casual entry of an Angel, who looks rather pale and worn out from prayer, coming into their cottage room where they lived at that time. It's not signed which is unusual. The picture frame is a lovely homemade one that Cecil did himself. He cobbled it together with bits of wood joined and then painted. It's enormous for a watercolour. It looks like he drew it, then painted it, then drew on top of it and hatched it over afterwards.

I remember that they still had various things in the painting at Paultons Square; the fire grate with the decorations on it, the chair and the table. What's interesting is the table legs are very similar to the one in the painting, *The Artist and His Wife*, of 1939. I wonder if it's the same square table. It's got that very particular reverse perspective where it's narrower at the front and goes out towards the back. He talked to me about its significance, but I can't remember what he said. It's as though it's seen through a fish-eye lens. There are things in the painting that I'm not sure what they are. I wonder what that oblong shape is on the shelf above the fireplace.

LM: I'd say it's a radio. And outside the window there's a lovely tree with leaves.

HM: The other picture that was left to me is an amazing dreamy nude by Cecil. It's very unusual, quite small, painted in 1939. I think this is probably his sexiest picture. It's a sort of composite of papers, one on top of the other. It's a mixture of various mediums. I love it. It's really unique.

We also have a painting he did in 1989 so they're fifty years apart. I said to Cecil, 'I'd like to commission a picture for Laura.' He asked, 'What would you like?' and I said, 'One of a Fool riding a bird.' He just got out a matchstick, dipped it into paint and painted it there and then while I was there. Cecil was technically very accomplished; he was a master technician, he could use anything.

I thought there was something innocent and unworldly about Cecil which he deliberately cultivated. He did not want to know about driving cars or any of that kind of thing. I think he wanted to preserve the Fool in himself because, for him, the Fool and the Angel met in innocence. They seem very different characters, but in fact they're very similar. I think they represent male and female archetypes that overlap in innocence. In Cecil's work, the Fool is male and the Angel is female. I don't know any male angels, although there's one scene of angels falling through the sky.

LM: Elisabeth did create the original Fool picture, didn't she?

HM: Yes. I remember Peter Levi quoting Picasso saying, 'I don't seek; I find.' Cecil would take what was necessary. Even when he paints himself and Elisabeth in *The Artist and His Wife*, in 1939, with the Egyptian crosses, the grail goblet and that very strange perspective of the table and those remarkable eyes of Elisabeth; she's an Angel and he is a bit of a Fool.

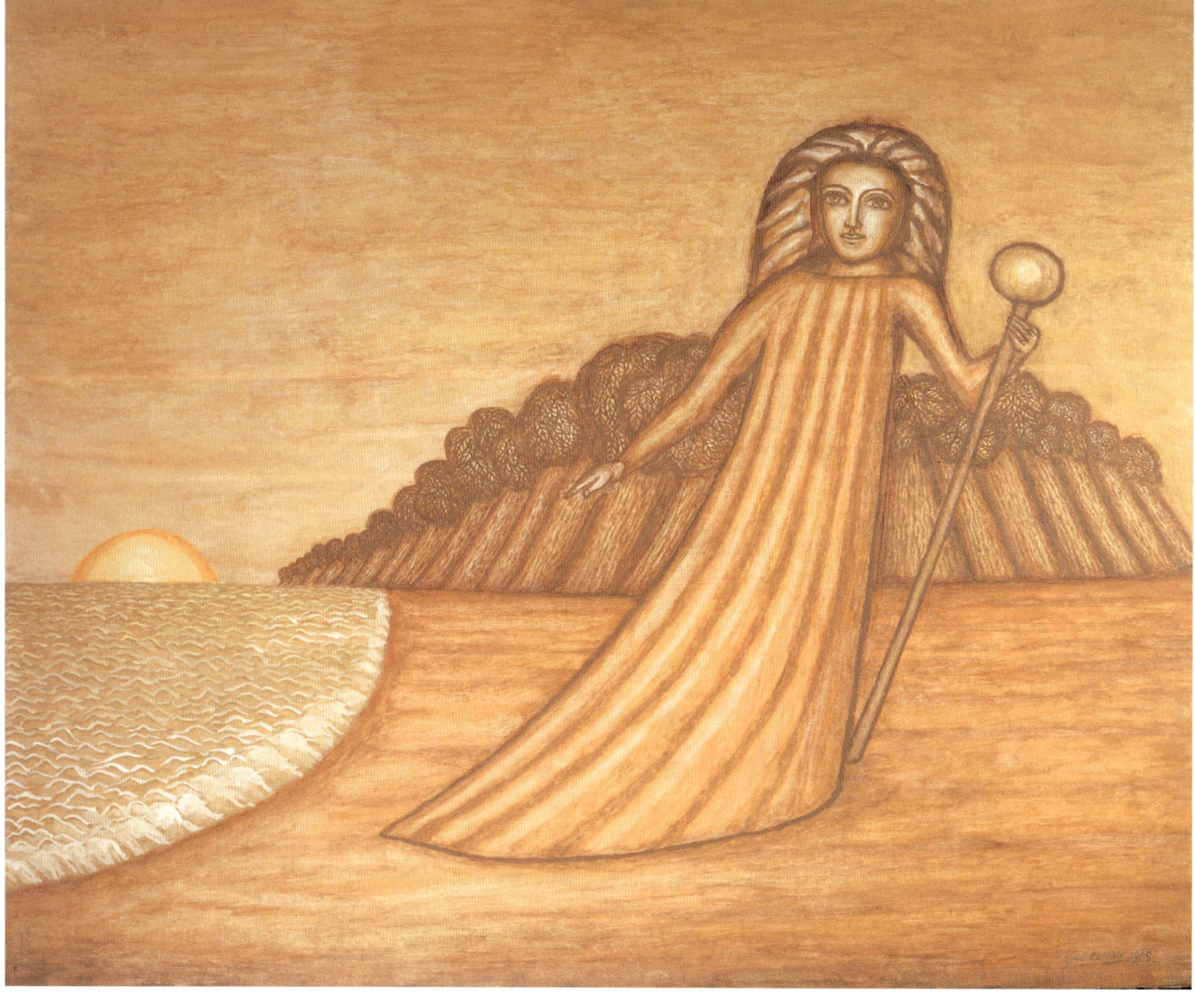

Cecil Collins
The Music of Dawn,
1988
Tempera on canvas
71 x 84cm

As mentioned earlier, what I've taken away from my friendship with Cecil and think about on a weekly basis, if not more often, is that everything is within us now. It is absolutely true; we don't need anything more than we have and we must make the best of what we've got. It's about finding the truth in what you have. Something that we talked about was the way in which this operated and how it was true of the entire universe. So everything that had ever happened at any time was not lost as it had all happened in the here and now and you just had to find that. You don't have to go to Jerusalem or the Himalayas to find your way to the truth. You find it in yourself and that you have it within you right now. To me that is so powerful, the notion of the unity of all time and space.

That realisation and the enormous power of the individual were for me the great message that came through Cecil. I think it is a truth that other artists, if they're good, also share. I remember going to a lecture by Joseph Beuys who began by saying, 'There is the power of a hundred nuclear bombs within this room, but you don't know it yet.' He and Cecil couldn't have been more unlike each other and yet I feel in their different ways they both recognised the importance of empowering the individual with their inner strength to develop their potential and allowing people to recognise that they didn't need any more than they actually had. When I think of Cecil, I remember his clothes: his shirts, the collars turned, and everything carefully mended by Elisabeth. He stepped very lightly on the earth. He didn't consume because he believed that which was important he had already.

DAVID MATTHEWS

David Matthews composes, edits, orchestrates, and writes. He has worked as Benjamin Britten's assistant at Aldeburgh. His publications include an introduction to the music of Sir Michael Tippett and since 1988 he has been Music Adviser to the English Chamber Orchestra. He has a special interest in the relationship between the visual arts and music and his composition *The Music of Dawn* was inspired by the Cecil Collins' painting of the same name.

THE MUSIC OF DAWN

In June 1989 I went to the Cecil Collins Retrospective exhibition at the Tate Gallery. I did not know that he had died, at the age of 81, shortly after the exhibition opened, until I saw the memorial bowl of flowers placed at the entrance. It was a shock: I had met Cecil Collins only once, but he had made a profound impression on me, and I had grown to admire his work more and more in recent years. I went round the exhibition in a state of heightened awareness, and when I reached the last room, with his very last paintings, I was taken aback by their beauty and the freshness of their vision. I was particularly struck by the painting called 'The Music of Dawn'. A priestess stands on the seashore, in soft dawn light, her right hand pointing down to the sun rising out of the sea. It is painted in tempera, and the colours are warm and glowing. It immediately suggested music as, from its title, it was obviously intended to do. Cecil Collins was the most musical of painters and I hope that he would have liked the idea of his painting being evoked in the medium of orchestral sound.

Of course one cannot literally translate a painting into music, or a seascape. My piece is also related to my own frequent experience of seeing the sun rising out of the sea at Deal in Kent, where much of the piece was written. The piece developed further when I had the idea of contrasting a static 'dawn' with a dynamic 'morning' music. This came after I saw another painting by Collins, his altarpiece of the sun, *Icon of Divine Light*, in Chichester Cathedral.

I did try to imitate the sound of the sea breaking over the shingle beach at Deal at one point near the beginning of the piece. I wrote down the rhythms I was hearing and then transcribed them for percussion instruments; a rain stick, small metal maracs, caxixi (special South American maracas) and a small sizzle cymbal. It is quite realistic.

The first part of my piece, slow and contemplative, evokes the pale dawn light, with its subtle shifts of colour and sense of expectation. What movement there is takes place against a background of sustained pedal notes. The intensification at the end of this section heralds the first real climax, for the rising of the sun. The remainder of the piece, which is fast and energetic, is a celebration of the morning, after the sun has gained strength. In form it is a scherzo in several sections, in the last two of which the music gradually slows towards a return of the opening of the piece; then a coda for the strings and a final blaze of midday light.

STEPHEN MCKENNA

Stephen McKenna, born in London, 1939, studied at the Slade School of Fine Art, London and became Senior Lecturer in painting, Canterbury College of Art (1965–1967) after which he was guest professor in Germany and he is currently president of The Royal Hibernian Academy, Dublin. He lives in County Carlow and Donegal, Ireland and is one of Ireland's foremost artists.

I think I originally met Cecil at a dinner at Richard Morphet's house. I knew about his work. I'd been vastly amused for years by a hanging in the Tate of two small pictures, one above the other. One was an extremely dull painting by Winston Churchill and above or below that was a painting by Cecil called *The Sleeping Fool*. I always enjoyed that; it was a wonderful touch. Some curator had a sense of humour. I didn't know Cecil's work very well, but I liked that picture and everything else I'd seen of his I found interesting.

My eyes were really opened to the work of Cecil once I met him. The man was so impressive that it encouraged you to look more carefully at work that you might otherwise have passed over. He had a way of talking about his own work, and work in general, which indicated that his was a very serious and complex mind. I'm not sure if you can talk about his subject matter because it was, in fact, quite varied, but I realised very quickly that, for all his other worldliness and concern with higher things, he was a master technician. He knew what he was doing. He got his hands dirty; he knew the technique of painting inside out, as well as being a very complex painter.

In a curious way, the same thing applied to him as a person. While he could talk very seriously and apparently without any humour about something extremely significant, he would suddenly break off and make a comment about somebody on the other side of the room which was an absolutely penetrating, incisive observation, often very funny and totally irreverent. He had a sense of humour and irony which he could turn on and off as he wished. It was part of his character. He was extremely sensitive to everything and his concern with what I call higher things. While this was probably central it was by no means the whole of his life and work. He was a man who enjoyed life.

Cecil was a great egocentric. It wasn't that he was selfish or arrogant; he was a modest, quiet man, but he had no doubts or false modesty about his position, his abilities and the importance of his work. He had a certain way of doing things, but he was also interested in other people and their art and was constantly interested in what was going on. He was a good teacher. I wasn't taught by him, but in conversation with him you were his student.

Cecil dressed in a somewhat eccentric manner, but his colour scheme was very carefully thought out. Elisabeth was an absolute beauty and had terrific elegance. I didn't know her as a young woman, but you don't remain an elegant lady if you've got a husband who doesn't appreciate it and Cecil was very proud of her appearance.

There's one very strange point here: I always saw them together; I very rarely saw one without the other. When Cecil died, I thought, and I think a lot of his friends thought the same, poor Elisabeth won't last long. What will she do without Cecil? She flourished. With the old tyrant out of the way, she became herself.

Stephen McKenna
Aiguablava
2007
Oil on canvas
150 x 200cm

She painted more, took herself seriously. She became a real person in her own right. When Cecil was alive, everything was centred around him in their house and in their work. Everything in their relationship was on Cecil's terms. He was old-fashioned and she always played the role of second fiddle. It wasn't absolutely in her nature perhaps, but she had decided she'd do that because she had a huge respect for Cecil as an artist. That's one of the problems with artists marrying each other. One of them always takes over, usually the man. In my generation, and even more in Cecil's, who was somewhat older than I was, it was almost part of the social mores: a woman expected the man to be the boss and the leader and if he wasn't, she would have thought, what have I got there? I haven't got a proper man, or something like that.

Elisabeth used to make cakes, but once Cecil died, she never made another one. All kinds of things suddenly became clear after his death. She had put on a show for Cecil and did it extremely well. Later, I saw quite a lot of Elisabeth's work. She was a very good artist. She probably wasn't on the level of Cecil. Whether she had been at the beginning, I don't know. It was her choice to give up her art to support Cecil and I think she probably had a happy life. It was nice that she returned to it finally but, putting it bluntly, it was too late. If you want to be a significant painter, you have to put in twenty years from 9am to 6pm; there's no way round that.

I started life as a professional soldier, but I soon gave that up. At the age of twenty, I went into painting. I studied at the Slade, but the teaching there was very poor. I did learn quite a lot from my tutor in the end, not so much about painting as about being a painter and being rigorous about what you were doing and looking at what you'd done. I'm still painting now; painters don't retire. I find that fashion comes and goes in the art market. If you stay where you are, it'll come back to you. Apart from the teaching I used to do, I just live from painting. I'm totally dependent on it.

Over the years, I've learnt that if you want to convince somebody of something such as to buy a painting or that there should or shouldn't be a new member of the Academy, you do it by rhetoric, not by rational logic. I remember Cecil saying to me once, 'You've got the right instrument for convincing people.' He said that I have a fairly deep, stentorian voice and he thought that was a useful attribute.

We used to talk about other painters sometimes and I remember him talking about Bacon. He regarded him as a decorative mannerist, pathological. He disapproved of that attitude to life; that was the core of it. I'd met Bacon once or twice and he was an extremely charming, courteous and cultivated man. I don't know if he and Cecil ever met. I think they must have done at some stage. I talked more with Cecil about the Italian Renaissance than the twentieth century. I was interested in the great muralists; that's what I was looking at the most. Leonardo never interested me as a painter. He had a great scientific mind, but he never finished a painting. *The Last Supper* was destroyed in the eighteenth century and then repainted half a dozen times. It's not his any more and there are only half a dozen paintings by him. I talked to Cecil about that, and about Giotto. Cecil was, of course, familiar with Giotto's paintings. Whether he'd actually seen them I don't know, but he would ask me what a painting was like, what condition was it in, and we'd talk about technical things. I've always been very interested in technique. When he talked about my work, Cecil would always make some pertinent and relevant remark, but I don't know if he ever came to any of my shows.

Cecil was interested in contemporary music; I was somewhat less so. I was certainly not interested in 1960s music, but I did like early twentieth-century music. In 1984 or '85, I'd finished building my studio in Donegal which had no electricity and I had a wind-up gramophone with very few records. I was discussing this with Cecil and he said, 'I've got a lot of records. Come and have a look.' I went to his studio in Chelsea, not Paultons Square, another studio round the corner from there. Paultons Square was the apartment. I think the studio belonged to the council, a real artist's studio. He may have worked there early on, but when I went there it was just a large storage room with stuff piled everywhere. He had his records there and we had a long conversation about them. They were all 78s, not even vinyl. It was an extraordinary collection. There were ten records for one symphony. He said, 'Why don't you have these? Those I want to keep, but take anything else you want.' I took a great many and I said, 'Cecil, I really feel I ought to pay you something for these.' He was not well off at all and it was an enormous gift. He could have sold them if he wanted to get rid of them. He said, 'What about £5?' I said, 'What about £50?' 'All right,' he said. I listened to those records a lot. I have them still. I'd never get rid of them because they were Cecil's.

Cecil and I used to talk about his system of teaching. Teaching was a very large part of his life as an artist and as a person, but it wasn't something he did only to earn money. There was a huge battle at City Lit because they were trying to get him to resign at the age of seventy, but he didn't want to stop. I think he felt that he had a very important message he needed to pass on to another generation of painters.

I spent a number of years teaching. I quite liked teaching, but I do not like institutions. I'm probably something of a rationalist, certainly in my language and the way I talk, and Cecil wasn't, although he did have a rational mind.

Cecil was not interested in people doing things like him. If they did, he stopped them very quickly. He had an obsession with his vision and his message and he wanted to pass that on. He knew that part of it would be embedded in the paintings, but not all of it. Some of it had to be done by showing and demonstrating and talking to young people; that was his interest in teaching. It was never about style.

Quite rightly, he deeply disapproved of the whole art education industry. To my shame, I was part of setting it up in the beginning, but by the late 1970s and '80s the art school system had got to the stage where nobody was teaching anything; they were just indulging themselves, teachers and students. It's become more and more like therapy, as far as I can see. Things have gone radically wrong in art schools and Cecil saw that. It's got worse since then. Fortunately, there are still a few people round who know something about art and about how to look at art. That's what Cecil and I talked about, the importance of looking and teaching people how to look. You have to learn this. I learned it from paintings, but I also learned it from a few painters I came across. They were usually a bit older than me. And I learned it from museums. That's where you educate yourself, in museums.

I think Cecil's teaching was really all about learning to see. The way he talked about how things were, one knew that there was more to be seen than appeared at first sight and I think that was his central message which was certainly useful to me, although I wasn't a student. Look at everything again and again. There's an inside and an outward shell.

BRYCE MCKENZIE-SMITH

Born in Australia, Bryce McKenzie-Smith read English at Melbourne in the late 1950s. He then taught briefly before he went to India in 1963 to search for a guru in which he was successful. Later, he proceeded to London to train as a psychotherapist. He found the cultural life of the metropolis, the historical associations and the British Museum Reading Room as well as the proximity to Paris appealing and settled in London. Since retiring in 2004, he spends a lot of time reflecting on life after death.

I met Cecil Collins at a meeting of an organisation called the Centre for Spiritual and Psychological Studies in 1965, just after I arrived in England. Cecil was on the council of the Centre which had been founded, and was run, by a remarkable woman called Alison Barnard in the early 1950s. For nine years attending their meetings, I knew Cecil simply as 'an artist' since he never spoke to me. Then in the summer of 1974, the Centre took over a hotel in Talloires on the banks of Lake Annecy in France. The hotel was near a château where St Bernard of Clairvaux had once lived. There must have been thirty or forty of us and Cecil gave a lecture with slides of his pictures. It was in the dark and I was extraordinarily moved by his talk. I actually found myself weeping. It was the cumulative effect and touched me somewhere very deeply. The same thing manifested in a different way in every picture. His work touched my soul.

I hadn't seen his pictures previously and didn't know anything about them or him. I had by then quite a good collection of modern British artists like Augustus John, Ambrose McEvoy and I had a little Rowlandson too, but after that, I sold them all and started buying Collins' work.

I bought quite a number directly from Cecil, mostly prints and lithographs; others I bought at auction. I also got the names of people who owned his work from the Whitechapel exhibition catalogue of 1959 and then went and asked if I could buy the paintings from them. None of them would sell, except for one I tracked down to the Imperial Tobacco Co. in Millbank. That had been bought by a discerning chairman who had since died. It had been put up in the attic that is where it was when I got there. The painting is called *Hymn* [1960]. It used to be called Death. Cecil told me later that the figure was neither a Sibyl, nor an Angel, but 'something new.' I used to have about twenty-five Cecil's. Now I have only six. Before I retired in 2004, I was an analytical psychotherapist and practised in various clinics in London, but mainly at home, as do most therapists.

I kept notes of my meetings with Cecil. I'm not capable of discussing paintings from a technical point of view so the notes are simply a record. I visited him a number of times and each time I came home from seeing him, I would make the notes while it was

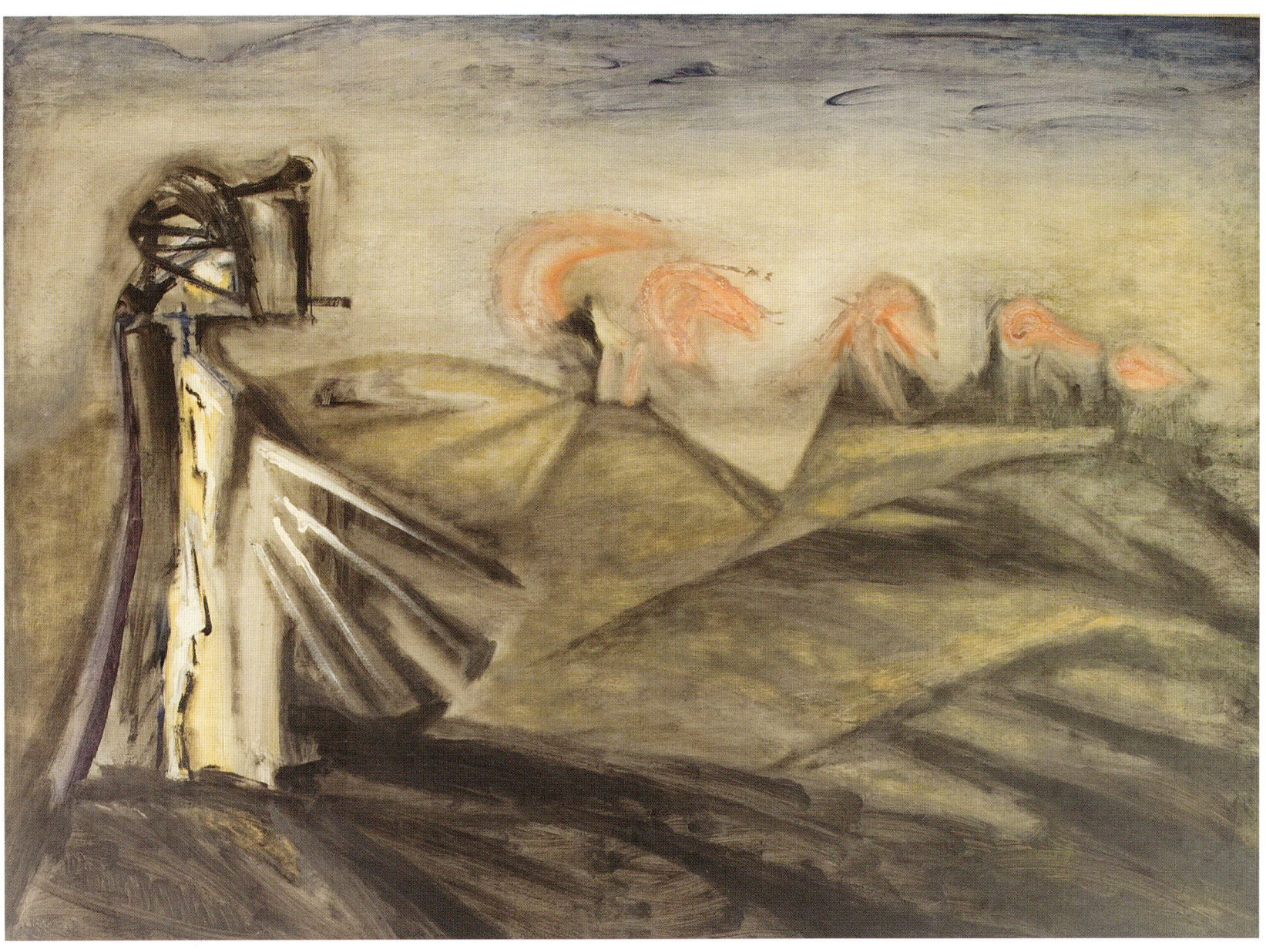

Cecil Collins
Hymn
1960
Oil on board
90.5 x 112cm

still fresh. He would talk about his work and himself, about religion and spiritual matters and all sorts of things. I felt I was treated as an equal, though when he got onto weighty spiritual matters he could be rather dogmatic. He obviously believed he was right and was sometimes intolerant of other people's views. He could be direct which I admired and he could also be a bit rude, but I didn't mind that. One time, Cecil was talking about how people weren't being taught to draw any more and how he used to go to life drawing and was considered very good at it, 'a prodigy'. I said, 'I haven't noticed any nudes amongst your work, Cecil,' and he said, 'Oh, there are plenty.'

Every November the Centre held a weekend conference at the Royal Albion Hotel in Brighton. Cecil was impatient of cant in spiritual matters and could be abrasive. At one of these conferences at the end of a morning's lectures, Cecil got up and said vigorously to the entire hall, 'I'm nauseated by all the talk about spirituality that we've had this morning.' A few hours later the chairman, Dr Michael Loewe from Cambridge, stood up and with a little twinkle in his eye, said, 'I'm going to nauseate Cecil Collins a little more, I'm going to talk about spiritual matters,' to the laughter of the afternoon discussion group.

Another time Laurens van der Post gave a lecture to the Royal School of Medicine in Wimpole Street, having just written a hagiographic biography of Jung, which I'd read and loathed. Van der Post was talking about the imitation of Christ and he was getting rather hoity-toity about people who couldn't be true to themselves, but just imitate Christ. I stood up and I said, 'I've heard that in various quarters there's an imitation of Jung.' Van der Post said, 'I can't give you any statistics on that, I'm afraid.' The moment Van der Post said that, Cecil, who was sitting opposite me, was up on his feet saying, 'I heartily endorse what the previous speaker said,' and then he held forth on the same theme of imitation of Jung and imitation in general.

When I visited Cecil in Paultons Square, I'd go straight up to his studio which was at the front of the house, on the third floor, overlooking the leafy square. It was a very crowded room with books, pamphlets and pictures strewn, stacked and piled haphazardly over the floor and the large cluttered table, leaving Cecil only a small, bare corner of the table on which to have his tea and toast. I would spend two or three hours with him and then afterwards there was always tea with the two of them upstairs in the living room.

He was a crafty old so-and-so, and rather mercenary too. He used to bring out the paintings he wanted me to buy, all his rubbish, as I called it. He'd try that on and that is why it took so long. I would say, 'Very interesting Cecil, lovely, but I don't think so,' and then he would gradually bring out better stuff and then when he got it down to two or three pieces that I liked, he'd come out with outrageous prices. I knew the fair price was about a third or a quarter. Then I'd spend the next hour or two saying, 'This is nice,' and how I couldn't make up my mind and so on. I'd wait for him to bring down the price and eventually he would get tetchy and say, 'Right, you can have it for that then.' I never paid unreasonable prices. Most of the time, though, Cecil talked about himself and his work and answered my questions. I bought a few of those little oils, four inches by three on board, that he had in a little box by the end of the table. Little gems, he called them. They were what I called the rubbish, but I liked a couple of them enough to buy them. Once he hesitated over a beautiful pen and ink drawing, that I loved, because he said it was one of Elisabeth's favourites and she'd be annoyed if he sold it, but finally he did and when I came upstairs for tea, she wasn't at all happy and she muttered something to Cecil. It was a pen and blue ink drawing of an Angel with wings facing you and it looked as if he'd done it in about a minute. He'd just gone zoom-zoom-zoom. My first impression was that it looked a terrific mess, but then after twenty or thirty minutes, the form emerged from the mass of cross-hatching and lines seemingly drawn at random, to reveal itself as a work of extraordinary richness. It grew on me enormously over the years.

I think he liked having an admirer. When I'd been visiting his studio for about a year, he told me I was beginning to 'read' his work. From then on after the Private View of each of his shows, he'd ring me up the next morning and ask me what I had thought of the pictures and every time I would say to him, 'Cecil, you know I can't talk about art.' He'd say, 'Forget all that, did you like it?' I would say something like, 'It was terrific,' and he'd say, 'That's all I want to hear, I want a direct response to my work.' He said regularly, 'Dealers and Private Views are the very devil.' He approved of us having a nineteenth century relationship when the collector visited the artist's studio, shared his mental world and attracted his pictures. He said I had the second biggest collection of his work. The Baring banking family had the biggest one and just behind me in third place was Canon Keith Walker.

Cecil sent quite a few of his students and others to have a look at the work in my house and it was a pleasure to show my Cecil pictures to those who came to see them. I also wrote to lots of people who had his pictures, some of them well known and famous, and almost without exception, they all welcomed me into their homes and were always delighted to show his pictures. I had the sense that there was this lovely feeling of community.

About two years after I'd been buying work from him, I wrote an essay on him and posted it to him. He rang the next day and said he had found the essay 'very sensitive' and that I had tried to do what no one else had attempted, to describe the effect of his work on the psyche. Others chart his images, but do not reach to the heart of him.

I was very fond of Cecil. He had a most mischievous schoolboy sense of humour. I got there one day and he could hardly wait. He said, 'I've got something terribly funny to tell you. A couple of Jungians came to see my work the other day and imagine, they told me what it meant.' He thought that was hilarious. Often it wasn't so much what he said, it was that wicked little smile he'd give when somebody said something pompous, just a little glint in his eye. Cecil was intelligent, but not cerebral and he wore his learning lightly. I was never sure how much he'd read. I know he and Elisabeth went to all sorts of lectures including RILKO (Research into Lost Knowledge Organisation). Elisabeth was most enthusiastic when that started. She said, 'It's a wonderful thing, you must go,' which I never did. There was so much going on in London; I had quite enough. I didn't say I wasn't going, but only 'That's very interesting, thank you for telling me.'

I never liked Elisabeth and I don't think she liked me. Often she said something to suggest that I was too serious. About others, too, she was quick to use the word earnest, always in a pejorative way. She had the manner of a lady of the manor and often spoke to me as though she was the one who knew how to live, that was the message she conveyed to me. Then I noticed her doing it to other people and that made me feel a little better. Cecil had a beautiful little notebook in which he did sketches in various media: pen and ink, pencil, wash; there must have been a hundred. He showed it to me two or three years before he died. It was the most beautiful book and when I asked him whether he'd sell it, he said, 'No.' About two years later was the last time I visited them; it was perhaps a year before he died. Cecil wasn't in the room and Elisabeth said to me, 'That little notebook has disappeared and we wondered whether you had stolen it.' I was so taken aback. I didn't know what to say.

On one of the last occasions that I saw him, at a Private View of his work at the d'Offay gallery, Cecil was wearing, on a very hot day, his usual heavy brown tweed suit and with both hands he held a camera attached to a cord round his neck. He looked at eighty, like a ten year old who had been given his first camera. For quite some time he leapt about, quirkily photographing everyone in the gallery, one by one. He struck poses, leaning on one leg, then the other, bending down, leaning back, clearly enjoying parodying the professionals and finally he turned his camera onto a man who was photographing him.

Cecil felt that few critics appreciated his work. Having grown into his world, I could see that it would take an exceptional critic who would have the time or the patience, being saturated with all the shows they see in a week, to enter into a Cecil picture and learn to 'read' it. Cecil put so much emphasis on the importance of learning to 'read' an image, not only his own, that he gave classes devoted to this art. I feel that if he could have gone on painting forever, we would eventually have had a map of the entire human psyche, of which each of his pictures is a part. To some extent he may have achieved this in his lifetime's dedication to what he believed was the function of the artist: to raise the consciousness of the world. He believed that his pictures were 'votive offerings' and hoped they would make people happy. He told me he was not conveying a message, but the experience of things that are there; then people might find these experiences within themselves. Bacon, he said, was the opposite, a therapeutic painter who squeezed out in his work the pus that was in him, as if from a pimple or a boil.

In my own experience a Cecil picture undeniably changes the atmosphere of a room, though how it does I do not know. Words that he used often to describe his pictures were 'absolutely un-analysable' and 'hypnotic', which they seem to many people to be. A 1958 watercolour study of *Three Seated Women* was meaningless for a time until suddenly it came to me or I had grown into the meaning. It became an ever more fruitful experience; a picture that still fascinates me, in the word's sense of irresistible enchantment. Three women are seated side by side, though clearly not together, representing as they do different aspects of consciousness: the figure on the right is an old woman composed of a mass of apparently chaotic black lines and splashes of paint, some form of original energy before it was worked on and given clearer definition; in the centre is a young woman with no facial features, a contemplative figure of the utmost serenity, one of those Cecil beings almost overwhelming in their gentleness. Finally, looking towards us from a doorway to the left is a woman akin to an Angel, an hieratic figure in which we see a fusion of the energy and poise of the other two women, a woman whose eyes flash out light towards us with tremendous, irresistible power. Apart from the pleasure I have in looking at this picture, and in being looked at, I feel that I receive from it a communication, although what that might be is, as Cecil says, 'beyond definition.'

It is his viewpoint which is so unusual. It is not, as with other artists' work, like looking at a picture screen from a seat in the stalls, but as though we have turned round in our seats to look towards the projector, our real self, on the dual side of which are angels, demons and all those other beings and forms since the dawn of creation.

Cecil said that he had seen angels and that in his work, they do not stand for something other than themselves. 'We cannot see them usually,' he said, 'because they are on a different level of intensity from that of our everyday life.' At almost any time he chose, he told me, he could change the level of intensity of his experience and enter the region where angels and other forms are found. His paintings show a real world, he said, he didn't make it up. Cecil said that Kathleen Raine had asked him whether he actually sees the angels he paints. 'I paint so that I can see them,' he had answered, 'The activity of painting brings them and that world into focus, though it is true that that world is, at times, clearly there without that activity.'

Cecil was much involved with 'vibrations' and 'intensity.' He once compared his 1974 lithograph, Anima, and his lithograph, Head of 1960, to a violin and a cello in intensity and said that Anima gave off remarkable vibrations. When I wasn't sure what he meant, he sounded a little irritated and said that he meant it gave the viewer a deep experience and filled the area in which it was hung with its essence. The special thing about his work, he believed, was that just as he incorporated a higher level in his pictures, so are those who look at them raised to that same level. There was no false modesty, which I liked.

He told me that he had tried to keep Cecil Collins out of his paintings and to provide objective works of art, but that he did it imperfectly; they were always attached to him by a string. I quoted Kathleen Raine's comment as the best thing I'd heard about him; that they are all aspects of the one world. 'Yes,' Cecil said. 'Variety in unity.'

JACINTA NADAL

Born 1923 in Madrid, Jacinta Nadal (née Castillejo) and her family fled Spain at the outbreak of the Civil War in 1936. She trained in modern dance with the Kurt Jooss Ballet in Cambridge (1942-1946). She has presented and acted in Spanish programmes for the BBC in television and radio. She studied drawing and painting with Cecil Collins and later sculpture under John Brown. In 1946 she married Rafael Nadal (1904-2001) who was lecturer in Spanish Literature, King's College, London and the de facto head of BBC broadcasts to Spain from the World Service (1939-1944). He then became Spanish correspondent for the *Observer* (1944-1953). He published extensively on Federico Garcia Lorca.

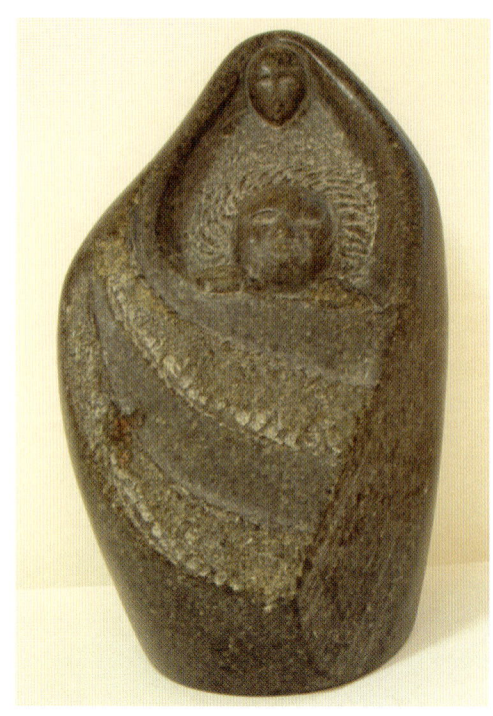

Jacinta Nadal
Creation
1998
Soap stone
33 x 19 x 20cm

I was born in Spain. My father, José Castillejo, was a Spanish intellectual and my mother was English. When Franco came to power, we had to leave Spain and came to my grandparents' house in England where we had come every year as children. Soon after, we went to Switzerland and then in 1940 during the Second World War, we returned to London to stay with my grandparents again. My father had a very difficult time because he couldn't get a proper job. He gave lectures, but the money wasn't enough to feed his family so he was in America half the time, lecturing. I met my husband, Rafael Martinez Nadal through my father.

Rafael, who was also in exile and the de facto head of the Spanish department of the World Service at the BBC called in my father to give a series of broadcasts to Spain about democracy; it was important for those in Spain to know that democracy still existed somewhere. My husband was nineteen years older than I was and I really jumped in at the deep end because he had to entertain politicians and all kinds of people in our flat. We let the basement to a Spanish couple and the woman helped with cooking and cleaning.

We may have come into contact with Cecil and Elisabeth through Stephen Spender as they moved in the same circle. Rafael, who was a great friend of Lorca's, instigated the first translations of Lorca's poetry by Stephen and Juan Gili. It was after one of Lorca's poetry readings in Madrid that he asked 'What do you think of my poems?' Rafael replied, 'I'm not sure whether they're really very good or whether you are just a fabulous reader of them.'

In fact, I think our first real meeting with Cecil and Elisabeth happened through my brother, David. He was a historian at Cambridge and had written a book on Newton and creativity. He had met the Collinses while they were living in Cambridge and then we all met at Cecil's Retrospective exhibition at the Whitechapel Gallery in 1959.

Rafael would have deep conversations with Cecil in his studio. Later, Rafael would also go once a month from King's College to the Central to meet Cecil and they would have tea or lunch with John Allitt, another tutor at the college and also Patrick Reytiens who was head of the fine art department there. Rafael wasn't an artist himself, but he had a strong sense of the theatre and they spoke the same language.

Cecil was very good at getting a crowd of his supporters to go to his exhibitions. He liked having this following; he enjoyed that. Sometimes he would like talking about what things were in his paintings, but other times he wouldn't necessarily explain. Cecil had a great sense of humour and of the absurd; he knew that he was part of the joke himself.

I went to Cecil's classes at the City Lit early on in our friendship. He was interested in how you go about your work, how your creativity comes, what you do with it and how you manage it. He wanted to know where it came from. I'm not sure that I managed to answer him. At the time I was going to his classes, Cecil borrowed one of my sculptures to have in his living room. He showed it to a few people to see if they wanted to exhibit my work. It was very supportive of him to do that, but nobody was interested so I took it back.

The tension with Kathleen Raine, who lived in the lower part of the house, was so sad because she was a great supporter of Cecil's. The whole thing was so childish. They had intended to share the house when it was bought and the flats weren't self-contained. Cecil and Elisabeth had to go past Kathleen's bedroom every time they went upstairs.

Cecil would visit Kathleen now and again because he had nothing against her. It's such a pity it developed in that way because it was very sad for everybody. It was one man and two strong women who were incompatible under the same roof. It built up slowly, a sort of rivalry. Cecil was very strong in one way, but not in others, so he was vulnerable. Once, I scolded Cecil, 'I think it's a disgrace that you should behave like that. Considering what you're interested in and the type of life you look as though you're aiming to live, I think behaving like that is outrageous.'

I remember an occasion when Kathleen was chairing some lectures and I thought perhaps I could take Elisabeth along, but Kathleen said, 'If Elisabeth comes, I'm not chairing the lecture.' The Collinses used to go out for meals because Elisabeth didn't want to cook. One had tea in their house, but not proper meals. There was a nice little French place just across the road so that's where we'd go. Kathleen would use the same restaurant and if she was already sitting there, we would have to go somewhere else. It was so absurd.

I got on well with Elisabeth and liked her. When Cecil was there, he dominated. However, she obviously inspired something in him because he drew and painted Elisabeth's face so often. They both had imaginations and could understand what that meant. If people haven't got imagination, they end up thinking everything you say is stupid. Artistic people understand each other and can understand these different levels. Cecil appreciated Elisabeth. She was lovely and a very interesting woman. Her first exhibition was in Cecil's lifetime, but she did a lot more after his death.

Elisabeth visited us not that long before both she and Rafael died. Somehow they knew it was going to be the last time. They didn't say anything about it, but I could feel what they both felt, that it was a sort of goodbye and they gave each other such a big hug.

ALICE OSWALD

Alice Oswald, born 1966 is an award winning British poet, including the T.S.Eliot Prize (2002) for her poem *Dart* and the Foreword Poetry Prize (2007) for *Dunt*. She read classics at New College, Oxford and is a trained gardener, having worked in the Chelsea Physic Garden and at Dartington Hall estate. She lives with her husband, the playwright Peter Oswald, and their three children in Devon.

ANGEL

In which an angel sees everything closing in on itself at the moment of dawn

Like glass, concealed but not lost in light,
contains in its light a certain unseeable thickness,
I saw the half moon sitting in a tree at dawn
lit with interior darkness.

I saw the ground was gone and all
along that gloom the little glows of cars
vanished away; a black unseeable bird
intermittently blew the infinite song in its centre.

I saw a woman in a shell;
I saw two people lying stony still
in the durable darkness of flesh
move their mouths as if to suck at darkness.

And when I touched their mouths,
I saw the outward closing its inward eye;
I saw the real unseeable sun in the sun, rise
in a region of shadow cut off from its own flames.

Alice Oswald
Dartington, 1997

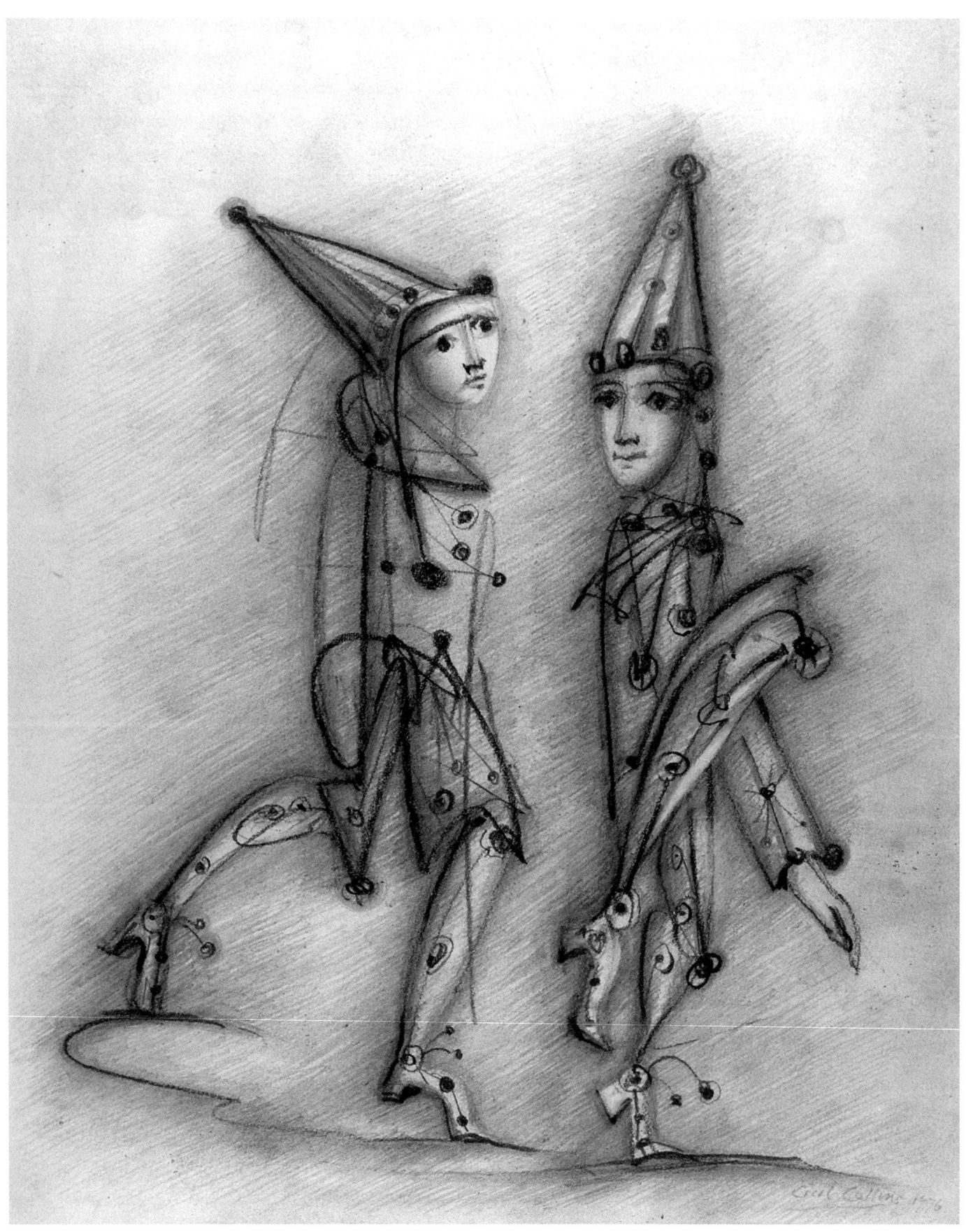

Cecil Collins
Two Fools Dancing
1976
Pencil
28 x 22cm

ALAN ROWLANDS

Alan Rowlands trained in three professions, scientist, musician and teacher of the Alexander Technique. He taught piano at the Royal College of Music and at Brockwood Park School for many years. His pioneering recordings of John Ireland's complete piano music and song accompaniments were issued for the first time on CD in 2008.

I got to know Cecil through Michel Langinieux, a French actor. I'd lived in Oakley Street in Chelsea for about thirty years before I met the Collinses who lived nearby in Paultons Square.

I'd met Michel years before in Switzerland, and then I met him again through his response to Douglas Harding's work. He was utterly inspired by it and he developed a one-man show which incorporated all of Harding's philosophical experiments and exercises, seeing out of nothingness, all that. He devised a show in which he played the character of the fool. He would don one disguise after another, sometimes in the character of a simpleton.

As a friend of Michel's, I was always trying to find him venues where he could put on his show. I think he must have met Cecil through Jane Hoare who taught art at Brockwood and also taught at the Central. Michel did his show at Jane Hoare's house and once Cecil had seen that show, he really took to it. He wanted his students to go and see it which was a great bonus for Michel. I distinctly remember Cecil also being at my friend Janice Hamer's house in Chiswick when Michel did the show there.

Janice, who's American, formed a very close friendship with Elisabeth. She's a composer who used to have a house in London and she was always over here for the summer. She tape-recorded a lot of Elisabeth's reminiscences because she was so interested in her. She said, 'Can we have some sessions with a tape recorder about your early life?' I think she found it difficult to persuade Elisabeth to do it and it wasn't all that easy, but they managed it in the end.

I would get asked to tea at the Collinses from time to time. The way I remember it was that one went up to their top room where Elisabeth would be welcoming and then at a certain point Cecil, who would have been having his rest in the room below, would come up and sit at the far end of the table. He would then start talking and hold forth most illuminatingly about everything: art and music and his own work.

Elisabeth introduced Saied to me. He was a student of Cecil's and a very skillful painter. She said, 'This young man is so interested in Krishnamurti. You must meet each other,' so I invited him to visit me at Oakley Street and we did hit it off straight away. When Saied was painting my portrait, I used to visit him at his house and studio in Greenwich.

I lived in very simple circumstances in those days, in just one room, but I had an upright Bechstein piano. It was a very nice piano and it was a marvellous place for easy access to the Royal College of Music because I could walk there in half an hour. I lived there for many years, but I needed to find somewhere secure for my old age because I was already sixty-eight. When I inherited the grand piano, I was either going to have to sell the piano or store it or move so that prodded me into action. I thought, I've got to take the bull by the horns and move now. I was seeing quite a lot of Elisabeth when I bought my flat and she helped me to choose the colours of my walls: apricot dawn in one room and what's called 'rise and shine', a cheerful yellow, in the kitchen.

Cecil loved Ravel. I remember him saying that Beethoven's music represented the ego and I remember thinking how true that was of the earlier and middle period Beethoven, the heroic Beethoven wrestling with his fate, determined that he would overcome all odds and saying that power was the morality of great men and it was his also. That was the tone of Beethoven's utterances in his earlier life. Those works such as the *Emperor Concerto*, the *Eroica Symphony* and the *Fifth Symphony* had this heroic caste, this defiance, which you could say represented the ego, but I could never get Cecil to accept the fact that Beethoven underwent a profound change after the *Hammerklavier Sonata*. There's a tremendous difference in Beethoven's so-called third period his last five piano sonatas, the *Ninth Symphony* and the last five string quartets. It's absolutely clear that he was letting go of his old attitude from his diary jottings of those years. At one point he says, 'God above all and live for your art alone. Nothing else is left for you.' It was a sort of giving in, an acceptance and submission to his death, to his suffering, to his loneliness and out of this came a new creative phase which transcends the ego.

It's so clear in, for instance, the last piano sonata. The first movement is stirring and heroic. You can hear that it's a final expression of the heroism of the ego and the embattled figure that Beethoven was, then in the last movement there is a total reconciliation and acceptance, utterly serene and celestial, ethereal writing of a kind that had never come out of him before. There's a lot of that sort of writing in his late music which I feel Cecil hadn't listened to.

Then the same thing arose with his friend, John Tavener. I went to a concert in St John's Smiths Square in which there were alternating pieces by Tavener and Handel. John Tavener spoke about his music and his feelings about music generally and he rather wrote off Beethoven. I don't know whether Tavener was influenced by Cecil but it seems likely to me. It was a similar point of view and he seemed to be exalting Mozart and saying that everything was in decline after that. Saied had heard an earlier talk given by John Tavener in which he expressed views which seemed to put down a lot of composers that we revere. Saied asked him, 'What about Bach?' Tavener said, 'He's too triumphalist.' So that was the end of Bach.

I must confess I'm not a follower of John Tavener's music, but when Elisabeth had her ninetieth birthday party in the Chelsea Arts Club, John Tavener wrote a special version of *Happy Birthday To You* which was quite simple and very nice. He'd made lots of photocopies and handed them round. There were many people there and at a certain point, we all sang Elisabeth 'Happy Birthday' to his tune, which was a very good idea.

From 1970, I taught piano every weekend at Brockwood Park School. The Head, Dorothy Simmons, had earlier run a school for intelligent delinquents with her husband near Cambridge. When I got to know Cecil, I started telling her various things about him and she said, 'That sounds like the painter we used to know when we were at Cambridge. I'd love to meet him again. We must ask him to come here and give a talk to the school and meet Krishnamurti.' So we set that up and Cecil was keen to go. He knew what Krishnamurti stood for, but he wasn't a wholehearted advocate of Krishnamurti's teachings which he felt were somewhat negative. He called it the *via negativa* which is a term for a philosophy which doesn't have ideals or aims or, in a sense, any positive context.

Dorothy said, 'We'll pick you up by car.' We met in London as arranged. She was driving and Cecil sat in the front and they got on famously. They talked and talked. On the motorway, they were so deep in conversation that she missed the vital turning off the motorway to get to Brockwood and went on quite a long way before she realised she'd made a mistake. Then she had to go further before she could turn round. I was in the back of the car with Elisabeth and didn't know the route. We were supposed to be having lunch with Krishnamurti at one o'clock and, when we got there, it was closer to two. It was a little embarrassing because he was always dead on time for everything, but he'd waited. Anyway, they did have lunch together and then Cecil gave a talk to the school. There was a bit of a hitch there too because they couldn't seem to make the projector work properly, but, even if it was a bit fraught, it was alright in the end. Cecil talked more about his vision than about his own painting.

I used to meet Cecil sometimes at a pub. He used to go to a pub at the bottom of Park Walk near the Kings Road for lunch until he got a tummy upset and then he said, 'They've got microbes in their food. Microbes with boots on.' After that, we had to abandon that pub and go elsewhere. We would meet sometimes at the Kings Head and Eight Bells on the embankment at the bottom of Cheyne Row.

It was wonderful that Cecil had his big show at the Tate gallery just in time. He was there at the opening in his wheelchair and he revelled in the appreciation and adoration of people who came. I found him totally endearing.

After Cecil died, I was doing a Schubert sonata, the G major, at the Purcell Room. I'd never played it in public before and the last of the four movements puzzled me. It gave me difficulty because it seemed almost trite. The last movement has a kind of popular dance quality which lacks Schubert's usual depth and warmth. I love the first three movements of the sonata and I thought, 'how am I to handle the last one as I don't feel in tune with its mood'. I was looking through the book on Cecil and I suddenly saw his picture of two Fools dancing and that absolutely captures the mood of this Schubert movement. There's a wonderful innocence in the expression in the eyes and a depth of feeling. Then a friend who knew the piece was tuning in to the same feeling and he said of the music, 'That's just a little procession and they're dancing up the street and beating their drums and dancing with innocent foolishness,' and suddenly the movement clicked with me and I rejoiced in it after that. Cecil's vision amplified an experience for me in my music and even elucidated it. There was something in that movement which I had missed and that drawing expressed it and brought it out so that I was able to find it in myself. Suddenly, I knew how to play it and it became marvellous to me. It was no longer trite or ordinary, it was just expressing this mood of innocent merriment.

I feared Elisabeth wouldn't be able to cope after Cecil died because she'd put everything into taking care of him, but it's quite astonishing what she did after his death. She was absolutely wonderful. She threw herself into all sorts of things, as well as painting, and she was very sharp. I used to go to Brockwood at weekends and once I was unwell and didn't go. I rang her up on Sunday evening and she said, 'Alan, why are you ringing me on Sunday? You should be in Brockwood.' She'd remembered that. She said, 'I've just spent the day with Pink Floyd.' She'd been up the river on a boat with them and I thought that was remarkable for a woman in her late eighties.

I have a painting of Elisabeth's that had stood on their mantelpiece for a long time. I always liked it and one day I thought, 'perhaps I could buy one of Elisabeth's. I would like to have something of hers'. I asked her to look for it. I said, 'You'll remember, the one I used to like.' Then she produced one, but it wasn't quite as I remembered it. I had it framed and then not long after that she rang me again and said, 'Alan, I've found the one you really did like. We made a mistake. You could change it for the other one and could put it in the frame.' Then I thought I'd like both and she practically gave it to me. I didn't really pay her very much more.

I have a marvellous letter she wrote to me, in her usual red ink, after she's heard me playing at a concert: *I must congratulate you again, and even again! for it was a most lovely concert. Your playing was a gift of happiness to a great many people in a way that can only happen sometimes when structure and passion and, for want of a clearer word, the Holy Ghost magically come together and the music "speaks". Ah well, I must not go over the top.*

When Elisabeth was dying, I went to the nursing home with the tape I wanted to play her of Allegri's Miserere. I'd been several times and used to massage her back a bit. I thought perhaps she'd like to hear this most wonderful music so I took it and found that she had died. Jeremy and Lily were there and we played it in her honour while she was lying there. Then they asked me round to Paultons Square and said, 'Would you like to take something?' So I have Elisabeth's rather striking teapot and one cup, one saucer, one small plate and one large plate. I thought, 'Here am I, living on my own. That's ideal for me, just one cup.'

NATASHA SPENDER

Lady Spender has spent her life immersed in the arts. She had a highly successful career as a concert pianist. For more than fifty years she was married to the poet, Sir Stephen Spender. She and her husband were friends with many of the most distinguished figures of the past century, including T S Eliot, Igor Stravinsky and Leonard Bernstein. She is writing her memoirs.

Stephen and I met Cecil when we were on our way back from our honeymoon in Cornwall in 1941. In the war one couldn't go abroad, but we thought we'd go as far as we could and stayed at a hotel near Carbis Bay. Then we stopped off at Dartington on the way back to London to stay with the Elmhirsts who were old friends of Stephen's. Cecil and Elisabeth lived in rooms overlooking the courtyard at Dartington. We were only there for a matter of days, but we saw quite a bit of them then. We used to go back there quite frequently to visit and always saw them too.

I was twenty-one when we married. Stephen was ten years older and very tall and handsome. Cecil painted a picture that was inspired by Stephen and me. It was called *The Fool and Child* in which I'm like a little lost figure, held by the hand and being led away from this conflagration. Stephen and I did indeed have the sort of relationship portrayed in that picture. We bought it from Cecil and owned it for a long time, but then came some financial crisis or other and we had to sell it. It's a beautiful picture and I loved it. As a result of us having it in our home, other people including my brother-in-law, Humphrey Spender, also bought Cecil Collins' paintings.

The zenith of our friendship with the Collinses was in the Dartington days. I didn't see them at all while they were in Cambridge, but once they moved to London, into the top half of Kathleen Raine's house, we had dinner with them once or twice. I think Sonia Orwell may have bought the house in Paultons Square for Kathleen Raine. Sonia had quite a bit of money, although she didn't know how much; she was being cheated by the people who administered the George Orwell estate.

Kathleen was connected to us because she had been married to Charles Madge who ran away with Stephen's first wife. I never met Charles Madge and only met the first Mrs Stephen Spender once. Stephen used to regard Kathleen as a kind of goody-two-shoes.

There was something rather like D H Lawrence about Cecil in the intensity of his vision and his belief that life signified in a certain way. Cecil's beliefs were very important to him and this partly decisive, partly mystical, view of life was particularly significant in the war because there was a sense in which everybody was surrounded by or fleeing from conflagration.

Cecil's friendship was much more with Stephen than with me, while Elisabeth was very much a womanly friend to women. She was much less a visionary; she was somebody who protected Cecil and looked after him and shared his views, but not in that sort of Lawrencean way. She managed Cecil's life almost like a stage manager. She was quite assertive. We all had rationing in the war and I had saved enough coupons to buy a beautiful red dress. Elisabeth managed to persuade me to swap my new red dress for a Paisley scarf. I knew I was being weak, but Elisabeth had such style and such panache that I assumed this scarf must somehow be very stylish.

FRANCES SPALDING

Art historian, critic and biographer, Frances Spalding is professor of Art History at Newcastle University and author of some fifteen books, including a centenary history of the Tate and *British Art since 1900* (Thames & Hudson). She co-curated with David Fraser Jenkins, *John Piper in the 1930s: Abstraction on the Beach*, an exhibition shown at Dulwich Picture Gallery and Djanogly Gallery, University of Nottingham in 2003.

Around 1980 I was invited by the Royal Academy Magazine to write an article on Cecil Collins. He was still teaching drawing at Central School of Art, and in addition to a brief interview with him in his home I attended one of his classes. I remember that he began the class by asking everyone to start drawing lying on the floor. This, I think, was to disable any well-tried skills or familiar habits we may have brought to the class. The atmosphere was one of complete respect for his words, so like others I dutifully lay on my front and attempted to draw, momentarily forgetting that I had dressed that morning in clean clothes, as I was going straight from Central to Paddington, to catch a train to Cornwall, to have dinner with Terry Frost and to spend a night in Jean Shrimpton's hotel. I seem to remember that I was wearing a pale, freshly laundered shirt. It looked different when I got up from the floor for I was liberally covered in charcoal dust.

A more significant anecdote is that told me by Judy Collins. At his Tate Retrospective, while being taken round in a wheelchair, Cecil Collins was heard to say aloud more than once, as he looked at his art, 'I have spoken truth.' Though something of an outsider in the art world, his convictions were unshakeable.

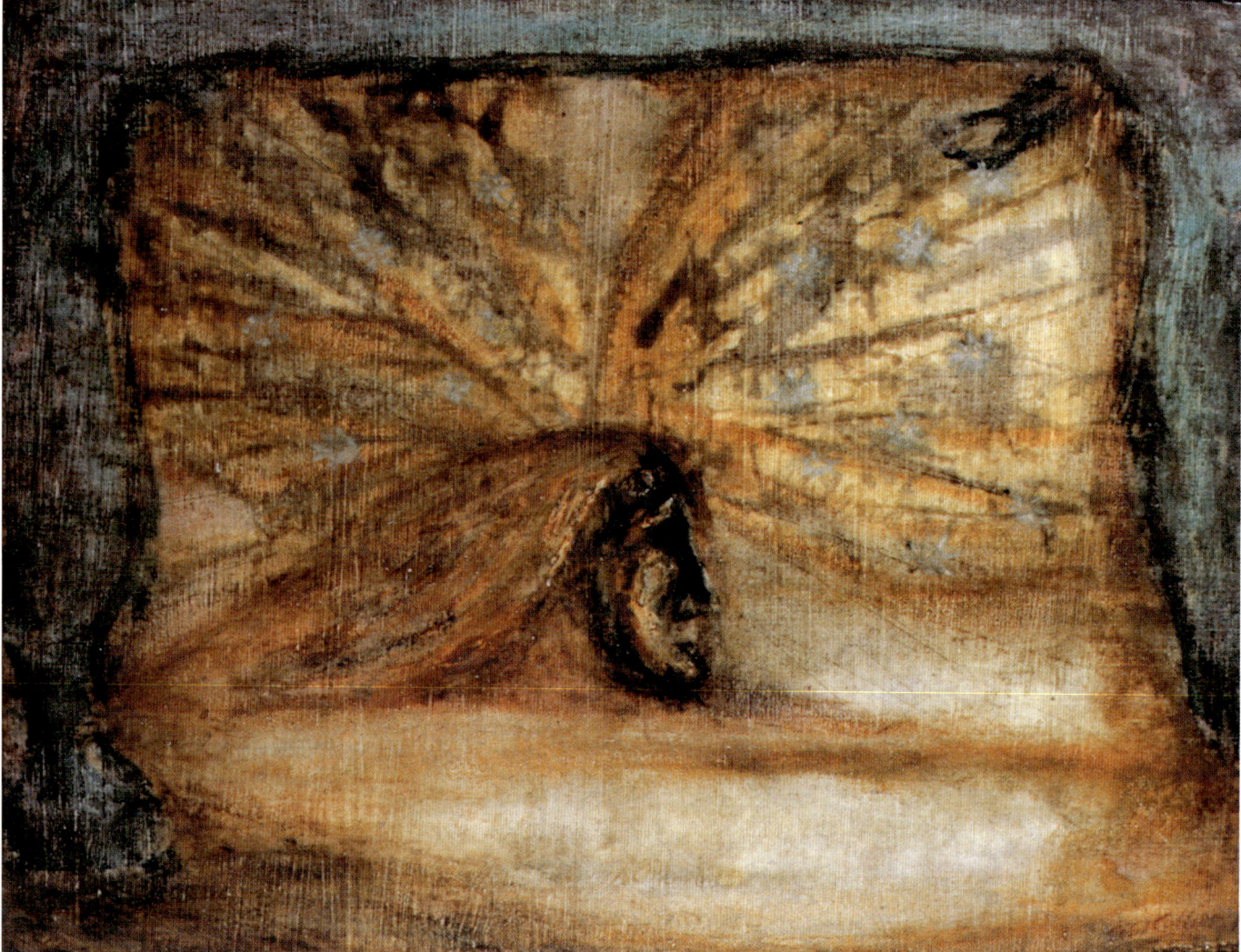

Cecil Collins
Head

GAY SCHROEDER

Gay Schroeder grew up in Cambridge, Massachusetts, USA and came to live in England in 1957 armed with an introduction from her father Eric Schroeder, to Elisabeth Ramsden Collins. The Schroeder and Ramsden families had grown up together in Yorkshire and Gay's father was godson of Elisabeth's mother. Gay remained in touch with Elisabeth and Cecil throughout their lives.

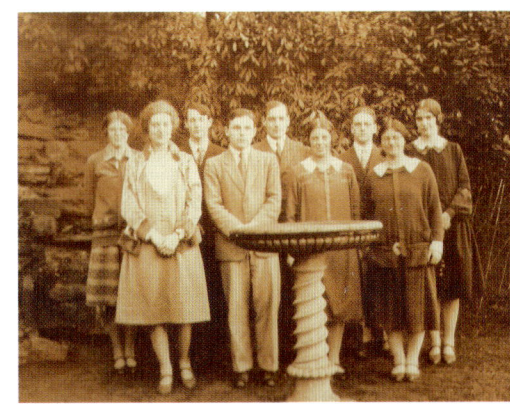

Photograph by Eric Schroeder
l-r front row: Elisabeth Ramsden with Ramsden and Schroeder siblings in Ramden's garden, Hollins, Yorkshire, 1920s

My father grew up in Yorkshire, not far from the Ramsden's, Elisabeth's family. There were four in my father's family and four in Elisabeth's: Elisabeth, Jinnie, Carolyn and their brother Charles. They were all of an age and romped on the moors together. My father studied History at Oxford and later he went to America and then met my mother there. I was born in America.

I was used to looking at paintings because my father had taught himself to paint in oils by copying Old Masters and then he branched out into watercolour which is much more difficult. When he became Keeper of Islamic art at a small museum in Cambridge [Massachusetts], dealers would advise him of new stock he should look at and so we had quite a lot of beautiful things on the walls in our house.

I was twenty-two when I came to England and went to live in Cambridge. My father had said, 'You must introduce yourself to Elisabeth, she has wisdom and that's a rare quality.' I've never forgotten that because it's absolutely true. Later, when I was trying to clear up in my father's house, I found a letter from my English granny, probably written to my father, saying something like, 'Elisabeth is marrying her artist friend, I don't think they have a penny to live on.'

I first met Elisabeth in 1947 when we came back to the UK after the war on a family visit. My father had two paintings by Cecil which he bought on a following visit. Much later Cecil gave Stephen and myself a copy of his etching, *The Kneeling Fool*; it was a present when we got married.

I used to play the viola, which Cecil teasingly referred to as my cello. I cycled around Cambridge with the viola strapped to my back and when I went to see Elisabeth, Cecil would always ask, 'How's the cello?' I rose to the bait every time.

They had no money in those years. Cecil was teaching part-time at the Central School in London, to-ing and fro-ing and I almost never saw him. I remember having tea with Elisabeth when Cecil was up in London teaching, and I became aware, without her saying anything, that she'd scraped together all she could to put tea on the table. On one occasion I brought along a Victoria sandwich cake that I'd made and Elisabeth told me that Cecil was very fond of them. Later, when Stephen and I went to live in Dublin we found a sensational old bakery which made all kinds of sandwich cakes, so whenever we came back to England, we would bring them one.

Elisabeth had a great gift for bringing people together and she had a very wide acquaintance. I remember going to a birthday party of hers in Cambridge and she'd invited three unattached men for me. I hadn't been in Cambridge that long and one of these young men proved to be a great treasure. He was a history don who liked to take people around and show them all the interesting places. I also bumped into one of the other men some months later and he said, 'I remember you from Elisabeth's. You don't by any chance sing do you? Because they need some more sopranos for the St Matthew Passion.' As it happened I had sung this at college so I went along and sang with the choir.

Stephen [Cross] and I met one Christmas through Elisabeth when she and Cecil were living in London at Paultons Square. Previously I'd spent Christmas in Cambridge with a friend, but Elisabeth used to phone me every year in November to say, 'If you're not going to your friend's come here.' That particular year I hadn't heard from my friend so Elisabeth said, 'Come here. We may have a friend coming. He says he's too busy because he's editing a film and can't leave the cutting room, but he might turn up.' That was Stephen. Later Elisabeth told me she'd sensed that he was interested in me, but said that she hadn't planned it.

Another Christmas I had a strange experience at their house. I was sitting on the staircase between Cecil's domain and Elisabeth's and Cecil had put on some music. I can't remember what the piece was, but opposite me on the stair was Cecil's drawing of two fools dancing and I suddenly saw that the rhythm of the music was the rhythm of this drawing. I told Cecil this and he said, 'Yes, you're right.'

JONATHAN STEDALL

Jonathan Stedall has been a documentary film-maker for over forty years, twenty-seven of which were spent with the BBC. He has worked on films with John Betjeman, Laurens van der Post, Malcolm Muggeridge, Fritz Schumacher, Mark Tully, Alan Bennett, Ben Okri, Ron Eyre, Bernard Lovell and Cecil Collins. He has also made films about the lives of several outstanding individuals including Leo Tolstoy, Carl Jung, Mahatma Gandhi and about the educational, curative and medical work inspired by the research and insights of Rudolf Steiner. His forthcoming book (2009), *Where on Earth is Heaven?* draws on all these experiences.

One of the things I loved about Cecil was his humour. He was a serious, intense person and that could have been a bit much if he didn't have the ability to laugh at himself. Cecil was certainly able to do that even about his appearance. He did look pretty scruffy, but he knew that. He had this appalling brown raincoat with patches and this battered old trilby. His shirts were patched by Elizabeth who redid the collars and cuffs because they were very hard up. He said to me once he thought that he looked like a Lebanese date trader which seemed to me a wonderful description.

Cecil painted beautiful pictures, but he didn't seem to have much interest in what surrounded him and I would say that extended to his clothing as well. I find that quite interesting and intriguing because I like the things around me to be beautiful, but Cecil wasn't bothered about that or his clothes as long as Elizabeth kept them clean and patched.

When I was working for the BBC at Kensington House in London there was a producer in the Arts Department called Mark Kidel. He said to me one day, 'You really should meet Cecil,' because Mark knew about my interests in philosophical and religious subjects as I'd made programmes in that area.

I went to Cecil's exhibition and met him and loved him and his pictures. The friendship really went from there. From the beginning, I used to often go and see them. Cecil would be in his studio. He listened to music when he was painting. I'd wave on the way up, but then go and have a lovely talk with Elisabeth.

I saw a great deal of them. They were my real companions in London for all the years that I knew them, so it was thirty years I knew Elisabeth and twenty years for Cecil. I think about them a lot. Obviously I had other friends and companions, but Cecil and Elisabeth offered me some sort of spiritual nourishment. When someone is a real companion, age is irrelevant, although I think that as a younger person one can gain from the insights and experience of older people, which I was aware of at the time with the Collinses.

I often went to supper at their place in Paultons Square and we'd also go out and eat. They introduced me to the Chelsea Arts Club which they loved and I became a member through them. Cecil was fond of eating in restaurants and I introduced them to one in Fulham called the Hungry Horse which Cecil enjoyed because it was English food and in particular English puddings. He liked what some people call school food, simple food, but very nicely done. He liked something we used to call at school 'dead man's leg' which is a sort of roly-poly pudding with raisins in it. I don't know why we called it that, but Cecil knew the name too. When one went out for meals with them, Cecil did tend to dominate the conversation, the way men often do, although it was wonderful to listen to him, but I think Elisabeth felt quite eclipsed by him in those situations.

Cecil and Elisabeth introduced me to the Centre for Psychological and Spiritual Studies run by Alison Barnard. It was a wonderful set-up that had evening lectures every few weeks in London. One of the things that was very good about it was that it wasn't under any particular banner so people came to it through all sorts of spiritual and religious interests.

Once a year, they had a weekend conference which usually took place in Hove in an English hotel. It wasn't exactly Fawlty Towers, but it was a seaside hotel where we all assembled on Friday afternoon and there was usually a talk that evening. At one particular conference, Cecil was going to speak on the Friday evening and Alison Barnard had given him strict instructions not to make it too long because everybody had just arrived. Cecil started his talk and it went on and on. He was a wonderful speaker but, like all of us, he could go over the top sometimes. You could sense people were getting restless, but Cecil wasn't sensing it at all. Alison, who was sitting at the back, was extremely aware that people had had enough. She made various gestures at him which he ignored so she finally stood up and said, 'Cecil, sit down,' and then he drew it to a close.

Sometimes people who are writers or painters aren't necessarily good at articulating their vision, but Cecil absolutely could. The other thing he could do which, in my experience is not that common, was that he was a very good self-publicist and very shrewd. He could sell his own work. Although there were some things very unworldly about him in the simple way he lived and his funny dress and seemingly no possessions, apart from what he

friends & other relationships

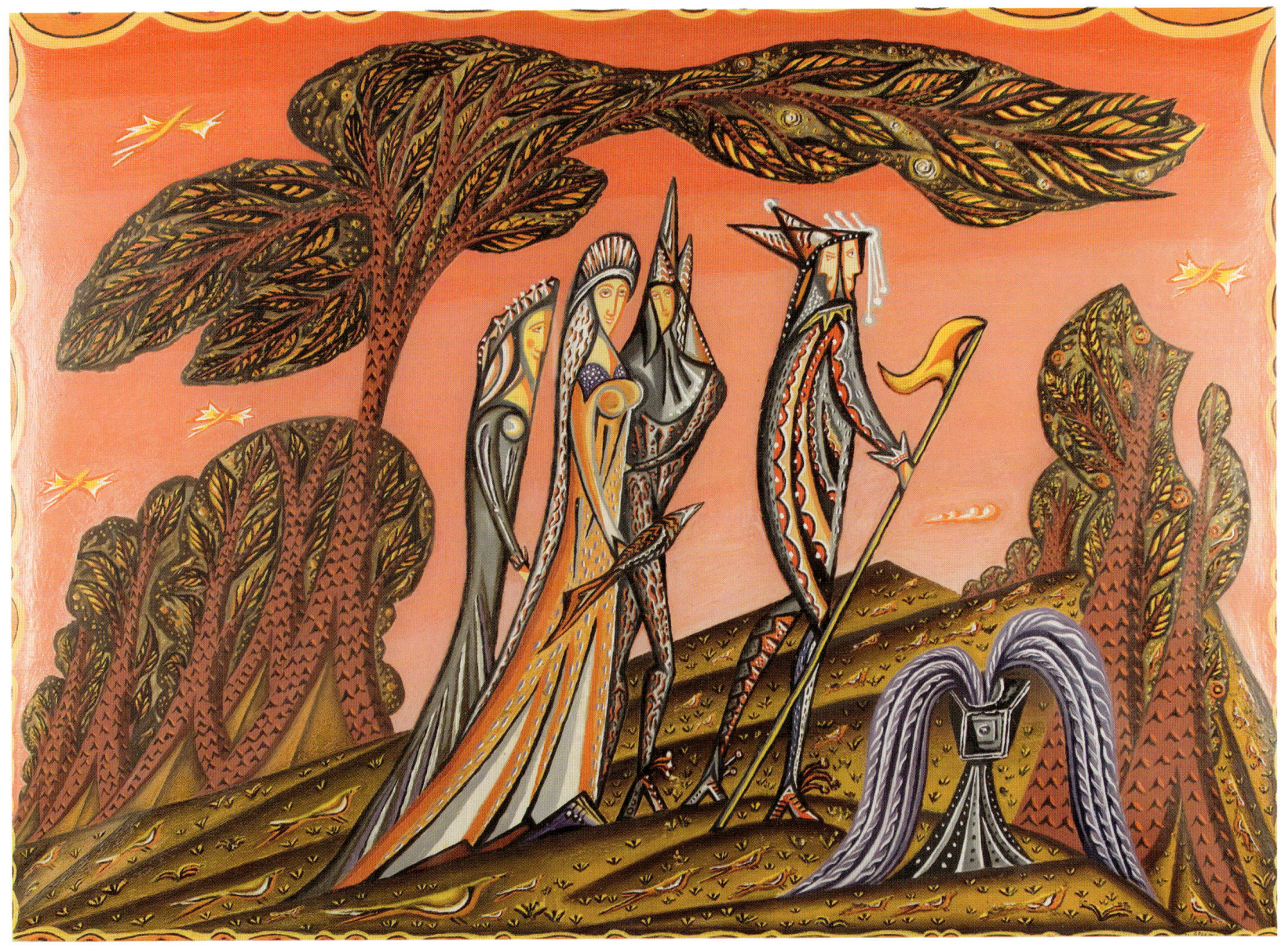

Cecil Collins
The Fools of Summer
1954
Tapestry design
53 x 38cm

needed to paint, he was very much living in his time. In that sense, he reminds me of Betjeman, a completely different character. People often think of Betjeman as being concerned with nostalgia and the Victorian age, but he was tremendously plugged into the here and now and so was Cecil.

Cecil didn't look at television much, but he certainly loved the cinema. He and Elisabeth always knew what was on and I often used to go to films with them. Part of being plugged into the present was an extreme sensitivity to what was both positive and negative. Cecil was, by temperament, a bit of an Eeyore. He was justifiably concerned about the contemporary world. He was very aware of what he would call 'the Philistines' and his great *bête noire* was Francis Bacon. He used to go on about him a lot and I think it irritated Elisabeth a little because she felt that he was overreacting. Bacon was an interesting artist and it may be that he was concentrating on the things that one would rather not recognise or see in the world rather than the angelic, the sacred.

Before I met Cecil and Elisabeth, I'd filmed the Camphill Communities in Aberdeen and Yorkshire in the late 1960s and been very touched by what I'd encountered, particularly with the village communities for handicapped adults. The characters I'd got to know there, in one sense, related to Cecil's theme of the holy Fool. Using the word 'fool' has to be done carefully because one doesn't want to make it sound derogatory but, in Cecil's eyes, it was a compliment that someone was a Fool. It's like Betjeman using the word 'dim' about someone or some building, which was a compliment in his eyes. He loved the word dim as it expressed his affection for what was neglected; he felt it was a word to be treasured. Cecil's connection with this image of the Fool, as I understand it, came from a similar kind of sensibility because when you meet a holy Fool, it affects you. It certainly affected me in that one's own masks fall away because Fools have no guile. That's one of their characteristics.

Sometimes handicapped adults are referred to as children, which is not right, I think. Children have that quality of innocence, but these adults are not like children, although they have the directness of children. Certainly my relationship with handicapped adults has been a very important influence in my life. What attracted and moved me so much was perhaps this encounter with the neglected or wounded part within myself. I tend to be too clever and scheming like most of us are in varying degrees.

Which leads me to the question: why was Cecil so interested in the Fool? Cecil may have looked quaint and I don't think that was a cultivated thing, but he himself was no fool. As I understand it, our sense of loss arises from this wounded or neglected part; hence the nostalgia for a golden age. However, I don't think with Cecil that there was a nostalgia or that he thought humanity should somehow go backwards. He was certainly aware of how unsatisfactory our own time is, but he knew the challenge is to move forward.

A similar question could be asked about Laurens van der Post's interest in the Bushman. There was a biography written about van der Post called *Walk with a White Bushman* which implied that he was like a Bushman, only white. It was a terrible title because Laurens was not like a Bushman. In fact, he couldn't be more different. It was that difference which made him so interested and touched by the Bushmen's way of life. I went to the Kalahari with Laurens van der Post to make a film about the mythology of the Bushman. By that time, the mid-1970s, they hardly existed in the way that van der Post wrote about them in the 1950s. However, we met a Bushman and he told their legends through images of the landscape and the animals. For the Bushmen, nature is like a mirror in which you learn to understand yourself. You could see aspects of yourself in nature and particularly with the animals, because of their different characteristics. In a sense this is true for all of us. Although van der Post greatly admired the Bushmen, I don't think he was saying, we all ought to go and live like Bushmen again.

Some people have horrible memories of their childhood, but assuming one's childhood was happy, perhaps even idyllic, I don't think it's helpful to think we can recapture that. You can't become a child again but, as an adult, you can consciously work at recapturing that kind of purity and innocence. This is where Cecil's work has been, and will continue to be, an enormous help to people because in our heart of hearts, we know how fallen we are. I think that one of the big challenges these days which Cecil was addressing in his work was that people need to be reminded of the essential purity that is in us. There's so much that conspires against that; such cynicism, every man for himself and survival of the fittest, but I think it's desperately important that we're also reminded we do have a divine origin. There's quite a battle going on at present. The idea of war in heaven becomes more real to me and Cecil was an important warrior in that war. That's why he could get on the phone and pester people and get support and not just quietly work away in his garret. He was a fighter, a warrior.

Most people who are creative feel quite modest about what they're doing, genuinely so, but Cecil had absolutely no qualms about saying his work was important and wonderful. If someone else said that, you'd think they were being pretentious, but he somehow got away with it. I never remember him being critical of anything he'd done. Years ago, I helped him catalogue all his paintings for insurance purposes. He was overwhelmed by the hugeness of the task and I offered to help him. We went through everything; it took days and days, and it was never, 'Oh that's not very good' or 'That's worth nothing.' They were all precious. Cecil was not modest about his achievements. Part of this process of cataloguing was putting a value on things and

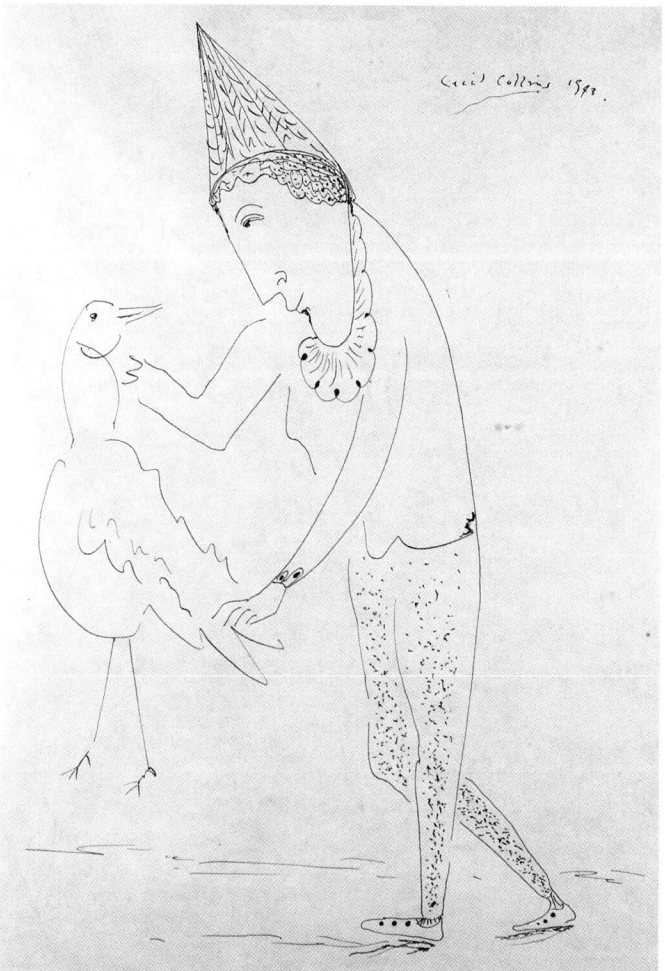

Cecil Collins
Fool with Bird
1943
Pencil on paper
35.5 x 23cm

it's hard to do that. Cecil certainly didn't undervalue them because I remember the total came out to something absolutely staggering which had to be modified for the insurance people. I think partly why he got away with beating his own drum was because you didn't feel that he was saying he was wonderful and marvellous, but what was important was what was trying to come through his paintings. That was worth shouting from the rooftops, not for the glory of Cecil Collins, but for the glory of God.

He was very interested in the period when artists were anonymous, when nothing was signed. We don't know who built Chartres cathedral and I think Cecil genuinely respected that. It's also important not to underestimate his courage and single-mindedness because he was not just poor, but also neglected. There's a wonderful phrase that Muggeridge used, 'Only dead fish swim with the stream.' Cecil certainly wasn't a dead fish. He swam against the stream and that took courage.

I deeply regret that I never directed a film on Cecil. I was producing the series *One Pair of Eyes* so I made it happen. I couldn't direct them all so I got someone else to do the one about Cecil. I kept an eye on it, but couldn't interfere with another director's work.

I was as close to Elisabeth as I was to Cecil, and I came to know her even better after Cecil's death when I saw a great deal of her. I and other friends felt that we wanted to help her because Cecil had done everything. She'd run the household, but Cecil dealt with the bank and money and paid all the bills, so cheque books were all a bit bewildering to her. It was quite touching in those last years of Elisabeth's life when she couldn't have coped with all that sort of thing without Robin's help.

Elisabeth had an allowance, nothing enormous, but what changed her fortune, apart from Cecil's pictures beginning to sell a bit more, was that she had shares in the family newspaper up in Yorkshire and there was a takeover. Suddenly she was quite a lot better off because of that. She could never quite come to terms with the fact that she could afford to write a cheque. It slowly dawned on her that she could go to a restaurant, that she wasn't stony broke. She was extremely generous to others, but she had always been used to having to count her pennies and mend Cecil's shirts rather than buying him a new one. It's like people who lived through the war. I was a child then, but I remember people saving string, saving paper bags, my mother using the paper the butter was wrapped in to oil the frying pan. Those things don't go away overnight.

It was interesting to experience Elisabeth after Cecil's death. The practical side was difficult for her, the missing him and feeling lonely, but I also sensed a kind of liberation, although that would be too strong a word. The last year or so of Cecil's life had been quite difficult for her. He was ill and needed caring for and she wasn't a natural nurse. That's no criticism whatsoever, but it was hard for her because of the whole messy business of his body not working properly any more. Another thing that came out quite strongly after his death was a feeling that there was an element of regret that they hadn't talked through a lot of things that couples tend to discuss these days. People of that generation didn't talk too much about intimate things. Elisabeth very much lived in the moment and therefore would probably have had a heightened awareness of how things had changed in her lifetime and how restrictive her own early life had been, not just because of the class she'd come from, but also because of the way Cecil was himself.

In my experience, neither of them had a particular connection with children. Elisabeth went so far as to say that she was rather frightened of them, which is quite interesting because this vision of the Fool is also an aspect of what I love about children, their directness. Elisabeth knew my children, in particular my daughter, Ellie, who is sensitive and with whom Elisabeth and I went to Paris twice. Elisabeth and Cecil came and stayed with us and Elisabeth stayed with us for Christmas a few times after his death. But I don't remember Cecil in relation to children at all.

I think there had been tricky times when Elisabeth perceived Cecil being enamoured with women who worshipped him. When they were still living in Cambridge and Cecil was working in London, he used to stay with Thetis. I think Elisabeth was worried about that, so she obviously felt a bit insecure about Cecil in relation to women.

Thetis was a real confidante to Kathleen Raine, but also very close to Elisabeth which was difficult as Kathleen and Elisabeth weren't speaking. My understanding is that the initial hostility came from Elisabeth. From what she said to me, it was clear that Kathleen had become a *bête noire*, because of Kathleen's bossiness. I can't remember anybody else who bugged Elisabeth particularly. I only knew Kathleen towards the end of her life, but she was a very powerful lady and Elisabeth was a powerful lady in quite a different way. These things are never sparked off by just one incident; there was obviously a build-up. I think it had to do with a party the Collinses were having to which Kathleen hadn't been invited, but she came up anyway; it was just the kind of thing she would do. She was very forthright, Kathleen, and not always terribly sensitive.

'Downstairs', Elisabeth called her. 'Did you see "Downstairs"?' I got to know Kathleen much better after Elisabeth died and I had inherited the flat. I knew her, not only through going to visit the Collinses, but also through Laurens van der Post. When I visited Elisabeth, I would say hello to Kathleen and exchange a few words, but wouldn't sit down for a big natter. I didn't feel I had to be secretive about it with Elisabeth. I would say if I'd been talking to her so I didn't have to pretend I hadn't seen her. Certainly, if ever I was either going in or coming out with Elisabeth, I was very aware how Kathleen would disappear so there was never an encounter on the staircase or in the hall.

Kathleen talked to me about it a bit after Elisabeth had died. Her understanding was always that it had come entirely from Elisabeth and, I think, probably that was quite genuine because people don't necessarily recognise the things in themselves that bug other people. Also, if you have a clash with somebody they can usually be avoided, whereas these two women were locked into the same building together for years. It was an interesting karma because it was quite a traumatic, unresolved situation. I believe this business of people not speaking to each other was much more common in the past when they were less mobile. I know my grandfather had a chauffeur who'd been his batman in the war and the chauffeur's brother was his head gardener, but the wives of these two brothers who lived in cottages on the estate never spoke to each other.

For Cecil I suspect it was slightly troubling that this situation had arisen between Elisabeth and Kathleen but it wasn't a problem for him in the way it was for Elisabeth. I'm sure he was aware that Kathleen could be a bit bossy, but he didn't have an antipathy as did Elisabeth. Her feelings became more conspicuous after he died when just the two women were in the house together.

Going back over my life and trying to write about it, as I am at present, the word I feel I want to use quite a lot is 'awakener'. If you look at your life, the really crucial moments are encounters with people and things that are awakeners for you. My meeting with the Collinses was a tremendous awakener, of what was dormant, within oneself. It was a confirmation of the hunches I was starting to have as a younger person. Such encounters are as though they're reminders of what your life is meant to be about.

James Hillman wrote a wonderful book called *The Soul's Code*. And he talks about the daemon of Socrates. Plato writes about the daemon as that which accompanies one through life and we need to listen to our daemon. That seems to me the same process really, of awakening to one's destiny. One thing that was very meaningful to Cecil was the spiritual discipline of Baha'i. Cecil didn't talk about it, but I know that for him it had been an awakener. At one point it was helpful and a great inspiration to him.

This interest in the spiritual dimension to life was the basis of our friendship. Cecil, Elisabeth and I came at these things from our own particular direction. For example, they knew of my deep interest in Rudolf Steiner. I talked about him sometimes and gave them the odd book. I remember Cecil, not in any critical sense saying, 'Tell me about Steiner. Explain about Steiner,' and then we'd talk about something else and later he'd put the same question again. I think Steiner's way of putting things in writing was not that helpful for Cecil. We all find what is meaningful for us, but Cecil did sense, I think, that what lay behind Steiner was absolutely in keeping with what he cared about most deeply. I know he and Elisabeth were both very touched by the films that I'd done about the Steiner work with handicapped people, although that was not something that made Cecil want to read a lot of Steiner. People come from different directions and therefore the language used is different too. Sometimes that can produce clashes between people, maybe simply because they're misunderstanding each other, but I never felt that with Cecil. There was an undercurrent a kind of an understanding and knowing at a deeper level that we were coming from the same place.

Cecil was his own person and that was what was very powerful about his vision. The problem with these awakeners, particularly if they're gurus like Steiner or Jung or whoever, is that people tend to repeat what the guru said, which might be helpful for them, but it's not very effective in terms of communicating their ideas to others. Whatever you receive, you have to make your own and I felt that whatever had inspired Cecil, he had absolutely made his own. He had his own particular way of expressing things that were meaningful to him.

Cecil left *The Praying Fool* to me in his Will. I was very touched that he'd remembered me. It's an example of his sensitivity, but also of him being on the ball in the sense of remembering that I'd helped him catalogue his work several years before and mentioned how much I admired that painting.

It's wonderful to have Cecil's paintings because the more you look at them, the more they mean. In making films, I've sometimes been frustrated with what I've done and felt I could have done more, particularly with ones I felt were important in terms of their content. Often, I've been very surprised by people's reactions to a film I've made: how much they seem to have got from a film which to me didn't seem to be there. This is relevant in relation to Cecil because when people are confronted by the result of a creative process, whether it's a film, a book or a painting, they have the capacity, in varying degrees, to not only see what's in front of them, but also to tap into the creative process itself so that all the things I wanted to put into my film, only a fraction of which could go in, somehow are accessible to people.

With a painter like Cecil who thought so deeply about things and then did what he could, when you see these paintings and look at them and look at them again, I find that you can tap into much more than what is on the canvas. I think that kind of accessing of all the things that have gone on behind the scenes is continually going on; we're much more in touch with this than we realise. I've always liked the definition of an icon as a window into heaven. An icon is a particular form of art, and Cecil's pictures are a kind of window into Paradise.

JOHN & MARYANNA TAVENER

Born in London in 1944, much acclaimed composer, John Tavener's first major work was the dramatic cantata, *The Whale*, based on the Old Testament story of Job. In 1977 he joined the Russian Orthodox Church and its mysticism became a major influence on his music. John was knighted in 2000. A three-day celebration of his music was held in Ireland, 2008. His wife, Maryanna, is a clarinettist and studied at Oxford. They have two daughters and one son.

JOHN

Cecil contacted me after he'd heard *Thérèse* at Covent Garden in 1979. I must have known him since then. I recall going to their place in Paultons Square and Elisabeth being on her own upstairs, then I heard the very slow sound of Cecil plodding up the stairs. It was always the same. I don't think he was ever there when I arrived; he was downstairs in the room he used as a studio. What he did in there when he wasn't painting, I was never quite clear, perhaps quite a bit of sleeping.

I very rarely saw any canvas of Cecil's on the easel. I did see one of the blue Angels in his studio, but whether he was actually working on it when I went down, I don't know. We'd go down to his studio a lot and spend a long time just talking, mostly about music because his records were all down there. I think Cecil often slightly elaborated the truth. He told me once that, apart from one critic, he and Elisabeth were the only people in the Queen's Hall to hear Stravinsky performing his piano concerto. I'm sure there was an element of truth to that, but whether there was literally one critic, I rather doubt.

Cecil did tend to get huge enthusiasms for people. Once it was for a French clown. I thought the clown was not a sympathetic character, but I remember traipsing down to some place in the East End where he was giving a show and then to some other place where he was doing something else. Cecil rang me up three or four times a day about this clown and said I could bring all my friends to see him. I thought the clown wasn't really worth it, but I went nevertheless. I suppose I believed in Cecil totally and thought if he was enthusiastic about this man, there must be something to him. Then suddenly he wasn't mentioned any more. Cecil's enthusiasms never lasted long. Another enthusiasm was the period when Cecil got very snap happy. He had this camera that developed prints immediately and whenever you entered the room, he'd take endless photographs. I wish I knew what happened to them.

Cecil was very funny in a wonderfully dry way. He had a tremendous sense of playfulness. Once when I was at the height of an Orthodox period in my life, and thought it was the only religion, he rang me up and pretended to be a Desert Father. He spoke in a very low gruff voice and had me fooled for a few seconds. Cecil did not approve of my Orthodoxy very much. I never knew what his religious affiliation was. He doesn't come across as a Christian painter in the way David Jones does. I think he was a Baha'i. Elisabeth said she would have converted to Orthodoxy if she'd been younger, but I never knew whether she really meant that.

The telephone was Cecil's way to communicate. Sometimes he would ring me four times a day just to talk. He'd make jokey remarks and one would always come away feeling better. He didn't actually tell me jokes; it was more a gentle mockery of things I felt strongly about that would always make me laugh. It wasn't offensive. Sometimes he'd ring me up and say, 'Nothing's happening here. Nothing at all,' in other words, 'I'm not working.' It didn't seem to bother him and I didn't understand that, although he was often quite melancholy so maybe it did trouble him.

Another interesting thing about Cecil was that he'd read people like Schuon and Guénon years before anybody else had. Cecil had a long correspondence with Karlheinz Stockhausen. I was interested in Stockhausen, but didn't share Cecil's passion for his music. However, I did share his passion for Arvo Pärt's. My first meeting with Pärt was quite a long time ago. He was brought to my house by a Russian Orthodox priest. He appeared to speak hardly any English and Father Michael was there as a kind of translator. When Father Michael had to go, I thought it was going to be a very difficult evening so I rang up friends of mine and said, 'Could I come down as I've got Arvo Pärt with me,' and they said, 'Yes, come and have dinner.' Arvo warmed enormously to the mixture of wine and feminine company; his English got a lot better and he opened up.

Cecil was a friend, or at least an acquaintance, of the Greek poet, George Seferis. When Cecil and Elisabeth went to Athens, it was August and appallingly hot but, according to Elisabeth, Cecil still wore his filthy overcoat and would never go out. She wanted to make a trip to the islands, but could not get him to leave the hotel. I think he was afraid of getting a chill. Elisabeth said she went out and enjoyed herself and just left him there. Cecil didn't like travelling at all.

I remember Cecil saying that Seferis looked like a second-hand date dealer. I think they came into contact with each other through Philip Sherrard. At the time, I was writing about Mary of Egypt, or wanting to, and Cecil thought that Philip might be helpful. He said, 'You'd better go and see the old rogue. He's hot on sex and on the Desert Fathers.' I was always astonished how Cecil knew where people were at and therefore how to communicate with them.

Some of his remarks about other people were quite extravagant. He called Beethoven 'that frightful tub thumper.' He didn't even like the late quartets which are very different from early Beethoven. In the late quartets, personal angst started to invade Beethoven's music. I found them extraordinary, but a lowering experience rather than a lightening one.

Cecil considered himself a composer. He couldn't play the piano and he just made a series of childlike noises on the bottom register of the piano and then played a few notes higher up. I'm sure there was a sincerity in what he did and he wanted me to sit there and listen to a piece that might have lasted half an hour and quite clearly could have been done by a child. Although one thought that Cecil himself had access to the 'childlike' and the 'great happiness', there was not a sign of a child in his life. I once said to Elisabeth, 'Did you ever think of having children?' 'Children?' she said. 'Cecil is a child.' She didn't like children.

I don't have a memory of Cecil listening to my music, but when he came to hear concerts of music I'd written, I presume he was listening. He did comment on them, but I can't remember exactly what he said. Occasionally he used the same words about my music as he did about his own paintings and about Arvo Pärt's music as well. He certainly liked pieces from *Thérèse* which is what he came to Covent Garden to hear.

I'd love to have a conversation with him now. He knew that I would probably go in a certain musical direction and that I would understand what he meant by the 'great happiness' which I certainly didn't at the time. When he spoke about the 'great happiness', it would almost always be in relation to a painting. I think particularly of his blue Angels. I have one that he painted late in his life.

Cecil always used to joke with me about Marco Pallis who was a Buddhist and very much a traditionalist. He would look at a painting of an Angel by Cecil and say, 'That's not an angel, not according to the iconography.' It always amused Cecil, that Marco couldn't see that it was an angel. Cecil thought tradition was very important but, on the other hand, he managed to get round it somehow, hence the whole business of not doing a traditional angel.

Cecil and I once talked quite seriously about collaborating on a ballet about the Fool, but it never happened. He wanted me to make the music and I did make a piece called *The Holy Fool*, but the ballet never got off the ground. He also encouraged me to write a quartet. I think he felt that one's more intimate thoughts should be in a smaller medium. I wrote three string quartets.

The Fool embodies a kind of illusion and I'm not sure that Cecil embodied an illusion. A Christian gets very hot under the collar if you start saying the world is illusory, but I think you can point out that the holy Fool, especially in eastern Christianity, is a very important figure who takes on an illusion to bring the world of illusion to reality.

All my paintings by Cecil were gifts from him. As he was doing his painting called *Dawn*, he couldn't see anything good about it; he said it looked like dog's turds. Once it was finished, however, he started to tell me how wonderful it was. *The Fool* print was a gift for my fortieth birthday.

Cecil was very pleased when he had that exhibition in Plymouth. He sat inside the train and said, 'It's very moving to be going back to the West Country, to be going west.' Maybe Cornwall, or wherever it was he originally came from, meant an awful lot more to him than he was usually able to say.

Elisabeth had a strange sense of humour. The rather charming drawing we have by her is of a figure and is inscribed, *He thinks he's a whirling dervish and he ain't*; very typical of Elisabeth. Then there's another one of a naked woman and Elisabeth wrote on it, *If you want to be naked, you have to have a beautiful body*. I don't know why she put that. I think it was very good that Elisabeth had that decade of being entirely herself after Cecil died.

There was a very haughty side to Elisabeth. You could do something that would slightly upset her and she would be quite sharp. It only happened to me once. A few days after Cecil died, my father and I decided to take her up to Yorkshire as she'd asked to meet Mother Thekla. When we got back at the end of that day, she said to my father, 'Thank you for everything and for being so wonderfully kind to me which is more than can be said for you, John,' and she mounted the stairs. I don't know what it was I had done, but it shows an aspect of her character.

I wasn't there when Elisabeth died, but I'd seen her a few days before. I was giving her little sips of champagne and she obviously enjoyed it. I think she regarded death as an exciting voyage. I don't think I've ever seen anyone die so beautifully as she did.

Elisabeth's funeral was in the Russian Orthodox Church and I remember Metropolitan Anthony saying to me, 'I respect Cecil Collins. I respect him very highly, therefore it's a great pleasure to have the funeral of his widow here.'

MARYANNA

John and I met through Cecil. Lots of people have met through Cecil and Elisabeth. She had a twinkle in her eye about those sorts of things. She didn't literally push us together. We actually met at a stained glass opening of Cecil's in Basingstoke, the second one I

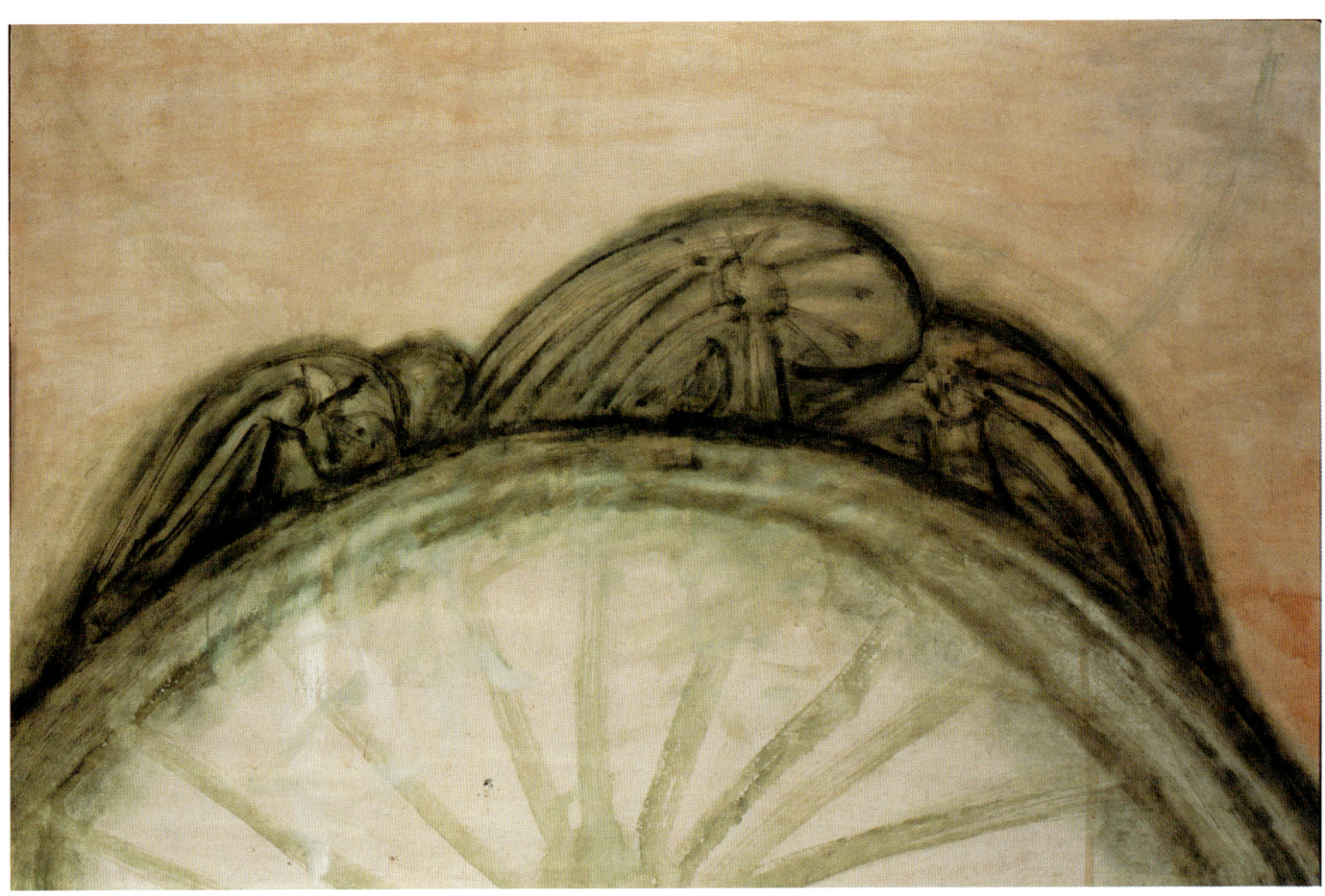

Cecil Collins
Landscape, Sunrise
1985
Mixed media
51.5 x 71cm

think. John had a piece of music performed there.

We went independently. I was just up at Oxford that term and I went with my father, Glen Schaefer, who was a great friend of Cecil's. I went to see Cecil's window and John and I met in the vicarage afterwards. John was the next youngest person there.

At one time, my father and Cecil had daily telephone conversations. I think they met when Cecil went to a talk my father gave at one of the meetings that Alison Barnard ran. My father was a brilliant speaker and would have absolutely fascinated Cecil, but I think the first time they met properly was when Metropolitan Anthony introduced my father at some other event at which Cecil was present

My father's world interested Cecil. It was so different, the world of science and technical physics. It fascinated Cecil because so many of the patterns that could be seen in those kinds of thoughts and realities transferred onto the patterns of other ideologies or thoughts about painting. There were discussions about whether there was one great Creator or one Truth, as it were, or if there was one Grand Unified theory of things. I grew up knowing all about metaphysics and people who have high ideals, who reach for the stars. Cecil and Elisabeth were completely devoted to Glen and vice versa. There was a passionate exchange of interesting ideas, particularly with Cecil.

When I went as a teenager with my father to see them, Elisabeth would make tea and Cecil would do all the talking and I would go downstairs and practise the clarinet in Cecil's studio which was occasionally rather frowned on. Elisabeth didn't like children very much.

Cecil was obviously difficult, but I don't think Elisabeth felt she had sacrificed herself to him. She loved being beautiful, always wearing those tremendous hats. She once asked me, 'How's the sex stuff?' She was curious, I think, whether or not there was any or if it was something that was normal, as it were. I think she would have been fascinated by John's positive reaction to our children.

JOHN

Now we have another baby, our third child, she would be surprised. Elisabeth once said to me, 'Maryanna must go off and find a young man. She's a young girl.' She was very hot on that. It wasn't that I was depriving her. It was because I had my work so she felt that Maryanna should be free to go off. I don't know whether she really meant it. I just listened without responding. I've always found that the erotic impulse transcends itself into work; for me, that's where it resolves almost in a tantric way.

For me, what was so life enhancing about Cecil was the understanding that he had, which you can only have intuitively. He believed that the human being is in the form that God created and has beauty in his innermost self. Cecil externalised this awareness. I've become more aware of this as I've grown older. Music must manifest above all and what Cecil called the 'Great Happiness.' If you met Cecil in person, you wouldn't think he manifested the Great Happiness which I understand as the God in us. I never had the feeling that he was a happy man, or that he was joyful and yet he could be so vivacious and funny. No-one has all the answers, but they were perhaps in his painting. He probably thought that that was the answer.

I remember Cecil saying very often that Elisabeth was by far the better painter, but he was the visionary. I don't think it was conceit; I think he really believed he was a visionary and he probably was. It's unfortunate that he had to keep saying it, but if he didn't say it, nobody would. The art establishment ignored him. If you're not in tune with his vision and if you're looking at his painting purely from a technical point of view, you might see faults in it. I always had the impression that painting for him was very slow and laborious, if not tedious. He didn't really want to paint, although Elisabeth said, or rather implied, that he should. She'd say to me, 'Can't you persuade him to paint? He doesn't want to paint any more'.

Visionary was a good label for Cecil to use for himself, but he didn't like being compared to Blake or even with David Jones. I don't madly like Blake as a painter, but I love him as a poet. Blake's very classical, very corporeal as a painter, whereas Cecil was absolutely not corporeal. He always called Francis Bacon his spiritual brother.

Cecil knew he had a vision and that only a few people were getting it and the art world wasn't having anything to do with it. I'll never forget the last telephone conversation I had with him from his hospital bed, just before he went into the operating theatre. He said he'd already had the anaesthetic. 'They still don't get it,' he said in this rather sleepy voice. 'They still don't know what I'm doing. The critics are the same.' It was a puzzle to him. I was amazed that it bothered him, even when he must have known he was dying, but I suffer from panning by critics so I know what it's like. The critics don't listen to what one is really doing. Then he just said, 'Look after Bell for me.'

I never knew what Cecil thought was beyond death or if he believed there was anything beyond it. He never said anything about that. I think he thought it was irrelevant, that it would be the manifestation of the 'Great Happiness', that we're part of an illusion here.

I was younger than Cecil and now that I know a lot more, I'd love to see him again. I understand many of the things he was talking about from my own experience and therefore it would be wonderful to have a communication with him. I used to think he and Elisabeth saw me as a son because, to some extent, we expressed the same vision, that same connection. That's why I'd love to see him and talk to him because I feel that I'm much closer to him now. I understand what he meant by the 'great happiness'; I understand the need for art to be blissful, rapturous and to be totally without pain. I think he wanted a world without anguish, without what you see on the news every single day or read in a newspaper. Art should be devoid of that. It shouldn't have any subjective deformation.

Some people know immediately what you're talking about. You don't have to struggle, and you become almost drunk in their presence. Cecil was one such person. I always felt very much better after being in his company.

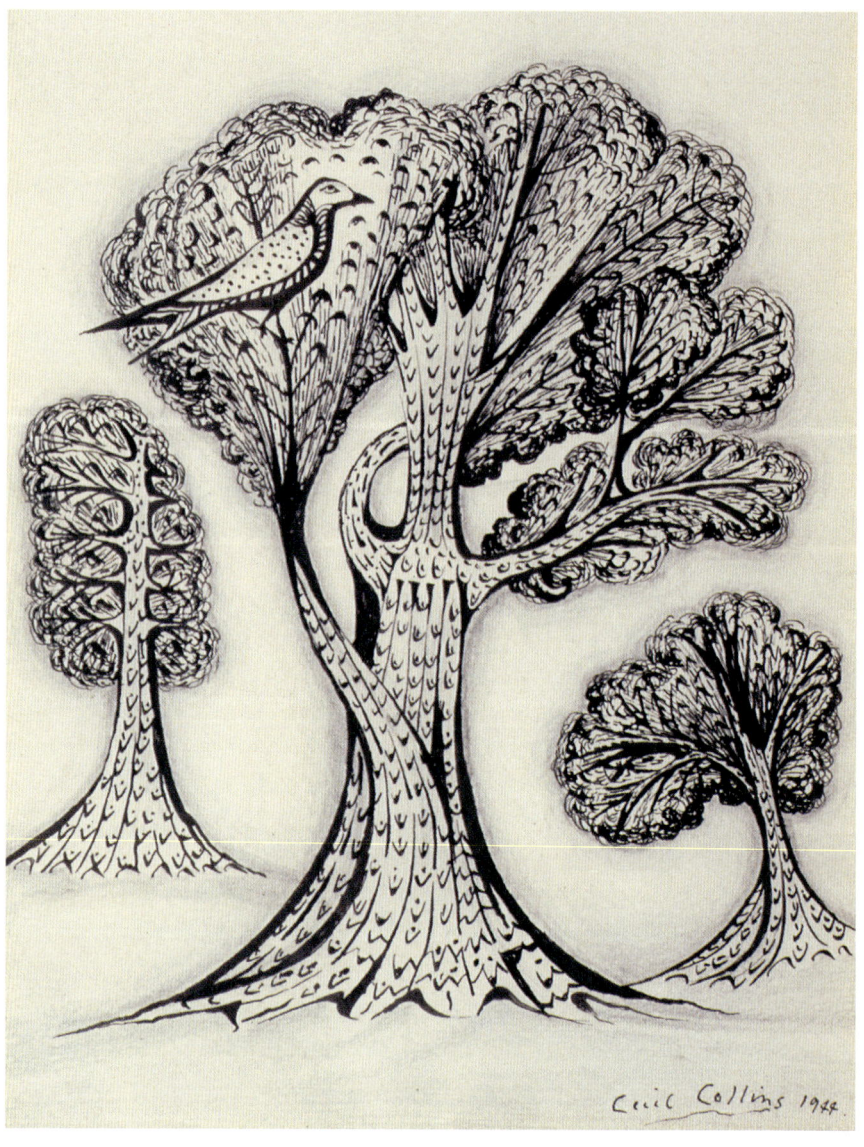

Cecil Collins
Bird Singing in Tree
1944
Ink and pencil on paper
19 x 14cm

OLIVIA TEMPLE

Olivia Temple is a writer and painter. She was not one of Cecil's pupils but met him and Elisabeth at the age of nineteen and their friendship continued until their deaths. Olivia has had several one-woman exhibitions, has written for many magazines and has co-authored two books with her husband, Robert, the latest being *The Sphinx Mystery*, published in February, 2009, by Inner Traditions. She also runs a theatrical design archive.

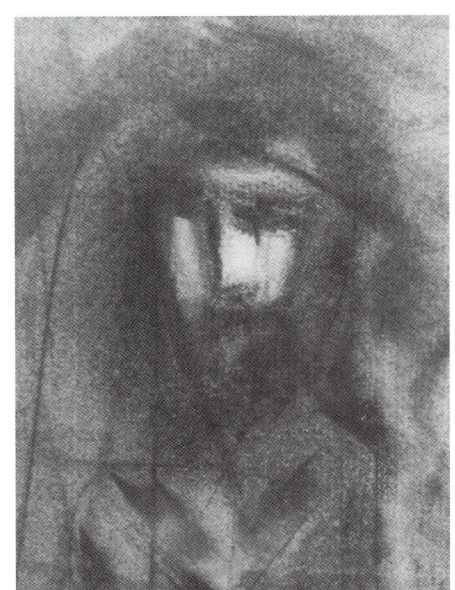

Cecil Collins
Head of Christ
1960
Charcoal on paper
22.5 x 15cm

When I think of Cecil now, so many years after his death, I am instantly with him and Elisabeth on the top floor of 47 Paultons Square in Chelsea. First, I see his wistful smile and feel his prickly three-day beard on my cheek. I see his layers of clothes, his thin neck and woollen tie which seemed somehow to hold his head onto the rest of his body. I wondered did Cecil really have a body or was he made of ectoplasm with folded wings, giving his back that slight hump? Was his fear of the cold and of catching a cold because he was only part human and therefore more vulnerable to earthly ailments? Sometimes I think he fooled us all.

Cecil's hands were very expressive, pale and slightly wafting, like water-lilies waving in a pond. Cecil's eyes missed nothing, but he kept most things to himself. Cecil's tweed jacket took on his persona and patina, as did his coat, hat and scarf. Cecil looked surprised when he laughed, as though he had not been allowed to when he was a boy. He reminded me of a brown hare, nibbling and sniffing secret scents in the air.

Sometimes after a supper of Cecil's favourite, shepherd's pie, served on Elisabeth's magical collection of assorted china, we would look at one of his paintings. He would point at the Angels treading clouds or a Fool leaning against a tree or leaving a city and say, 'They've just had supper,' or 'He's seen a thing or two,' or 'Do you think they like each other?' I think Cecil inhabited his paintings and knew his Angels and his Fools. It was as if, were one to peel away the layers of pigment, blow away the trapped light, scratch gently down layer after layer, the Fool and the Angels would be revealed as living, moving entities who would nod at Cecil and murmur, 'Good evening.' His technique, his mastery of glaze, pigment and depth was alchemical.

Cecil liked jokes and often described his Angels and Fools as ethereal furniture: 'moving furniture' or 'feeble furniture', as he called it. He loved to make you guess which novel's title he was miming. He would stick one elbow out at an angle and wave at it, then he would raise the other elbow and wave at that, struggling to control his laughter. 'Give up?' he'd ask and add, *'A Farewell to Arms!'* Then he would laugh and laugh until his eyes filled with tears. He loved Marcel Marceau who represented the archetypal fool and his favourite film was *Les Enfants du Paradis*.

Unlike my husband, Robert, I was never invited into the inner sanctum of the studio, down a floor from the living area, although I did go in once when they didn't come upstairs for supper after Elisabeth called. I was so disappointed to see that all the paintings were facing the wall and could only be imagined.

When we first met the Collinses, they lived in Cambridge where we visited them once or twice, but after they moved into the top half of Kathleen Raine's house in Chelsea, our visits were more frequent. An Indian cotton bedspread acted as a curtain across the stairs between floors and, from then on up, you entered the magical world of Cecil and Elisabeth, every inch crowded with much loved things. On the stairs and overseeing it all was Cecil's huge painting which now hangs in Tate Britain, *Portrait of the Artist and his Wife*. Everything about Cecil and Elisabeth is in that painting: the golden fount of inspiration flowing from Elisabeth's breast, the fruit on hand-made plates, the leaves and peach kernels scattered on the table, the sacred geometry of the goblet, the magical landscape of the secret garden, the swans on the lake, the crazy legs of the table and chairs, each part representing the whole.

After helping Elisabeth with the washing up in the tiny landing kitchen, I remember sitting in front of the gas fire, a little bowl of water placed near it, listening to Cecil talk about his struggles with some of the faculty at Central who hated his type of art and tried

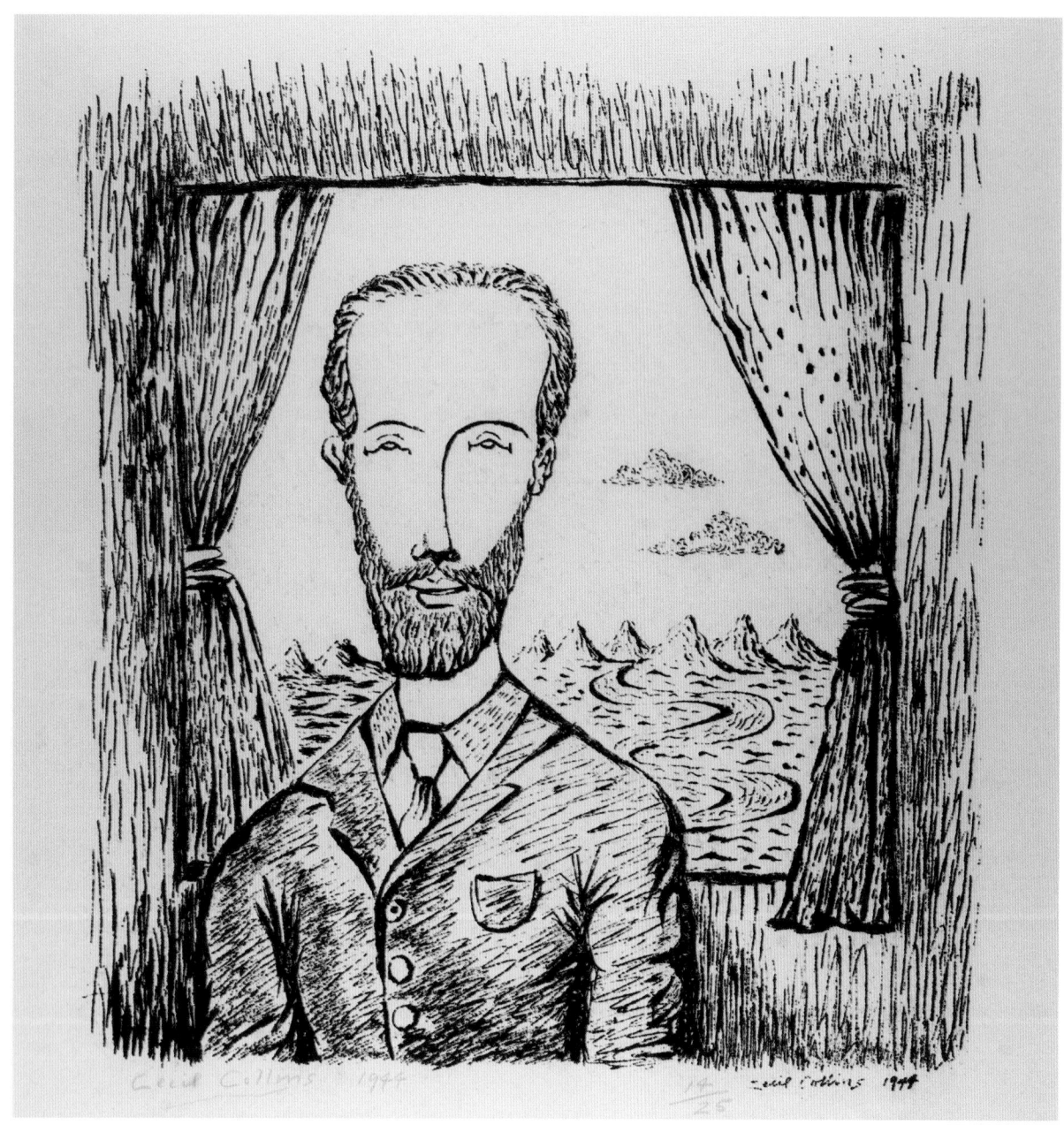

Cecil Collins
Self Portrait
1944
Roneo stencil
22.8 x 20.3cm

to get him dismissed; about how much he loved his students, got succour from them and respected them as artists and how he loved to teach. As he talked, little still-lifes caught my eye and a hypnotic trance came over me: the little bundle of twigs tied up with string, the Angel face fresco on the wall like a sunburst, the folded paper figures that Elisabeth had made and balanced on the mantelpiece, her pleated paper lampshades, the pebbles, comfortable cushions, Elisabeth's long feet clad in pointed slippers.

Elisabeth always had a pile of hardback books beside her chaise longue and another heap of exhibition catalogues and invitations to private views. She would suggest which exhibitions to go to, whose work she liked, which composers, Arvo Pärt and John Tavener among others. Sometimes we all went to a recital or concert. At one of these, Elisabeth introduced us to the composer, Sir Arthur Bliss.

She was not painting much then, hardly at all, but her creativity glowed in everything she wore and had around her. Natural objects, her collection of hats in a colourful heap in the bathroom, pure fabrics, wool and cotton or silk and lovely woody, mossy colours streaked with a flash of bird-feather brightness. She had style.

Like a slowly turning kaleidoscope, I can bring up images of my two friends until everything is merged into a sparkling, jewelled landscape where the Fools are waving with Cecil's wan smile and the Angels with Elisabeth's unwound hair are floating.

ROBERT TEMPLE

Author of fifteen books, translated into forty-five languages, Robert Temple has presented and produced for television. His translation of the Epic of Gilgamesh was performed at the National Theatre. He has edited a magazine, been a science reporter for Time-Life and has recently produced nine classical music CDs. He met Cecil and Elisabeth in 1966 and his friendship with Cecil was based on their shared sense of humour and wonder.

'It should really be *In riso veritas* (rather than *In vino veritas*), for nothing so reveals us as our laughter.' James Joyce

It all began in October 1966 when I arrived in England from America as a PhD student in Hindu Philosophy. Within weeks, I was invited as a 'promising young person' by the organiser, Alison Barnard of *The Centre for Spiritual and Psychological Studies*, to her annual Brighton conference where Cecil was one of the speakers.

I noticed a strange, silent man in a thick tweed jacket, scuffling around like a mouse. He had a hunched back and I realised he wore this bulky garment to soften the outlines of his back. He and I did not fall into each other's arms the first minute by any means; Cecil was an introvert. You had to approach him. He was gregarious, but would not initiate contact.

During the conference Inayat Khan talked about his Sufi movement, Chogyam Trungpa Rimpoche, a famous lama fresh from Tibet, stood smiling in saffron robes, speaking a few words of hesitant English, the actor Sir John Sinclair elucidated the nature of the Beyond and Major-General Scott-Elliot talked about his obsession with Atlantis.

The quietest talk was given in a half whisper by the very shy Cecil Collins. I moved forward several rows because I could not hear him when he started. I was then near enough to hear the marvellous things he was saying. I was overwhelmed by his speech and congratulated him at the coffee break, but he mumbled and looked embarrassed.

When I told Alison I thought he had given the best speech at the conference, she was dumbfounded. Cecil Collins? She had never met anyone before who thought he was that good. She thought I was a strange fellow to settle on Cecil like that. What became clear was that no one at the conference was interested in cultural matters. They were interested in the esoteric, whereas what I'd thought most appealing about Cecil's talk were his comments as they related to culture. I was interested in the esoteric, but it was for culture that I had a proper passion.

Over the years, Cecil gave many talks to the Centre which were circulated in mimeographed copies which I valued highly. His talks were about the nature of reality, super-reality and what lay behind art. He was always talking about the spiritual dimension as it impinged upon creativity and individual life.

WHISTLER'S CLUB

Before the first conference ended, I had bonded with Cecil and he and his wife, Elisabeth, decided we would see each other again. It was difficult because they were living in Cambridge at 35 Selwyn Gardens. Their house in this quiet, obscure little street was peaceful and light, but they were out of the main currents of events, being neither part of the Cambridge establishment, nor sufficiently often in London to be part of anything in the capital. They were living a life of extraordinary cultural isolation which is one of the reasons why they returned to London.

When the Collinses moved to Chelsea, my wife, Olivia, and I visited them often. They would take us to the Chelsea Arts Club for lunch or give us dinner in their flat. In those days, the club was for genuine artists and their friends and was rather spare. The meals were one step up from public school food: silverside of beef, overboiled potatoes, soggy sprouts and custard on a jam tart. Cecil loved all that kind of food and could never get enough of it.

He recommended me for membership, Kathleen Raine seconded me and so I joined that august club founded by Whistler. Whenever Cecil went there, he always mentioned Whistler with reverence, lowering his voice and glancing superstitiously at his portrait.

The food is now superb, but the conversation is no longer about Surrealism, Elizabeth Frink's latest sculpture or what Virginia Woolf and Lytton Strachey had been like.

THE WHITE WITCH

The Collinses had bought the top two floors of a house at 47 Paultons Square and on the two floors below lived the poet, Kathleen Raine. The relationship between the Collinses and Kathleen began sweetly, but soon soured as she was outstandingly arrogant and had a foul and remorseless temper.

Open warfare broke out over a silly dispute precipitated by Kathleen. There was one stairway for them all and the Collinses had to walk past Kathleen's bedroom. As the door was usually open, the intimacies of her daily living were obvious. Kathleen was a formal and fastidious person, but also passionate and relentlessly unforgiving.

The Collinses had crossed Kathleen by not taking sufficiently seriously her absurd complaints about something to do with the stairway. From the moment of that quarrel until the day Elisabeth died, Kathleen refused to speak a single word to either of them and refused to look at them when they brushed past.

Although I had, for years, been one of Kathleen's protégés, she never spoke to me again after my first book was published in 1976, without her prior approval. It contained an appendix on the Neoplatonic philosopher Proclus whom she considered her territory.

Kathleen was convinced she was a witch and told me so many times. She was so enraged at having been romantically rejected by Gavin Maxwell who was ninety percent gay that she 'cursed him under the rowan tree'. Kathleen was convinced that her curse had been effective as various catastrophes happened to him afterwards. This meant she could indulge herself for decades afterwards in a masochistic Roman Catholic hot-bath of delicious guilt for, as a white witch, she had misused her powers to commit a black act. While atoning for an injury to this one man, she did not neglect to berate men in general. Kathleen's love/hatred of men was never focused on Cecil as she considered him entirely sexless.

ANCIENT SPRINGS SOCIETY

Before the break with Kathleen, Olivia and I had formed *The Ancient Springs Society* for young people who were serious about poetry or pretended to be. We took the title from one of Kathleen's most fascinating books, *Defending Ancient Springs*, and Kathleen was the first speaker. We held our meetings in Alison Barnard's house in Wimpole Mews surrounded by her elegant inlaid eighteenth-century furniture.

The most fascinating talks given to the Society were by Cecil. He spoke with such imagination and intensity about the numinous world which he portrayed in his paintings: of the higher things, of meaning and love and the divine, of his Fools and his Angels. Cecil was as warm and confiding in these cosy surroundings as he was in one-to-ones with his students. Cecil adored the company of intelligent young people but, although he loved them, he and Elisabeth had taken the decision not to have children of their own. This was primarily Elisabeth's decision. She told Olivia that she had never wanted them.

MYSTERIOUS NAMES

Elisabeth always called Cecil 'Parc' (pronounced *parse*). I asked her why and she said it was short for 'parson' and it went back to the days when they were courting and she used to tease him about being as sober as a parson when he met her family.

Cecil always said it was a mysterious name. He would smile enigmatically and could not be drawn on the subject. Elisabeth later said it was because Cecil, when young, reminded her of a badly tied-up parcel. I am inclined to suspect that both were cover-stories because she was so private about their personal life that she simply wished to fob off enquiries.

I believe the true meaning of 'Parc' was as an abbreviation for one of those French words they bandied about between themselves when they were young. I think Elisabeth had been annoyed by Cecil's niggardliness with money. (Many of us were astonished to find out, after his death, that he left £1.4 million of his own assets.) He had acted the pauper with the greatest conviction all his life and everyone had felt sorry for him for being penniless.) I believe Elisabeth accused him of being parsimonious and to soften the accusation, they agreed that he was *parcimonieux* (stingy). The nickname then became 'Parc'. It is obvious that Elisabeth would never wish to mention this to anyone, as it reflected unfavourably on Cecil.

From the time we got to know him well, Olivia and I always called him 'Cecil the Pestle', or simply 'Pestle'. Cecil loved that. It appealed to the child in him. He would have loved any other silly nickname just as much. We never dared to call him 'Parc' as that was the private name used only by Elisabeth and would have been an infringement of her proprietorial rights.

He craved to be known by nicknames, to be thought of as endearing to young people. Whenever he saw us, he glowed visibly, nearly humming with happiness. He adored being adored, although it wasn't really being adored which Cecil wanted. It was rather to be thought of as a cosy type of fellow.

THE WOOING OF THE ANGEL

The wooing of the Angel, Elisabeth, by her Fool, the young Cecil, was a romantic epoch in their lives. Elisabeth gave Olivia the wonderful photo of them in the 1930s standing side by side at a cottage gate. It was taken at a place in Buckinghamshire called Springhill, Highwood Bottom. (I can just imagine Cecil's jokes about high bottoms.) Cecil always referred to that time with something approaching ecstasy. He was one of the most romantic of men, whereas Elisabeth was far more practical. She was a very earthed angel. Somebody had to get the supper.

There is no doubt that, to Cecil, the young Elisabeth was a vision of beauty on a cosmic scale, nor did he ever change his view in later life. I believe his almost excessive adoration of her placed her on a pedestal from which it was difficult for her to extricate herself so that she ended up having to be rather condescending to Cecil as she was not allowed to be anything less than a divine archetype.

Something of the romance of their wooing days came across very strongly to me when Cecil told me his charming story about

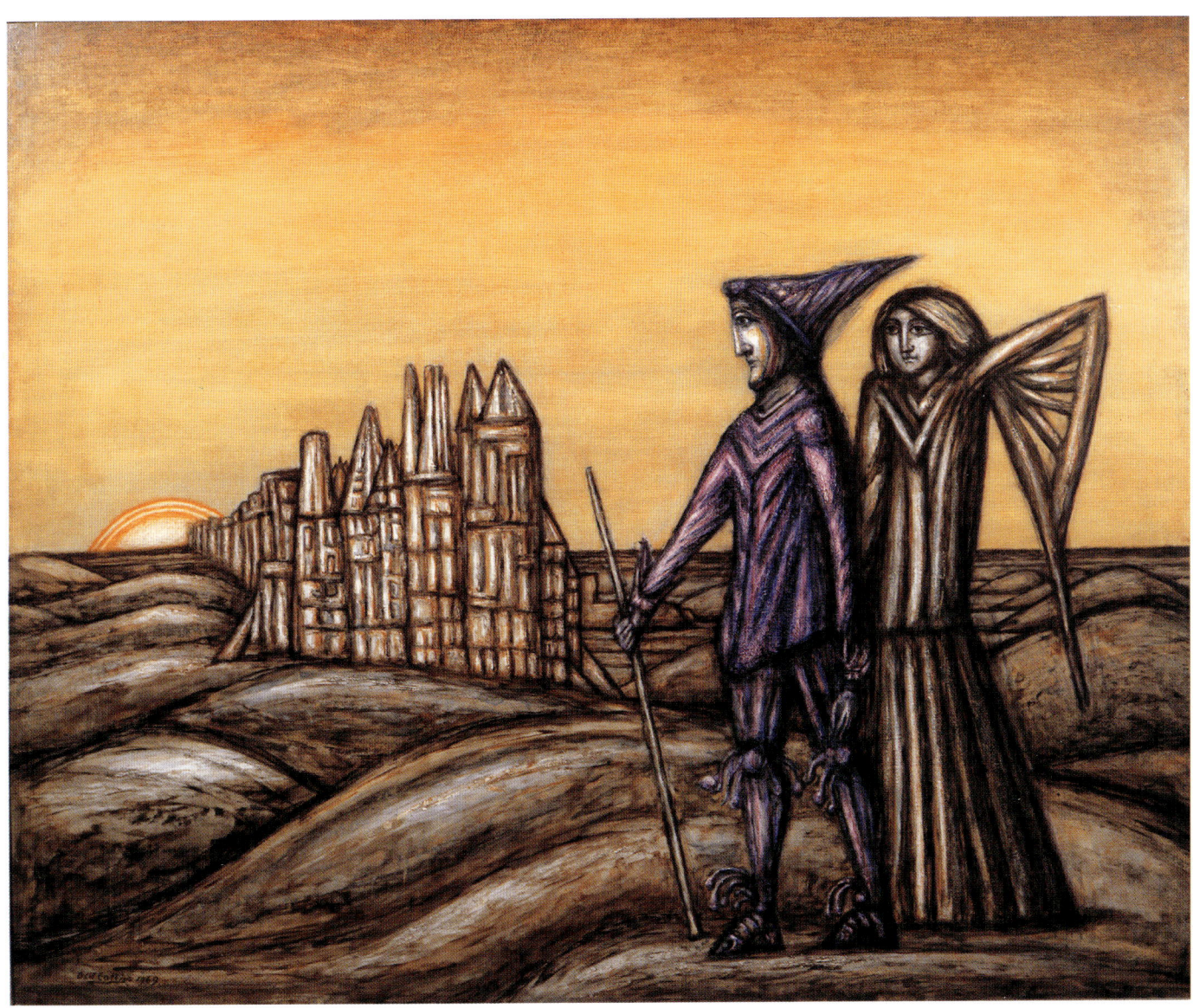

Cecil Collins
Angel and Fool Entering a City
1969
Mixed media on board
75 x 90cm

the Brontës. They had lived at Howarth where Elisabeth came from. Cecil told me that on one of his trips to Howarth when they were courting, Elisabeth mentioned that the little lady they had just passed on their walk was so old that she had known the Brontës. Cecil, true romantic that he was, was thunderstruck. 'Do you mean to tell me that I have just looked into the eyes of someone who looked into the eyes of the Brontës?' Elisabeth answered yes and wondered what was so special about that. Cecil made her promise to contrive for him to meet the woman.

When they later managed this, Cecil asked the old lady, 'What were the Brontës like? Can you describe them? What was your impression of them?' The old lady thought for a moment and, still annoyed eight decades later, blurted out, 'Hummphhh! Them girls in them hats!' After telling me this, Cecil and I laughed and giggled until we had tears in our eyes. 'Them girls in them hats!'

PRIVATE PLEASURES

Cecil loved all things which were cosy. One of his favourite and deeply secret habits was to go to one of the many old-fashioned Bloomsbury hotels in the vicinity of the Central School and have traditional high teas. He always did this alone, except in the most exceptional circumstances. As he and I became more intimate, he could not resist telling me of this private vice.

He would go into long descriptions about real scones, proper Cornish clotted cream, real strawberry jam, genuine cucumber sandwiches with ultra-thin bread and his great passion for Patum spread on hot buttered crumpets with cucumber. He would talk dreamily of bloaters and quality kippers, not the ones found in supermarkets, but from Harrods or the fishmonger on Fulham Road.

He also loved smoked salmon sandwiches, trimmed ham sandwiches with cress, a good Welsh rarebit, *mille feuilles*, custard tarts and Bakewell tarts, but had difficulty finding anywhere which prepared them to the correct standard. He revelled in such things. It was his glittering vice! That shows just how innocent Cecil was, if he could not do anything more wicked than have tea and scones alone as a consenting adult in the privacy of a small hotel lounge.

Finally, the day came when he said he would like me to join him. By the time he got around to extending this invitation, I had moved to the country and it never proved possible to arrange a tea during one of my London visits.

Another of his secrets was to indulge in the gluttony of a traditional roast lunch, then to shuffle on his great overcoat, rub his scruffy, unshaved chin and scuttle out onto the street like a naughty little mouse who had just stolen some cheese.

RELEGATED TO THE BASEMENT

The first time I saw Cecil's paintings was at an exhibition I was taken to by Alison Barnard in March 1967 at the Crane Kalman Gallery. It was where I began to creep into his magical world of Angels and Fools and commenced the process of understanding the way he saw the universe. The show was shared with Winifred Nicholson who had, for a time, been one of the inhabitants of Kathleen's basement.

Although Winifred was a charming woman, I found her paintings pale, feminine and lacking in firm structure and as if they might drip off the surface, being merely pools of water held vertically against the paper or canvas, ready to drain away. Cecil's pictures, on the other hand, were extraordinary and made a bizarre first impression upon me. I had trouble coming to terms with them because I had never seen anything like them before.

Cecil was present, head down, shyly drifting around in his tweed jacket, and Elisabeth, head erect as usual, was energetically

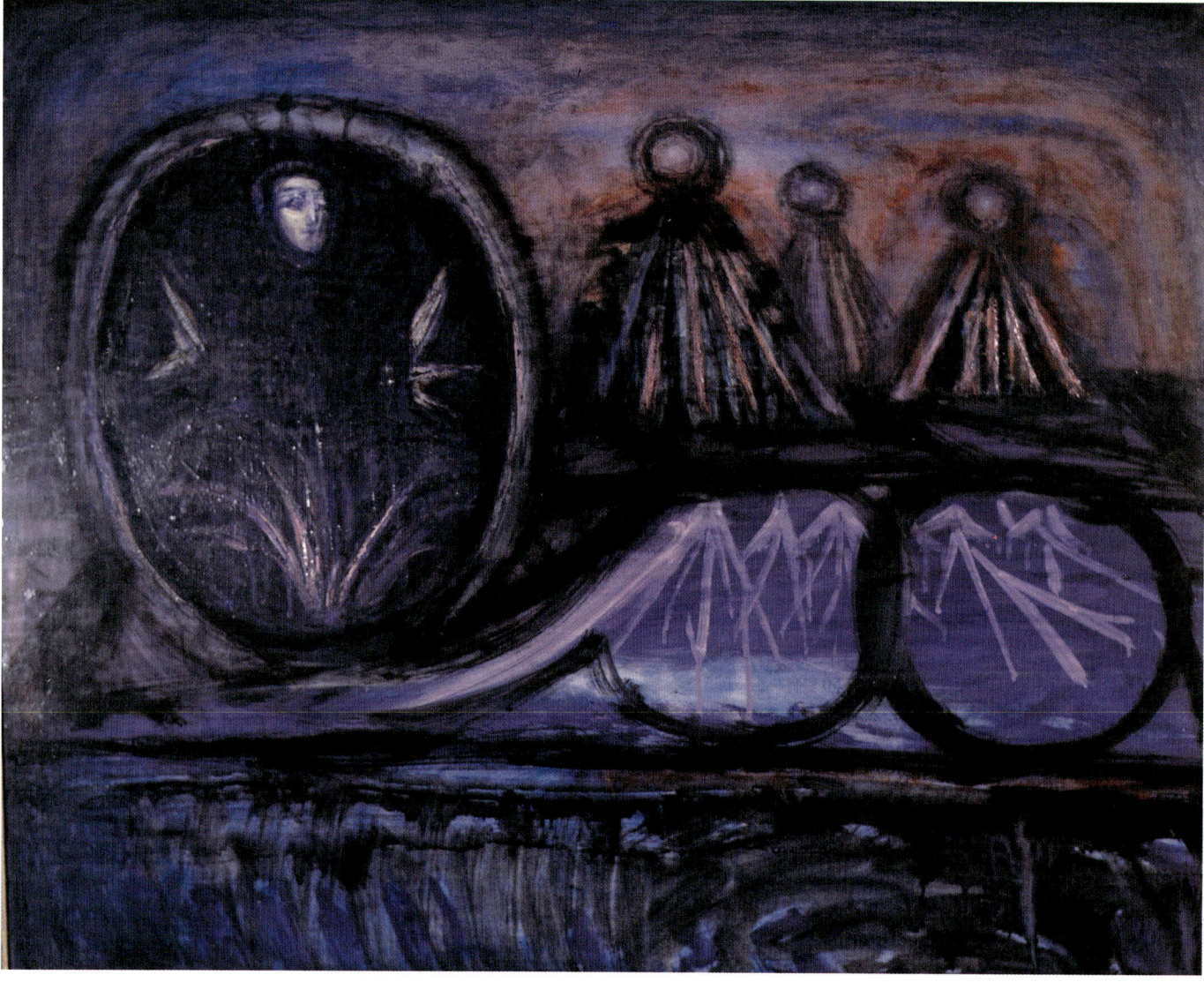

Cecil Collins
The Sacred Mirror
1966
Mixed media on board
75 x 90cm

making her points, smiling in her magical way. This was more effective than finger-jabbing would have been. She was dressed, as she always was at these events, in some long and languid manner, with a fine brooch, restrained and tasteful as befitted a Ramsden married to a slightly wacky painter. Elisabeth had perfected the art of being Cecil's wife in public and adjusted her appearance to the timbre and tone required.

I managed to find a girl to chat to, Cecil's student, Anne Kendall, who later became an archaeologist in the Andes, discovered lost Inca ruins and proved herself to be a most impressive and dynamic person. On this occasion, she was accompanied by her academic mentor, the popular author on pre-Columbian antiquities, Cottie Burland. Since I had studied Meso-American archaeology not long before, most of our conversation was on that subject.

Cecil spent some time with us, encouraging Anne in her Peruvian interests and praising her work as he was always keen to do with his students. He exchanged a few amusing asides with Cottie Burland, then moved on to other arrivals.

I remember being impressed that Cecil was so caring about his student which raised my opinion of him immensely. His passion for his students always came from the heart and was in no way an affectation or mere politeness.

Many fascinating people were there, some of whom I met for the first time that evening, such as Rafael and Jacintha Nadal. Rafael had been a friend of Garcia Lorca which amazed and excited me. Rafael was one of the most passionate collectors of Cecil's work and he bought at least nine of Cecil's oil paintings and various prints.

Cecil was relegated to the basement as a kind of footnote to Winifred's exhibition. It was Winifred who had all the glamorous and attentive people round her because she had once been married to Ben Nicholson who had become famous by then which gave her cachet in the art world. Cecil was considered merely a quirky painter who had once been a Surrealist for a few months in the 1930s. There was simply no one at that time who recognised Cecil Collins as a major artist, although there were people who loved his work. Elisabeth was having to work really hard that evening to get anyone to pay any attention to Cecil who kept hiding in the basement, chortling in his beard to a few intimates.

Cecil's fellow council members from the Centre for Spiritual and Psychological Studies turned up in his support as they did whenever he had an exhibition. It was seen as a way of advancing the cause for greater spirituality in modern life. On this occasion, the two fiery Blacker sisters were there. The more interesting of the two, Thetis, was a highly-gifted designer of batiks and a great supporter of all spiritual causes. She was exotic, funny and outrageous and could do a brilliant and rather hair-raising impersonation of a Mafia female assassin in dark glasses.

CECIL'S SECRETS

I never studied art and the basis of the friendship with Cecil had very little to do with art, although we did discuss art endlessly. Not the history of art, but his art.

As I came to know Cecil better, he would tell me more and more of his secrets. I would discuss with him his mixed egg-tempera technique and his reverence for the book, *The Materials of the Artist*, by Max Doerner which became available in English in 1963. He was also keen on Cennino Cennini's *Craftsman's Handbook* which first appeared in English in 1933.

Among the secrets of his craft which Cecil imparted to me was that he painted to music. In those days, people had vinyl records and used record players or gramophones. Cecil had one in his studio and was technologically advanced because attached to it he had headphones, which few people owned then. With these on, he would stand for hours painting visions of paradise, inspired by the music.

The symphonies of Bruckner were his favourite music for this purpose. With passionate excitement, he invited me to listen so I put on the headphones and heard Bruckner for the first time.

SEVEN SWANS A-SWIMMING

The painting of Cecil's that Olivia and I loved the most was *Portrait of the Artist and His Wife* (1939). It represented Cecil and Elisabeth as an enchanted couple in a magical world and hung on the stairs as you went up to see them.

This painting probably has more symbols in it than any other single work of Cecil's and they are more overt. For instance, Cecil and Elisabeth are sitting with Egyptian ankhs in their hands, the symbol of eternal life. These were not a joke. Cecil believed deeply in the ankh, though to my knowledge he only ever painted one again, in *Dawn* of the same year.

I remember scrutinizing *The Artist and His Wife* with Cecil one day and said of the swans on the lake in the background, 'Those are seven swans a-swimming!' He congratulated me on recognising the swans from one of his favourite songs, 'The Twelve Days of Christmas' which starts with

> On the first day of Christmas,
> my true love gave to me
> A partridge in a pear tree.

Cecil was fascinated by the concept of a partridge in a pear tree. This idea inspired his various pictures of birds, some of them in trees. The splendid print, *The Joy of the Fool* (1944), showing a Fool with raised arms gazing ecstatically at two hearts in a tree, which he gave to Olivia and me for our wedding present, also had a resonance of this same partridge in a pear tree, but the bird had turned into a pair of hearts instead. Even a bird of paradise or a phoenix was, to Cecil, a more resplendent form of partridge. He was never an ornithologist.

The 'seven swans a-swimming' were, for Cecil, not just a picturesque image. They have a long pedigree and are first mentioned by the Greek poet, Callimachus, in his "Hymn to Delos". The poet wrote of this isle sacred to the ancient Greeks, 'The swans went round Delos seven times... and they had not yet sung the eighth time when Apollo was born.' In the Greek esoteric tradition, the seven circlings of Delos by the swans represented the notes leading to the perfection of the musical octave. Apollo was not only god of the lyre, but was frequently depicted riding on a swan.

These swans are also related to the seven eagles of alchemy which represent the seven sublimations required in the Great Work. In Islam, devout pilgrims are required to make seven circumambulations, or circlings, of the *Kaabah* shrine at Mecca, which is a survival of a mystical tradition unappreciated by the majority of pilgrims today.

Perhaps the most intriguing symbol in *The Artist and His Wife* is the one absolutely central to the smaller *Dawn*. It is often referred to as a chalice, but this strangely shaped object is clearly meant to be the *vas spirituale* or vase containing the spirit of things.

The Litanies claim the Virgin Mary is this *vas spirituale* which is also one of the central symbols of the alchemists. In the eighteenth century the French esotericist Jean-Baptiste Alliette gave a curious recipe of what this vase held, '... a vase full of celestial-astral liquid, consisting of one part wild-honey, one part of terrestrial water and a third part of celestial water.' He added mysteriously, 'The secret, the mystery was therefore in this vase.'

This is precisely the sort of esoteric notion to have delighted Cecil's mystical and humorous inclinations. He often did not know whether to laugh or to pray and his paintings often contain both states. Cecil would have loved the newly-rediscovered *Gospel of Judas* which portrays a laughing Jesus who shocks his disciples by his constant mirth.

Cecil and I agreed that it is the humourless people who cause all the trouble and if they were to be killed by laughing gas one day, the world would probably have no more wars. Fools are incapable of warfare. How dreary Cecil thought those people were who grimly fixated on some mystical experience which did not feature laughter as one of its chief elements. If you cannot laugh at yourself, as Cecil frequently did, then you can easily become insufferably vain. The importance of humour cannot be overestimated. As far as Cecil was concerned, laughter was the very essence of paradise.

COLLECTING CECILS

Olivia and I bought six pictures from Cecil during the time we knew him including a wonderful self-portrait of him in front of an open window, dated 1944. We were given a seventh as a wedding present. With great reluctance and simply because I was a soul-mate, Cecil sold me what he described as his only charcoal drawing, a portrait of Christ. Cecil commented on how surprised he had been to achieve such a satisfactory effect in what was, to him, a strange and unfamiliar medium.

Similarly, he described at great length and in some rapture, his first encounter with the lithograph process, the result of which was *The Great Happiness* (1965). I bought this from him, took it home, but became disenchanted by it because it was too abstract. I returned it to him and swapped it for two smaller prints. I was very happy with the transaction, having effectively gained an extra piece of his magical art, whereas Cecil thought that he had won because he had avoided a partial cash refund, as parting with money was unendurable to him.

Cecil's little studio was filled with pictures facing the wall in vertical heaps, at least two hundred of them leaning inwards. There would normally only be one picture visible, sometimes not even one. This was not only to stop them fading, but because they were his secrets.

When Cecil dragged me down to his studio, leaving Olivia and Elisabeth upstairs for an hour, or even two, he would be in a state of overwhelming mystical exaltation. With glowing eyes, he would extricate a picture and reveal it like a god unveiling the creation of a new world in a faraway galaxy. The novelist, John Cowper Powys, communicated a similar intense feeling in his visionary novels. Cecil had known slightly, and deeply admired, Powys who, through his novels, spoke of being in direct communication with the earth spirit. Cecil also believed himself to be literally in personal communication with the earth spirit.

The painting which I hoped to buy one day, and discussed most often with Cecil, was *Angel and Fool Entering the City* (1969), wrongly titled in the Tate Gallery's Retrospective catalogue of 1989 as Fool and Angel Entering a City. Never at any time did Cecil speak of the Fool before speaking of the Angel. Cecil seemed almost as excited as I was about my getting this newest of his large paintings at that time, but was psychologically incapable of making any concession on the price.

Sometimes Cecil and I would jointly fantasise about my getting another new lustrous green painting of his which he kept touching up. It showed three female figures rising from a calm sea at dawn. This painting was listed in the Tate Retrospective catalogue as *Daybreak* (1971), but when discussing it with me Cecil called it *The Goddesses of Creation Arising from the Sea*. 'Look,' he said. 'One of the goddesses is holding a flowering branch which symbolises the dawn of creation. I'm wondering if I should change the title to *The Dawn of Creation*. What do you think?'

Cecil worked for months to enhance the magical effect of this painting by applying new glazes to it. On one occasion, he said he had already applied thirty-two layers of glaze to that picture and was continuing to do more, a very slow process. He used to tell me at length about how the light got trapped within the molecules of the glazes, refracting internally in a strange and miraculous way. He thought of this painting in particular as a light-trap. Cecil's eyes would sparkle maniacally and he would say, 'This results in light emanating from the painting itself which has become its own source of light and is no longer reflected light.' He considered that to be a divine and numinous quality.

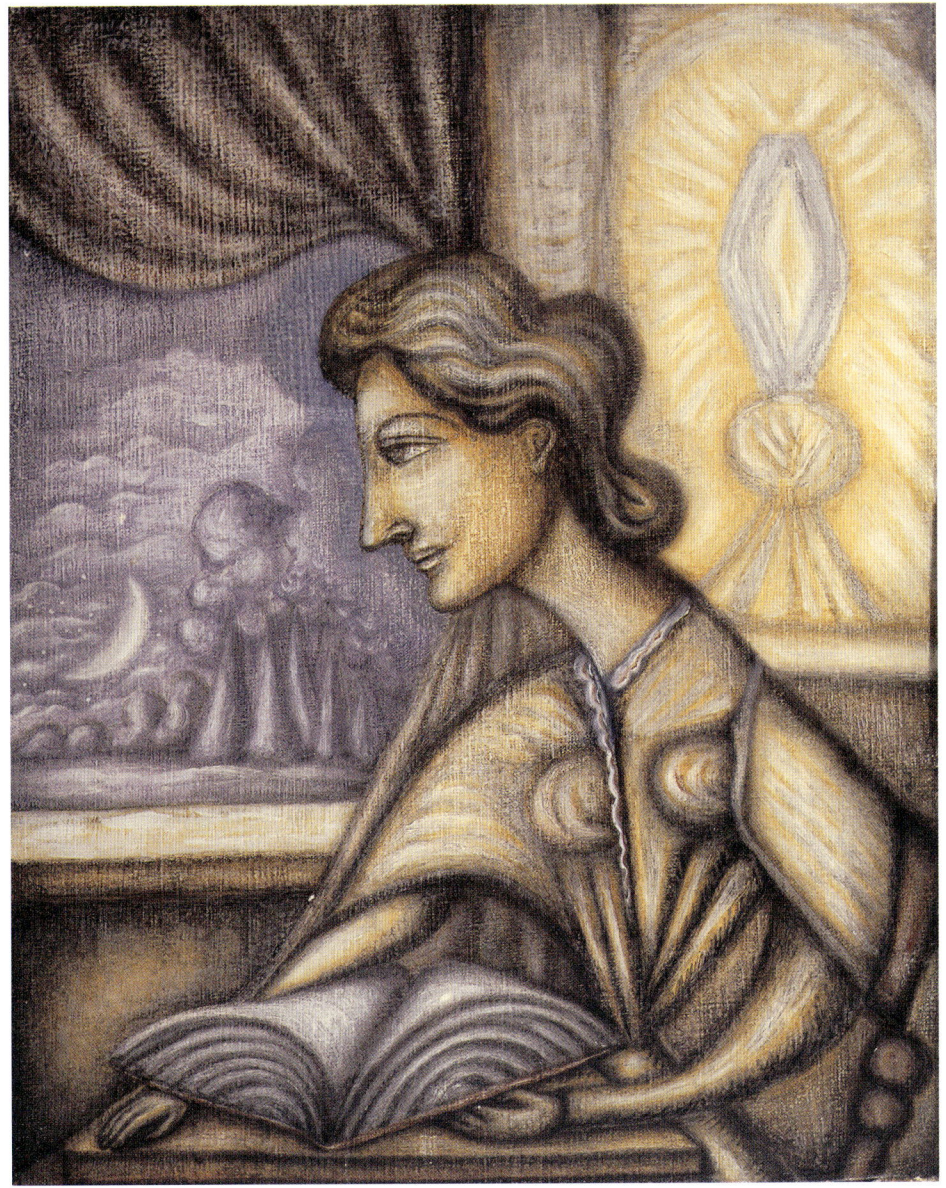

Cecil Collins
Elisabeth, the Artist's Wife
1950
Oil on canvas
43 x 33cm

Together, we would gaze closely at the green painting and allow the light from it to irradiate our faces, at least in our imaginations. He was tempting me to prefer this painting to *Angel and Fool Entering a City* which he readily admitted had far less light emerging from it having fewer glazes. It was a sunset painting so this would have been inappropriate as the whole effect was meant to be one of oncoming dusk.

It may seem strange that we spent so many hours exploring his paintings together and discussing the ones I would finally have, considering that he never made any hint of a price reduction. I did have a sense of depressing powerlessness and it was one of my greatest disappointments in life that I could never afford to buy a painting by Cecil and had to make do with the monochrome visions, rather than one in full colour. What I paid for those works from Cecil came out of our food money. It was many years before we could afford the cost of frames for those visions of paradise, but it was a sacrifice we never regretted.

Occasionally, when he was feeling relaxed and happy, Cecil would let me fish around in the piles of pictures and turn some round. He was always deeply apprehensive when I did this, but he tolerated it as one tolerates a baby pulling at one's trouser leg.

At that time, Cecil was inclined to regard his earlier paintings as much less important than his more recent work, because it had all been ignored for so long and was associated in his mind with decades of humiliation and neglect. I, however, did not view the early works like that at all. My many passionate speeches of praise and joy at the revelations of all those magical visions were met with annoyance or at other times with a mixture of delight and a sigh of resignation or despair.

He was never completely happy when Olivia raved about the small painting now called *Elisabeth, the Artist's Wife* (1950) that she would like to have one day, apart from *Portrait of the Artist and His Wife*. He felt uneasy we devoted so much attention to this early work, but forgave us as he understood Olivia longed to have it because of our fondness for Elisabeth. I shared the deep admiration for that picture, not because it represented Elisabeth, but because of the magnificent achievement of colour balance, composition and magic.

He constantly enjoyed tempting a fellow spirit with his visions and wanted me to step into their worlds. Often he would speak of the lovingly portrayed characters as his dear friends. They were, of course, dream-friends. Cecil unquestioningly considered that the Fool represented himself and had an equal certainty that the Angel represented Elisabeth. He was her Fool. She made the shepherd's pie. That is what Angels do for Fools. It stands to reason.

SPEAKING WITH THE ANGELS, LAUGHING WITH THE FOOLS
Cecil would often laugh and make little noises representing how his

odd figures might sound if we could hear them. Sometimes he would gurgle, at other times he would say, 'Boop! Boop!' Sometimes he would make Marcel Marceau hummings and whimpers or he might lower his voice into a deep bass and mumble something semi-coherent and buffoonish. He would imitate the cry which one of his birds might make or pretend to chew or peck or move like a creature. He would point at them and grin, looking at me conspiratorially in merriment.

I would rarely join in because they were his creatures and it would have been presumptuous for me to attempt to speak for them, though I occasionally would add a chorus or amplify a mode. For instance, if he was cheeping, I might cheep in reply in a quieter voice, allowing him to remain the chief cheeper. After all, there is an etiquette in these things.

Once in a while, he would point at an ominous creature or shape and growl menacingly, voicing the danger. It was all a bit like watching the *Teletubbies* where the innocent little creatures do not speak, but make sounds which one more or less understands. Perhaps we were communicating in the alchemical language of the birds. Saint Francis of Assisi would have understood us.

You can see how impossible it would have been for anyone without the same mischievous sense of humour and delight in whimsy to share these experiences with Cecil and why it meant so much to him to have found someone who knew what he meant when he gabbled in painter's gibberish, rocking with laughter when he hit on a particularly salubrious sound which perfectly expressed what we thought of a particular fool or other creature.

Angels are too holy and sublime to boop and cheep, but Cecil very rarely made a single sound of a particular tone expressing wisdom, surprise or despair for an angel. Cecil was well aware that the angels despair of us and the mess we are making of things. However, we had an implicit agreement between us that the angels were to remain generally silent.

Another picture Cecil and I used to look at and discuss a lot was the one now called *The Sacred Mirror* (1966). To me, he called it *The Magic Mirror* or *The Mysterious Mirror*. I never liked the surroundings, but I loved the mysterious figure inside the mirror. Sometimes Cecil would make an ominous humming noise about that mirror, as if a hive of bees were inside and might suddenly swarm out or he might make some modest screeches, like little owls at night. We would have long sessions talking about what lay behind that mirror and about the worlds behind our world. I cannot count the hours during which Cecil and I gazed together into that mirror in that particular painting, both of us trying to figure out what it meant, for he did not know any more than I did. He had only painted it because he had seen it, not because he understood it.

It is important to realize that Cecil believed literally in other and higher dimensions of reality, divine dimensions. Although he respected

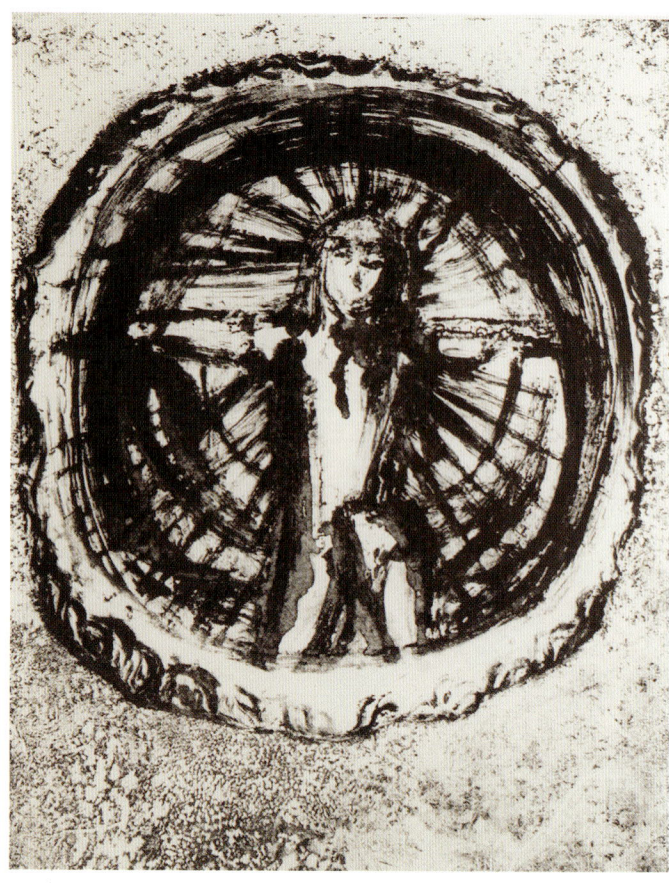

Cecil Collins
The Eternal Sun
1961
Lithograph
56.8 x 40.7cm

Jung, Cecil did not believe these visionary realms were anything like the mythical images called by Jung, the Archetypes which resonate in the Collective Unconscious, a kind of mass shared unconsciousness. Cecil did not believe any of his individual visions really existed anywhere, even in another dimension. His Angels and Fools were emanations of symbolic forces which transcend our world.

Cecil believed he was communing with these deeper, divine realities and his paintings were indicators of these ultimate realities which he struggled to portray symbolically. There was not one instant in his mature creative life when he doubted that he was speaking with the angels or laughing with the fools. He considered himself a joyous fool. His heart was singing; his brush was singing; his soul was on fire.

There was nothing affected about Cecil's attitude. He never appeared pious in any way or tried to put on airs. He had only pity and a gentle contempt for people who behaved like that.

ELISABETH'S BIN BAG

Cecil's one major fault was a quiet, stubborn egotism. It was this that led him to be insensitive on numerous occasions to Elisabeth's talent and needs. She became embittered and resentful of this in her later years. Cecil and Elisabeth often snapped at one another. As she entered her seventies and saw that she had never achieved recognition as an artist in her own right, Elisabeth became deeply alarmed and occasionally despondent. She would get out her old paintings and look them over, then wish to throw them away.

On one occasion when Cecil was not at home, Elisabeth took the opportunity to do a big clean-out of the flat. Olivia volunteered to help. There were some black plastic rubbish sacks already filled. Before Olivia left, Elisabeth asked her if she would mind carrying one down for the rubbish collectors. Olivia agreed, but when she got downstairs, she looked inside and saw that it contained a large bundle of about one hundred water colours. Thinking they were no good, Elisabeth had decided to discard them.

Olivia did not throw them away; she put the bag into the boot of her car and tucked them away at home to await a change of the artistic climate. Years later, when Elisabeth was achieving recognition with an exhibition of her own and selling her work, Olivia went round and handed her the huge pile of her old work which she had thought destroyed years earlier. Elisabeth was thrilled and put them into her exhibitions and sold them.

NOT A SURREALIST

One might think that Cecil would have had sympathy with Surrealism, but he did not, although in the great 1936 Surrealist Exhibition in London he showed two rather inferior paintings which were of a Surrealist nature, *Angel Images and Negative Spectres in Conflict* (1933) and *Virgin Images in the Magical Processes of Time* (1935). These were hung between paintings by Salvador Dali and Giorgio de Chirico. André Breton and his wife attended, along with other Parisian Surrealist dignitaries, wearing raw beefsteaks on their shoulders.

All his life Cecil retained friendly relations with Julian Trevelyan who also exhibited then, but I believe the other British Surrealists did not like Cecil because he was inclined to revere the divine, the existence of which they furiously denied.

Cecil could have advanced his career if he had played along, but he was repelled by the disturbing and nightmarish images of painters like Yves Tanguy which seemed like visions of hell rather than glimpses of heaven. Cecil also became severely disenchanted by the political activities and leanings of the French Surrealists who had all adopted Communism. Cecil was deeply opposed to Communism, as well as to Fascism. He opposed all political movements and doctrines which attempted to enslave the spirit of man within false, materialist visions. It was impossible for Cecil to remain a Surrealist which he could only be said to have been for a few months.

THE VISION OF THE FOOL

Cecil would often show me a copy of his only book, *The Vision of the Fool*, which was published in 1947. It was impossible to borrow because even Cecil himself never found a way to obtain a second one. He would handle and speak of it with reverence. Until recently, when I obtained a rare, signed copy of the original edition, I had never read it. It is truly magnificent. It says so much so eloquently, but in those early years before his recognition, people tended to laugh about it and few, if any, had ever read it. Desperate for encouragement, Cecil used to look at me and Olivia and say, 'T S Eliot told me he liked it.' He often said that; he needed to say it because he felt, quite rightly, that the precious book had fallen on stony ground.

Kathleen Raine viciously ridiculed this purported pretension of Cecil's. She used to say, 'Cecil is always claiming that T S Eliot liked his pathetic little book. What nonsense that is! I can't believe that Eliot was being anything other than polite.' However, in 1979, Kathleen Raine overcame her personal prejudices sufficiently to write a fine booklet in praise of Cecil.

FESTSCHRIFT FOR A FRIEND

In 1972, Olivia and I appeared in a little book with Cecil. It was entitled *Festschrift for KFB* edited by our Sinhalese friend, Tambimuttu, known as Tambi. Olivia had both a drawing and a poem in it and I had a poem beautifully illustrated by Olivia's drawing. KFB stood for Kathleen Falley Bennett, a rich American woman from Chicago called Kay who was sponsoring Tambi's publication efforts and whom he wished to thank in this exuberant manner.

We worked with Tambi for months to put that book together. Olivia went to Stephen Spender's house to pick up his contribution and I went to see William Empson in Hampstead to get his. Spender was a great admirer of Cecil's and had written an article, "The Work and Opinions of Cecil Collins", praising him for 'creating a genuine poetic world of his own' and reproducing *The Pilgrim Fool* (owned by Spender) and *The Sleeping Fool*, both painted in 1943. Other contributors to the Festschrift included Laurence Durrell, David Gascoyne, Shusha Guppy, Michael Hamburger, Marcel Marceau, Iris Murdoch, Ezra Pound, Kathleen Raine and her daughter, Anna Madge Hopewell, Feliks Topolski and Julian Trevelyan.

One of Cecil's prints was reproduced as a full page and he drew a special bird with a birthday inscription, dated 1972, for Kay. I believe it was never reproduced except in that little book and I do not know what happened to the original. Probably Tambi kept it or gave it to Kay.

Olivia and I were not considered distinguished enough to have our names advertised on the back jacket with the other contributors and being in it was a real honour. It gives me an eerie feeling now to look at the book, seeing us there tucked between the same covers as our old friend Cecil the Pestle, just where I feel we belong, in my case as a Fool, in Olivia's case, as an Angel.

PHILIP VANN

Philip Vann is a writer on the visual arts. He is author of *Face to Face: British Self-Portraits in the Twentieth Century*, and books on modern and contemporary artists including William Crozier, Dora Holzhandler, Cyril Power, Greg Tricker and Joash Woodrow. He lives in Cambridge.

I was born in Leeds in 1958. I was always very interested in literature and read voraciously as a child. I did very well at school in creative writing and in all the arts. I read English Literature in the late 1970s and then I moved to London. I worked for the BBC for a time; it was quite a lowly job, but they allowed me to do some research on an arts programme on the World Service. I always wanted to write and I thought maybe I'd go into publishing or be a novelist or something.

My love of art and writing came together and in about 1984 I was drawn to write about mystical art. Something in me responds to it very deeply in a timeless way. There were a few artists I really wanted to meet at that time: Cecil Collins, John Craxton and Dora Holzhandler. I'd seen an illustration of the *Sleeping Fool* and it immediately awakened something in me, just as the works by Chagall that I'd seen in galleries and reproductions when I was about twelve had also resonated with me. Chagall's painting in the Tate is of a sleeping poet and there's a parallel with Cecil's *Sleeping Fool*. Each artist has a unique resonance, but Chagall and Cecil both had universal visions.

What impressed me about Cecil's work was that it was a purely poetic way of looking at the world and one could write about it, hopefully, in an equivalent, poetic way. Cecil was very clear, very lucid, without being prescriptive. The two good teachers I'd had in my life, at school and university, were like that too and let you discover for yourself.

Meeting Cecil for the first time was for me quite a release, a sense of coming home, because here was a rare person with whom you could communicate in a natural and easy way without any self-consciousness. Through his paintings, there's a return to your primordial mind which is probably what all good art and poetry and music aspires to. Otherwise, as Cecil used to say, 'It's just confectionary; just journalism.'

I told him I'd been a student at Cambridge and he told me that he'd lived there. He felt that the academic mind in Cambridge was about analysis, conceptualising things, not about intuitive responses. Things have changed now and there's Kettle's Yard which has a picture by Cecil. It's a very small ink drawing. I suppose Cecil would have known Jim Ede. Cecil talked about the loneliness of the role as an artist in our society and about how lonely his life had been. He used the word lonely several times. There was a certain amount of anger and depression about his own life.

I visited the Collinses three or four times in Paultons Square. I remember climbing all the stairs and being very intrigued by the cooking arrangements on the landing of the staircase. Cecil and Elisabeth both made me very welcome and I was struck by how youthful they were, but I often find that with artists. I always thought of them as my contemporaries. Cecil said as an appraisal of me as a writer, 'That's your task in life: to explain art to people.'

I remember visiting Cecil in his flat in 1985. We had a cup of tea in the living room. There was a mural on the wall. The Collinses were very amusing and making jokes about the narrowness of the Tate Gallery. Then I went with Cecil to the studio and I remember it being quite dark compared to the lightness and the vivacity of the living room. It was a more philosophical kind of space. He showed me his paintings which were very beautiful. I remember standing in front of the small, icon-like paintings which had a subtle burnished, layered effect. Cecil talked about the climate and atmosphere, which he referred to as the perfume, of the paintings. I'd never thought of art in that way or had never heard it articulated quite like that.

To me, it was so refreshing to be with someone with whom I could be totally open about my response to mystical painting. My response to Cecil's work was partly physical, partly spiritual. Painting is a physical medium, but it affected me in a primordial way and I felt an expansiveness of perception being with him. As I was looking at the pictures Cecil said, 'You're a real fool.' No one likes to be called a fool so I found myself inwardly bristling. At the time the ego was resistant, but I've come to understand since more consciously that he was actually being very positive and giving me a huge compliment.

Cecil expanded on his comment afterwards when he talked about the harsh society we live in which is anti-civilisation in so many ways with its very narrow focus on the brash and the splash of the moment. He said we're all wounded souls and that there's great pain in self-knowledge. It wasn't simply about those who are cultured and aware and those who are not. He didn't think in such simplistic terms, but he was saying that those who are aware carry the grief and the burden of society as part of their consciousness, simply because they're aware of it. Cecil spoke of the music of Mozart and Chopin as being double edged in its evocation of paradisical merriment and what he called subtle melancholy. He believes this

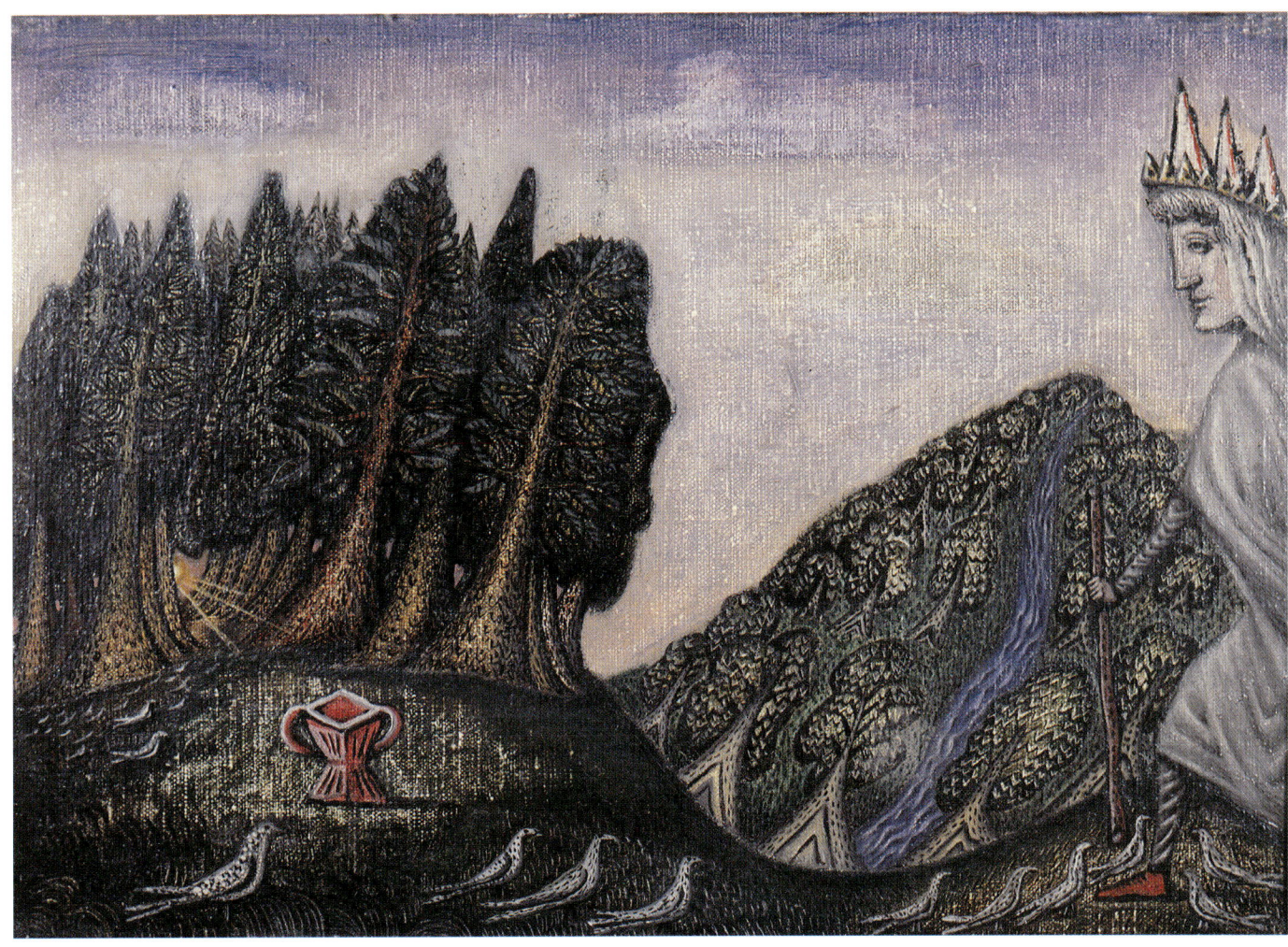

Cecil Collins
The Return
1943
Oil on canvas
24.5 x 33cm

serves only to make paradise more beautiful and more human. Cecil commented, 'I haven't finished with my Fools yet. After all, their innocence and sorrow are inexhaustible.' It's slightly uncanny and maybe a bit eerie the way that Cecil sums up through his medium a universal enigma. The object is inseparable from the mystery; the painter and paint; the seer and the object have become inseparable. There is a unity, but it's not one we can ever fully know.

I remember Cecil's very thin, ageless, face as he talked about those moments of greater consciousness and about religious consciousness while I was peering at these small pictures. There was an atmosphere in the paintings that at one moment I became part of, showing how ultimately we are all inseparable. I've had, in my own experience, such times of what I can only describe as expansiveness where suddenly the 'I' moves to something much larger and grander. One doesn't want to judge or pigeonhole, but there's an insatiable desire in contemporary society to box things in and to place them as one might place a bet.

Cecil said, 'My life has not followed the usual order. As a young man, I lived a retired country life absorbed in my work. Now I lead a busy life in the city.' He lived off the King's Road, which was full of youthful energy. He quite enjoyed the liveliness, the colours and the fashions. It can be seen as a lot of tat in some ways, but I prefer to see it as exuberance. One time, I made some comment about people on the Underground and he said, 'They're like the living dead. They're sleepwalkers.' He was very fresh, very witty. I've seen photographs of him as a young man, but as a middle-aged man he had virtually the same appearance, quite sage-like, like a wise fool.

The second time I visited the Collinses, my article about Cecil had been published in *The Artist* and they invited me round. I had put all my feelings and thoughts into the article and Cecil said he liked it, but I got a sense from Elisabeth that she didn't want Cecil to be over-adored. She may have thought that I was just another adulating young person, as I was then, though when I reread the article now, I think it's pretty objective. I remember Elisabeth started talking about a lowbrow thriller writer on this initial encounter, perhaps to bring down the somewhat high-flown atmosphere. Elisabeth would deflate any pomposity. She never accompanied me to the studio when we went down to look at Cecil's work in his studio on the floor below. That evening, they took me to have supper in a lovely house around the corner with some neighbours, who were a very cultured, youngish German couple in their thirties; one was an illustrator. There was a lot of laughter at the supper table and I was slightly taken aback by it, the utter youthful spirit of it.

Another memory I've got is of an autumn evening. Cecil was wearing his overcoat and we were walking through the streets of Chelsea. I can't now remember where we were going or exactly what he said, but I can recall the atmosphere which was jokey, humorous, affectionate and spontaneous. Cecil was like a teenager. There was a lightness, a sparkling merriment about the way he just stopped in the street and suddenly started laughing about something, defying any preconceptions of an old man.

Years later in the 1990s, after Cecil died, when Elisabeth had restarted her painting career and I interviewed her for her exhibition catalogues, I really began to appreciate her work. I think it's beautiful. We don't have to compare her and Cecil's work or put them in a league table. I think they're both wonderful in their own right and quite unique, quite different, though there are many affinities. Once we were talking about biography and Elisabeth said, 'If you looked into our lives, what you'd come up with would be shocking. It would be very surprising. There are all kinds of secrets in people's lives.' They led, in many ways, very unconventional lives, especially in the 1930s when they lived at Dartington Hall. Society was so much more conventional then.

Elisabeth was very encouraging and warm about my writing. She was always very kind. She said that this was, in many ways, a really wonderful period to be alive because nowadays people were so much more open than she remembered in her youth, even in the circles that she mixed in. Personal freedom was very important to her. She said, 'There is something about this age, a great freedom between people.' There was a sense of wishing that she could have lived like that and a touch of regret in her voice that she had given up her painting career to look after Cecil. Although her response when I asked why she hadn't practised consistently as a painter throughout her life, was answered immediately and with certainty, 'Living and people come first.' Looking after Cecil as a true artist came first for her.

Elisabeth and Cecil were such distinct, strong personalities, as well as being very gentle and open towards each other and to others, but they were also quite strict in their views. They wouldn't allow any nonsense. Everything was definite and specific and they had strong opinions on society, art and life, not in a prescriptive way, just born out of their own experience which had became their philosophy.

Elisabeth and Cecil were conscious that they weren't burdened with education. They saw it as a virtue, yet he was extremely erudite and both of them would come up with amazingly learned references. They were self-cultured and thought intuitively for themselves.

Cecil once talked to me about the different levels of happiness: the lesser happiness, the ordinary happiness and the great happiness. The greater happiness has to do with the feeling of total openness and vulnerability that is connected both to human tragedy and comedy, which come together in a Shakespearean sense. The feeling I get from Cecil's paintings is the same feeling I get from the Fool in King Lear.

As I conjure up memories of Cecil and looking at paintings with him, my response is exactly the same as it was in 1984. Yet there's also a paradox there. Because of the unending mystery of what he was painting, it's open to new feelings and interpretations each time you look at it because we're all endlessly changing. It's about the ever-changing and the unchanging. Looking at his work is a living experience. As with any good painting, sculpture, poem or piece of music, you return to it and you see or hear it refreshingly anew and yet it's always speaking to something beyond change.

Cecil was very shrewd, very aware of the world. He was dealing with mystical areas of consciousness and philosophy, but what he was expressing at the same time was very real. He was aware of the mystical tradition in poetry and art. He said to me, 'People think I am a cerebral person, but I am a man of pure feeling.' We're now in an age where knowledge is endlessly regurgitated and we lose the freshness of discovery in the moment of revelation.

Cecil once asked me, 'Why are you interested in art? Where does it come from?' There were so many possible answers, but I related it to my family background and how various relations of mine had some rather wonderful modern British paintings in their houses, including pictures by Mary Newcomb, Alan Lowndes, Jacob Kramer and David Bomberg. My mother's two brothers and their wives were very visually aware and I used to love looking at these beautiful paintings as I was growing up. Cecil told me that people should have art in the home, original paintings, not prints, and that this was so important for the family and for the whole of society.

I don't think we ever talked about the history of art. We just looked at his paintings, I responded and he made his comments to my response. He was very interested in how I was responding. It was a genuine dialogue, like a dance of thought. It wasn't as if I was visiting a grand old artist who would talk at me; it was a living experience with an eternally youthful old painter.

I remember references to Indian and Persian art and to Coomaraswamy who Cecil said I should read. I remember him also talking about *mudra*, the hand gestures. That was in his art and also in his person. Cecil's hands were bony and elongated, very gestural. He used them a lot and they were very expressive. It somehow all connected with what he was talking about, the *mudra* in art, an evocative gesture.

I'm a great lover of authentic naïve, self-taught painting and Cecil and I discussed this a bit. In the spring of 1986 I went to Hungary and visited museums of folk art and also looked at a lot of naïve art which was still thriving there then. When I met Cecil in the autumn of 1986 he asked, 'Did you come across any wonderful contemporary folk artists?' I said, 'I did.' He said those artists would have had a totally pure vision.

When there was an exhibition at the Tate of some Anthony Caro sculptures, Cecil expressed to me his sense of bewilderment as to what these works were about. Cecil got quite passionate talking about Anthony Caro. He was completely mystified by his art. I get very little resonance from these sculptures. My mind draws a blank and I intuited Cecil had exactly the same reaction.

Francis Bacon was Cecil's antithesis, but I think Cecil really rated Bacon as a great painter in his own way. He said, 'Francis Bacon is an artist looking at darkness with great scrutiny, whereas I am turned to the dawn.'

There's a famous phrase by Matisse that art should be like a comfortable armchair. Cecil Collins quoted that and said, 'That just won't do. It has to be much, much more than that.' I take it in a different way; it may read differently in the original French. In English we think of the old-fashioned cliché, sitting comfortably in an armchair with pipe and slippers, but in the French original it's more like when you're ensconced in the most comfortable armchair, you're totally at ease and at one with your life.

I went to the opening of the Basingstoke stained glass windows. It amused me because Cecil was always speaking against the established church and organised religion and then suddenly there he was, in a church. He was quite subversive, quite wicked, in the things he would say. This attitude can be clearly seen in his painting of the Fool picking his nose in front of an archbishop. Cecil once said, 'Theology is a quest for security on the part of the male. There are no feminine theologians.' Since there are feminine theologians, that was mischievous. Cecil also talked about the saga at the art college and the fact that they tried to make him retire because he was over sixty. He talked about the cultural bureaucrats with a vested interest in the system. He said they were 'The avant-garde of the Sixties, the failed artists.'

I visited Cecil Collins at the Anthony d'Offay Gallery during his exhibition there. He was holding court to quite a lot of young art students. One of them was having a discussion with Cecil. There were two strands to it. The student was very doubtful that painting could communicate something universal and Cecil was adamant that it could. Cecil and I had been talking about Ken Kiff and how we both admired his qualities as a painter, but we both expressed the opinion that he touched the mythical and not the archetypal, though the student disagreed with us.

The Vision of the Fool is the most amazing piece of writing. It's exactly the same spirit as Cecil's drawings of fools; there's a feeling of gaiety, abandon and liberating foolishness. I think it does resonate with a later generation, rather than the generation of the Forties. It relates very much to the hippy consciousness that grew up in the Sixties. Occasionally, I see in his work an iota of religious sentiment, less purity of consciousness and more stylisation, but then he was a fallible human being and, as an artist, would pick up the vibrations of the time. I don't hold that against him because there's so much that's wonderful and original.

I get pristine sensations of awe and wonder when I look at his work, which moves us because it's both physical and metaphysical and there's no contradiction between the two. In *Head of an Angel*, Cecil felt he'd actually got to another level. He was very excited. After years of searching, he felt that he'd found something exciting and original. It was a radical new departure for him. It's got some wonderful elements to it and there's a rather amazing shape in the sky, an abstraction of a cloud, but it's that kind of stylisation which does make you think of 'religious art.' I remember we talked about the cloud in one of his other pictures and he said, 'Clouds have a special meaning to me.'

The Agony in the Garden is one of my favourite pictures. I remember seeing it in the Barbican show, *A Paradise Lost*. Also *The Pilgrim Fool* is a great comment on the apocalyptic realities around him with the bombing of Plymouth in the background. It sums up the agony of war and the compassion that you need to deal with it. It's a marvellous painting, Cecil at his best. The girl in the picture looks young, but also quite ageless. Her eyes are closed, or in reverie, and she's clearly looking to the future. It's the antithesis of the brutality of those times and it's also a different vision of maleness in the world that's very important to bear in mind. It's not an effete vision of maleness. It's very powerful, very protective, but it's also incredibly gentle and I think that's something Cecil realised we need to cultivate. There is now a growing awareness through ecology and the resurgence of green thinking that it is the only way we can survive the potential of this terrible conflagration.

Cecil and Elisabeth were like mirrors through which people could see aspects of themselves clearly. People sometimes lost faith in Cecil and that's very sad, but it makes you wonder how authentically they were touched in the first place. I can understand people reacting against him and being dismissive of what they may take to be a cosy English cultural tradition, but he portrayed the originality of his vision. Blake came up peripherally now and then in my conversations with Cecil, but I got the impression he didn't want to go down that route. He may even have deflected my questioning on Blake.

Cecil is classified as a modern Blakean which is no bad thing. Blake talked about not being a slave to any other man's system and both he and Cecil were immensely powerful individualists that went their own way. Maybe Cecil was wary of being enslaved by the Blakean tag. I think there are many parallels, even though they're different artists from different centuries. They were both working in the mystical tradition and, in many ways, they were saying the same thing. Blake's paintings and poems give you a spiritual sensation and people respond to Cecil Collins' work in the same way. There's a great gentleness in Cecil Collins' work, but there's a great fierceness as well and Blake had that too. They both had that feeling of merriment: the innocence of Blake is very close to the foolishness of Collins. There's great movement in the flow and the rhythm, but Cecil also talked about Byzantine icons so maybe the stillness that you get in the figures of icons is important. They both seemed to have a natural mystical facility, an access to mystical awareness. As a child, Blake saw angels in trees and Cecil Collins also had very early mystical experiences. There's a wonderful story Cecil told of how, in his twenties, he had a vision of a bird in a tree whose song was equivalent to the form of the tree.

True painters like Cecil are immensely self-assured, but essentially they're not arrogant people. They may have doubts and can be very vulnerable in other ways, but they have this amazing perseverance and dedication. They see their own way through all the worldly problems, difficulties and anxieties and even though they may be feeling incredibly lonely and get no response for years on end, there's an innate self-assurance that sees them through to the end.

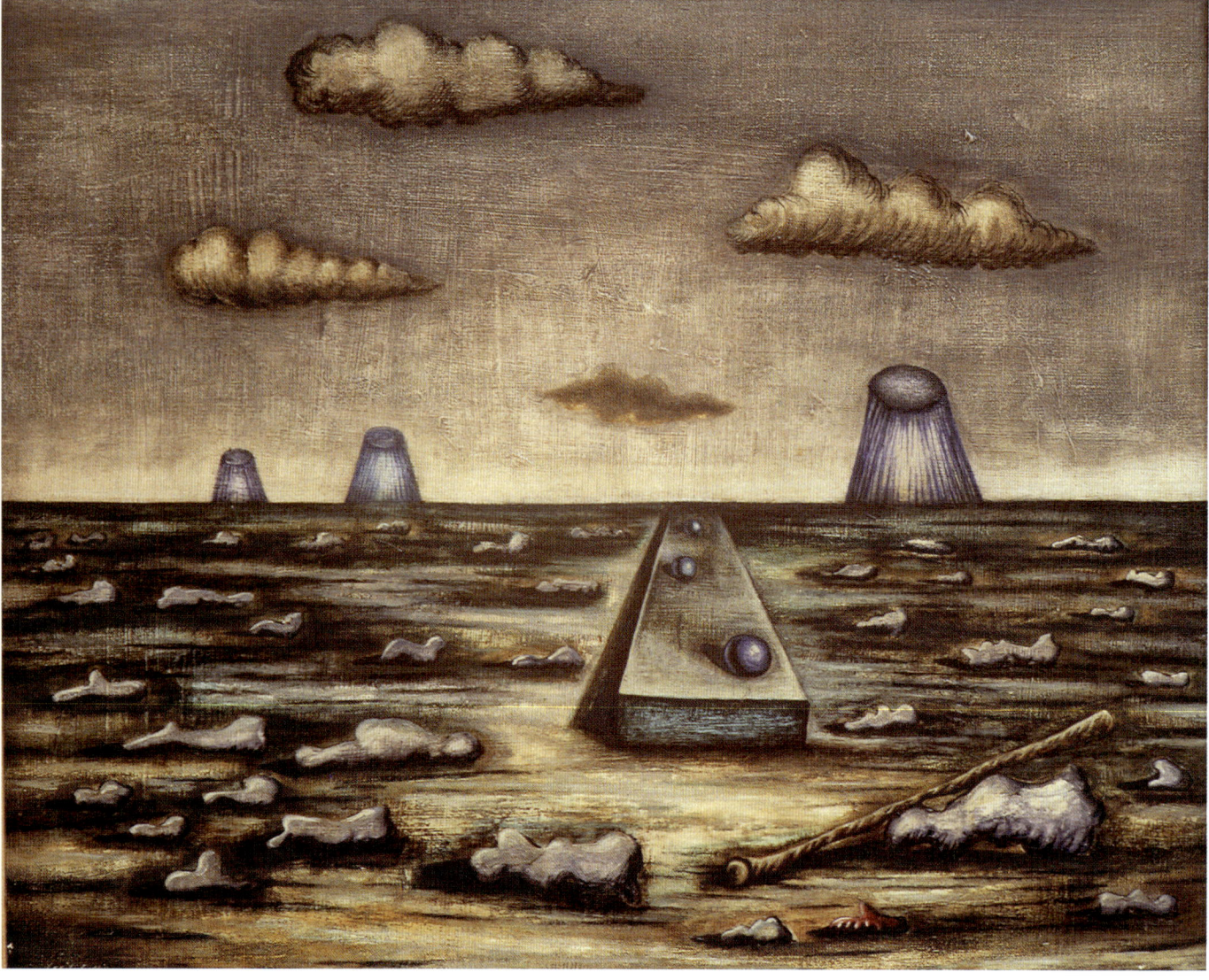

Cecil Collins
Landscape: The Approach
1940
Oil on canvas
51 x 61cm

KEITH WALKER

Keith Walker has served the Church as Vice-Dean of Chichester Cathedral, residentiary Canon at Winchester Cathedral, librarian at Winchester Cathedral and is author of *Images or Idols, the Place of Scared Art in Churches Today*. He has commissioned or was responsible for obtaining many notable pieces of contemporary art for the Church including the Cecil Collins and Patrick Reyntiens Angel windows, *The Mystery of the Holy Spirit* window, as well as Elisabeth Collins' design for an altar rail cushion. He and his Dutch wife divide their retirement time between England and Holland.

I first came into contact with Cecil when I was the Precentor at Chichester Cathedral, which really meant Deputy Dean or Sub-Dean. The Dean was Walter Hussey who was very keen on art and obtained some wonderful commissions: Henry Moore, Graham Sutherland in St Matthew's Church, Northampton, and then Chichester Cathedral.

There was a gentleman who lived in Chichester whose wife was an artist, although not renowned. They had seen a painting by Cecil Collins in, of all places, the Cairo Art Museum. She was thrilled with this. It moved her very deeply, as Cecil's paintings can. When she died, this gentleman, who was not impecunious, felt he wanted to memorialise her by commissioning a work by Cecil for the cathedral. This was the altar frontal, the *Icon of Divine Light*, painted on a wooden panel in St Clement's Chapel. That was my first encounter with Cecil's work. I didn't meet him in person till a blessing of the work during Evensong which was a very important occasion for Cecil.

Cecil, being Cecil, didn't produce a study for what he proposed to do for a long time. When eventually he did, it was of a very poor nature. It was difficult to determine what he intended from such a rough sketch. I suppose it's fair to say that it had a sort of sun image on a background, but from my standpoint it was very much the introvert expecting the world to understand him on the his own terms. Cecil knew what he wanted to do in his head and heart, but what he showed us was absurd. He just hadn't thought it through in terms of getting it accepted by a committee and that was, I'm afraid, typical of Cecil.

Walter Hussey had to take this sketch through a Chapter meeting. Before the meeting, Walter asked me how I felt about it all and having recently seen an exhibition of Cecil's work and been very moved by it, I said, 'I feel very strongly that this has the makings of a wonderful work of art.' The Chapter was very kind to approve it because I don't think anyone was very keen, apart from the Dean and myself.

From this awkward beginning, the sketch went on to its superb, consummated end. The finished work is painted on panel and you can see it as a great star among the stars or you can see it as a large flower among little flowers. It works both ways. The point about the latter interpretation is that in the paintings by the patron's wife, flowers and petals were very important so it was a kind of secret message to the patron and, in another world, to his deceased wife. I don't know if Cecil had ever seen any of the wife's paintings, but the widower spoke to Cecil about them and may have shown him photographs. Cecil certainly knew what he was doing when he painted it to allow one interpretation as a large flower.

I went to look at the altar on my own after the ceremony of introduction. My little daughter, Sarah, came with me. She could only have been about three at that time and I was holding her hand. I just stood silently looking at the frontal because it's a superb piece of sacred art. Then Sarah loosened her hand from mine and went forward. I let her because who is more innocent than a child? She sat down beside the painting and stroked it. I told Cecil this and he said, 'Ah, now I know it's all right.'

I was speaking with Patrick Reyntiens at a later date when I had moved from Chichester Cathedral to All Saints Church, Basingstoke, and he said, 'I'd be prepared to make a window for nothing if Cecil was the designer.' He tossed off this remark when we were in the south presbytery aisle and I thought, 'I'll remember that.'

All Saints is a very beautiful church, but the glazing in the west end was plain because the money had run out. The first piece that came in with my patronage was Elisabeth Frink's *Head of Christ*. It's one of her very good works. I then went to see Patrick to talk about a stained glass window. He said he couldn't remember his earlier remark and there would be a charge. I thought, never mind. I felt I had to be the mean instrument of a great patronage for the church and so I went to see Cecil. Patrick and Cecil then came down to Basingstoke; they liked the church and the site that was proposed. Cecil sat in the choir and said to Patrick, 'It's already working within me.'

The Church Warden and I had the authority to use a particular fund as we wanted which was quite unusual. This was the early 1980s when the markets were favourable and we raised the money. I more or less did it on my own and the Church Warden, who was totally in favour of the project, checked everything through. We raised over £47,000 without depleting the capital sum. We did the side windows first, what we call the 'angel windows', which are straight out of paradise. Cecil told me he had to go back to Byzantine work to get the image he wanted and they're just magnificent. After we did the side windows, there was sufficient money left to embark on the central window, the *Mystery of the Holy Spirit*.

We went to Cecil again and he produced a study, but it was difficult dealing with him. I once drove all the way from Basingstoke to Cecil's house after he said he was ready to meet me, but he'd done nothing so I had to turn round and come back again. However, I didn't stand on my dignity. I knew I wanted this work of art from Cecil. It is curious that Cecil longed for a commission within the church, both he and his wife told me so, but he was at the same time doing everything he could to spoil it. I can only interpret this as the action of an introvert. Cecil just couldn't come to terms with the outside world.

After quite a lot of awkwardness, Cecil did produce a sketch and it was, in fact, a brilliant one. I took it to the relevant church committee, but they turned it down and I thought I'm not taking this so I appealed against it. They said it wasn't a Christian image. Funnily enough, my wife and I, with our daughter Sarah, were on holiday in Venice and there were sun images all over the place. I decided to challenge them and they allowed me, which was unusual, to come back to the authorising committee. I took the precaution of going to see a professor in Cambridge who looked at the image and then wrote a statement for me. Patrick Reyntiens also wrote a statement which I took with me to the committee. I was there for about three quarters of an hour and, reluctantly, they did let it go through so it went ahead. I think the initial rough sketch went to Patrick, but I would have loved something as a remembrance.

Patrick is a very fine glass artist, very dedicated. He went to Germany for the glass because they made it in the medieval way with all the air bubbles locked in. This means that light passes into the glass and is refracted in a certain way which makes it more luminous.

When the committee saw the result of what they'd agreed to, they were pleased and that's to their credit. Cecil, at his best, is a great sacred artist and I think he was at his best with those windows, both the side windows and the central one; they all go together obviously. It represented for me the mystical dimension of his work.

John Tavener's music was played at the dedication of the big window, *The Mystery of the Holy Spirit*. I went to Tavener and told him the subject of the window was angels and would he compose a piece for the dedication. He said he would and I said, 'I'll get some words from one of the poets.' I went through Vaughan, the whole lot, but I couldn't find any that were appropriate so I sat down and wrote something myself and posted it to him. Tavener rang shortly after and said, 'I've done it.' I couldn't believe it. It's funny how these things happen. I think that if things work like that, it is the Holy Spirit.

One of Cecil's images is very roughly a chalice with a great circle in the chalice and three eyes. That came from me commissioning Cecil when I was a member of the Chichester Chapter, Spirit of God. Cecil wanted tremendously to fulfil the commission. He came to Chichester and then produced this extraordinary very original design. It's Trinitarian: each of the three eyes is a little different from the other. It's a drawing which shows Cecil's love of the Trinity. There is also the circle and all that that means, both in Christian terms and in terms of other religions.

This was turned down by the Chapter which was a great sorrow to Cecil. His design for St Clement's Chapel had already been achieved, but he very much wanted this commission for St Richard's shrine too. He wanted the Church to acknowledge him, to recognise him for the spiritual artist he was.

I know many people who have no patience with the kind of person Cecil was; they erase him from their memory, people who could have helped him artistically. One gallery owner told me very explicitly that he'd have nothing more to do with Cecil because he was such a very difficult person to deal with.

Anthony d'Offay once commissioned an exhibition of pencil drawings from Cecil. The drawings all had to be of a certain size to fit some frames. Cecil immediately produced nearly all of them bigger than the agreed size and d'Offay prevented the exhibition from going ahead. It was in Cecil's own interests for it to happen, both to propagate his art and to earn money, but he insisted on doing it on his own terms, even though it had all been agreed. I got the story from Cecil and his version went something like this: 'These rogues, these gallery owners, what do they want? The skin off your back and forty per cent of the proceeds.' Then it came out what had actually happened. In fact, Cecil had a number of exhibitions with Anthony d'Offay, both before and after this incident. They were quite marvellous shows and Cecil was shrewd enough to know how valuable they were. I wouldn't want his behaviour to be seen in terms of pride and selfishness. As I understand it, it was some complication of his introvert personality.

The first time I went to tea with Cecil and Elisabeth, we met in Kathleen Raine's flat which was underneath Cecil's, but Kathleen wasn't there. Cecil and Elisabeth may have been looking after it while she was away. Most of the time, Cecil just sat and looked at me. Elisabeth had to bridge the gap. Cecil was trying to decide whether I had the Spirit inside me or whether I was another clergyman fake. It seems he decided the former. Thereafter we always met in Cecil's own flat, though I felt he was keeping me out of the sanctum, the sacred place, of his studio. When I went to the flat, Elisabeth would let me in and we would sit and talk, maybe even have a cup of coffee and then his lordship would arrive. I think this was a ceremonial entry. It was what the great artist does.

Cecil Collins
Angel Window
1987
All Saints Church, Basingstoke
Stained glass (realised by Patrick Reyntiens)
15 x 30ft

friends & other relationships

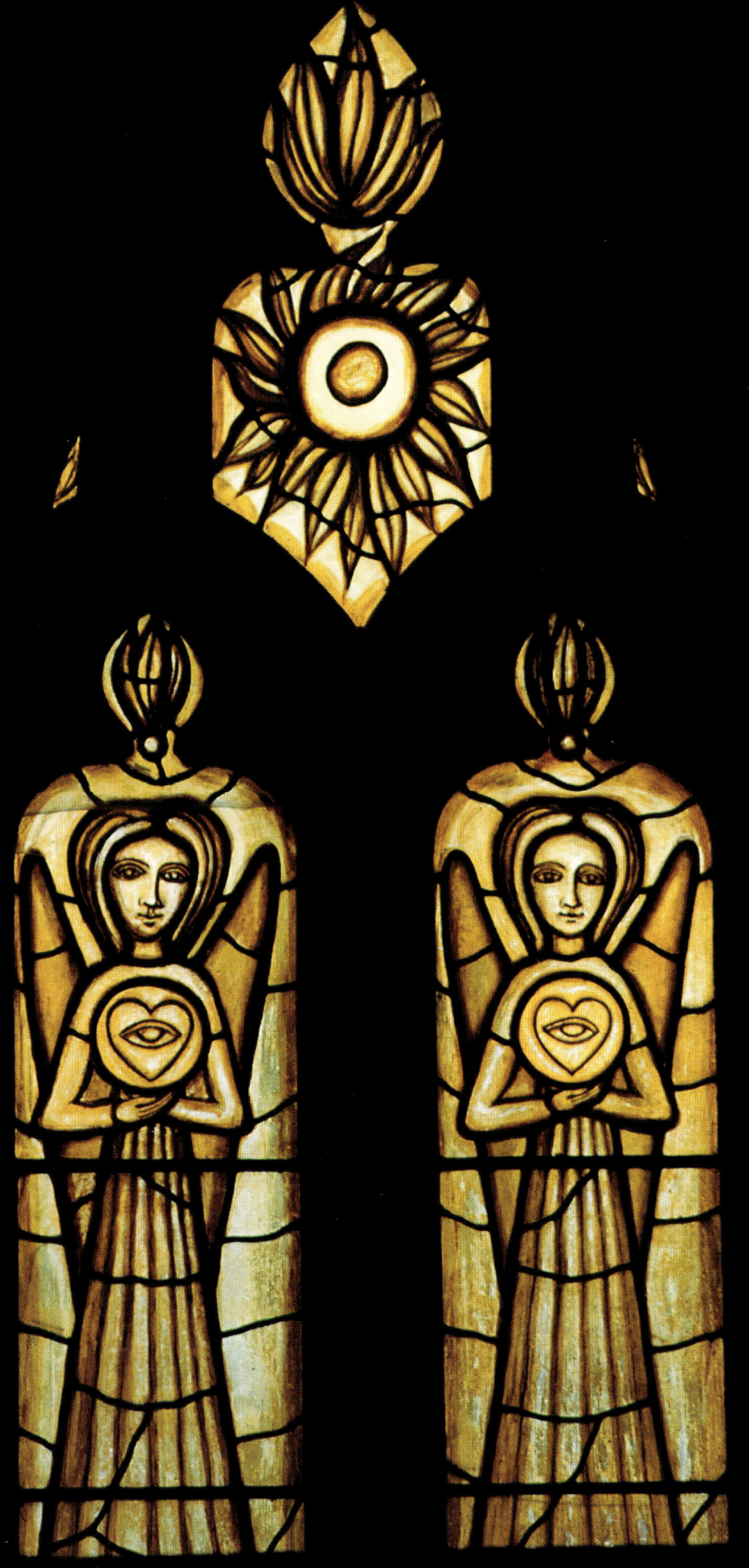

I think Cecil thought that I had the makings within me of a genuine enlightened person. It was a big compliment. They don't come too often and I was very grateful for it. He had the idea that all religions are tribal and that what matters is the universal vision which is what he was dedicated to. If he had to, he could work within the parameters of a particular religion and was more touched than he was able to say by the figure and person of Jesus Christ. I don't say this because of my own understanding. Sometimes he used to try and goad me. It was when we talked about God. He loved to say something that might make some clergymen react strongly, such as, 'All great religious gurus, whether it's Buddha or Mohammed or Christ or Moses, are really the same,' or 'The institution is corrupt, get out of it.' There was a twinkle in his eye, but I didn't rise to the bait.

Cecil was a very intelligent man; there's no question about that. He had shrewd insight into the personalities of other people. I wouldn't describe him as selfish, but he was self-absorbed and he was very uncertainly related to the world around him. He could be as humble as a child and was very open to the spirit of God, but he had this awkward personality. When Elisabeth had to have a replacement hip operation, she went down to a hospital in Kent and eventually Cecil went to see her, having commandeered a student to take him there. When Cecil got to the hospital, he sat next to the bed and began a long, bemoaning lament about his own difficulties having to live on his own. He didn't notice the woman in a hospital bed before his eyes. For once, Elisabeth erupted and absolutely shred him to pieces. When Cecil came back, he said he felt like a cockerel that had been plucked. He was smiling at that point. In the way he told the story was an implicit acknowledgement that perhaps his behaviour had been inappropriate.

One fascinating anecdote about Cecil concerns a small, exquisitely painted *Head of an Angel* from his last period. I commented in my ignorance, 'Why is the angel sad-looking?' Cecil looked at me in deep pain and said, 'This world in a graveyard of angels!' He went on to speak about the cosmic conflict in which we are all involved.

Another story about Cecil concerns the television programme about him, the one that begins with Cecil and Elisabeth sitting at a table. I got hold of the film and brought it down to Chichester. Cecil was to give a speech and then the film was to be shown. It was quite a large audience and two young men were in charge of the technical side, but the sound malfunctioned and the showing of the film was a bit of a disaster. Afterwards Elisabeth sat there looking subdued, but Cecil played the fool acting out a joke he used to tell about a sailor at sea trying to find something on the horizon. He picked up someone's cap, put it on back to front and placed his hand above his eyes and said, 'I can't see it.' Antics like that were his way of dispelling grief or unhappiness and inviting us to be more light-hearted.

When I was a member of the General Synod of the Church

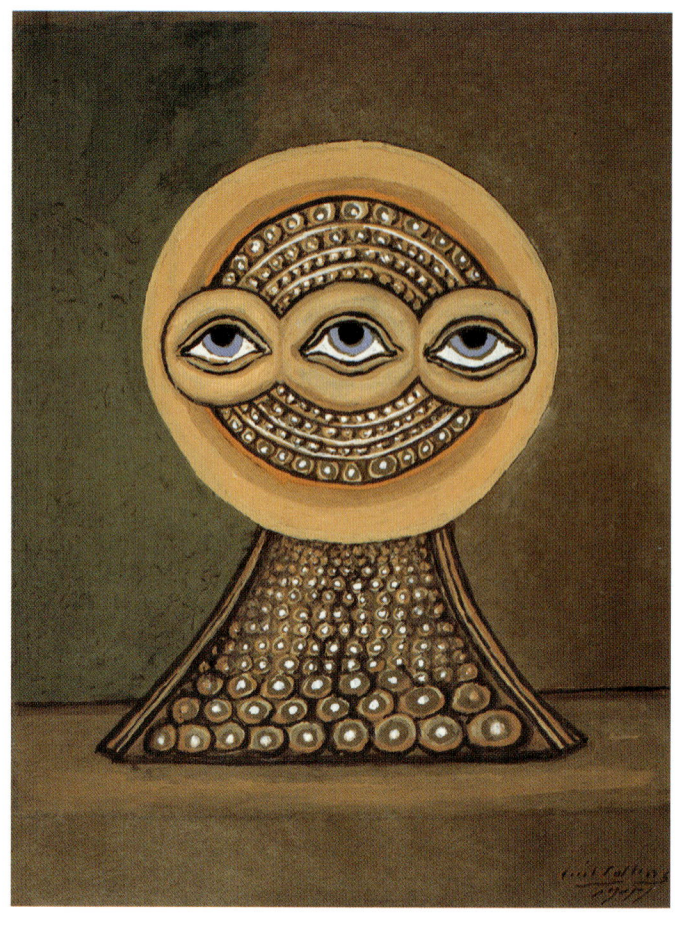

Cecil Collins
The Vision of the Trinity
1977
Gouache
22 x 17.4cm

of England, I used to have to go up to London three or four times a year and I always spent time with Cecil. We spoke very easily about the sacred and the reality of the spiritual world which is more real than the physical world. Cecil understood that too.

Cecil was totally against incarnation which is from the Latin meaning 'enfleshment', which for Cecil, was not the way forward. That's another reason why he couldn't properly be a Christian. Cecil's temperamental disposition was away from the flesh, away from the body, a bit like Plato seeing the body as a tomb. He looked for the eternal world as something spiritual and radiant, transcending the body. Temperamentally I think he found nauseating, the mystery of spirit engaging with matter and being enriched by that engagement. Cecil's perception was more Greek, or Platonic, let's say. I think he wanted to reach beyond the body, the tomb, and his physical disability. His hunchback was a kind of token of this, a reminder. Seeing himself as a fool fits with all of that. He was, as it were, a neo-Platonist, a mystic born into a very secular worldly culture and, to that extent, he was a fool in relation to the culture because he was at variance with the main beliefs of his time. He was a visionary. He didn't belong to any formalised scheme of religion, but he was deeply spiritual. I think he was wrong to scorn the idea of incarnation. What does an artist do but incarnate spiritual vision?

About three years before he died, he said in conversation that he sometimes saw angels. The only way he could communicate the meaning of this was to say that angels moved at a great speed and sometimes his inner perception could match this speed. On another occasion at about the same time he said to me that we need a category of knowledge he called 'atmosphere'. By this I think he meant developing awareness and that our organ of perception is 'the eye of the heart'.

I would say, if one has to use a technical language, that Cecil was really a Gnostic. It was partly a sort of escape from the prison house of this world, an escape from the limitations of ugly matter and so on. Part of it was, no doubt, a result of clear thinking and spiritual feeling, but part of it was his own physical condition. He had a very frail physique but, as many frail people are, he was very tough. He was pale and thin and I wouldn't have thought he could lift heavy objects, but he lived on in the world till he was about eighty-one, probably thanks to Elisabeth who took such good care of him. During Cecil's lifetime, Elisabeth was always in the background. She looked after Cecil as her vocation, but her life's task wasn't fulfilled simply by that. She had her own artistic vocation. After his death, she blossomed as an artist.

I think Elisabeth learned to deal with the frustrations which anyone would have living in constant close contact with someone like Cecil and she managed very well. I remember one time I was with Cecil down in his studio and we were looking at works of art and Elisabeth rang through to say, 'Tea's ready,' and he said, 'We'll come straight away.' He put the phone down and immediately continued with what we were talking about. It was more than half an hour before we went up so these small, but important, domestic matters he didn't manage very well.

I was at the opening of Cecil's great Retrospective exhibition at the Tate held shortly before he died. He sat there in his wheelchair with Judy Collins on one side holding his hand and me holding the other. He was very frail, but whether he knew that he was being called to another world, I don't know. When he was in hospital during the last week of his life, he used to phone me virtually every night. Elisabeth asked me afterwards in a gentle way, 'What did he say?' I said it was simply conversation, without any particular edge; he was just wanting to find fellowship. I think the fact that, in however poor a way, I was trying to relate to God struck a chord with Cecil and perhaps for him the strange experience of finding a clergyman who actually liked art had that mystical strain which you intuit in another person. I could see it in him and he could see it rather dimly in me. On his death, I took the funeral in the St Thomas More church at the bottom of Paultons Square.

I visited Elisabeth soon afterwards and as we walked through a room in the house, she in front and I behind, she turned to the left, not looking at me, but looking over her shoulder and in the corner was Cecil's trilby set on a chair so that it looked as if it was being worn. There were some other garments that he normally wore there too. I think it was to help her keep the sense of his presence; it's a whole way of being. That proved to be a rich seam which was fascinating for me to explore.

I studied Marxist literary theory for my first degree and was still carrying all that Marxist baggage and not quite sure what to do with it. Applying all that hardcore leftwing theory to Cecil Collins was an intellectual experiment and a funny thing to do to, I suppose.

TOM & ODETTE WORRELL

Tom Worrell Junior is a maverick businessman, philanthropist and preservationist. He and his wife, Odette, have set up a number of charitable foundations and have made significant contributions to humanitarian causes worldwide. His most ambitious project is El Monte Sagrado Living Resort in Taos, New Mexico, which embraces innovative solutions for green building, construction, water purification and recycling, serving as a model of sustainability for homes, schools, even towns

TW: We first saw Cecil Collins' work at the Anthony d'Offay gallery in London. There were about ten or fifteen paintings there, but the one that jumped out was *Tabla Rasa* and we fell in love with it. It's about inward looking.

OW: We purchased our first pieces of Cecil's work from Anthony, but Peter and Renata Nahum had *The Voice* in their gallery and that's another of our favourite pieces. It was Peter who orchestrated having tea with Elisabeth and Cecil. I was struck by the large number of books in their flat, so many books that I don't recall seeing a stick of furniture. Books were piled on top of each other for seats and there was a glass tabletop with books underneath and tea on top of it. Even though we were indoors, Elisabeth was wearing a beautiful sun hat, not with fabric flowers, but with real ones on it. The whole afternoon was beautiful.

TW: We found that we had a lot of spiritual things in common. He had studied a lot about Native Americans and one of my great life teachers is a Native American, Oren Lyons, Chief of the Onondaga, one of the six nations of the Iroquois. He has become an un-elected spokesman for Native American and ecological causes.

OW: At that time, my husband and I were involved in trying to help Native American tribes. Cecil was very quiet and thoughtful. Everything Cecil said mattered, otherwise it didn't come out of his mouth. He was a man of few words. Two of the quotes that Cecil shared with us was 'The pain stops here' and 'Whatever befalls the earth befalls the sons of the earth.' That has been my husband's mission for his entire life: to take care of the earth. We smiled and knew right away that we were going to get along.

TW: We immediately felt connected and there was another natural connection: Elisabeth's family was from Virginia and I had lived in Virginia for thirty years. During our visit, Cecil gave us a little pen and ink painting. It's not even as big as a postcard and has an image of Elisabeth.

OW: We were instantly drawn to a painting of Cecil and his wife sitting down titled *The Artist and His Wife*. It's absolutely remarkable. I thought that the vista behind them was their life leading up to this beautiful place where they were sharing a meal together and all that they had experienced. Cecil looked at me and said, 'No, it's quite the opposite. We're about to begin our journey. It's the end of our life that we have to look forward to.' I thought this was a beautiful way of looking at things. My husband and I also purchased *The Pilgrim Fool* of a Fool leading a young girl away from a fire.

TW: To me, *The Pilgrim Fool* is a very powerful anti-war statement.

OW: Another picture we love is *The Voice*, an image of this wise face within waves that are crashing. My husband had it on the wall behind his desk for many years; it was the only piece of art in his office. He has dedicated his last fifteen years to getting water clean, with the necessary science and the emotional reasons for doing this. Native Americans believe that we are part of the earth and not on top of the earth. Cecil's *The Voice* goes back to Native Americans and water. When Tom was a young child, he was taken into the woods and taught that everything is a part of God so when we hurt the earth, we're hurting ourselves. Water is the basis for life like the air we breathe. Tom's passion has led him to create beautiful spaces and always with water. All of our businesses are based around a sacred circle with water running through it. *The Voice* resonated deeply with Tom and he chose it, whether consciously or unconsciously, to be his motivating image.

TW: We saw the Collinses just that one time, twenty years ago, but it had a permanent effect on us. We bought work by Cecil over a period of about five years. I think he was a very old soul and his work was an expression of knowledge from his soul, not from his ego or his intellect.

OW: What Cecil was trying to share with those that were attracted to his work was that you can put your energy into what's wrong or you can put your energy into what's right. You can be gracious and do something from the point of inspiration rather than desperation. We should never get so comfortable with our lives that we stop growing; that's why we're here. When you live your life without being conscious of decisions that you make, then you're making them from both a mental standpoint and a perfunctory one. Living with these paintings, there are several that have been more of a comfort than daily inspiration, like the Angel comforting the Fool. Every time I look at it, I think of the intense love between Cecil and Elisabeth, how he spoke of her as if he were seeing her for the first time, the way he would portray her as an Angel, as something beyond beautiful and he's often the innocent Fool who, of course, is not a fool at all. It reflects the feelings that my husband and I share. When things have been difficult in our marriage, or when times have been just difficult in general, that painting has been a good friend, helping to put things into perspective.

We started collecting art when we first married twenty-one years ago and we've moved home many times since then, however we've never once considered selling any of our pieces by Cecil Collins. It's never even entered our minds, yet we've sold some of the pieces that would seem more important to most collectors' minds. For example, we owned some Turners and we were very moved by them and yet, when we made changes to our home, the Turners were among the first paintings we wanted to sell, not just for monetary reasons, but because it was time to move on and because Turner was more of a technician the way he studied light.

friends & other relationships

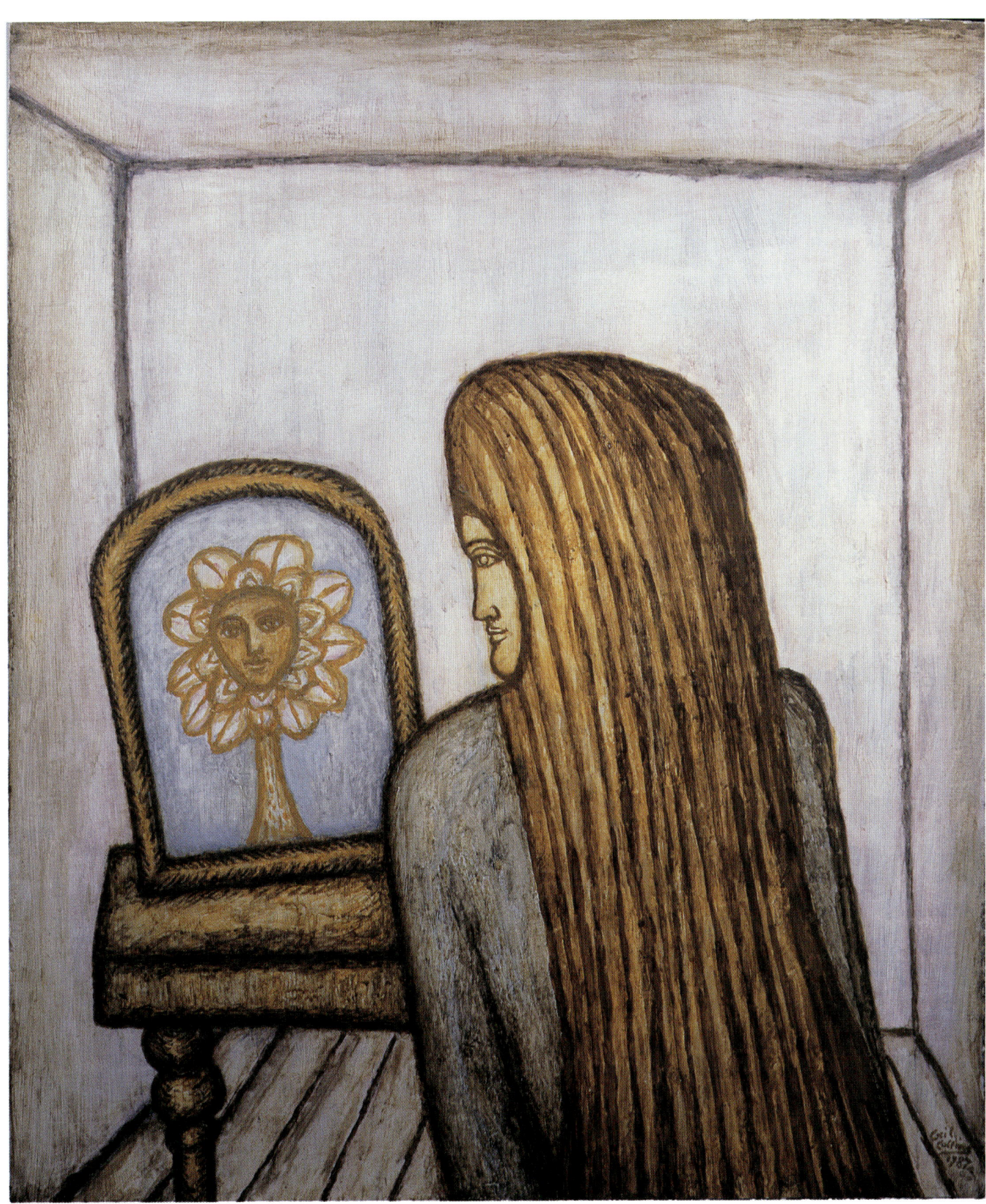

Cecil Collins
Tabula Rasa
1987
Tempera
61 x 51cm

INDEX

A

Ackling, Roger 98, 99
Adams, Ruth 247
Agar, Eileen 48
Albemarle Gallery 40, 267
Allen, Clare 54-5
Alley, Anthea (Oswald) 57
Alley, Melissa 57-9
Alley, Ronald 42
Alliette, Jean-Baptiste, (1738 – 1791) Parisian occultist, originator of the Tarot cards as used today, 300
Allitt, Eleanor 203, 208-10, 226
Allitt, John 107, 136, 163, 202, 208, 209, 211, 226, 241, 252, 22276
Allitt, Lucy 210-11
Allitt, Mary 210, 215
Allitt, Nicoletta 210, 211, 214-15
Anderson, Jennifer 217, 251
Anderson, William, (1936-1997) author, *Cecil Collins: The Quest for the Great Happiness*, 71, 153, 204, 217, 222, 242, 250, 251
Anthony d'Offay Gallery 36, 54, 103, 180, 215, 261, 275, 307, 313
Antrim, Alexander R. M. McDonnell, 9th Earl of Antrim, (b.1935) chief picture restorer, National Gallery and Tate Gallery, 238
Arthur Tooth & Sons 39, 239
Astor, Stella 60-1, 68
Audergon, Arlene, American born therapist, trained in 'Process Work' (process orientated psychology), 178

B

Bach, Johann Sebastian 195
Bacon, Francis, (1909-1992) 39, 44, 47, 62, 70, 73, 98, 103, 153, 202, 236, 258, 265, 266, 271, 275, 285, 307
Ball, Lawrence 218-19, 240
Ballantine, Sherry 62-3, 98
Ballet Jooss, established by Kurt Jooss and Sigurd Leeder, Germany (1933), with Hein Heckroth as theatre designer, best known for their anti-war ballet, *The Green Table* 44, 179, 240
Barber, Samuel 97, 150
Baring, Anne (née Gage) 92, 220-8
Baring, Francesca 225
Baring, The Hon. Robert 71, 100, 101, 220-8, 256, 265
Barnard, Alison, founder of Centre for Spiritual and Psychological Studies, 132, 236, 272, 284, 291, 295, 296, 297, 298
Barnard, Julian 229-31

Beckmann, Max, (1884-1950) German artist associated with Neue Sachlichkeit, 'New Objectivity', 252
Beethoven, Ludwig van, (1770-1827) 150, 279, 290
Beeton, Rosalind 62, 65-6
Benjamin, George 218
Bennett, Kathleen Falley 303
Berlin, Isaiah 222
Bernac, Pierre, (1899-1979) French baritone and teacher, 150
Bernstein, Elmer, (1922-2004) film score composer, 48
Betjeman, John, (1906-1984), English poet, writer and broadcaster, 285
Bird, Paul 200, 203
Bjornson, Maria, (1949-2002), theatre stage designer, 253
Blacker, Thetis, 226, 233-6, 287, 299
Blake, William, (1757-1827) British visionary poet and print maker, 18, 72, 111, 162, 172, 176, 195, 202, 236, 237, 249, 253, 255, 257, 292, 308
Blakenham, Viscountess, Marcia 40, 68-72, 86, 228, 252
Blakenham, Viscount, Michael 40, 68, 72
Bliss, Sir Arthur, (1891-1975) British composer, 294
Block, Deborah 73, 74
Block, Raphael 73-4
Bloom, Archbishop (Metropolitan Anthony), 93, 203 290, 291
Bloomsbury Gallery 16
Boehm, Jacob, (1693-1781) German Christian mystic, founder of Theosophy, 92
Boulanger, Lili, (1893-1918) French composer, winner of the Prix de Rome in 1908, sister of Nadia, Boulanger, 240
Boulanger, Nadia (1887-1979) conductor and music teacher, 93, 131
Bould, Martin 75
Bowles, Peter 50, 71, 82, 237-8
Bowles, Susan 237, 238
Bowness, Sir Alan, Director of the Tate Gallery (1980-1988), 42, 239
Brancusi, Constantin, (1876-1957) Romanian sculptor, domiciled in Paris, 18
Breton, André, (1896-1966) French author and founder of Surrealism (1924), 31, 303
Britten, Benjamin, (1913-1976) British composer, 225
Brown, Robert David, (1925-2002) initially veterinary scientist, became Assistant Keeper, Tate Gallery, (now Tate Britain) 42
Bruce, Anne 200-1

Bruckner, Anton, (1824-1896) Austrian composer, 299
Brunskill, Ann 76-7
Burland, Cottie 299
Burr, James 82, 146

C

Callimachus, Greek architect and sculptor, 5th century BC, 39
Caro, Anthony, (b. 1924) British sculptor, 307
Carter, Lucy (née Rothenstein) 238
Castillejo, David 276
Castillejo, José 276
Cézanne, Paul, (1839-1906) French artist, 25
Chagall, Marc, (1887-1985) Belorussian-French painter, 99, 304
Chaitow, Michael 78-9, 81, 112, 123, 229
Chopin, Frédéric, (1810-1849) Polish composer and virtuoso pianist, 25, 131, 304
Cina, Colin 131
Clark, Lord, Kenneth (1903-1983). Director, National Gallery (1933-1946) and writer-presenter of TV series, *Civilisation*, 16, 50, 238, 239, 240
Clatworthy, Bob (Robert) 92, 93, 94, 195, 196, 222
Claude Gelleé (called Claude Lorrain) (c.1600-1682) French classical landscape painter, 89
Coleridge, Samuel Taylor, (1772-1834), English poet and philosopher, 153
Collins, Elisabeth 16, 17-18, 19, 28-32, 36, 38, 39, 40, 42, 95, 96, 98, 101, 106, 110, 111, 112, 113, 114, 116, 117, 130, 147, 165, 167, 176, 180, 182, 192, 200, 201, 204, 208, 209, 210, 214, 215, 217, 221, 225, 226, 227, 228, 229, 230, 233, 234, 241, 245, 246, 248, 251, 252, 253, 254, 256, 261-3, 265, 266-7, 268, 270-1, 274-5, 277, 279, 280-1, 283, 287, 290, 291-2, 294, 296-7, 298-9, 301, 302-3, 305-6, 310, 312, 313, 314
Collins, Dr. Judith 17, 38, 42, 43-5, 49, 124, 234, 248, 282
Collis, Maurice, (1889-1973) writer and administrator in Burma, 233
Colonna, Vittoria, (1490-1547) Italian noblewoman and poet, 204
Comfort, Alex, 1920-2000, physician, poet, novelist, pacifist, best known for *The Joy of Sex*, (1972), 19, 259
Cook, Gary 80-81,

Coomaraswamy, Ananda, (1877-1947) metaphysician and pioneering art historian and neo-Platonic philosopher of Indian art, 137, 306
Corbett, Lily 60, 82-6, 98, 106, 164, 178, 186, 189, 228, 281
Cortot, Alfred, (1877-1963) Franco-Swiss pianist and conductor, 150
Crane Kalman Gallery 298
Cranswick, David 71, 87-90, 103, 105, 106
Craxton, John, (b.1922) British neo-Romantic painter, 304
Crisp, Quentin, (1908-1999) British writer, model, and raconteur, 190
Critchlow, Keith, co-founder of the journal *Temenos*, authority on sacred geometry and architecture, Professor Emeritus at The Prince's School of Traditional Arts, London and former professor of Islamic Art at the Royal College of Art, London, 90, 229
Cross, Stephen 202, 218, 229, 239-42, 283
Crouch, Christopher 22
Crowns of Happiness, The (play for children by Cecil Collins) 211-12, 214
Cuthbert, Caroline 44
Cuthbert, Rosalind 91-4

D

Dai, Saied 95-7, 122, 123, 279
Dali, Salvador, (1904-1989) Spanish Catalan surrealist painter, 31
Dante Alighieri, (c1265-1321) Italian poet, 203, 204
Darlington, Steven 265
Dartington Hall 19, 31, 38, 47, 50, 200, 221, 240, 241, 248, 245, 256, 262, 281, 306
Daumier, Honoré, (1808-1879) French artist, 241
Davie, Alan, (b. 1920), Scottish painter and musician, 195
Dinesen, Isak, pseudonym of Baroness Karen von Blixen-Finecke (1885-1962) Danish author, 129
Doerner, Max 130, 299
d'Offay, Anne 225
d'Offay, Anthony 8, 46, 71, 225, 238, 242, 310
d'Offay, Timothy 8
Donizetti, Gaetano Maria, (1797 – 1848) *Il Borgomaestro di Saardam*, 209
Drysdale, Alexandra 98-9, 101
Drysdale, Andrew 100, 101
Drysdale, Helena 245

Drysdale, Merida 100-1, 238
Duchamp, Marcel, (1887-1968) French artist, 25
Duparc, Henri, (1848-1933) French composer, 150
Durrell, Laurence, (1912-1990) British author, 303

E

Ede, Jim, (1895-1990) British art collector and patron, 304
Eisenhart, Ruth 18, 58, 68, 86, 88, 102-3, 124, 125, 154, 164, 178, 180, 184, 185, 198
Electra, 1962 Greek film based on Euripides' play (*Elektra*), director-producer, Michael Cacoyannis; music Mikis Theodorakis 202
Elgar, Sir Edward, (1857-1934) English Romantic composer 150
Eliot, T.S. (1888-1965) poet, dramatist and Nobel Laureate, 263, 303
The Wasteland 149
Elmhirst, Dorothy Whitney (1887-1968) and Leonard (1893-1974), founded Dartington Hall, important artistic centre in the 1930s, 191, 281
Empson, William (1906-1984) English literary critic and poet, 303
Engel, Dr Werner, Jungian analyst, 112, 113, 114
England, Jane 72, 235
Erasmus, (1466/9 1536) Dutch Renaissance humanist and theologian, 247
Evans, Merlyn 220
Eye of the Heart, The, (1978) film about Cecil Collins, (transcript of Cecil Collins' commentary) 242-4

F

Fedden, Mary, OBE, RA (b.1915) British artist, 246
Fiennes, Susanna, (b. 1961), artist 184
Fludd, Robert, (1574-1637) prominent English physician and mystic, 18
Freedman, Miriam 105-6, 112, 115
Freud, Sigmund, (1856-1939), Austrian psychiatrist 225
Frink, Dame Elisabeth, (1930-1993) British sculptor, 265, 309
Fuller, Peter, (1947-1990) art critic and founder, 1987, *Modern Painters*, 99

G

Gage, Anne see Baring, Anne
Gagaku, ('elegant music') Japanese classical music style, 218
Gale, Jeremy 86, 106, 107-11, 178, 186, 228, 281
Gardiner, Charles Wrey, (1901-1981) Welsh poet, editor and publisher, 32
Gascoyne, David, (1916- 2001) British poet, 303
Ghosh, Amal 124, 125, 193-7
Gill, Eric, (1882 – 1940) British sculptor, typographer, 30, 43, 90, 200, 241, 257, 266
Gilmour, Dave, (b.1946) lead singer of Pink Floyd, psychedelic rock band, 113
Gilmour, Ginger 98, 106, 112-14
Giotto di Bondone, (c 1267 – 1337) Florentine painter and architect, 271
Gluck, David 198-9
Graves, Morris, (1910 – 2001) American artist, co-founder with Mark Tobey of Northwest School, 257
Green & Stone frames, London, 223, 224
Greene, Graham, (1904-1991) British author, 17
Griffin, Sheila 105, 115
Guénon, René, (1886-1951) French author of metaphysics, sacred science and symbolism, 289
Guppy, Shusha, (1935-2008) Persian (Iranian) writer, editor and singer, 303

H

Hamburger, Michael, (1924-2007) British translator and poet, 303
Hamer, Janice 279
Hamet Gallery, London 39
Harding, Douglas, (1909-2007) British author and spiritual teacher, 279
Hauser, Kitty 247-9
Haydn, Joseph, (1732-1809) Austrian composer, 203
Heckroth. Hein, (1901-1970) German theatre designer, 19
Heffer Gallery, Cambridge, 20, 32
Henderson, Catherine 73
Hepworth, Dame Barbara, (1903-1975) British sculptor 57
Herbert, Dr Jack 249
Heron, Patrick, (1920-1999), British painter, writer and designer, 220
Hicks, Clive 250-1
Hirst, Desirée 249
Hitchins, Ivon, (1893-1979), British artist, belonged to the London Group, 200
Hoare, Jane 279
Hoare, Meriel 116-17
Holzhandler, Dora, (b.1928), British artist, 304
Hoole, John, first Director of the Barbican Gallery (1982 – 1996), 46
Hopewell, Anna Madge, daughter of Kathleen Raine and Charles Madge, 303
Hopton, Ian 118-21
Hotter, Hans, (1909-2003) German operatic bass-baritone, 150
House, Adrian, publisher with William Collins, author of an outstanding life of *Francis of Assisi*, 265
Hovhaness, Alan, (1911 – 2000) (born, Alan Vaness Chakmakjian), mystic American composer of Armenian-Scots ancestry, 218
Howells, Lynnette, Australian born artist, 73, 115
Humperdinck, Engelbert (1854-1921) German composer, best known for the opera *Hänsel and Gretel*, (c.1891), 240
Hussey, Walter, (1909-1985) Anglican clergyman and art patron, 309
Hutchings, Gay 122-5
Hutton, John (1906-1978) New Zealand born artist and glass engraver, 182
Hutton, Marigold 182
Hyman, Timothy 252-3

J

Jane England Gallery 18, 58, 86, 101, 110, 226
Jencks, Maggie Keswick 68
Jennings, Humphrey, (1907-1950) British film-maker, founder, 1937, Mass Observation social research organization, (Sussex University Library), 48
Johnston, William 20, 26, 100
Johnstone, Gwynneth 100
Jones, David, (1895-1928) Welsh born, British artist and modernist poet 33, 182, 233, 257
Jooss Ballet see Ballet Jooss
Joseph, Sir Keith, (1918-1994) British barrister and Conservative Cabinet Minister, widely regarded as the 'power behind the throne' in the creation of what came to be known as Thatcherism, 222
Josipovici, Gabriel, (b.1940) Writer and philosopher, 252
Jung, Carl Gustav, (1875-1961) Swiss psychiatrist, 93, 195, 202, 225, 251, 274, 302

K

Kandinsky, Vassily, (1866-1944) Russian artist and art theorist, 93
Keeble, Brian, author and editor, founder, Golgonooza Press and a co-founder of the *Temenos Review* and Temenos Academy, 236, 242
Kendall, Anne 299
Kenton, Warren (b.1933) (Z'ev ben Shimon Halevi) architect and authority on the Kabbala, 229
Kestelman, Morris 92, 193, 220
Khan, Pir Vilayat Inayat, (1916-2004), Sufi leader and teacher, 22, 295
Kidel, Mark, British documentary film maker, 254, 284
Kiff, Ken, (1935-2001), British artist, Associate Artist, National Gallery (1991-1993). The *Narrative Paintings*, ICA (1979), curated by Timothy Hyman, included Kiff's series *The Sequence*, 98, 253, 307
Kingston, Alex (Alexandra), British actress, 155, 179, 183-5
Klee, Paul, (1879-1940) Swiss-German painter 94, 99
Knight, Jonathan 126-8
Krishnamurti, Jeddu, (1895-1986), Indian philosopher and speaker on spiritual subjects, awarded the UN Peace Medal, 1984, 280

L

Lancaster, Maria 22, 80, 129-32, 218
Lane, Danny 123, 124, 134-7, 200
Lane, John 253, 254-8
Lane, Truda 254-8
Langinieux, Michel, eccentric actor who waged a long personal campaign to have all the asbestos removed from the Sorbonne. 279
Lannoy, Richard 259-60
Latham, Shelley 102, 138-40
Leach, Bernard, (1887-1979) British studio potter and teacher, 19
Leanse, Robin 252, 261-263
LeBoulanger, Sylvie 141-5
Lefevre Gallery 32, 195
Leicester Galleries 32, 49
Leonardo da Vinci, (1452-1519) Italian artist and polymath 202, 271
Levi, Peter, (1931-2000) British poet, sometime Jesuit priest, Professor of Poetry, Oxford University (1984-1989), 265, 268

INDEX

Lodge, Diana Violet Irene Maud, née Uppington, (1906-1998) Welsh artist and second wife of Oliver W. Lodge (married 1932) She answered his advertisement for a nude model and had modelled for Eric Gill (1882-1940) and Duncan Grant (1885-1978), 182
Lodge, Oliver William Foster, (1878-1955) British poet and artist, renowned for developing wireless telegraphy and his interest in spiritualism, 182
Loewe, Dr Michael 273
Lorca, Garcia, (1898-1936) Spanish poet, dramatist and theatre director, 299
Loydell, Rupert 264
Ludgate, Ruth 146-7
Lyons, Orega 314
Lyth, Claire, theatre designer, formerly Head of Design, Liverpool Playhouse & Lyceum theatre, Edinburgh, 240

M

MacDonald, John, art critic, journalist and past Curator of the Australian Department in the National Gallery, Australia 261
MacDonald, Stephanie 261
MacDonald, Duncan 32
MacGregor, Neil 72
Machiavelli, Niccolò, (1469-1527) Italian Renaissance diplomat, political philosopher, musician, poet and playwright, 170
McKenna, Stephen 270-2
McKenzie-Smith, Bryce 272-5
Maclagan, David 253
Madge, Charles 281
Marceau, Marcel, (1923-2007) French mime artist, 293, 302, 303
Marchant, Leonard 172
Marks, Lord Michael, (1920-998), philanthropist, poet, artist and collector of Cecil Collins work, 180
Marshall, Harry and Laura 265-8
Masson, André, (1896-1987), French artist, 259
Matisse, Henri, (1969-1954), French artist, 307
Matthews, David 269
Maufroy, Muriel 147-8, 154
Marx, Karl (1818-1883) German philosopher, political economist, historian, and revolutionary, 248
Maxwell, Gavin 249, 296
Mayne, Tim 190-2
Mayr, Simon, (1763-1845) born Bavaria, Germany, settled in Bergamo, Italy (1802) Gaetano Donizetti's music teacher, 204
Meister Eckhart, (c. 1260–c. 1328), German theologian and mystic, 92
Mellor, David 46-8, 248
Menuhin, Yehudi, (1916-1999), American-Jewish (later Swiss, then British) violinist and conductor, 131
Messiaen, Olivier, (1908-1992) innovative and influential French composer, organist and ornithologist and inspiring teacher, 218, 219
Michelangelo Buonarroti (1475-1564), Italian artist and poet, 202, 204
Miró, Joan, (1893-1983) Spanish Catalan painter, sculptor and ceramist, 99
Monk's Cottage, Highwood Bottom, near Speen, Buckinghamshire, 30
Moore, Henry, (1898-1986) English sculptor, 28, 43, 173, 221, 309
Moore, Nicholas, British poet, 32
Morphet, Richard 8, 39-42, 43, 44, 49, 200, 228, 234, 255
Morris, Isobel 186-9
Mozart, Wolfgang Amadeus (1756-1791), Austrian composer, 303
Murdoch, Iris, DBE, (1919-1999) Irish-born novelist and philosopher, Fellow of St Anne College, Oxford (1948-1999), 265, 303
Musil, Robert, (1880-1942), Viennese author, 252

N

Nadal, Jacinta 226, 276-7, 299
Nadal, Rafael 203, 226, 227, 2276, 277, 299
Nahum, Peter 49-51, 237, 313
Nash, Paul, (1889-1946), British artist, 257
Newman, Barnett, (1905-1970) American artist, 51
Nichol, Gail 126
Nicholson, Ben, (1894-1982) British abstract painter, 299
Nicholson, Winifred, (1893-1981) British artist, 8, 33, 45, 226, 235, 256, 257, 258, 298, 299
Norland, Brigitte 149-53

O

Oliver, Mervyn 100
Orwell, Sonia, 1918-1980, second wife of George Orwell (pen-name of Eric Arthur Blair, 1903-1950), 281
Oswald, Alice 277
Ouspensky, P.D. (1978-1947) Russian philosopher, 131

P

Paich, Slobodan 80, 81, 129, 130, 131, 132, 218
Palmer, Samuel, (1805-1881) British artist, 18, 46, 72, 162, 236, 237, 255
Pallis, Marco, (1895-1989) British-born mystic, mountaineer and author affiliated to the Traditionalist School, 290
Pärt, Arvo, (b. 1935) renowned Estonian composer in minimalist style, frequently set to sacred texts. 21, 45, 89, 218, 289, 294
Patrick, Michael 198
Peake, Mervyn Laurence, (1911-1968), British artist, poet and author, best known for his illustrations and the *Gormenghast* novels, 20, 100, 163, 182
Perls, Fritz, (1893-1970) noted German-born psychiatrist and psychotherapist 62
Picasso, Pablo, (1881-1973) Spanish artist, 99, 170, 236, 250
Piero della Francesca, (c1412-1492) Italian artist, 96
Plath, Sylvia, (1932-1963) American poet and author, *The Bell Jar*, 195
Plumb, John 92, 93
Pollack, Framers, St James, London 223
Pollock, Jackson, (1912-1956) American Abstract Expressionist artist, 39
Poulenc, Francis, (1899-1963) French composer, 150
Powys, John Cowper, (1872-1964) Welsh author of *A Glastonbury Romance, Owen Glendower* and *Weymouth Sands*, 252, 253, 300
Proctor, Maxwell 197

Q

Qu, Lei Lei 154-5

R

Rachmaninov, Sergei, (1873-1943) Russian composer, virtuosic pianist and conductor, 138, 166
Raine, Kathleen, (1908-2003), British poet, scholar and co-founder, *Temenos Review* (1981), then Temenos Academy, (1990) 8, 18, 32, 40, 45, 72, 86, 151, 156, 203, 217, 226, 233, 235, 236, 239, 241, 246, 249, 254, 258, 259-60, 262, 263, 275, 277, 281, 287-8, 295-6, 303
Ramsden, Clifford, Elisabeth Collins father, 28
Ramsden, Elisabeth see Collins, Elisabeth
Ravel, Maurice, (1875-1937) French composer and pianist, 150, 163, 279
Read, Herbert, (1893–1968) British anarchist poet, art and literature critic, 31, 241
Redon, Odilon, (1840-1916) French Symbolist artist, 239
Reid, Sir Norman, Director of the Tate Gallery (1964-1979), 42
Rembrandt, (1606-1669) Dutch artist, 85, 89, 99, 231
Reynolds, Alan 221
Reyntiens, Patrick 80, 94, 134, 136, 160, 161, 196, 198, 200-1, 203, 265, 267, 276, 309, 310
Ridley, Philip 156-9
Rilke, Rainer Maria, (1875-1926) German poet, 225
Robertson, Bryan, OBE (1925-2002), curator and arts manager, 16, 20, 32, 36, 43, 234, 256
Rodin, Auguste, (1840–1917) French sculptor, 102
Roszak, Theodore, *Unfinished Animal* 257
Rothenstein, Sir John Knewstub Maurice, (1901-1992) art historian, Director, Tate Gallery (1938-1964), 32, 42, 100, 200, 237, 238
Rothenstein, Lucy 100, 237
see also Carter, Lucy
Rothenstein, Sir William (1872-1945) Principal, Royal College of Art (1920-1935), 16, 18, 32
Rothko, Mark, (1903-1970), American Abstract Expressionist artist, 51
Rowe, Nomi 15-23, 86, 190, 191, 192
Rowlands, Alan 279-81
Rubbra, Edmund, (1901-1986) British composer. His work included ballet music for Margaret Barr, Director, School of Dance and Mime at Dartington Hall. Lecturer, Worcester College, Oxford and Professor, Guildhall School of Music and Drama, London, 241
Ruhemann, Helmut, chief picture restorer, National Gallery (1946-1967) under Director Sir Philip Anstiss Hendy (1900-1980), 238
Rumi Jalaluddin, (1207-1273) Persian poet, Sufi spiritual teacher and mystic, 22

S

St John Perse, pseudonym for M R A Alexis Léger, (1887-1975). Poet and diplomat, Nobel Prize winner for Literature, 1960, 62
Samuels, Bernard 255
Satie, Erik, (1866-1925), French (French-

Scots parentage) composer and pianist, associated with Dada and precursor of minimalism and repetitive music. He said of himself, 'I came into the world very young, in an age that was very old', 218

Schaefer, Glen, W., (1930-1996), Canadian-born ornithologist, pyhsicist and cosmologist, (father of Maryanna Tavener) 18, 85, 163, 226, 291

School of Economic Science 118, 119

Schroeder, Gay 239, 240, 283

Schubert, Franz Peter, (1797-1828) Austrian composer, *G major sonata* 280

Schumann, Robert, (1810-1856), German composer and pianist 195
 Kinderscenen 169

Schuon, Frithjof, (1907-1998) mystic German philosopher, 289

Seferis, George, pseudonym of Georgios Seferiádes, (1900-1971) Greek poet and Nobel Laureate, also career diplomat, Ambassador to UK (1957-1962), 289, 290

Segovia, Andrés, (1893-1987) Spanish classical guitarist, 131

Senat, Conrad, composer and publisher 19

Serota, Sir Nicholas, Director, Tate Gallery, 36-8, 42, 44

Seymour, Anne, formerly Curator, Modern Collection, Tate Gallery, married Anthony d'Offay (1977), 42

Sherrard, Philip, (1913-1995) author, translator and scholar in metaphysics, theology, art and aesthetics 18, 226, 260, 290

Shostakovich, Dmitri, (1906-1975) Russian composer, 150, 157

Sibelius, Jean, (1865-1957) Finnish composer, 138

Simmons, Dorothy 280

Smirnov, Dimitri, Russian composer, 176

Spalding, Frances 16, 282

Spall, Timothy 181

Spence, Basil Urwin, OM, OBE, RA, (1907-1976) Scottish architect including, Coventry Anglican Cathedral, begun in 1956 completed 1962. President of the Royal Institute of British Architects (1958-1960) and Professor of Architecture, Royal Academy, 182

Spencer, Stanley, (1891-1959) British painter. His 2001 Tate Retrospective was curated by Timothy Hyman, 200, 236, 237, 247, 248, 255, 257

Spender, Humphrey 281

Spender, Lady Natasha 31, 50, 281

Spender, Sir Stephen, (1909-1995) British poet, novelist and essayist, 16, 31, 281

Stedall, Jackie 226

Stedall, Jonathan 182, 226, 235, 284-8

Steiner, Rudolf, (1861-1925) Austrian philosopher and educationalist, founder of Anthroposophy, 288

Stockhausen, Karlheinz, (1928-2007) German composer, 18, 93, 131, 209, 218, 222, 240, 263, 289

Stravinsky, Igor Fyodorovich, (1882-1971) Russian composer, pianist and conductor. His ballet music, *The Rite of Spring*, 1913, one of three commissioned for Diaghilev's *Ballets Russes* caused a riot when first performed in Paris, 89, 218, 222, 289

Su Dong Po 154

Surrealist Exhibition, London, (1936) 303

Sutherland, Graham 224, 309

Swan, Oliver 235

Sylvester, David, (1924-2001) British art critic, curator and collector, 45

T

Tagore, Rabindranath, (1861-1941) Indian poet, philosopher and artist 19, 196, 252

Tambimuttu, Meary James Thurairajah, (1915-1983), Tamil poet, editor and critic, 303

Tanguy, Yves, (1900-1955), French Surrealist artist, 303

Tassie, Nicola 124, 160-5

Tavener, John 18, 44, 45, 71, 85, 114, 218, 226, 255, 263, 265, 267, 279-80, 289-92, 294, 310

Tavener, Maryanna 226, 289-92

Temple, Olivia 293-4, 295, 296, 301, 303

Temple, Robert 130, 295-303

Thatcher, Margaret, Prime Minister of the United Kingdom (1979-1990), 49, 204, 222

Thekla, Mother 290

Thierry's restaurant 72, 235

Thompson, Lewis, (1909-1949) British poet, traveller and mystic, 259, 260, 261

Tibetan trumpets 150

Tippett, Sir Michael Kemp (1905-1998) British composer, 86

Tobey, Mark, (1890-1876) American mystical artist, known for his 'white writing' pictures, follower of the Baha'i faith and interested in eastern philosophy, art and religions, co-founder of the US Northwest School 18, 19, 31, 44, 83, 195, 221, 222, 240, 241, 253, 256

Topolski, Feliks, (1907-1989) Polish-born British artist, 303

Traherne, Thomas, (c.1636-1674) metaphysical poet and religious author, 202, 203

Trevelyan, Julian, (1910-1988) British artist, founder member, British Surrealists (1930s), 182, 246, 303

Turnbull, William, British sculptor, 195

Turner, Evan 50

Tweedie, Mrs Irina, (1909-1999) first Western woman to receive spiritual training in the Sufi Naqshbandi system in India. She had a group in north London. The diary of her training, *Daughter of Fire*, 1995, reprinted by The Golden Sufi Centre, USA 22, 54, 65, 66, 71, 73, 74, 83, 87, 88, 105, 112, 113, 114, 129, 130, 131, 132, 134, 137, 141, 142, 218, 219

U

Uccello, Paolo, (1397-1475) Italian artist, 153

Uglow, Euan, British artist, 98

V

Van der Post, Laurens, (1906-1996) Afrikaner author, political adviser, philosopher and explorer, 132, 149, 163, 202, 273-4, 286, 287

Van Gogh, Vincent, (185-1890) Dutch artist, 25

Vann, Philip 304-8

Vaughan, Keith, (1912-1977) British artist, 220

Vaux, Mark 92, 196

Vermeer, Johannes, (1632-1675) Dutch artist, 89

Vie, Howard 166-7

W

Wagner, Wilhelm Richard, (1813-1883) German composer, conductor, theatre director and essayist, *Parsifal* 138, 139

Waley, Arthur, (1889-1966) British Orientalist, Sinologist and translator, 19, 31, 241

Walker, Anne 167-8

Walker, Canon Keith 265, 274, 309-313

Ward, Nellie 28

Warhol, Andy, (1928-1987) American artist, 25, 39

Warner, Jacqueline 20, 169-71

Wellington, Irene 100

Welsford, Enid 32

Whistler, J.A.M. (1834-1903), American-born British artist, 295

Whone, Herbert, (b 1925) violinist, artist and author, including a series of essays, *The Hidden Face of Music*, (1974), 218

Williams, Charles, (1886-1945) British poet, novelist, theologian and literary critic, author of *The Figure of Beatrice* (1944), 203

Wilson, Simon 42

Winston, Willow 123, 124, 172-7

Wisner, Jane 177

Wood, Edward, nephew of Elisabeth Collins, 228

Worrell, Tom and Odette 313-14

Wright, Joe, (b.1972) English film director, 180, 181

Wright, John, (1908-1991) puppeteer, co-founder, with Lyndie Wright, Little Angel Theatre, London (1961), 178

Wright, Lyndie 178-81, 183, 184

Wright, Sarah, puppeteer, 184

Y

Yeats, William Butler, (1865-1939) Irish poet, 19

Young, Peter 247, 248

Z

Zienko, Kate 151, 152

ACKNOWLEDGEMENTS

The truth of existence can only be apprehended by love, knowledge is always relative.
Cecil Collins

First and foremost to Cecil and Elisabeth Collins. At the mention of their names, strangers opened their homes and hearts to me. I was astonished and enchanted that the charm and wisdom of these two people is still as potent for everyone I contacted as it is for me.

I am deeply indebted to the following for their good will and expertise:
All the contributors, my profound gratitude for their infinite patience, hospitality and generosity in sharing their memories of Cecil and Elisabeth. Thanks to Robin Vousden who kindly made time for me in his busy life. It was a pleasure to listen to his knowledge of Cecil and Elisabeth, but sadly my equipment was foxed by the acoustics of the Gagosian Gallery's magnificent proportions. Although the tape was sent to three different specialists, it could not be rescued. There was never another opportunity to record again which is a real loss. Anne Aylor for being the most inspiring teacher of writing in the same spirit as Cecil taught art. I deeply appreciate the enormous care and time she lavishes on her students. Her faith and assistance in this project has encouraged me to keep going against the odds. I value highly her perfectionism, sense of humour and insistence on clarity of thought. Also for being a constantly available friend. Brita Pouget for encouraging me at the very beginning by her impeccable transcriptions. Irene Boston for being such a reliable and highly professional transcriber, not to mention being the only one to understand what I needed when I tore a knee ligament. Slavica Savic for so kindly putting me in touch with Irene. Diana Davies for her enthusiasm and rigorous editorial skills, for knocking the Chronology into shape and for becoming an appreciated new friend. Elisabeth Russell Taylor, widow of Tom Fairs (colleague of Cecil), good new friend for most generously introducing me to her invaluable editorial friends, including Elisabeth Ingles and Jill Foulston. Naomi Gryn who worked her 'elf' magic on my 'old cobbler work' at every stage, for polishing the Chronolgy and for becoming an admired new friend. Judy Goldhill for introducing her gifted friends to me. For being a responsive student and delightful friend herself, also a superb photographer. Jasmine Lawrence whom I've been fond of since she was a child, for her quiet meticulousness and being willing to do the donkey work. Daniel Kirkpatrick for suggesting Gordon Lee in an emergency and thanks to Gordon himself. David Wilson for his good natured willingness to do whatever I asked, even the impossible. Maria Lancaster for being a true friend indeed and for all her wonderful practical help and support. I couldn't have done without her dynamic energy. Luska Mengham for her excellent work on the Chronology.

David Mellor for his supportive understanding and introducing me to Luska. Ursula Esling for her superlative proofing and at such speed. Ann Wroe for recommending Ursula and for helping beyond her knowledge. She has been a mentor and model. Also to Malcolm Wroe for his warmth and welcome. Saba Milton and Richard Braude for their valuable help. Ellie Stedall for lending a hand. Marie-Claire Koralek for being a very precious friend and stepping in at the last minute with her habitual brilliance and incredibly generous nature. All my friends for their forbearance and love while I was absorbed in bringing this book to completion. Dearest daughter, Olivia, for her excellent research on the Chronology and for taking over the management so magnificently, beyond the call of filial love, when all seemed lost. Beloved husband, Oscar, for his encouragement and support when I was low and for being there always even when I was absent. Last, but certainly not least, Jonathan Raimes for his endless patience and brilliant creative adaptability. This complex book is testament to his impeccable design skill.

PERMISSIONS AND CREDITS

Brancusi – *Kiss* (1907); The Bridgeman Art Library, © ADAGP, Paris and DACS, London 2008

Sienese unknown Master of the Osservanza - *The Meeting of Saint Anthony and Saint Paul* (c.1420s-1440s); National Gallery of Art, Washington, H. Kress Collection (with special thanks to Barbara Goldstein Wood)

Lewis Thompson – *The Fool at Morning; The Fool in the Forest*, from series The Fool (to Cecil Collins in gratitude for his pictures); Lewis Thompson papers, Washington State University Libraries, manuscripts, archives and special collections

Cecil Collins – *Morning* (1943); Christie's Images Ltd

Mark Tobey – *Portrait of Cecil Collins*; The Dartington Hall Trust Archive (with special thanks to Yvonne Widger)

In Concordiam Populo, reproduced by kind permission of the Bodleian Library, Oxford

Pictures belonging to the Cecil Collins estate copyright Tate